PREHISTORIC

INVESTIGATIONS 2

THE *IN SEACH OF* OMNIBUS

Christopher Seddon

Copyright notice

GLANVILLE PUBLICATIONS

Published by Glanville Publications, London, UK

ISBN: 978-1-7392519-9-4

Contents

Introduction

This work brings together my twelve *In Search of … a Prehistoric Investigation* series of Kindle Short Reads into a single printed omnibus edition. The series explores key aspects of the evolutionary, cultural, and technological development of our species. It is intended as a follow-up to my earlier work, *Prehistoric Investigations*, and like it, I try to present each topic in the context of the overall big picture of the human past.

Each chapter corresponds to a Short Read from the *In Search of* series. Some chapters focus on particular species or particular periods in hominin evolutionary history. The hominins are a group comprising anything more closely related to a present-day human (*Homo sapiens*) than it is to our closest living relatives, the chimpanzees (*Pan troglodytes* and *Pan paniscus*). Other chapters focus on culture and technology. In both cases, I often take a historical perspective.

As each of the Short Reads was a self-contained work, this has meant that there is a certain amount of duplication between the chapters of this work. I have tried to keep this to a minimum, but it will invariably be more noticeable in an omnibus volume. It does mean that the chapters may be read in any order. For anybody wishing to do so, a brief description of each chapter follows this introduction.

As with my other work, *Prehistoric Investigations 2* attempts to strike a balance between the needs of the general reader and those of the academic. For the latter, a comprehensive bibliography is provided.

Chapter descriptions

- *The first hominins.* Before the first humans came the age of the australopithecines – apes that walked upright like humans, but with brains no larger than those of chimpanzees. The famous 'Lucy' is a near-complete skeleton of an australopithecine, but her discovery came half a century after an equally epoch-making discovery. Whereas Lucy became a global sensation, the fossil known as the Taung Child was generally dismissed as the fossil of an ordinary ape. It was only because of the persistence of anthropologists Raymond Dart and Robert Broom that was it eventually accepted as a human ancestor - but how and why did apes begin walking upright in the first place?

- *Homo erectus.* In the late nineteenth century, Dutch anthropologist Eugène Dubois believed that he had found the missing link. His quest took him to the island of Java, then part of the Dutch East Indies. He found the first example of an extinct human that had lived significantly before *Homo sapiens* – but for all his protestations, it was not the missing link. However, Dubois's then-novel approach of seeking human origins through fossil hunting arguably gave birth to the discipline of palaeoanthropology.

- *The Acheulean hand axe.* A multifunction tool that remained in use, more or less unchanged, for 1,750,000 years. Ubiquitous in the archaeological record of Africa and western Eurasia, this most distinctive of prehistoric artefacts outlived the human species that invented it, *Homo erectus*, and it endured five times longer than *Homo sapiens* has existed. It was not the first tool to be made and used by early hominins, but it was the first to be recognised as a prehistoric implement. It played a pivotal role in demonstrating that humanity had existed for far longer than nineteenth-century scholars had believed.

- *Piltdown Man.* The story of the most notorious hoax in the history of palaeoanthropology. Early in 1912, Charles Dawson, a respected Sussex solicitor and keen amateur archaeologist, showed palaeontologist Arthur Smith Woodward two skull fragments he had found in a gravel pit near the village of Piltdown, Sussex. Piltdown Man became a scientific sensation. It was the subject of hundreds of articles in scientific journals. Books and, indeed, entire careers were devoted to its study. Then, in 1953, forty-one years after its discovery, it was exposed as a forgery. Who was the hoaxer, what were their motives, and how did the hoax go undetected for so long?

- *Muddle in the middle.* For many years, palaeoanthropologists believed that human evolution was a straightforward progression from the ape-like australopithecines, to the more human but still small-brained *Homo erectus*, to the larger-brained Neanderthals and *Homo sapiens*. But by the 1990s, it was becoming clear that this scenario was massively over-simplified and hid the true complexity of what became referred to as the 'muddle in the middle'. Genetics and the many fossil discoveries of the early twenty-first century have begun to clarify human evolution in the Middle Pleistocene and explain how *Homo sapiens* emerged into a world it shared with Neanderthals, Denisovans, and 'hobbits'.

- *First use of fire.* The ability to produce fire on demand is one that humans share with no other species in the world. Its importance to humanity is underlined by its recurrence in traditions around the world: the well-known story of how Prometheus stole the secret of fire from the gods for the benefit of humanity is only one such example. This is hardly surprising for a discovery that Darwin described as "*probably the greatest, excepting language, ever made by man*" - but how was it made?

- *Neanderthals.* The term 'Neanderthal' has been used in a negative context for decades, but why do Neanderthals get such a bad rap? Nineteenth century texts show that Neanderthals were studied in the context of then-current (and long-discredited) views about 'race'. The reputation of Neanderthals further suffered when French anthropologist Marcellin Boule published an influential study of a well-preserved skeleton of an elderly male from La Chapelle-aux-Saints and failed to recognise that his stooped posture was due to age-related osteoarthritis. How all of this came about, how Neanderthal reputations have slowly recovered, how it has been shown that they certainly were not dimwits, and how they live on in present-day populations is the subject of this chapter.

- *Early funerary practices.* Mourning and remembering the dead is a very ancient part of the human condition, but it may not be confined to modern or even archaic humans. Human funerary traditions could represent a pattern of behaviour with roots that lie millions of years in the past. Controversially, it has been suggested that ritual cannibalism may have been a frequent element of these early traditions.

- *The origins of Homo sapiens.* How our understanding of human origins has developed over the centuries, from the Great Chain of Being to modern theories. We still tend to think we are very different to anything else living on the planet Earth, even if we now recognise that we are indeed part of the animal kingdom. Evolutionary biologists, supported by genetic evidence, tell us that humans are closely related to African apes, as Darwin suggested in the nineteenth century. Since the publication of Huxley's *Evidence as to Man's place in Nature* and Darwin's *The Descent of Man* a century and a half ago, we have learned that we were not even the first human species, but comparative newcomers. In the last forty years, theories have come and gone as to our origins. Only now, helped by accurately dated fossils and more powerful genetic techniques, are palaeoanthropologists beginning to learn the real picture.

- *Prehistoric Art.* The discovery of the first cave art shattered nineteenth-century perceptions that the people of that era were primitive savages. More recently, archaeologists have discovered the existence of an even earlier cave art tradition, far from Europe in Southeast Asia. Did the two traditions have a common origin, still further back in time, or did they arise independently? Predating these two cave art traditions are two separate abstract graphic traditions from South Africa. Did figurative art arise from these or similar abstract traditions, and how did the abstract traditions themselves arise?

- *Early seafarers.* The oldest-known boats are only around 12,000 years old, but seafaring could predate the emergence of modern humans. This chapter investigates the possible use of boats by Neanderthals, the first settlement of Australia, the Bronze Age boats discovered at North Ferriby, Yorkshire, Polynesian voyaging in the Pacific, and how Bronze Age travellers might have deduced that the Earth is not flat.

- *Early metallurgy.* Only a few metals are commonly found in the native state. In antiquity – and indeed for centuries after – only seven were known: gold, silver, copper, lead, tin, iron, and mercury. Of these, only gold, silver, and copper occur in significant quantities in the native state, and of these, only copper is suitable for toolmaking. Nevertheless, it was these seven metals that were responsible for the technological and economic systems upon which the ancient world was built.

Dramatis Personae

Svante Arrhenius	(1859-1927)	Swedish chemist.
Davidson Black	(1884-1934)	Canadian anthropologist at the Peking Union Medical School, Beijing.
Jacques Boucher de Perthes	(1788-1868)	French customs official.
Marcellin Boule	(1861-1942)	French anthropologist, Professor of Palaeontology at the Muséum National d'Histoire Naturelle, Paris.
Henri Breuil	(1877-1961)	French archaeologist.
Robert Broom	(1866-1951)	Scottish palaeontologist.
George Busk	(1807-1886)	British surgeon and palaeontologist, Hunterian Professor of Comparative Anatomy and Physiology at the Royal College of Surgeons.
Guy Callendar	(1898-1964)	British engineer.
Alexander Cave	(1900-2001)	British anatomist.
Jean Clottes	(born 1933)	French prehistorian.
Carleton Coon	(1904-1981)	American anthropologist, Professor of Anthropology at the University of Pennsylvania.
Yves Coppens	(1934-2022)	French palaeontologist and member of the International Afar Research Expedition.
Raymond Dart	(1893-1988)	Australian anatomist and anthropologist, Professor of Anatomy at the University of the Witwatersrand in Johannesburg.
Charles Dawson	(1864-1916)	British solicitor and amateur archaeologist.
Charles Darwin	(1804-1892)	British naturalist, co-proposer of the theory of evolution through natural selection.
Marcelino de Sautuola	(1831-1888)	Spanish archaeologist, discoverer of Altamira.
Robin Dennell	(born 1947)	British archaeologist

Eugène Dubois	(1858-1940)	Dutch physician and palaeoanthropologist.
Sir Grafton Elliot Smith	(1871-1937)	Australian anatomist, Professor of Anatomy at University College London.
Sir John Evans	(1823-1908)	British businessman and scholar.
John Frere	(1740-1807)	English landowner and local politician.
Johann Carl Fuhlrott	(1803-1877)	German schoolteacher and amateur naturalist.
William King Gregory	(1876-1970)	American palaeontologist, Da Costa Professor of Zoology at the American Museum of Natural History, New York.
Ernst Haeckel	(1834-1919)	German zoologist.
Christopher Henshilwood	(born 1951)	South African archaeologist.
Aleš Hrdlička	(1869-1943)	Czech anthropologist, Curator of Physical Anthropology at the United States National Museum (now the Smithsonian Institution), Washington, DC.
Thomas Henry Huxley	(1825-1895)	British biologist, Professor of Natural History at the Royal School of Mines (now part of Imperial College London).
Donald Johanson	(born 1943)	American paleoanthropologist and member of the International Afar Research Expedition.
Charles Keeling	(1928-2005)	American climate scientist.
Sir Arthur Keith	(1866-1955)	Scottish anatomist and anthropologist, Hunterian Professor and conservator of the Hunterian Museum of the Royal College of Surgeons of England.
William King	(1809-1886)	Anglo-Irish geologist.
Ralph von Koenigsberg	(1902-1982)	Dutch palaeontologist.
Sir Edwin Ray Lankester	(1847-1929)	British zoologist and evolutionary biologist.
Louis Leakey	(1903-1972)	Kenyan-British palaeoanthropologist.
Mary Leakey *nee* Nicol	(1913-1996)	British palaeoanthropologist.
Richard Leakey	(1944-2022)	Kenyan palaeoanthropologist and conservationist, son of Louis and Mary Leakey.
Sir Wilfrid Le Gros Clark	(1895-1971)	British palaeontologist, Professor of Anatomy at the University of Oxford.

Carl von Linné *styled* Carolus Linnaeus	(1707-1778)	Swedish naturalist.
Richard Lydekker	(1849-1915)	British palaeontologist
Sir Charles Lyell	(1797-1875)	Scottish geologist
Owen Lovejoy	(born 1943)	American anthropologist and anatomist at Kent State University, Ohio.
Léonce-Pierre Manouvrier	(1850-1927)	French anthropologist.
Othniel Charles Marsh	(1831-1899)	American palaeontologist, Professor of Palaeontology at Yale University.
Sir Paul Mellars	(1939-1922)	British archaeologist.
Gerrit Smith Miller, Jr.	(1869-1956)	American zoologist, Curator of Mammals at the United States National Museum (now the Smithsonian Institution), Washington, DC.
Steven Mithen	(born 1960)	British archaeologist.
Ashley Montagu *born* Israel Ehrenberg	(1905-1999)	British-American anthropologist.
Hallam Movius	(1907-1987)	American archaeologist.
Kenneth Oakley	(1911-1981)	British anthropologist and geologist at the British Museum (Natural History), London.
Henry Fairfield Osborn	(1857-1935)	American palaeontologist, President of the American Museum of Natural History, New York.
Charles Phillips	(1901-1985)	British archaeologist.
Joseph Prestwich	(1812-1896)	British businessman and scholar.
John T. Robinson	(1923-2001)	South African palaeontologist.
Vincent Sarich	(1934-2012)	American molecular biologist at the University of California, Berkeley.
Hermann Schaaffhausen	(1816-1893)	German anatomist, Professor of Anatomy at the University of Bonn.
Gustav Schwalbe	(1844-1916)	German anthropologist, Professor of Anatomy at the University of Strasburg.
Ralph Solecki	(1917-2019)	American archaeologist.
William Sollas	(1849-1936)	British anthropologist and geologist.
William L. Straus, Jr	(1900-1981)	American anatomist.
Christopher Stringer	(born 1947)	British palaeoanthropologist.
Maurice Taieb	(1935-2021)	French geologist and member of the International Afar Research Expedition.

Nainoa Thompson	(born 1953)	Polynesian navigator.
Philip Tobias	(1925-2012)	South African anthropologist.
Philip Tobias	(1925-2012)	South African anthropologist.
Sir Arthur Smith Woodward	(1864-1944)	British palaeontologist, Keeper of Geology at the British Museum (Natural History), London.
Edward Wright	(1918-2001)	British businessman and archaeologist.
Lucilio Vanini *styled* Giulio Cesare Vanini	(1585-1619)	Italian philosopher.
Rudolf Virchow	(1821-1902)	German pathologist.
Alfred Russel Wallace	(1823-1913)	Welsh naturalist, co-proposer with Darwin of the theory of evolution through natural selection.
David Waterston	(1871-1942)	Scottish anatomist, Professor of Anatomy at King's College, London.
Franz Weidenreich	(1873-1948)	German anatomist.
Joseph Weiner	(1915-1982)	South Africa-born biologist, Reader in Physical Anthropology at the University of Oxford.
Tim White	(born 1950)	American palaeoanthropologist.
Allan Wilson	(1934-1991)	New Zealand molecular biologist at the University of California, Berkeley.
Richard Wrangham	(born 1948)	British primatologist.
Solly Zuckerman	(1904-1993)	British zoologist and government advisor.

01: The first hominins

Part I: The Taung Child

"A scorn for accepted opinion"

Not yet out of his twenties, Dart was highly regarded as an anatomist but, by his later own admission, "*not only controversial, but upsetting and potentially dangerous*"[1]. Anatomist Sir Arthur Keith, who had recommended him for his new position, did so with "*a certain amount of trepidation*" and said, "*Of his knowledge, his power of intellect and of imagination, there could be no question; what rather frightened me was his flightiness, his scorn for accepted opinion, the unorthodoxy of his outlook*"[2].

Dart had made a fossil find that would eventually be regarded as one of the most important in the history of palaeoanthropology. He had found the skull of an ape that walked upright; a transitional form between small-brained, arboreal apes and large-brained ground-living humans. He had found a possible 'missing link' between apes and humans and fired the starting gun on an as-yet unresolved battle between South and East Africa to be recognised as the cradle of the human lineage.

But the announcement of this epoch-making discovery was met with near-total disbelief.

Dart

Raymond Dart was born in 1893 in Toowong, a suburb of Brisbane, Australia. He was the fifth of nine children born to farmer and trader Samuel Dart and Eliza Dart (*nee* Brimblecome). The young Dart was an able student who gained a scholarship to Ipswich Grammar School before studying geology and zoology at the University of Queensland. He then went on to study medicine at the University of Sydney, where he studied under the Scottish anatomist James Wilson. Dart completed his studies in 1917 and enlisted in the Army in 1918. He was assigned to the Australian Army Medical Corps with the rank of Captain and posted to Britain in July. He arrived in London in September, although the Armistice just three months later meant that he never saw any action[3].

However, the end of the war did not mean the end of Dart's military service. As a doctor, he was sent to France to attend to the medical needs of the army personnel still there in large numbers. This was a source of growing frustration for Dart as he had by now been offered a position as an anatomy demonstrator by anatomist and fellow Australian Grafton Elliot Smith as the latter prepared to take up the post of Professor of Anatomy at University College London. Dart notes that when asked if he would accept the post, "*my knees went weak at the thought*". The Army bureaucracy involved in being demobilised in Britain rather than

Australia was considerable, but Dart eventually returned to civilian life on 18 October 1919[3,4].

At UCL, Dart described working under Elliot Smith as *"my student dream come true"*[4]. He soon immersed himself in a wide range of problems allotted to him by Elliot Smith, but in September 1920 he was awarded a one-year Rockefeller Foundation fellowship in the United States. He was granted an unpaid leave of absence for the 1920-21 academic year and left for the United States on 24 September. The twelve-month program of studying and teaching took Dart to Washington University in St Louis, MO, the Woods Hole Marine Biological Station at Cape Cod, MA, the American Association of Anatomists in Philadelphia, PA, and the anatomy departments of the major medical schools in the Midwest and the Northeast United States and Canada. The latter included Cincinnati Medical School, where Dart met medical student and anatomy demonstrator Dora Tyree. The couple were married on 3 September 1921, just before Dart was due to return to Britain. Back in London with his new wife, Dart resumed his work at UCL in October. He must have felt his career as an anatomist was moving in the right direction, but it would take an unexpected turn a year later[3].

The newly founded University of the Witwatersrand in Johannesburg had a vacancy for the Professor of Anatomy, and Elliot Smith intimated that he was putting Dart's name forward for the position. Dart, horrified at the idea, immediately turned down the offer but Elliot Smith, his former mentor James Wilson, and Sir Arthur Keith eventually persuaded him to reconsider. Arriving in South Africa early in 1923, Dart found that the facilities at his new post were basic, to say the least: the Anatomy Department's student labs lacked gas, electric plugs, water taps, and compressed air. The Medical School did not possess a library, and the dissecting room had been used as a sports hall. Cadavers lay on dissecting tables, only partially covered[3].

Dart recalled that *"Our first inspection of these conditions left my wife, who I had taken from her medical studies at Cincinnati, in tears – a woman's prerogative I rather envied at that moment"*[4]. It certainly was not what he was used to at UCL, but not being one to feel sorry for himself, Dart set to work to improve matters in the Anatomy Department. He obtained funds to redecorate the Department premises and pitched in with his students to clear weeds away from the entrance to the Medical School. Meanwhile, Dora set to work with a sewing machine to make proper shrouds for the cadavers. Finally, he set to work to try to establish a library for the Medical School[3].

An important discovery

The lack of equipment and medical literature at the University led Dart to revive his interest in anthropology, which he had first developed when working with Elliot Smith at UCL. In July 1924, he encouraged his students to bring in any fossils they came across during their summer vacation, offering a five-pound prize (worth about £120 today) from his own pocket for the most interesting discovery[4].

Although it did not win her the prize (which was voted on by the students rather than awarded by Dart), anatomy demonstrator and medical student Josephine Salmons brought in the fossilized skull of a baboon that had been found at the Buxton Limeworks near the town of Taung (then known as Taungs). Dart noted that *"this valuable fossil had been blasted out of the limestone cliff formation – at a vertical depth of 50 feet* [15 m] *and a horizontal depth of 200 feet* [60 m] – *at Taungs, which lies 80 miles* [130 km] *north of Kimberley on the main line to Rhodesia, in Bechuanaland, by operatives of the Northern Lime Company*"[5].

The notable South African palaeoanthropologist Philip Tobias, who later studied under Dart, has filled in some detail on the find and the momentous sequence of events it set in motion[6]. Tobias notes that fossil baboons had been found at Taung as early as 1919, although Dart was unaware of this at the time. In the southern hemisphere winter of 1924, E.G. Izod, a director of the Northern Lime Company, visited Taung and noted the fossilised monkey skull in the office of site manager A.E. Spiers. Izod took the specimen back to Johannesburg and his son Pat Izod subsequently showed it to his friends at the University of the Witwatersrand, including Salmons. Dart[4] gives a slightly different version of events: "*The previous night she* [Salmons] *had visited a family friend, Mr E. G. Ezod, a director of the Northern Lime Company, and had noticed a fossil skull on the mantel above the fireplace. It had come from the Company's mine at Taungs in the Bechuanaland Protectorate*".

After "*careering down the hill in my model-T Ford*", Dart discussed the find with geologist Robert Young, Professor of Geology at the University, who in turn asked A.E. Campbell, general manager of the Northern Lime Company, to arrange for any fossil-bearing rocks to be kept for Dart. Young was due to investigate further lime deposits in the Taung region in November 1924, and he agreed to visit Spiers and see if anything of interest had been found. Among the specimens that Spiers passed to him was a skull noticeably larger than that of a baboon, which had been found by a quarryman named M. De Bruyn. While there is some uncertainty surrounding the exact circumstance of the find, it seems that both De Bruyn and Spiers realised that the skull was not just another baboon[4,6].

The skull was, however, almost entirely encased and rock. Dart had neither the experience in preparing fossils nor the necessary tools to do so. Nor were there any local experts to assist. He procured a hammer and chisel from a local hardware shop and borrowed one of his wife's knitting needles. Thus equipped, he set about as best he could to extract the fossil from the rocky material[4].

After several weeks of work, Dart was able to see that the skull had belonged to a juvenile anthropoid ape[1], not a monkey. The remains comprised the face, part of the skull, the complete lower jaw, and a brain endocast (a cast of the inside of the braincase that had formed naturally when material within the skull hardened to rock). The brain was small, like that of an ape, but the teeth were more humanlike than apelike. Even more remarkably, the foramen magnum (the opening in the skull through which the spinal column passes) was located centrally at the base of the skull. This central placement is an adaptation for walking upright that is seen only in humans. In present-day apes, the foramen magnum is located at the rear. This meant that the fossilised ape must have been a biped – an ape that walked on two legs. Early in 1925, Dart submitted his conclusions to the journal *Nature*, naming the species represented by the Taung fossil skull *Australopithecus africanus* ('Southern ape of Africa'). It was of importance because "*it exhibits an extinct race of apes intermediate between living anthropoids and man*"[5].

The Taung skull would become known as the Taungs Baby, although from the start it was

---

[1] Anthropoid apes, commonly known as the great apes, include chimpanzees, bonobos, gorillas, and orangutans. The group does not include gibbons (lesser apes).

known that it represented an individual that was beyond infancy. Sir Arthur Keith believed that the individual was *"in the fourth year of growth"*[7], which is in full agreement with present-day estimates that it was 3.73 – 3.93 years old at death[8]. More recently, it has become known as the Taung Child. By whatever name, the Taung fossil is what was then called a *hominid* and is now called a *hominin*. A hominin is defined as a human or anything that is more closely related to a human than to an anthropoid ape. The definition of the old term, hominid, has now been expanded to include anthropoid apes.

Dart discussed the upcoming announcement with his friend B. G. Paver, a news editor for the *Star* newspaper in Johannesburg who had a keen interest in science. Paver agreed to embargo the story until after the article had appeared in *Nature*. In the 1920s, and indeed for decades after, long-distance mail was sent by ship, and mailboats from South Africa took around three weeks to reach London. Adding to the confusion, journals published in London took a similar amount of time to find their way to South Africa although news of important announcements would generally precede them. Such lags are difficult to imagine for anybody used to email and online publications. When the publication date for Dart's article drew near, Paver cabled *Nature* to enquire as to whether they had received it, and if so, did they intend to publish it. He was advised that the article had been received, but that the claims it made were so far-reaching that it had been referred to various experts in Britain to see if it was suitable for publication. Paver replied that he would not embargo the story beyond the *Star's* evening edition of 3 February[4].

The *Star* duly broke the story on the evening of 3 February, and morning papers around the world the next day reported the discovery of the 'missing link' in South Africa. Dart soon received congratulatory messages from Elliot Smith and his staff in London, the former (and future) South African Prime Minister Jan Smuts, and Scottish palaeontologist Robert Broom, now based in Cape Province[4]. Broom would go on to become a redoubtable ally of Dart.

A sceptical reception

Its hand presumably forced, *Nature* published Dart's article on 7 February, but in contrast to the reaction to the report in the *Star*, the reception was lukewarm. One week after Dart's letter appeared in *Nature*, the journal published the responses of four leading anatomists, including Keith and Elliot Smith.

Sir Arthur Keith praised Dart's clear descriptions and the accuracy of his drawings, but he reserved judgment until more details were available. He was sceptical of Dart's claims and said that *Australopithecus* was probably more closely allied to chimpanzees and gorillas than to humans[9]. Anatomist Wynfrid Duckworth was also dubious. He was *"fairly certain"* that some of the humanlike characters Dart had emphasised were *"related preponderantly to the youthfulness of the specimen"*[10]. Palaeontologist Sir Arthur Smith Woodward, who had announced Piltdown Man as *Eoanthropus dawsoni*, could see nothing *"in the orbits, nasal bones, and canine teeth definitely nearer to the human condition than the corresponding parts of the skull of a modern young chimpanzee"*. He even criticised Dart for introducing the term *Australopithecus*, which he complained was a *"barbarous"* mishmash of Latin and Greek[11].

Dart's former mentor Grafton Elliot Smith was more sympathetic. He cautioned that *"it would be rash to push the chain of support of the South African anthropoid's nearer kinship with man"* and that "*Many of the features cited by Prof. Dart as evidence of human affinities, especially the features of the jaw and teeth mentioned by him, are not unknown in the young of the giant anthropoids and even in the adult gibbon*". His overall view, though, was that when further evidence was available, he would be "*quite prepared to admit that an ape has been found the brain of which points the way to the emergence of the distinctive brain and mind of mankind*". He concluded that an African origin for humanity would only be a surprise "*to those who do not know their Charles Darwin*"[12].

In an article appearing in the *British Medical Journal* on the same day as the *Nature* responses, Keith[13] expressed doubt over Dart's claims that *Australopithecus* was a biped. "*We cannot be certain of posture until we find a bone of the lower limb. One cannot see any character in the skull which justifies the supposition of an erect posture*", he wrote. He nonetheless stressed the importance of the find and was full of praise for Dart: "*it is not only a missing link but a very complete and important one, but it lies altogether at the anthropoid end of the chain which culminated in man. It is a discovery which places Professor Dart's name in the front rank of students of the evolution of man and anthropoid*".

Dart was up against the problem that his claims contradicted the then-prevalent but incorrect 'brains first' model, which stated that large brains were the defining feature of humanity and must have emerged before any other aspects, including bipedalism[14]. Just over twelve years earlier, the discovery had been announced of *Eoanthropus dawsoni* ('Dawson's dawn man'), commonly known as Piltdown Man[15]. As required by the 'brains first' model, *Eoanthropus* was a being with a large, humanlike brain and an apelike jawbone. Not until 1953 would Piltdown Man be exposed as a forgery[16]. A second erroneous notion was that the origins of humanity were very ancient and that the divergence from the anthropoid apes had occurred at the start of the Miocene epoch[17,18], or even earlier[19]. Radiometric dating techniques[2] in the 1920s were crude by today's standards, but the then accepted date of 19 million years ago for Eocene/Miocene boundary[18] was reasonably accurate. The currently accepted date is 23 million years ago. The third then-prevalent misconception was that the origins of humanity were to be found in Asia rather than Africa. Although Darwin had proposed an African origin for humanity[20], his view had fallen out of favour by the early twentieth century. A popular model was that successively more 'advanced' humans had spread out from a 'centre' somewhere in Asia, displacing more primitive types to peripheral regions, including Africa[21]. Consistent with this view, the earliest-known fossil humans at this time were *Pithecanthropus erectus* from Java (Java Man) and *Sinanthropus pekinensis* from China (Beijing Man). Both are now classed as *Homo erectus*.

However, the main problem for Dart was his location, far from the world-class facilities that he had enjoyed access to while he was in London. South Africa at that time was largely lacking the resources that would typically be used to study a fossil find of such potential importance. There were no comparative anatomical collections comparable to those of the Hunterian Museum in London, or the Natural History Museum in Paris, nor were there any major reference libraries. Palaeontology is a discipline that relies heavily on comparative studies and these issues were clearly of concern to the four anatomists who haired their views

---

[2] All radiometric dating techniques work on the same basic principle, i.e., the decay of radioactive isotopes such as radiocarbon (^{14}C). The rate of decay is known and by comparing the abundance of the isotope with that of its decay products or its expected initial abundance, the age of a sample can be determined. Examples of such techniques include radiocarbon (^{14}C), argon-argon ($^{40}Ar/^{39}Ar$), potassium-argon ($^{40}Ka/^{40}Ar$), uranium-series (U-series), and cosmogenic nuclide ($^{26}Al/^{10}Be$) dating.

in the 14 February edition of *Nature*[14]. Keith, for example, had noted that Dart *"regrets he has not access to literature which gives the data for gauging the age of young anthropoids"*[9] and in his BMJ article had said that *"those who have charge of much larger collections than were at the disposal of Professor Dart have a somewhat unfair advantage over him"*[13]. Similarly, Duckworth stressed the need for a *"thorough survey of a collection of immature (anthropoid ape) crania"*[10].

Some of the issues could have been resolved by sending the Taung skull to London, where they could be studied by others with the aid of the reference collections and literature that Dart was lacking. But Dart was unwilling to do so. Since the end of World War I, there had been a strong emphasis on nation-building and self-determination among South African citizens and a desire for a more independent position for the Union of South Africa[3] within the British Empire[4]. Science played a major role in this ethos, and while sending the Taung skull to London would have been considered to be best practice at the time, it would have gone against this evolving local tradition[14]. One option would have been for Dart to travel to London with the Taung skull and avail himself of the collections and other resources there. The University of the Witwatersrand offered to pay for his passage – but only in exchange for the fossil. Dart declined the offer because he did not want to give up the fossil, and he did not want a lengthy absence from his new department (again, we must remember that regular long-haul air travel was still decades in the future)[4]. Another option would have been to have sent a plaster cast of the Taung skull to London in lieu of the fossil itself and Keith – realising that the fossil would not be coming to London – wrote to Dart on 3 June enquiring about purchasing such a cast. Here again, though, Dart was up against the difficulties of being so far from the academic establishment of Europe. In London, there were companies that specialised in making anatomically accurate plaster casts. In Johannesburg, there were none[14].

In the meantime, Dart had been contacted by the organisers of the South African delegation to the British Empire Exhibition, held at Wembley from 23 April to 1 November 1924. The Exhibition was intended to showcase the diversity of the cultures and industries of the countries making up the Empire and to promote understanding and commerce within it. Dart was invited to put together an exhibition featuring the Taung skull. He agreed and engaged a local artist to produce a passable model of the skull, sculptures illustrating Dart's impression of what the Taung Child would have looked like, and diagrams showing the place of *Australopithecus* in the human family tree[4]. Robert Broom, mistakenly believing that Dart intended to send the skull itself, urged him to reconsider. *"Send a cast if you like, but don't let the skull out of your hands and I really think you should not send it to London at all"*, he wrote. *"After the sneers of the English I don't think you ought to favour them by* [sending] *anything but casts or photographs"*[14,22].

Unfortunately, this early attempt at science outreach backfired rather badly. Keith, having

---

[3] The predecessor state to the present-day Republic of South Africa, the Union of South Africa came into existence in 1910 with the unification of the former British colonies of Cape, Natal, Transvaal, and Orange River into a single state. It became a republic in 1961.

[4] The British Empire would become the British Commonwealth of Nations in 1931 following the Balfour Declaration of 1926. The latter proclaimed that the United Kingdom and the Dominions (Australia, New Zealand, South Africa, Canada, Newfoundland (which did not become a province of Canada until 1949), and the Irish Free State (now the Republic of Ireland or officially, simply Ireland)) were autonomous and equal communities.

viewed the exhibit at Wembley, wrote a letter in the 4 July edition of *Nature*. He noted that he and others had preferred to reserve judgment on *Australopithecus* "*to await an examination of the fossil remains, or failing such an opportunity, to study exact casts of them.*" He complained that "*students of fossil man have not been given an opportunity of purchasing these casts; if they wish to study them they must visit and peer at them in a glass case which has been given a place in the South African pavilion*". Of Dart's claims that the Taung skull represented an intermediate between anthropoid apes and humans, Keith said, "*An examination of the casts exhibited at Wembley will satisfy zoologists that this claim is preposterous*". He then reiterated his earlier view that the skull had belonged to a young anthropoid ape, which "*at the most represent a genus within the Gorilla – Chimpanzee group*". He noted that Robert Broom had estimated that the skull was from "*probably not earlier than Pleistocene*[5]"[26] and stated that "*Students of man's evolution have sufficient evidence to justify them in supposing that the phylum*[6] *of man had separated from that of anthropoid apes early in the Miocene period. The Taungs ape is much too late in the scale of time to have any place in man's ancestry*" and as a result, Dart's proposed family tree could be likened to claiming "*a modern Sussex peasant as the ancestor of William the Conqueror*"[7].

Relations between Dart and Keith had hitherto remained cordial, despite the latter's scepticism[14], but now they began to deteriorate. In the 26 September edition of *Nature*, Dart complained that Keith, in his 4 July article, had "*attempted to show first that I called the Taungs skull a 'missing link' and secondly, that it is not a 'missing link'. As a matter of fact, though I undoubtedly regard the description as an adequate one, I have not used the term 'missing link'*". Dart went on to note that not only had Keith used the term himself in his 14 February article in the *British Medical Journal*, but he had stated that the skull was a very complete and important 'missing link'. "*After stating his views so definitely in February, it seems strange that, in July, he should state that "this claim is preposterous"*". Dart maintained that Keith, in any case, was wrong. His views only went to show "*how unsatisfactory the study of the replica can be in the absence of the original*"[27].

Keith hit straight back, claiming that Dart was "*under a misapprehension in supposing that I have in any way or at any time altered my opinion regarding the fossil ape discovered at Taungs*". He reminded readers that in the 14 February edition of *Nature*, both he and Elliot Smith had expressed the view that the Taung ape belonged to the same group as the chimpanzee and gorilla. He now reiterated this viewpoint and that it was "*preposterous*" to create a new grouping for it. As to it being a 'missing link', Keith wrote, "*The position which Prof. Dart assigns to the Taungs ape in the*

---

[5] The Pleistocene is the geological epoch preceding the current Holocene. It began around 2.580 million years ago and ended around 17,000 years ago. The boundary between it and the preceding Pliocene epoch is currently defined by the Global Stratotype Section and Point (GSSP) of the Gelasian Stage at Monte San Nicola in Sicily, currently dated at 2.580 million years ago. This followed a redefinition of the boundary in 2009 from the GSSP of the Calabrian Stage at Vrica, Calabria, Italy, which is dated at 1.806 million years ago. The change was made so that the onset of major glaciation, previously referred to as Plio-Pleistocene, could be accommodated wholly within the Pleistocene[23]. However, prior to 1948, the Calabrian Stage (1.806 million to 774,000 years ago) was considered to be part of the Pliocene and was so defined in 1910[24,25]. Note, however, that the type sections used to define these geological stages are not the same as those that were used in the early twentieth century, and radiometric methods used to date them were crude by today's standards.

[6] The term phylum is being used to mean 'race' or 'stock' rather than in the taxonomic sense, where it is a ranking between Kingdom and Class. For example, humans (and indeed all vertebrates) belong to the Phylum *Chordata*. Chordates are animals with a *notochord* (a stiffening rod such as a spinal column) at any stage of their life cycle.

genealogical tree of man and ape has no foundation in fact"[28].

Broom

Robert Broom was 27 years older than Dart. He was born in Paisley, Scotland, in 1866. After qualifying as a medical doctor at the University of Glasgow in 1889, he twice visited the United States to explore opportunities for a career in medicine. He then developed an interest in the anatomy and embryology of Australian monotreme and marsupial mammals and moved to Australia in 1892 where he combined medical practice with zoological studies. He collected plant, animal, and fossil specimens and his publications concerning the anatomy and embryology of Australian mammals established him as a comparative anatomist. In 1896, Broom, while on a visit to London, had a chance to examine some fossil reptiles at the British Museum (Natural History)[7] that had been unearthed in the Karroo region of South Africa. These fossils showed peculiar mammal-like characteristics, that had led some to suspect that they might hold clues to the evolutionary origin of the mammals. We now know that these mammal-like reptiles were indeed the ancestors of modern mammals. Both belong to a group known as the therapsids, early fossil examples of which have been found in the fossil sequence of the Karroo. The mammal-like reptiles lived during the Late Permian (260 million years ago), predating the dinosaurs[29].

Broom now decided that he wanted to move to South Africa to study the Karroo fossils while continuing to practice medicine. He moved there in 1897, but he was unable to secure a medical post in the Karroo region and with his wife unhappy with the situation, returned to Britain in May 1898. It was only a few months before Broom soon tried again. He set up a medical practice in Port Elizabeth but soon took over a practice in Pearston, a small town in the eastern Karroo. Here he had the opportunity to collect and study fossils, and he uncovered a large number of important specimens that confirmed the link between mammal-like reptiles and modern mammals. In 1903, he was appointed Professor of Zoology and Geology at Victoria College, Stellenbosch, Cape Provence. He worked closely with the South African Museum in Cape Town, providing them with many fossils, and was made an honorary curator there in 1905. However, by 1910, his relationship with the Museum had deteriorated after the government revoked a rail pass that he had used on his fossil-collecting expeditions to the Karroo. The pass had been provided on the condition that any fossils he found were donated to the Museum, albeit the latter was not government-run and was not involved in the decision to revoke his pass. Broom nevertheless stopped providing the Museum with fossils. He resigned from his position at Victoria College and returned to medical practice, this time in Springs, to the east of Johannesburg[22].

This did not mean an end to Broom's fossil-collecting activities. He established relations with local collectors, whom he paid to bring him specimens. These he would describe in

---

[7] Until 1963, the Natural History Museum in Kensington, London was a department of the British Museum. It was officially known as the British Museum (Natural History), commonly abbreviated to BM(NH). It became an independent museum in 1963, but it retained the original name until 1992, by which time it had merged with the neighbouring Geological Museum. The formal name was rarely used outside academia and the museum was generally referred to as the Natural History Museum. Here, I follow common practice in referring to the museum by what was its official name at the time.

print and sometimes sell, on occasions, to overseas buyers. His principal source was a man named Rev. J. H. Whaits, for the services of whom he often competed with his former colleagues at the South African Museum. On one occasion, in 1911, the BM(NH) sent a representative to South Africa to purchase fossils with funds that could comfortably outbid Broom. Whaits sold his entire collection at a price Broom had no hope of matching, infuriating the latter who now had no opportunity to study and describe the material before it left South Africa[22].

The episode left Broom with an enduring dislike of the British scientific establishment, which goes a long way to explaining why he so strongly opposed the idea of Dart sending the Taung skull to London. He also found a way to outmanoeuvre both the South African Museum and the BM(NH). He had previously corresponded with and eventually met American palaeontologist Henry Fairfield Osborn, President of the American Museum of Natural History, New York, and he had travelled to New York to study their collection of Permian mammal-like reptiles from Texas. In 1912, with the AMNH now interested in obtaining South African fossils, Broom persuaded Osborn to hire a local collector. Whaits was duly engaged on the provisor that Broom was given priority in describing the finds. Unfortunately, this deepened Broom's rift with the South African Museum to the extent that by the early 1920s he had been banned from studying fossils there and was generally *persona non grata* with the South African Association for the Advancement of Science[22]. However, his reputation remained high in Britain, and he was elected a Fellow of the Royal Society in May 1920.

In his congratulatory letter to Dart on 8 February, Broom expressed a desire to see the Taung skull for himself and proposed to make the trip up to Johannesburg. He gave no date for doing so, and on 20 February he turned up in Dart's laboratory unannounced. According to Dart[4], Broom completely ignored him and his staff, made straight for the fossil skull, and dropped to his knees in front of it before looking up at the stunned onlookers. Nobody, least of all Dart, seems to have been troubled by this entrance. He and Dora were happy to host Broom over the weekend while the latter made his first study of the Taung skull[3].

A few days after his visit, Broom submitted an article to *Nature*, which appeared in the 18 April edition of the journal[26]. In his 4 July letter to *Nature*, Sir Arthur Keith had been happy to cite the Pleistocene date from this article, but he conveniently ignored that Broom's article also contained the same family tree as the one he had so strongly objected to at Wembley. Broom's article was the first wholly positive appraisal to appear since the initial announcement ten weeks earlier. It should be noted that at this point he was the only person other than Dart to have seen the actual skull as opposed to drawings and the unsatisfactory cast exhibited at Wembley.

Frustration

Dart's reluctance to allow the Taung skull to travel meant that only one other Northern Hemisphere scientist examined it during the 1920s. This was Czech anthropologist Aleš Hrdlička, Curator of Physical Anthropology at the Smithsonian Institution in Washington, DC. Dart also arranged for him to visit the Buxton Limeworks, where he spent three days. Hrdlička's article appeared in the October 1925 edition of the *American Journal of Physical*

Anthropology, shortly after Dart and Keith's spat in the 26 September edition of *Nature*. But in it, he chose to reserve judgement: "*Just what relation this fossil form bears, on one hand, to the human phylum, and on the other to the chimpanzee and gorilla, can only be properly determined after the specimen is well identified, for which are needed additional and adult specimens*"[30]. As Broom later noted, "*his conclusions do not help us very much*"[31].

In London, resistance to Dart's conclusions continued. Solly Zuckerman, famous for his research projects for the British government during World War II, was working as an anatomist at the London Zoological Society from 1928 to 1932. With access to a reference collection that included 120 chimpanzee skulls, including 40 subadults, he concluded "*It is unreliable to draw hard-and-fast conclusions from Professor Dart's excellent plaster cast, and therefore difficult in the face of these conflicting views, to make any statement. I may mention, however, that in the cast the canines in no way differ from those of any of the young anthropoids*"[32].

For his part, Dart continued his restoration work on the Taung skull and wrote a monograph about it[4]. But he published nothing further on *Australopithecus* for the remainder of the decade. Broom, returning from a visit to the United States and Britain, wrote, "*I do not know what he intends to do*". He noted in frustration that "*the scientific world has apparently quietly dismissed any claims the Taungs Anthropoid Ape might have to be near the point of the origin of Man, and the general opinion seems to be that it is only a Chimpanzee*". He continued to maintain "*that Australopithecus is not a Chimpanzee, and that it is an Anthropoid Ape very much nearer to the form which gave rise to Man than either the Chimpanzee or the Gorilla, and that it is thus by far the most important fossil ever discovered*". He noted that the milk teeth of the Taung skull resembled those of a human infant than an infant chimpanzee[31].

Further 'man-apes' are found

What was needed was more fossil evidence, and as a seasoned fossil hunter, Broom was well-placed to obtain it. But he remained firmly out of favour with the South African scientific community, and to make matters worse, his medical practice was in decline. By 1933, now struggling to make ends meet, he was practising medicine at Maquassi in Transvaal. His fortunes turned a year later when Jan Smuts, after lobbying from Dart, pressured the government into providing funds for him to be appointed Keeper of Vertebrate Palaeontology and Anthropology at the Transvaal Museum in Pretoria. At the same time, the University of the Witwatersrand awarded him an honorary science doctorate, and the Medical School there appointed him Lecturer in Comparative Anatomy. He was now 68[3].

In 1936, he instigated new searches for early human fossils. In late July that year, he visited the limestone caves at Sterkfontein near Krugersdorp, 25 km (15 miles) northwest of Johannesburg. "*Mr. G. W. Barlow, the very understanding manager of the lime works there and on whom I had impressed the importance of keeping his eyes open for a Taungs ape, handed me the brain cast of what appeared to be a large anthropoid*". Over the next few days, assisted by workers at the site, Broom recovered the greater part of an adult skull, including the upper part of the face, the detached right upper jaw with three teeth, and a detached upper third molar (M_3). No lower jawbone or lower teeth were found. Broom noted that "*the newly-found primate probably agrees fairly closely with the Taungs ape*" but there were sufficient differences for him to place it in a new species, which he named *Australopithecus transvaalensis*[33]. A few weeks later, having had time to reconstruct the dentition of the new find, he reported that the upper dental arcade was humanlike and U-shaped, nothing like the V-shaped dental arcade of a chimpanzee or a gorilla. He concluded that "*the Sterkfontein ape at least is not a chimpanzee, and that it approaches man in quite a number of characters*"[34].

Finds continued. By 1938, finds at Sterkfontein included a lower third molar (M3), second premolar (P2), a canine, and the incisor portion of a lower jawbone. From the small lower jawbone portion, Broom now claimed that *Australopithecus transvaalensis* should be placed in a new genus, *Plesianthropus* ('near man'). Writing in the 27 August edition of *Nature*, he also reported the discovery of a skull, a right portion of a lower jawbone, and several teeth at Kromdraai, a fossil-bearing breccia-filled cave a short distance from Sterkfontein. The discovery was made by a schoolboy, who noticed the remains in a rocky outcrop at the top of a hill. After making enquiries with the boy's mother, Broom "*found the boy with four of what are perhaps the most valuable teeth in the world in his trouser pocket*". The boy later led Broom to the site, where he recovered the other remains. The skull was of another anthropoid ape, midway in size between that of a chimpanzee and that of a gorilla but resembling neither. From the preserved portion of the braincase, he estimated the cranial capacity to have been around 600 cc. The dentition was humanlike in shape, but much larger. The second premolar (P2) differed "*very markedly*" from that of *Plesianthropus* and was fifty per cent larger, so Broom assigned the remains to a third species, *Paranthropus robustus* ('robust alongside-man'), in recognition of it being apparently more powerfully built than *Plesianthropus*[35].

Broom and Dart now invited two anthropologists from the AMNH to visit, Da Costa Professor of Zoology William King Gregory and Milo Hellman. The pair spent two months in South Africa and "*were given every facility for the study of the original fossils*", which they believed were "*all probably of Pleistocene age*". They claimed that *Australopithecus*, *Plesianthropus*, and *Paranthropus* were survivors of diversified *Dryopithecus* stock. *Dryopithecus* was a genus of late Tertiary apes that ranged from Spain to India, and East Africa. Gregory and Hellman concluded that the 'man-apes' were "*cousins of the contemporary human branch*". Their "*numerous transitional conditions*" connected "*the families of apes and men at no very distant geological date (perhaps the lower Pliocene)*". The remains gave "*no support*" to the prevalent view of humans separating from apes in the early Tertiary[36].

The tide seemed to be turning at last, but then World War II intervened. A fall in the price of lime caused the Sterkfontein quarry to shut down. That and Barlow's death more or less halted excavations for the duration of hostilities. The only work carried out was a brief excavation at Kromdraai in 1941, where Broom was joined by his new assistant, palaeontologist John T. Robinson. The war years were largely spent preparing a monograph on his finds[4].

Post-war acceptance

Broom's monograph appeared early in 1946[37] and was praised by British palaeontologist Sir Wilfrid Le Gros Clark, who said that Broom had "*very considerably enhanced the prestige of South African science in the eyes of the world generally*" and expressed the hope that funds would be made available to continue the work at Sterkfontein and elsewhere[38]. At the Pan-African Congress on Prehistory held in Nairobi in January 1947, Le Gros Clark paid tribute to Dart and Broom and said that they had "*certainly not over-estimated the significance of the Australopithecinae*", and that their interpretations of the fossils "*were entirely correct in all essential details*"[39]. Shortly after this, Sir Arthur Keith wrote to *Nature* to concede defeat. "*Like Prof. Le Gros Clark, I am now convinced, on the evidence submitted by Dr. Robert Broom, that Prof. Dart was right and I was wrong; the Australopithecinae are in or near the line which culminated in the human form*"[40].

With these endorsements, the anthropological community finally accepted that the australopithecines were bipedal apes. Jan Smuts, now in his second term as Prime Minister, answered Le Gros Clark's call for funding. At the start of 1947, he asked the now-octogenarian Broom to resume his excavations. Assisted by Robinson, Broom worked at Kromdraai for three months, but only one possible australopithecine bone was found. On 1 April, the pair moved to Sterkfontein and were at once rewarded with "*sensational discoveries*". After finding the fragmentary remains of a juvenile aged around three, a subadult, and some isolated teeth, they recovered the nearly complete adult skull of an adult *Plesianthropus*, albeit with the lower jawbone missing[41,42]. The skull, which belonged to a middle-aged female[43], became popularly known as Mrs. Ples. The formal name is Sts 5. The cranial capacity was later estimated to be around 415 cc[44].

Discoveries continued through 1947, including a pelvis and other postcranial[8] remains[45,46]. By March 1948, eight skulls in various states of preservation had been found[44]. In November 1949, Broom and Robinson began working at another fossil-bearing breccia-filled cave site, Swartkrans, a mile from the Sterkfontein caves. They soon discovered a lower jawbone with the premolars and molars still in place, as well as several isolated teeth. These remains were described as *Paranthropus crassidens* ('thick-toothed alongside man')[47]. The site yielded further fragmentary remains over the following months, enabling sketches to be made of the skull form[48]. Another discovery made in 1949 was a lower jawbone that Broom and Robinson described as *Telanthropus capensis* ('Entry man from the Cape')[49,50]. The affinities of this fossil are disputed, but it is now generally assigned to *Homo erectus*[51].

By 1950, in a classic case of 'splitting'[9], Broom was arguing that the Taung, Sterkfontein, Kromdraai, and Swartkrans fossils should be assigned to five separate species in four genera and three subfamilies[52]. His scheme was not widely accepted. *Plesianthropus transvaalensis* is now regarded as the same species as *Australopithecus africanus*, and *Paranthropus crassidens* as the same species as *Paranthropus robustus*. As early as 1951 it was argued that *Paranthropus* should be subsumed into *Australopithecus*[53]. However, many retain the two genera, informally referring to *Australopithecus* and *Paranthropus* as gracile and robust australopithecines, respectively.

Sterkfontein, Kromdraai, and Swartkrans have continued to yield hominin fossils and they are now part of the Cradle of Humankind, a World Heritage Site named by UNESCO in 1999. The fossils from these sites continue to be a source of national pride in South Africa. In 2004, Mrs. Ples made the Top 100 in SABC3's television series *Great South Africans*, placing her in the company of Nelson Mandela, Steve Biko, and Dr. Christiaan Barnard. Rather unfairly, neither Dart nor Broom made the list. While neither was born in South Africa, this was also the case for some who were included.

---

[8] Postcranial remains are any remains from below the skull and lower jawbone.

[9] So-called 'splitters' are prone to assign new species and genera for almost every new fossil find. The opposite of splitting is 'lumping'; lumpers tend to cram as many fossils as possible into existing species and genera. Broom was, by his own admission, a splitter.

Robert Broom died in April 1951, aged 84. In an obituary published by the Royal Society, zoologist David Watson wrote: *"Broom's scientific career was thus unlike that of any other man. He revolutionized our knowledge in two fields of comparative anatomy, the first between the ages of thirty-four and forty-four, the second from the age of seventy to his death at eighty-five. And for the greater part of his life, for forty years, he made his living by the practice of medicine. His published papers are unlike those of all his contemporaries, in every respect"*. Broom was, Watson concluded, *"a man unique, who in his work showed himself to be possessed of genius"*[54].

Raymond Dart died in November 1988, aged 95. His former student and long-term friend Philip Tobias wrote *"On one hand, to few men of the 20th century, in this or any other country, has it been given so greatly to expand the frontiers of humanity's understanding of itself and its origins. On the other hand, Dart was the most human of human beings, the most gentle and genial. Growing old gracefully, he fulfilled Cicero's ideal: for this was a man who grew old in body, but never in mind. For him, old age was the crown of life, our play's last act. His enthusiasm remained undimmed; his zest for ideas undiluted. We are all the poorer for his having died; we and countless others are the richer for his having lived"*[55].

Part II: Lucy

The International Afar Research Expedition

By the end of the 1960s, the focus of the investigation of human origins had shifted from South Africa to Ethiopia, Kenya, and Tanzania. In the quarter century since the publication of Broom's decisive monograph, many important discoveries had been made at Olduvai Gorge, a dry valley on the western margin of the Eastern Rift Valley in northern Tanzania. British anthropologists Louis Leakey and his wife Mary Leakey *nee* Nicol had been working there since the early 1950s. In 1959, Mary found an almost -complete skull hominin skull that Louis described as *Zinjanthropus boisei* (Boise's man from East Africa). Zinj is the ancient Arabic name for East Africa; Charles Boise was an American mining engineer who had financially assisted the Leakeys' work since 1948[56]. Informally named 'Nutcracker Man' by the press, it was soon 'lumped' into *Paranthropus* by John T. Robinson[57].

Late in 1960, the Leakeys' eldest son Jonathon, now working with them in the field, discovered a juvenile jawbone, several skull fragments including matching left and right parietals, and some hand, wrist, and finger bones. These remains were eventually described as a new human species, *Homo habilis* ('Handy man'), a name suggested by Raymond Dart. It was claimed that *Homo habilis* was an earlier, smaller-brained, and more primitive human species than *Homo erectus*[58,59], although all of these claims have been disputed[60–62].

So it was that in the late 1960s, French geologist Maurice Taieb was studying the evolution of the Awash River valley in the southern part of the Afar region of Ethiopia. In 1969, he discovered a geological formation near the Hadar River, a tributary of the Awash, which contained hitherto unknown Pliocene and Pleistocene sedimentary deposits. These were rich in well-preserved, diverse mammalian fossils, raising the possibility of finding hominin remains. Taieb now wanted to organise a survey expedition to the Afar Region to evaluate the potential there for more extensive paleoanthropological fieldwork, but he found that all the leading figures in the field were either sceptical or busy with other projects. However, he did meet American anthropologist Donald Johanson, who at the time was still completing his PhD. He had nevertheless already begun to make a name as an adept fossil hunter, and he was enthusiastic about an expedition to the Afar region. Early in 1972, Taieb organised a six-week expedition to Hadar with Johanson, French palaeontologist Yves Coppens, and American geologist Jon Kalb. On their return, Taieb invited prominent scientists to join the International Afar Research Expedition, a multi-national, transdisciplinary team that would explore the Hadar Formation in greater depth with the objective of recovering hominin fossils[63,64].

Taieb and Johanson worked to recruit a Franco-American team of scientists. They agreed that Taieb would be the expedition's chief geologist, Johanson the chief palaeoanthropologist, and Coppens the chief palaeontologist. Taieb recruited botanist Raymonde Bonnefille, geologist Nichole Page, and an artist named Guillemot and Johanson recruited archaeology graduate students Gene Dole and Tom Gray[65]. This eight-strong team would discover what is probably the most famous fossil ever found – Lucy.

Technical Interlude 1: Dating *Australopithecus*

One of the main problems facing anthropologists during the first half of the twentieth century was the lack of a reliable means of dating more recent artefacts or fossil remains. The only radiometric method available at the time was the uranium-lead method, which relies on the decay of uranium to lead. As noted, the dates of the Miocene epoch were known with reasonable accuracy by the 1920s, and the age of the Earth was accurately determined at 4.55 billion years old in 1956[66]. Unfortunately, this method is far less useful for anything less than a few million years old and consequently, more recent prehistoric timescales were only poorly understood. Robert Broom, for example, had estimated that the Taung skull was from no earlier than the Pleistocene, although in the 1920s, the base of the Pleistocene was taken to be the end of the Calabrian Stage (774,000 years ago by today's estimates). Writing in 1959, Dart[4] noted that he, Broom, and others originally believed that the skull was about one million years old, but based on then-recent geological work he suggested that the australopithecines had probably lived 750,000 years ago.

In the 1950s, two new radiometric methods came into use – radiocarbon (^{14}C) dating and potassium-argon dating. The familiar radiocarbon dating method is useful for dating samples up to around 50,000 years old, and potassium-argon dating relies on the decay of radioactive potassium isotope ^{40}K to argon and can be used to investigate Pliocene and Pleistocene (and indeed earlier timescales). The use of radiocarbon dating is limited to organic materials, while potassium-argon dating is restricted to fossils and artefacts associated with minerals containing potassium, for example, volcanic tephra.

Nutcracker Man (or OH 5 to give the skull its official name) was best guessed to be around half a million years old[67], but Louis Leakey realised that the new potassium-argon method could be used to obtain accurate dates for the volcanic tephra of Bed I[68]. Work over the next few years showed that it and the hominin fossils it contained were far older than these guestimates and were actually 1.75 million years old[69–71]. *Homo erectus* remains, found in the upper part of Bed II, were found to be 490,000 years old[71].

Unfortunately, the limestone context of the South African australopithecine fossils and the absence of volcanic material generally in South Africa meant that the potassium-argon method could not be used to obtain dates directly. An alternative method that was tried is faunal correlation, where a fossil of unknown age is dated by reference to associated fauna. If fossil X is associated with faunal remains of species Y and occurrences of species Y elsewhere can be dated accurately (e.g., by the potassium-argon method), then this will give an approximate date range for fossil X. Based on dates obtained by this method and the uranium-lead method, the Sterkfontein fossils were long believed to be around 2.9 to 2.3 million years old[51]. In 2013, the Taung skull was estimated to be 2.6 – 3.0 million years old[72]. These dates correspond to the Late Pliocene.

In the last twenty years, several new dating techniques have come into use. One of these is cosmogenic nuclide dating. This technique relies on the constant bombardment of Earth by cosmic rays causing the production of very small quantities of radioactive isotopes of aluminium (^{26}Al) and beryllium (^{10}Be) in rocks and minerals on the surface. When sediment from these materials becomes buried, exposure to cosmic rays and the consequent production of these isotopes will cease. Over time, the quantities present will fall due to radioactive decay. By measuring the quantities remaining in sediments associated with a fossil, the time the fossil has been buried can be determined. This method showed that the Sterkfontein fossils were considerably older than had been estimated, dating from 3.41 to 3.67 million years ago[73,74].

Discoveries at Hadar

The International Afar Research Expedition's field season at Hadar began in the autumn of 1973. On 30 October of that year, towards the end of the first season of excavation, the team discovered a fossil knee joint. Based on biostratigraphy, it was estimated to be more than three million years old. The knee joint and associated proximal femoral elements had indisputably belonged to an upright-walking hominin[63,75,76]. Encouraged by this discovery, they returned for a second season in 1974.

On 24 November, Johanson and Gray were returning to camp in a Land Rover, having spent the morning surveying. Finds had been modest: teeth from an extinct horse, the partial skull of an extinct pig, some antelope molars, and a partial monkey jawbone. In the heat of noon, it had become too hot to continue. Then Johanson, feeling 'lucky', decided to double-check a small gully that other members of the team had already twice investigated without finding anything. This time, however, their luck was in. Johanson spotted a hominin elbow bone, and he and Gray soon found other fragmentary remains dotted around on the surface, including the back of a skull, a partial thighbone, a partial pelvis, and some vertebrae. Understandably excited, they returned to camp. After three weeks of excavation, several hundred bone fragments had been recovered. The finds represented 40 per cent of a single female hominin skeleton, which remains one of the most complete hominin fossils ever found. Her remains were given the official designation AL-288-1 (the first fossil to be discovered at Afar Locality 288), but she is far better known by her nickname 'Lucy'. The name comes from the 1967 Beatles song *Lucy in the Sky with Diamonds*, which was played repeatedly at a party held at the campsite to mark her discovery[65].

At 3.2 million years old, Lucy was thought to have wrested the crown for the oldest hominin yet found from *Australopithecus africanus* although we now know that the two were contemporaries. She stood a diminutive 1.1 m (3 ft 7 in) tall and weighed an estimated 29 kg (64 lb)[77]. Although her brain was only a little larger than that of a chimpanzee, her pelvis and lower limbs were almost identical in function to those of modern humans, showing that she was a biped. However, Johanson, Coppens, and anthropologist Tim White felt that Lucy was distinct from any previously found or described australopithecine species, and accordingly described her as *Australopithecus afarensis* ('Southern ape from Afar')[78]. Under an agreement with the government of Ethiopia, the skeleton of Lucy was taken out of the country to be reconstructed by anthropologist Owen Lovejoy at the Cleveland Museum of Natural History in Ohio. It was then returned to Ethiopia[65]. More than four decades after the discovery, it was suggested that Lucy had died from multiple injuries incurred from falling out of a tall tree[79]. The report attracted a degree of scepticism, but if true it would have been an ironic fate for a biped ape noted for living on the ground.

Lucy was not the last major discovery made by the International Afar Research Expedition. During the 1975 season, the team found over two hundred separate fossil bone fragments at a single fossil bed known as AL 333. The remains represented at least thirteen individuals of *Australopithecus afarensis*. The group, which became known as the First Family, included adult males and females, and four or more infants. For a long time, it was believed that they were all members of a single relatively large social group who were the casualties of a catastrophic event, possibly a flash flood[63].

However, later reconstructions of the local environment cast doubt on the hypothesis. Although the channel had flooded at one stage, the event was less catastrophic than had been supposed. The site was a shallow depression and not a deep gully in which the group could have become trapped. Investigation of the sediments in the channel suggested that the flow of water had been quite gentle, and insufficient to overwhelm the group[80]. This left open the question of how the remains had reached the site. There is no evidence that they were attacked by a predator[81].

One controversial suggestion by British archaeologist Paul Pettitt[82] is that the remains were intentionally left elsewhere by other group members following their deaths before being swept to the findspot by the flooding. Pettitt described this as 'archaic mortuary behaviour'. This, he argues, was a stage in the development of mortuary practices that preceded rituals such as formal burials. It is easy to be sceptical of this suggestion, but it certainly cannot be dismissed. It should be noted that numerous studies have shown that non-human primates have an awareness of death and will respond in various ways to the deaths of other group members. For example, mothers will carry the bodies of deceased infants for long periods after their deaths. Even more strikingly, high-status group members have been known to 'guard' the body of a fellow high-ranking individual, denying access to younger or lower-ranked group members. Such behaviours have been observed among a wide range of primate species[83].

The work of the International Afar Research Expedition continued until 1981. In September 1974, a few weeks before the discovery of Lucy, a Soviet-backed military coup deposed Emperor Haile Selassie. The resulting political instability worsened towards the end of the 1970s, and in 1982 a moratorium on field research in the country was imposed by the government. An American team that arrived in August of that year spent three weeks in Addis Ababa trying to obtain permits, only to be turned back. The authorities were said to be unhappy that foreign expeditions had removed fossils from the country and contributed little in return to local institutions and scholars. The ban on field research lasted until 1990, when the Hadar Research Project was able to resume work. The military dictatorship fell a year later. Despite ongoing conflict in the region, research work continues to this day[63,64].

Technical interlude 2: When did we diverge from apes?

Even after it became accepted that australopithecines were bipeds and likely a transitional form between anthropoid apes and humans, the view persisted that the split between apes and humans was very ancient. As late as the 1960s, the fossil ape *Ramapithecus*, discovered in 1932 in the Siwalik Hills of India[84], was being claimed as one of the earliest hominins, or broadly ancestral to them[85]. The genus *Ramapithecus* was later subsumed into *Sivapithecus*, an extinct genus of apes that lived 12 million years ago[51].

However, it was around this time that the new science of molecular biology changed the picture dramatically. Following the discovery in the 1950s of the role of DNA in inheritance, it was discovered that the genetic material of all living organisms undergoes occasional random changes known as mutations, often through DNA copying errors during cell division. If a mutation occurs in reproductive cells, it will be passed on to the next generation. Consequently, over many generations, mutations will accumulate in genetic sequences. These mutations occur at a roughly constant rate, so differences between equivalent genetic sequences in two species – the genetic distance – will be related to the time since the two species last shared a common ancestor. This is known as the divergence time.

To obtain actual divergence times in calendar years, it is necessary to calibrate this 'molecular clock', i.e., determine the rate at which genetic distances increase with time. These days, genetic sequencing enables direct comparisons between the genetic sequences of children and parents to obtain intergenerational mutation rates. Originally, genetic distances were obtained for species where actual divergence times are known from the fossil record, from which divergence times could be calculated for other species. This method had the drawback that it relied on accurately dated fossil records.

Before DNA sequencing became practical, researchers used proteins as a proxy for DNA sequences. Serum albumin is produced by the liver and is the most abundant protein found in the blood of vertebrates. In 1967, molecular biologists Vincent Sarich and Allan Wilson obtained and purified serum albumen from humans, chimpanzees, bonobos, gorillas, orangutans, gibbons, siamangs, and six species of Old World monkey, and produced the corresponding antisera (antibodies) by immunising groups of rabbits. They then reacted various serum/antiserum combinations together and measured the strength of the reactions: the stronger the reaction, the more closely related the sources of the serum and antiserum. Human serum produced stronger reactions with the antisera of African apes than that of Asian apes. Furthermore, serum/antiserum reactions were far stronger between any combination of human, chimpanzee, bonobo, or gorilla than any of these with orangutans. The implication was that Darwin had been right all along: humans were more closely related to African apes than to Asian apes and must, therefore, have evolved in Africa. Moreover, they were more closely related to African apes than any of the latter were to orangutans. It was orangutans and not humans that were the outliers. However, the most dramatic part of the study was the conclusion that assuming humans diverged from Old World monkeys 30 million years ago, then the divergence from African apes had occurred just 5 million years ago[86].

As might be expected, this challenge to the ancient split orthodoxy was met with scepticism and downright disbelief, but further work by Sarich and Wilson confirmed the original findings[87]. The serum/antiserum method was not sensitive enough to determine which of the African apes was our closest relative, but later work showed that it was the two species of chimpanzee ('common' chimps and bonobos)[88]. Modern estimates, relying on intergenerational mutation rates and factoring in differences between the rates for humans and apes, suggest that humans diverged from chimpanzees 6.6 million years ago[89]. The 'missing link' can be defined as our last common ancestor (LCA) with chimpanzees.

The Laetoli footprints

Although Ethiopia was off limits to palaeoanthropologists, this was not the case further south in Tanzania. In 1975, a team led by Mary Leakey was investigating Laetoli, 45 km (28 miles) south of Olduvai Gorge. Expedition members were taking part in a dried elephant dung fight when one of the participants ducked into a gully and noticed some animal tracks in a layer of fossilised volcanic ash. An immediate ceasefire was called and the tracks of numerous animals were investigated. The question was immediately asked: could the ash also contain the footprints of hominins[64]?

It was not until 1978 that geochemist Paul Abell found the first hominin footprint at Site G Locality 8. The trail now referred to as the Laetoli Footprints is 27 m (88 ft) long and includes around 70 hominin footprints. The footprints, preserved in volcanic ash for 3.66 million years, were made by three bipedal individuals, designated G1, G2, and G3, and thought to be *Australopithecus afarensis* all walking in the same direction[90].

The trio was walking through muddy ash following the eruption of a volcano, and their footprints were captured like plaster casts. The mud had time to harden before further eruptions covered the footprints in a layer of ash, from which they would not emerge until the present day. The scene is depicted in the Hall of Human Origins at the AMNH, where a life-sized male is displayed with a protective arm around the shoulder of the female while a volcano smoulders menacingly on the horizon. The volcano responsible for preserving the footprints is unknown. It had long been assumed to be Sadiman, 20 km (12 miles) away, but a study in 2011 showed that the footprint tephra shares no similarity with any rock type found at Sadiman[91].

The footprints tell us that in terms of their locomotion at least, the Laetoli hominins were humanlike. They had humanlike arched feet with an inline big toe, unlike the opposable big toe of anthropoid apes[92]. The deep heel impressions in relation to those made by the toes suggest that they were walking fully upright, and a comparison of the footprints with those of anthropoid apes and modern humans confirms that they most closely resemble the latter[90]. The humanlike gate was further demonstrated by an experiment in which subjects made footprints by walking through a sand trackway. The footprints resembled those at Laetoli, suggesting that the Laetoli hominins walked with extended hind limbs like humans, rather than with flexed hind limbs like apes[93].

Part III: Ardi

Our latest earliest ancestor

During the mid-1990s and into the early 2000s, the australopithecine family grew, with several new species reported from East Africa[94–96], Chad[97], and South Africa[98]. The finds suggested that the gracile australopithecines (*Australopithecus*) had inhabited a range stretching from South Africa to the crossroads of North and Central Africa. Conceivably, they could have extended their range into the grasslands of Asia[60], although there is as yet no fossil evidence to suggest that they did so. The gracile australopithecines had lived from 4.2 million[99] to 2.0 million[100] years ago and the robust australopithecines (*Paranthropus*) might have lasted until as recently as one million years ago, well into the era of *Homo*[51]. The australopithecines were a highly successful, long-lived, and wide-ranging hominin group, occupying the middle third of the era since humans had diverged from apes. But what of the hominins that had lived during the first third of this era?

In 1992, a research team headed by American palaeoanthropologist Tim White began investigating the Middle Awash study area. White had worked as an assistant to anthropologist Richard Leakey before joining Mary Leakey's team at Laetoli. In 1978, he co-authored the paper in which *Australopithecus afarensis* was described as a new species of hominin, and it had been his idea to give it the specific name *afarensis*[65].

Between 1992 and 1993, White's team made the first discovery of a pre-australopithecine hominin near the small village of Aramis. They recovered the fragmentary remains of around seventeen individuals, which appeared to be more primitive and apelike than any previously known australopithecine. The 4.4 million-year-old remains were initially described as *Australopithecus ramidus*, but they were later assigned to a new genus, *Ardipithecus*. 'Ardi' means 'ground' or 'floor' in the Afar language and 'ramid' means 'root'. White believed that *Ardipithecus* represented an earlier hominin adaptive plateau than the australopithecines, lying near to the ancestry of all later hominins[101,102]. But this discovery was only the beginning.

In November 1994, White returned to the Middle Awash. Work had commenced at Locality 6, near Aramis, when one of White's students, Yohannes Haile-Selassie, found what he immediately recognised as a hominin second metacarpal finger bone. At first, it was thought to be just an isolated discovery, but a few days later the team found another metacarpal and soon it became clear that they had multiple elements of a skeleton. The bones were extremely and on exposure to the atmosphere began to dry and crumble, so chemical hardeners had to be applied immediately. White decided to remove some fossils while still encased in blocks of sediment, cover them in plaster, and take them to the National Museum of Ethiopia in Addis Ababa where they could be cleaned and preserved in the Museum's laboratory. After ten days of excavation, White realised that no bones were duplicated. They all came from the same individual. All told, the team recovered 125 pieces of the skeleton, including the skull, teeth, hands, arms, pelvis, legs, and feet. Like Lucy, the skeleton was of a female, only a million years older and even more complete. However, the work of reconstructing the individual who became known as 'Ardi' would be painstaking and would take many years[64].

In the meantime, Haile-Selassie was involved with further discoveries of *Ardipithecus* remains between 1997 and 1997. These remains, which were also found in the Middle Awash region, were older than the 1992 – 1994 findings. At 5.2 – 5.8 million years old, they dated to the Early Pliocene/Late Miocene. Their dental characteristics were more primitive than *Ardipithecus ramidus* and they were assigned to a new species within the *Ardipithecus* genus, *Ardipithecus kadabba*. The specific name means basal family ancestor in the Afar language[103].

As years passed, White came under increasing pressure to publish his full set of data. He was threatened with loss of funding, being told that his fossils were of limited value until they became accessible. White refused to be hurried. He would not publish until the research had been completed, and if funds ran out, it would only delay matters further[64]. However, by this time, even earlier fossil finds were being claimed as possible hominins.

Technical interlude III: the third chimpanzee?

Having established that the 'missing link' was our last common ancestor (LCA) with chimpanzees, anthropologists tended to assume that it was physically and behaviourally similar to a chimpanzee or bonobo. Indeed, biologist and science writer Jared Diamond went so far as to describe humans as no more than a third species of chimpanzee[104]. Anthropologists frequently used the two chimpanzee species as a proxy for the LCA, in attempts to predict how it might have behaved and interacted with its environment.

Chimpanzees and bonobos live in communities that vary in size from 20 – 25 to as many as 120 and comprise multiple males and multiple females[105]. Their mating behaviour is polygamous, and any male will mate with any female. Females tend to disperse from the group into which they are born, but males usually remain with the group for life[51]. Their social organisation is known as 'fission-fusion', where individuals forage in parties that vary in size and composition[106]. However, there are some behavioural differences between the two. Female chimpanzees, who are unrelated to one another, tend to forage small territories either alone or with dependent young, but the closely related males tend to form bands that patrol the territories of the females and fend off males from neighbouring groups. The environment is highly competitive for the males, who need not only to maintain their own status within the group but also to keep outsiders away from the group's females. However, because they are all closely related and because they share the common goal of keeping outsider males away, there is a degree of cooperation between the males in a group[51].

By contrast, bonobos tend to forage in small mixed-sex groups. Bonobo society is based on strong ties between the females and weaker ties among the males, despite the former being unrelated to one another[51]. Bonobos indulge in a wide range of sexual activities matched only by humans, including face-to-face copulation (in contrast to the 'doggie-style' mating favoured by chimpanzees), tongue kissing, oral sex, and same-sex genital rubbing. It is thought that they use sex as a means of diffusing tensions rather than resorting to conflict[105].

In sexually reproducing species, sexual dimorphism refers to the physical differences between the two sexes. It is common among primates: in many primate species, the males are larger than the females and have enlarged canine teeth. These are used for threat displays in order to gain social dominance. Chimpanzees exhibit a moderate degree of sexual dimorphism. The males are about 35 per cent larger by body weight than females[107] and also have enlarged canine teeth in comparison to females[51].

Among existing primate species there is a strong correlation between mating strategy and sexual dimorphism. This is related to male-on-male aggression, which is limited in monogamous species such as gibbons but is far more pronounced in polygamous species. With the latter, where males are competing for access to females, natural selection will favour the larger, more powerful males, and those with enlarged canine teeth.

Humans are only mildly sexually dimorphic, from which it can be predicted that they are primarily if not entirely monogamous. Indeed, human society is based around what might be termed 'serial monogamy': a tendency to remain with the same partner for an extended period of time, if not for life. Relationships can break up, but infidelity, while in one, is generally frowned upon. Anthropologists asked, how did such a condition arise from a more strongly dimorphic and polygamous ancestor? It turned out that they had been asking the wrong question.

Original Man

Orrorin tugenensis ('Original Man of Tugen' in the local Tugen language and nicknamed 'Millennium Man') was discovered in 2000 in central Kenya by French palaeontologist Brigitte Senut and British palaeontologist Martin Pickford. The fossils were discovered in 6 million-year-old sediments at four localities in the Lukeino Formation of the Tugen Hills, a series of hills in Kenya's Baringo County. The finds comprised twenty fossils belonging to at least five individuals. The bones included a fragmentary lower jawbone, teeth, a right upper arm bone, and two left and one right thigh bones. Computerised tomography scans and other studies of the thigh bones suggested that *Orrorin* was a biped, although it was also a good climber[108–110].

Senut also suggested that the thigh bone was more humanlike than that of both *Ardipithecus* and the australopithecines. Similarly, the small and thick-enamelled molar teeth were more humanlike than either the thin-enamelled molars of *Ardipithecus* or the thick-enamelled but large molars of australopithecines. Accordingly, she suggested both were off the line of evolution leading to humans and that *Ardipithecus* was on the evolutionary line leading to chimpanzees. *Orrorin*, she argued, led to *Homo* via an intermediate genus, *Praeanthropus*, with *Ardipithecus* and *Australopithecus* branching off before *Praeanthropus* arose[109].

Praeanthropus was first proposed in the 1950s. It has never been widely accepted, but there have been suggestions that it be revived to accommodate *Australopithecus afarensis*[111–113]. Thus, it was only some australopithecines that were bumped from the line leading to *Homo*; Lucy and her kin were not excluded. The claim nevertheless attracted heated criticism from Tim White at a conference held at the Académie des sciences in Paris[114,115]. Later work tended to support White. One study concluded that the *Orrorin* thigh bone most closely resembles those of the australopithecines, confirming that *Orrorin* was indeed a biped, but rejecting the suggestion that it was more closely related to humans than were australopithecines[116]. Other work, focusing on cranial and dental characteristics, confirmed *Ardipithecus's* place in human ancestry[113,117].

Hope of life

A year after *Orrorin* was first described came reports of an even earlier hominin, this time from the Djurab Desert in northern Chad. The discovery was made by French palaeontologist Michel Brunet and comprises a near-complete skull, fragmentary lower jawbone, and several teeth. The skull was nicknamed Toumai, meaning 'hope of life' in the local language, and described as *Sahelanthropus tchadensis* ('Sahel Man of Chad')[118].

Faunal correlation suggested that Toumai was 6 to 7 million years old[119]. Subsequent finds of teeth and a fragmentary lower jawbone were associated with fauna that suggested a date range of 6.5 to 7.4 million years ago[120]. This earlier date range was later supported by a cosmogenic radionuclide date of 6.8 to 7.2 million years ago[121], although the reliability of this was challenged[122]. These dates were at odds with estimates that the LCA had lived just five million years ago. There was a suggestion that after the human/chimpanzee split, members of the two lineages continued to interbreed for a while, before separating for good. The genetic date would then reflect the latter event rather than the former[123]. However, the later estimate of 6.6 million years ago for the LCA is more compatible with Toumai's hominin status if the lower/mid-range of the faunal dates is accepted.

The addition of the teeth and the fragmentary jawbone enabled a virtual cranial reconstruction to be attempted[124]. One problem was the lack of any postcranial remains, but morphological comparisons of the reconstructed cranial features with those of anthropoid apes and hominins suggested that the affinities of *Sahelanthropus* lay with the latter[125]. However, there were also suggestions that *Sahelanthropus* was an early gorilla[126]. Another suggestion was that a non-bipedal primate partial thighbone discovered in 2004 could be assigned to *Sahelanthropus*, throwing its hominin status into doubt[127]. Postcranial remains were finally reported in 2022 from the site of the original discovery, including a left thighbone and a pair of forearm bones. Analysis of the thighbone confirmed that *Sahelanthropus* was a biped[128].

Given that the material from both *Orrorin* and *Sahelanthropus* is very fragmentary, some argued that it is too soon to be drawing anything other than tentative conclusions[129] and it cannot be ruled out that bipedalism evolved more than once[130]. Even assuming that *Orrorin* and *Sahelanthropus* are indeed hominins, are they sufficiently distinct from *Ardipithecus* and from each other to justify placing them in two new genera? It's lumping versus splitting again, and in a classic case of the former, Tim White claimed that a comparison of the dentition of *Orrorin* and *Sahelanthropus* with that of *Ardipithecus kadabba* cast doubt on whether they represented three distinct genera or even three distinct species[131].

Technical interlude IV: the origin of bipedalism

Until recently, it was generally thought that five million years ago, our ancestors inhabited continuous forests in the tropics of Africa, but their way of life was changing. The Late Miocene was a period of global cooling, in part due to the uplifting of the Himalayas and the Tibetan Plateau as the Indian subcontinent continued its slow collision with southern Asia. The weathering of the freshly exposed rocks resulted in a significant reduction of atmospheric CO_2, causing a drop in global temperatures[132–134]. In East Africa, meanwhile, the uplifting of the Ethiopian Plateau had blocked moisture from the Atlantic Ocean, casting a 'rain shadow' across much of East Africa[135–137]. The cooler and more arid conditions caused the continuous forests to break up and be replaced by more open woodland and grassland savannah[135].

When the forests began to break up, our ancestors had to adapt to life on the savannah. The view was that when it was on the ground, the LCA – in common with present-day chimpanzees – could walk upright but more usually got around on all fours by knuckle-walking. This is a form of locomotion in which the forelimbs hold the fingers in a partially flexed posture that allows body weight to press down on the ground through the knuckles, with the back of the middle phalanges bearing the weight[138]. There were several reasons why bipedalism was seen as advantageous in a savannah habitat, for example, improved predator avoidance by being able to see further across an open savannah than a quadruped[135]. One suggestion was that it arose from the need for early hominins to reduce exposure to the Sun while foraging. When upright, hominins had less of their body surface exposed than those going about on all fours, and they could continue to forage when the Sun was high in the sky. They could also benefit more from cooling breezes[139]. The problem with these theories was that paleoenvironmental studies suggested that early hominins inhabited wooded rather than savannah environments[140,141]. If they spent relatively little time in open environments, exposure to the Sun could not have been a major factor in selecting for bipedalism[142].

However, the 'Efficient Biped' model is one savannah model that circumvents some of these difficulties. In 1980, anthropologists Peter Rodman and Henry McHenry suggested that Late Miocene forests shrank, sources of food became more thinly dispersed and apes would have had to travel further to obtain the same amount of food. Natural selection would tend to favour more energy-efficient ways of getting about. Rodman and McHenry noted that firstly, humans are at least as energy-efficient as conventional quadrupeds at walking speeds, although they are less efficient runners, secondly, the bipedal gait of humans is much more energy-efficient than either the knuckle-walking or upright walking of chimpanzees, and thirdly, knuckle-walking and upright walking incur similar energy costs for chimpanzees, but the latter leaves the forelimbs free for food collection. Hence, natural selection would favour more energy-efficient bipedal locomotion over quadrupedal locomotion[143]. The theory has the attraction that in regions where the environment was becoming more open, bipedalism would have been effective for moving through open patches, but forest/woodland living could have been maintained[142]. A weakness of the theory is that its energy calculations are based on chimpanzee locomotion, and it cannot be assumed that the energy efficiency of quadrupedal versus bipedal locomotion for the LCA was equivalent[144].

The 'Man the Provisioner' model was a rather different model proposed by Owen Lovejoy in 1981[145]. As with the 'Efficient Biped' model, Lovejoy saw the switch to bipedalism as an evolutionary response to the need to forage further afield due to food sources becoming more dispersed due to Late Miocene climate change. The difference is that the evolutionary focus was on liberating the forelimbs. This enabled males to carry food back to a home base and share it with females and their offspring. This afforded a three-way benefit to the females. Firstly, it ensured that they and their offspring were well-fed, secondly, it gave them more time to devote to parental care, and thirdly, being well-fed reduced the time between successive pregnancies.

For the males to benefit in terms of reproductive success, they needed to provide solely their own offspring. To be reasonably certain that they were doing so, they needed to be in a monogamous relationship. This pair-bonding was reinforced by females remaining continually sexually receptive and concealed ovulation meant that regular copulation was necessary in order to conceive. Concealed ovulation is an unusual feature of human reproductive biology. Females of most mammal species are only sexually receptive when ovulating and able to conceive; at such times, they give visual, olfactory, or other cues to advertise their condition to the males. For example, with both 'common' chimpanzees and bonobos, the genitals turn bright red. There are no equivalent cues in our species, but copulations take place throughout a woman's menstrual cycle, and she has no need to advertise when she is ovulating.

Lovejoy's theory did not gain widespread acceptance because it was assumed that the LCA was similar in appearance and behaviour to non-monogamous chimpanzees, and estimates at the time suggested that australopithecines were even more sexually dimorphic than chimpanzees[107]. Hence, it was believed that the mating strategy of the LCA was polygamous.

Ardi revealed

In October 2009, after fifteen years of study, Tim White and his colleagues published their long-awaited report on *Ardipithecus ramidus*. The report ran to 108 pages. At the same time, a collection of eleven articles appeared in the journal *Science*. The work largely centred around the skeleton discovered by Haile-Selassie, now nicknamed 'Ardi' and believed to have been female. White's collaborators in this lengthy project included Owen Lovejoy, who years earlier had reconstructed Lucy.

Ardi was about the same size as a chimpanzee, weighing around 50 kg (110 lb), with a height of 1.2 m (4 ft 0 in)[141], and her brain, with a cranial capacity of 300 to 350 cc, was similar in size to that of a chimpanzee[146]. She was a facultative biped, meaning that she was capable of walking on two legs, but also spent time in the trees. As with the australopithecines, the foramen magnum was positioned in the centre of the skull. What was lacking were some of the more advanced adaptations to bipedalism that are seen in later hominins, and consequently Ardi was a less efficient walker than a human. Her thigh bones and pelvis were adapted for upright walking, but also retained apelike adaptations for climbing. The most significant apelike retention was an opposable big toe[101,147–149].

Opposable thumbs and big toes are a common primate feature, as they are essential for climbing and living in trees. Australopithecines and humans later lost the opposable big toe, because an inline is more efficient for a habitual biped. The opposable thumb, on the other hand, is useful for grasping things, and so it was retained. Ardi had 'dual-purpose' feet for upright walking on the ground and climbing in the trees: the opposable big toe was pre-hominin retention to aid climbing but they also had humanlike adaptations to aid walking on the ground – the metatarsals were shortener than those of present-day African apes. The morphology of her hands, arms, feet, pelvis, and legs imply that Ardi moved in the trees on her feet and palms rather than clinging to the undersides of branches like modern apes. Her movement in the trees had more in common with monkeys and the early ape *Proconsul* than with modern apes[141,147,150,151]. Ardi had none of the features that have evolved in modern apes to stiffen their hands for suspension and vertical climbing. Her locomotion did not resemble that of modern apes – and, probably, this was also the case for the LCA[148]. This more or less ended the notion of the LCA being chimplike[141], and this was not the only major surprise to emerge from the *Ardipithecus* data.

The body size of *Ardipithecus* was only slightly dimorphic[141], and its canine teeth were only slightly more dimorphic than those of humans. All known apes possess what is known as a honing C/P3 dental complex where the pointed-shaped upper canine fits in with the lower canine and lower third premolar in a way that it is constantly sharpened. This feature is more developed in males than in females because the dagger-like upper canines are important in male-on-male aggression. However, with *Ardipithecus*, not only were male and female canines similar in size, but the male canine had been dramatically 'feminised' in shape. The crown of the upper canine was altered from the pointed shape seen in apes to a less threatening diamond shape in both males and females, and there was no sign of a honing complex[152]. This suggested a reduction in male-on-male aggression, implying a humanlike largely monogamous mating strategy. In turn, this suggests that the LCA was monogamous, and the polygamy of modern apes was a later development.

A monogamous LCA lent support to Owen Lovejoy's 'Man the Provisioner' model, but there was still the problem of the supposedly high sexual dimorphism of australopithecines. This objection disappeared in 2003 when a reassessment of Lucy and the First Family suggested that *Australopithecus afarensis* was no more sexually dimorphic than modern humans, and had probably been monogamous[153].

Conclusion

We have not and probably never will find the ape species that begat the two lineages that led to humans on one side and chimpanzees on the other. It has been estimated that only around seven per cent of all primate species that have ever existed are known from the fossil record[154]. The surprise is that in its behaviour and social structure, the LCA was probably more humanlike than chimplike. Further support for the mating strategy of the LCA being humanlike has been provided by comparative studies of the human and chimpanzee Y chromosomes. The Y chromosome is one of the two sex-determining chromosomes in most mammals, containing the SRY (sex-determining Y) gene that triggers the development of male gonads. Given the close evolutionary relationship between chimpanzees and humans, it might be expected that there would be little difference between the Y chromosomes of the two species, but studies have shown otherwise. Comparisons of the MSY (male-specific region) of the two suggest the human version has been more highly conserved, whereas around a third of the equivalent genes in the chimpanzee version have sustained inactivating mutations. Other changes have led to a complete restructuring of the chimpanzee MSY. Overall, the human version appears to have been closer to that of the LCA and, by implication, to the basal hominin condition. The changes may reflect the effects of natural selection driven by the importance of sperm competition in a promiscuous species[155,156]. These results imply that it is the chimpanzee mating strategy rather than the human mating strategy that has changed the most since the time of the LCA.

It should be noted that bipedalism was not the only possible solution to the problem of shrinking forests. Another was to forage in smaller groups: studies have shown that the daily travel distance of chimpanzees varies with party size and that individuals or members of smaller foraging parties travel shorter distances than those in larger parties. This might have been the origin of the fission-fusion society of chimpanzees. Thus, we might envisage that in the late Miocene, the LCA could have existed as a series of isolated populations. As the forests broke up, one or more populations could have solved their feeding problem with bipedalism leading to humans while others could have solved it with small group sizes and a fission-fusion social organisation leading to chimpanzees[106].

All the evidence suggests that the emergence of the hominins was an evolutionary adaptation to the climate change of the Late Miocene. Climate change has been our constant companion ever since, continuing through to the end of the last ice age 11,650 years ago. There is, however, an important difference between this climate change and the current climate emergency in that the latter is of our own making. Geological events and cyclical variations in the Earth's orbit, axial tilt, and spatial orientation drove climate change up to the start of the Industrial Revolution, but it has been subsequently driven by anthropogenic CO_2 emissions. The hominin story began with climate change; we must ensure that climate change does not also bring it to an end.

02: *Homo erectus*

Death of a palaeoanthropologist

The death in late 1940 of the 82-year-old Dutch palaeoanthropologist Eugène Dubois produced a flurry of obituary notices in the scientific journals of the day[1,2]. Writing in the 1942 edition of *The Rationalist Annual*, anatomist Sir Arthur Keith later noted that Dubois was "*an idealist who held his ideas so firmly that he tended to bend the facts rather than alter his ideas to fit them*"[3]. Keith was not noted for pulling his punches, but was he being harsh on Dubois? Half a century earlier, Dubois had found the first example of a human that had lived significantly before *Homo sapiens* and was significantly smaller-brained. He believed that it was, in the parlance of the time, a 'missing link', an evolutionary halfway house between apes and modern humans. Although the scientific community was intrigued by Dubois's claims, scientists were generally sceptical. It was not the first time, nor would it be the last time, that an epoch-making discovery in the field of human origins would be met with disbelief. The popular view was that he had withdrawn access to his fossil finds for nearly a quarter of a century and spent the last four decades of his life in a sulk.

How much, if any, of this was true?

Dubois

It was on the island of Java in October 1891 that a Dutch army doctor named Eugène Dubois made the discovery for which he is best remembered. Marie Eugène François Thomas Dubois was born in 1858 into a Catholic family living in Eijsden, a village close to the Belgian border in the south of the Netherlands. His father was apothecary Jean Joseph Balthazar Dubois, an émigré from Thimister-Clermont, Wallonia, who later became Mayor of Eijsden. As a boy, he developed a keen interest in fossil collecting and the natural world. At the age of twelve, he asked his father to send him to the State HBS, the technical high school in Roermond, rather than a Catholic school. At the State HBS, there were excellent facilities for studying chemistry, zoology, botany, and mineralogy. The elder Dubois, mindful of the views of other Catholic families in Eijsden, was hesitant, but eventually agreed. He had entertained hopes that his son would choose apothecary as a career, but he was to be disappointed. Eugène chose medicine over apothecary as a career, beginning his medical studies at the University of Amsterdam in 1877 at the age of nineteen. He soon came under the influence of the German anatomist Max Fürbringer, who offered him a coveted position as his anatomy assistant in 1881. Dubois continued to flourish at the University of Amsterdam. He qualified as a medical doctor in 1884 and was promoted to lecturer in comparative anatomy in 1886[4].

Dubois had been interested in the subject of human origins from an early age, attending lectures on the subject whenever possible. He believed that fossils represented the best means of exploring evolutionary history, and although it might sound strange now, this approach was uncommon at the time. Evolutionists including German zoologist Ernst Haeckel, 'Darwin's Bulldog' Thomas Henry Huxley, and Darwin himself viewed comparative anatomy and embryology as providing crucial evidence for evolution. Haeckel believed that in developing from a single cell to an adult, an embryo passes through all the stages of its evolutionary ancestry. His approach was summed up by the phrase "*Ontogeny recapitulates phylogeny*", i.e., the biological development of an organism (ontogeny) repeats its evolutionary development (phylogeny). Under this approach, fossils were largely redundant in demonstrating the descent of humans from apes. Dubois's mentor Max Fürbringer had been a student of Haeckel and an exponent of his teachings, so he would have unlikely to have emphasised the importance of fossils in the quest for human origins. A possible inspiration for Dubois's approach was German pathologist Rudolf Virchow, who suggested that a single fossil discovery in the tropics could change the whole picture[4–6].

Dubois resolved to find that single fossil, a missing link, which he believed might be found in the Dutch East Indies (now Indonesia). He argued that humans must have evolved in the tropics, where present-day apes live. Unlike Darwin, who suggested that humans might be most closely related to African apes[7], Dubois believed that humans are most closely related to gibbons. Dubois also read the reports of the British palaeontologist Richard Lydekker about the discovery of a fossil ape in the Siwalik Hills in India, and those of German geologist Karl Martin in which he noted similarities between the fossil fauna of the Dutch East Indies and that of the Siwalik Hills. Fossil apes – and, it was to be hoped, fossil humans – were likely to be found there also. There are many caves in the Dutch East Indies, and at that time, human fossils in Europe had nearly always been found in caves. Finally, searching for the missing link in a Dutch colony would pose fewer problems than a search in the then-British Raj[4].

The Missing Link

Although Darwin's view that humans had evolved from apes was generally accepted in Dubois's day, it was not yet clear how close the relationship is. It was thought that the Great Apes (chimpanzees, gorillas, and orangutans) are more closely related to each other than any of them are to humans. The Great Apes and the gibbons were all thought to belong to the taxonomic grouping Family *Simiidae* and humans to another, Family *Hominidae* (the hominids). Dubois believed that these two families were linked by a third, now-extinct family that was transitional between the two: the so-called missing link.

Dubois was building on the theories of Ernst Haeckel, who believed that human evolution had taken place in 22 stages, beginning with very simple lifeforms, and ending with humans. The antepenultimate stage was the apes, and the penultimate stage – lying midway between apes and humans – was *Pithecanthropus alalus* ('speechless ape-man'), "*whose body was indeed formed exactly like that of Man in all essential characteristics, but who did not as yet possess articulate speech*". That the missing link was speechless was a logical deduction from the principle that ontogeny recapitulates phylogeny: human infants lack articulate speech at birth, so the missing link must also have lacked it[8]. Haeckel set out his theories in his 1868 work *Natürliche schöpfungsgeschichte*, which was translated into English as *The History of Creation*. Among the more speculative ideas put forward was the suggestion that humans had originated in Lemuria, a now-sunken continent that supposedly existed in the Indian Ocean between India, Indonesia, and Madagascar.

In the late 1960s, molecular biologists discovered that humans were most closely related to African apes, as Darwin had suggested[9]. Indeed, they found that African apes and humans are more closely related to each other than any of them are to orangutans. This meant that it made no sense to place them in a group that included orangutans but not humans. Accordingly, the hominid family was expanded to include the Great Apes, although it does not include the more distantly related gibbons.

The notion of a single 'missing link' between apes and *Homo sapiens* is now known to have been over-simplistic. The fossil record has revealed a great diversity of now-extinct hominids that were more closely related to us than to the African apes. These include archaic human species such as the Neanderthals and the smaller-brained but biped australopithecines. This subfamily grouping is known as the hominins; this term is gradually replacing 'hominid' in common usage. The still-unidentified Last Common Ancestor (LCA) of humans and present-day African apes probably resembled *Ardipithecus*, a small-brained ape that could walk upright but retained opposable big toes for climbing[10].

Odyssey

Dubois's approach was unique in his day. No other scientist of the late nineteenth century conceived an expedition with the expectation of finding a particular fossil hominid in a particular location. Unsurprisingly, he failed to persuade the Dutch government to fund an expedition. He then had the idea of joining the Royal Netherlands Army and having himself posted to the Dutch East Indies as a medical officer, in the hope of finding sufficient time for fossil hunting away from his army duties. It was a risky endeavour that meant abandoning a promising career in anatomy, and he was strongly advised against it. However, he disliked teaching, and he had come to distrust Fürbringer, whom he (quite unfairly) suspected was trying to take the credit for his work concerning the comparative anatomy of the vertebrate larynx. Unfounded fears over others stealing his intellectual property became a recurring theme of Dubois's career[4,6].

On 11 December 1887, accompanied by his wife Anna, whom he had married a year earlier, and his newborn daughter, he arrived in Padang, Sumatra. Unfortunately, the demands of his day job as a medic left him very little time for fossil hunting. In May 1888, he had himself transferred to Paja Kombo in western Sumatra, where he was better placed to investigate caves and where his medical duties were less onerous. In July, he began exploring Lida Ajer, a small cave system in the Padang Highlands, located to the south of Paja Kombo. Within weeks, he had found the remains of orangutans, gibbons, and other mammals. Armed with this evidence in support of his claims, Dubois appealed to Dutch national pride and persuaded the government to relieve him of his medical duties. In March 1889, he was reassigned to the Department of Education, Religion, and Industry for the purpose of pursuing the fossil-hunting project. He was also given the services of two members of the Engineering Corps and fifty forced labourer convicts to help him with his excavations[4].

Unfortunately, this first excavation project was not a success. One of the engineers died of fever and Dubois had to dismiss the other for incompetence. Many of the convict labourers either deserted, were dismissed for misconduct, or fell ill, and Dubois himself was plagued with bouts of malaria. The few fossils that were found were very recent, suggesting to Dubois that what he was looking for would not be found in Sumatra, and his attention turned to the neighbouring island of Java. In October 1888, a mining engineer found a fossil human skull in marble outcrops near the village of Wadjak. The skull, though primitive[10], appeared human, but it suggested to Dubois that Java was the logical place to continue his quest[4]. The Wadjak skull, while thick-walled, is now widely regarded as representing a modern human[11].

In April 1890, Dubois received permission to transfer his operations to Java, where he was again assigned two engineers and a team of convicts. The engineers proved to be considerably more able than their predecessors in Sumatra. Dubois continued to focus on cave sites, and soon located a second skull at Wadjak, albeit more fragmentary than the first. Once cleaned and prepared, it was apparent to Dubois that it belonged to the same 'race'[11] as the first skull and was not a missing link. Although the caves were productive, Dubois soon realised that exposed riverbeds could also yield fossils. He had been hidebound by European notions of where fossils were to be found, and such notions did not apply in Java. The topography is completely different, with few lowland caves. The island comprises lowland plains, punctuated by towering volcanos that lack foothills. Dubois switched his attention to the Bengawan Solo, one of Java's major rivers, where underlying sediments would be exposed in the dry season[4].

This move paid off, and large numbers of animal fossils were recovered. Crucially, these were slightly younger than those from Siwalik Hills, dating to the Late Pliocene/Early Pleistocene. It was at this period when Dubois believed that the missing link must have lived, raising hopes that it would soon be found. In November 1990, a partial human jawbone was discovered in deposits at Kedung Brubus, but it was too fragmentary for Dubois to draw any conclusions. In August of the following year, Dubois moved operations to the village of Trinil. Discoveries soon followed: in September, an upper right third molar (M3) from a large primate, and then, in October, a fossilised human skullcap. While the face and lower cranium were missing, it was clearly more primitive than the Wadjak skull, and associated fossil fauna indicated that it was far more ancient. It was long and low rather than domed, thick-walled, and the browridges were pronounced and shelf-like. It was more apelike than a Neanderthal but more humanlike than an ape. The rainy season then intervened, and Dubois was stricken by a further bout of malaria, but in August 1892, a nearly complete human thighbone was discovered. The thighbone was morphologically modern, and Dubois was convinced that he had discovered an upright-walking transitional form between apes and humans – the missing

---

[10] In this context, 'primitive' simply means closer to the ancestral condition or sharing more features with ancestral populations. The opposite of primitive is 'derived' – a derived feature is one not shared with ancestral populations.

[11] At the time and for some decades afterwards, it was generally believed that humanity comprised several distinct 'races', some of which were more developed than others. It has long been accepted that the race concept has absolutely no validity.

link[4].

Dubois initially proposed to name his find *Anthropithecus erectus* ('erect man-ape'), based on the apelike proportions of the brain (which he estimated at 700 cc) and the modernity of the thigh bone. However, in November 1892, he revised the cranial capacity upwards to 900 cc, closer to that of a human than an ape, though at the low end of the modern range. Accordingly, he renamed the fossil *Pithecanthropus erectus* ('erect ape-man')[5]. The name was probably a homage to Haeckel's hypothetical *Pithecanthropus alalus*[15].

A battle for acceptance

In his third quarterly report of 1892, Dubois included a preliminary description of his discovery. Things got off to a bad start when an editor appended the comment, "*This last conclusion* [that the Dutch East Indies was the cradle of humankind] *really does seem to have been made rather hastily*". The local newspaper *Bataviaasch Nieuwsblad* published a critical letter (probably written by the editor P. A. Daum under a pseudonym) concluding that "*the esteemed Mr. Dubois, prejudiced because he has completely swallowed Darwinism, has gone too far, and has constructed a connection between the human femur and the monkey skull and molar where none ever existed*". Ironically, the letter, which was published on 6 February 1893, was signed "*Homo erectus*", the name by which *Pithecanthropus* would eventually come to be known[6]. Dubois published a monograph entitled "*Pithecanthropus erectus: Eine menschenähnliche Uebergangsform aus Java*" in 1894[16]. He made no further discoveries in Java, and in 1895, he and his wife returned to the Netherlands.

He returned home to find that European scientists had mostly failed to back his conclusion that he had found the missing link. German zoologist Paul Matschie only read Dubois's third quarterly report of 1892, but he suggested that the Trinil skullcap, molar tooth, and thighbone had originated from three separate species. Anatomist Wilhelm Krause attributed the skullcap and molar tooth to an ape and the thighbone to a human. Rudolf Virchow was critical of Dubois's evolutionary model and attributed the skullcap to a gibbon and the thighbone to a human. Other sceptics included French anthropologist Paul Topinard and Dutch anthropologist Herman ten Kate[6].

In Britain, Richard Lydekker claimed that the Trinil skullcap belonged to a modern human afflicted by microcephaly[17]. More than a century later, Indonesian anthropologist Teuku Jacob proposed the same explanation for the remarkable 'hobbits' (*Homo floresiensis*) from the island of Flores to the immediate east of Java[18]. Scottish anatomist David John Cunningham[19] noted that the skullcap and the molar tooth "*present no such characters as would warrant the formation of a new family. The cranium at least is undoubtedly human. Most certainly they are not derived from a transition form between any of the existing anthropoid apes and man… The so-called Pithecanthropus is in the direct human line, although it occupies a place on this considerably lower than any human form at present known*". Cunningham also asserted that the thighbone's "*form and proportions are more those of a modern than of a prehistoric thigh-bone*" and that it was unlikely to have originated with the same individual as the skullcap. Fellow Scot Arthur Keith agreed that the remains were "*indicative of a human race more primitive than any hitherto discovered*"[20]. Anatomist Sir William Turner said that "*there is nothing in the configuration of the skull-cap to place it in a different category from those remains of human Quaternary Man* [i.e., Neanderthals] *obtained in Europe, which have already been referred to as possessing similar characters*"[21].

Dubois's claim that his fossils represented a transitional form between humans and apes was supported only by Ernst Haeckel[22], French anthropologist Léonce-Pierre Manouvrier, and American palaeontologist Othniel Charles Marsh. Manouvrier was unconvinced that the skullcap, molar, and thighbone had originated from the same individual, but he was otherwise supportive, and his estimates of the cranial capacity agreed with those of Dubois[23]. Marsh said that Dubois had *"proved to science the existence of a new prehistoric anthropoid form, not human indeed, but in size, brain power, and erect posture, much nearer man than any animal hitherto discovered, living or extinct"*. Marsh also noted that *"Dr. Dubois's discovery was not received with great favor, and the facts and conclusions stated in his memoir were much criticised. Among a score or more of notices of this elaborate memoir which appeared subsequent to my review, I do not recall a single one that, in attempting to weigh the evidence presented, admitted the full importance of the discovery made by Dr. Dubois. The early conclusions seemed to be that the various remains discovered were human, and of no great age; that they did not belong to the same individual; that the skull apparently pertained to an idiot; and that both the skull and femur showed pathological features. In fact, the old story of the distrust aroused by the discovery of the Neanderthal skull, nearly forty years before, was repeated, although in a milder form"*[24].

Dubois cannot be faulted for his initial response to the lukewarm reception his claims received. Within weeks of his return to Europe, he embarked on a tour to promote his claims[25]. He attended numerous conferences and symposia and lectured at nearly every major institution in Europe between 1895 and 1896. He exhibited his fossils and permitted others to examine them, arguing his case in person. His promotional tour took in Leiden, Liège, Brussels, Paris, London, Cambridge, Edinburgh, Berlin, and Jena. He provided additional information about the geology and fauna of Trinil, and he made comparative studies of the Trinil thighbone against anthropological collections in Paris. This campaign won Dubois a significant number of converts, and the position of *Pithecanthropus* in human evolution became a topic of considerable interest. In the five years following his return, Dubois published 19 articles on *Pithecanthropus*, while others published just under a hundred. On average, such articles were appearing almost fortnightly. Dubois gained considerable recognition for his work: in 1886, he was awarded the Prix Broca for contributions to anthropology, and a year later, he was awarded an honorary doctorate in botany and zoology by the University of Amsterdam[5,6]. At the Fourth International Congress of Zoologists, held at Cambridge on 22 - 27 August 1898, Ernst Haeckel spoke in support, stating that the Trinil fossils were *"a relic of that extinct group intermediate between man and ape to which as long ago as 1886 I gave the name Pithecanthropus. He is the long-sought 'missing link' in the chain of higher primates"*. He noted that the estimated cranial capacity of 900 to 1,000 cc was about two-thirds the human average and twice that of the apes, placing *Pithecanthropus* midway between the two[22].

A year later, just when Dubois seemed to be winning the argument, he accepted a comparatively minor role as Professor of Geology at the University of Amsterdam. Just as the importance of fossils was becoming appreciated in the quest for human origins, Dubois withdrew from the debate. Between 1900 and 1922, he published just five articles about *Pithecanthropus*. He withdrew all access to his fossils, refusing to allow anybody to examine them until 1923[5,6].

Withdrawal

The conventional view is that Dubois was acting out of pique. He was not satisfied with the honours that had come his way: he wanted complete uncritical acceptance that *Pithecanthropus* was the missing link. After all the initial scepticism he faced, nothing else would do. This view makes very little sense, given that the tide was clearly turning his way. In the 1920s and 1930s, there were suggestions that he had suffered a breakdown, but there is little evidence for this. During this self-imposed exile, Dubois published a total of 116 papers on geology and hydrology, and he was the sole author of all but one of these papers. It is difficult to see how he could have accomplished this with serious mental health issues[6].

Another suggestion is that the issue was Dubois's overbearing anxiety about his intellectual property. In May 1897, Dubois invited German anatomist Gustav Schwalbe, Professor of Anatomy at the University of Strasburg, to study the Trinil fossils. Two years later, to Dubois's dismay, Schwabe published a detailed analysis of *Pithecanthropus* without first seeking his permission. The monograph[26] took up over 200 pages of the first edition of a new journal, *Zeitschrift für Morphologie und Anthropologie* ('Journal of Morphology and Anthropology'), which Schwalbe himself had launched. The journal was intended to promote the theory of evolution in Germany, and also, in the first edition, Schwalbe[27] emphasised the importance of the fossil record to the field of comparative anatomy. In subsequent editions, Schwalbe outlined an evolutionary scheme encompassing apes, humans, *Pithecanthropus*, and Neanderthals[6]. The journal remained in print for just over a century, finally ceasing publication in 2001. The imagined episode with Fürbringer a decade earlier must have been on Dubois's mind as he saw Schwalbe building his reputation on the very fossils that he had given him access to in 1897[5,6].

In the meantime, Dubois was now in his relatively unimportant professorship at the University of Amsterdam, and his status depended primarily on his being the custodian of the Trinil fossils. He saw Schwalbe and others receiving credit for the fossils and reasoned that if matters were allowed to continue, there would be little to be gained by producing a new and more detailed description. Accordingly, he decided to deny access to the fossils until he was ready to publish, but this would take many years. Dubois was particularly interested in the evolutionary development of brains, and he actually published far more extensively on this subject than he did on *Pithecanthropus*. He developed a theory that related the evolutionary development of mammals to increases in brain size, which stated that for every evolutionary advance, the brain size doubles in size relative to the body. Thus, human brains are four times the size of great ape brains, eight times the size of carnivore and ungulate brains, and sixteen times the size of rabbit brains[5].

The problem for Dubois was that the theory predicted that *Pithecanthropus*, lying halfway between humans and apes, should have a brain that was half the relative size of a human. But it did not. At 900 cc, its brain was nearer two-thirds the size of a modern human brain. For the theory to work, *Pithecanthropus* would have to be rather more massive than a modern human, whereas the thighbone suggested that its stature was comparable. To get around this difficulty, Dubois postulated that the relative proportions of the limbs and the torso were more apelike, i.e., *Pithecanthropus* had relatively shorter limbs than a human. The larger torso gave *Pithecanthropus* the extra weight needed to make the theory work and had the added advantage that its locomotion was now still partially apelike. Dubois now likened

Pithecanthropus to a giant gibbon, leading to another popular misconception, that he had repudiated his claim that it was the missing link. This is not so: recall that Dubois believed that humans evolved from gibbonlike ancestors. *Pithecanthropus* would, therefore, be more gibbonlike in form than humans[5].

This was clearly what Sir Arthur Keith had in mind when he said that Dubois "*tended to bend the facts rather than alter his ideas*", but the main problem with the model was a flawed underlying premise. Humans are not more 'advanced' than rabbits, because evolution does not work that way. Natural selection favours the organisms that are most effective at reproducing and passing on their genes. Rabbits, as is well known, are supremely effective at this. Larger brains are only one adaptive solution; there are many others. In the case of rabbits, it is sheer fecundity.

While Dubois worked on his theory, which would not be complete until 1928, irritation at the lack of access to his fossils grew. In 1922, Henry Fairfield Osborn, President of the American Museum of Natural History, New York, delivered an international protest about the situation to the Koninklijke Nederlandse Akademie van Wetenschappen (Royal Dutch Academy of Sciences), who in turn put pressure on Dubois to allow any qualified scientist to study his fossils[6]. In July of the following year, Dubois invited Czech anthropologist Aleš Hrdlička, Curator of Physical Anthropology at the United States National Museum (now the Smithsonian Institution), to examine the fossils. He also provided plaster casts to the Koninklijke Nederlandse Akademie van Wetenschappen, the United States National Museum, and the American Museum of Natural History[28].

Black and Weidenreich in China

In 1899, a European doctor found a human tooth among fossils being sold for use in traditional medicine in a Beijing drugstore. Palaeontologists eventually traced the tooth's origin to a complex of fossil-bearing limestone caves at Longgushan ('Dragon Bone Hill') near the village of Zhoukoudian (then known in the West as Chou Kou Tien), located 40 km (25 miles) southwest of Beijing. In 1921, the Swedish geologist Johan Gunnar Andersson began excavating a collapsed cave at Zhoukoudian. The site became known as Locality 1, to distinguish it from other caves in the area. In 1923, Anderson and Austrian palaeontologist Otto Zdansky found a human molar at Locality 1. A second human molar was subsequently found in 1926 among fossils that had been shipped back to Sweden[11].

These discoveries attracted the interest of Davidson Black, a Canadian anthropologist at the Peking[12] Union Medical School[29]. Black sought support from the Rockefeller Foundation for more extensive excavations, which granted him $80,000 (equivalent to about $1.35 million in 2022) to establish the Cenozoic Research Laboratory at the Peking Union Medical School. Excavations commenced in 1927 at Locality 1 under Swedish palaeontologist Anders Birgir Bohlin, and a further human molar was discovered[30]. Black described the teeth as *Sinanthropus pekinensis* ('Chinese man of Peking')[31]. While it was arguably premature to erect a new species and genus based on three teeth, more substantial finds soon followed[32]. In 1928, two partial human jawbones and skull fragments were recovered[33], and in 1929, the

---

[12] Beijing was known in the west as Peking or Pekin until the mid-1980s, although the BBC held out until 1990. The old name survives in such forms as the Chinese dish Peking Duck and the dog breed Pekinese.

new field director Pei Wenzhong found a skullcap. There was now ample fossil evidence for what became popularly known as Peking Man[11,34].

In March 1934, Black died suddenly from a heart attack, four months short of his fiftieth birthday. He was succeeded by German anatomist Franz Weidenreich from the University of Chicago. Weidenreich, who was Jewish, had moved to the United States after Hitler came to power. Work continued at Zhoukoudian until the Japanese invasion in 1937, by which time it had produced a total of five more or less complete skullcaps, nine large skull fragments, six facial fragments, 14 partial jawbones, 147 isolated teeth, and eleven postcranial bones. These represented more than forty *Sinanthropus* individuals, of both sexes, and all ages[11,35,36].

The similarities between *Sinanthropus* and *Pithecanthropus* were soon noticed[37]. Weidenreich had no doubt that *Sinanthropus* was a hominid (as then defined), a member of Family *Hominidae*. He said that the similarities were so close that "*there cannot remain the slightest doubt that Pithecanthropus is a real hominid belonging to the same primitive group as Sinanthropus*"[36].

Dubois was furious, and while accepting that *Sinanthropus* was a human species, this was emphatically not the case for *Pithecanthropus*, which he maintained was more apelike. If *Pithecanthropus* was a member of the human family, albeit a primitive member, it could not be the missing link. It could not be a member of the transitional family Dubois believed to exist between humans and apes. Hence, he would fight tooth and nail against suggestions that it belonged to Family *Hominidae*. In 1935, he published an article entitled *On the Gibbon-like Appearance of Pithecanthropus erectus*[38]. But he was fighting a rearguard action, and developments in Java itself were about to add to his difficulties.

Von Koenigswald in Java

While Weidenreich was making discoveries at Zhoukoudian, Dutch palaeontologist Ralph von Koenigswald made a further discovery in Java. He arrived in Java early in 1931 to study animal fossils discovered at multiple locations in Java and stored at the Dutch Geological Survey in Badung. In August of that year, a geological surveyor discovered a fossil-rich terrace on the Solo River, near the small village Ngandong in central Java. The following month, the Dutch Geological Survey began excavating the terrace. Within days, fossil human skulls began turning up. Von Koenigswald was not initially involved with the excavations, but he was interested in human evolution and was quick to investigate reports that human skulls had been found[5].

Von Koenigswald had hoped that the new finds would be *Pithecanthropus*, but the cranial vault and browridges appeared more modern, and the extensive faunal remains suggested a more recent origin. Excavations at Ngandong continued until November 1932, by which time twelve human skulls and two shinbones had been found, along with extensive faunal remains. The average cranial capacity was around 1,100 cc – less than a modern human but greater than *Pithecanthropus*. The remains came to be known as Solo Man, and their age and affinities would be disputed for many years[5,11]. Dubois, for his part, wasted little time in dismissing any connection between Solo Man and *Pithecanthropus*[39].

However, von Koenigswald's hopes of finding fossils more closely resembling *Pithecanthropus* were soon to be realised. Excavating near Mojokerto, eastern Java, in 1936, a member of von Koenigswald's team named Andojo[13] recovered a partial juvenile skull[5]. The skull later became known as the Mojokerto Child, and it belonged to a child originally believed to have been aged four to six years old at death. Computerised tomography has since shown that the development of the Mojokerto Child is more consistent with an age of one year to 18 months old at death. Their brain had attained 72 to 84 per cent of adult size, similar to a chimpanzee, but far more than the figure of just 50 per cent for a modern infant[40]. To von Koenigswald, the skull was clearly human, but he named it *Pithecanthropus modjokertensis*. This drew an angry rebuke from Dubois, so in the hope of pacifying him, von Koenigswald renamed the juvenile fossil *Homo modjokertensis*. Privately, he continued to refer to it as *Pithecanthropus*[5].

Beginning in September 1937, von Koenigswald made further discoveries at Sangiran, central Java, after promising to pay local people 10 cents for each find. The finds included three partial craniums, some partial jawbones, and a large number of isolated teeth. Von Koenigswald's delight at these discoveries was somewhat tempered when he learned that his helpers had broken the most complete cranium into smaller pieces to maximise their bounty. The reconstructed cranium was nevertheless decisive. It contained the region of the ear and the region where the cranium articulates with the jawbone. Both regions were humanlike, not apelike. There could be no doubt: *Pithecanthropus* was human[5]. In 1939, von Koenigswald and Weidenreich suggested that *Pithecanthropus* and *Sinanthropus* were "*related to each other in the same way as two different races of present mankind*"[41].

Dubois was having none of this and continued to reject any comparison between his find and von Koenigswald's. In a trilogy of papers published in the journal of the Royal Dutch Academy of Sciences[42–44], he accused von Koenigswald and Weidenreich of allowing themselves to be guided by preconceived opinions rather than studying the material in an unbiased way. He died on 16 December 1940, just weeks after the last paper in the series was published and having spent the final years of his life locked in a bitter feud with von Koenigswald. The latter, for his part, remained critical of Dubois and his work until his death in 1982[6].

It is now generally accepted that von Koenigswald and Weidenreich were right and *Pithecanthropus* and *Sinanthropus* belong to the same species. In 1950, as part of an attempt to tidy up the bewildering plethora of hominin genera, the German biologist Ernst Mayr reclassified both as *Homo erectus*. The logic was that if a species was human, then it should be included in *Homo*. The view that the Javanese and Chinese populations could represent different 'races' is also thought to be likely. Multiple evolutionary lineages could have existed in East Asia, and some populations could have retained primitive features that were lost in other populations[45,46].

Loss of the Zhoukoudian fossils

Unfortunately, the Zhoukoudian fossils were lost during World War II. Work at the site had been halted by the Japanese invasion in 1937, but the fossils remained at the Cenozoic Research Laboratory of the Peking Union Medical College until 1941. As the fighting intensified, an attempt was made to transfer them to the American Museum of Natural

---

[13] Many, though not all, Indonesians are known only by a single name.

History for safekeeping. The fossils were entrusted to a group of US Marines, who were to transport them by rail to the Marine base at the port of Qinhuangdao, 300 km (185 miles) east of Beijing. From there, they were to be shipped to the United States aboard the SS *President Harrison*. But on the morning of 7 December, the Japanese attacked Pearl Harbor, bringing the United States into the war. The SS *President Harrison*, after being pursued by Japanese warships, was deliberately run aground to prevent her from falling into enemy hands, and never reached Qinhuangdao[14]. The fossils were never seen again, and their fate remains a mystery to this day.

Fortunately, Weidenreich had made plaster casts, now kept at the American Museum of Natural History, and copies of the casts are held by the Institute of Vertebrate Palaeontology and Palaeoanthropology (the successor to the Cenozoic Research Laboratory) in Beijing. After the war, excavation resumed at Zhoukoudian, and several discoveries have been made since, including two skull fragments. Zhoukoudian became a World Heritage site in 1987[11].

Theories abound as to the fate of the fossils. One theory was that they went down with the *Awa Maru*, an ocean liner requisitioned by the Japanese military and sunk by the US submarine *Queenfish* in March 1945. In the 1970s, the Chinese located the wreck and spent five years searching for the gold, platinum, and diamonds that were supposedly on board. Neither the fossils nor any treasure was found.

In 2010, Paul Bowen, the son of a former US Marine, contacted American anthropologist Lee Berger and claimed his father had come across the fossils in 1947 during the Chinese Civil War[47]. Cpl. Richard M. Bowen was with a group of Marines in Qinhuagdao that came under fire from advancing communist forces. While digging foxholes for shelter, the group dug up a footlocker containing bones. They promptly reburied the box and were safely evacuated back to the United States shortly thereafter. A likely scenario is that the fossils did indeed reach the Marine base at Qinhuangdao, but not in time to be loaded onto a ship. In the undoubtedly chaotic evacuation of troops from China, the officer in charge of the fossils took the decision to bury them for later retrieval. It must be assumed that nobody involved in the burial survived the war.

Berger procured two 1930s maps of the Marine base, and Paul Bowen was able to identify a stone barracks where the 1947 incident took place on both maps. In November 2010, Berger and two Chinese colleagues from the Institute of Vertebrate Palaeontology and Palaeoanthropology visited Qinhuagdao in the hope of locating the burial site. A Mr Wang, who had been a child in 1947, remembered both the US Marines and the stone barracks highlighted by Paul Bowen. The area was heavily built-up in the 1970s, but some World War II-era landmarks were still visible. From these, and the details provided by Paul Bowen and Mr Wang, Berger and his colleagues were able to pinpoint the site of the long-demolished barracks to within an area measuring 200 × 200 m (220 × 220 yards). Unfortunately, the area now holds warehouses and parking lots. Recovery of the fossils, assuming the footlocker survived the 1970s construction work, will be impossible until the site is redeveloped. This presupposes the fossils were even there in the first place, which is by no means certain. The fact remains that the last definite sighting of the fossils was when they left the Peking Union Medical School aboard a USMC vehicle.

---

[14] The Japanese nevertheless managed to salvage the wreck. After repairs, the ship was renamed the *Kachidoki Maru*.

From Asia to Africa

After World War II, there was a shift in emphasis from Asia to Africa as the 'cradle of mankind'. British archaeologist Robin Dennell[48] has given four main reasons for the change. The first of these is that the australopithecines were now being accepted as human ancestors. The first example had been discovered by the Australian anthropologist Raymond Dart at Taung, South Africa, in 1924. Dart[49] described the juvenile cranium as having belonged to an ape that walked upright like a human, despite being only slightly larger-brained than a chimpanzee. Thanks to the efforts of Scottish palaeontologist Robert Broom[50], Dart's conclusions were eventually accepted, and longstanding sceptic Sir Arthur Keith conceded that he had been wrong and Dart had been right all along[51].

The second reason was the belated proof that the notorious *Eoanthropus dawsoni*, better known as Piltdown Man, was a forgery[52]. A large-brained but apelike hominid fitted early twentieth-century 'brains-first' models, which stated that large brains were the most important feature distinguishing humans from apes and must have begun to develop before any other distinguishing features. But it was completely at odds with the picture that had subsequently emerged from the fossil evidence. The globular braincase was at odds with the long, low braincase of Neanderthals and *Homo erectus*; the large brain was at odds with the chimpanzee-sized brains of the australopithecines.

The third factor was that the Old Guard, who had argued strongly for an Asian origin, were now dead: in addition to Dubois, they included the British trio of Sir Arthur Keith, Sir Grafton Elliot Smith, and Sir Arthur Smith Woodward, all of whom had died by the mid-1950s. Black had died before the war, and Weidenreich lived only until 1948. Only von Koenigswald lived into 1980s. In most cases, these men left no trained successors to continue their work.

The fourth factor was the work of British palaeoanthropologists Louis and Mary Leakey, who began excavating at Olduvai Gorge, Tanzania, in the early 1950s. In 1959, Mary found an almost-complete australopithecine skull that Louis described as *Zinjanthropus boisei* (Boise's man from East Africa). Zinj is the ancient Arabic name for East Africa; Charles Boise was an American mining engineer who had financially assisted the Leakeys' work since 1948[53]. The next year, the Leakeys' son Jonathon found a juvenile jawbone, several skull fragments, and some postcranial remains. Formally designated OH (Olduvai Hominid) 7, they were eventually described as a new human species, *Homo habilis* ('Handy man'), a name suggested by Raymond Dart. It was claimed that *Homo habilis* was an earlier, smaller-brained, and more primitive human species than *Homo erectus*[54,55]. Louis Leakey's larger-than-life personality made him a household name and helped to ensure that Olduvai Gorge took centre stage. At the same time, fieldwork in China was halted for three decades following the communist takeover and the establishment of the Peoples' Republic of China.

Date of the Mojokerto Child

The date of the Mojokerto Child has long been a source of controversy. The first attempt to date the skull was made in 1969 by American geochronologist Garniss Curtis using the potassium-argon method[15], a technique he helped to develop. Curtis collected volcanic rock samples from the site where the cranium was supposedly found, which he assumed would be the same age. He was shown the spot by Teuku Jacob, a former student of Ralph von Koenigswald. He obtained a date of 1.9 million years, albeit with some uncertainty. Even the lower range of his estimates made the Mojokerto child far older than the one million years most believed it to be, and very few experts accepted it[5].

In 1990, Curtis re-dated his 1969 samples using the more accurate argon-argon technique that had been devised in the intervening years. This time, he obtained an age of 1.7 million years, with a lower degree of uncertainty. This was still 'too old', but there was now a feeling that it was worthwhile obtaining more samples. In 1992, Curtis returned to Java with a team from the Geochronology Centre at the Institute of Human Origins, Berkeley, California, including geologist Carl Swisher. They were joined by Jacob and collected volcanic pumice samples from several sites where fossils had been found, before reaching Mojokerto. There, Jacob led the team to a different site than the one he had taken Curtis to in 1969. He claimed that a few years after Curtis's first visit, he had met Andojo and asked to be shown the spot where he had found the Mojokerto cranium. The Berkley team began to suspect that nobody really knew the exact spot where the discovery was made[5].

The new samples gave an age of 1.81 million years[56], which was still 'too old'. By now, it was generally accepted that humans had originated in Africa rather than Asia, but in the early 1990s, no significantly earlier examples of *Homo* had been found in Africa. If the Mojokerto Child really was that old, it would reopen the possibility of an Asian origin. Knowing that such a date would certainly be controversial, the team delayed publishing their results. Swisher had a possible solution to the problem of the uncertainties surrounding the cranium's findspot. The cranium itself was packed with volcanic pumice, meaning that a date obtained from this material would almost certainly be correct. The only difficulty was persuading Jacob, who was known to be very protective of the fossils in his care, to agree to the extraction of sufficient pumice from the fossil to allow it to be dated[5].

In the book *Java Man*, Swisher[5] claimed that Jacob was initially agreeable, and the Berkley team travelled to Yogyakarta to carry out the work. At first, Jacob wanted to start immediately, but Swisher and his colleagues were exhausted from an overnight flight. By the time they had set up a camera and lighting to document the pumice removal, they were too tired to continue. After agreeing to meet Jacob at his lab the next morning, the team arrived only to find he'd gone to Jakarta for a pre-arranged meeting and would be gone for three days. They spent three days collecting samples near Mojokerto for palaeomagnetic analysis[16], before returning to Yogyakarta. This time, Jacob had left a note saying that he was too busy

---

[15] All radiometric dating techniques work on the same basic principle, i.e., the decay of radioactive isotopes such as radiocarbon (^{14}C). The rate of decay is known and by comparing the abundance of the isotope with that of its decay products or its expected initial abundance, the age of a sample can be determined. Examples of such techniques include radiocarbon (^{14}C), argon-argon (^{40}Ar/^{39}Ar), potassium-argon (^{40}Ka/^{40}Ar), uranium-series (U-series), and cosmogenic nuclide (^{26}Al/^{10}Be) dating.

[16] Palaeomagnetic dating relies on periodic changes in the polarity of the Earth's magnetic field. During intervals of 'reversed' (as opposed to 'normal') polarity, a compass needle will point south rather than north. Ancient polarities can be detected in volcanic rock and fine-grained sediments that settled into place relatively slowly. Ferromagnetic particles in these materials will preserve a record of the polarity at the time of cooling or settling. The last reversal occurred 780,000 years ago.

to do the work, and that he could not see them. The team left Java empty-handed, and the index of *Java Man* notes this bizarre episode as "*Jacob, Teuku, obstructive behaviour of, 86-89*". Jacob's side of the story is not known.

Nevertheless, Swisher and his colleagues decided to publish the 1.81 million year date in the journal *Science* and announced their results at a packed news conference. The story made the front page of the *New York Times*, but as they feared, the anthropological community remained sceptical. By now, though, they had a possible solution to Jacob's 'obstructive behaviour'. After coming across a 1937 photograph of the Mojokerto findspot in the archives of the American Museum of Natural History, they contacted various institutions worldwide and obtained six additional photographs taken between 1936 and 1938, showing the findspot from various angles. In 2000, they returned to Java but found that extensive farming and changes in vegetation in the intervening decades made it impossible to pinpoint the exact spot shown in the photos to within more than a few tens of metres. However, this was sufficient to show them that it was not the spot that Jacob had shown them in 1992.

The matter was partially cleared up in 2003, when a team led by New Zealand anthropologist Michael Morwood adopted a slightly different approach. Morwood's team considered the geological horizons within the Mojokerto study area, several of which contained volcanic pumice. Pumice Horizon 5 underlies the area of the Mojokerto findspot by 13 metres (42 ft 7 in) and must be older than the fossil. The pumice was not mixed with gravels or other materials, suggesting that it had been deposited soon after it was formed. The horizon was thus the same age as its constituent pumice material. Morwood and his colleagues then dated the pumice by fission track dating, which relies on counting tracks left in crystalline material by the particles emitted when atoms undergo radioactive decay. A date of 1.49 million years ago was obtained, meaning that the Mojokerto child could be no more than this[57]. By this time, the Sangiran fossils had been dated to 1.51 million years[58], meaning that the Mojokerto Child was possibly not even the oldest fossil human in Java. However, later work suggested that the Sangiran fossils are no more than 1.45 – 1.3 million years old[59]. Given that the Mojokerto date is a maximum, it now seems likely that *Homo erectus* reached Java much later than was believed in the 1990s. A more precise date for the Mojokerto Child will have to await the extraction of pumice from it. Almost three decades after the 'obstructive behaviour' debacle, this has not been attempted.

Homo erectus in Africa

Possible examples of what is still generally referred to as *Homo erectus* began to turn up in Africa within a few years of the end of World War II, although the tendency to erect new genera for each new find continued unabated. The first of these was a partial lower jawbone found by Robert Broom and his assistant John T. Robinson at Swartkrans, a limestone cave near Krugersdorp, 25 km (15 miles) northwest of Johannesburg, South Africa. Broom and Robinson described the jawbone as *Telanthropus capensis* ('Entry man from the Cape')[60,61]. Its affinities are disputed, but later finds including a partial adult skull suggested that the jawbone should be assigned to *Homo erectus*[11].

Between 1954 and 1955, the French palaeontologist Camille Arambourg found two partial lower jawbones in North Africa. The first of these was found at Tighennif, a sandpit 20 km

(12 miles) east of Mascara, Algeria. Arambourg noted similarities between his find and *Pithecanthropus* and *Sinanthropus* – still using the terminology that Mayr had attempted to deprecate. Inevitably, he described his find under another new genus, *Atlanthropus mauritanicus* ('Atlantic man from Mauritania'[17])[62]   The Tighennif jawbone has been estimated to be 700,000 years old[63], but it could be as old as 989,000 years[64]. Although generally included in *Homo erectus*, its affinities are uncertain[64,65]. The second jawbone was discovered at the site of Sidi Abderrahman, southeast of Casablanca, Morocco, and was described as being very similar to *Atlanthropus*[66]. It is likewise now considered to probably be *Homo erectus*.

The first example of a fossil with unequivocal affinities to the Javanese and Chinese *Homo erectus* to be found in Africa was a skullcap excavated by Louis Leakey at Olduvai Gorge in 1961. Leakey referred to the fossil as 'Chellean Man' because it was found in association with what was then referred to as Chellean stone hand axes[67].   The Chellean tool tradition was named for Chelles in France, but such hand axes are now generally referred to as Acheulean (for Saint-Acheul, France). The skullcap was later given the designation OH 9, and it is estimated to be 1.2 million years old[11].

Many African finds have since followed, but some argue that African examples should be classed as a separate species, *Homo ergaster* ('working man'), with the term *Homo erectus* reserved for the Asian fossil remains. Proponents of this view argue that there are subtle but significant differences between the Asian and African fossils. The skull of *Homo ergaster* (Africa) has a higher-domed cranium, fairly thin cranial bones, weak browridges, and a lightly built face, whereas *Homo erectus* (Asia) has a long, low cranium, a low forehead, thick cranial bones, a massive face and browridges[68–70]. There are also dental differences between the two populations, with the lower premolar root and crown morphology of the African population said to be more primitive than that of the Asian population[71]. Some even argue that *Sinanthropus pekinensis* should continue to be recognised as a separate species in the guise of *Homo pekinensis*[70]. It remains disputed as to whether or not these differences justify the recognition of two or more separate species[72]. Some prefer to view *Homo erectus* as a widespread and diverse species known from Africa and Eurasia[73].

About a boy

Most hominin fossil finds comprise skull fragments, partial jawbones, or teeth. As we have seen, even the latter is sometimes sufficient to erect new species. Reasonably complete skulls are rare, as are any postcranial bones (i.e., from below the neck). Near-complete skeletons are excessively rare. Examples include the world-famous 'Lucy' discovered in the 1970s. Not so well-known, but even more complete is the Turkana Boy, a subadult male *Homo erectus* found on the south bank of the Nariokotome River, 5 km (3 miles) west of Lake Turkana, Kenya. The Turkana Boy is more complete than any human fossil prior to 130,000 years ago, with only a few bones missing from the hands and feet[74].

We know nothing about the circumstances of the Turkana Boy's death. That he failed to live to adulthood was almost certainly the rule rather than the exception, but were others left

---

[17] The name here references the ancient Roman province of Mauritania, corresponding to Algeria and Morocco, rather than the present-day country of that name. It is the Roman province that gave its name to the legendary Cunard ocean liner RMS *Mauretania*.

to mourn him? We simply do not know, and never will know. All we know is that he died, and he was rapidly buried by natural processes on the edge of a marsh. In August 1984, his remains were revealed when fossil hunter Kamoya Kimeu was prospecting for fossils. Kimeu was a long-time assistant of Kenyan anthropologists Richard Leakey and his wife Maeve Leakey *nee* Epps. The team was planning to move camp the next day after failing to discover any hominin remains. While conducting a final search of the area on his own, Kimeu came across a small skull fragment that he recognised to be of human origin. Working with British anthropologist Alan Walker, the Leakeys spent the next four years excavating the findspot. They eventually recovered a complete skull and most of the skeleton of the individual who became popularly known as the Turkana Boy or the Nariokotome Boy. The remains are officially known as KNM-WT-15000 (Kenya National Museum – West Turkana)[74].

The stratigraphic position in which the Turkana Boy was found is bracketed by volcanic tuffs that were potassium-argon dated at 1.65 million years and 1.33 million years. Assuming that the deposits between the tuffs accumulated at a consistent rate, the Turkana Boy lived around 1.60 million years ago[75]. Based on dental development, he was initially estimated to be 11 to 13 years old at death, and his height was estimated to be 1.64 – 1.68 m (5 ft 4.5 – 5 ft 6 in)[75].

The Turkana Boy's arms were short in relation to his legs, unlike those of an ape. His pelvis was narrower, increasing the energy efficiency of his legs. The lower part of his ribcage was also narrowed, but the upper part was expanded to compensate in terms of chest volume and lung function. This gave him the characteristic barrel-shaped chest of a modern human. There is no doubt that the Turkana Boy was committed to the terrestrial habit and had abandoned any residual reliance on tree-climbing[74].

Although only a few of the Turkana Boy's foot bones were found, it is likely that his feet were essentially modern. Human footprints have been found preserved in two sedimentary layers near the town of Ileret, Kenya, and at around 1.51 – 1.53 million years old, they are similar in age to the Turkana Boy. The prints were made by around twenty individuals with modern, humanlike feet, arched with in-line big toes. They reflect movement and pressure distribution that is characteristic of modern human walking, and the size of the prints is consistent with the stature and body mass estimates of *Homo erectus*[76,77].

However, the Turkana Boy was not entirely like a modern human, and he possessed some archaic features. His brain, though close to adult size, was only about two-thirds the average size of that of a modern human. He lacked the globular braincase of a modern human, his forehead was flat and receding, and his browridges were prominent. He completely lacked a chin, with massive, forward-jutting jaws. He had a pronounced occipital torus or horizontal ridge at the back of the head, where the neck muscles are attached[11,74].

The Turkana Boy's overall rate of ontogenetic development and maturation was more rapid than for a modern human. In primates, there is a strong correlation between the rate of dental development (ages when the crown formation and root formation are completed) and overall development (characteristics such as adult brain weight, age of sexual maturity, and lifespan). Modern humans have a more prolonged dental development than other primates. They reach sexual maturity later and live longer[78]. Dental enamel on a growing tooth is laid down in a 24-hourly growth cycle that remains preserved in the hard tissues of the crown and roots, rather like the growth rings of a tree[79,80]. With techniques such as a scanning electron microscope, the growth increments can be counted and used to determine the time since eruption[80,81].

This technique has been used to show that early hominins had faster, more apelike rates of dental enamel growth than modern humans. Crown formation times for the Turkana Boy's back teeth were similar to those of the australopithecines and more rapid than those of modern humans. Once these faster growth rates were taken into account, it was estimated that the Turkana Boy was only eight years old rather than 11 to 13 years old as first thought[82].

It was originally estimated that Turkana Boy would have attained an impressive adult height of 1.85 m (6 ft 1 in) and weight of 68 kg (150 lb)[83]. These figures assumed that he was on the cusp of a humanlike 'adolescent growth spurt', but they were later challenged after the dental evidence showed that his rate of development and maturation had been more apelike. The 'growth spurt' of chimpanzees is less pronounced than that of modern humans, and by assuming that that of the Turkana Boy was intermediate between the two, his adult height was re-estimated at a rather less than strapping 1.68 m (5 ft 6 in) [84]. However, it was later suggested that this figure understated the chimpanzee 'growth spurt', and when this was taken into account, the adult height of the Turkana Boy was estimated to be still-respectable at over 1.75 m (5 ft 9 in)[85].

The crossroads of Europe and Asia

Lying on the eastern shores of the Black Sea, Georgia was in classical antiquity the destination of Jason and the Argonauts in their quest for the Golden Fleece. In the 1980s, evidence emerged that it was a stopping point for a much earlier human migration, from Africa rather than Ancient Greece. The ruined medieval fortress of Dmanisi lies 93 km (58 miles) southwest of the capital, Tbilisi, and it has been of interest to archaeologists for many years. During the course of one such excavation, archaeologists broke through the foundations of a medieval structure into an ancient river deposit, where simple flaked stone tools were found with faunal remains[74].

During the 1990s, fossil human remains were recovered, including two partial crania (D2280 and D2282)[86] and a lower jawbone[87]. Subsequent excavations have revealed further fossil human remains. These include the cranium (D2700), lower jawbone (D2735)[88], and partial skeleton of an adolescent[89], the cranium (D3444) and lower jawbone (D3900) of an elderly male[90], an entirely complete adult cranium (D4500) and jawbone (D2600)[91], and the postcranial bones of three adults[89]. Palaeomagnetic, potassium-argon, and argon-argon dating suggests that the site was first occupied shortly after 1.85 million years ago, and repeated occupations continued until around 1.77 million years ago[86,88–90,92,93].

The elderly male had lost all but one of his teeth in the years before his death. He could not have survived on his own and must have been cared for by others during his later years[90,92]. The most recent skull to be discovered at the site, the fifth, known as Skull 5, is characterised by a large face and thick browridges. It is complete and undeformed – the only known fully preserved adult hominin skull from the early Pleistocene[91].

From this substantial assemblage of fossil remains, it has been estimated that the Dmanisi ranged from 1.45 – 1.66 m (4 ft 9 in – 5 ft 5 in) tall and weighed 40.0 to 50.0 kg (88 to 110 lb). The cranial capacities of the five skulls range from 546 to 730 cc, only about half that of a modern human, and lower than the subadult Turkana Boy[89,91].

The Dmanisi people were initially assigned to *Homo erectus*[88], then put forward as a new human species, *Homo georgicus*[94]. This proposal was then retracted, and the rather cumbersome designation *Homo erectus ergaster georgicus* was proposed instead[91]. For all these proposals, their small body and brain sizes suggest that the Dmanisi people were simply an early form of *Homo erectus*. It could be that early *Homo erectus* was not only quite widespread geographically, but highly variable in both body and brain size, and less modern than sometimes supposed. The Dmanisi D2700 adolescent cranium is similar in size and shape to KNM-ER 42700, a partial cranium from Lake Turkana, that has been dated to 1.55 million years ago. Its cranial capacity is only 691 cc, but it is typical of larger *Homo erectus* crania when adjusted for size. The Dmanisi and early African *Homo erectus* fossils could represent different populations of a single, highly variable species[95].

When did humans first leave Africa?

Were the Dmanisi people the first humans to leave Africa? The date of 1.85 million years ago predates any of the Javanese dates. The earliest Chinese human fossil is a partial *Homo erectus* cranium that was found at the village of Gongwangling, Shaanxi Province, in 1964. Originally thought to be 1.15 million years old, it was later found to be much older at 1.63 million years. It thus slightly predates the fossil remains from Java[96]. The date was also consistent with those obtained for stone tools found at the sites of Xiaochangliang and Majuangou in the Nihewan Basin, 150 km (90 miles) west of Beijing. The earliest of these date to 1.66 million years ago[97,98].

These dates supported a picture of early humans reaching Georgia 1.85 million years ago and dispersing east towards Java and China over the next twenty millennia. However, in 2018, significantly earlier artefacts were reported from Shangchen, a newly discovered site not far from Gongwangling. Seventeen artefact layers have been identified in a largely continuous sequence. Palaeomagnetic dating shows that the most recent layer is 1.26 million years old, some 370,000 years more recent than the Gongwangling cranium. But the earliest layer is 2.12 million years old, predating the skull by 490,000 years and the Dmanisi people by 270,000 years[99]. While we do not know anything about the hominins predating the Gongwangling *Homo erectus* cranium, it is clear that Dmanisi does not represent the earliest hominin migration from Africa.

We cannot even be certain that the earliest Shangchen toolmakers were *Homo* and not australopithecines. We know that australopithecines were making stone tools 3.3 million years ago[100]. It is generally accepted that they never left Africa, but this could simply reflect a lack of preservation or even a lack of fieldwork in such a vast area. For millions of years, Africa and Eurasia have formed a single landmass, and it is only by convention that we regard Europe, Asia, and Africa as being separate continents. Early hominins are unlikely to have made the distinction. Three million years ago, the grassland savannahs of Africa extended from West Africa to northern China, and there is no obvious reason why the australopithecines could not have expanded their range there[101].

Late survival of *Homo erectus* in Asia

It is assumed that *Homo erectus* persisted in Africa until around 600,000 years ago, at which point larger-brained hominins began to emerge[11]. However, this is by no means definite. The Daka cranium, a *Homo erectus* skullcap found at Middle Awash in 2002, is one of the most recent examples, but it is around one million years old[102]. As previously noted, the Tighennif jawbone could be as recent as 700,000 years old, but its affinities are uncertain. *Homo erectus* apparently persisted in Asia until far later than it did in Africa, though by just how long remains uncertain. In 1996, it was reported that the fossil remains recovered by Von Koenigswald in the 1930s at Ngandong and a fossil skullcap found at the nearby site of Sambungmacan in the 1970s were no more than 27,000 – 53,000 years old[103]. However, subsequent studies reported rather earlier dates. One gave minimum dates of at least 143,000 years and possibly as much as 546,000 years ago[104]. More recently, a date range of 108,000 – 117,000 years was reported for the Ngandong remains[105].

However, isolated populations of Asian *Homo erectus* might have survived into the Holocene epoch and interbred with modern humans. Fossil human remains outside the range of variation of early East Asian *Homo sapiens* have been reported from three sites in southwestern China: Longlin Cave in Guangxi Province, Maludong ('Red Deer Cave') in Yunnan Province, and Dushan Cave in Changshou District. The Longlin fossils included a partial skull, a temporal bone fragment probably belonging to the skull, a partial lower jawbone, and some fragmentary postcranial bones. The cheekbones of the skull are broad and flared sideways, giving it a strong facial resemblance to *Star Wars* villain Darth Vader. Features reminiscent of archaic hominins include conspicuous browridges and a less prominent chin than that of a modern human. The Maludong remains include a skullcap, two partial jawbones, and a partial thighbone. The two sites are located 300 km (185 miles) apart, and radiocarbon dating has yielded an age of 11,500 years for Longlin and 14,000 years for Maludong[106].

The Longlin and Maludong hominins were popularly reported as the Red Deer Cave people. At first, it was thought that they represent a single population, but later work suggested that the 'Darth Vader' Longlin skull has affinities to early *Homo sapiens*. The bony labyrinth (the bony outer wall of the inner ear) of the temporal bone fragment resembles that of a modern human. The skull's unusual shape could have resulted from interbreeding between archaic and modern humans. Possibly, Longlin was a 'hybrid zone' located on a border between relict archaic and modern populations. Such hybrid zones are known to occur with some present-day non-human primate populations[107], and occurred between Neanderthals and Denisovans[108]. On the other hand, the Maludong thighbone has affinities to archaic humans, in particular those from the Early Pleistocene such as *Homo erectus*. The thighbone has not been assigned to a particular human species, but *Homo erectus* is certainly likely[109].

The fossil remains found at Dushan Cave are 15,850 – 12,765 years old. They include a partial cranium, fragments of a lower jawbone, and a complete set of teeth except for a left third molar (M_3). All these remains were associated with the same individual, known as Dushan 1. Although the remains were assigned to *Homo sapiens*, the dentition is a mosaic of archaic and modern features. The dentition of Dushan 1 could simply represent a high degree of regional variation. Alternatively, Dushan 1 could be a late surviving descendant of one of the earliest modern human groups to settle in what was an isolated region of southern China. It could have retained primitive dental traits that typically occur in Middle Pleistocene archaic humans. There is also the possibility that these features were the result of interbreeding with a late-surviving archaic population in the region[110]. The findings from these three Chinese sites suggest that isolated populations of archaic humans, possibly *Homo erectus*, could have still been living in China as late as 11,500 years ago and that some of them interbred with modern humans.

One species or many

By the early 1980s, a picture of early human evolution was beginning to emerge. *Homo habilis*, initially controversial, was now becoming accepted as the earliest, most primitive, and still quite apelike human species. Some have argued that it should be classed as an australopithecine (*Australopithecus*) rather than a human (*Homo*)[101,111]. The estimated cranial capacity of no more than 600 cc[71] is way below even the 750 cc human minimum Sir Arthur Keith proposed in the late 1940s[112]. The apparent apelike features such as proportionately long arms and short legs, and curved, sturdy hand bones suggested that *Homo habilis* had retained some tree-climbing ability[113,114]. Against this, it was argued that there is insufficient fossil evidence to infer apelike limb proportions[115,116]. Even now, the only postcranial remains to have been found are hands, portions of a right arm and both legs, and a reasonably complete foot (OH 8)[11]. It should be remembered that near-complete skeletons such as the Turkana Boy are very much the exception. There is no example of *Homo habilis* in anything like such a state of preservation.

Despite these concerns, *Homo habilis* became widely accepted as the earliest representative of our genus, *Homo*. Compared to the australopithecines, the skull was less massively built, and the upper and lower jaws were within the size range of both *Homo erectus* and modern humans. The feet were humanlike, as were the thumb joints[117]. Analysis of the skull characteristics of *Homo habilis* in comparison to those of other hominins suggests that it does indeed belong within *Homo*, albeit the most basal member of the genus[118,119].

The 1980s view was that *Homo habilis* evolved from an australopithecine ancestor; in turn, *Homo habilis* evolved into *Homo erectus*, and *Homo erectus* evolved into a larger-brained, but still archaic, form of *Homo sapiens*. These 'archaic *Homo sapiens*' included subspecies such as Neanderthals, and from them eventually arose wholly modern *Homo sapiens sapiens*, which was itself regarded as a subspecies. The so-called 'robust' australopithecines (*Paranthropus*) were thought to be an extinct side-branch from this sequence[120].

This simple, unilinear scenario turned out to be a massive oversimplification. How *Homo sapiens*, Neanderthals, and Denisovans (whose existence was unsuspected in the 1980s) emerged from the Middle Pleistocene 'muddle in the middle' I have discussed elsewhere. However, the evolutionary history of earlier *Homo* is no less complex. That the scenario outlined above might not be the full picture first became apparent in the mid-1980s. Overall, there was found to be a large degree of variability within the fossil material assigned to *Homo habilis*. This was commonly attributed to a high degree of sexual dimorphism, or physical differences between the sexes[121], but some suspected that the 'male' and 'female' fossils might actually represent two different species. Soviet anthropologist Valery Alekseyev proposed assigning KNM-ER 1470, a well-preserved *Homo habilis* cranium from Koobi Fora, a site on the eastern shores of Lake Turkana, to a new human species, *Homo rudolfensis*. The name refers to the original European name for the lake, Lake Rudolf. The cranium was discovered in 1972 and assigned to *Homo habilis*, but Alekseyev noted that it has a flatter, broader face, and larger teeth than are typical for *Homo habilis* and proposed a new designation for it[71,117]. KNM-ER 1470 is now thought to be 2.03 million years old[122]. Following Alekseyev's proposal, several fossils were reassigned to *Homo rudolfensis*, although none were postcranial remains[68,71].

The existence of *Homo rudolfensis* as a separate species remained controversial, not least of all because there was no real agreement on which (if any) of the recognised *Homo habilis* fossils should be reassigned to the new species[117,123]. However, in 2012, fossils were found at Koobi Fora that supported the distinctiveness of *Homo rudolfensis* from *Homo habilis*. The new fossils range in age from 1.78 to 1.95 million years old and include the well-preserved face of an adolescent, one nearly complete and one fragmentary lower jawbone. The face shares many of the features distinguishing the original 1972 cranium from other specimens of early *Homo*, and the dental arcade of the jawbones differs in shape from that of *Homo habilis*[124].

A 2015 reconstruction of the lower jawbone of the OH 7 *Homo habilis* further supported the two-species scenario. It was found that the jawbone was surprisingly apelike, with a long and narrow dental arcade closer to *Australopithecus afarensis* than to the parabolic arcades of *Homo sapiens* or *Homo erectus*. The overall shape of the arcade was not compatible with the specimens assigned to *Homo rudolfensis*, again suggesting that the latter is a separate species[125].

It was suggested that *Homo habilis* is bracketed in time by AL 666-1, a 2.33-million-year-old upper jawbone recovered at Hadar, in the Afar region of Ethiopia[126] and by KNM-ER-42703, a 1.44-million-year-old partial upper jawbone from Koobi Fora, Kenya[72], but doubts later emerged that either fossil represents *Homo habilis*. If AL 666-1 is excluded, then the oldest uncontested *Homo habilis* remains are only 1.9 million years old[95]. If KNM-ER-42703 is excluded, the most recent example of *Homo habilis* lived 1.65 million years ago[125].

Problems began to arise with the reconstruction of the OH 7 lower jawbone. It was more primitive than the AL 666-1 upper jawbone, despite being 500,000 more recent. If hominins with a more humanlike jawbone morphology already existed 2.33 million years ago, then the origin of *Homo habilis* must lie even further back in time. AL 666-1 also lacked any features in common with *Homo rudolfensis*[125], and the researchers noted an earlier suggestion that AL 666-1 shows similarities to early *Homo erectus*[91]. If correct, it made the first occurrence of the species 680,000 years earlier than the 1.65 million-year-old KNM-ER 3733 cranium from Koobi Fora, East Turkana[127], then recognised as the earliest African example of *Homo erectus*. In 2020, a 2.04 million-year-old *Homo erectus* cranium (DNH 134 skull) was found Drimolen, South Africa[128]. Even this was older than the earliest uncontested example of *Homo habilis*.

The authors of the OH 7 study also challenged the long-standing view that the brain of *Homo habilis* was significantly smaller than that of *Homo erectus* and obtained a range of 730 – 825 cc for the OH 7 individual based on a reassessment of two parietal bones. This figure lies within the range for *Homo erectus*, albeit at the lower end. The results were consistent with a view that early humans were distinguished more by facial morphology than they were by differences in brain size. Rather than one evolving from another, *Homo habilis*, *Homo rudolfensis*, and *Homo erectus* coexisted in East Africa two million years ago. Their differing facial morphology probably reflected adaptations to different environments[125].

A more radical suggestion is that *Homo habilis* and *Homo rudolfensis*, in common with the Dmanisi people, were no more than early forms of *Homo erectus*. On this view, early *Homo* is seen as a single evolving lineage rather than multiple species. Proponents of this view claimed that shape variation within the five Dmanisi crania is roughly the same as that within the various early *Homo* crania from East Africa, even though the former are recognised as belonging to a single species, and the latter are generally recognised as representing several[91]. The suggestion that such conclusions can be drawn from a consideration of cranial shapes alone has been questioned[129], especially given the supposed retention of tree-climbing adaptations by *Homo habilis*[114]. However, as noted, very little postcranial *Homo habilis* and *Homo rudolfensis* material has been found, so this counterclaim itself may be questioned. Regardless of whether *Homo habilis*, *Homo rudolfensis*, and *Homo erectus* are regarded as one species or several, the likelihood is that they all could interbreed in the same way that *Homo sapiens*, Neanderthals, and Denisovans could all interbreed.

Toolmaking abilities and symbolic behaviour of *Homo erectus*

The signature tool of *Homo erectus* was the Acheulean hand axe, flat cobbles or large flakes that were completely flaked over on both sides to produce a sharp edge around the entire periphery. They were commonly teardrop-shaped, narrowing from a broad base at one end to a rounded point at the other. Other common shapes include ovals and triangles. Acheulean hand axes are one of the most distinctive, commonest, most widely distributed, and longest-lasting of all prehistoric artefacts. Several hundred thousand have been recovered from sites in many regions of Africa and Eurasia[74].

The longstanding view is that *Homo habilis* and the earliest *Homo erectus* made only simple flake stone tools (Oldowan, or Mode 1), but *Homo erectus* soon graduated to the more sophisticated Acheulean hand axes (Mode 2), supposedly reflecting their greater cognitive abilities. In fact, hand axes were not adopted everywhere, even by *Homo erectus*. In particular, they are rare east of the so-called Movius Line[18] in East Asia. It seems likely that economic rather than cognitive factors led to the invention and use of the hand axes. The earliest manufacture of these tools coincides with a long-term drying period 1.7 million years ago, which resulted in the expansion of grasslands and grazing bovid species in East Africa. The hand axes could have been better suited to the butchery of large herbivore carcasses than sharp Oldowan flakes[130].

Another longstanding view is that *Homo erectus* was incapable of symbolic thought[131], but tantalising evidence emerged to the contrary in 2015. Researchers were studying freshwater mussel shells collected by Eugène Dubois at Trinil in 1891, which now form part of the Dubois Collection in the Naturalis Biodiversity Centre in Leiden. The shells are 430,000 – 540,000 years old. The researchers found that a geometric pattern of grooves had been engraved into one of the shells. The pattern was probably made with a shark's tooth and appears to have been intentionally created. It consists of a zigzag line with three sharp turns

---

[18] Named for American archaeologist Hallam Movius, who first drew attention to the apparent absence.

producing an 'M' shape, a set of more superficial parallel lines, and a zigzag with two turns producing a back-to-front 'N'. Another shell had been sharpened and polished for use as a cutting tool: the earliest-known example of the use of shells for toolmaking. The engraved geometric pattern suggests that at least some capacity for symbolic thought was already present in early humans 500,000 years ago[132].

Despite this, it is unlikely that *Homo erectus* was capable of modern speech. The thoracic vertebral canal of the Turkana Boy is much narrower than that of a modern human and closer in relative size to that of a non-human primate. The nerves passing through this region control breathing, and *Homo erectus* might have lacked the fine breathing control necessary for modern speech. Without it, early hominins would only have been capable of short, unmodulated utterances, like those of extant non-human primates[133].

Use of fire

There is no doubt that mastery of the use of fire was a breakthrough for early humans. A fire can deter predators, provide heat and lighting, and be used for cooking. It would have allowed activities to be performed after dark and would certainly have been a major asset in colder regions of Eurasia.

British primatologist Richard Wrangham[134] has suggested the invention of cooking food played an important role in human evolution. Cooking food makes it more palatable and increases the available nutrient. Wrangham suggested that cooking food enabled the gut to become smaller. Guts and brains are the two most energetically 'expensive' organs in the human body, and the energy saved by shrinking the former enabled the latter to become larger. Wrangham's model predicts that the first evidence for fire use should coincide with the emergence of the first hominins with brains significantly larger than those of the australopithecines – but clear evidence does not appear in the archaeological record until much later. Finding incontrovertible evidence for fire use is more difficult than finding stone tools: a fire is transient and can only be inferred from clear evidence that combustion has occurred. There is also the issue of distinguishing the controlled use of fire from natural wildfire. In Africa, the latter is commonly started by lightning. However, the importance of the early use of fire is such that the evidence must indeed be incontrovertible to be accepted[135]: for example, evidence for hearths. Unfortunately, this is lacking from the earliest candidate sites.

The earliest evidence from Africa is inconclusive. Localised red patches of oxidised sediment found at Koobi Fora site FxJj20 are around 1.6 million years old and are thought to be the remains of fire use by early humans. Similar evidence has been reported from the slightly more recent Kenyan site of Chesowanja. Stronger evidence has been found at Swartkrans, which is about 1.0 to 1.5 million years old, where archaeologists have recovered 270 burned animal bones from a gully in the uppermost level of the cave, Member 3[136]. The problem is that it cannot be ruled out that wildfire ignited inflammable material, including animal bones lying on the floor of the cave mouth, and that these were later washed by rainfall deeper into the gully where Member 3 formed[135]. The counter-argument is that the burned bones are found throughout the 6 m (19 ft 8 in) thick Member 3, but hardly any have been found in the earlier Members 1 and 2. The latter two also contain animal remains in large quantities, and if wildfire had been responsible for the burning, then burned bones would have been found in all three levels.

Conclusive evidence does not emerge until one million years ago. Wonderwerk Cave is a cave site in Northern Cape Province, South Africa. Archaeologists investigated a habitation layer known as Stratum 10. They found ash, minute bone fragments, and complete or fragmented bones that show signs of burning. The material, which was associated with stone tools, persists throughout the whole of Stratum 10. It suggests that fires were occurring in the cave too frequently to be explained by natural causes. Furthermore, the fires were occurring 30 m (100 ft) from the mouth of the cave (even further away at the time Stratum 10 was laid down.) – much too far for the burnt material to have been blown in or washed in from outside. Even the possibility of spontaneous combustion of bat guano was ruled out. Though rare, this has been known to occur in caves[137].

What we do not know is if Wonderwerk Cave people were actually producing fire, as opposed to simply making use of wildfire to start their own fires. The evidence from Eurasia suggests the latter. Humans had widely dispersed across Eurasia one million years ago, and the ability to control the use of fire in the colder environment would have obvious advantages. In reality, habitual fire use did not become widespread until 400,000 years ago and later, with only limited evidence for it before then. The implication is that humans were able to occupy higher latitudes without habitual as opposed to opportunistic use of fire[138–141].

Therefore, the Wrangham cooking hypothesis looks improbable. Notably, by 400,000 years ago, *Homo erectus* had given way to the larger-brained humans, suggesting that bigger brains led to the use of fire, rather than the other way around. Rather than cooking enabling smaller guts, experimental work has suggested that the use of stone tools to slice meat and pound root vegetables might have been the key. Without any cooking at all, food so processed requires less mastication and reduced metabolic demands[142].

The real 'missing link'?

Eugène Dubois sought a 'missing link' between apes and humans, a genus intermediate between *Homo* and apes. *Pithecanthropus erectus*, now recognised as *Homo erectus*, clearly was not such a missing link. While the term 'missing link' has largely fallen out of use, most would now consider it to be our Last Common Ancestor with African apes, which lived millions of years before *Homo erectus*. But was Dubois entirely misguided in his ideas? The australopithecines, though they walked upright, were apes, not humans. Their brains were only slightly larger than those of present-day chimpanzees at around 450 cc. If we accept the revised cranial capacity of *Homo habilis* at 730 – 825 cc, there is a significant jump in brain size between *Australopithecus* and *Homo*. The idea of an intermediate genus between the two is not far-fetched. Indeed, the suggestion has actually been made for *Homo habilis*[143], though the assumptions that it 1) predated *Homo erectus*, 2) retained tree-climbing abilities, and 3) was smaller-brained than *Homo erectus* have all been shown to be suspect.

In 2015, it was claimed that the origins of *Homo* had now been pushed back to 2.75 – 2.80 million years ago. LD 350-1 is a partial lower jawbone with molar, premolar, and canine teeth *in situ*. It was found at Ledi-Geraru, in the Afar region of Ethiopia[144]. Although the external surface of the jawbone resembled that of *Australopithecus afarensis*, it otherwise lay outside the range of variation for most other diagnostic traits for an australopithecine. Its discoverers did not assign it to any recognised species of *Homo*, nor did they propose a new specific name for the jawbone. However, they did suggest a possible connection to KNM-ER 5431, a group of isolated molar and premolar crowns discovered at Koobi Fora in the 1980s. These teeth, which are around 2.7 – 3.0 million years old, were described as exhibiting a mixture of australopithecine and early *Homo* characteristics and could represent the same transitional form as LD 350-1[145]. The authors of the OH 7 study stated that LD 350-1 is more primitive than any lower jawbone assigned to *Homo habilis*[125].

The authors of the LD 350-1 report noted that "*In the majority of traits that distinguish it from this species [Australopithecus afarensis], LD 350-1 presents morphology that we interpret as transitional between Australopithecus and Homo*"[145]. The interesting word here is 'transitional'. At the moment, very little is known about the hominins represented by LD 350-1 and KNM-ER 5431. However, we can be hopeful that cranial parts will at some stage turn up, and it will enable the cranial capacity to be estimated. My guess is that it will lie midway between *Australopithecus* and *Homo erectus*. In that event, there would be a very strong case for placing the LD 350-1 hominins in their own genus rather than in *Homo*. While it is likely that some other name will be chosen, and it could in any case break the rules on taxonomic nomenclature, but it would be a nice touch if the name *Pithecanthropus* could be revived.

Legacy

Dubois's reputation undoubtedly suffered through his stubborn insistence that his Trinil fossil was the missing link and his rejection of any evidence contracting that view. Yet it is inescapable that he was a pioneer in the field of palaeoanthropology and should be considered to be one of the founding fathers of the discipline. Palaeoanthropology came into its own at the turn of the last century, as may be appreciated from the founding of journals, the holding of conferences and symposia, and the unprecedented number of books and other publications on human evolution intended for both academics and the lay public. The rate of hominin fossil discoveries increased, as did the attention paid to them. Dubois's perseverance in promoting his discoveries was a major factor in establishing palaeoanthropology as a scientific discipline. In the face of the harsh criticism that his ideas faced following his return to Europe in 1895, a less stubborn and determined man might have given up[6].

Epilogue

In June 2009, fellow Dutchman Marco Langbroek named the asteroid (206241) Dubois in honour of Eugène Dubois. The asteroid was discovered by Langbroek in 2002 in data collected at Mount Palomar, California, as part of the Near-Earth Asteroid Tracking (NEAT) program[146]. The International Astronomical Union citation in the journal *Minor Planet Circulars* read, "*Dutch anatomist, surgeon and palaeontologist Marie Eugène François Thomas Dubois (1858-1940) was the 'founding father' of palaeoanthropology. His dedicated search culminated in 1891 with the discovery of the first Homo erectus fossils in a bank of the Solo river near Trinil, Java. The name was suggested by M. Langbroek*"[147].

03: The Acheulean hand axe

The Swiss Army Knife of the Palaeolithic

The Swiss Army Knife is a multifunction pocketknife that has been manufactured since the late nineteenth century and has long been a byword for adaptability. In the last fifteen years, the smartphone has taken on a similar role, combining a camera, satnav, music player, and handheld computer in addition to its function as a communication device. There is an important difference between the two, however. The technology in a smartphone is ephemeral. For tech enthusiasts, the launch of the latest Apple iPhone or Samsung Galaxy is one of the most keenly awaited events of the year. These devices typically cost four-figure sums yet are destined to be superseded within a year. Speculation as to what features will be included in the next-generation model typically begins within a few weeks of the launch of the current model. By contrast, and notwithstanding the wide range of models produced, the basic functionality of the Swiss Army Knife has remained unchanged for decades. A basic 13-function knife is very little different to one that could have been purchased in the 1950s. The original Soldier's Model 1890 Model was first issued in 1891 and underwent no major redesign until 1951.

Now imagine a multifunction tool that remained in use, more or less unchanged, not for decades, but one and a three-quarter million years. The earliest-known examples of the teardrop-shaped Acheulean stone hand axe are 1,760,000 years old[1], and the most recent examples are around 55,000 years old[2]. Ubiquitous in the archaeological record of Africa and western Eurasia, this most distinctive of prehistoric artefacts outlived the human species that invented it, *Homo erectus*, and it endured five times longer than *Homo sapiens* has existed. As a single object or achievement to represent humanity, the Acheulean hand axe stands alongside the Moon landing, the Pyramids, or the works of Shakespeare. It was not the first tool to be made and used by early hominins[19], but it was the first to be recognised as a prehistoric implement. It played a pivotal role in demonstrating that humanity had existed for far longer than nineteenth-century scholars had believed.

A very remote period indeed

John Frere was an English landowner and local politician who served as High Sheriff of Suffolk in 1776. He was the father of the Napoleonic-era diplomat John Hookham Frere. He took an interest in antiquaries and was a Fellow of both the Royal Society and the Society of Antiquities of London. In 1797, Frere investigated a discovery of flint tools by workmen

---

[19] A hominin is a human or anything more closely related to a human than it is to an ape.

at a brickyard near Hoxne, Suffolk. In a letter published three years later in the journal of the Society of Antiquities' journal *Archaeologia*, Frere[3] suggested that the tools were "*weapons of war, fabricated and used by a people who had not the use of metals*". They "*lay in great numbers at the depth of about twelve feet, in a stratified soil, which was dug into for the purpose of raising clay for bricks*" and noted that the gravelly soil in which they were found was overlain by a stratum of sand containing "*extraordinary bones, particularly a jaw-bone of enormous size, of some unknown animal, with the teeth remaining in it*"[3]. Frere also appreciated the stratigraphical significance of the tools being found beneath water-laid deposits that now lay well above the flood plain of the River Waveney to the north. The landscape must have undergone considerable alteration since the manufacture of the hand axes[4]. This led him, famously, to claim that "*The situation in which these weapons were found may tempt us to refer them to a very remote period indeed; even beyond that of the present world*". He noted that it would otherwise be difficult to account for them being found below a stratum that had "*been once the bottom, or at least the shore, of the sea*".

Similar flint stone tools had been known since Roman times, but their significance was not widely appreciated. Indeed, some believed they were associated with thunderbolts rather than objects of human origin[5,6]. It was not until the late seventeenth century that a clear association between stone artefacts and extinct fauna was demonstrated. In 1679, antiquarian John Conyers found a hand axe opposite Black Mary's Hole, a well near Gray's Inn Road, London. The hand axe was associated with the tooth of either a mammoth or a straight-tusked elephant (*Palaeoloxodon antiquus*). Some years later, in 1715, the antiquarian John Bagford suggested that the elephant had probably been brought to Britain by the Romans, but he also accepted that the hand axe was of human origin[7]. The Gray's Inn hand axe is now in the British Museum, but it was largely ignored by the antiquarian world of the day. Frere was probably unaware of its existence.

Frere submitted the flint tools to the Society of Antiquaries of London, together with his conclusions. In doing so, he became the first to use archaeological context to attest to their great antiquity and – by implication – that of humanity. The hand axes are now known to have been associated with the Hoxnian Industry and are thought to be 315,000 - 350,000 years old[4]. It would take more than sixty years for Frere's radical suggestion to become widely accepted. During the eighteenth century, most people believed that the Bible and the works of Classical scholars contained everything there was to know about the origins of humanity. Few doubted that the Earth and all life had been created by God and the date of the Creation was widely thought to be in 4004 BC. This date was computed by Archbishop James Ussher of Armagh in 1650 from purely Biblical sources. In Frere's time, these views were only slowly beginning to come under scrutiny as geologists began to understand the processes that had shaped the surface of the Earth. Hence, the majority of his contemporaries still preferred to hold on to Biblical explanations for human origins.

It was not until 1859 that two British scholars, Joseph Prestwich and John Evans, visited former customs official Jacques Boucher de Perthes at Abbeville in northern France. By now, the intellectual climate was very different to that at the turn of the century. Geology – in its infancy then – was now a mature discipline thanks to the efforts of Scottish geologist Sir Charles Lyell, who had popularised the hitherto largely ignored work of fellow Scot James Hutton. It was now clear that the Earth had been shaped by geological processes that could not be accommodated in the 6,000-year timescale proposed by James Ussher, and evidence had continued to accumulate for greater human antiquity than that allowed by the Ussher chronology.

In 1813, the Danish historian Lauritz Schebye Vedel-Simonsen observed that the earliest inhabitants of Scandinavia had used weapons and implements made from wood and stone. These were followed by later artefacts of copper, and only the latest were made from iron. The picture this suggested was a lengthy period of gradual technological advance. This notion was taken up by Christian Jürgensen Thomsen, who was appointed Curator of the Northern Museum of Antiquities (now the National Museum of Denmark) in 1816 and held the position until his death in 1865. Thomsen faced the task of putting the museum's large and growing collection into order, and he arranged them by the now-familiar Ages of Stone, Bronze, and Iron. The system was proposed by Thomsen in 1836, in a preface to his guidebook to the museum's collection[8]. In January 1837, Thomson published a short essay in which he divided prehistory into the Stone Age, Bronze Age, and Iron Age. This Three Age system was widely adopted, especially after the essay was translated into English in 1848[9].

Although what had become known as the 'Antiquity of Man' was no longer the outrageous idea it had once been, decisive evidence was still lacking. It was the possibility of finding such evidence that brought Prestwich and Evans to Abbeville. Prestwich had been interested in geology from childhood and pursued his interest at University College, London. Despite his passion for geology, it became purely a leisure activity as he became involved full-time in the management of his father's wine import business. Prestwich nevertheless published his first paper in 1834 at the age of 22, and a further 27 papers between 1840 and 1855. Most of these papers related to British coalfields or the Tertiary geology of Britain and northern Europe. A chance meeting on a train with antiquarian John Evans in 1857 would lead to a friendship and collaboration in an endeavour to find proof of the Antiquity of Man[10].

Evans, like Prestwich, was not a full-time scholar. He worked as a partner in John Dickinson Stationery Ltd, a papermaking business established by his uncle and later father-in-law, John Dickinson. He was nevertheless a distinguished antiquarian, whose interests also included the coinage of Iron Age Britain. He was the father of Sir Arthur Evans, who is best known for his excavation of the Palace of Knossos and the discovery of the Minoan civilisation of Crete.

Boucher de Perthes had spent much of his life working in the French customs service, finally succeeding his father Jules-Armand as Director of Customs at Abbeville in 1825. He held this post until it was abolished in 1852. He became interested in the Antiquity of Man after meeting Casimir Picard, a medical doctor who moved to Abbeville in 1828. Probably around 1842, soon after Picard's early death from pneumonia, Boucher de Perthes began collecting stone tools recovered from gravel pits in the Somme Valley. He noticed that the tools were sometimes associated with the remains of elephants and rhinoceros, which had long been extinct in France. In 1847, he published his conclusions in a three-volume work entitled *Antiquités celtiques et antédiluviennes* (Antiquities of the Celtic and Antediluvian peoples). Antediluvian ('before the Flood') was the term then used to describe the geological epoch we now know as the Pleistocene. He made the mistake of illustrating the work himself, although he could easily have afforded the services of a professional engraver. His illustrations were of poor quality. Worse, though, was the work's mystical speculations about reincarnation. All of this detracted from its more valuable findings, and it found little favour with the French Académie des Sciences. It did not help that the possibility of an antediluvian origin for humanity went against the prevailing opinion at the academy. The work was also poorly received in Britain, and Darwin dismissed it as 'rubbish'[14].

However, the work did attract the interest of Marcel-Jérôme Rigollot, a medical doctor who lived a short distance away in Amiens. Though initially sceptical, Rigollot began to explore the river gravels in the Saint-Acheul, a suburb of Amiens, 40 km upstream from Abbeville, and he soon discovered similar artefacts. Rigollot was a no-nonsense, hands-on researcher, who avoided Boucher de Perthes' speculations. His report, published in 1854, was straightforward and well-illustrated. Unfortunately, he died in 1854, soon after the publication of his report. The artefacts recovered by Boucher de Perthes and Rigollot included the teardrop-shaped hand axes we now know as 'Acheulean'. Encouraged by Rigollot's findings, but concerned about a possible loss of priority, Boucher de Perthes published the second edition of his book in 1857. Much of the new content consisted of correspondence, newspaper articles, and short essays intended to establish his priority, and it fared no better than the first edition[10,14].

Boucher de Perthes' luck finally changed in 1858 when he met the Scottish palaeontologist Hugh Falconer, who in turn persuaded Prestwich and Evans to investigate the findings at Abbeville and Saint-Acheul. In April of the following year, the pair met with Boucher de Perthes and – apparently to their surprise – they were convinced by the evidence. It has been suggested that the decisive moment came when the pair were invited to photograph a hand axe lying *in situ* in the wall of a gravel pit at Saint-Acheul[10,14].

On their return to Britain, Prestwich and Evans gave a series of presentations at the Royal Society and the Society of Antiquaries of London, in which they publicly supported Boucher de Perthes' claim. Ironically, before any of these lectures took place, Evans stumbled upon John Frere's letter to the Society of Antiquaries. The circumstances by which it came to his attention are not known – possibly he saw one of the hand axes in the Society's collection. He would have seen at once that it closely resembled the Acheulean hand axes that he and Prestwich had examined in France, and learned about the missed opportunity of more than six decades earlier. He and Prestwich rushed to Hoxne to investigate, and the Hoxne hand axes featured prominently in the papers they presented to the two learned societies. It was the final proof of the Antiquity of Man because it repeated the same set of discoveries that had been made on the Somme. Shortly thereafter, Prestwich and Evans arranged for Sir Charles Lyell, the leading British geologist of the time, and a longstanding sceptic of the Antiquity of Man, to visit the Somme. More hand axes were found at St Acheul, and Lyell was now convinced. At a packed session of the British Association for the Advancement of Science held at Aberdeen in September 1859, in the presence of Prince Albert, he added his support to the case. The mainstream Victorian scientific establishment finally came to accept the Antiquity of Man. Some years later, in 1872, the French archaeologist Gabriel de Mortillet used St Acheul as the type site for the stone hand axes, giving them the name by which they have since been known: Acheulean[15]. But had Frere not been ignored for sixty years, they might now be known as Hoxnian.

Introducing the Acheulean hand axe

Acheulean hand axes are flat cobbles or large flakes that are completely flaked over on both sides to produce a sharp edge around the entire periphery. They are sometimes referred to as bifaces, though strictly speaking a biface is any piece that has been worked on two sides. Many are teardrop-shaped, narrowing from a broad base at one end to a rounded point at the other. Other common shapes include ovals and triangles. Acheulean hand axes are one of the most distinctive, common, widely distributed, and longest-lasting prehistoric artefacts. Several hundred thousand have been recovered from sites in many regions of Africa, Europe, and Asia. Although the hand axes are the defining feature of the Acheulean stone tool industry, it is important to note that they are not its sole artefact. Some tools have a sharp edge rather than a point opposite the base and are referred to as cleavers rather than hand axes. Picks are large trihedral (three-sided) cutting tools with a thick, pointed lip. Other Acheulean artefacts include cores, flakes, and flake tools[16-18].

The Acheulean is chiefly associated with *Homo erectus*, although it continued into the Middle Pleistocene/ Chibanian (774,000 – 129,000 years ago), when larger-brained hominins emerged. The earliest hand axes, from Kokiselei, West Turkana, Kenya, are around 1.76 million years old[1]. Acheulean hand axes were not the first stone tools to be produced by humans, but unlike earlier artefacts, they were the first tools that were beyond the abilities of non-human apes to manufacture. To make one, the toolmaker had to think ahead about the overall shape of the finished artefact. Instead of simply producing sharp flakes, they had to trim the hand axe to produce cutting edges, and sides that converged to a pointed tip[19]. Finally, the steps involved in producing a cleaver are different from those required for a hand axe, so the toolmaker had to decide before starting which tool type they were going to produce[20].

Although there is no consensus on all the uses to which Acheulean hand axes were put, one of the principal uses was likely to have been the butchery of large herbivore carcasses[21]. Hand axes from the Late Acheulian site Revadim, on the southern coastal plain of Israel, have been found to bear preserved fat residues and were associated with cut-marked animal bones[22]. Another probable use was for working wood and other vegetal materials such as sedge[23]. It has been suggested that the ovate examples could be used as discuses for bringing down prey[24], though some feel that this is unlikely[25]. As we shall see, there are other even more controversial suggestions. Overall, though, it might indeed have been the Swiss Army Knife of its day, useful for a multitude of tasks.

Origin of the Acheulean

The Acheulean tradition is known as a Mode 2 tool type on a classification devised by British archaeologist Sir Grahame Clark in 1969 that is still used today. In Africa, its appearance followed the Oldowan, a tool tradition based on pebble cores and flakes, which is classified as a Mode 1 industry on Clark's scale. The Oldowan was named by British palaeoanthropologist Louis Leakey, who discovered large numbers of stone tools at Oldoway Gorge (now Olduvai Gorge), Tanzania, in 1931. Leakey's finds included a stone chopping tool now on display in the British Museum, which, at 1.8 million years old, is one of the oldest objects in the museum's collection.

Initially, Oldowan artefacts were categorised by British palaeoanthropologist Mary Leakey into a range of types including bifacial choppers, core scrapers, flake scrapers, and hammerstones[26]. However, experiments with replicating Oldowan artefacts showed that all of these supposed 'types' can result from flaking stone cobbles to produce sharp stone flakes. The same experiments showed that the flakes are useful cutting tools, probably used for butchery, but the cores were no more than leftover by-products. The hammerstones were used for breaking open bones to extract marrow, and might also have been used to detach flakes from cores[27,28]. In all probability, the Oldowan was not a single 'industry' as such and was independently invented on multiple occasions[29,30].

The Acheulean is commonly thought to have emerged about 1.75 – 1.70 million years ago from the Oldowan via a transitional industry known as the Developed Oldowan. This industry comprises two sub-types, the Developed Oldowan A (DOA) and the Developed Oldowan B (DOB). From a typological and technical perspective, the hand axes are seen as a logical development from bifacial choppers[26]. The main problem with this view is that it assumes that the bifacial choppers were an actual Oldowan tool type. In addition to the experimental evidence noted above, it has also been argued that many of the 'developed' tool types of the DOA are reflections of flaking characteristics of raw material types and original shapes of cobbles used rather than evidence for technological change. The DOB, for its part, contains many artefacts that are Early Acheulean in character, and it appears in the archaeological record at around the same time. Thus, the DOA and the DOB should more properly be considered to be part of the Oldowan proper and the Acheulean, respectively[31].

In 1969, South African archaeologist Glynn Isaac suggested that striking the large flakes used for making bifaces involved the formulation of a set of deliberate techniques quite separate from those used in the flaking practised during the Oldowan. It was this novel knapping strategy that heralded the appearance of the Acheulean[32]. More recently, Isaac's conclusions have been borne out by brain imaging studies, in which subjects performed toolmaking tasks. The results showed that more areas of the brain are involved in Acheulean toolmaking than are with Oldowan toolmaking[33–35]. Surprisingly, though, studies in which the hand movements of subjects were recorded by a wired-up glove suggest that making an Acheulean hand axe requires no greater levels of manual dexterity than those needed to make the far simpler Oldowan tools[36]. Taken together, these results suggest that the transition from Oldowan to Acheulean traditions was associated with enhanced cognitive ability rather than manual dexterity.

Currently, the oldest fossil remains recognised as belonging to *Homo* are a partial lower jawbone and three teeth from the site of Ledi-Geraru, in the Afar region of Ethiopia. These remains are 2.75 – 2.80 million years old[37,38]. The origins of African *Homo erectus* (sometimes referred to as *Homo ergaster*) date to at least 2.04 million years ago[39], and possibly as far back as 2.33 million years ago[40]. Along with *Homo habilis* and *Homo rudolfensis*, it is one of at least three hominin species that arose from the earliest *Homo*[40], but it is the only one associated with the Acheulean tradition.

Homo habilis persists in the fossil record until at least 1.65 million years ago[40], meaning that it probably persisted after the appearance of the Acheulean hand axes. If a cognitive threshold had to be reached for the Acheulean tradition to emerge, does this mean that *Homo erectus* took 300,000 years to reach it, and *Homo habilis* never reached it at all?

Homo habilis has long been thought to be smaller-brained than *Homo erectus*[26,41], though recent work has cast doubt on this view[40]. It was also claimed in a report published in 2021 that the brains of early *Homo* remained a primitive apelike organisation of the frontal lobe.

Not until 1.7 – 1.5 million years ago did the frontal lobe of *Homo erectus* undergo reorganisation to the humanlike condition, by which time, the first hominins had left Africa. Over forty hominin skulls were considered, ranging in age from 2.03 million to 70,000 years old[42].

If this conclusion is correct, then the answer to the above question is 'yes', and the authors of the report suggested that there might be a link between the frontal lobe reorganisation and the emergence of Acheulean technology. However, a note of caution should be sounded. *Australopithecus sediba*, a late species of australopithecine[20] that lived in South Africa two million years ago, reportedly shows possible development towards humanlike frontal lobes, suggesting that this reorganisation might have preceded the appearance of *Homo*[43]. Notably, the 2021 study described as 'indeterminate' the status of KNM-ER 1470, a 2.03 million-year-old *Homo rudolfensis* skull that had previously been described as humanlike in its brain organisation[44].

As interesting and potentially far-reaching as this study is, it is probably best to remain sceptical for now and look for other explanations for the delay before Acheulean technology emerged. Purely economic rather than cognitive factors could have led to the development of the new tool technology. The earliest Acheulean hand axes coincide with a long-term drying period 1.7 million years ago, which resulted in the expansion of grasslands and grazing bovid species in East Africa. The hand axes could have been better suited to the butchery of large herbivore carcasses than sharp Oldowan flakes[21]. As noted above, there is evidence from the site of Revadim, Israel, that Acheulean hand axes were used for butchery. Although the Revadim hand axes are far more recent than the earliest East African examples, the almost unchanging nature of the Acheulean hand axe tradition means that it is likely that both were used for similar purposes.

Acheulean hand axes did not completely replace Oldowan tools in Africa. Tools of both types have been found in association with *Homo erectus* crania at two sites in the Gona region of Ethiopia: Busidima North (BSN12), dating to 1.26 million years ago, and Dana Aoule North (DAN5), dating to 1.6 – 1.5 million years ago. The association with hominin remains is rare, but the co-occurrence of the two tool types has been documented at many early Acheulean sites. At some sites, Oldowan tools unaccompanied by Acheulean tools persisted until as late as 500,000 years ago[45]. The co-occurrence of Oldowan and Acheulian artefacts in Africa shows that the two toolmaking traditions were not mutually exclusive time-successive components of an evolving cultural lineage[1].

Invented once or many times?

Was the Acheulean hand axe invented once or on multiple occasions? On the face of it, given its extraordinary longevity, it is difficult to imagine that after its initial invention, nobody ever again came up with the idea. If so, it would make the inventor the most important individual in human history; beside them, Galileo, Newton, and Einstein would pale into insignificance. Had this one individual died in childhood – a far from unlikely possibility – the Acheulean

---

[20] The australopithecines were small-brained bipedal hominins that lived in Africa from around 4.2 to 2.0 million years ago. They include the famous 'Lucy' (*Australopithecus afarensis*) and are thought to have made and used simple stone tools.

hand axe might never have been invented, and the whole history of the last 1.76 million years would have been entirely different. Even now, human technology might not have progressed beyond Mode 1 Oldowan flakes and cobbles. The possibility of parallel universes in which the Acheulean hand axe was never invented makes good science fiction, but the idea can safely be dismissed because there is a major weakness in the scenario.

We can categorically rule out the possibility that the Acheulean hand axe was invented by an individual who sat down one day with a block of suitable raw material, began chipping away, and had a eureka moment that changed the course of the next 1.76 million years. Experiments have shown that if novices are provided with suitable raw material but no instruction, and are then shown a finished hand axe, they will struggle to replicate it. Compared to experienced stone knappers, novices will use a greater variety of methods, only to produce a far cruder result[46]. When, on the other hand, a novice is shown a hand axe being made (again without verbal instruction), performance improves markedly[47].

Lower Palaeolithic Oldowan toolmakers would not have the advantage of knowing what a hand axe looked like, much less how to make one. Possibly, it was noticed that 'bifacial choppers' could be put to a greater variety of uses than other stone tools, and toolmakers began intentionally producing them. Over time – possibly many centuries or even millennia - the classic hand axe form emerged as an optimal form and knapping techniques developed. To a present-day archaeologist, such a timescale would be no more than a blink of an eye. The relevant knowledge would not be confined to one individual, but would be shared across hominin groups over a reasonably wide area.

Could such a process have happened more than once, with multiple convergences on the form of the Acheulean hand axe? There are two reasons why it might not have. As noted above, the invention of the Acheulean hand axe might have been driven by environmental conditions in East Africa, which were not replicated elsewhere. Such 'bifacial choppers' as were produced were not exceptionally useful, and there was no motivation to develop them further. The other possibility is that once the hand axe had been invented, knowledge of it spread before it could be invented elsewhere.

The archaeological evidence does point to the initial spread of the Acheulean hand axe being a single invention. The earliest hand axes, from Kokiselei, West Turkana, Kenya, are 1.76 million years old[1], and slightly younger (1.75 – 1.70 million years old) Acheulean stone tools have been found at two other East African sites, Konso, Ethiopia[16] and FLK West, Olduvai Gorge, Tanzania (part of the Frida Leakey Korongo site)[48]. Dates for these three East African sites, which lie less than 1,000 km (620 miles) apart, were obtained by argon-argon dating of underlying and overlying volcanic material, and by paleomagnetic dating[21]. In South Africa, the earliest appearance of the Acheulean is around 1.6 million years ago, with dates obtained by a range of radiometric techniques including cosmogenic ^{26}Al/^{10}Be dating of deeply buried material[49,50].

The earliest-known non-African examples are those from Attirampakkam in southeastern India. Palaeomagnetic considerations give a minimum date of 1.07 million years ago, and

---

[21] Palaeomagnetic dating relies on periodic changes in the polarity of the Earth's magnetic field. During intervals of 'reversed' (as opposed to 'normal') polarity, a compass needle will point south rather than north. Ancient polarities can be detected in volcanic rock and fine-grained sediments that settled into place relatively slowly. Ferromagnetic particles in these materials will preserve a record of the polarity at the time of cooling or settling. The last reversal occurred 780,000 years ago.

cosmogenic ^{26}Al/^{10}Be dating gives a weighted mean date of 1.51 ± 0.07 million years ago[51].

Three sites on Spain's Mediterranean coast have yielded the earliest European dates: La Solana del Zamborino, Cueva Negra del Estrecho del Río Quípar, and Barranc de la Boella. All lie in a range of 960,000 to 780,000 years ago. These dates were obtained by a combination of palaeomagnetic and faunal[22] considerations and cosmogenic ^{26}Al/^{10}Be dating[52,53]. Hand axes appeared in northern Europe 650,000 to 670,000 years ago, near the end of the cold Marine Isotope Stage[23] (MIS) 16. The date ranges were obtained using electron spin resonance[24] and uranium-series dating for Acheulean artefacts found at the site of Moulin Quignon in the Somme Valley, which was one of the sites investigated by Boucher de Perthes[54].

The Acheulean tradition reached Britain 620,000 – 560,000 years ago. Around 330 Acheulean hand axes were recovered during industrial quarrying at Fordham, Kent, in the 1920s. Recent work at the site using infrared-radio fluorescence (IR-RF) dating of feldspar has shown that artefacts still *in situ* come from levels dating to at least 570,000 – 513,000 years ago. These levels were deposited during the glacial MIS 14, so the artefacts themselves probably date to the preceding warm interglacial MIS 15 from 620,000 to 560,000 years ago. No hand axes were recovered during this excavation, but those recovered in the 1920s are believed to be the same age[55].

In each case, core and flake tools precede the appearance of Acheulean hand axes in the archaeological record, so the spread of the latter occurred after the first arrival of toolmaking hominins in the region. Albeit there are considerable uncertainties in some of the dates, there is a relationship between the first appearance of Acheulean hand axes in a region and its distance from East Africa. For multiple inventions of the Acheulean hand axe, such a relationship would not be expected[47]. That does not mean that local independent inventions of hand axes can be ruled out, and as we shall see, this might have happened on one or more occasions in East Asia.

---

[22] Faunal dating relies on finding faunal remains in the same context of the artefacts or fossils under consideration. Knowing the dates that a species or a characteristic feature of a species (for example, dentition) were current implies a date range for the artefacts or fossils.

[23] Marine Isotope Stages (MIS) are alternating cold (glacial) and warm (interglacial) climatic episodes, determined by the ratios of the two principal isotopes of oxygen ^{18}O and ^{16}O in ancient ice core samples, plankton, or marine sediments. They are numbered back in time from the present day (MIS 1). Even-numbered stages correspond to glacial periods and odd-numbered stages (including the present) to interglacial periods.

[24] Electron spin resonance and luminescence dating are techniques that rely on the exposure of buried crystalline minerals to low levels of natural radioactivity, causing electrons to become trapped in their crystal structure. By measuring the quantity of trapped electrons and the exposure rate ('dose'), the time since burial can be determined. The quantity of trapped electrons can be measured by one of three methods, the choice of which will depend on the type of material to be dated. Thermoluminescence (TL) involves heating a sample to expel the trapped electrons, which emit light as they escape; this provides a measure of their quantity. Optically Stimulated Luminescence (OSL) works on the same principle except the electrons are expelled by an intense light source. Electron Spin Resonance (ESR) involves direct measurement of the magnetic 'signal' of the trapped electrons. Infrared-radio fluorescence (IR-RF) is a new technique which relies on the emission of infrared photons by the trapped electrons when exposed to ionizing radiation.

Were Late Acheulean hand axes more refined?

By 600,000 years ago, larger-brained hominins start to appear in the fossil records of Africa and Eurasia[56,57]. The expansion of brain size was probably an evolutionary response to the Middle Pleistocene Transition, a process which began 1.25 million years ago, and was largely complete by 700,000 years ago[58]. Climatic cycles changed from low amplitude, high-frequency swings (periodicity 41,000 years) to swings of high amplitude but lower frequency (periodicity 100,000 years)[59,60]. Hominins would have faced much greater environmental disruption, with the distribution of animal and plant resources subject to greater latitudinal shifts. Consequently, they would have required better means of obtaining food, maintaining social networks, and surviving in harsh environments[61].

The larger-brained hominins are conventionally lumped together as *Homo heidelbergensis*, though they were almost certainly not a single species and the more general term 'Middle Pleistocene *Homo*' is used here. The lineages leading to Neanderthals, Denisovans, and *Homo sapiens* had by now diverged from their common ancestor and were likely to have been present in Europe, Asia, and Africa, respectively. Other large-brained hominin lineages could also have existed, but ultimately died out[62]. Smaller-brained hominins also persisted: *Homo naledi*[63] in Africa, *Homo floresiensis*[64] in Flores, *Homo luzonensis*[65] in the Philippines, and *Homo erectus* might have survived in Java until as late as 120,000 years ago[66].

Larger brains might also be expected to have enabled the development of new tool technologies to meet the more challenging conditions. Is such a change seen in the archaeological record of the Middle Pleistocene? Middle Pleistocene *Homo* would continue to make **Acheulean** hand axes for another 300,000 years or so, but could later examples be of a higher quality than earlier ones?

It has been argued that Late Acheulean hand axes are thinner, more extensively trimmed, and more symmetrical both in plan form and in edge view. The shaping process was more complex than that for earlier hand axes, entailing at least two major stages: roughing out and finishing. Roughing out is broadly comparable to Early Acheulean shaping, but it involves the specific aim of establishing a centred, bifacial edge with a geometry suitable for the subsequent finishing operations. Finishing involves detaching flakes to thin the core and regularise its shape through often complex and repeated flaking. The process generally requires the use of 'soft hammers' (bone, antler, or wood), though experimental work shows that satisfactory results can be achieved with suitable preparation of the surface to be struck (the striking platform). The preparatory work entails small-scale chipping and/or abrasion of edges to alter their sharpness, bevel, and placement relative to the midline. Finishing, in any case, can require extensive preparation of the striking platform. The finished product is a relatively thin, lightweight hand axe with sharp, regular bifacial edges[34].

The 3d symmetry of the Late Acheulean hand axes suggests a cognitive advance whereby a toolmaker could hold a mental image of the finished tool while it was still a block of unworked stone, and 'rotate' it in their mind's eye. But does the notion of refinement hold up to scrutiny? If there is a link between this refinement and brain expansion, one could expect to see two periods of stasis representing Early and Late Acheulean, with a period of rapid change 600,000 years ago corresponding to the onset of the Middle Pleistocene *Homo*[17,19].

Identifying such a change in the archaeological record is difficult because most artefacts are only weakly dated[17]. Various studies have yielded contradictory results: some claim that later hand axes are indeed more refined and symmetrical than earlier examples[16,67,68], but others claim that there is no evidence for an increase over time in refinement and symmetry[69,70]. In some cases, European hand axes that were assumed to be Late Acheulean based purely on refinement have turned out to be much older and predated the emergence of Middle Pleistocene *Homo*[52].

Glynn Isaac studied the Acheulean artefacts from the Olorgesailie Formation in the Olorgesailie Basin, southern Kenya, which documents the Acheulean from 1,200,000 to 499,000 years ago[71]. He noted that the Acheulean displays a *"variable sameness"* and strikes *"even enthusiasts as monotonous"*[72]. By this, Isaac meant that changes in hand axe form appear largely random from layer to layer and over time, without any obvious long-term trend. If the hand axes in one assemblage appeared more refined than those in another, it could be attributed to the raw materials used and differences in the fracture mechanics of these raw materials. For example, flint and chert are easier to work than volcanic material, and consequently flint or chert hand axes can appear to be more finely made[17,73].

Many of the European assemblages are small, and any inferences drawn can be problematic. The site of La Noira in central France and Boxgrove, West Sussex, both have extensive assemblages of hand axes. The earliest artefacts at La Noira have a minimum age of 700,000 years. The use of morphometric techniques to quantify hand axe symmetry shows that the early La Noira artefacts already display a high degree of refinement relative to early Acheulean hand axes, albeit slightly less so than later hand axes from that site or the 480,000-year-old hand axes from Boxgrove. The inference is that while there was a trend to more refined hand axes over time, the transition appears to have begun well before 600,000 years ago. By the time Acheulean technology reached Europe, hand axe makers already possessed the necessary cognitive and motor capabilities to produce more refined and symmetrical hand axes[74].

This does not mean that there is no link between brain size and hand axe refinement. We should bear in mind the incompleteness of the fossil records of Africa and Eurasia. The brain size of *Homo erectus* ranged from 650 to 1,200 cc, with an average of around 950 cc. The larger-brained hominins known from around 600,000 years ago are around 1,230 cc[75]. Unfortunately, the fossil records of Africa and Europe are very sparse for the period from 1 million to 600,000 years ago. However, beginning in 1993, hominin fossils have been excavated from the cave site of Gran Dolina in the Sierra de Atapuerca, northern Spain. Based on uranium-series and electron spin resonance dates, the remains are around 770,000 – 950,000 years old[76,77]. In 1997, the fossils were described as a new hominin species, *Homo antecessor*, which based on estimates from the best-preserved cranium had a brain size greater than 1,000 cc[78].

This is above the average size for *Homo erectus*. The problem is that although around ten individuals have been found at Gran Dolina[79], *Homo antecessor* fossil remains have not been found elsewhere, so we have but a single datapoint. Furthermore, associated stone artefacts are core and flake tools; no hand axes have been found at this site[80]. However, *Homo antecessor* is thought to lie close to (albeit not on) the line of evolution that led to later Middle Pleistocene hominins[81]. The process of brain expansion might have already been underway, and hence preceded the La Noira artefacts.

A long production run

Although certainly not conclusive, the evidence points to two phases in the life of the Acheulean hand axe: its initial development 1.75 – 1.70 million years ago in East Africa driven by economic factors and/or enhanced cognitive abilities, and its refinement 700,000 – 500,000 years ago driven by enhanced cognitive abilities. It's the equivalent of Apple keeping the same iPhone in production for a million years before upgrading it to an 'S' model. How can we explain such an extraordinarily long production run, with only a minor upgrade in the middle?

American cognitive archaeologists Frederick Coolidge and Thomas Wynn note that although methods of tool production had become more sophisticated than those of *Homo erectus,* the range of tasks performed did not change. Middle Pleistocene *Homo* had become more efficient at carrying out these tasks, but the role technology played in its way of life did not change significantly. Coolidge and Wynn believe that while Middle Pleistocene *Homo* was able to fine-tune the technologies and expertise of *Homo erectus*, it was not able to advance them significantly, and its ability to innovate was still lacking. They note that the imposed shape of the hand axe was in great contrast to tools used by apes to crack hard-shelled nuts or access foods such as termites and honey from well-defended nests. This suggests that *Homo erectus* had a very different relationship with tools than do apes. On the other hand, the "*dogged conservatism*" of the hand axe suggests that that relationship was also very different to that of present-day humans with tools[19].

The implication here is that the thought processes of *Homo erectus* and Middle Pleistocene *Homo* were very different to our own and that the supposed 'lack of innovation' is more a product of our expectations than an unexplained phenomenon. A harsher interpretation is that *Homo erectus* was limited from a cognitive point of view and unable to come up with anything better, while for its part, Middle Pleistocene *Homo* could only make an incremental improvement. There are several explanations for hand axe conservatism that focus on cognitive limitations. Coolidge and Wynn emphasise a lack of 'working memory' compared to modern humans[19].

Another suggestion is that *Homo erectus* had a shorter childhood than *Homo sapiens*. In the latter, there is a development window between the ages of 3½ to 10 years old, when many cognitive abilities are formed, but the shorter childhood of *Homo erectus* might have limited its ability to innovate[82]. This is similar to the abilities of modern people to learn languages. Children have no difficulty mastering their mother tongue, but older people can never entirely master the grammar and sound patterns of other languages. The ability to do so declines past the age of six, and it is usually completely lost shortly after puberty. These 'critical periods' for specific kinds of learning are common in the animal kingdom, because the resources that would be needed to keep dedicated 'learning systems' in operation past a certain age are better utilised elsewhere[83].

These explanations sound perfectly reasonable, but I will admit to being wary of them if only because the cognitive abilities of early humans have been badly underestimated in the past. Neanderthals, all too often characterised as dimwits, appear not to be obviously inferior to contemporaneous *Homo sapiens* in terms of technology, diet, hunting techniques, capacity for innovation, or social networking abilities[84]. Until the early part of this century, it was argued that *Homo sapiens* also lacked behavioural modernity until as recently as 50,000 years ago[85,86]. This viewpoint, based on a misreading of the archaeological record, was largely refuted by a landmark paper published in 2000 by American anthropologists Sally McBrearty and Alison Brooks[87].

There is also evidence for symbolic behaviour by Middle Pleistocene *Homo*. Twin Rivers is a complex of caves near Lusaka in southern Zambia. British archaeologist Larry Barham investigated the site in the late 1990s, and he recovered over 300 pieces of haematite, limonite, and specularite. These minerals are known as ochres and can be used to produce a range of colours including red, yellow, brown, and purple. The Twin Rivers pieces range in age from 266,000 to 400,000 years old. These minerals do not occur naturally around the site and must have been brought to it from elsewhere. Some of the specularite pieces showed signs of grinding, and a quartzite cobble, recovered by an earlier expedition in 1954, was found to be stained with traces of specularite. The hardness of specularite is greater than other ochres and a commensurately greater effort is required to obtain powder for pigments. Simple utilitarian explanations cannot be ruled out, such as use for medicinal purposes or hide processing. However, the range of colours seen at Twin Rivers and the effort required to obtain and grind the different materials suggest that these explanations are inadequate. Barham suggests that the ochres were used primarily for ritual body painting and possibly even for cave painting[88].

Finally, evidence for symbolic and other advanced behaviours in *Homo erectus* was identified when archaeologists studied a group of freshwater mussel shells excavated by Dutch anthropologist Eugène Dubois at Trinil, Java, in 1891 and found that one shell had been engraved with a geometric pattern and another sharpened and polished for use as a cutting tool. Also notable is that the assemblage contained a large number of large adult mussels, suggesting that they had been intentionally collected as food. The use of seafood was once thought to be exclusive to modern humans, beginning as late as 165,000 years ago, but this find suggests that it was a much earlier dietary adaptation[89].

Even the simple fact that *Homo erectus* and Middle Pleistocene *Homo* were able to migrate from Africa and adapt to diverse environmental and climatic conditions in Eurasia suggests that these hominins could not have been without some ability to innovate. How, then, to explain the gap between this and the apparent 'stagnation' in Acheulean hand axe technology[90]?

One suggestion is that the ability to make them was at least partially 'under genetic control', in other words, a hard-wired rather than culturally transmitted (taught) behaviour. There are parallels in the avian world, most notably nest building. Many species build intricate nests, the construction of which entails the use of specific materials and lengthy hierarchical sequences. The required behaviours involve little if any cultural transmission and are thought to be a combination of innate instructions and individually acquired knowledge. On this view, once they became advantageous, good hand axe-making genes would be selected for, and once they were fixed in the population, they would account for the extraordinary conservatism and lack of variability of the Acheulean industry, and its sameness across a wide range of environments[18].

Critics argue that so-called imitation learning is adequate to explain the intergenerational transmission of Acheulean technology. Young hominins would have been familiar with the sight and sound of individuals making hand axes from their earliest childhood. They would be exposed to the technological processes and the associated social contexts in which the hand axes were made, and would grow up familiar with the processes and products of hand axe production as expressed by their elders and peers. Hence, it is unnecessary to postulate an innate ability to make hand axes[91].

Likewise, the lack of significant variation across a wide range of environments does not require complex explanations. Modern hunting knives, notwithstanding extensive cultural variations in shape and appearance, all have the same basic form, *i.e.*, a handle to hold them and a blade for cutting. Similarly, a tool used primarily by hunter-gatherers for butchery would not be expected to show variation in response to environmental change. Regardless of any changes in hunting strategy, the basic functions and design of a hand axe would remain unaltered[91].

Even the view that hand axes were as invariant as Isaac claimed has been queried, with the argument advanced that it is "*a gross oversimplification of the archaeological record*". Sites in southern England display considerable variability in hand axe shape both on the landscape scale between different sites and at the same site over geological timescales. Assemblages dominated by ovate or pointed hand axes may represent the toolmaking practices of hominin groups at different times and places. Longer-term trends in British hand axe assemblages have also been discerned across multiple marine isotope stages. Those from MIS 13 have been described as "*crude, narrow ovates*" or "*well-made, rounded ovates*", from MIS 11 as "*squat, broad-pointed handaxes with a strong ovate element*" or "*pointed ovates with a twisted ovate component*", and from MIS 9 "*pointed handaxes with cleavers*" or "*pointed plano-convex forms*" (Britain was probably depopulated during the cold MIS 12 and MIS 10). Again, these variations may represent the varying toolmaking repertoires of hominin groups at different times and places within a broader Acheulean tradition, which would not be expected if hand axe-making was a hard-wired rather than taught tradition[91].

It could be that the key to the longevity of the Acheulean technological tradition was nothing more than its flexibility of adaptation to different subsistence niches; a case of 'it ain't broke, don't fix it'[70]. However, archaeologists Meir Finkel and Ran Barkai[90] go further, and believe that the hand axes played an additional, social role. They suggest that innovations only evolved and spread in fields of human behaviour where they were advantageous, but that this was not the case for hand axe technology, where conservatism was preferred. Finkel and Barkai suggest that the hand axe served a dual function, serving on one hand as an essential tool for butchery and other tasks such as woodworking. However, producing hand axes also acquired a secondary meaning as a social norm analogous to that of chopsticks in China, Mongolia, Korea, and Japan. To the people of this part of the world, chopsticks are far more than just eating utensils. In Japan, they are referred to as 'the sticks for one's life', and in much of Asia, they are regarded as a symbol of life. They are commonly used for marking occasions such as birthdays, weddings, or funerals. Sometimes, they are made of luxury materials such as gold, silver, copper, rhinoceros horn, deer antler, ivory, ebony, mahogany, or jade – the latter being particularly prized.

Similarly, Finkel and Barkai see the Acheulean hand axe as the "*flagship of Acheulean adaptation and way of life*". In a hunter-gatherer world that was liable to change, the ever-present tradition of the Acheulean hand axe provided reassurance. There was little incentive to experiment with other tool types.

The Movius Line

As noted above, Acheulean technology reached the southeast of India 1.51 million years ago, and the hand axes are as abundant in Southwest and South Asia as they are in Africa and Europe. What is surprising is that they are very rare east of the Indian subcontinent, where Oldowan-type core and flake artefacts predominate. The boundary between the two regions is known as the Movius Line after the American archaeologist Hallam Movius, who first noted an east/west discontinuity in the archaeological record in 1948[92]. This demarcation was later dubbed the Movius Line by the American anthropologist Carleton Coon[93], and it has been widely accepted ever since. British archaeologist Robin Dennell described Movius' proposal as *"one of the most enduring contributions to palaeoanthropology"*[94].

Movius took the view that there was a fundamental distinction between the 'progressive' societies of Africa, Europe, and West Asia and their backward counterparts to the east. He viewed East Asia to be a *"quiet conservative corner amidst the fast advancing human world"* and *"a region of cultural retardation"*. Its lithic assemblages were *"monotonous and unimaginative"*. This negative assessment was based primarily on the absence of the Acheulean hand axes.

For his part, Coon was a polygenist who believed that present-day human populations are made up of separate races that evolved in parallel from *Homo erectus*. Each race had crossed the *sapiens* threshold at a different time, and this was reflected in differing levels of 'cultural achievement'[95]. Polygenism was a product of nineteenth-century European colonial thinking[96], but it was widely accepted by anthropologists until the 1930s[97]. Coon's endorsement of Movius has, understandably, left many modern scholars uncomfortable with the concept of the Movius Line, at least *sensu stricto*[98]. The idea that the ancestors of present-day East Asians were less 'progressive' than those in the West is no longer regarded as an acceptable viewpoint[99,100].

It should be noted that the Movius Line is not inviolable: since Movius' study, bifaces have been found in various parts of East Asia, including the Bose Basin in southern China, Danjiankou and the Luonan Basin in central China, Dingcun in northern China, and the Imjin-Hantan River Basin on the Korean Peninsula. They tend to be thicker, heavier, and less intensively knapped than those to the west of the Movius Line, and no cleavers have been found. Also, they are far less abundant than in the West. For example, in the Imjin-Hantan River Basin, where they have been reported at higher frequencies than elsewhere in East Asia, they still represent less than 5 per cent of the total stone artefacts found. The likeliest explanation is that they represent the independent invention of large bifacial cutting tools, possibly more than once. Alternatively, the bifaces could genuinely belong to the Acheulean tradition, but with cleavers being lost. However, this would not explain the limited knapping, which is less than even the earliest Acheulean artefacts[47,98].

Four main explanations have been proposed for the Movius Line.

1. *Hominin dispersal into East Asia predates the advent of Acheulean technology.* If the Movius Line is accepted as genuine, the simplest explanation for it is that the ancestors of those living east of the Movius Line left Africa before the advent of Acheulean hand axe technology[101,102]. Until the 1990s, this scenario would not have been considered: the hand axes were thought to have come into use around 1.5 million years ago, and *Homo erectus* was not thought to have left Africa until around one million years ago. But in 1994, a much earlier date of 1.81 million years ago was then obtained for the earliest *Homo erectus* in Java[101], making the scenario a possibility.

Since then, the situation has become less clear-cut. The Java dates were found to be inaccurate: the earliest dates for Java are now no more than 1.51 million years old[103], and even this could be an overestimate[104]. The earliest dates for fossil *Homo erectus* in Eurasia are 1.77 million years old for the extensive remains recovered at Dmanisi, Georgia[102] and 1.63 million years old for a skull from Gongwangling, China[105]. As noted above, the date for the earliest hand axes has been pushed back to 1.76 million years ago. This date suggests that the Acheulean hand axe first appeared at around the same time or possibly slightly before the first dispersals of *Homo erectus* into Eurasia. However, the earliest archaeological evidence for a hominin presence at Dmanisi and Gongwangling is rather earlier: 1.85 million years ago for Dmanisi[106] and 2.12 million years ago for Gongwangling[107]. The latter predates Dmanisi by almost 300,000 years, suggesting that toolmaking hominins left Africa long before the invention of the Acheulean hand axe.

Even earlier dates have been obtained for Oldowan tools from the Dawqara Formation in the Zarqa Valley, Jordan, predating Dmanisi by 630,000 years[108], but it should be noted that hominins could have crossed Sinai into the Levant during a period of warm, wet climate, At such times, Sinai greens and the Levant becomes a northeasterly extension of Africa[109,110].

Overall, it does seem likely that the first hominins dispersed into Eurasia before the first appearance of Acheulean hand axes, but does this account for the Movius Line? The problem with this viewpoint is that it assumes that Acheulean hand axe use never spread to the descendants of groups that had already left Africa. Acheulean technology spread into Europe, Southwest Asia, and India[51,52,111,112]. Even if we accept that the earliest hominins to disperse from Africa were less cognitively advanced than those who came later (which is far from proven), this theory fails to explain why Acheulean technology did not also spread fully into East Asia[98].

2. *Lack of suitable raw materials.* Movius noted that the raw materials used to produce Lower Palaeolithic tools in East Asia were often low-quality quartz and quartzite. Therefore, it is argued, that the lack of suitable raw materials made impossible the manufacture of refined Acheulean implements. Against this, experimental work by American archaeologist Kathy Schick has shown that it is possible to make a large hand axe, using locally available limestone from Zhoukoudian, near Beijing, which was the site where 'Peking Man' was discovered in the 1930s[113]. The use of such material is documented from Acheulean sites in India, suggesting that *Homo erectus* recognised its suitability for hand axe manufacture[98].

However, the lack of raw materials theory cannot be entirely dismissed. As noted above, among the group of mussel shells collected by Eugène Dubois at Trinil, Java was an example that had been sharpened and polished for use as a cutting tool. The availability of local raw materials for stone toolmaking is poor[89], and the scarcity might have prompted the use of alternatives. The question is, are such cases sufficient to account for the scarcity of Acheulean hand axes east of the Movius Line?

The theory is also favoured by proponents of the 'hard-wired' hand axe-making theory. It is suggested that when migrating hominins reached places where suitable raw materials were once again available, they were able to immediately start making hand axes again. Otherwise, it is argued, the knowledge of how to make them would have long since been forgotten[18].

3. *The bamboo hypothesis.* Complimentary to the lack of raw materials hypothesis is the suggestion that human groups in East Asia began to use materials other than stone for toolmaking, possibly driven by local scarcities of suitable raw material. Bamboo has often been suggested as an alternative[114,115]. It can be used to make sharp knives suitable for butchery and other tasks. Such tools are far less durable than those of stone, but they are far easier to make, and the raw material is far more widely available[26].

Proponents of what has become known as the 'bamboo hypothesis' argue that unlike the grassland and savannah environments of Africa and western Eurasia, the environment of Pleistocene Southeast Asia would have been predominantly made up of tropical lowland evergreen rainforest. This would have prompted hominin populations to adopt novel economic and technological strategies. These would have included broad-spectrum hunter-gathering and high mobility due to edible plants being scattered and game animals being small and elusive. Based on ethnographic evidence, it is argued that rainforest-dwelling hominins would have manufactured sophisticated 'extractive' tools (projectiles, snares, traps, etc.) for obtaining resources directly from the environment. These would have been produced almost exclusively from plant materials such as bamboo, which were always to hand and enabled the hominins to remain mobile. Large, heavy stone tools would have been far less important in the dense tropical forest. Their main function would have been for manufacturing and maintaining the plant-based tools, for which simple core and flake-based stone tools would suffice[99].

Bamboo knives and other plant-based tools could have been the world's first disposable technology but if so, they would be archaeologically invisible as they are also a biodegradable technology and would be unlikely to survive for over a million years[98]. Experimental work has shown that cutmarks on bone produced by bamboo can be distinguished from those produced by stone tools by using a scanning electron microscope (SEM), raising the possibility of testing the bamboo hypothesis against the archaeological record[116]. To date, no such evidence has emerged[98].

However, there are objections to the bamboo hypothesis. The first is the presupposition that the climate of East Asia has always been hot and humid, and hence conducive to the growth and spread of bamboo. When first proposed, it was believed that Pleistocene climate change had had very little impact in Southeast Asia. Since then, studies have shown that rainforests have been significantly affected by the cycling between warm, wet and cold, arid climate[117–119]. The assumption that early hominins in Southeast Asia lived in an environment of unchanging rainforest, which is crucial to the bamboo hypothesis, is suspect[99].

Another suspect notion is that complex stone tool technologies are not found in rainforest habitats. This view is contradicted by archaeological evidence from Central and South America (fluted and stemmed bifacial points hafted as projectiles), Island Southeast Asia (ground/polished adzes, geometric microliths, bifacial projectile points), northern Queensland, Australia and Papua New Guinea (hafted axes), and Central Africa (finely-shaped lanceolate bifaces, bifacial core-axes, prepared blade-core technology, points, and backed artefacts). Overall, the bamboo hypothesis is unlikely to account for the Movius Line[99].

4. *Demographics and social transmission.*

It has been suggested that the Movius Line is the result of factors involving the social transmission of the techniques and traditions of knowledge associated with Acheulean technologies. For example, a migration into a new area where local knowledge about sources of raw material was lacking might lead to an intergenerational break in the transmission of knowledge about hand axe manufacture[98]. Another possibility is that population sizes at the extremities of migrations from Africa were too low to keep the skills necessary for hand axe production alive from one generation to the next[112]. In small, dispersed populations, opportunities to meet practitioners skilled in particular crafts will be significantly fewer than in large, non-dispersed populations. In such cases, the skills required to complete a given task will be learned imperfectly, or not at all by the next generation. This effect will be more pronounced for complex tasks requiring high skill levels. Hence, it is argued that the skills required to make Acheulean hand axes eventually died out. On this view, the Movius Line, *senso lato*, is purely a demographic phenomenon[120].

Of these possible solutions to the Movius Line problem, the fourth is the most attractive, but at this point, we should ask ourselves if it is a solution to a problem that does not exist. Is the Movius Line a real phenomenon, even *senso lato*? Robin Dennell[121,122] argues that it is not and that the concept is "*a house built on sand that should be forgotten*". He suggests that East Asia during the Lower Palaeolithic was not an isolated backwater and not inherently different from the rest of Eurasia.

Dennell notes that there is no unambiguous evidence that any of the Mainland Southeast Asian core and flake industries cited by Movius are from the Middle Pleistocene and contemporaneous with Middle Pleistocene Acheulean assemblages in South and Southwest Asia. Indeed, there is no convincing evidence that hominins were in Mainland Southeast Asia at all before one million years ago, and very little prior to 100,000 years ago. The rarity of hand axes in China could be apparent rather than actual and could be a reflection of an incomplete archaeological record.

Movius regarded Zhoukoudian as a prime exemplar of East Asian simple core and flake industries. The problem is that Acheulean artefacts are typically found in open-air settings rather than caves, and Zhoukoudian is a cave site. Many cave sites across Eurasia lack bifaces. Dennell argues that there needs to be greater recognition that caves and open-air sites can contain very different kinds of information. Like-for-like comparisons need to be made between cave sites in Europe and East Asia, or between open-air sites in Europe and East Asia, and not by mixing the two types of sites. Dennell also notes that while 'textbook' hand axes and cleavers are unmistakably Acheulean, this is not always the case. There is a "*surprisingly large*" grey area and objects originally classed as cores and choppers have been later reclassified as hand axes. Similarly, the definition of 'Acheulean' is open to interpretation: for example, whether or not the Developed Oldowan B should be subsumed into the Acheulean.

Rather than monolithic, mutually exclusive cultures of Acheulean hand axe users in Europe, Southwest and South Asia and Oldowan tool users in Southeast and East Asia, Dennell suggests that the true picture is a more complex mosaic in which Oldowan and Acheulean technologies were both in use in the same regions. Unstandardised flake assemblages are common in East Asia, but they also occur in Europe, Southwest, and South Asia while bifacial assemblages are common in Europe, Southwest and South Asia, but as noted they are also present in limited quantities in East Asia.

Even the broad categorisation of stone tools from East Asia as simple Mode 1 Oldowan could mask considerable variability. There are assemblages from the 1.1 million-year-old site of Donggutuo in the Nihewan Basin of northern China, which demonstrate innovative flaking methods, using hard hammers to manufacture pre-determined core shapes, small flakes, and finely retouched[25] tools[123]. The view that hand axes are better/more advanced than core and flake tools is implicit in Sir Grahame Clark's scheme, but it is becoming clear that this is not necessarily the case. The importance of finding hand axes in Lower Palaeolithic assemblages might have been overplayed[99].

As previously noted, Acheulean hand axes did not completely replace Oldowan tools in Africa; the two co-occurred at some sites, and the latter occurred on their own at others. The variability of tool technology in Africa was probably a reflection of many different factors including tool function, distances to sources of raw material, environmental variability, population sizes, and the degree of contact with other hominin groups[45]. Similar factors could have operated in Eurasia. The Clactonian is a British core and flake industry named for Clacton-on-Sea, Essex, where it was first identified in 1911[124]. It is associated with the warm MIS 11 interglacial period[125] from 424,000 to 374,000 years ago[126]. The traditional view is that the 'simple' core and flake Clactonian preceded the 'advanced' Acheulean. But, as noted above, Acheulean hand axes reached Britain much earlier during MIS 15, at least 560,000 years ago. Other work shows a broad variation in British Lower Palaeolithic assemblages and the Acheulean and Clactonian are distinguished only by the presence or absence of hand axes. At Barnham, Suffolk, an industry traditionally interpreted as Clactonian has also been shown to be contemporary with biface manufacture. This strongly challenges the notion that the Clactonian and Acheulian are culturally distinct. That the former industry lacked hand axes might simply reflect the quantity, quality, and location of raw material, and the desired uses of that raw material by toolmakers[127].

We should also note that although there is as yet no evidence for the use of bamboo implements, there is the shell-cutting tool from Trinil, Java. This find demonstrates that eastern *Homo erectus* populations were capable of utilising raw materials other than stone for toolmaking where necessary. Even if the Movius Line *senso lato* is accepted, it is not credible to dismiss the hominins of East Asia as the 'backward cousins' of hand axe-using populations to the west.

The 'sexy hand axe' theory

For all the decades of study, much about the possible functions of these often beautifully crafted artefacts remains speculative. At some sites such as Melka Kunture in Ethiopia, Olorgesailie in Kenya, Isimila in Tanzania, and Kalambo Falls on the border of Zambia and Tanzania, hand axes occur by the hundreds, often in dense scatters – but they appear to have been discarded soon after manufacture. They show no obvious signs of wear, suggesting that they were never used[17]. At the British site of Boxgrove, no hand axe excavated to date shows any signs of macroscopic edge damage through use[128]. Another puzzle is that some hand axes are too large and unwieldy to be useful. The Furze Platt hand axe on display at the Natural History Museum in London is a fine example of an 'XXL-sized' hand axe. Found at Furze Platt, Berkshire, in 1919, it measures 300 mm (1 ft) in length and weighs 2.8 kg (6 lb 2 oz).

British researchers Marek Kohn and Steven Mithen[129,130] posed the following five questions:

---

[25] Intentional reshaping of a stone flake.

1. Why are hand axes so ubiquitous in the archaeological record?
2. Why are they often found in such large numbers at individual sites?
3. Why was time invested in making hand axes, when simpler tools would suffice for tasks such as butchery?
4. What was the value of imposing such high degrees of symmetry in hand axe manufacture?
5. Why are some hand axes too large to be of any practical use?

The pair sought to explain the above in terms of sexual selection, a mode of selection proposed by Darwin in *Origin of Species*[131] and developed in his later work, *The Descent of Man*[132]. Sexual selection occurs either when members of one biological sex choose mates of the other sex (intersexual selection) or compete with members of the same sex for access to members of the opposite sex (intrasexual selection). As a result of this selection, some individuals within a population enjoy greater reproductive success than others. Successful males benefit from frequent mating opportunities and controlling access to females whereas females maximise the return on the resources they invest in reproduction by mating with the best males.

Kohn and Mithen focused on intersexual selection with an emphasis on the classic example of the peacock's tail. The large tail is resource-intensive to grow, and when peahens see a male sporting a healthy, elaborate tail fan, they will see it as a sign of good genes and be more likely to choose him as a mate. The male is signalling that he can maintain himself in a healthy condition and is good enough at finding food, fighting parasites, and avoiding predators to be able to afford the extra expense of growing an elaborate tail fan.

By analogy, Kohn and Mithen proposed that hand axes were similarly made to signal to prospective mates. Making a high-quality hand axe requires suitable raw materials (high-quality flint, chert, quartzite, etc), and hammers (stone and/or bone) for shaping it. Depending on local conditions there will be degrees of difficulty obtaining these materials, and that is before the labour-intensive process of making the hand axe can even begin. The theory was that when a female was presented with a large, difficult-to-make, symmetrical hand axe, she would conclude that its maker possessed the right attributes to father successful offspring. Symmetry is seen as a desirable attribute by many primates, including humans. Single genes control the development of features on both sides of organisms, including humans. Near-perfect symmetry is uncommon, and factors such as mutations, pathogens, or stress during development may lead to a degree of asymmetry.

The hand axe, having served its purpose (or not), would be discarded. An important difference is that while a peacock's tail remains permanently attached to its owner, a hand axe does not. There is the possibility of cheating by acquiring a better quality hand axe than one could make for oneself. Accordingly, it is suggested that the hand axes were made in the presence of the prospective mate, explaining why they occur in such prolific numbers at individual sites.

The making of hand axes was not necessarily confined to males, but while males made large, showy, but impractical hand axes, those made by the females were smaller, less refined, and more utilitarian. Males, in turn, might have been attracted to females making symmetrical hand axes. Although hand axes were made for utilitarian purposes, this was not their primary function. Kohn and Mithen suggest that there were two technologies in use. The hand axes were a 'social' technology, related principally to the social world. The other technology was 'functional', and related to the natural world. It comprised tools such as cores and retouched flakes, used for plant processing, woodworking, and animal butchering. Some functional tools could have been made from organic materials (wood, bone, horn, etc).

The sexual selection hypothesis can be seen in the context of Mithen's earlier theory of 'cognitive fluidity', proposed in 1996[85]. Mithen suggested that the brains of archaic and indeed early modern humans comprised several cognitive 'domains': a 'linguistic intelligence' for language, a 'social intelligence' for managing social interactions, a 'natural history intelligence' for dealing with such matters as animal behaviour, weather, and local geography, and a 'technical intelligence' for toolmaking. These specialist intelligences were underpinned by a core of 'general intelligence'. In present-day people, the various intelligences are linked by what Mithen terms 'cognitive fluidity'. However, Mithen suggests that this was not always the case and that early humans were literally incapable of joined-up thinking.

The modular view would see the 'social intelligence' responsible for making hand axes, whereas the 'technical intelligence' would be used for all other toolmaking. Academic journals refer to Kohn and Mithen's proposal as the sexual selection hypothesis, but it has inevitably become known as the 'sexy hand axe' theory. It has been widely cited and discussed at conferences. However, American anthropologists April Nowell and Melanie Lee Chang[133] have raised several objections to it. Their main criticisms are as follows:

1. The hypothesis overplays the importance of symmetry in mate selection. The social complexity of early hominin societies must have been at least comparable to that of present-day chimpanzee or bonobo societies, and personality and the capacity for intra-group politics must have been at least as important as the ability to make a symmetrical hand axe.
2. Hand axes are more durable, easier to use, and better suited to a wide range of tasks than are easier-to-make flakes. Symmetry allows force to be delivered more evenly and makes the tool less likely to twist during use. Perfectly symmetrical hand axes are rare and what symmetry does exist may be explained by function, efficiency, precision, and safety.
3. Sites at which hand axes occur in great numbers are rare; they are far less abundant at most sites. Furthermore, the large accumulations at some sites probably took place over many centuries.
4. Evidence that most hand axes were never used is suspect: very few sites have been investigated for use-wear analysis of hand axes, and most finds are unsuited to such analysis having been subjected to processes that have erased signs of use-wear, for example, at Boxgrove, small movements in silts in which they are buried.

In summary, Nowell and Chang argue that the ubiquity of unused hand axes may be more apparent than actual, and that there are more parsimonious explanations for their symmetry. However, they leave unexplained the very large hand axes such as that from Furze Platt. This axe is around 300,000 years old. In addition to being impractically large, it is highly symmetrical, and it may have some symbolic or ritual importance[134].

The end of the Acheulean

The lengthy Acheulean age finally drew to a close with the advent of the Middle Stone Age in Africa and the Middle Palaeolithic in Europe. Hand axes and other Mode 2 technologies gave way to prepared core industries such as the Mousterian, a tradition principally associated with Neanderthals in Europe. Prepared core techniques, which are classified as Mode 3 in Sir Grahame Clark's scheme, entail shaping a stone core to a pre-planned form, from which flakes of a desired size and shape are then struck and, if necessary, retouched. Such techniques make better use of raw materials because many flakes may be struck from the same core. Unlike the multi-purpose Acheulean hand axe, they enable tools to be produced for specific purposes such as cutting, scraping, or piercing. They are third-generation stone tool industries lying midway in complexity between the earliest Oldowan-type tools and those of late prehistory.

Predetermination, or the production of standardised flakes by pre-shaping a core, is assumed to require a degree of preplanning and a certain level of cognitive attainment. Predetermination is expressed in prepared core industries through the use of methods such as the Levallois technique, which is named for the Parisian suburb of Levallois-Perret where examples of such prepared cores were discovered in the nineteenth century. Prepared-core methods involve multiple separate stages, each of which requires careful preplanning. Some scholars consider the use of predetermination to be one of the main characteristics differentiating Middle Palaeolithic stone tool industries from those of the previous period[135]. Prepared-core industries might have come about when toolmakers realised that the debitage of flakes produced as a by-product of hand axe manufacture could sometimes be useful as tools in their own right. Gradually, the emphasis shifted to the flakes themselves becoming the main product[136].

If one accepts that Late Acheulean technology represents an advance over that of the Early Acheulean, then the 'proto-Levallois' methods of the Late Acheulean may be seen as transitional to subsequent prepared core methods: a 'Mode 2.5' technology[137]. Early examples of such predetermined flake production are claimed for the early part of the Yabrudian, one of three industries making up the Acheulo-Yabrudian complex of the Levant. A study of Yabrudian assemblages recovered from Tabun Cave, Israel, dating from 415,000 to 320,000 years ago, is said to have demonstrated a calculated and pre-planned flake production, albeit less complex and elaborate than full Levallois technology[135].

Regardless of such considerations, the transition to the Middle Stone Age in Africa began at least 320,000 years ago and was largely completed before 200,000 years ago[71,87]. In Europe, the transition occurred slightly later, 270,000 – 240,000 years ago[138]. Hand axe usage persisted in some parts of Asia until as late as 55,000 years ago[2].

Epilogue

Some years ago, the BBC ran a series entitled *Today's Phrase* on their website. On 12 September 2012, the phrase 'end of an era' was featured. "*When a period of time, which is marked by a significant event, comes to an end, we say it is the end of an era*". The piece gave three examples, the last of which was "*Most people choose to download music nowadays. It's the end of an era for CDs.*"

The compact disc first appeared thirty years earlier, in October 1982. In this day and age, thirty years is a respectable run for any technology, but in comparison to the remarkable longevity of the Acheulean hand axe, it really is rather insignificant. The transition from the Acheulean hand axe to prepared core industries was an end of an era like no other.

04: Piltdown Man

A repellent idea

On 30 July 1953, delegates to an international conference in London on *Research on Fossil Homininidae in Africa* organised by the Wenner-Gren Foundation visited the British Museum (Natural History) to view the remains of the world-famous *Eoanthropus dawsoni* ('Dawson's dawn man'), better known as Piltdown Man. Since its announcement forty-one years earlier, *Eoanthropus* had spawned hundreds of articles in scientific journals. For decades, it had figured large in books about human origins. Entire careers had been devoted to its study. Breaking the story of its discovery shortly before the official announcement, the *Manchester Guardian* (now the *Guardian*) described Piltdown Man as "*one of the most important prehistoric discoveries of our time*". The British press had long been envious of the string of fossil human remains discovered in France and Germany, and they delightedly hailed Piltdown Man as 'the first Englishman'.

Among those present at the BM(NH) viewing was South Africa-born biologist Joseph Weiner, a Reader in Physical Anthropology at the University of Oxford. Piltdown Man had hardly figured in the conference deliberations, but at dinner that evening, Weiner was seated with geologist Kenneth Oakley from the BM(NH) and American anthropologist Sherwood Washburn. The visit had stimulated discussion of the previously ignored Piltdown Man, and it had left Weiner troubled. That evening, he was unable to sleep as his "*cogitation had occupied the small hours on my return to Oxford after the Wenner-Gren dinner*". Weighing up a range of hypotheses for Piltdown Man, there was only one that could not be ruled out. It was a "*repellent*" idea with far-reaching implications, but it was the only one that made any sense[1]. Weiner would later recall Sherlock Holmes' maxim: "*When you have eliminated the impossible, whatever remains, however improbable, must be the truth*".

Piltdown Man was a forgery.

PART I: Dawson's dawn man

41 years earlier

Accounts vary as to how solicitor and amateur archaeologist Charles Dawson acquired two skull fragments that attracted the attention of Arthur Smith Woodward at the British Museum (Natural History). Even the dates of events prior to 1912 are uncertain[2–5]. According to Dawson, the events leading to the discovery of Piltdown Man were set in motion when he was walking along a farm road close to Piltdown Common, Uckfield, Sussex and noticed that the road had been repaired with brown flints of a type uncommon in the region.

Dawson was born into a successful family in 1864. His father, Hugh, was a barrister. His two younger brothers, Hugh and Trevor, both attended university. Hugh became Vicar of Clandown, near Bath, while Trevor served in the Royal Navy and later became Managing Director of the engineering company Vickers. He was knighted in 1909. For his part, Charles did not attend university and followed his father into the legal profession, joining the law firm Langhams in 1880. In 1890, after several years based at the firm's head office in London, he was made a partner and moved to the branch at Uckfield. In 1900, he took over a long-established Uckfield law firm and in 1906, with business partner George Hart, renamed it Dawson Hart & Co Solicitors. The still-existent firm has retained this name ever since. Dawson was closely involved in the civic affairs of Uckfield and served as Clerk to the Urban District Council and Clerk to the Uckfield Justices. He was Secretary of the Uckfield Gas Company, Solicitor to the Uckfield Building Society, and a trustee of the Eastbourne Building Society. Now aged forty, Dawson married Hélène Postlethwaite, a widow with two adult children, in 1905. The couple had no further children[1,5].

However, Dawson's great interest was the natural world. He had collected fossils since his youth and had been encouraged by the now-elderly fossil collector Samuel Beckles. In 1885, aged only 21, he was elected a Fellow of the Geological Society. He submitted many fossils to the British Museum (Natural History), which awarded him the title of 'honorary collector'. Three of his many discoveries bear his name: the dinosaur *Iguanadon dawsoni*, the Lower Cretaceous mammal *Plagiaulax dawsoni*, and the fossil clubmoss *Selaginella dawsoni*. In 1889, he co-founded the Hastings and St Leonards Museum Association, and in 1892, he joined the Sussex Archaeological Society. About this time, he began to make a name for himself with spectacular discoveries. These included a Roman statuette made from cast iron, a prehistoric stone axe with its wooden haft still intact, and bricks dating to the very end of the Roman period in Britain. Recognition for his endeavours came in 1895 when he was elected a Fellow of the Society of Antiquaries of London, still aged only 31. Meanwhile, in his day job as a solicitor, Dawson acted for several prominent local antiquarian collectors[5].

By the turn of the century, Dawson possessed an imposing CV, but was everything as it seemed? Between 1883 and 1909, he wrote or co-authored more than 50 archaeological, historical, and palaeontological publications – but as impressive as this total sounds, none of these publications greatly furthered his career. Late in 1909, just weeks after Trevor received his knighthood, Hélène wrote to Home Secretary Herbert Gladstone, suggesting that her husband be made a Companion of the Bath[26]. Nothing came of the suggestion. In any case, Dawson was probably more interested in academic recognition, which, for all his efforts, seemed to be eluding him[6].

So it was, on that day in question, Dawson claimed to have been out for a walk near Piltdown Common. If we take his account at face value, his enquiries revealed that the flints

---

[26] To those unfamiliar with the arcanities of the British honours system, the Companion of the Bath (CB) is the lowest of the three classes within the Most Honourable Order of the Bath. Unlike the other two classes, the CB is not a knighthood/damehood. Possibly Mrs Dawson felt Gladstone was more likely to recommend a CB for her husband than a full knighthood. Dawson's undoubted contributions to the local community would probably now earn him an MBE (Member of the Most Excellent Order of the British Empire, or in common parlance, a 'gong'), but this Order was not established until the year after his death.

that had drawn his attention had come from a gravel pit on a neighbouring farm. The gravel pit was of Pleistocene origin. He enquired there for fossils and asked the workmen to save anything they could find. On one of his subsequent visits to the gravel pit, Dawson was given a piece of an "*unusually thick human parietal bone*".

When this sequence of events occurred is uncertain. In an account of the discovery published in the *Hastings and East Sussex Naturalist* in 1913, Dawson recalled that his walk was "*just at the end of the last century*". He had been presiding at a Court Baron of Barkham Manor, Piltdown, and when the meeting ended, he went for a stroll on the road outside the manor house. In his 1955 book *The Piltdown Forgery*, Joseph Weiner states that he obtained permission from Sir Percy Maryon-Wilson, Lord of Barkham Manor, to examine the records of the Barkham Manor Estates. He found that Dawson had assumed Stewardship in 1898 and presided over the Court Baron for the first time in 1899. Meetings were also held in 1904 (apparently postponed by a year), 1907, and 1911[1]. The 1899 meeting would fit Dawson's recollection in the *Hastings and East Sussex Naturalist*. However, in the March 1913 edition of the *Quarterly Journal of the Geological Society*, he states that the walk was "*several years ago*"[2], suggesting that it was more recent than what by then would have been almost a decade and a half previously. As to when Dawson was given the skull fragment, 1908 is generally accepted, but this is based solely on a reference in the *Times* the day after *Eoanthropus* was officially announced in December 1912, where it is stated to have been "*four years ago*". But this rather crucial date was never mentioned in any subsequent report; it could have been any time after the walk, which itself could have been as early as 1899[5].

To add to the confusion, a different version of the discovery was given by Woodward in his book *The Earliest Englishman*, published in 1948 four years after his death. According to this account, Dawson made visits to the site, but eventually, the workmen he had spoken to reported that they had dug up what they thought was a coconut, which they thought might be of interest to Dawson. As it was too bulky to keep, they broke it up with a shovel and kept one piece before discarding the rest. When Dawson was shown the piece, he recognised that it was a piece of a human skull rather than a coconut[10]. There are obvious problems with this version of events: why would the workmen think that a coconut would be of any interest to Dawson, and if they did, they could surely have found somewhere to keep it to await his next visit.

At all events, Dawson continued his investigation of the gravel pit, but it "*was not until some years later, in the autumn of 1911*" that he found another, larger piece of the same skull, belonging to the frontal region[2]. Early in 1912, Dawson contacted Woodward at the BM(NH). Woodward, like Dawson, was from a well-to-do background. He was born in Macclesfield in 1864, and several generations of his family had worked in the silk industry. His boyhood was spent in an intellectual environment, and he took an interest in the natural world from an early age. After studying chemistry, physics, mineralogy, petrology, and geology at the newly established Victoria University of Manchester, he joined the British Museum (Natural History), aged 18[11].

According to the Natural History Museum's website, Woodward joined the Department of Geology as a 2nd class assistant on 24 August 1882, having beaten 13 other candidates. He was promoted to Assistant Keeper on 23 March 1892, and to full Keeper on 19 December 1901. He became a Fellow of the Royal Society in 1901 and was awarded the Royal Medal in 1917 for his contributions to palaeontology. Other awards included the

Geological Society's Lyell Medal in 1896 and Wollaston Medal in 1924, the Prix Cuvier of the French Académie des Sciences in 1918, the Linnean Medal of the Linnaean Society and the Hayden Medal of the Philadelphia Academy of Natural Sciences in 1940, and the Mary Clark Thompson medal of the National Academy of Sciences, Washington in 1942. He also held honorary doctorates from the universities of Glasgow, St Andrews, Tartu, and Athens. He was knighted in 1924, following his retirement from the Museum. Woodward's principal area of expertise was fossil fish, and his four-part *Catalogue of the Fossil Fishes in the British Museum (Natural History)* was published between 1989 and 1901. His research of fossil fish collections around the world for this project took him to Denmark, Sweden, Finland, Russia, the United States, Canada, and Lebanon. His obituary, following his death in 1944, said of the catalogue that "*It is still of immense value and no subsequent work has approached it in scope*"[11].

Woodward had known Dawson since 1891, when the latter had reported the discovery of a fossil mammalian tooth in a quarry in Hastings. Woodward believed that the tooth provided the earliest evidence for mammals in Europe during the Cretaceous period, when dinosaurs were still the dominant form of life. Based on the large size of the tooth and the shape of its crown, Woodward claimed that it derived from a new species of multituberculate[27] mammal, for which he proposed the name *Plagiaulax dawsoni*[5].

Now, more than two decades later, Woodward recognised the importance of the discovery and was anxious to investigate. Unfortunately, the gravel pit was subject to flooding for five or six months of the year, and it was not until the spring that the pit was dry enough to commence excavations. Dawson obtained permission to do so from George Maryon-Wilson, Lord of Barkham Manor and Robert Kenward, a tenant farmer. Neither was told the full purpose of the investigation. Dawson and Woodward hired one labourer for the heavy digging and were joined by Jesuit priest Pierre Teilhard de Chardin.

Teilhard, born in Auvergne, central France, was like the other two from a prosperous background. He took his first vows as a Jesuit in 1901 but moved to Jersey the following year in response to the anti-clerical agenda of Émile Combes. After continuing his studies in Jersey between 1902 and 1905, he taught physics at the Collège de la Sainte Famille in Cairo. In 1908, he came to Hastings to complete his theological training at the Ore Place Jesuit seminary, and he was ordained in 1911. In common with Dawson, however, his main interest was natural history, and when the two met in 1909, it was unsurprising that they became good friends.

The team made a systematic search of the undisturbed gravel pit and the surrounding spoil heaps, with fieldwork continuing through the summer. Several additional skull fragments were recovered, closely associated with the right side of a lower jawbone. The latter had two molar teeth remaining *in situ*. Along with Dawson's earlier finds, the remains comprised the larger part of a remarkably thick human braincase and an apelike partial lower jawbone.

---

[27] The multituberculates are an extinct order of mammal that first appeared during the Jurassic period. They were small, rodent-like animals, once thought to give birth to helpless underdeveloped young as do present-day marsupials. However, it is now believed that their gestation period was comparable to that of present-day placental mammals.

Other finds included nine Chellean or pre-Chellean[28] stone tools, numerous 'eoliths'[29], and several animal teeth and other remains[30]. All the finds were heavily mineralised with iron oxide. As the excavation season drew to a close, Woodward felt they had enough material to publish the first account of their discoveries in December 1912[2,3,12].

Dawson and Woodward go public

Woodward formally described the Piltdown remains at a packed meeting of the Geological Society in Burlington House, London, on 18 December 1912. To his annoyance, the story had been broken almost a month earlier by the *Manchester Guardian* on 21 November and further reported by the *Times* two days later. However, the press speculation concerning the find stimulated both public and academic interest, and this certainly contributed to the full house[5,12].

Presentations were given by Dawson, Woodward, and Grafton Elliot Smith, then Professor of Anatomy at the Victoria University of Manchester. Dawson spoke first, describing the circumstances of the initial discovery, the excavations to date, and the geology of the Piltdown gravel pit. The stratified gravel of the latter was "*of Pleistocene age but that it contains, in its lowest stratum, animal remains derived from some destroyed Pliocene deposit probably situated not far away, and consisting of worn and broken fragments*", and the Piltdown cranium and jawbone could not "*safely be described as being of earlier date than the first half of the Pleistocene Epoch*". The Piltdown individual probably lived "*during a warm cycle in that age*"[2].

Woodward spoke next, providing a detailed description of the cranium and the jawbone. The latter, he claimed, was "*in the same mineralised condition as the skull, and corresponds sufficiently well in size to be referred to the same specimen without any hesitation*". The jawbone appeared to be "*almost precisely that of an ape, with nothing human except the molar teeth*". The enamel and dentine of two heavily worn molar teeth had been "*equally worn down by very free movements in mastication, and such a marked regular flattening has never been observed among apes*". Woodward described the braincase as having an estimated capacity of "*at least 1,070 cc, while a consideration of the missing parts suggests that it may have been a little more*", although it was "*much below that of the Mousterian* [Neanderthal] *skulls from Spy and La Chapelle-aux Saints*". Woodward noted that the discoveries of *Pithecanthropus* (*Homo erectus*) and "*several skulls of the Mousterian (Neanderthal) type*" had led to the view that "*early man was characterised by a low, flattened forehead and a prominent bony brow*". But the Piltdown specimen, despite being "*certainly the oldest typically-human brain-case hitherto found, exhibits no anterior flattening, but has the frontal eminence* [forehead] *as steep as in modern man, without any prominent supraorbital ridge* [browridge]". Woodward proposed that the Piltdown individual belonged to a new species, to be named *Eoanthropus dawsoni* ('Dawson's dawn man') in honour

---

[28] Chellean (for Chelles, near Paris) was the name given to the stone hand-axe industries of Lower Palaeolithic Europe and pre-Chellean refers to earlier/contemporaneous core and flake industries. These stone tool industries are now generally referred to as Acheulean (for Saint-Acheul, France) and Oldowan (for Olduvai Gorge, Tanzania), respectively.

[29] Eoliths ('dawn stones') are naturally shaped flint pieces once thought by some to be very early stone tools.

[30] Two small broken pieces of a molar tooth of a Pliocene elephant, a mastodon molar, two hippopotamus teeth, two molar teeth of a Pleistocene beaver, part of a red deer antler, a Pleistocene horse tooth, and a partial deer metatarsal.

of Dawson[2].

The final speaker was Smith, who described the brain of *Eoanthropus dawsoni*. This was "*the most primitive and most simian human brain so far recorded*", but it was showing some early signs of expansion in the regions associated with "*the power of spontaneous elaboration of speech and the ability to recall names*"[2].

After the presentations had finished, there was a discussion at which several of the most prominent scientists of the day spoke. The importance of the remains seemed beyond doubt, but not everybody accepted that they dated to the Pleistocene. Arthur Keith believed that the "*very simian characters*" of the sub-symphysial region of the jawbone (*i.e.*, the region below the ridge formed by the fusion of the two halves of the jawbone in early life), the "*undoubtedly large anterior teeth*", and the "*primitive characters of the skull and brain*" suggested an earlier much date, possibly the Pliocene. Keith was influenced by a thick, chinless lower jawbone discovered in a sandpit in the village of Mauer, near Heidelberg, Germany, in 1907. The Mauer jawbone was "*of early Pleistocene date, the symphysial region of the jaw was essentially human in its markings and characters; whereas the same features in the remains just described were simian, and therefore presumably much earlier*". Keith also expressed concerns about the reconstruction of the jawbone, which he thought "*approached too nearly the characters of the chimpanzee*". Palaeontologist Edwin Tulley Newton drew attention to the "*highly-mineralised condition of the specimens*" and likewise favoured the Pliocene. Conversely, geologist Clement Reid argued that the gravel deposits in which the remains were found were "*not pre-Glacial or even early Pleistocene – they belong to an epoch long after the first cold period had passed away*"[2].

One dissenting voice was Scottish anatomist David Waterston, Professor of Anatomy at King's College, London. He noted that the cranium was "*human in practically all its essential characters*", whereas the jawbone "*resembled, in all its details, the mandible of the chimpanzee*". It was "*very difficult to believe that the two specimens could have come from the same individual*"[2].

Cricket bats, Piltdown II, and Dawson's death

Excavations continued at the Piltdown gravel pit during the 1913 and 1914 excavation seasons. During the summer of 1913, Teilhard found a mandibular right canine tooth. The "*remarkable*" tooth was "*certainly that of a Primate Mammal, and may therefore be referred without hesitation to Eoanthropus*". Dawson found two human nasal bones and fragments of a turbinated bone lying together. The latter fell apart when touched, but the fragments were recovered by sieving and pieced together by Woodward's wife Maud. Other finds included fragmentary teeth of rhinoceros, stegodon, and mastodon, all of which were "*highly mineralised*"[13]. No further remains were found at the gravel pit after 1913, and the finds from there became collectively known as Piltdown I. At the end of the 1913 excavation season, Teilhard returned to France[5].

However, during the summer of 1914, as Europe slid inexorably towards war, came the discovery of a remarkable bone implement supposedly made and used by *Eoanthropus*. Dawson and Woodward described the find in a presentation to the Geological Society in December 1914[14]. It had been found about a foot below the surface in dark soil beneath a hedge bordering the gravel pit and was covered with pale yellow clay like that at the bottom of the gravel pit. It could not have been buried for any length of time and had presumably been thrown there by workmen digging for gravel. When cleaned, it was found once again to be mineralised on the surface with iron oxide. Unfortunately, it had been accidentally broken in half by a workman's pick during the excavation.

The implement was described as "*a stout and nearly straight narrow plate of bone, 41 cm. long and varying from 9 cm. 9 to 10 cm. in width, with the thicker end artificially pointed or keeled, the thinner end artificially rounded…. The bone at the pointed end measures 5 cm. in maximum thickness, while the thickness at the rounded end scarcely exceeds 8 cm*". It appeared to have been made by flaking a longitudinal strip from a limb bone, comparable to the way in which stone tools are flaked from cores. The two ends of the implement were shaped by cutting rather than grinding and polishing, and the bone had been worked "*when it was in a comparatively fresh state*". Dawson and Woodward noted that the only known Pliocene or Pleistocene limb bones large enough to make such an implement from were those of Proboscidcans (elephants and mammoths). The bone was possibly from a woolly mammoth (*Mammuthus primigenius*) or southern mammoth (*Mammuthus meridionalis*).

As to the probable use of the implement, "*it can only be remarked that we have no evidence to guide us. Its shape is unique, and an instrument with a point would be serviceable for many purposes*". Antiquarian George Fabian Laurence and a Mr E. A. Martin both suggested that it was used as a club. Geologist Samuel Hazzledine Warren thought it might have been a "*hacking-tool*". Archaeologist Reginald Smith told the meeting that he "*could not imagine any use for an implement that looked like part of a cricket-bat*"[14].

The presentation to the Geological Society would be Dawson's last. Late in 1915, he was taken ill and spent the spring of 1916 convalescing at home in Lewes. After being treated with a course of serum injections, he returned to work in Uckfield. However, his condition significantly worsened in June, and he was bedridden throughout July. On 10 August, he died, aged just 52. The cause of his death is not known, though it has been suggested that he was suffering from pernicious anaemia[5]. In an obituary that appeared in the *British Medical Journal* on 19 August 1916, Dawson was described as "*a splendid type of that great class of men who give the driving power to British science the thinking, observant amateur*"[15]. Dawson's wife Hélène, who was five years older than him, survived him by only a year.

Early in 1917, Woodward announced the discovery of two pieces of a second human cranium and a molar tooth. These comprise the Piltdown II skull. Woodward claimed that the remains were found by Dawson in a large field about two miles from the Piltdown gravel pit. He and Dawson had searched it several times without success during 1914. "*When, however, in the course of farming, the stones had been raked off the ground and brought together into heaps, Mr. Dawson was able to search the material more satisfactorily; and early in 1915 he was so fortunate as to find here two well-fossilised pieces of human skull and a molar tooth, which he immediately recognised as belonging to at least one more individual of Eoanthropus dawsoni*". The first and most important cranial fragment was "*part of the supra-orbital region of a right frontal bone adjacent to the middle line*" which as in "*exactly the same mineralised condition as the original skull of Eoanthropus, and deeply stained with iron oxide*". It was "*similarly thickened*" and it provided "*a portion* [of the skull] *that was absent in the first specimen*". The second cranial fragment was "*the middle part of an occipital bone, which is also well fossilised, but seems to have been weathered since it was derived from the gravel*". Though it was "*still stout, it is thinner than the corresponding bone of Eoanthropus from Piltdown*". However, this fragment duplicated a part of the skull that was present in Piltdown I. The lower left first molar tooth agreed "*very closely with that of the original specimen of Eoanthropus dawsoni, but more obliquely worn by mastication"*. It was *"equally well fossilised, and stained brown with oxide of iron in the usual manner"*[16].

The announcement of a second *Eoanthropus* fossil won over many doubters, and it might be asked why there was a two-year delay between Dawson's discovery and the by-now posthumous announcement. Though Dawson wrote to Woodward about the cranial fragments early in January 1915 and about the molar tooth on 30 July, Woodward apparently did not inspect these new remains until after Dawson's death. Nor, it seems, did he ever knowingly visit the spot where the finds were made. In 1926, in a personal communication to Aleš Hrdlička, Woodward admitted that Dawson had told him that he had found the Piltdown II remains on the Sheffield Park Estate (now a National Trust property) but would not reveal the exact spot. This was confirmed in 1954 after the forgery was exposed. When Joseph Weiner questioned Lady Maud Smith Woodward about her late husband's relationship with Dawson, she said that he had pressed Dawson over the Piltdown II discovery spot without success. Dawson's illness had made the enquiries *"fruitless"*, and despite searching for the site himself, he was never able to find it. This uncertainty as to the location of the Piltdown II find might explain Woodward's delay in announcing it[5].

In addition to the Piltdown II remains, there was another find that Woodward never announced at all. In July 1913, Dawson wrote to Woodward, claiming to have found the frontal part of a human skull at another site, now thought to be at the village of Barcombe Mills, which roughly lies midway between Piltdown and Lewes. Dawson never named the find spot in any report, but after his death, Woodward recorded the Barcombe material as being derived from Pleistocene gravel in a field near Barcombe Mills railway station. Letters suggest that he was aware of Dawson's interest in the site, and the pair may have visited it in late April 1913. Woodward received the Barcombe material from Dawson's widow Hélène in January 1917. The material included several skull fragments, apparently from two individuals. It is not known for certain why Woodward never made a formal report, but as the remains bore little resemblance to those from Piltdown and were generally unremarkable, he probably concluded that they were not from *Eoanthropus* and were of little scientific value[5].

The 'hurly-burly' is slow to die down

In 1914, Arthur Keith noted that the *"dust raised by the hurly-burly which followed the famous discovery at Piltdown is only in process of settling"*[17], but it would continue for several years, and Keith was rarely far from the epicentre. Born and raised in Aberdeen, Keith studied medicine at the University of Aberdeen. After undertaking fieldwork in the Malay Peninsula for the Royal Botanical Garden, he studied anatomy at University College London and at the University of Aberdeen. In 1894, he was elected a fellow of the Royal College of Surgeons of England, and in 1908, he was *"placed in charge of the vast treasury of things housed in the Museum of the Royal College of Surgeons of England"* where his interests turned towards *"the machinery of human evolution"*[18]. Keith was knighted in 1921.

David Waterson, who had expressed doubts about the Piltdown jawbone after the initial announcement, later wrote to *Nature* magazine with his concerns. Citing radiograms (X-ray photographs) of the Piltdown jawbone and that of a chimpanzee that had been published in the 1 October 1913 edition of *The British Journal of Dental Science*, he superimposed tracings of the radiograms. These showed views from sideways and above, and Waterston noted that the two sets were "*practically identical*". He also noted that the molar teeth not only "*approach the ape form, but in several respects are identical with them*". The Piltdown cranium, on the other hand, was "*essentially human*"[19].

Waterson was not alone: in November 1915, American zoologist Gerrit Smith Miller, Jr. observed that "*Deliberate malice could hardly have been more successful than the hazards of deposition in so breaking the fossils as to give free scope to individual judgment in fitting the parts together*". In a report published by the Smithsonian Institute in Washington, DC, he noted that by this time, no fewer than three reconstructions of the braincase had been attempted. Miller did not accept that the pattern of wear of the molar teeth was necessarily unique to apes and claimed that "*among nine chimpanzees with teeth at nearly the same stage of wear as in the type, the smooth condition shown by the fossil is closely approached by one individual and exactly matched by another*". Miller went on to propose that the jawbone had belonged to an extinct British species of chimpanzee, for which he put forward the name *Pan vetus* ('old chimpanzee')[20].

Miller was supported by William King Gregory, who said that Miller was "*fully justified in holding that the lower molars of the Piltdown jaw are those of a chimpanzee and not those of an extinct genus of Hominidae*"[21]. Gregory had earlier noted suggestions that the Piltdown remains "*may represent a deliberate hoax, a Negro or Australian skull and a broken ape jaw, artificially fossilised and planted in the gravel-bed to fool the scientists*", although he personally endorsed the find[22]. Woodward was understandably unhappy, and he wrote to Dawson saying that he was "*surprised that the Smithsonian will publish such nonsense*"[5]. Keith subsequently maintained that the teeth were "*as unlike chimpanzee teeth as teeth can well be*"[23].

William Plane Pycraft, an osteologist at the BM(NH), was even less impressed than the other critics. He maintained that the jawbone was "*well within the limits of human variation*" and that it was "*idle indeed to pretend that the molars of the chimpanzee are indistinguishable from those of the Piltdown jaw*". In a withering assessment of Miller's arguments, he said that "*they are based on assumptions such as would never have been made had he not committed the initial mistake of overlooking the fact that these remains - which, by the way, he has never seen - are of extreme antiquity, and hence are to be measured by the standards of the palaeontologist rather than of the anthropologist. This unfortunate lack of the right perspective has caused him to overlook some of the most significant features of these remains, and has absolutely warped his judgment in regard to the relative values of the likenesses between these fragments and the skulls the chimpanzee which he has so woefully misread*"[24].

Pycraft was clearly not one to pull his punches, but after reviewing the criticisms, Miller saw no reason to change his views. He noted that "*there was no sufficient reason for treating the jaw otherwise than as that of a chimpanzee accidentally washed into proximity with a human skull*". He conceded that the strongest argument against his viewpoint was "*the improbability that the first trace of a primate representing a group not hitherto known in the Pleistocene of Europe should have been found within a few feet of complementary parts of an unusual human brain case*" but noted that there were considerable "*divergences of view*" as to whether unknown types of ape might have lived in Europe during the Pleistocene and that "*no definite conclusion can be based on the fact that the fragments were found near together*"[25].

That no fossil apes had been found in Europe later than the Early Pliocene was invariably a hindrance to the view that the cranium and jawbone were not from the same individual[3]. Some even believed that a more accurate reconstruction of the jawbone would reveal it to be human rather than apelike[3]. For example, anatomist Andrew Francis Dixon thought that it was "*very doubtful if the remarkable features which it exhibits are sufficient to support the claim that Piltdown man belonged to a genus different from modern man*"[26].

The 'dualistic' (as opposed to 'monistic') interpretation suffered a body blow with the announcement of the second *Eoanthropus* fossil. Piltdown II won over many of the doubters. The objections of Waterston and Miller could now be dismissed. Critics including Gregory now accepted the association of the Piltdown I cranium with the jawbone[12,27].

However, the doubters had always been in a minority. In the foreword to his 1915 work *The Antiquity of Man*, Keith wrote, "*No discovery of recent date has had such a wide-reaching effect as that made by Mr Charles Dawson at Piltdown, Sussex. Hence the reader will find that a very considerable part of this book is devoted to the significance of that specimen of humanity which Dr Smith Woodward named Eoanthropus dawsoni*"[28]. Piltdown Man also featured prominently in the second edition of *Ancient Hunters and their Modern Representatives*, by British anthropologist and geologist William Sollas[29]. The first edition had only appeared in 1911, and one can only imagine Sollas' frustration when *Eoanthropus* was announced a year later. *Diversions of a Naturalist*, by zoologist Sir Edwin Ray Lankester, while covering topics as diverse as grouse and jellyfish, devoted a chapter to the "*Missing Link*" in which Eoanthropus took centre stage[30].

It would be a mistake to think that even the 'monists' had all been singing from the same hymn sheet. As early as April 1913, the Danson Company of Weymouth was offering plaster casts of *Eoanthropus* to order, for a price of £9 17s (£9.85), about £1,500 at today's prices. Keith ordered a completed skull and a disassembled cranium and jawbone[5]. Having already expressed concerns about Woodward's reconstruction, he attempted his own, which increased the height of the braincase by "*nearly half an inch*" and the cranial capacity to just under 1,500 cc[28]. In his autobiography, published in 1950, Keith reflected that he had "*fitted the various fragments of the skull into what I believed to be their proper places, and became convinced that Smith Woodward, in his reconstruction, had deprived Piltdown man of some 250 or 300 c.c. of his brain-space. The errors made in reconstruction seemed to me patent to the practised eye of an anatomist*"[31].

Keith's reconstruction of the remains displeased Grafton Elliot Smith, who described it as "*this disgusting mess*"[5]. In August 1913, an International Congress of Medicine met in London, and visitors from abroad were shown Woodward's reconstruction of Piltdown Man at the BM(NH). Keith later recalled that "*when they assembled in the theatre of the College of Surgeons I did not hesitate to point out the anatomical impossibilities of that reconstruction. Had I not done so I knew that German anatomists would. I also wrote an account of my criticism and sent it to The Times, where it duly appeared. The fat was now in the fire. Elliot Smith poured the vials of his wrath on me – through the post. He carried the controversy to the pages of Nature (September, 1913)*". Matters came to a head at a meeting of the Royal Society in February 1914, after Smith had read a paper to the Royal Society on the brain of Piltdown Man. Keith "*attended that meeting, and in the discussion which followed I did not mince my words in pointing out the glaring errors in the reconstructed brain-cast he exhibited to the meeting. It was a crowded meeting, and it so happened that he and I filed out side by side. I shall never forget the angry look he gave me. Such was the end of a long friendship. He must have felt I was in the right, for he never published the paper he read to the Royal Society, and when, at a later date, he and Dr. John Beattie made a reconstruction of the Piltdown skull, their result did not differ materially from mine. Nevertheless the Royal Society looked on me as a brawler, and continued to frown on me for my outspoken criticism*"[31].

For the purposes of an exhibition held at the Royal College of Surgeons in August 1913, Keith also dispensed with the name *Eoanthropus dawsoni* and renamed the Piltdown Man *Homo piltdownensis*. As might be expected, the scientists at the BM(NH) were unhappy[5], but Keith held his ground. His view was that the Piltdown skull was human in every respect bar the jawbone, and it should therefore be reclassified as *Homo*. Present-day rules do permit a species to be moved to another genus, but the specific name is not changed. If Keith's proposed transfer to *Homo* had been accepted, then the correct name would have been *Homo dawsoni* ('Dawson's man'). However, Keith later backed Woodward's creation of a new genus for Piltdown. Noting the "*anthropoid characters of the mouth, teeth, and face, the massive and ill-filled skull, the simian characters of the brain and its primitive and pre-human general appearance*", he now accepted that Woodward was "*absolutely justified*" in placing it in a separate genus to *Homo*[32].

Discussion on the Piltdown Skull, by John Cooke is a 1915 painting that still hangs on the walls of the Geological Society of London. The Society's website describes it as "*One of the Society's most popular paintings*". The work depicts a meeting at the Royal College of Surgeons on 11 August 1913. Lying on a table is a reconstruction of the Piltdown skull, accompanied by human and chimpanzee remains for comparison. Dawson, Woodward, Pycraft, and Smith are among those gathered around the seated Keith, who is wearing a lab coat. Any differences they had over the various reconstructions were of far less importance than one overriding factor.

For Keith and the others present at that meeting, *Eoanthropus* had ticked a lot of boxes.

Early twentieth-century perspectives on human evolution:

The modern view is that humans (Genus *Homo*) are most closely related to chimpanzees and that our last common ancestor with them lived comparatively recently, about 6.6 million years ago according to a recent estimate[33]. Any primate on our side of the human/chimp split is known as a hominin. This has replaced the older term hominid, which, as now defined, also includes the anthropoid apes (chimpanzees, gorillas, orangutans, and many extinct apes). Fossil evidence for the earliest hominins is confined to Africa; there is no evidence that they lived elsewhere until much later. The earliest hominins (*Ardipithecus* and *Australopithecus*) were bipeds like us, but their brains were no larger than those of chimpanzees. Larger-brained hominins – the first humans – emerged around 2.75 – 2.80 million years ago, again in Africa[34,35].

The contrast between what we know now and what was widely believed during the first half of the twentieth century could not be greater. The suggestion that humans are closely related to apes was proposed by Darwin's advocate Thomas Henry Huxley in his 1863 book *Evidence as to Man's Place in Nature*[36]. Huxley's work, the first ever to be devoted to the topic of human evolution, was followed eight years later by Darwin's *The Descent of Man*[37]. Here, Darwin speculated that humans might have evolved in Africa from apes closely related to chimpanzees or gorillas. We now know that Darwin was right, but his view had fallen out of favour by the start of the twentieth century.

At the time, there was very little fossil evidence concerning the ancestry of *Homo sapiens*. Neanderthals were identified in 1856 and described as a separate species in 1864, but for some time, they were widely thought to be a 'lower race' of our own species. In *The Descent of Man*, Darwin mentions them just once. 'Java Man' (*Pithecanthropus erectus*) was discovered at Trinil, Java, in 1891 by Dutch anthropologist Eugène Dubois. It was markedly smaller-brained than modern humans, but claims by Dubois that it was a 'missing link' between humans and apes were generally dismissed. 'Heidelberg man' (*Homo heidelbergensis*) was known only from a thick, chinless lower jawbone discovered in a sandpit in the village of Mauer, near Heidelberg, Germany, in 1907. In the 1920s, excavations in China revealed human fossils, which Canadian anthropologist Davidson Black described as *Sinanthropus pekinensis* ('Chinese man of Peking'). Similarities between *Sinanthropus* and *Pithecanthropus* were soon noted, although Dubois was sceptical. The only fossil ape then known was *Dryopithecus*, which had lived in Eurasia, not Africa. Indeed, Darwin[37] noted this as a caveat to the African origins theory.

By the turn of the century, anthropologists were being heavily influenced by three paradigms, all of which would turn out to be incorrect. The first of these was a widespread belief that humans had evolved in Asia rather than Africa. Present-day apes live in the tropics, so it was reasonable to assume that humans had evolved in the tropics – but the scant fossil evidence for *Pithecanthropus* suggested the Asian tropics rather than the African tropics. It was not until 1924 that the first African hominin, *Australopithecus africanus*, was discovered by lime quarry workers at Taung, South Africa and described by Australian anatomist Raymond Dart[38]. Unfortunately, Dart was reluctant to allow his fossil skull to be sent to London, where there were extensive reference collections with which it could be compared. It was, therefore, much easier for anatomist Sir Arthur Keith and others to dismiss his claims that *Australopithecus* was a bipedal ape[39].

The Asian origins paradigm, however, was not based solely or even primarily on a lack of African fossil evidence, but on something rather more sinister. There were two underlying assumptions. Firstly, there was a 'centre' where the first humans had evolved and from where they had radiated. As they did so, more primitive hominins were displaced, with the most primitive living furthest from the centre. On this view, *contra* Darwin, chimpanzees and gorillas were no more than primitive forms, displaced to Africa by more advanced types originating in Central Asia[40]. The second assumption was that humanity itself was made up of distinct 'races', some of which were intrinsically superior to others. 'Lower races' included Aboriginal Australians, Andaman Islanders, and Negros (Blacks), all of whom – like the African apes before them – had been pushed to the peripheries of human affairs by the 'higher races'. These included Mediterranean, Nordic, and Alpine (Central Europeans and Western/Central Asians) 'races', with 'Mongols' (East and Southeast Asians, Arctic peoples, Native Americans, and Pacific Islanders) lying midway between the 'higher' and 'lower' races[41].

Unfortunately, this racist nonsense was all too common (though by no means universal) in anthropological thinking for decades. British archaeologist Robin Dennell[40] has described the period from 1870 to 1930 as "*the Age of Prejudice*". But while such thinking prevailed, Africa was seen as no more than a periphery to which the more primitive races had been displaced. Accordingly, *Australopithecus* could have had nothing to do with human origins and could be ignored. The claims of *Eoanthropus*, as a European hominin, were far stronger.

The second of these three paradigms was the 'brains first' paradigm: the view that since large brains were the most important feature distinguishing humans from apes, they must have been a very early development, preceding mandibular development or the transition to bipedalism. Proponents of this view included Keith and Elliot Smith[39]. The latter noted that "*It was not the adoption of the erect attitude that made Man from an Ape, but the gradual perfecting of the brain and the slow upbuilding of the mental structure, of which erectness of carriage is one of the incidental manifestations*"[41]. A small-brained bipedal ape such as *Australopithecus* was completely at odds with this view, whereas the larger-brained but otherwise ape-like *Eoanthropus* supported it.

The third erroneous paradigm was that the split between apes and humans was very ancient. American palaeontologist Henry Fairfield Osborn placed the split in the Oligocene (33.9 – 23.03 million years ago)[42]. Sir Arthur Keith and American palaeontologist William King Gregory favoured a split at the start of the Miocene (20.03 – 5.33 million years ago)[32,43]. In 1919, British anatomist Frederick Wood Jones proposed the 'tarsioid hypothesis', which linked human origins to tarsiers[44]. This implied an even earlier split, in the Eocene (55.8 – 33.9 million years ago). In various guises, the 'early origins' view was dominant until the 1960s. Swiss anatomist Adolph Schultz based his models on embryological evidence, British palaeontologist Sir Wilfred Le Gros Clark relied on comparative anatomy, and American palaeontologist William King Gregory relied on dental evidence[45].

Part of the rationale for the 'early origins' viewpoint was again racist. The differences between the various 'races', now recognised as trivial, were thought to be so significant that they implied a great time depth. For example, Sir Arthur Keith believed that "*The whole length of the Pleistocene does not seem sufficiently long*" to differentiate Blacks from Europeans[28]. Phylogenetic trees depicting human origins from this period commonly show a very long history of modern human 'races'[41,42]. In one of the most egregious examples of this thinking, British politician and science writer Samuel Laing maintained that "*if there is any truth in evolutions, then the Negro type must be one of the oldest, as nearest to the animal ancestor, and this ancestor must be placed very far back before the Quaternary period* [began 2.58 million years ago], *to allow sufficient time for the development of such entirely different and improved races*". He went on to claim that "*the Negro and the European stand further apart than those anthropoids* [chimpanzees and gorillas] *do from one another, and no naturalist from Mars or Saturn, investigating the human family for the first time, and free from prepossession, would hesitate to class the white, black, yellow, red, and perhaps five or six other varieties, as different species*"[46].

Such views began to fall out of favour in the 1930s[40], but it took the horrors of Nazism to finally discredit them. The early post-war period saw the emergence of the New Evolutionary Synthesis, which combined Darwinian natural selection with Mendelian genetic inheritance. This new paradigm enabled established views on species and populations to be examined and revised[47]. Between 1950 and 1964, UNESCO issued three Statements on Race, affirming just how wrong Laing and others had been. *Homo sapiens* is a single species; its populations differ from one another by far less than what they have in common[48].

PART II: Exposed

Post-war difficulties for *Eoanthropus*

As the world emerged from World War II, Piltdown Man came to be seen as an anomaly, and non-British researchers largely ignored it[49]. Indeed, it is questionable as to how widely it was ever accepted outside Britain[39]. In a review article entitled "*The Riddle of Man's Ancestry*", American anthropologist William L. Straus, Jr. made no reference to it whatsoever[50]. Even Sir Arthur Keith admitted that "*If we could get rid of the Piltdown fossil fragments, then we should greatly simplify the problem of human evolution*"[18].

By the end of the 1940s, Raymond Dart's *Australopithecus* had been accepted as a human ancestor, with Keith recanting his earlier opposition[51]. By this time, more African hominins had been discovered, including *Homo rhodesiensis* ('Rhodesian Man', 1921), *Plesianthropus transvaalensis* ('Near-man from the Transvaal', 1947), and *Paranthropus robustus* ('robust alongside-man', 1938). The latter two were discovered by Scottish palaeontologist Robert Broom, a long-time supporter of Dart. German American biologist Ernst Mayr led a general tidying up of the plethora of species now populating the human family tree. *Pithecanthropus erectus* and *Sinanthropus pekinensis* were recognised as belonging to the same species, which Mayr designated *Homo erectus*. *Australopithecus africanus*, *Plesianthropus transvaalensis*, and *Paranthropus robustus* were all lumped into *Homo transvaalensis*[31].

The emerging picture was of small-brained biped apes in Africa (*Homo transvaalensis*), followed by smallish-brained humans with low, flattened foreheads and prominent browridges (*Homo erectus*), followed by larger-brained humans retaining the long, low cranial shape and prominent browridges of *Homo erectus* (Neanderthals) and modern humans (*Homo sapiens*). This model asserted the primacy of bipedalism over brain enlargement as the hallmark of early human evolution[49]. With its globular cranium, large brain, and apelike jaw, *Eoanthropus* was becoming ever harder to fit into the picture.

In 1944, Sir Arthur Smith Woodward died, aged 80. He was survived by his wife Maud. His death meant that the Piltdown remains at the BM(NH) were no longer considered untouchable. Given the increasingly problematic status of *Eoanthropus*, the Museum authorised tests to be conducted on the remains, in the hope of clarifying the age of the remains and whether the cranium and jawbone genuinely belonged to the same individual[5].

Radiometric dating techniques had existed since the early twentieth century, but until radiocarbon dating became practical during the 1950s, such methods could only be used to date samples that were millions of years old. One dating technique that was available was fluorine dating. Originally developed in the nineteenth century, the method relies on measuring the quantity of fluorine absorbed by a fossil. The quantity present increases over time, and hence is a measure of how long the fossil has been buried. Unfortunately, the chemistry of groundwater and soil will vary from site to site. This limits the use of fluorine

---

[31] Today, all three are classed as australopithecines. *Plesianthropus transvaalensis* is classed as the same species as *Australopithecus africanus*, although *Paranthropus robustus* is accepted as a separate species and by some as belonging to a separate genus, the 'robust' australopithecines.

dating to fossils from the same site, where it can be used to determine their relative ages. The technique was never widely used and had fallen into obscurity by the early twentieth century. It was revived by Kenneth Oakley in the 1940s. Oakley was able to take advantage of the considerable advances in analytical chemistry since the nineteenth century. He first used the technique to try to verify the antiquity of a human skull from Kanjera, Kenya. Unfortunately, it was found to have been saturated with fluorine from the volcanic deposits in which it was found[52].

Undeterred by this initial setback, Oakley turned the unsolved problem of Galley Hill Man, a skeleton that was discovered in the late nineteenth century in Middle Pleistocene gravels at Galley Hill, Swanscombe, Kent. It had been the subject of a long-running controversy over whether it dated to the Pleistocene, as Sir Arthur Keith believed, or whether it was a recent intrusive burial. Oakley was able to show that it was the latter, more recent than fossil animal bones from the gravels, and almost certainly less than 10,000 years old. To demonstrate the validity of the fluorine test, Oakley applied it to the Swanscombe skull, the skull of a young female early/proto-Neanderthal found in the same gravels in the 1930s. It had been found in association with Acheulean hand axes, and it was generally accepted to be the same age. The skull was found to contain far higher levels of fluorine than the Galley Hill remains, so confirming both its Pleistocene age and the validity of the fluorine dating method[53].

Oakley now applied his updated fluorine dating methods to the Piltdown cranium and jawbone, as well as other faunal remains from the gravel pit. The results were not consistent with a Pleistocene origin for *Eoanthropus*. The fluorine content of animal remains of undisputed Early Pleistocene age was, as expected, far higher than later Pleistocene age. However, the *Eoanthropus* remains all showed very little fluorine and could not, therefore, date to the Early Pleistocene. Oakley suggested that "*they date from the time of final settling of the gravel, which from physiographic and other evidence is now considered to be not earlier than the last interglacial period*". He speculated that *Eoanthropus* was "*a specialised forest type which evolved in isolation and became extinct at the beginning of the last glacial period, less than 100,000 years ago*"[53]. In other words, far from being a distant ancestor of humanity, *Eoanthropus* was nothing more than a recent, extinct side branch in which the jawbone had somehow made an evolutionary reversal to an atavistic apelike condition.

The study failed to resolve the question of whether the cranium and jawbone were part of the same individual. Noting the limited resolution of fluorine dating, Oakley remarked that "*It is still open to anatomists to argue about the naturalness of the association of an ape-like mandible with a typically human brain-case, but in the light of the new dating evidence it appears more probable that they belong to the same creature*"[53] – and continue to argue they did. In 1951, British-American anthropologist Montague Francis Ashley Montagu highlighted "*a striking disparity*" that "*does not appear to have been sufficiently emphasised*", this being that "*while the cranial bones of Piltdown I and II are extraordinarily thick the mandible is comparatively remarkably thin, the latter being of about the same general thickness as that of the average mature female chimpanzee*". Ashley Montagu noted that such a disparity between the thickness of the cranial bone and jawbone was unknown in any primate, living or extinct. For this reason, "*it would seem highly improbable that the gracile mandible found with the Piltdown cranium bones belonged to the same individual*".

This, then, was how matters stood in July 1953, when Joseph Weiner had his "*repellent idea*".

Eliminating the impossible

Weiner saw that there were only two 'natural' explanations for Piltdown Man, "*i.e. that Piltdown man was in fact the composite man-ape of Woodward's interpretation, or that two distinct creatures, fossil man and fossil ape, had been found side by side*". But he realised that neither explanation was satisfactory. On one hand, "*on evolutionary grounds alone, a late Dawn Man stood out as an obvious incongruity*". On the other hand, what were the feasible explanations for the "*two-creature*" alternative? "*If the jaw and the cranium had not come together by nature or by blind accident then could they have got there by human agency? This would mean that someone by mischance or error had dropped a fossil jaw in the pit (perhaps used as a rubbish dump) dug in gravel which happened to contain fossil remnants*"[1].

Not only was this unlikely in the extreme, but it left unexplained how the same could have happened for the Piltdown II cranial fragment and molar tooth. Possibly, they could have been brought across in gravel from the original Piltdown gravel pit. The hypotheses were becoming ever more elaborate. If the jaw was from a fossil ape, then what fossil ape was it? Postulating that the jaw was not a fossil but from a modern ape was equally problematic, because the teeth possessed features unknown in modern apes. Weiner was led inexorably to the conclusion: "*A modern jaw with flat worn molars and uniquely worn-down eye tooth? That would mean only one thing: deliberately ground-down teeth. Immediately this summoned up a devastating corollary – the equally deliberate placement of the jaw in the pit*"[1].

The Piltdown hoax is revealed

Weiner discussed his suspicions with Wilfrid Edward Le Gros Clark, his department head at Oxford. Le Gros Clark in turn contacted Oakley and asked him if he thought that there was any possibility that the Piltdown jawbone could be a forgery. Oakley said that he thought that artificial abrasion had been applied to the teeth. The three men agreed that the BM(NH) should be actively involved in the investigation and that until this was completed, there was a need for strict secrecy. The areas investigated were as follows: the abrasion of the teeth, a retesting of the fluorine levels, measurement of organic content, and the surface staining[5].

On 20 November 1953, Weiner, Oakley, and Le Gros Clark released a paper entitled "*The Solution of the Piltdown Problem*"[54], which was circulated to the press. The results of their investigation "*demonstrated quite clearly that the mandible and canine are indeed deliberate fakes.*" Consideration of the molar teeth attached to the Piltdown jawbone identified eight points of suspicion:

1. The occlusal surfaces (biting surfaces), particularly of the M_2 molar, were planed down over almost their whole extent to a flatness far greater than that normally produced by natural wear.
2. The borders of the flat occlusal surfaces, particularly at the sides, were sharp-cut and lacked the bevelling that might be expected from natural wear.
3. The centre of the talonid basin (a low shelf at the posterior end of the tooth) in the M_2 molar was not worn and was bounded by a sharp-cut and unbevelled border of the planed surface of the crown. This could be produced by artificial abrasion but would not be expected from natural wear.

4. The surface of the areas of dentine exposed on the anteromedial cusps of the two molars was flat, and it was flush with the surrounding enamel instead of forming a depression, as would be expected from natural wear.
5. In both molars, far more dentine had been exposed on the anterointernal cusps than the anteroexternal cusps. During natural attrition, the lateral cusps of lower molar teeth are normally worn down more rapidly; hence, there is usually a greater exposure of dentine than for the medial cusps.
6. The degree of wear in the two molars, M_1 and M_2, was almost identical. However, in the early stages of natural attrition, M_1 is typically worn than M_2.
7. The planes of the flat occlusal surfaces of the two molars did not fit together to form a uniform contour. Unless the teeth were displaced from their natural position after death, this is difficult to explain in terms of natural wear.
8. Inspection of the Piltdown II molar tooth with a binocular microscope showed that the occlusal surface of the enamel had been finely scratched, as though by an abrasive.

For the Piltdown I canine tooth, discovered by Teilhard de Chardin in 1913, four points of suspicion were identified:
1. The mode of wear of this tooth was unlike that found normally in the canines of either apes or humans. The abraded surface had exposed the dentine over the entire lingual surface from medial to distal border, and at one point this reached the apex of the pulp cavity.
2. The condition of the apex of the root, and the wide and open pulp cavity seen in an X-ray photograph, indicated that the canine was either incompletely erupted or had only just recently completed its eruption. This was inconsistent with the severely abraded condition of the crown.
3. X-ray examination showed no evidence for the deposition of secondary dentine, as might have been expected if the severe abrasion of the lingual surface of the crown were the result of natural attrition.
4. Under a binocular microscope, the abraded surface of the crown showed fine vertical scratches, which suggest the application of an abrasive.

Moving on to the fluorine tests, Weiner, Oakley, and Le Gros Clark noted that the tests carried out in 1949 and reported in 1950 had established that the Piltdown cranium and jawbone were more recent than Early Pleistocene but could not establish whether they were the same age. However, improved techniques were now available, and it was thought worthwhile to repeat the analysis. The results left no doubt that *"whereas the Piltdown cranium may well be Upper Pleistocene as claimed in 1950, the mandible, canine tooth and isolated molar are quite modern."*

The team next reported on a new technique that had been used to estimate the age of remains from early occupation sites in North America. Nitrogen dating relies on the gradual loss of nitrogen from bone as collagen is broken down into amino acids and leached away. As collagen decomposes, it releases nitrogen at a reasonably uniform rate, so providing an indication of age. The rate of decay is dependent on the burial environment, so like fluorine dating, nitrogen dating is only useful for determining the relative ages of material from the same site. However, the team noted that the method was a useful supplement to fluoride dating and was also useful for dating specimens too recent to be dated by the fluorine method. The results agreed with all the other evidence indicating that *"the Piltdown mandible, canine and isolated* [Piltdown II] *molar (II) are modern. (The possibility that the Piltdown specimens were steeped in a gelantinous preservative has been borne in mind; if this had been the explanation of their nitrogen-content, the cranial bones which are porous would have shown more nitrogen than the highly compact dentine of the teeth; whereas the reverse is true.)"*

Finally, the team reported on the colouring of the Piltdown specimens, beginning with the Piltdown I canine. Noting that the black coating had been described as *"ferruginous"* by Dawson and Woodward, they noted that when Oakley had sampled the teeth in 1948, he had found that "below an extremely thin ferruginous surface stain the dentine was pure white, apparently no more altered than the dentine of Recent teeth from the soil." The current analysis demonstrated that *"the coating on the canine is in fact non-metallic, it is a tough, flexible paint-like substance, insoluble in the common organic solvents, and with only a small ash-content. The extreme whiteness of the dentine and the nature of the black skin are thus both consistent with the evidence presented above for the essential modernity of the canine"*.

Moving on to the jawbone, it was *"of a reddish-brown colour which, though rather patchy, matches closely enough that of the cranial fragments to raise no suspicion that all the remains (from the original Piltdown site) might not belong to one skull. The frontal fragment stated to have been found at a second site (Piltdown II) is also of a similar brown colour but differs noticeably from the darker greyish-brown occipital fragment from the same site. That the colour of all these fragments is due to iron oxides has been confirmed by direct analysis in the Government Laboratory. But whereas the cranial fragments are all deeply stained (up to 8% of iron) throughout their thickness, the iron staining of the mandible is quite superficial. A small surface sample analysed in 1949 contained 7% iron, but, when in the course of our re-examination this bone was drilled more deeply, the sample obtained was lighter in colour and contained only 2-3% of iron. The difference in iron staining is thus also in keeping with the other evidence that the jaw and the cranium are not naturally associated"*.

Woodward had recorded that *"the colour of the* [cranial] *pieces which were first discovered was altered a little by Mr. Dawson when he dipped them in a solution of bichromate of potash* [potassium bichromate] *in the mistaken idea that this would harden them."* Chemical analysis and X-ray spectroscopy confirmed that the cranial fragments seen by Woodward in the spring of 1912 (before he commenced excavation work) contained chromate, but none was found in the cranial fragments found that summer. This would have been as expected if Woodward had stopped Dawson from dipping them in the chromate solution. Similarly, it would have been expected that the jawbone – excavated later, in the presence of Woodward – would not contain chromate. But chemical analysis revealed otherwise. *"The jaw does contain chromate. It is clear from Smith Woodward's statement about the staining of the cranial fragments of Piltdown I (which we have verified), that a chromate staining of the jaw could hardly have been carried out without his knowledge after excavation. The iron and chromate staining of the Piltdown jaw seems to us to be explicable only as a necessary part of the deliberate matching of the jaw of a modern ape with the mineralised cranial fragments"*.

Weiner, Oakley, and Le Gros Clark concluded: *"From the evidence which we have obtained, it is now clear that the distinguished palaeontologists and archaeologists who took part in the excavations at Piltdown were the victims of a most elaborate and carefully prepared hoax. Let it be said, however, in exoneration of those who have assumed the Piltdown fragments to belong to a single individual, or who, having examined the original specimens, either regarded mandible and canine as those of a fossil ape or else assumed (tacitly or explicitly) that the problem was not capable of solution on the available evidence, that the faking of the mandible and canine is so extraordinarily skilful, and the perpetuation of the hoax appears to have been so entirely unscrupulous and inexplicable, as to find no parallel in the history of paleontology discovery"*.

Aftermath

Later editions of the *Times* on Saturday, 21 November 1953 reported the *"startling discovery"* that the Piltdown skull was a forgery. Under the headline *"Piltdown Man Forgery – Jaw and Tooth of Modern Ape 'Elaborate Hoax'"*, the newspaper's Museum Correspondent outlined the findings of Weiner, Oakley, and Le Gros Clark. Turning to the inevitable question of the identity of the perpetrator, the article noted that Dawson was *"an amateur collector of fossils"* who had died *"highly regarded by scientists, in 1916, aged 52"*. Woodward was described as *"an authority of international reputation and unassailable integrity"*. The report also mentioned Teilhard de Chardin, noting that he and Woodward were *"two witnesses of the highest character" who "either found, or helped to find, the bones now known to be spurious"* and suggested that the remains had been planted by a third party for them to *"unimpeachably discovered"*. Should that third party have been Dawson, *"it would be but one more instance of desire for fame (since money was certainly not here the object) leading a scholar into dishonesty"*. In conclusion, the article paid tribute to the *"persistence and skill of modern palaeontological research"*.

The exposure was widely reported. In London, the *Star* headlined with *"The Biggest Scientific Hoax of the Century!"* Across the Atlantic, under the headline *"Piltdown Man Hoax Is Exposed: Jaw an Ape's, Skull Fairly Recent"*, John Hillary of the *New York Times* reported that *"Part of the skull of the Piltdown Man, one of the most famous fossil skulls in the world, has been declared a hoax by authorities at the British Natural History Museum"*. He noted that *"This declaration in the current issue of the museum's bulletin has been made after twenty years of rumors and uneasy speculation among European paleontologists about the authenticity of the bones"*.

When Weiner and Oakley visited the now-elderly Sir Arthur Keith, he said that he had heard the news on the radio and wearily conceded that *"I think you are probably right, but it will take me some time to adjust myself to the new view"*[12]. Though Keith had by now accepted that *Eoanthropus* was problematic, the revelation that he had devoted so much of his career to a forgery must have been devastating. He died just over a year later, aged 88.

Not everybody was ready to concede that Piltdown Man was a forgery. The *Times* devoted extensive column inches to the story in the week following the exposure, and on 26 November, it reported that Dr Alvan Theophilus Marston, the dental surgeon and anthropologist who discovered the Swanscombe skull, had protested *"the attack which has been made against Mr. Dawson in The Times and in the B.B.C. broadcast on Saturday"*. Marston had attended a meeting of the Geological Society of London where Oakley had explained why he and his fellow investigators had concluded that the jawbone of a modern ape had been faked to match a genuine cranium from the Upper Pleistocene. Marston complained that *"It has been very strongly hinted, if not definitely stated, that Mr. Dawson took the canine tooth and lower jaw of a modern ape…"* before being interrupted by geologist William King, presiding, who said that *"it was not a case of trying to justify or to condemn anything that had appeared in the newspapers or on the B.B.C."* and that they were hoping to get Marston's views on the jawbone itself. Marson replied that he had received a letter from Barkham Manor confirming Dawson's integrity and that *"they should not attack this man – it is so simple to prove that the canine tooth is not modern"*.

Dawson's stepson, Captain F.J.M. Postlethwaite, while on leave from serving with the British Camel Corps in Sudan, was also quick to come to Dawson's defence. He wrote to the *Times* on 23 November in robust terms, describing his late stepfather as "*an unassuming and thoroughly honest man*". Postlethwaite said that it "*would surely be absurd*" to suggest that Dawson had the expertise to produce a fake that could "*deceive his partner, a scientist of international repute*". He was also "*at all times far too honest and faithful to his research to have been an accessory to any faking whatsoever*".

While popular interest might have focused on the identity of the perpetrator, questions were being asked in scholarly circles as to why it had taken more than four decades for the hoax to be discovered. Weiner[1] suggested that "*the skill of the deception should not be underestimated*". William Straus[3], reflecting on the affair, noted that until the fluorine tests had shown the "*relative recency of all the specimens*", nobody had had any reason to suspect forgery. He added that "*methods for conclusively determining whether the specimens were actual fossils or faked ones, short of their wholesale destruction, were developed only in recent years*". The "*ready initial acceptance of the Piltdown discovery at its face value*" Straus attributed to "*the philosophical climate that invested the problem of human evolution at that time*", i.e., the then-prevalent 'brains first' paradigm, as supported by Elliot Smith and others. Sherwood Washburn[55], on the other hand, recalled Gerrit Miller's "*Deliberate malice*" observation in 1915 and suggested that had Miller had access to the original specimens rather than plaster casts, he might have identified the forgery much earlier. Washburn also noted that "*there never was enough of the fossil to justify the theories built around it*".

American anthropologist Earnest Hooton was critical of this latter assertion, noting that Eugène Dubois and Raymond Dart had relied on equally scant evidence to make claims about human evolution that were now widely accepted. Hooton nevertheless professed continued support for the 'brains first' paradigm. Though praising Weiner, Oakley, and Le Gros Clark for their "*skill and their thoroughness*", he expressed a degree of reservation over their evidence and said that he "*would not be surprised to live to witness the discovery even of an authentic Eoanthropus – jaw, brain case, and all*"[56]. Archaeologists Robert Heizer and Sherbourne Cook noted that "*a large amount of investigation by the fluoride method appears to support the validity of the technique*". Recalling that the technique had been known since the nineteenth century, they regretted that nobody "*until the time of Oakley, saw in the fluoride technique a ready means of solving the most difficult single problem of the Piltdown remains, which was the matter of the association of the mandible with the skull*"[57].

The exposure of the hoax did not end the investigation of the Piltdown material, and in 1955, Wiener, Oakley, Le Gros Clark, and others published their findings in the *Bulletin of the British Museum (Natural History) Geology*. These further revelations were surely enough to convince even the few remaining die-hards like Marston and Hooton. The Museum's Director, Gavin de Beer, gave a summary of the report: "*We are now in a position to give an account of the full extent of the Piltdown hoax. The mandible has been shown by further anatomical and X-ray evidence to be almost certainly that of an immature orang-utan; that it is entirely Recent has been confirmed by a number of microchemical tests, as well as by the electron-microscope demonstration of organic (collagen) fibres; the black coating on the canine tooth, originally assumed to be an iron encrustation, is a paint (probably Vandyke brown); the so-called turbinal bone is shown by its texture not to be a turbinal bone at all, but thin fragments of probably non-human limb-bone; all the associated flint implements have been artificially iron-stained; the bone implement ['cricket bat'] was shaped by a steel knife; the whole of the associated fauna must have been "planted," and it is concluded from radioactivity tests and fluorine analysis that some of the specimens are of foreign origin. The human skull fragments and some of the fossil animal bones are partly replaced by gypsum, the result of their treatment with iron sulphate to produce a colour matching that of the gravel. Not one of the Piltdown finds genuinely came from Piltdown. These latest investigations have demonstrated the methods now available which will not only make a successful repetition of a similar type of forgery virtually impossible in the future, but will be of further value in palaeontological research"*[58].

As to the perpetrator, Weiner[1] said that the forgery could have been produced by anybody with a reasonably sound knowledge of archaeology, palaeontology, geology, and chemistry. With these technical skills, they would also be able to place secondary fossils consistent with the era in which *Eoanthropus* supposedly lived (for example, the rhinoceros and mastodon teeth were authentic Red Crag fossils from East Anglia). From a practical point of view, as the excavations progressed, they would need to be able to follow progress so that they could place further faked material in places where it was likely to be found. They were likely to have been an established fossil collector, able where necessary to source specimens from other collectors either by purchase or exchange.

Investigation of the Piltdown material has continued to the present day, though nothing has been learned that significantly affects the conclusions drawn in 1953 and 1955. Radiocarbon dates of 500 ± 100 years old for the jawbone and 620 ± 100 years old for the cranium were obtained in 1959[59], but these were contradicted by dates obtained by the Oxford AMS lab in 1989, which were 90 years old for the jawbone and 970 ± 140 years old for the cranium[60]. A more recent attempt to date the remains was unsuccessful due to contamination and lack of datable material[6].

A 1982 study using immune reactions to proteins extracted from the jawbone suggested that it was indeed from an orangutan[61]. A more recent multidisciplinary study confirmed by morphometric analysis that the Piltdown molar and canine teeth were from a subadult orangutan. The Piltdown II molar appeared to be an M_1 and was the antimere (mirror image) of the Piltdown I M_1, hence both originated from the same animal. Mitochondrial DNA analysis showed that the Piltdown I canine and the Piltdown II molar both belonged to the same haplotype, consistent with them both being from the same animal. Phylogenetic analysis of the mitochondrial DNA showed that the teeth originated from a Bornean orangutan (*Pongo pygmaeus*)[6].

The same study found that consistent methods had been used to produce the fakes, suggesting that the forgery was the work of a single individual (regardless of whether others had collaborated in the hoax). However, they were not a trained conservator. Some aspects of the work were found to show inexpert skills. There was a crack running through the alveolar trabecular system (the bony ridge holding the tooth sockets) that had probably occurred when the initially intact jawbone was broken in two at the mandibular symphysis. The two molars, removed for filing down, had had their root tips damaged during the removal, and they had been improperly re-seated due to the putty holding them in place having set too rapidly[6].

Part III: Whodunnit?

Dawson: did he have 'form' before Piltdown?

The objections of Marston, Postlethwaite, and others notwithstanding, suspicion invariably fell on Dawson, and has continued to do so ever since. Joseph Weiner's 1955 account[1] stated that "*it is not possible to maintain that Dawson could not have been the actual perpetrator*". Contrary to Postlethwaite's protestations, "*he had the ability, the experience, and whatever we surmise may have been the motive, he was at all material times in a position to pursue the deception throughout its various phases*". It is important to note that Weiner chose his words carefully. He did not say that Dawson *was* the perpetrator, only that it is not possible to rule him out. Dawson certainly meets the criteria Weiner outlined for being a suspect.

Dawson also had a motive, albeit one that I will question. He desired recognition by academia, and there is little doubt that his ambition was to be elected a Fellow of the Royal Society. He might also have been motivated by the knighthood awarded to his younger brother Trevor in 1909, though that could have been of more interest to his wife Hélène than to Dawson himself. Dawson was indeed nominated for Fellowship in 1913 and continued to be every year until his death, though without success. However, failure to be elected at the first attempt was not unusual: even Arthur Keith's election in 1913 followed rejections in 1911 and 1912[4].

Dawson "*died too soon to be given any special award from a scientific body*"[1], but had he lived, *Eoanthropus dawsoni* might have enabled him to achieve his ambition. He had everything to gain from the forgery and, it is argued, nothing to lose. If he was to become a Fellow of the Royal Society, he needed the major discovery that had so far eluded him[4,6]. But is it true to say that Dawson had nothing to lose? Let us not forget that Dawson was not just plodding along in some day job; he was the senior partner in a long-established law firm, and he was deeply involved in local civic matters. He was, in every sense, a pillar of the local community in Uckfield. Weiner[58] suggests that "*Dawson's heart did not seem really to be in legal activities*", but this is speculation on his part. Could Dawson have achieved the above without throwing himself into it wholeheartedly? Was he so desperate to become a Fellow of the Royal Society that he was prepared to stake his personal reputation on a forgery that would be subjected to the highest level of scrutiny both in Britain and abroad?

Archaeologist Miles Russell[5,62] has brought a comprehensively researched case against Dawson alleging that many of his supposed discoveries were either dubious or out-and-out fakes and that Piltdown Man was no more than the culmination of a life's work of forgery and deception. Below, I discuss a few of the cases of possible deception investigated by Russell. For the full details, the reader is referred to Russell's *Piltdown Man : The secret life of Charles Dawson & the world's greatest archaeological hoax* (2003) and *The Piltdown Man Hoax: Case Closed* (2012).

One set of artefacts made with obvious intent to deceive is the Pevensey bricks, three fragmentary bricks supposedly found by Dawson at the Roman fortress at Pevensey, East Sussex, between 1902 and 1906, though not reported until 1907. The bricks bear the stamp of the emperor Honorius, during whose reign the Romans withdrew from Britain and if genuine, they would have dated to the very end of the Roman period in Britain. However, modern thermoluminescence dating techniques have shown that the bricks were fired no earlier than the beginning of the twentieth century. There is no doubt that they were a deliberate fake, but was Dawson responsible? Between 1906 and 1907, the Pevensey site was the subject of an archaeological excavation conducted by historian Louis Salzman under the auspices of the Sussex Archaeological Society. It cannot be ruled out that the bricks were manufactured and planted by Salzman or a member of his team, hoping to add a major discovery to what would otherwise turn out to be an unexceptional list of finds.

Russell claims that the *Plagiaulax dawsoni* tooth Dawson reported to Woodward in 1891 was artificially abraded, like the Piltdown teeth. He suggests that the tooth could have been filed down from a multituberculate fossil taken from Samuel Beckles' personal collection. However, palaeontologist William Clemens, writing in 1963, would go no further than noting that the tooth's similarities to the genus *Plagiaulax* were *"neither numerous, detailed, nor fully convincing"*. He suggested that *"The presence of a single pulp cavity in the root reduces the probability that the tooth is a plagiaulacid molar, which has two roots, and strongly suggests that it is not the tooth of a mammal"*[63]. This was a decade after the Piltdown exposure and Clemens would surely have been alert for any possibility of forgery.

A problem common to many of Dawson's supposed discoveries is that their provenance is generally vague; they were not always found by Dawson himself, and they were often reported many years after their supposed discovery. For example, the Beauport Park statuette was reportedly found in 1877 beneath a slagheap from the Roman ironworking site. The finder was a workman named William Merritt, who was digging for material for road surfacing. Dawson did not acquire the statuette from Merritt until 1883, when still aged only nineteen. A further decade passed before he showed it to Augustus Wollaston Franks, President of the Society of Antiquaries, and it was exhibited at a meeting of the Society in May 1893.

The small, corroded statuette is Roman in style, but Dawson believed that it was made from cast iron rather than wrought iron. To produce cast iron requires temperatures of around 1,200°C, which is thought to have been beyond the technologies of Roman ironworkers. Many of those attending the meeting were dubious about the claimed antiquity of the statuette. There were suggestions that it was a modern replica, possibly produced as a souvenir. In a letter to William Crake, secretary of the Hastings Museum Association, Dawson claimed that after the Society of Antiquaries disputed the statuette, he tracked down Merritt and obtained more details of the discovery. The statuette had apparently been found with coinage from the emperor Hadrian's reign, which linked it to an earlier, authenticated discovery of Roman coins made in the 1870s in similar circumstances. This strengthened Dawson's case that the statuette was of Roman origin, but another decade passed before he exhibited it again in a display of Sussex ironwork held in Lewes in 1903 that Dawson organised on behalf of the Sussex Archaeological Society.

Was Dawson using these decadal time-lapses to cloud the specifics of the discovery and provenance of the statuette? Possibly, but it could be that in both cases, he had other, more pressing matters to attend to; in 1883, he was only just establishing himself in the legal profession, and in 1993, he was busy with a wide range of extramural activities. Having gained information that lent some credibility to the statuette's supposed provenance, Dawson might simply have put it aside until an opportunity arose to put it on display again. As for the statuette, it is clearly not a genuine Roman object, but it is more likely that it was produced as a souvenir rather than as a deliberate fake. The discovery of Roman coins might have inspired Merritt to try and pass the statuette off as a genuine Roman object.

In some cases, Dawson never even saw the objects he was reporting on when they were intact. In 1893, he examined a collection of prehistoric stone tools belonging to Stephen Blackmore of Eastbourne with a view to acquiring it for the Hastings Museum Association. He noticed a drawing of a hafted axe, which was of considerable interest. At that time, no intact wooden hafts of prehistoric stone axes were known. Blackmore claimed to have found the axe some years earlier, and that the haft was carbonised and crumbled away at the touch. Fortunately, he had been able to make a drawing of the axe with its haft still intact. Blackmore's collection never appeared in the Hastings Museum. This *could* mean that it never existed at all – or quite simply that Dawson had failed to persuade Blackmore to sell it.

In 1894, an article by Dawson regarding the discovery appeared in *Sussex Archaeological Collections*, the journal of the Sussex Archaeological Society. The article was accompanied by an artist's impression of the hafted axe rather than Blackmore's drawing. Dawson has been criticised for not using the original drawing – but if he was unsuccessful in purchasing Blackmore's collection, he would not have had access to his drawing. From the axes with intact hafts that have since been recovered in northern Europe, we now know that the various methods of hafting were quite different to that depicted in the article. But all this proves is that either Blackmore's reconstruction was inaccurate, or Dawson's subsequent recollection of it was.

Dawson has also been accused of plagiarism in his 1910 book *The History of Hastings Castle*, as well as in various articles written between 1898 and 1911. These works do contain large quantities of other people's work, but in all cases, these elements are suitably referenced, albeit Russell suggests *sometimes rather vaguely*. He notes that if Dawson had been credited as editor rather than author, the allegations of plagiarism might not have arisen.

In all these cases, and the others investigated by Russell, Dawson comes across as somewhat naïve, and his methods and documentation haphazard and amateurish. But even where there is clear evidence for forgery, there are other suspects. Nowhere is there conclusive evidence for Dawson's dishonesty. We should not forget that Dawson *was* an amateur; it would be a mistake to hold him to the exacting standards expected of professional archaeologists today. That is not to say that Dawson was not the perpetrator of the Piltdown forgery, or even that the issues Russell raised surrounding his discoveries all have innocent explanations. But as far as suggesting that Dawson had 'form' before Piltdown, the case remains unproven.

With Piltdown, we see a now-familiar pattern of vagueness. Dawson's account begins with a walk that could have taken place as early as 1899 or as late as 1907. Again, though, this could be attributed to sloppiness rather than a deliberate smokescreen. Dawson was central to the discoveries; he was in the right place at the right time to be the hoaxer, he had the skills, and the means to acquire the fossils and other materials used. He arguably also had the motive. But we must at least examine other possibilities.

If not Dawson, then who?

In an afterword to Joseph Weiner's 1955 book, re-released in 2003 to mark the fiftieth anniversary of exposure of the forgery, British palaeoanthropologist Chris Stringer noted a longstanding joke that 'Chipper', a white goose prominent in a photograph of the Piltdown excavation team is the only one in the picture *not* to have been named as a suspect. In addition to Dawson, those named as possible suspects include Woodward, Teilhard de Chardin, Keith, Elliot Smith, and Sollas. Other names mentioned over the years have included zoologist Martin Hinton and even Sir Arthur Conan Doyle. None of the cases really stand up to scrutiny.

Sir Arthur Smith Woodward had known Dawson for many years and was his principal collaborator with Piltdown. But if a craving for recognition could be argued as a motive for Dawson, this is less obviously the case for Woodward. To recap, he was acknowledged as an authority on fossil fish, and he had been a Fellow of the Royal Society since 1901. It is certainly true that Woodward was a beneficiary of Piltdown, but the case against him rests largely on his failure to clarify with Dawson the exact circumstances in which the first cranial fragment of *Eoanthropus* was found, as well as his failure to spot some of the more obvious aspects of the forgery. But, with *Eoanthropus* now widely accepted, would he have continued excavations at Barkham Manor until 1938? During this 21-year period, of course, no further remains were found. It seems unlikely that he would devote more than two decades to such an endeavour if he did not intend to plant any further fakes, or he knew that no more were going to be planted. That he did so makes it unlikely that he was involved in the forgery[5].

Pierre Teilhard de Chardin was named as a suspect by American palaeontologist Stephen J. Gould in 1979[64]. Gould suggested Teilhard collaborated with Dawson and that rather than being a malicious forgery, Piltdown Man was intended as a practical joke that went too far. Though he became a more serious figure in later life, the young Teilhard was known as a joker who had known Dawson for some years. Gould suggests that it was Teilhard who obtained the secondary fossils that the 1955 study showed had originated from overseas. He could "*easily imagine*" that Dawson and Teilhard hatched the plot for their own different reasons: "*Dawson to expose the gullibility of pompous professionals; Teilhard to rub English noses once again with the taunt that their nation had no legitimate human fossils, while France revelled in a superabundance that made her the queen of anthropology*". They probably never expected the scientific community to fall so readily for the wheeze and might have thought about owning up but could not.

Having returned to France in the autumn of 1913, Teilhard was called up for war service in December 1914 and served as a stretcher bearer with the 8th Moroccan Rifles. He was decorated for valour and did not return to Britain until after the war. Dawson persevered with the plot and planted the Piltdown II fakes in 1915. But then he died unexpectedly the next year, and by the end of World War I, three of Britain's leading scientists – Woodward, Keith, and Elliot Smith – had backed Piltdown. It would have been professional suicide for Teilhard to confess now. As it was, he went on to play a major role in describing (the *bona fide*) *Sinanthropus pekinensis*.

The main weakness of this theory is that it presupposed that Dawson could not have perpetrated the hoax on his own. Indeed, Gould poses the Teilhard hypothesis as nothing more than a "*much more interesting*" alternative to that of Dawson acting alone, after stating that the latter possibility is "*the most probable in my view*".

Gould nevertheless went on to expand on the theory a year later[65]. He obtained a copy of a letter written by Teilhard to Oakley on 28 November 1953, a week after the hoax was exposed. Teilhard, who was by now the only one of the Piltdown excavators still living, congratulated Oakley for his role in discovering the forgery, before vehemently protesting the innocence of Dawson and Woodward. He put forward the suggestion – previously dismissed by Weiner – that a collector had inadvertently dropped the ape jawbone into the gravel pit, where it had rapidly become stained by iron in the local water. In addition to its extreme unlikelihood, this suggestion failed to explain the jawbone's filed-down molars. However, it was with his attempt to explain Piltdown II that Teilhard made his "*fatal error*", or so Gould claims. The letter claims that Dawson "*just brought me to the site of Locality 2 and explained me* [sic] *that he had found the isolated molar and the small pieces of skull in the heaps of rubble and pebbles raked at the surface of the field*". However, as Gould points out, nothing was found at the second site until early 1915, by which time Teilhard was serving with the French army. Gould suggests that Teilhard could not have seen the Piltdown II remains unless he and Dawson manufactured them before he left for France. Oakley picked up on the inconsistency, and when he wrote back to Teilhard, the latter realised his error, and Gould suggests that his reply on 29 January 1954 was an attempt to recover.

"*Concerning the point of 'history' you ask me, my 'souvenirs' are a little vague. Yet, by elimination (and since Dawson died during the First World War, if I am correct) my visit with Dawson to the second site (where the two small fragments of skull and the isolated molar were found in the rubble) must have been in late July 1913*". In a postscript to this letter, he added, "*When I visited the site no. 2 (in 1913?) the two small fragments of skull and tooth had already been found, I believe. But your very question makes me doubtful! Yes, I think definitely they had been already found: and that is the reason why Dawson pointed to me the little heaps of raked pebbles as the place of the 'discovery'*".

On 2 March 1954, Teilhard also wrote to Robert Kenward's daughter Mabel, claiming that "*Dawson showed me the field where the second skull (fragments) were found. But, as I wrote to Oakley, I cannot remember whether it was after or before the find*".

It should be remembered that Teilhard was now in his seventies. His health began to fail early in 1954, and he died in April 1955. Philip Tobias claimed that Gould's case against Teilhard was "*seriously weakened*" by this fact alone. Tobias suggested that "*the site of Locality 2*" that Teilhard referred to was the site near Barcombe Mills and not the Piltdown II site at Sheffield Park Estate, as Gould assumed. Forty years after the event, and under the influence of ageing, Teilhard could have confused the Piltdown II remains with the frontal bone Dawson found at Barcombe Mills in July 1913. Teilhard was in Hastings during August 1913, and Dawson would almost certainly have taken him to the Barcombe Mills site. Tobias also questioned whether such an elaborate hoax could be intended as a joke, or whether Teilhard would even have had the requisite knowledge of human and primate anatomy, palaeoanthropology and palaeontology, geology, and archaeology as he was still completing his theological studies. He concluded that the case that Teilhard was Dawson's co-conspirator was weak[4].

Tobias[4] went on to name Sir Arthur Keith as a suspect, with Dawson as an accomplice. On the face of it, Keith seems an unlikely suspect. As one of the leading anthropologists of his day, he had no need for deception to advance his career. However, Tobias notes that in 1912, Keith's knighthood was over a decade in the future, the publication of his book *The Antiquity of Man* was three years in the future, and his candidature for Fellowship of the Royal Society had been rejected twice. Keith was clearly irritated by the rejections. Tobias notes that in his diary entry for 25 March 1911, Keith refers to being given "*a slap in the face*". A year later, on 2 March 1912, after being turned down for the second time, he wrote, "*Royal Society still left me out so I have made up my mind to be content without it. Rather foolish a man at 46 needing qualifications and fellowships. Besides I don't think the men already elected are really quite capable of judging good and bad work*". Keith was elected a Fellow a year later. In his autobiography, Keith admitted that he had been impatient, perhaps unreasonably so, at "*being kept waiting so long*", and that "*one of the goals I expected to reach ten years ago comes now*". Tobias also highlighted the importance of *The Antiquity of Man* to Keith, who described it as "*my chief claim to recognition as a man of science*".

Clearly, Keith was an ambitious man, and at 46 he felt that he was still short of his career goals. As also noted, Piltdown Man fitted his 'brains first' model, whereas *Australopithecus* did not. But would personal ambition and a particular model of human evolution drive him to commit an act of fraud? Tobias cited "*nine pointers to Keith's guilt*", which he claimed were "*parts of such a pattern*" of cover-ups on Keith's part. I summarise them below, along with what I believe are the explanations in each case.

1. Keith wrote an editorial for the *British Medical Journal* (BMJ), which appeared on 21 December 1912, three days after the announcement at Burlington House, in which he gave details about the Piltdown site and the history of the discoveries that were supposedly not discussed at the 18 December meeting. Furthermore, his diary suggests that he wrote the article three days before the meeting. The latter detail is probably not relevant; he could have sketched out the article with what he knew before the meeting and then revised it before the journal went to press. It has also been claimed that full details of the whereabouts of the site were in fact revealed at the 18 December meeting; Tobias is assuming Dawson and Woodward's 1913 article is an accurate transcript of *everything* that was discussed at the meeting.

2. Keith supposedly visited the Piltdown site with his wife on 4 January 1913. They were unable to find the site and returned to London. Tobias argues that this was a smokescreen to hide the fact that he was familiar with the site and that it was also suspicious that he failed to make a prior arrangement to meet Dawson. Equally, though, it could have been a spur-of-the-moment visit because his wife wanted to see the site, and he happened to have the time (4 January 1913 was a Saturday).

3. In his autobiography, Keith claimed to have first met Dawson "*early in 1913*". In fact, he must have met Dawson earlier on at least two previous occasions. The first was when Keith was one of three guests of honour at an event hosted by Dawson, Lewis Abbott, and W.R. Butterfield in Hastings in July 1911. The second was an episode when Dawson visited the Royal College of Surgeons (see 6 below). When talking to Weiner in 1953, Keith said that he'd met Dawson "before the famous meeting of 1912", then corrected himself and said that it was after then. He subsequently checked his diary and confirmed that the date was 28 January 1913 (just over three weeks after his abortive trip to Piltdown). Keith was 84 when he wrote his autobiography, and he died just over a year after his discussion with Weiner. As with Teilhard, this is more readily explicable in terms of lapses in memory.

4. Czech anthropologist Aleš Hrdlička wrote to Keith late in October 1912 asking him what he knew about the soon-to-be-announced Piltdown discovery. Keith did not reply until after the 18 December meeting, claiming the delay was because he had not

seen the Piltdown material before then. In fact, he twice viewed it at the BM(NH) earlier in December. This is hardly significant – Keith could easily have forgotten to write back to Hrdlička, and when he finally did so, he excused the delay with a small diplomatic lie.

5.   After Piltdown was exposed, Keith systematically destroyed all his extensive correspondence with Dawson and his notes about Piltdown. My reaction here is, can you blame him? He had devoted much of his professional life to a fossil that had turned out to be a forgery. Hardly *"remarkable and suspicious"*, as Tobias asserts.

6.   On 12 May 1912, Dawson wrote to Woodward with the manuscript of a paper on 13th thoracic vertebrae in humans (the normal number is 12). In an accompanying letter, he said that he had visited the Royal College of Surgeons to study skeletons in Keith's collection. He was *"very anxious to get it* [the paper] *placed at once because I have had to work the photographs under the nose of Keith and his assistant. I gather from the latter that Keith is rather puzzled* [about] *what to make of it all, and I want to secure the priority to which I am entitled"*. Tobias notes that Dawson had no qualifications or experience as an anatomist and that he would not normally have been given access to the collection unless Keith was satisfied with his credentials. That he was given access Tobias takes as evidence for collusion between Keith and Dawson. He suggests that the real purpose of the visit could have been to procure fossil material to be used at Piltdown and that the 13th vertebrae paper was just a ruse to which Dawson had been put up by Keith. Again, though, it could be that Dawson's account is true, and that he simply smoozed his way past Keith's assistant and got his photographs. Keith probably forgot all about the incident.

7.   Keith repeatedly asserted that Dawson was an honest man, long before the forgery was exposed, and indeed afterwards. Tobias again views this as part of a coverup: the more he emphasised Dawson's honesty, the less likely it was that anybody would question the legitimacy of Piltdown. Again, it is more likely that Keith wanted to speak well of somebody whom he liked and respected, who had died before his time.

8.   Tobias finds suspicion in Keith's repeated assertions that Piltdown was genuine – but Keith's theories depended on it being genuine, so it is hard to agree.

9.   In July 1913, pathologist Samuel George Shattock presided over a conference on pathology held as part of the 17th International Congress of Medicine in London, and he presented a paper on cranial thickening in some modern people and in *"certain Pleistocene crania"*. He claimed that the cranial thickening was a pathology rather than a normal condition of the latter. But in his 1915 book *The Antiquity of Man*, Keith stated of *Eoanthropus*, *"The bone is naturally formed; there can be no question of disease. My colleague Mr. Shattock definitely settled this point"*. This was certainly reprehensible, but hardly proof that Keith was complicit in the Piltdown forgery.

Russell[5] dismissed this *"pattern"* as *"lacking in anything but the most circumstantial detail"*, and I am inclined to agree. Keith can only be faulted on the last point and even then, it only shows that Piltdown was important to his theories. This is not disputed, but it is certainly not tantamount to saying that he was responsible for the forgery.

Ronald Millar[12] suggested that Sir Grafton Elliot Smith was a suspect. He would have had a motive, because *Eoanthropus* fitted his theories about migration from a 'centre' as waves of more advanced races drove out the more primitive ones. Elliot Smith believed that the centre was in the Middle East, and the presence of a more primitive being in Britain was consistent with this view. Another possible motive is that Elliot Smith was after Woodward's job at the BM(NH). He knew that Woodward's main field was fossil fish and not human anatomy, and that once Piltdown was exposed as a fraud, his position there would become untenable. But as the forgery remained undiscovered and Elliot Smith's own career flourished, he let matters lie.

As an anatomist and an expert on prehistoric skulls, Elliott Smith would certainly have had the expertise to perpetrate the hoax. He would also have had very little difficulty in procuring the skulls and other material to be used in the hoax. Though working in Egypt in what Millar thought "*might be considered a backwater appointment in Cairo*" at the time of the Piltdown discoveries, "*his tumultuous appearances in England coincide remarkably with the turn of events in Sussex*". He would, of course, have to explain why he, too, had been fooled by Piltdown when it was exposed, but here he could blame the fact that he had based his findings on plaster casts of the Piltdown remains, and that these were inaccurate.

Weiner[66] gives short shrift to Millar's arguments. Noting that Elliot Smith was not even based in Britain at the time, he asked, "*Where are the proofs that Elliot Smith made the many repeated visits to the Barkham Manor site or the Sheffield Park site that would have been needed? How did he manage to arrange that Dawson followed him at the appropriate times to find the planted material and to make the announcements to the British Museum or the public? In fact, the events of the 1915 finds alone are so complicated that for Elliot Smith to have been tied up in these let alone with events before he even got to England, I find completely incredible*".

The case against William Sollas was brought by James Douglas, a former Professor of Geology at the University of Oxford. Shortly before his death in 1978, Douglas made a tape recording in which he claimed that Sollas had collaborated with Dawson to perpetrate the hoax. He was motivated by his dislike of Sir Arthur Smith Woodward, and wished to discredit him. On the tape, Douglas claimed that he could remember a packet of potassium bichromate being delivered to Sollas, and that Sollas borrowed ape teeth from the Department of Human Anatomy at Oxford. Weiner[67] dismissed the allegation. He notes that the potassium bichromate could hardly be taken as positive evidence, and in any case, everybody was aware at the time that Dawson had used bichromate solution in a misguided attempt to preserve the specimens. Moreover, as the 1953 report had shown, Dawson had used a variety of methods to darken his specimens and there was no evidence that he had learned about any of these methods from Dawson. Of Sollas borrowing ape teeth, Weiner said, "*If Douglas had remembered Sollas borrowing an ape's jaw or even better, an orang's jaw, that would have been rather more interesting*". As to the motive, if Sollas wished to humiliate Woodward by exposing his gullibility and incompetence, then why did he firmly support *Eoanthropus dawsoni* in the first place? Why did he not take his revenge by exposing the hoax after Dawson's death? Weiner concluded that Douglas had "*certainly added a mystery of his own devising to the Piltdown saga – why should Douglas on such incredibly weak evidence take the trouble to besmirch Sollas' reputation?*"

Martin Hinton, a zoologist who worked at the BM(NH), was known to be a prankster, and he is said to have disliked Woodward. The case against him seems to rest largely upon a canvas trunk bearing his initials that was found in the loft space of the Museum during a clearout in the mid-1970s. Therein were bones of unknown origin, some of which had been chemically treated. All this proves is that Hinton might have been experimenting in ways of reproducing the fake staining of the Piltdown remains. There is no evidence that he ever visited Piltdown during the excavations[5]. Another suggestion is that Hinton realised that the Piltdown material was faked and, far from wanting to humiliate Woodward, tried to lead him into discovering the hoax for himself by leaving objects that he would be sure to identify as fake. These included the Piltdown I canine and the 'cricket bat'. The fake canine was based on Woodward's original reconstruction of Piltdown, which Keith had rejected. Unfortunately, the plan failed because both were accepted as being genuine[27].

Finally, we come to Sir Arthur Conan Doyle, who was named as a suspect by popular science writers John Winslow and Alfred Meyer in 1983[68]. In addition to his talents as an author, Conan Doyle was a medical doctor with a knowledge of human anatomy, chemistry, geology, and archaeology, and a keen collector of fossils. He lived in Windlesham, just 13 km (8 miles) from the Piltdown site, and he was known to take long walks in the area. He knew Dawson and Woodward, and during the Piltdown excavations, he supposedly visited the site regularly. On his honeymoon in 1907 following his second wedding (his first wife died), he spent two months in the eastern Mediterranean and in 1909, he went on a cruise to the western Mediterranean. On these trips, he probably visited Malta, Algeria, and Tunisia, where he could have obtained the fossil teeth used in the Piltdown hoax. Finally, it is alleged that as a Spiritualist, he had a grudge against Darwinian advocate Sir Edwin Ray Lankester. Lankaster was a leading critic of Spiritualism, who had exposed the American spirit medium Henry Slade and had him prosecuted for fraud. Slade was convicted and jailed for three months but released on a technicality and fled to the United States. Spiritualists believe it is possible to communicate with the spirits of the dead and that spirit mediums can conduct such communication through séances. They also believe that spirits are capable of evolving and progressing through higher spheres or planes of existence.

Conan Doyle is thus alleged to have had the means and motives to have perpetrated the Piltdown hoax. However, the evidence that he did is unconvincing. In his 1912 novel *The Lost World*, it is suggested that Conan Doyle dropped hints that Piltdown was a forgery. In the book, there is an exchange in which the character Tarp Henry observes that "*if you are clever and you know your business you can fake a bone as easily as you can a photograph*". Another character, Summerlee, says that such a practical joke "*would be one of the most elementary developments of man*". Conan Doyle began planning the novel in August 1910 and completed it in December 1911. It was serialised in *The Strand Magazine* starting in April 1912, a few months before Dawson and Woodward went public with *Eoanthropus*. None of this seems to add up to very much. Equally, that the geography of *The Lost World's* fictional plateau bears a striking resemblance to the Weald is unsurprising, given that Conan Doyle lived and took long walks there.

The case against Conan Doyle was dismissed by Australian anthropologist Ian Langham[69] as "*the latest (and flimsiest) of a number of recent attempts to implicate a famous or eminent person through the assembling of purely circumstantial evidence*". Langham noted that contrary to Winslow and Meyer's account, Conan Doyle was on good terms with Lankester. Indeed, Lankester is said to have been the inspiration for *The Lost World's* lead character Prof. George E. Challenger. Another obvious question is, why did he never admit to the hoax? As a publicity stunt, it was surely second to none. Langham also noted that Conan Doyle's 'informed interest' in palaeontology was actually very naïve: many of his supposed fossils turned out to be oddly shaped rock formations, concretions of sand and iron oxide, etc. It would therefore not have been as straightforward for him to 'salt' the Piltdown gravel pit with convincing fossils as Winslow and Meyer suggested, and in any case, there is no definite proof that he ever even visited the site. As a further example of Conan Doyle's gullibility, Langham cited his belief that a photograph taken by two young girls in 1917 demonstrated the existence of fairies. In 1983, the two now-elderly women concerned admitted that the photograph was faked.

This list of suspects is by no means exhaustive; Tobias noted[4] that at least 21 people had been named over the years "*on circumstantial evidence of varying degrees of confidence*". In most cases, the alleged motive was either personal advancement or a grudge against somebody in the scientific establishment, with Woodward as a common target. But suppose the target was not part of the scientific establishment. Supposing that the target was Dawson?

Dawson the intended victim, not the perpetrator?

Dawson, as we have seen, was a major figure in the Uckfield community, and he seems to have been generally well thought of. However, his relationship with the Sussex Archaeological Society was largely ended by what Weiner[1] referred to as the 'Castle Lodge episode'. Since 1885, the Society had been based at Castle Lodge, a townhouse in Lewes owned by the Marquis of Abergavenny. In the autumn of 1903, the property was sold to Dawson, who gave the Society notice to quit by midsummer 1904. The Society was completely taken by surprise at the purchase, as it had been given to believe that it would be given the first option to buy in the event of the property being sold.

Noting that the Piltdown discovery had been largely ignored by the Society, Weiner spoke to Louis Salzman, now President of the Society. Salzman had been a member at the time of the 1904 debacle, and it was largely for this reason that Dawson's subsequent activities had been treated with scepticism. Although Weiner initially supposed that Dawson had purported to have opened negotiations on behalf of the Sussex Archaeological Society, Salzman clarified via the *Sunday Times* that at no time had this been the case, and Weiner set the record straight in the second impression of his book. However, the vendors may have erroneously believed so, possibly due to Dawson's use of Sussex Archaeological Society headed notepaper[5]. At all events, Dawson still appears to have been in the doghouse over the episode four decades later. Russell[5] notes that in 1946, Salzman commented that "*his name was later given to the 'Pilt Down Man' [sic] (Eoanthropus dawsoni), the lowest form of human being, with the discovery of whose remains he was associated*".

Salzman, as previously noted, was leading Pevensey excavations of 1906-07, where the bricks supposedly bearing the stamp of the Roman emperor Honorius were found. If he or a member of the team was responsible for that forgery (rather than Dawson), could they not also have been behind the Piltdown forgery? Alternately, if a small number of members of the Sussex Archaeological Society became aware of the Pevensey forgery, could that not have inspired one or more of them to perpetrate the Piltdown forgery with the intention of discrediting Dawson? There would have been members of the Society with the ability to do so. Again, the question must be asked, why do the forger(s) never go public? The answer here might be that with Dawson's unexpected death in 1916 they decided to let the matter drop.

Contra Miles Russell's second Piltdown book[62], the Piltdown case is not closed. The case against Dawson is stronger than that against any of the other usual suspects; for that reason, he must remain the prime suspect. However, the case against him is certainly not conclusive, and we should be open to the possibility that the perpetrator was a low-profile individual, now long dead, and whose identity we are unlikely ever to learn.

Epilogue

Following Charles Dawson's death in 1916, no further examples of *Eoanthropus dawsoni* were ever found. On 23 July 1938, just two months before the Munich Agreement, Sir Arthur Keith unveiled a sandstone monolith to mark the spot where Dawson had found the Piltdown I cranium and jawbone. Before unveiling the monument, he said, "*So long as man is interested in his long past history, in the vicissitudes which our early forerunners passed through, and the varying fare which overtook them, the name of Charles Dawson is certain of remembrance. We do well to link his name to this picturesque corner of Sussex – the scene of his discovery. I have now the honour of unveiling this monolith dedicated to his memory*". The monolith bears the inscription "*Here in the old river gravel, Mr. Charles Dawson, FSA found the fossil skull of Piltdown man 1912-1913. The Discovery was described by Mr. Charles Dawson and Sir Arthur Smith Woodward in the Quarterly Journal of the Geological Society 1913-15*". The monument, its inscription barely visible through a covering of lichen, stands there to this day. In the village of Piltdown is the *Piltdown Man* pub, renamed from *The Lamb* in the 1920s. In 2011, it briefly reverted to its original name. But as of 2022, it is once again serving pints as the *Piltdown Man*.

05: Muddle in the middle

Bigger brains

By the early twentieth century, a picture of human evolution was starting to emerge. The first example of *Pithecanthropus* (now known as *Homo erectus*) had been discovered by the Dutch physician and anthropologist Eugène Dubois at Trinil, Java, in 1891, and Neanderthals had been known since the 1850s. In 1902, German anthropologist Gustav Schwalbe proposed two evolutionary schemes: one postulated that *Pithecanthropus* was the direct ancestor of modern humans, and Neanderthals were an extinct side branch on the other. The second postulated a line of evolution from *Pithecanthropus* to Neanderthals to modern humans without branching[1]. He was on the right lines with his first scenario, although the emerging science of palaeoanthropology would be wrong-footed for more than four decades by the Piltdown Man forgery in 1912.

The sequence of events leading from the relatively small-brained *Homo erectus* to the larger-brained Neanderthals and modern humans remains uncertain to this day. Early humans were larger-brained than the australopithecines, whose cranial capacity was typically around 450 cc[2,3]. The adult cranial capacity of *Homo erectus* averaged 975 cc, though with considerable variation. Brain size increased slightly in specimens from later times[4], but it was still rather less than the 1,350 average of modern populations[5]. The fossil record shows that around 600,000 years ago, there was a substantial increase in brain size with the appearance of hominins with a typical cranial capacity of around 1,200 cc[4], about 90 per cent of the modern figure.

The appearance of these larger-brained hominins coincides broadly with the end of the transition from the Early to Middle Pleistocene. The Middle Pleistocene Transition (MPT) saw the swings between a warm, wet climate and a cold, arid climate decrease in periodicity from 41,000 years to 100,000 years. There was a commensurate increase in intensity as ice sheets in higher latitudes had much longer to build up. The transition began around 1.25 million years ago and was completed by 700,000 years ago[6].

The Mauer mandible

The first discovery of a hominin fossil from the Middle Pleistocene was made in 1907. The Mauer mandible is a virtually complete lower jawbone that was found in a sand quarry at the village of Mauer, 10 km (6.2 miles) from Heidelberg. The discovery was made on 21 October 1907 by Daniel Hartmann, a 52-year-old quarry worker, at a depth of 24.63 m (80 ft 10 in) from the surface of the quarry. The jawbone was described by Otto Schoetensack, a retired industrialist turned Professor of Palaeontology at the University of Heidelberg. Schoetensack had long been aware of the possibility of finding fossils at the site since the discovery of a fossilised elephant skull fragment in 1887, and he had asked quarry workers to keep a lookout. Hartmann duly contacted Schoetensack, who assigned the jawbone the specific name *Homo heidelbergensis* ('Heidelberg man') in a monograph entitled *Der Unterkiefer des Homo Heidelbergensis Aus den Sanden von Mauer bei Heidelberg* ('The lower jaw of *Homo heidelbergensis* from the sands of Mauer near Heidelberg')[7].

The jawbone possesses a mosaic of features intermediate between *Homo erectus* and *Homo sapiens*. The mandibular body is robust and the chin receding like *Homo erectus*, but the size and shape of the teeth are within the range of modern humans[8–10]. The Mauer mandible is 609,000 ± 40,000 years old[11], making it the oldest-known example of the species it defines. However, the lack of comparative material at the time it was found and the fossil itself being a lower jawbone with no cranial parts made it difficult to diagnose the species and position it in the hominin phylogeny. The specific name *Homo heidelbergensis* was largely forgotten for much of the twentieth century[10].

The Kabwe cranium

Almost a decade and a half after the discovery of the Mauer mandible, a near-complete cranium was found at a lead and zinc mine at Broken Hill (now Kabwe) in Zambia (known before independence as Northern Rhodesia. On 17 June 1921, a Swiss miner named Tom Zwigelaar and an African worker made the discovery. Czech anthropologist Aleš Hrdlička later investigated the site, hoping to learn more about the circumstances of the discovery. He interviewed Zwigelaar, who was still working at the mine and described him as "*a serious middle-aged man, not highly educated but of good common sense*". Zwigelaar and a young African (whom he never named) had been working at 10:00 PM in a "*pocket where there was much lead ore*". Zwigelaar recalled, "*the digging was not hard, not like stone, more loose. After one of the strokes of the pick some of the stuff fell off, and there was the skull looking at me. It was very strange and with some of the matter adhering to it looked so unlike an ordinary human skull that I thought it was a big gorilla*". Zwigelaar showed the cranium to the mine officials, one of whom – a Mr. McCartney – photographed Zwigelaar holding the skull, with the place where it was found in the background. Hrdlička included the photograph in his report[12].

Soon after its discovery, the Kabwe cranium, which lacks its lower jawbone, was donated to the British Museum (Natural History)[32] by the Rhodesia Broken Hill Development Company. British palaeontologist Arthur Smith Woodward described it as *Homo rhodesiensis* ('Rhodesian man') in the 17 November 1921 edition of the journal *Nature*[13], although as with *Homo heidelbergensis*, this name was not widely adopted. In common with *Homo erectus*, the Kabwe cranium is long and low, with massive, continuous browridges[5]. The cranial capacity is around 1,280 cc[14], well within the modern range and far greater than that of *Homo erectus*.

---

[32] Until 1963, the Natural History Museum in Kensington, London was a department of the British Museum. It was officially known as the British Museum (Natural History), commonly abbreviated to BM(NH). It became an independent museum in 1963, but it retained the original name until 1992, by which time it had merged with the neighbouring Geological Museum. The formal name was rarely used outside academia and the museum was generally referred to as the Natural History Museum. Here, I follow common practice in referring to the museum by what was its official name at the time.

The circumstances of its recovery meant that until recently, there were only very rough estimates of its age. However, sediment scraped off the skull has now yielded a combined uranium-series and electron spin resonance age of 299,000 ± 25,000 years old[15].

Zambians have been seeking repatriation of the Kabwe cranium from Britain for decades. It has been claimed that the cranium may have been exported illegally. The Bushman Relics Proclamation was enacted under the Northern Rhodesia Ordinance No. 15 of 1912 and was in force at the time of the discovery nine years later. Under this legislation, an export permit was required for the cranium, and it is alleged that the Rhodesia Broken Hill Development Company failed to obtain such a permit[16]. In recent years, there has been a growing tendency for former colonial powers to return cultural artefacts and human remains to Indigenous peoples. The United Kingdom has been notoriously reluctant to consider returning antiquities acquired during its imperial past, most notably the Elgin Marbles acquired from Greece by the Seventh Earl of Elgin in the early nineteenth century. However, we should bear in mind that it would now be inconceivable for such an important fossil to leave the country of its discovery. For this reason, serious consideration should be given to returning the Kabwe cranium to Zambia.

Muddle in the middle

Following these discoveries, many similar finds were made in Europe and Africa. European finds include Steinheim, Germany (1933), Swanscome, England (1935), Petralona in northern Greece (1960), and Arago in southern France (1964). African examples include Bodo, Ethiopia (1976), which at 600,000 years old, is the oldest larger-brained hominin so far found in Africa[17]. More recently, finds have been made at Narmada, India (1982), and at several sites in China including Dali (1978), Jinniushan (1984), and Xujiayao (1974). These Asian finds are all more recent than the European and African examples, dating from 200,000 to 370,000 years old[18–20].

The cranial capacity of Middle Pleistocene *Homo* was greater than that of *Homo erectus* and only slightly less than that of Neanderthals and *Homo sapiens*, and the dentition was more modern than that of *Homo erectus*. However, the cranium retained the long, low aspect of *Homo erectus* rather than the globular aspect of *Homo sapiens*, and the lower jawbone lacked the well-developed chin of *Homo sapiens*[5]. Middle Pleistocene *Homo* also lacked many of the features associated with Neanderthals. The Neanderthal cranial vault did not resemble the modern globular form, but it also differed from those of Middle Pleistocene *Homo*. It was larger and the cranial vault higher and more rounded, with laterally projecting parietal bones and a rounded and projecting occipital bone, or 'occipital bun'. The browridges, though prominent in both cases, differed in shape. Neanderthals had distinct tori above each orbit rather than a single, shelflike structure, and the orbits themselves were rounder rather than more rhomboidal[21].

Until the middle of the 1990s, Middle Pleistocene *Homo* was typically referred to as 'archaic *Homo sapiens*', reflecting the persistence of archaic features. On this view, modern humans in Africa and Neanderthals in Europe were simply regarded as later subspecies of *Homo sapiens*: *Homo sapiens sapiens* and *Homo sapiens neanderthalensis*, respectively. Subsequently, however, the tendency was to regard Middle Pleistocene *Homo*, Neanderthals, and modern humans as separate species, and revive the name *Homo heidelbergensis* for Middle Pleistocene 'Archaic *Homo sapiens*'. On this scheme, *Homo heidelbergensis* was viewed as the common ancestor of a Eurasian lineage leading to Neanderthals and an African lineage leading to modern humans. This view was little more than a change in the bookkeeping[22] as both schemes proposed that Neanderthals and modern humans evolved from the same earlier group regardless of how the latter was named. The case for adopting the new scheme rested on the assumption that the differences between the three were sufficient to justify classifying all of them as separate species. We have since learned that the Eurasian lineage later underwent at least one further split between Neanderthals and Denisovans[23,24].

The problem with *Homo heidelbergensis* is that as Archaic *Homo sapiens*, it came to be used as a dumping ground for any Middle Pleistocene hominin that could not be classed as *Homo erectus*, a Neanderthal, or modern *Homo sapiens*[21]. Consequently, it tended to be defined in terms of features intermediate between *Homo erectus* and later humans, whereas a species should be defined in terms of unique traits[25]. There was also much debate as to whether *Homo heidelbergensis* is indeed a single species, with some also reviving the name *Homo rhodesiensis* for the African examples. In the late 1990s, anthropologist Phillip Rightmire described this confused situation as the *"muddle in the middle"*[23]. However, at the time Rightmire was writing, important evidence was emerging from two cave sites in the Sierra de Atapuerca, a large limestone hill in northern Spain, near the city of Burgos. The two sites dated to either side of the critical period 600,000 years ago.

The Pit of Bones

The first of these two sites is the human burial pit known in Spanish as Sima de los Huesos, meaning rather appropriately 'the Pit of Bones'. The burial pit is a small muddy chamber with a floor area of just 17 sq. m (185 sq. ft), which lies at the bottom of a 13 m (43 ft) vertical shaft. This in turn is located more than 500 m (⅓ mile) from the entrance to the cave system. Such an inaccessible site would probably have remained undiscovered had the cave system not long been a target for cavers from Burgos. Graffiti found in the pit suggests that explorers reached it as long ago as the late thirteenth century. In the mid-1970s, one such group of cavers told palaeontology student Trinidad Torres that bones of cave bears were so abundant in the pit that it had been named Sima de los Huesos. Subsequently, investigators found a human lower jawbone there, but the site was so challenging that they did not return until 1982. Two human teeth were found, and systematic excavation commenced in 1984. Work has continued ever since[26]. Over 6,500 fragmentary hominin fossils have been recovered from the pit, including seventeen skulls. In total, the remains are thought to represent at least 28 individuals of both sexes[27]. Curiously, though, the only stone artefact to be found is a single hand axe[28].

The circumstance by which the corpses reached the pit remains uncertain. Physically, they could only have done so via the vertical shaft[29], suggesting that the individuals either fell or were dropped into the chamber[30]. Many of the remains are of adolescents and young adults, and it could be that the deaths did not result from everyday events[31]. On the other hand, the pattern of mortality was probably quite normal for the time. Notably, a similar peak in adolescence has been found at the Neanderthal site of Krapina in Croatia. The deaths could simply have been the result of hunting accidents and childbirth complications. The former were probably not uncommon among inexperienced young hunters[32,33].

One individual is known to have met a violent death. Cranium 17 is a largely complete skull recovered in 52 pieces. Although most of the breakages occurred long after death, researchers identified two unhealed depressed fractures consistent with blunt force trauma from the same weapon, resulting in penetration of the bone-brain barrier. Either injury would likely have been fatal, and two suggest deliberate intent. That the injuries were both caused by an impact with the same object rules out the possibility that the damage to the skull was caused by the body landing on a hard object when it was dropped into the pit. Cranium 17 thus represents the earliest reasonably clear-cut case of lethal violence between humans and shows that this rather depressing aspect of human behaviour had a very early origin[30]. Age estimates for the Sima hominins ranged from 350,000[34] years to 600,000 - 530,000 years[35] before being shown to be around 430,000 years[27].

The study of this huge collection of bones is still ongoing and could be for some time yet as the site has continued to yield further fossils. However, it has become clear that the fossils consistently show a mixture of *Homo heidelbergensis* and Neanderthal characteristics. Neanderthal-like features are present in the face and the front of the cranial vault, many of which are related to the jaws and other elements of the masticatory apparatus. This suggests that facial modification was the first step in the evolution of the Neanderthal lineage and indicates a mosaic evolution, with different features evolving at different rates[27]. The question remains as to whether the Sima hominins are 'proto-Neanderthals' or a sister group to the Neanderthals, i.e., part of a European clade[33] that includes Neanderthals but not actually Neanderthals themselves[24]?

The pioneers

Another possible new human species entered the fray in the second half of the 1990s. The Gran Dolina ('Great Depression') is another cave site in the Sierra de Atapuerca. It is one of several that were discovered during the construction of a railway for the transport of minerals at the end of the nineteenth century. The systematic excavation of the site started in 1978, but it was not until 1993 that a survey pit was started, and the layer known as TD6 was reached the following year[36]. In 1994, excavations of Layer TD6 began to reveal hominin remains and stone tools, which palaeomagnetic considerations suggested were more than 780,000 years old[37]. The 1994-95 excavation season yielded around 90 fossil fragments corresponding to a minimum of six individuals[38]. In addition, 268 flaked stone artefacts were reported over the next few years[39]. By 2008, fossils associated with ten individuals had been identified[38]. A date range of 770,000 – 950,000 years ago for the TD6 fossils and stone

---

[33]A clade is any group of living organisms possessing a set of characteristics and sharing a common ancestor that itself possessed these characteristics. The term comes from the Greek *klados*, meaning a branch. Characteristics are described as either primitive or derived. 'Primitive' does not mean backwards or poorly adapted. It simply means that it arose before a clade's common ancestor and thus is not unique to that clade. 'Derived', on the other hand, refers to traits that are unique to a particular clade and arose no earlier than that clade's common ancestor. Most species possess a combination or 'mosaic' of primitive and derived characteristics.

artefacts was obtained by uranium-series and electron spin resonance methods[40,41].

It was suggested that the TD people had a cranial capacity of over 1,000 cc, based on a large cranial fragment, ATD6-15. Notably, this individual is thought to have been around 11 years old at death; the adult cranial capacity would have been still greater. Even 1,000 cc is higher than the typical values for *Homo erectus*[37,42]. ATD6-69 is a juvenile upper jawbone and partial face that might have belonged to the same individual as ATD6-15. It revealed a modern-looking midface, tucked in rather than jutting forward. Other specimens revealed dental traits that differ from African *Homo erectus*. In 1997, the TD6 hominins were described as a species, *Homo antecessor* ('Pioneer Man') and claimed to be a possible common ancestor of Neanderthals and modern humans[42]. This claim was later withdrawn, although it was still maintained that *Homo antecessor* was distinct from *Homo erectus* and closely related to the lineage leading to Neanderthals, *Homo sapiens*, and Denisovans (the latter were not known in 1997)[43]. The distinctive, modern-like facial anatomy of *Homo antecessor* is absent from *Homo erectus* in both Africa and Asia[44].

In 2007, a fragment of a lower jawbone and an isolated tooth from the same individual were recovered from layer TE9 of the nearby Sima del Elefante ('Pit of the Elephant') site. These remains were dated using palaeomagnetic and cosmogenic radionuclide techniques and are approximately 1.22 million years old[45]. They were provisionally assigned to *Homo antecessor*, but it was later decided not to include them in any named species and identify them only as *Homo* with species indeterminate[46]. It is now thought that there was no lineal relationship between the TE9 individual and *Homo antecessor*[47].

Although no *Homo antecessor* remains have been found elsewhere, it was possibly widespread in Europe. In May 2013, human footprints were discovered on the beach at the coastal village of Happisburgh, Norfolk (pronounced 'Hazebrough'). The footprints briefly emerged at low tide, having been exposed by rough seas. Within a few days, they had vanished again, but not before a team from the British Museum had obtained plaster casts and 3d images. A total of 152 footprints were recorded, of which twelve were complete enough for analysis. It is thought that they represented five individuals ranging in height from 0.93 to 1.73 m (3 ft. 0 in. to 5 ft. 8 in.), suggesting the presence of both adults and children. The estimated foot size, foot area, and stature of the Happisburgh people were consistent with estimates for *Homo antecessor*[48].

The footprints are thought to be the same age as a group of flint artefacts found at Happisburgh three years earlier, estimated to be at least 780,000 years old and possibly as much as one million years old[49]. This makes the Happisburgh footprints the earliest known direct evidence for a human presence in northern Europe. The Happisburgh people lived on the edges of a conifer forest close to where the Thames flowed into the North Sea, about 150 km (95 miles) north of the present estuary. Animal remains from stone tool findspot suggest that they lived towards the end of an interglacial period, although which is uncertain. There were warm periods between 866,000 and 814,000 years ago, and between 970,000 and 936,000 years ago[49], although either would be broadly consistent with the age of the TD6 remains.

But what of the TD6 people? It has been suggested that Early Pleistocene hominins outside of Africa were constrained by latitude, with any occupation of regions north of the 40th Parallel (the latitude of Valencia, Sardinia, and Ankara) occurring only during warm interglacial periods[50]. In the case of the TD6 people themselves, they appear to have suffered a grim fate. Around 25 per cent of the bones found at Gran Dolina show signs of damage including chop marks and cut marks, peeling where bones have been broken and bent, and marks where bones have been splintered for marrow extraction. This all adds up to a compelling case for cannibalism. The extent and pattern of the damage marks suggest butchery for food purposes rather than ritual cannibalism[51]. Did conditions become so harsh for the TD6 people that they ended up eating each other?

Four scenarios

Four scenarios have been proposed to resolve the muddle in the middle[52,53]. The first is the 'mid-Middle Pleistocene' model, which views *Homo heidelbergensis* as a single species that evolved from *Homo erectus* and spread widely across Africa and into western Eurasia at the beginning of the Middle Pleistocene. Subsequently, around 300,000 years ago, *Homo heidelbergensis* differentiated into Neanderthals (and Denisovans) in Eurasia and modern humans in Africa. This is the straightforward change in bookkeeping from 'Archaic *Homo sapiens*' as noted above. One possible version of this scenario is that *Homo heidelbergensis* spread from Africa or Southwest Asia during a warm interglacial when populations were increasing. When glacial conditions returned, some of the Eurasian populations were able to survive in refugia where conditions were less harsh. Thus isolated, they began to diverge from the African populations[54].

The second scenario is the 'early Middle Pleistocene' model, which proposes that *Homo rhodesiensis* evolved from *Homo erectus* in Africa. A single population of *Homo rhodesiensis* then migrated to Europe, diverged from the African populations, and subsequently became *Homo heidelbergensis*. As with the second scenario, *Homo heidelbergensis* was the ancestor of Neanderthals, and *Homo rhodesiensis* was the ancestor of *Homo sapiens*. Alternatively, *Homo heidelbergensis* can be simply viewed as an early form of Neanderthal and the stay-at-home African *Homo rhodesiensis* as very early *Homo sapiens*.

The third scenario is the 'late Early Pleistocene' model, which proposes that *Homo antecessor* was the common ancestor of *Homo heidelbergensis* and *Homo rhodesiensis*. These two species appeared around 600,000 years ago in Eurasia and Africa, respectively. Subsequently, *Homo heidelbergensis* was ancestral to Neanderthals, and *Homo rhodesiensis* was ancestral to *Homo sapiens*. Rightmire[52] considered this scenario to be problematic because *Homo antecessor* has not been found in Africa. There was also a view that *Homo antecessor* was no more than an offshoot of African *Homo erectus* that died out after a failed migration to southern Europe[26].

The fourth scenario is the 'late Middle Pleistocene' model, proposed by paleoanthropologists Marta Mirazón Lahr and Robert Foley[55]. The model envisaged a much later divergence between Neanderthals and *Homo sapiens* around 250,000 years ago. They linked this development to the emergence of prepared-core (Mode 3) stone tool technologies, which eventually replaced Acheulean hand axes. This in turn they related in turn to an African species they termed *Homo helmei* ('Helme's man'). This name was originally assigned to a 260,000-year-old partial skull found at Florisbad, Bloemfontein, South Africa, in the 1930s, and named for expedition sponsor Robert E. Helme. Lahr and Foley suggested that *Homo helmei* dispersed to Europe and gave rise to Neanderthals; those remaining in Africa gave rise to *Homo sapiens*.

The evidence from Sima de los Huesos disposes of the Lahr and Foley model. The Sima hominins were already displaying incipient Neanderthal characteristics 430,000 years ago, well before the hypothetical dispersal of *Homo helmei*. Other Middle Pleistocene hominins, such as the Swanscombe cranium, also show emerging Neanderthal characteristics[56]. However, the limited amount of fossil material available made it very difficult to obtain a definitive answer as to which, if any, of the other scenarios is correct. Matters were further complicated by the need to consider the Denisovans, confirmed fossil evidence for which is limited to a lower jawbone and a few teeth.

It has been suggested that as *Homo heidelbergensis* is so poorly defined and problematic, the species classification should be retired. European fossils defined by the Mauer mandible should be reclassified as early Neanderthals. The authors of this proposal suggested that *Homo rhodesiensis* should also be retired, as the classification has never been widely used as an alternative to African *Homo heidelbergensis*. Like *Homo heidelbergensis*, *Homo rhodesiensis* is poorly defined, and some also feel uncomfortable about the connection of the specific name with the controversial figure Cecil Rhodes. Accordingly, it was proposed that a new species defined by the Bodo skull, *Homo bodoensis*, should replace *Homo rhodesiensis*[57].

British palaeoanthropologist Chris Stringer has criticised the suggestion of using the name *Homo bodoensis*. He notes that under the rules set out by the International Commission on Zoological Nomenclature, established names take priority over new ones. Hence, because *Homo rhodesiensis* has already been formally described, it must be used unless the original description was incorrect. He points out that the name was derived from Northern Rhodesia, not Cecil Rhodes himself. Even if an exception was to be made for *Homo rhodesiensis*, other established names have precedence. Stringer notes that the Saldanha skull, found at Saldanha Bay Local Municipality, South Africa, in the 1950s, was one of the fossils included in *Homo bodoensis*. At the time of its discovery, the skull was described as *Homo saldanensis*, but it is now widely accepted as belonging to the same species as the Kabwe skull. Regardless of whether the Kabwe skull is classed as *Homo heidelbergensis* or *Homo rhodesiensis*, these names have priority and *Homo saldanensis* is generally regarded as a 'junior homonym'. But were they to be retired, *Homo saldanensis* and not *Homo bodoensis* would be the correct name for the Bodo skull[58].

With these difficulties in mind, the situation has become a little clearer with the recovery of ancient DNA from Neanderthal and Denisovan remains. Analysis of the genetic data suggests that the ancestors of *Homo sapiens* diverged from the common ancestor of Neanderthals and Denisovans (informally dubbed 'Neandersovans') 765,000 years ago[59] and Neanderthals and Denisovans diverged from one another 737,000 years ago[60,61]. An earlier date of 800,000 years ago, based on dental characteristics, has been proposed for the split between Neanderthals and *Homo sapiens*[62].

These dates are too early for either the single-species *Homo heidelbergensis* ('mid Middle Pleistocene') model or the *Homo rhodesiensis* migration to Europe ('early Middle Pleistocene') model. The divergence of *Homo sapiens* from the Neanderthal/Denisovan common ancestor and the subsequent divergence of Neanderthals from Denisovans from one another predates the earliest fossil evidence we currently have for either *Homo rhodesiensis* or *Homo heidelbergensis* by over 100,000 years. Earlier fossil evidence could be found, of course, but for now, we are left with Rightmire's 'problematic' 'late Early Pleistocene' model and *Homo antecessor*.

Despite the fossil evidence being restricted to the one site in northern Spain, there is genetic evidence to support a close relationship between it and 'Ancestor X', the common ancestor of 'Neandersovans' and *Homo sapiens* presumed to have lived in Africa 800,000 - 750,000 years ago. No DNA has been recovered from any of the TD6 hominins, but researchers were able to obtain the dental enamel proteome (i.e., the proteins expressed during tooth formation) by recovery of specific peptide sequences from a *Homo antecessor* molar tooth (ATD6-92). The results suggest that *Homo antecessor* is a close sister lineage to later Middle and Late Pleistocene hominins rather than ancestral to them as first claimed, but this is consistent with it being closely related to Ancestor X[63].

To make the 'late Early Pleistocene' model work requires Ancestor X to have been broadly contemporary with *Homo antecessor* at Gran Dolina and the Happisburgh footprints. On this model, a population of Ancestor X migrated to Europe around 800,000 – 750,000 years ago, and Neandersovans are descended from it. However, *Homo heidelbergensis* (*sensu stricto*) is defined by the Mauer mandible, which postdates the Neanderthal/Denisovan split. Therefore, it cannot have been a 'Neandersovan'. Also, given that the African and Eurasian lineages must have been separate no later than 750,000 years ago, hominins such as those represented by the Kabwe and Bodo skulls cannot have been *Homo heidelbergensis*. *Homo rhodesiensis* must have been a separate species, descended from a stay-at-home population of Ancestor X. But what was Ancestor X?

If *Homo antecessor* was indeed a European sister species to African Ancestor X, it could have shared the same distinctive facial anatomy. Stringer suggests that it might not have been entirely lacking in derived traits that supposedly first appeared in the later lineages and could have been a mosaic of primitive and derived traits. Some of the latter might have entered the Neandersovan lineage and others the *Homo sapiens* lineage. Thus, the face could have *antecessor*-like features and be retained in the *sapiens* lineage in Africa, while the teeth were Neanderthal-like and became increasingly *sapiens*-like over time. Meanwhile, in Europe, the face became increasingly Neanderthal-like over time[64].

However, there is also the issue that the massive facial morphology of the Kabwe and Bodo skulls is very different to that of both *Homo antecessor* and *Homo sapiens*, and it has been suggested that this excludes them as possible ancestors of the latter. Yet other Middle Pleistocene hominin fossils conventionally lumped into *Homo heidelbergensis* and *Homo antecessor* have a more *sapiens*-like midface. These include the partial crania from Thomas Quarry (Morocco) and Ndutu (Tanzania) and Chinese examples including Dali and Jinniushan. Regardless of what species the Kabwe and Bodo crania might have belonged to, they might well not be ancestral to *Homo sapiens*. Instead, our species might descend from something more closely resembling *Homo antecessor*[65].

This complex situation, where there is no clear-cut geographic relationship between hominins possessing and those lacking *sapiens*-like facial morphology, might be resolved with a paradigm shift. Instead of successive human species dispersing from Africa and then evolving, a 'shuttle dispersal' model has been proposed, where there are bidirectional exchanges between Africa, Asia, and Europe. A study claimed that Africa has been the biggest net donor of human populations, with 40 per cent of total dispersal events starting from there. Africa received 24 per cent of total dispersal events. Asia was the biggest net recipient, receiving 42 per cent of total dispersal events. Only 24 per cent of dispersal events to other continents started from Asia. This model could explain the seemingly complex phylogenetic connections among African and Eurasian *Homo* species and populations[66].

Sources and sinks in Europe

In Europe, the Sima de los Huesos possessed a mixture of *Homo heidelbergensis* and Neanderthal characteristics, but 'classic' Neanderthals or those possessing the full suite of Neanderthal characteristics do not appear in the fossil record until 130,000 years ago. It has been suggested that these characteristics appeared gradually over time, in a piecemeal fashion[67,68], resulting in a gradual transition by accretion from European *Homo heidelbergensis* to Neanderthal. This model explains the 'proto-Neanderthal' features of the Sima people and other fossils from the period prior to the appearance of the 'classic' Neanderthals. These include a 400,000-year-old fragmentary skull from Swanscombe in England, the 225,000-year-old Steinheim skull from Stuttgart, Germany, the 400,000-year-old Aroeira 3 skull from Gruta da Aroeira, Portugal[69], and the six hominin remains from the Aniene Valley near Rome, which are 295,000 to 220,000 years old[70].

Some of the distinctive Neanderthal features might have resulted from the effects of genetic drift on small, isolated populations[71]. Genetic drift refers to random inter-generational changes in the frequency with which characteristics (hair colour, blood group, etc.) occur in a population. Even if none confer any particular advantage, the changes will occur because some individuals will have more children than others. In a small population, this can result in some characteristics becoming very common, and others disappearing completely.

However, matters may be more complex than implied by the accretion theory. If no other factors were operating, later fossils would always be more derived in the Neanderthal direction than earlier ones. But this is not always the case. Overall, European *Homo heidelbergensis* is highly variable in terms of its skull, lower jawbone, dentition, and postcranial[34] anatomy. Fossils exhibit a mosaic of primitive and derived characteristics that cannot be consistently organised along a chronological scale of 'increasingly Neanderthal'[72]. One possibility is that the Neanderthals were just one of several human species living in Europe during the Middle Pleistocene, only gaining sole possession of the continent 200,000 years ago[73]. On this view, the Sima people, while closely related to Neanderthals, were not 'proto-Neanderthals'. There are also fossils that are intermediate between *Homo erectus* and *Homo heidelbergensis*. These include the human skullcap found near the Italian town of Ceprano, which exhibits a combination of primitive *erectus*-like and derived *heidelbergensis*-like traits[74], and is thought to be 385,000 – 450,000 years old[75,76]. A partial lower jawbone from Mala Balanica, Serbia, exhibits a similar combination of primitive and derived traits[57]. It is about the same age as the Ceprano skullcap at 397,000 - 525,000 years old[77].

The solution to these issues might be the 'sources and sinks' model, which proposes that Europe was a population 'sink' that became largely depopulated during adverse climatic episodes. Each time the climate improved, the continent was repopulated from 'sources', or refugia that had remained habitable. The refugia were only capable of supporting their existing populations: they could not serve as 'arks' where other populations could seek refuge, with the consequence that these died out. During glacial periods, distinct demes[35] emerged within the isolated populations. In addition to the effects of natural selection, these

---

[34] Postcranial remains are any remains from below the skull and lower jawbone.

[35] A regional population of a species exhibiting morphological differences from other, similar populations of the same species.

populations would have experienced genetic drift. During warmer spells, populations expanded and came into contact with one another to produce a 'mix and match' of morphological characteristics. The sources and sinks model would allow multiple species including some more archaic than others (or simply populations with different anatomical characteristics) to come into contact and interbreed. Over time, more and more of the characteristics associated with 'classic' Neanderthals would have accreted in the population at large, until the full suite of Neanderthal characteristics was acquired[72].

Meanwhile, in Africa

In Africa, the date of the earliest fossil *Homo sapiens* has been gradually pushed back over the years. Jebel Irhoud is a cave site in Morocco located about 100 km (60 miles) west of Marrakech. During mining operations in the area in 1961, an almost complete adult cranium (Irhoud 1) was found. This prompted excavations between 1967 and 1969 that recovered an adult braincase (Irhoud 2), a juvenile lower jawbone (Irhoud 3), a juvenile upper arm bone (Irhoud 4), a juvenile hipbone (Irhoud 5), and a fragment of a lower jawbone (Irhoud 6). Unfortunately, only the precise location of the upper arm bone was accurately recorded, which made dating the remains problematic.

The more intact of the two adult skulls, Irhoud 1, has primitive features including moderately developed browridges and a long, low cranial vault. However, the forehead is within the modern range, and the estimated cranial capacity of 1,300 to 1,480 cc also falls within the modern range. The Irhoud 2 braincase, though less complete, is broadly similar to that of Irhoud 1. The facial morphology of both skulls is almost modern, as is that of the jawbone. The cranial vault morphology, though outside the modern range, is closer to it than *Homo erectus*, *Homo heidelbergensis*, or Neanderthals. Irhoud 3, the juvenile lower jawbone, is more robust than that of present-day people, but it has a distinct, modern-like chin. It lies within the range of early modern humans, but outside the area where this overlaps with recent modern humans[21,78–80].

Interpreting the Jebel Irhoud fossils has long been complicated by the persistent uncertainty over their age. They were originally thought to be no older than 40,000 years and possibly an African offshoot of Neanderthals. Such affinities were challenged in the 1980s and faunal evidence suggested that the site dated to the Middle Pleistocene. In 2007, they were estimated to be around 160,000 years old[81], but this date was problematic because the Jebel Irhoud fossils are more primitive than supposedly older remains from two sites in East Africa: Herto and Omo[80].

The Herto remains were discovered in 1997, and at the time were thought to be the earliest fossil remains of *Homo sapiens*. They were discovered in the Upper Herto Member, a geological stratum in the Bouri Formation at Middle Awash, Ethiopia, and comprised three well-preserved skulls plus fragmentary remains[82]. These were found to be around 154,000 – 160,000 years old[83]. All three of the skulls show cutmarks indicative of some form of mortuary ritual: the earliest example of such practice documented for modern humans.

Two of the skulls belonged to adult males, and the third to a six-year-old child. The cranial capacity of the better-preserved adult skull is 1,450 cc, which lies at the upper end of the modern human range. Although close enough to present-day humans to be classed as *Homo sapiens*, they still possess some primitive features including more robust facial features and a longer braincase. Accordingly, they were classed as a new subspecies, *Homo sapiens idaltu*. The word *idaltu* means *elder* or *first-born* in the Afar language. It was claimed that *Homo sapiens idaltu* had evolved from *Homo rhodesiensis* and was the ancestor of fully modern *Homo sapiens*[82].

Omo 1 and Omo 2 are a pair of crania that were discovered in 1967 at two sites on opposite sides of the Omo River in southwestern Ethiopia, albeit both are believed to be part of the same geological stratum[84]. Both crania are modern in appearance. The fragmentary Omo 1 cranium has a globular braincase and a steep forehead. It has a prominent chin, small browridges, a rounded occipital region at the back of the skull, and the teeth are modern in shape and size. Although it is still more robust than many modern skulls, it is unmistakably *Homo sapiens*. The cranial capacity of the more intact Omo 2 is 1435 cc, larger than the present-day average. The braincase is long but domed, and the browridges are small. However, Omo 2 retains some primitive features, notably a more receding forehead, a more angular occipital region, a prominent occipital bun, and a slight ridge along the midline of the braincase known as sagittal keeling[85].

The pair were originally believed to be around 130,000 years old, but in 2005, they were found to be far older. It turned out that the geological stratum in which the fossils were found was sandwiched between two layers of volcanic tuffs (ash) from nearby eruptions, and both fossils had lain just above the lower layer of tuff. Volcanic ash can be readily dated by the argon-argon method, and the lower ash layer, the Nakaa'kire Tuff in Member I, was found to be 196,000 years old. As the Omo crania could only be slightly more recent, they had to be far older than the Herto remains[84].

The two Omo individuals were probably not exact contemporaries and could have lived centuries apart. This would still not be long enough for significant evolutionary change to have occurred, but Omo 1 and Omo 2 could have belonged to two different populations, each of which lived in the region at a different time. Omo 1 represents the modern or near-modern condition, but Omo 2 probably represents a more archaic lineage[86]. The redated Omo skulls were now the earliest-known examples of *Homo sapiens*.

However, there was some doubt as to the stratigraphic relationship between the Nakaa'kire Tuff and the hominin remains. Accordingly, the focus shifted to the KHS Tuff, another widespread deposit of fine ash fallout, more than 2m (6 ft 6 in) thick, lying at the base of Member II. As this tuff overlies Member I, it is clearly younger than the Omo skulls, and obtaining a date for it would provide a minimum age for the Omo skulls. Unfortunately, the fine grain size of this tuff means that it could not be directly dated by the argon-argon method. In 2021, researchers obtained a date for the KHS Tuff by comparing its chemical signature with those of ignimbrites from the caldera-forming eruptions of the Shala and Corbetti volcanoes. These are the only Main Ethiopian Rift volcanos known to have produced major eruptions between 170,000 and 250,000 years ago. A match was found with material from the Qi2 eruption of Shala, and argon-argon dating yielded a date for the eruption and, hence, the KHS tuff of 233,000 years old, meaning that the Omo skulls are at least this old and almost twice as old as originally believed[87]. By this time, though, the origins of *Homo sapiens* were known to be even earlier.

Between 2004 and 2011, new excavations were carried out at Jebel Irhoud, and a further sixteen human fossils were discovered, along with a large number of associated stone artefacts. The finds allowed secure dates of 315,000 ± 34,000 years old to be obtained, and the age of the Irhoud 3 lower jawbone to be re-estimated at 286,000 ± 32,000 years old[88]. The revised date not only pushed back the earliest examples of *Homo sapiens* by at least 90,000 years, but it also explained why the Jebel Irhoud remains were more primitive than Omo 1 and the Herto remains. It suggested that as with the Neanderthals, facial modification had been the first step in the evolution of the *Homo sapiens* clade. The transition from the long, low to globular braincase was a later development.

The earlier dates for the Jebel Irhoud fossils put the spotlight on other African human fossils from the period 250,000 – 300,000 years ago. These include a partial skull found in the hot spring at Florisbad, some 50 km (30 miles) from Bloemfontein, South Africa. The town takes its name from Floris Venter, a local entrepreneur who, in 1912, enlarged the pools at the spring for use as a spa. Later that year, an earthquake caused a new spring eye to open up, revealing stone tools and fossils[89,90], which were later described in a paper by Raymond Dart's future ally, Robert Broom[91].

In 1932, zoologist Thomas F. Dreyer and his assistant Alice Lyle carried out new excavations in the vicinity of the spring. The work was funded by Cambridge-educated Robert Edgerton Helme, who served with the Royal Field Artillery during World War I and attained the rank of Captain. In the early 1920s, he moved to South Africa because the British climate disagreed with his asthma[92]. According to one account, Venter feared a loss of revenue if his baths were temporarily drained, meaning that Dreyer and Lyle had to wade around in the waters and grope for bones. On one such occasion, Dreyer plunged his hand into the spring deposits underwater and found a partial human skull, with his fingers stuck between its eyes.

The skull comprises the right side of the face, most of the forehead, portions of the roof and sidewalls, and a single upper right third molar[5]. A date of 259,000 years old was obtained for the skull in 1996[93]. In 1935, Dreyer described the find as *Homo helmei* ('Helme's Man'), to mark its distinctiveness from other fossil *Homo sapiens* then known and to acknowledge Helme's sponsorship[94]. *Homo helmei* was never widely accepted as a species, and the Florisbad skull is typically referred to as *Homo heidelbergensis*. However, it differs in many aspects. In comparison to the skull of a present-day human, it is thick-walled, the face is broad and massive, and the braincase is long and low. However, the browridges are less prominent than those of *Homo heidelbergensis*, the forehead is relatively steep rather than low and flattened, and the face is flat and tucked in beneath the front part of the cranial vault[5,86,95].

Although the Florisbad skull is too incomplete to be certain, it seems likely that it is also a part of the early *Homo sapiens* clade[56]. Similarly, a case could also be made for KNM-ER 3884, a 270,000 – 300,000-year-old partial skull found in 1971 in the Guomde Formation of East Turkana, Kenya[96], and also ES-11693, a skull found in 1986 at Eliye Springs, West Turkana, Kenya. The ES-11693 skull was described as 'archaic *Homo sapiens*' and grouped with Omo 2, although no direct date is available[97].

This fossil evidence, from North Africa, East Africa, and South Africa, suggests that the characteristics associated with present-day humans emerged only gradually in Africa after splitting from the archaic Eurasian populations, and was a pan-African accretional process. However, variation across the African later Middle Pleistocene/early Late Pleistocene fossils shows that there was not a simple linear progression towards later *Homo sapiens* morphology, and there was chronological overlap between different 'archaic' and 'modern' forms[64]. Overall, there appears to be much in common with Neanderthal evolution in Europe.

Modern facial and near-modern jawbone characteristics emerged around 300,000 years ago, but the modern globular cranial vault does not appear until 233,000 years ago (Omo 1). At this stage (assuming it is the same age), the Omo 2 cranium suggests that populations with the archaic cranial vault form still existed then. At this stage, populations represented by the fossil remains were still more robust than any living population, and it is not until 35,000 years ago that people with the more gracile, fully modern skeletal form make their appearance[80,86,98]. Even the Omo 1 cranium was outside the present-day range of variation, which was not reached until between 100,000 and 35,000 years ago[99].

The question, perhaps, is at what point could humans first be described as 'modern'? Is it with the Jebel Irhoud and Florisbad hominins, or is it not until later? Although the Jebel Irhoud remains are quite distinct from *Homo heidelbergensis* or *Homo rhodesiensis*, the cranial vaults of Irhoud 1 and Irhoud 2 lie outside the present-day *Homo sapiens*. There is a case for classifying the Irhoud remains as a separate species, possibly *Homo helmei*. However, Chris Stringer has argued that such splitting would be unhelpful, as there are already difficulties in differentiating *Homo heidelbergensis* and *Homo rhodesiensis* from the earlier stages of evolution towards Neanderthals and modern humans. Accordingly, Stringer suggested reviving the term archaic *Homo sapiens* for early members of the modern human lineage[64]. This recognises that the Jebel Irhoud and Florisbad hominins are part of the *Homo sapiens* clade, even though there are significant differences between them and later *Homo sapiens*. It would also imply that 'modern human' and *Homo sapiens* are not necessarily synonymous[100].

Denisovans

While Neanderthals have been known since the nineteenth century, the existence of Denisovans was entirely unsuspected until March 2010. The discovery came two years after a distal phalanx (fingertip) bone from a hominin little finger was recovered from Denisova Cave in the Russian federal subject of Altai Krai. The cave is named for a hermit called Dionisij (Denis), who is supposed to have lived there in the eighteenth century, but if this is true, then he was only the latest in a long line of inhabitants.

The small finger bone is around 30,000 – 48,000 years old. It was at first thought to have belonged to a child aged from five to seven years old, but this was later revised to an adolescent aged 13.5 years. Due to the cold, dry climate, the bone was sufficiently well preserved to extract DNA from it, isolate mitochondrial DNA fragments, and sequence the entire mitochondrial genome. It was assumed that the bone had belonged to either a Neanderthal or a modern human, but neither turned out to be the case. Instead, the sequencing revealed that it had belonged to a hitherto-unknown species of human that had last shared a common ancestor with Neanderthals and modern humans about a million years ago[101].

The next step was to obtain a nuclear genome sequence, which was completed in December 2010. This showed that the previously-unknown hominins, now dubbed 'Denisovans', had diverged from Neanderthals 640,000 years ago, and from present-day Africans 804,000 years ago. The two Eurasian species (Denisovans and Neanderthals) were thus more closely related to each other than they were to modern humans (an African species), as might be expected[60]. The date of the Denisovan-Neanderthal split was later revised upwards to 737,000 years ago[61].

The unexpected development was the finding that 4.8 per cent of the nuclear genome of present-day Papuans derives from Denisovans, greater than the Neanderthal contribution of 2.5 per cent[60]. The finding came just months after the headline-making discovery that our ancestors had interbred with Neanderthals. It implied that the Denisovan range had once extended from the deciduous forests of Siberia to the tropics, which is wider than the range of any hominin species apart from our own. Denisovan-derived genes were later identified in present-day populations of the Wallacea archipelago lying to the east of Borneo, the Philippines, Fiji, Polynesia, and in Aboriginal Australians[102]. Denisovan ancestry has since been found in populations from central and East Asia, the Himalayan region, and southern and central India, though in far lower percentages than has been found in the Pacific and Australian populations[103,104]. Denisovans also interbred with Neanderthals: a bone fragment has been found at Denisova Cave that belonged to a thirteen-year-old girl with a Neanderthal mother and a Denisovan father[105]. That the small number of individuals identified at Denisova Cave should include a first-generation hybrid implies that such interbreeding was very common.

The Denisovans themselves have still not been formally named or described as a species. Physical remains that have been definitely identified as Denisovan are limited to the bone fragments and teeth from Denisova Cave and a 160,000-year-old partial lower jawbone from Xiahe on the Tibetan Plateau. Denisovan molar teeth are very large, above the typical size range for those of Neanderthals or Homo sapiens and share no recent features with them. There is apparently no connection with the teeth of the very few Middle Pleistocene hominin fossils known from Southeast or East Asia[60,106]. Conversely, the small Denisovan finger bone whose DNA identified the species is indistinguishable from that of a modern human. Neanderthal-specific characters of the phalanx must have evolved after Neanderthals diverged from Denisovans, and the *Homo sapiens* form represents the original primitive condition[107].

The jawbone was found in 1980 at the Baishiya Karst Cave, Xiahe (3,280 m (10,760 ft) altitude) and uranium-series dating suggests that it is at least 160,000 years old. No DNA has been obtained from it, but proteins recovered from dentine were found to match those of Denisovan teeth. The teeth themselves, like those from Denisova Cave, are extremely large[108].

There have been suggestions that the late archaic fossil hominins from Narmada in India and from Jinniushan and Xujiayao in China could be Denisovans. They are far more recent than western *Homo heidelbergensis*, but as no genetic material has been recovered from them, there is no proven connection[24,109]. Two hominin crania from Lingjing, in Xuchang County (Henan Province), could also be Denisovan. The crania have archaic long, low cranial vaults but also have more modern reduced browridges. Again, no genetic material has been obtained[110].

Dragon Man

The debate over the place of these late archaic Asian fossils in the human story took a new twist in 2021 when the pre-World War II discovery of an exceptionally well-preserved archaic human cranium was reported in the city of Harbin, in the province of Heilongjiang, northeast China. The cranium was found by Chinese labourers in 1933, during the Japanese occupation of Manchuria. The labourers were building a bridge over the Songhua River in Harbin. One of the labourers concealed the cranium in an abandoned well to keep it from the Japanese. It was then safeguarded by three generations of the man's family until 2018, when they donated it to the Hebei GEO University Museum, Shijiazhuang.

The cranium was studied by an international team led by Qiang Ji, Professor of Palaeontology at the Hebei GEO University. Chris Stringer, who was involved with the study, claimed that the Harbin skull was the most important fossil he had seen in 50 years. The cranium is thought to have belonged to a male aged about fifty. It is massive in size, larger than those of all other known archaic humans. The braincase is relatively long and low, the browridges are massive, and the one remaining tooth – a left molar – is massive. However, the face, wide, flat, and tucked in below the browridges, is modern in appearance, as are the flat, low cheekbones. The cranial capacity of 1,420 cc is comparable to that of *Homo sapiens* or a Neanderthal. With its mosaic of primitive and derived characteristics, the Harbin cranium is distinct from *Homo sapiens*, Neanderthals, *Homo heidelbergensis*, or *Homo rhodesiensis*, and it was described as a new human species, *Homo longi*. The specific name is derived from Long Jiang, which is a common name for the Heilongjiang Province and means 'Dragon River'[111]. The cranium soon gained the nickname 'Dragon Man'.

The circumstances of the excavation make dating the skull problematic, as there is no clear archaeological context. However, the Hebei GEO team managed to constrain the age of the skull by optically stimulated luminescence to 138,0000 – 309,000 years old, and uranium-series dating gives a minimum age of 146,000 years. Accordingly, the skull could be anything from 146,000 to 309,000 years old, a date range that lies within the Middle Pleistocene[112]. The cold climate of northeastern China means that there is a good chance that DNA has been preserved in good condition and could possibly be recovered from the skull, although this has not yet been attempted.

The Hebei GEO team conducted a cladistic analysis to establish relationships between the Harbin cranium and 95 cranial, mandibular, or dental fossils of archaic and early modern humans[66]. The closest related fossil to the Harbin skull was found to be the Xiahe partial jawbone, which has been genetically identified as Denisovan. The large molars of the Harbin skull are consistent with it being Denisovan, though confirmation must await the recovery of DNA from the skull. While we cannot assume that the Harbin skull necessarily represents a Denisovan, it does seem to be the most likely possibility.

However, the team also made the controversial suggestion that *Homo longi* is a sister group to *Homo sapiens* and is more closely related to modern humans than are Neanderthals. Their results showed that *Homo sapiens* diverged from *Homo longi* 948,000 years ago and from Neanderthals 1,007,000 years ago. The proposed date of the Neanderthal-*sapiens* split is more than 200,000 years earlier than those obtained from genetics. Another early date was 770,000 years for the divergence of the Jebel Irhoud people, considered to be basal *Homo sapiens*, from other *Homo sapiens* fossils. This would suggest that the *Homo sapiens* clade is much older than previously believed[66].

There is no particular reason to favour results obtained from DNA over those obtained from fossils where the two differ, but sometimes the implications of the differing conclusions make one seem more probable than the other field[113]. In this case, it seems less likely that

Homo longi (a Eurasian species which may or may not be Denisovan) would be a sister species to *Homo sapiens* (an African species) than it would be for it to be a sister species to Neanderthals (another Eurasian species). It should also be borne in mind that several genetic studies have reached the same conclusion. For this reason, it is as well to be sceptical as to whether this cladistic study challenges the prevailing view that Denisovans are more closely related to Neanderthals than to modern humans.

One question is, should the Harbin cranium eventually prove to be Denisovan, what would happen to the name 'Denisovan'? The short answer is that the correct name for the species would be *Homo longi*, a name which, unlike *Homo neanderthalensis*, bears no resemblance to the informal name. The problem is that 'Denisovan' has been in both scientific and lay use for over a decade, and it is certainly easier on the tongue than what would be the scientific name. It is difficult to see it ever disappearing from use.

Hobbits

The human family that emerged from the 'muddle in the middle' was not just made up of Neanderthals, Denisovans, and *Homo sapiens*. In addition to the possible late-surviving *Homo erectus* in East Asia, three further human species are known to have existed since the time of the earliest recognised representatives of *Homo sapiens*, the Jebel Irhoud people.

The Indonesian island of Flores is part of the Lesser Sunda, an archipelago stretching from Bali to Timor. The name comes from the Portuguese word 'flowers' and is a legacy of Portugal's colonial influence in the region between the sixteenth and mid-nineteenth centuries. The first modern human settlers of Australia are believed to have 'island hopped' through the Indonesian archipelago. In 2003, a joint Australian and Indonesian team of anthropologists was investigating Liang Bua, a limestone cave in the western part of the island. Instead of evidence for this migration, they discovered a largely complete skeleton now known formally as LB1, but almost immediately nicknamed Flo. The skeleton was accompanied by a complete lower jawbone (LB2). Remarkably, the 30-year-old female had stood no more than 1.06 m (3 ft 6 in) tall. Her weight was estimated to lie between 36 and 16 kg (79 and 35 lb). She had a cranial capacity of just 380 cc, no greater than that of an australopithecine. Yet she was fully human: she lacked the large back teeth of an australopithecine, her facial proportions were human, and she appeared to be a fully committed biped. Accordingly, her discoverers classed her as belonging to a new human species, *Homo floresiensis*. Small though her brain was, relative to her size, it was comparable to that of *Homo habilis* and *Homo erectus*[114]. Later work revised Flo's cranial capacity upwards to 426 cc[115]. Further remains, representing at least nine individuals, were recovered in 2004[116,117]. LB1 and the other *Homo floresiensis* remains, initially thought to be as recent as 18,000 years ago, are now thought to range from 60,000 to 100,000 years old[118].

The small size of *Homo floresiensis* is thought to be a result of a phenomenon known as insular dwarfism. If animals live on an island where there are few predators but food is also scarce, they will 'downsize' over many generations. Natural selection favoured the smaller animals in each generation because they require less food, and in the absence of predators, there is no advantage to being any larger. On Flores, there is relatively little animal life, and the only predator is the Komodo dragon.

The only other large animal species on Flores was an elephant known as *Stegodon sondaari*, which underwent insular dwarfism before becoming extinct (these animals were still quite large, comparable in size to a water buffalo). If hominins such as *Homo erectus* had reached Flores, then possibly the same could have happened to them, eventually leading to *Homo floresiensis*. Simulations suggested that dwarfing could have occurred in as little as 360 generations[119].

The announcement of the discovery attracted considerable publicity, and *Homo floresiensis* was immediately nicknamed the Flores Hobbit. However, some were sceptical as to whether it was genuinely a new human species. Teuku Jacob claimed that Flo was a modern human suffering from microcephaly, echoing Richard Lydekker's rejection of *Pithecanthropus* a century earlier[120]. Jacob's theory received only limited support[121], although it was later revived in a modified form. A few years after his death in 2007, Jacob's former co-workers claimed that Flo had suffered from Down syndrome[122,123].

Despite this, most accepted *Homo floresiensis* as a new human species[124–127]. Studies mainly considered the metrics of Flo in comparison to microcephalic humans, pygmies, early human species, and australopithecines. The general conclusion was that *Homo floresiensis* showed a better fit with the various extinct hominins than it did with the microcephalic or normal modern humans: for example, Flo's long, low braincase is not a feature shared with modern humans, microcephalic or not[128], and her wrist was more primitive that of a modern human[129]. Comparisons of Flo's skull with those of modern humans with Down syndrome showed that there were significant anatomical differences between the two, ruling it out as an explanation[130].

Other pathological explanations were also rejected, such as Laron syndrome (a form of dwarfism related to a genetic disorder) and cretinism (severely stunted physical and mental growth due to a congenital deficiency of thyroid hormones)[128]. Landmark analysis of Flo's skull shows that it is distinct from those of modern people affected by these conditions. Landmarks are anatomical points that are equivalent for all the specimens under consideration[131].

X-ray CT scans of Flo's cranial bones show a distribution of bone thickness and arrangements of cranial structures that are primitive traits for hominins and differ from the derived condition of modern humans both healthy and microcephalic[132]. Dental studies have shown that in comparison to *Homo floresiensis*, the teeth of *Homo sapiens* are derived for 9 out of 26 character-states[127]. Overall, the pathologically deformed modern human theory could be dismissed.

The next question is, what did *Homo floresiensis* evolve from? The most obvious possibility is *Homo erectus*, chiefly because we know that it was present in Asia. Dental studies do support this view: molar, premolar, and canine teeth of *Homo floresiensis* were compared against an extensive sample of teeth from present-day modern, prehistoric modern, and archaic humans. Researchers concluded that the dentition of *Homo floresiensis* shared derived characteristics with those of Early Pleistocene *Homo erectus* from East Africa and Java, and with the Dmanisi hominins, but they found that none of the 'hobbit' teeth exhibited the very primitive dental morphology associated with *Homo habilis* or the australopithecines[127].

However, studies considering the possible effects of insular dwarfism on brain size have suggested that a simple downsizing from *Homo erectus* cannot fully account for the small brain size of *Homo floresiensis*. It was suggested that the smaller-brained *Homo habilis* or the Dmanisi people are more plausible ancestors than *Homo erectus*, although this presupposes that *Homo habilis* actually was smaller-brained[115,133]. One suggestion is that the evolution of brain size under insular dwarfism was independent of the evolution of body size. This is the case for fossil dwarf hippopotamus from Madagascar, where the brains were found to have been 30 per cent smaller than predicted by the simple insular dwarfing model[134].

Researchers have also noted that while the cranial metrics are consistent with *Homo erectus*, the limb proportions of *Homo floresiensis* have more in common with *Australopithecus garhi*[126], and the feet are a mosaic of primitive apelike and derived humanlike features. The big toe is fully in-line, if short, and the metatarsals follow a humanlike sequence in which the 1st (innermost) is the most robust, followed by the 5th (outermost), then 4th, 3rd, and finally 2nd. The foot, though, is disproportionately long compared to that of a modern human. The lesser metatarsals (2nd to 5th) are long, and the outer toes are long and curved, unlike the short, straight toes of a modern human[135]. The fact that the feet and limb proportions of 'classic' Asian *Homo erectus* were modern suggests that *Homo floresiensis* evolved from a species that was more primitive, such as *Homo habilis*[136].

The most recent work, considering cranial, dental, and postcranial characteristics, has rejected a close relationship between *Homo floresiensis* and *Homo erectus*. Instead, it suggests that *Homo floresiensis* is either a sister species to *Homo habilis* or a sister species to a clade containing *Homo habilis* and later human species. It is nevertheless part of the human rather than australopithecine lineage[137]. The likeliest scenario is that *Homo floresiensis* is descended from a very early human migration that predates *Homo erectus* in Asia.

The next big question is how did these ancestors – whatever species they were – reach Flores in the first place? Unlike Java and many other islands in the Indonesian archipelago, Flores has never been connected to the mainland, even during the maximum extent of ice ages, when sea levels fell substantially. Consequently, it has been suggested that Flo's forebears were able to build boats[138]. However, there is no direct evidence in the form of artefacts to suggest that humans constructed boats until very late in prehistory. We know that modern humans must have used boats to cross the sea from the Island Southeast Asian archipelago to Australia, but could earlier hominins have made sea crossings by boat? The construction of a suitable watercraft and the navigational skills required to make a voyage across the open sea are commonly believed to have been beyond the abilities of early *Homo*[139]. In the case of early migrations from Africa, most anthropologists take the view that purely overland routes were used, but no overland route has ever existed to Flores.

Could Flo's ancestors have reached Flores using some form of primitive watercraft – possibly logs lashed together – or are there other possibilities? The answer is 'yes': they could have been swept out to sea and stranded on Flores by a natural occurrence such as a flash flood or a tsunami, possibly surviving on a raft of matted vegetation until they made landfall. This is believed to have been how the ancestors of the New World monkeys reached South America from Africa, and we can safely say that these early monkeys did not use boats.

We do not know when the first hominins reached Flores, but the site of Mata Menge in central Flores has yielded a 700,000-year-old fragmentary adult hominin lower jawbone and six teeth[140]. These fossils have been described as '*Homo floresiensis*-like', though they are even smaller than those of their Liang Bua counterparts. The Flores hominins were thus already downsized by this time, suggesting an arrival much earlier than 700,000 years ago[141] – but how much earlier? It has been suggested that stone tools from Mata Menge and another central Flores site, Wolo Sege, show technological continuity with the *Homo floresiensis* artefacts from Liang Bua. Although they cannot tell us anything about the size of their makers, the Mata Menge artefacts are 880,000 years old, and those from Wolo Sege are at least a million years old[142,143].

It remains an open question as to whether other humans came into contact with these diminutive beings or were connected in any way to the demise of the 'hobbits' after their million-year sojourn on Flores. Parts of Southeast Asia may have been inhabited by Denisovans during *Homo floresiensis'* latter days, and modern humans had reached Australia by 50,000 years ago. There is evidence for controlled usage of fire at Liang Bua between 41,000 and 24,000 years ago, suggesting that modern humans in Flores at that time[144].

The Philippines

In 2007, a 67,000-year-old human third metatarsal was found at Callao Cave in northern Luzon, the largest island of the Philippines. The bone is gracile, suggesting that it belonged to a small-bodied modern human possibly ancestral to the indigenous Aeta people who now live in the region. However, it also lies within the range of *Homo habilis* and *Homo floresiensis*, and it could not be ruled out that the bone was evidence that similar archaic humans had reached the Philippines[145].

Subsequently, twelve fossil hominin elements representing at least three individuals were found in the same stratigraphic layer of the cave. They include teeth, finger bones, toe bones, and a partial juvenile thighbone. The remains exhibited a mosaic of primitive and derived features not seen in other human species. The teeth show a puzzling mixture of archaic and modern human features. The toe bones and finger bones are curved and show similarities to the australopithecines (despite being separated from them by millions of years of evolution), suggesting adaptations to climbing. The Callao Cave remains were according described as a new human species, *Homo luzonensis*[146].

The evolutionary relationship of this new species to other humans has yet to be determined, but the discovery of 57 stone tools and a butchered rhinoceros in the nearby Cagayan Valley suggests that hominins were on Luzon prior to 700,000 years ago[147]. It should be noted that the Philippines, like Flores, has always remained insular during ice ages, raising similar questions as to how early humans got there.

The Rising Star people

Even more mysterious than the 'hobbits' of Flores and *Homo luzonensis* are Rising Star cave people of South Africa. They were discovered in 2013 by members of an expedition led by American palaeoanthropologist Lee Berger, a former student of Philip Tobias. Berger already had one major discovery under his belt, the australopithecine species *Australopithecus sediba*. Following this discovery, he felt that other South African cave systems had the potential to yield hominin fossils, so earlier in 2013, he had recruited cavers Steve Tucker and Rick Hunter to search the Rising Star cave system, located in the Cradle of Humankind World Heritage Site near Krugersdorp.

Although the cave had been well explored over the years, Tucker and Hunter came across a narrow shaft that dropped vertically for 12 m (39 ft) into an unexplored chamber. Tucker descended into the chamber, where he found and photographed a fossil skull and jawbone lying on the floor of the cave. From the photographs, Berger could see that the remains were too primitive to be those of a modern human. Convinced that Tucker had found important fossils, he wasted no time in obtaining *National Geographic* funding for an expedition.

Funding, however, was not the major problem. Before they could even attempt the narrow drop into what became known as the Dinaledi Chamber ('chamber of stars'), researchers would have to pass through another tiny shaft known as Superman's Crawl, and then climb a steep section known as Dragon's Back. For claustrophobics, it was the stuff of nightmares. Thus, on 7 October 2013, Berger posted an unusual appeal on the Facebook page of the American Association of Physical Anthropologists. He was seeking a small group of individuals with excellent professional and team skills for a short-term excavation project, but there was a catch: applicants had to be 'skinny and preferably small'. He believed that there were at best three or four people in the world who would fit the criteria. In the event, within days 57 suitable candidates had applied from which he chose six, all women.

A month after the Facebook appeal, on 7 November, Berger's expedition set up camp at the Rising Star cave system, and three days later, the 'underground astronauts' (as Berger termed them) entered the cave. Working in six-hour shifts, they soon recovered more fossil material than had been found in the whole of South Africa in the previous 90 years. On the surface, a large team prepared and catalogued the fossils as they were brought out of the cave and social media was used extensively to report progress. On 21 November, the number of fossils recovered reached 500, and the 1,000 mark was reached on 25 November. The expedition's final haul was 1,550 fossils comprising 15 individuals, including males, females, and infants. The fossil remains of juvenile hominins are extremely rare, and their discovery opened up the possibility of gaining new insight into the maturational processes and life history stages of extinct hominins[148].

In an unusual move, Berger then invited thirty young postdoctoral researchers from fifteen countries to help him evaluate the massive fossil collection at a workshop in Johannesburg. They were accompanied by twenty of Berger's more senior colleagues, who had collaborated with him on the *Australopithecus sediba* discovery. Not everybody was happy about entrusting such important fossils to inexperienced researchers, but for the latter it was a fantastic opportunity.

In September 2015, Berger and his colleagues announced their findings[149,150] and described the remains as a new human species, *Homo naledi* ('naledi' means 'star' in the Sotho language). With multiple examples of almost every bone in the skeleton, it was possible to describe the new species in great detail. *Homo naledi* was comparable in height and weight to a small-bodied modern human or a large australopithecine, with an estimated stature of around 1.5 m (5 ft) and weighing 40 to 55 kg (88 to 121 lb). The brain was extremely small for a hominin, ranging from 465 to 560 cc, overlapping with the range of values known for australopithecines, and exceeding only the cranial capacity of the Flores 'hobbits'. The reconstructed skeleton exhibited both humanlike and apelike features, but in a mosaic combination that had not been seen with other hominins.

The feet and lower limbs are humanlike, but the upper thighbone, pelvis, and shoulders are apelike. The upper limbs retain a morphology adapted to climbing, and lack many of the derived features of other early humans[151]. The hands and wrists are humanlike, though the fingers are curved suggesting *Homo naledi* spent time in the trees as well as on the ground[152]. Although the feet are modern, the toe bones are more curved, and the inner longitudinal arch is reduced. These features suggest that bipedal locomotion of *Homo naledi* was unique to it[153].

Overall, *Homo naledi* is the most primitive, small-brained hominin ever to have been included in *Homo*, but the dentition, the shape of cranium, and the shape of the lower jawbone have more in common with *Homo* than with *Australopithecus*[149].

Primitive characteristics such as small brains suggest that the *Homo naledi* emerged early in human evolutionary history, but it has a mosaic anatomy of primitive and derived features that makes it difficult to assign it a definite place in the human family tree. It shares with *Homo erectus* and *Homo sapiens* many derived features of the hand, foot, and lower limb that are not present in *Homo habilis*, *Homo floresiensis*, and *Australopithecus sediba*, but it lacks several derived traits of the shoulder, trunk, and hip that are shared by *Homo erectus* and *Homo sapiens*. There are some cranial similarities to *Homo erectus*, but there are also significant differences, and the lower jawbone appears to be more primitive. No cladistic interpretation of this anatomy can eliminate the need for reversals (reversion of characteristics from the derived to the ancestral state) or parallelisms (where similar traits emerge independently in two closely related lineages). One possibility is that *Homo naledi* was the result of hybridisation between apelike and humanlike hominin lineages[154,155].

Tucker and Hunter continued their investigation of the Rising Star cave system, and they discovered a second fossil-bearing chamber. Named Lesedi Chamber ('chamber of light'), it lies 30 m (100 ft) below ground and is not connected to the Dinaledi Chamber. Subsequent excavations recovered 133 hominin fossils representing at least three individuals: two adults and a juvenile, all assignable to *Homo naledi*. The most significant discovery was a near-complete cranium with an estimated cranial capacity of 610 cc. This lies within the range of other early humans, but it is still less than half of the modern average[156]. Finds continue to be made, including a juvenile nicknamed 'Leti' ('lost one'), who was aged four to six years old at death[157].

Calcium carbonate flowstones in the chamber were found to have been contaminated with materials from associated muds, meaning that uranium-series dating would be challenging. With no dates initially available for the fossils, attempts were made to date them by comparisons with other hominin fossils, with estimates ranging from one to two million years[158,159]. A date for the fossils was finally obtained in 2017, using a combination of uranium-series and electron spin resonance techniques. The result was an unexpectedly recent value of 236,000 – 335,000 years[160], later revised to 241,000 – 355,000 years ago[161]. Up until then, it was thought that only large-brained hominins more closely related to early *Homo sapiens* had existed in Africa at this late stage, although this conclusion was based on a very sparse fossil record. It is now clear that hominins in Africa were very diverse, and that *Homo naledi* represents the survival of at least one lineage from the earliest era of *Homo*[154].

No less intriguing than the origin of *Homo naledi* is the question of how the fossils reached the two underground chambers in the first place. There are hardly any non-hominin fossils in Dinaledi Chamber, although they are abundant in the adjacent Dragon's Back. This eliminates the possibility of the remains having been swept into Dinaledi Chamber by a flash flood, as it would have left a mixture of hominin and non-hominin remains in both chambers. Carnivores are also unlikely out: even if a carnivore had preyed exclusively on

Homo naledi, why would it drag its prey into such an inaccessible location? In any case, none of the bones showed any signs of gnawing by carnivores[150,162]. It has been suggested that the surface preservation of the bones is too poor to rule out carnivore involvement[163], but this does not address the other problems with the carnivore theory.

One suggestion was that the chambers had once been connected to the surface by a narrow fissure, and hominins had fallen through it to their deaths. A comprehensive survey of the cave system later found that the only other route into the chamber was a crack that became filled with flowstone more than 600,000 years ago, long before the fossils were deposited[164]. In any case, such a 'death trap' would not account for the lack of non-hominin faunal remains[162].

The only obvious explanation that avoids all of these issues is that the remains were deliberately placed in these chambers by fellow group members. Once again, we must fall back on Sherlock Holmes' observation that when you have eliminated the impossible, whatever remains, no matter how improbable, must be the truth. It seems inescapable that the Rising Star people deliberately placed the remains of deceased group members in the caves. This explanation seems particularly applicable to Leti, who was found alone and *sans* postcranial body parts in a narrow fissure[157]. The Rising Star people were no larger than Lee Berger's 'underground astronauts' and would have been able to negotiate the Rising Star cave system with greater ease than most modern people. British archaeologist Paul Pettitt has suggested that 'archaic mortuary behaviour' was a very early hominin development, citing the AL 333 australopithecine 'First Family' fossil deposit found in the Afar region of Ethiopia in 1975 as evidence[165]. If he is correct, then there is no reason to suppose that the Dinaledi Chamber and Lesedi Chamber remains could not be an example of what he terms funerary caching: the deliberate placing of corpses in natural fissures or caves. Pettitt has said that he is almost but not quite ready to accept this possibility[166].

Conclusion

The gradual progression from australopithecine to *Homo habilis*, then *Homo erectus*, and finally archaic *Homo sapiens* from which emerged Neanderthals and modern people was a compellingly simple and elegant scenario that featured in museum displays for many years. What we now know is not only far more complex but, I'd argue, far more interesting. Rather than an orderly procession of ever-more 'advanced' species, leading inexorably towards *Homo sapiens*, the hominin family tree has been likened to a 'tangled bush'[167].

Despite the climatic upheavals of the Middle Pleistocene transition, smaller-brained hominins continued to flourish. While the Flores 'hobbits', the Luzon people, and possibly others lived in isolated habitats, this was not the case with the Rising Star people. Krugersdorp, as we have seen, has hosted hominins for millions of years, some of which must surely have been contemporary with *Homo naledi*. The date range for the Dinaledi Chamber overlaps with that of the Florisbad cranium, found 400 km (250 miles) to the southwest. Meanwhile, we have seen evidence that *Homo erectus* might have survived until as recently as 11,500 years ago in China and interbred with modern people (see Chapter 2).

We now know that many useful genes in our makeup were 'imported' from Neanderthals and Denisovans; for example, present-day Tibetans have several unusual genetic variants of

Denisovan origin that have helped them to adapt to the low oxygen levels on the Tibetan plateau[168].

It now seems that the large-brained humans diversified into three populations, from which arose Neanderthals in Europe and western Asia, Denisovans in East Asia, and *Homo sapiens* in Africa. Characteristic features of the three types 'accreted' over time until recognisably modern *Homo sapiens*, 'classic' Neanderthals, and presumably an equivalent Denisovan phenotype emerged. When these populations came into contact, they interbred. Surviving 'super-archaic' populations also contributed to the mix. In this respect, humans are no different from any other species of primate. Our closest living relatives, chimpanzees, appear to have undergone the ancient introgression of an extinct ape lineage[169], and natural hybridisation has been reported for around 10 per cent of non-human Old World and 7 per cent of New World primates[170].

Rather than a tangled bush, where spreading branches can never reconnect, hominin evolution might be better likened to a braided stream where rivulets in a valley repeatedly divide and reconnect. Multiple hominin lineages diverge, become isolated, but later come into renewed contact to form a single hybrid lineage. The analogy is not perfect, because dividing rivulets within a braided stream never flow into a cul-de-sac, whereas many hominin populations of the past did become extinct. The technical term for this process is reticulate evolution, from the Latin word *reticulum* meaning 'little net'. As we have seen, there is strong evidence that it played a significant role in hominin evolution.

It is remarkable how much we have learned from genetics. That Denisovans existed, much less interbred with our ancestors, was unsuspected until a little over a decade ago. Nevertheless, there is still much to be learned about the human past. We can be hopeful that through genetics and new fossil discoveries, our knowledge will continue to increase.

06: First use of fire

Introduction

The theft of fire from the gods for the benefit of humanity is a recurring theme in many traditions around the world. Commonly, the perpetrator is a trickster who steals fire from a supernatural being who has withheld its use out of a mistrust of humanity. Thieves include ǀKaggen (San people of South Africa), Mātariśvan (the Rigveda), Māui (Polynesia), dogs, rabbits, hares, opossums, crows, and spiders. One of the best-known legends is that of Prometheus, first recorded by Hesiod in the eighth century BCE in *Theogony* and *Works and Day*. Prometheus, son of the Titan Iapetus, stole fire from Olympus and hid it in a fennel stalk. He was already out of favour with Zeus after tricking him into allowing humans to keep meat for themselves and sacrifice only the bones wrapped in fat to the gods, and this latest misdemeanour was the final straw. He was chained to a rock, and his liver was gnawed each day by an eagle, only to grow back overnight. Zeus eventually relented and allowed Heracles to kill the eagle and release Prometheus.

Fire can be used to provide heat and lighting, for cooking, and to deter night-time predators. Smoke signals, used by Native Americans, Aboriginal Australians, and other traditional societies, were undoubtedly used by prehistoric peoples. Human activities can be performed through the hours of darkness, and fire would certainly have been an asset to early humans migrating from Africa into higher latitudes. That the theft of fire occurs in so many world mythologies underlines its importance in human societies. Darwin[1] described the discovery of fire as "*probably the greatest, excepting language, ever made by man*". There is little doubt that the mastery of fire was a vitally important breakthrough for early humans, but how, where, and when did it occur?

What is fire?

The phenomenon we describe as 'fire' is a self-sustaining exothermic reaction between oxygen and organic or other combustible materials, which liberates heat and light, and requires ignition to start it going. The 'fire triangle' of oxygen, heat, and fuel must all be present for fire to exist. Natural fires can be ignited by lightning, volcanic activity, sparks from rockfalls, or spontaneous combustion. Of these, lightning strikes are by far the most important, causing 5,000 fires annually in the US National Forest alone[2]. Natural wildfires occurring deep in geological time can be identified by the presence of fossil charcoal in sedimentary rock, which preserves plant anatomy in pieces over a few microns in size[3]. Such evidence is very ancient: fossil charcoal representing vegetation charred by a low-intensity fire has been identified in siltstone deposits dating to the Silurian period (443.8 – 419.2

million years ago), two hundred million years before the age of the dinosaurs[4].

Evidence for wildfire nevertheless remains scarce during the Devonian period (417.2 – 458.9 million years ago), with only scattered charcoal records from the Late Devonian despite the appearance of extensive forests. Not until the Carboniferous period (458.9 – 298.9 million years ago) is there extensive evidence for widespread fire systems[2,5]. During the Carboniferous, oxygen levels were higher than those of the present day, leading to fires that were more frequent, more extensive, and more intense than those of the present day[2,6–8]. The greater prevalence of wildfires, relative to today, is probably why the evidence for them is so widespread.

Wildfires can be devastating and as concern grows over climate change, they regularly feature in news reports from around the world. Equally, though, they are part of the natural cycle of death and regeneration. Some plants (e.g., *Ulex*) rely on fire for seed germination: heat from the fire cracks the seed coat and releases the seeds. Some trees, notably some conifers, have a fire-resistant bark that protects the vulnerable cambium tissue layer. They may shed their lower branches to reduce the risk of surface fires spreading upwards. Some plants (e.g., *Eucalyptus, Sequoia, Betula*) may regenerate or produce new shoots from burnt trunks. The burning of plants releases nutrients into the soil and dramatically affects its structure. Plant communities can simply regenerate in *situ*, or their destruction can result in a new plant succession, where an area is colonised first by so-called 'pioneer species' (annual forbs and grasses), followed by perennial forbs and grasses. Eventually, 'climax' vegetation (trees and shrubs) colonises the once burnt-out area, which may eventually become a woodland[2].

Fire and early hominins

Fire was a part of the landscape inhabited by the earliest hominins, long before they learned how to produce it for themselves. What was their awareness of fire, and what, if any, use were they able to make of it? The ability to conceptualise a fire is a prerequisite to the use of fire. Conceptualisation may be defined as an understanding of how fire behaves under varying conditions that would enable the prediction of its movement, hence permitting activity in close proximity to it. Field studies of savanna chimpanzees (*Pan troglodytes verus*) at Fongoli in Senegal suggest that they are able to predict the behaviour of wildfires of various intensities. The grassland/woodland home range of the chimpanzees is constantly affected by wildfires, which begin in October each year and burn more than 75 per cent of it annually. This is probably a greater incidence of wildfire than that experienced by the earliest hominins, but it gives an insight as to how apes with a comparable brain size respond to it. If present-day chimpanzees possess the cognitive abilities to accurately predict and exploit wildfire behaviour, it suggests that relatively small-brained early hominins were capable of safely navigating wildfire and understanding its behaviour[9].

Although the apes tended to avoid most of the wildfires, they met even the most intense fires with relative calm and seemingly calculated movement. After fires, they spent more time foraging and travelling in burned areas than they did in partially burned or unburned areas. These findings support the hypothesis that hominin fire use was an early development. Assuming that early hominins had similar abilities, then rather than simply fleeing from a wildfire, they would have understood it as a force shaping their local ecology. They would have factored its effects into their daily activities, for example, continuing to forage and travel within areas in proximity to wildfires as long as resources remained[9].

There are three possible reasons why early hominins might have been attracted to fire-modified landscapes: changes in the distribution of and access to food, greater ease of travel, and a reduced threat of predators. The majority of important chimpanzee dry-season foods (defined according to time spent feeding on these species) are tree fruits, such as baobab fruit, which is rarely affected by fire. They also feed extensively on Vigna vine legumes. Although fire destroys these plants, in the long term it promotes greater propagation. Other important dry-season chimpanzee foods include honey (almost always harvested from a tree hollow and frequently from baobab trees), and *Macrotermes* termites (protected from wildfire by large termite-mound refugia). Fire eases travel by removing thick undergrowth and aids predator detection by removing vegetation that could otherwise provide cover for ambush predators. That chimpanzees favoured burned over partially burned or unburned areas suggests that they are aware of and are exploiting these advantages, suggesting in turn that early hominins did also[9].

The Wrangham cooking hypothesis

British primatologist Richard Wrangham[10] believes that the ability to cook food played a crucial role in human evolution. Cooked food is not only more palatable but the available nutrient is increased. Wrangham claims that once humans learned how to cook food, the gut could become smaller. Another change is that *Homo erectus*, Neanderthals, and modern humans show a marked reduction in molar size compared with earlier hominins, which cannot be explained simply in terms of craniodental and body size evolution. Modern humans also spend far less time eating than comparably sized primates[11].

Why might a smaller gut be desirable? Early *Homo* represented an advance in brainpower over pre-human hominins. This, in turn, poses the question of why this extra brainpower was needed. Oversized brains might sound like a good idea, but the same could be said of owning a Rolls-Royce. The problem in both cases is that they are expensive to run, and there is a pretty good case for trying to make do without. In humans, brain tissue requires over 22 times as much energy as an equivalent amount of muscle tissue; in modern humans, this amounts to around 16 per cent of the body's energy budget despite the brain making up just 2 per cent of the body's overall mass[12]. While the energy costs were less for the smaller brains of early *Homo*, they were still considerable – but the benefits apparently outweighed the costs. What could these have been?

Originally proposed in the 1980s, the social brain hypothesis states that the large brains of primates enable them to use knowledge about the social behaviour of their fellows to predict their likely future behaviour and base their relationships upon these predictions[13]. Later work suggested that there was a long between primate brain size and not only group size, but also the size of 'grooming cliques' within an overall group[14–16].

Living in larger social groups might have facilitated the brain enlargement of early *Homo* as cooperative behaviours would have reduced food costs. However, this does not explain how and why larger social groups came about in the first place. Were smaller group sizes no longer adequate, and if not, then why not? The earliest fossil remains associated with *Homo* date to around 2.75 million years ago[17,18], and remains identified as early *Homo erectus* date to around 2.33 million years ago[19–21]. This timescale is close to the onset of the Quaternary Ice Age, which followed 50 million years of climatic downturn. Cooler, more arid conditions alternated with warm, wet conditions as ice sheets ebbed and flowed in higher latitudes. Even before the onset, East Africa was experiencing a long-term increase in overall aridity, punctuated by more humid episodes[22]. These climatic fluctuations would have put increasing pressure on pre-human hominins as traditionally favoured food items became only sporadically available. Cooperative behaviours would have been essential for survival. It is surely no coincidence that larger-brained early *Homo* emerged around this time.

The onset of the Quaternary Ice Age, the first full-blown ice age for a quarter of a billion years, provides a plausible explanation for the larger brains of early *Homo*, but how was such an expansion possible in the first place? We now come to the expensive tissue hypothesis, which states that to compensate for the energy used by an oversized brain, another part of the body must cut down its energy consumption. The brain is not the only 'gas-guzzling' organ in the human body: the heart, liver, kidneys, and gut also consume disproportionally large amounts of energy. There is no scope for downsizing the heart, liver, or kidneys: their size is more or less determined by the size of the organism. This leaves only the gut. In simple terms, you can have a big brain or a big gut, but you cannot have both[12].

Animals with a diet of low-quality hard-to-digest foods require large guts with complex fermenting chambers, and large brains are not an option. Only animals with diets that are high in sugars and proteins can get by with smaller simpler guts, and so sustain the energy costs of a large brain. This, in turn, implies a diet of high-quality, easy-to-digest foods, and the ability to cook food would have been a major asset.

Evidence for early fire use

On the Wrangham view, we would expect the first evidence for the use of fire to coincide with the emergence of *Homo erectus*, but clear signs of the use of fire do not show up in the archaeological record until much later. Palaeontologist Travis Pickering has noted that the initial harnessing of fire was "*such an extraordinary accomplishment that any claim of that achievement requires extraordinary evidence for its acceptance*"[23]. To find such evidence is far harder than finding evidence for stone tool use. The latter, regardless of age, are still readily accessible to us by sight and touch. Fire, on the other hand, is ephemeral. After a fire has burned itself out, it can only be identified by trace evidence. Distinguishing the controlled use of fire from natural wildfire is also a problem, at least in parts of the world where lightning-induced wildfires are common. Evidence for hearths would certainly meet Pickering's criteria, but unfortunately this is lacking from the earliest candidate sites.

Patches of reddened sediment found at site FxJj20 AB, Koobi Fora, Kenya, are around 1.5 million years old and have been claimed as remains from fire use by early humans since the early 1970s. Further excavations were carried out at the site in 2010, yielding new material. Studies conducted in 2016 suggested that knapped stone fragments associated with the sediments had been exposed to high temperatures[24]. Possible evidence for fire use has been reported from other sites of comparable age: 40 pieces of discoloured clay aggregates associated with stone tools and faunal remains from the 1.42 million-year-old site of GnJi 1/6E, Chesowanja, also in Kenya[25]. From the roughly one million-year-old site of Gadeb 8E, Ethiopia, are stones showing differential dark grey and red discolouration, suggesting that they may have been burned in a fire. The stones were found to exhibit thermoremnant magnetisation[36], consistent with being heated[26,27]. This evidence is by no means conclusive, and relatively speaking, it is quite late in the hominin story.

What might be considered stronger evidence was found in the late 1980s at the cave site of Swartkrans, South Africa, dating to about 1.0 to 1.5 million years ago. There, archaeologists have recovered 270 burned animal bones from a gully in the cave's uppermost level, known as Member 3. Hominin remains found at the site include both *Homo erectus* and the australopithecine species *Paranthropus robustus*, and while it is generally assumed that only the former was responsible for the fires, there is no evidence that this was definitely the case[28]. However, Pickering has noted that the burned bones were probably moved a short distance away from where they were burned. Therefore, it cannot be ruled out that wildfires ignited flammable material, including bones which were lying on the floor of the cave mouth, and that these bones were later washed by rainfall deeper into the gully where Member 3 formed[23].

Against that, at the time of the discovery, palaeontologist Bob Brain[28] had argued that while the burned bones are found throughout the 6 m (19 ft 8 in) thick Member 3, hardly any have been found in the earlier Members 1 and 2, despite these containing vertebrate fossils in large quantities. If wildfire had been responsible for the burned bones, then they would have been found in all three levels and not just Member 3. On the balance of probabilities, the Swartkrans evidence does seem to demonstrate fire use – but it does not do so beyond reasonable doubt.

The earliest currently known evidence for fire use that could be considered 'extraordinary' is that from Wonderwerk Cave, a site in Northern Cape Province, South Africa, which is around one million years old. Archaeologists investigated a habitation layer known as Stratum 10, which was found to contain ash, minute bone fragments, and complete or fragmented bones showing signs of burning. This material was associated with stone tools, and it persists throughout the whole of Stratum 10. Overall, it suggests that fires were occurring in the cave at a frequency too great to be accounted for by natural causes. Any lingering doubts were banished by the location of the excavation area, 30 m (100 ft) from the cave entrance. The latter was still further away at the time Stratum 10 was laid down – much too far for the burnt material to have been blown in or washed in from outside. Berna's team was even able to rule out the possibility of spontaneous combustion of bat guano, which though rare has been known to occur in caves[29].

This evidence tells us that *Homo erectus* was making use of fire in Africa at least one million years ago, and probably earlier. What remains unknown is whether these early humans knew how to actually produce fire, or if they were simply making opportunistic use of wildfire to start their own fires. The picture outside Africa suggests the latter. By one million years ago, humans were already widely dispersed across Eurasia and the controlled use of fire would have been a powerful resource in higher latitudes. Therefore, it might be expected that signs of fire use would be widespread.

---

[36] When a rock cools, it acquires thermoremanent magnetisation from the Earth's field.

However, until 400,000 years ago, the evidence is very limited: a handful of sites in Asia and none at all in Europe[30]. Locality 1 at Zhoukoudian is a much-investigated cave site near Beijing, with archaeological layers that accumulated between 592,000 – 417,000 and 256,000 – 230,000 years ago[31]. Layer 10, the earliest layer, has yielded burnt bones and stone tools, and the presence of hearths has been claimed for decades. The problem is that there are no traces of the wood ash and charcoal that might reasonably be expected to be associated with a hearth[32]. However, more recent work has identified clear-cut evidence for fire use in the more recent Layer 4 using measurements of the magnetic susceptibility, colour, and diffuse reflectance spectra of sediments. Layer 4 dates to around 300,000 years ago. The long-running debate over this site could potentially be resolved if future research reveals similar evidence from Layer 8-9 and Layer 10[31].

More conclusive evidence has been reported from two sites in Israel: Gesher Benot Ya'aqov and Evron Quarry. Gesher Benot Ya'aqov is a 790,000-year-old site on the shores of the now-drained Lake Huleh. Burned wood and small burned flint fragments have been found at the site and may indicate the locations of hearths. Although Gesher Benot Ya'aqov is an outdoor site, wildfire is unlikely to account for the burning. Electrical storms in the region mainly occur during the wet season, making lightning-induced wildfires uncommon. Hence, human fire-starting is thought to be the most probable explanation[33].

Roughly the same age as Gesher Benot Ya'aqov at 1.0 – 0.8 million years old, Evron Quarry is also an open-air site, on the coastal plain of western Galilee. A suite of spectroscopic methods has recently been used to demonstrate that closely associated faunal remains and stone tools were exposed to high temperatures. This approach has the advantage of being able to identify burning in the absence of visual signatures of fire. It does offer hope that similar evidence might be identified at other sites where it has hitherto been overlooked[34].

For now, though, these three sites represent the sole evidence for fire use in Eurasia during the Early and Middle Pleistocene[37]. There is no evidence at all at any European site until around 400,000 years ago. Two sites, Schöningen, in Lower Saxony, Germany, and Beeches Pit, Suffolk, England, provide the earliest evidence. At Schöningen, the evidence consists of some heated flints and charred wood, including a wooden tool, and the possible remains of hearths. At Beeches Pit, located on the bank of a pond, the evidence consists of heated lithics and heated sediments, interpreted as the remains of hearths. There is also credible evidence from the sites of Terra Amata, near Nice, France and Vérteszöllös, 45 minutes to the west of Budapest, Hungary, but the dating of these sites is imprecise, with estimates ranging from MIS 11 (424,000 – 374,000 years ago) to MIS 9 (337,000 – 300,000 years ago)[30,36].

Thereafter, evidence for fire use is seen increasingly throughout Europe, Asia, and Africa. That it does not seem to have become a maintainable technology until between 400,000 and 200,000 years ago suggests that early humans, such as *Homo erectus*, were able to live in northern latitudes without it[30]. The timing is a problem for Richard Wrangham's cooking hypothesis. Middle Pleistocene humans such as *Homo heidelbergensis* and Neanderthals (and presumably Denisovans) were larger-brained than *Homo erectus*, suggesting that bigger brains led to the widespread use of fire, rather than the other way around.

---

[37] The Pleistocene is divided into Early (2.580 million – 774,000 years ago), Middle (774,000 – 129,000 years ago), and Late (129,000 – 12,700 years ago) stages[35].

Keep the home fires burning

Of course, as proponents of the cooking hypothesis remind us, an absence of evidence is not the same as evidence of absence[37]. Direct evidence for fires only survives under exceptional circumstances, and the earliest such evidence cannot reliably tell us when fire was first used[38]. Activities relating to fire use could be spatially distinct from those leading to large assemblages of stone tools and faunal remains, and could be missed[39].

It has been argued that the ability to produce fire is less crucial to the use of fire than is generally assumed. If early humans could not ignite fires for themselves, they would need to be able to maintain them, especially in winter/during the wet season, when wildfire would not normally be available[40]. Indeed, fire-making is viewed as only the final stage in the transition from no fire use through opportunistic use to controlled use of fire[38]. The latter would require a good knowledge of slow-burning materials such as animal dung, which can frequently be seen smouldering after a wildfire front has passed, and would likely have been noticed by early humans[40,41].

Could humans without the means to produce fire become obligate fire users? Theoretically, once a fire has been lit using a natural source, it can be kept going indefinitely. In practice, this is far from straightforward. Keeping the fire supplied with fuel is a task that has to continue alongside other activities such as hunting, gathering, and toolmaking. The fire has to be kept going in wet weather, which means it would have to be set in a cave, rock shelter, or artificial shelter. Finally, the fire has to be transported when a group relocates. The further a group moves, the longer the fire has to be kept going, the greater the risk is that it will go out. Inevitably, a fire would go out from time to time, and no wildfire would be available to replenish it. A functional social network with other fire-using groups would have been a necessity, so that the fire could be relit with the aid of a neighbouring group[38,40].

Were early humans capable of the complex behaviours required for this degree of fire maintenance, which would have entailed considerable levels of cooperation and social networking, the ability to plan ahead, and to conceptualise 'delayed returns' where time and effort expended do not produce immediate rewards? In the case of *Homo heidelbergensis* and Neanderthals, the answer, probably, is 'yes'. For smaller-brained hominins such as *Homo erectus*, it seems less likely. The cognitive requirements do not seem to be that much less onerous than those required to actually produce fire.

Criticisms of the Wrangham model

Middle Pleistocene humans such as *Homo heidelbergensis* and Neanderthals (and presumably Denisovans) were all larger-brained than *Homo erectus*, which hints that bigger brains might have led to the widespread use of fire, rather than the other way around. If so, then how is the downsized gut of early *Homo* to be explained? One possibility is that rather than cooking, the key to more efficient food processing was the use of stone tools to slice meat and pound root vegetables. Even without roasting (which is the most basic cooking method), food that has been processed in this way requires less masticatory effort and reduces metabolic demands. Tool use rather than controlled fire use could have enabled reductions in the size of the molar teeth and jaw musculature of *Homo erectus* and enabled brain expansion[42].

Wrangham[43] rejects this view and suggests that slicing and pounding might have had limited benefits. He notes that 'raw foodists' (people who choose to live for long periods on a diet of exclusively raw foods) suffer energy deficiencies despite using electrical blenders to process food. The problem with this argument is that raw foodists typically live in industrial societies and eat store-bought foods. Indeed, Wrangham notes this. I would question whether people following what dieticians have described as a fad diet are even a reliable proxy for early *Homo erectus* of at least 2.33 million years ago. Interbreeding between *Homo sapiens* and Neanderthals and Denisovans resulted in the transfer of many genes that survive in present-day populations. While many of these genes were beneficial, some were not. These include genes implicated in type 2 diabetes and Crohn's disease[44], smoking addiction, increased risk of depression, incontinence, bladder pain, urinary tract disorders, protein-calorie malnutrition, LDL cholesterol and vitamin D levels, rheumatoid arthritis, visceral fat accumulation, schizophrenia, and actinic keratosis (precancerous skin lesions resulting from exposure to the Sun)[45,46]. Many of these genes were probably once advantageous, but adverse effects were triggered by the changes in diet following the coming of agriculture in Neolithic times. Modern humans diverged from *Homo erectus* long before they did from Neanderthals and Denisovans, and metabolic differences are likely to have been correspondingly greater. Wrangham also notes that there are no known ethnographic examples of people processing raw foods, but this is only to be expected. Nobody (barring the raw foodists) doubts the advantages of cooking. What is disputed is that it was a prerequisite for brain expansion. There is an important difference between 'limited benefits' and 'insufficient'.

Gut size reduction is not the only evolutionary change that Wrangham has attributed to the use of for. He has noted that without fire to deter not just predators but also large mammals such as elephants and rhinos, sleeping on the ground in the African woodlands and savannahs would have been dangerous. He suggests that it might have been knowledge of fire that made *Homo erectus* finally abandon any residual dependency on tree-climbing[10,43]. There is no doubt that knowledge of fire would have reduced the risks of sleeping on the ground, but that is not to say that these would otherwise have been insurmountable. An obvious solution would be for individuals to take turns to stay awake and keep watch. Even without a system of watchkeeping, people sleeping in groups would likely comprise individuals of different 'chronotypes', i.e., with different wake-sleep cycles. At any given time, if the group was large enough, at least one individual would almost certainly be awake and could sound the alarm if necessary[47] *Homo erectus* is believed to have lived in groups with an overall size of one hundred or more[48]. These would be dispersed into smaller sleeping groups to reduce the risk of the entire group being overwhelmed by a concerted attack, either by human enemies or a pack of predators[47].

Another evolutionary change that Wrangham[43] has attributed to fire use is endurance running, an ability that is unique to humans among the primates. Humans are mediocre sprinters: the world record for the 100-metre sprint is 9.58 seconds, set by Jamaican sprinter Usain Bolt in 2009. This corresponds to a speed of 37.5 km/hr (23.3 mph). For comparison, lions have a top speed of 81 km/h (50.3 mph) and can run a 100-metre sprint in 4 seconds. On the other hand, humans are excellent endurance runners, able to cover long distances over extended periods. At the London 2012 Olympics, British gold medallist Mo Farah recorded a time of 27 min 30.42 sec in the 10,000 metres, or just over 6 m/sec (13.4 mph). Even an amateur jogger can average 3.2 to 4.2 m/sec (7.2 to 9.4 mph) for 10 km (6.2 miles) or more. This ability is rare among quadrupedal mammals: even horses cannot sustain anything better than a canter at 5.8 m/sec (13 mph) over long distances. For endurance running to have evolved suggests that it gave early *Homo* a significant survival advantage.

Endurance running might have enabled hunters to run down their prey before killing it with close-range weapons. Although endurance running is uncommon among present-day hunter-gatherers, it would have been necessary before the invention of projectile weapons such as the throwing spear. Endurance running might also have helped early *Homo* to compete more effectively with scavengers, including pre-human hominins. These possible advantages were noted by biologists Dennis Bramble and Daniel Lieberman[49], who observed that modern humans possess many skeletomuscular features not shared with apes that adapt them for endurance running. These adaptations are associated with energy efficiency, shock absorption, stability, and temperature regulation, and nearly all of them were also present in *Homo erectus*. They include features that promote stabilisation of the head and trunk and shock absorption in the foot, although some, such as the presence of a long Achilles tendon, cannot be verified due to incomplete fossil evidence.

Wrangham argued that without a reduction in body hair, *Homo erectus* would not be able to lose body heat efficiently when running, but that this reduction meant that they could not keep warm when sleeping without fire. He cited an estimate[50] that the human public louse diverged from its closest relative, the gorilla louse, 1.84 – 5.61 million years ago in support of an early reduction of body hair in *Homo*. Clothing would be a solution, but Wrangham suggested that this was a much later development. He cited an estimate[51] that the human head louse and body louse diverged from one another 83,000 – 170,000 years ago, which has been claimed to represent an upper limit for the invention of clothing. The problem with this line of reasoning is that there are many occasions when it is not possible to keep warm by either endurance running or sitting by a fire, especially in higher latitudes. Neanderthals were fire users, but even during warm interglacial periods, they would have faced a considerable heat-loss problem if they had gone hunting and gathering stark naked in the middle of winter. Accordingly, it is argued that they must have had clothing to keep out snow and water and cope with even averagely cold winter temperatures[52]. The head louse/body louse studies related to the adoption of clothing by *Homo sapiens* in Africa[53,54], and are not necessarily informative about humans who left Africa much earlier.

These objections would also seem to dispose of another claim made for fire: that *Homo erectus* could not have occupied the temperate latitudes of Eurasia without it[38]. Even Neanderthals might have had to rely on cape-type rather than tailored clothing[55], and the production of this simpler clothing could well have been within the cognitive abilities of *Homo erectus*. Clothing would have been essential in Eurasia, but fire – while desirable – might have been a resource that was utilised only seasonally. It has been suggested that Early Pleistocene humans were not able to occupy regions north of the 40th Parallel (the latitude of Valencia, Sardinia, Ankara, and Beijing) outside warm interglacial periods[56].

There is no doubt that control over fire was a very important development, but there is a danger of it becoming an evolutionary 'theory of everything'. The fact remains that evidence for widespread fire use is not seen until 400,000 years ago – a time at which humans were not undergoing large-scale evolutionary change. A possible scenario for early fire use is that it occurred as early humans adapted to an increasingly fire-prone landscape in Africa. Between 3.6 and 1.4 million years ago, open grassland environments expanded, and wildfires became more frequent. As we have seen, chimpanzees are able to exploit fire-modified landscapes, so we can be reasonably certain that *Homo erectus* also could. Human fire control could have been driven by a focus on foraging benefits provided by naturally occurring wildfires. Burning off the surface vegetation made the location of high-value food items (small burrowing animals, reptiles, insects, seeds, tubers, etc) easier, and some food items, such as tubers, were naturally cooked by the fire[57].

Australian ethnographic studies suggest benefits such as prey density and habitat diversity depend on a history of regular burning[58]. Such practices by present-day hunter-gatherers are widespread across almost all biomes worldwide[59]. Compared with undisturbed woodland, the grow-back vegetation following a fire contains a far greater range and quality of edible plant foods for both humans and potential prey animals[60]. Hunter-gatherers also burn off vegetation for a variety of other reasons, such as clearing passageways, hunting along the fire front, or signalling to distant groups[61].

For early *Homo*, the next step was actual fire control by using the burning vegetation from the natural fire to start fires elsewhere. Purposeful cooking then evolved by using fire to cook tubers that were too deep-rooted to be heated by surface fires. This scenario of early fire use would not leave archaeological evidence such as hearths and would be indistinguishable from ordinary landscape fires[57]. On this view, fire is viewed as a seasonal resource, with only limited maintenance. The reliance on fire as a seasonal resource does not constitute year-round obligate cooking, as envisioned by the Wrangham cooking hypothesis. Enhanced maintenance of fires would require base campsites, which do not become evident in the archaeological record until 400,000 – 200,000 years ago, i.e., when widespread fire use becomes evident in the archaeological record[39].

Neanderthal fire production and use

The breakthrough that enabled humans to produce fire for themselves – the real gift of Prometheus – might have been the advent of hafted tools. The basic kindling technique of rubbing a stick in a groove in a wooden hearth closely resembles hafting as a process: both involve two components and the use of an intermediate. For hafting, this is some sort of connective (adhesive or twine) to join the two components and for kindling it is tinder[40]. It may be significant that the first archaeologically attested adhesives required the use of heat[62–64] (see below). Hafted tools first appeared around 500,000 years ago, and their use was widespread in Europe and Africa after 300,000 years ago[65]. Hafting appeared at a time when the multipurpose Acheulean hand-axe was being replaced by specialist stone tools. These were manufactured by prepared-core methods where stone cores are shaped to a pre-planned form, from which flakes of a desired size and shape are then struck[66,67]. The final retirement of the venerable Acheulean hand axe marks the transition from the Lower to the Middle Palaeolithic period – but does it indeed mark the beginning of a Promethean age when humans were freed from the need for helpful lightning strikes and could produce fire for themselves?

There is no doubt that Neanderthals used fire, with evidence that includes hearths and burned bones. Such evidence is seen at several sites in the period from 400,000 to 245,000 years ago, although it is absent from many others[68–70]. There is a body of evidence to show that Neanderthals made use of fire for toolmaking. Several fragmentary boxwood (*Buxus sempervirens*) sticks have been found at the site of Poggetti Vecchi in Tuscany, Italy. The 171,000-year-old sticks are over 1 m (3 ft 3 in) long, rounded at one end, and pointed at the other. They have been partially charred, possibly to reduce the effort of scraping boxwood, which is a very tough wood. The sticks have the size and features of multipurpose tools known as digging sticks, the use of which is ethnographically recorded in many hunter-gatherer societies[71].

Chemical analysis of organic residues attached to stone artefacts has shown that Neanderthals used distilled birch bark pitch for hafting them to spears or handles. Such evidence has been found at several sites in Germany and Italy, with dates ranging from around 125,000 to 50,000 years ago[64,72–74]. At the cave sites of Grotta del Fossellone (55,000 – 40,000 years old) and Sant'Agostino (120,000 – 112,000 years ago), both in Latium, Italy, conifer resin was mixed with beeswax to improve its adhesive properties. Ethnographic evidence shows that resin, which dries when exposed to air, has to be warmed over a small fire to soften it, before moulding and pushing into position in the haft[63]. The distillation of birch bark pitch is a complex process[64], and it is perfectly reasonable to suppose that if Neanderthals mastered it, they could also have mastered the secret of fire production.

It has been argued that tar could have been produced by simply burning birch bark near a hard surface, from which it can readily be scraped off for use. While such a process is very wasteful, the abundance of raw materials could have made the more complex technique of distillation unnecessary[75,76]. However, experimental work suggests that such methods would be suitable only in situations where small quantities of tar were required. Researchers tested four increasingly complex methods of tar production: simple condensation, heating a roll of bark in an ash mound, heating a roll of bark in a pit with a collecting vessel below, and a raised structure comprising heating a roll of bark surrounded by a screen in a raised earthen mound with a collecting vessel below. It was found that the more complex methods give better tar yields: the four methods yielded 0.646, 0.877, 1.579, and 13.772 cc of tar, respectively. All these methods could be used to produce the amount of tar found at Neanderthal sites, but the simple methods would take considerably longer and require up to forty times as much bark[64].

Neanderthals might also have made use of fire to stimulate the growth of edible plants. High-resolution paleoenvironmental and archaeological data dating to around 125,000 years ago have been obtained at the site of Neumark-Nord, 35 km (22 miles) west of Leipzig, Germany, which was then located by the side of a lake. Among the factors influencing plant succession were clear signs of fire use as identified by charcoal particles. During a largely continuous 2,000-year period of human presence, the area was an open landscape. Comparison with other lake basins in the region during the same period strongly suggests that human activities were a contributing factor. As noted above, present-day hunter-gatherer groups worldwide regularly burn off vegetation to increase habitat diversity and prey density. However, it is not possible to determine whether the fires at Neumark-Nord were intended to open up the landscape or simply represent small-scale activities such as repeatedly lighting campfires around the lake[77].

The question is, though, at what point was fire produced for these purposes instead of simply being harvested or conserved from convenient wildfires? The oldest-known wooden tools in Europe are around 337,000 – 300,000 years old[78], and it would not be an unreasonable hope for the remains of fire drills to appear in the archaeological record. In the event, the earliest such evidence (from Peru) is only 10,000 years old[40]. The other classic way of producing fire is to strike a light using flint and steel. Neanderthals could have generated sparks using iron pyrites (crystalline iron disulphide) as a substitute for steel. As the name implies, sparks are produced when a piece of iron pyrites is struck with a flint, or when two pieces of iron pyrites are struck together. Such usage is ethnographically reported throughout the New World, in Australia, Melanesia, and Siberia, although it is uncommon in Africa. Microscopic and macroscopic striations and polish on bifacial tools from several Neanderthal sites in the Dordogne region of France have been interpreted as the result of repeated striking with iron pyrites to generate sparks. Similar makings were obtained by experimentally striking the flat or convex side of a biface with fragments of iron pyrites[79].

This research followed suggestions that Neanderthals used powdered manganese dioxide as a combustion aid. Blocks of manganese dioxide have long been known at several Neanderthal sites, also in the Dordogne region, with discoveries going back to the 1950s. The conventional view is that it was used as a pigment, but collecting it would have required considerable effort, whereas soot and charcoal were equally suitable and far more readily available. Accordingly, it has been suggested that the real use was as a combustion aid. Though it is not inflammable, manganese dioxide is a powerful oxidising agent. Experiments with commercial manganese dioxide compositionally similar to the Neanderthal blocks show that it lowers the ignition temperature of wood turnings and increases the completeness of combustion[80].

These results add up to a very strong case for Neanderthal fire production, but the Neanderthal bifaces and manganese dioxide blocks are all only around 50,000 years old, very late in the Neanderthal era and at a time when the first modern humans had already begun to move into Europe[81]. If the Dordogne material really does represent the earliest Neanderthal fire production, then it is even possible that Neanderthals learned about it from the incoming modern humans as a 'bow wave' of technology and culture diffused from modern humans in North Africa and Asia in advance of a large-scale dispersal into Europe[82].

In fact, by 90,000 years ago, sites like Gruta da Oliveira, a cave system in Torres Novas, Portugal, have yielded dense, hearth-focused scatters of stone tools and burnt bones in occupation layers that are too ubiquitous to be explained by anything other than regular, consistent use of fire. The date is early enough to rule out the bow wave theory. The patterns of cave usage are essentially the same as those of Upper Palaeolithic modern humans at Gruta do Caldeirão, 40 km (25 miles) to the north of Gruta da Oliveira, 50,000 years later[83].

One method by which we distinguish between natural and artificially produced fires is by studying polycyclic aromatic hydrocarbons (PAH), which are organic compounds produced during the combustion of plant material[38]. Light PAHs (comprising 3 – 4 rings) are a major component of wildfire PAH emissions and disperse widely during natural wildfire events, whereas heavy PAHs (5 – 6 rings) are a major component of particulate emissions of burned wood. The abundance of the two in sediments is informative of fire use: if Neanderthals

---

[38] A PAH molecule comprises two or more conjoined aromatic rings (each comprising six carbon atoms). Examples include naphthalene (two rings), anthracene (three rings), and phenanthrene (three rings).

were relying on wildfire, it would be expected that an increase in the abundance of heavy PAHs would be matched by an increase in light PAHs. Lusakert Cave (LKT 1) is a Middle Palaeolithic site in the Armenian highlands with 18 layers of occupation dating from 60,000 to 40,000 years ago. No correlation was found between the abundance of heavy and light PAHs. Instead, the abundance of heavy PAHs was proportional to the density of artefacts in each occupation layer at the site. This would suggest that the occupants of the cave were able to control fire and utilise it regardless of the variability of wildfires in the local environment[84].

Again, though, the dates from LKT 1 are relatively late. Also, data from two French sites, Pech de l'Azé IV. (occupied 100,000 – 50,000 years ago) and Roc de Marsal (occupied 85,000 – 45,000 years ago) suggests that fire usage was at its greatest during warm periods. Well-preserved hearths are evident during the warm MIS 5 (130,000 – 74,000 years ago), but there is much less evidence for fire usage during the later MIS 4 (74,000 – 59,000 years ago) and MIS 3 (59,000 – 24,000 years ago). This is the opposite of what would be expected if the occupants of the sites were able to make fire for themselves. It is more consistent with a reliance on natural fire sources, which would be scarcer during cold periods[85].

In summary, there is no strong evidence that Neanderthals were able to make fire for themselves until 90,000 – 50,000 years ago and even then, only regionally. Either the ability to produce fire was lost by some populations, or it was independently invented by multiple populations[84]. Both possibilities seem likely: it is difficult to believe that fire production was only invented once. Conceivably, it was invented on multiple occasions well before 90,000 years ago, but on each occasion, the secret was eventually lost as already small Neanderthal groups contracted or died out[86]. Neanderthal groups are known to have suffered such a fate during adverse climatic episodes[87,88].

Hobbits, *Homo naledi* and fire

Two of the most remarkable paleoanthropological discoveries of the present century have been those of *Homo floresiensis* in 2004 and *Homo naledi*, announced in 2015. Though classed as human and accordingly placed within *Homo*, both species had brains closer in size to those of the more apelike australopithecines. The diminutive *Homo floresiensis* from the Indonesian island of Flores stood no more than 1.06 m (3 ft 6 in) tall, with an estimated weight of 36 – 16 kg (79 – 35 lb) and an estimated cranial capacity of just 426 cc[89]. The modern average is around 1,350 cc.

Originally, it was believed that these hominins, which were immediately nicknamed 'hobbits', had survived on the island of Flores until as late as 12,000 years ago[90,91]. Despite their tiny brains, it was suggested that *Homo floresiensis* was able to plan, respond to situations, use memories, and communicate information among group members[92]. In support of these claims, the discovery of charred animal bones, reddened rocks, and several burnt pebbles was cited as evidence that *Homo floresiensis* had used fire[91].

However, in 2016, revised dates were obtained for the hominin remains. It was found that they ranged from 60,000 to 100,000 years old, and associated stone tools ranged from 50,000 to 190,000 years old[93] – but the evidence for fire use dated to between 41,000 and 24,000 years ago. This date was far too recent to have been associated with known *Homo floresiensis* remains, and it is now thought more likely that the fire was produced by modern humans[94].

Homo naledi was reported by American-South African palaeoanthropologist Lee Berger in 2015. The announcement followed the recovery of 1,550 fossils representing at least 15 individuals from a highly inaccessible chamber within the Rising Star cave system, located within the Cradle of Humankind World Heritage Site, South Africa[95,96]. *Homo naledi* had an estimated average adult height of around 1.45 m (4 ft 9 in) and weighed 33 to 43 kg (73 to 95 lb), comparable to a very small-bodied present-day human. The brain was extremely small, ranging from 465 to 560 cc, overlapping entirely with the range of values known for australopithecines[97,98]. No dates were initially available for the fossils, but based on its seemingly primitive characteristics, *Homo naledi* was thought to have lived around 1 – 2 million years ago[99,100]. However, the fossil remains were subsequently found to be just 240,000 – 335,000 years old[101,102], bringing *Homo naledi* into the era of archaic and early *Homo sapiens*.

Among the many questions raised by the discovery was how did the fossil remains reach what became known as the Dinaledi Chamber ('chamber of stars'), which lies 30 m (100 ft) below the surface and 80 m (260 ft) in a straight line from the nearest entrance? To reach it, present-day cavers must negotiate a complicated set of passages and fractures for 120 m (395 ft) and pass through a narrow access point known as Superman's Crawl, so called because cavers can only pass through it by extending one arm in front of themselves like Superman in flight. Superman's Crawl leads into a large antechamber known as the Dragon's Back Chamber. The next leg is a 15 m (50 ft) climb up the side of the Dragon's Back, a sharp-edged dolomite block that has dislodged from the roof. This is followed by a 12 m (39 ft) vertical drop known as the Chute into the Hill Antechamber, which leads via a passageway into the Dinaledi Chamber proper. The Chute is in places as narrow as 0.2 m (7.9 in). The main passage of the Dinaledi Chamber is 10 m (33 ft) long, but its minimum width is just 0.25 to 0.5 m (10 in – 1 ft 8 in)[95,103].

The Rising Star fossils were not the first hominin remains to be discovered in an inaccessible location, but usually such discoveries are made in chambers linked by a shaft to the surface. Such finds might represent unfortunate individuals falling into a shaft, as seems to have been the case for Burger's earlier fossil hominin discovery, *Australopithecus sediba*[104,105]. However, no such explanation seems to be applicable to the Rising Star hominins. A comprehensive survey of the cave system showed that there was no other route into the chamber, apart from a crack that became filled with flowstone at least 600,000 years ago – well before the *Homo naledi* fossils reached the cave[106]. In any case, had there been such a 'death trap' leaving into the Dinaledi Chamber, it would be expected that non-hominin faunal remains would have been found alongside the *Homo naledi* fossils – but they did not. The Rising Star hominins were unaccompanied by any other fossil remains. This absence also ruled out the possibility that a flash flood had swept the hominins into the chamber from the adjacent Dragon's Back, where non-hominin fossils are abundant[95,107].

In the absence of any other obvious possibility, it has been suggested that the *Homo naledi* remains were deliberately placed in the chamber by fellow group members. It has even been claimed that some of the remains were intentionally interred in purpose-dug 'burial features'[108] and that geometric patterns were intentionally engraved on the walls of the chamber[109]. As might be expected, these claims have met with considerable scepticism. Nevertheless, the presence of the *Homo naledi* remains in the Dinaledi Chamber requires explanation, and all plausible explanations point to the hominins intentionally negotiating the cave system to reach the chamber. In turn, this implies a means of illumination and the use of fire[110]. Or does it? Critics point out that no evidence has been found of fire use, and that there are alternative means of navigating within the cave system, such as by sense of touch or smell, or by following air currents. While it could be argued that this sounds harder to believe than the use of fire, the cave might have been more accessible before the Dragon's Back block became dislodged[111]. It has been suggested that this occurred after the *Homo naledi* fossils were deposited in the Dinaledi Chamber[102].

Despite their small brains, *Homo floresiensis* and *Homo naledi* likely possessed similar levels of encephalisation to *Homo erectus* after their smaller overall body size is taken into account[112]. Therefore, the probability that they used fire is comparable, and the search for evidence should continue.

Fire use in the African Middle Stone Age

The first *Homo sapiens* are now known to have lived around 286,000 years ago[113]. These early *Homo sapiens* were not yet fully modern and are sometimes referred to as 'archaic *Homo sapiens*'[114,115]. Modern features, such as our distinctive globular skull shape, emerged around 230,000 years ago[116,117]. Although early *Homo sapiens* fossils have been found in Europe dating to 210,000 years ago[118], our species did not leave Africa in large numbers until around 84,000 years ago[119].

In terms of tool technology, the period from 320,000 to 40,000 years ago in Africa is known as the Middle Stone Age. It is known for bursts of innovation followed by a reversion to supposedly more conservative technologies, although these supposed fluctuations might have been a series of adaptations to changing environments rather than being 'more advanced' or 'less advanced' than their predecessors[120]. The earliest examples of innovative technologies have been found at Pinnacle Point, a golf course near the coastal town of Mossel Bay, Western Cape Province, South Africa. In 2000, as part of the preparatory work for the construction of the golf course, a survey was made of a group of nearby caves, in which were found many artefacts and animal remains going back to the early part of the Middle Stone Age. Subsequently, a team of archaeologists investigated the caves and made a series of discoveries in the lowest levels of the caves, which are 164,000 years old. These included just under sixty pieces of ochre, carefully selected for the reddest, most chromatic hues, and a total of 1,836 flaked stone artefacts, including a significant number of small blades less than 10 mm (0.375 in) in width known as microliths[121]. These were once thought to have been a much later development[122] and were commonly used in hafted tools and weapons, or set into bone or wooden handles, or the shafts or tips of spears[123]. Other stone artefacts found at Pinnacle Point included many made from silcrete, a concrete-like material formed from silica and soil grains. Silcrete is a fine-grained high-quality material that is typically very workable in its natural state.

However, experimental work using silcrete obtained from sources near Mossel Bay showed that in its raw quarried form, the local material was difficult to flake consistently into usable tools. Researchers drew on ethnographic data from Australia, where Aboriginal Australians apply heat treatment to silcrete to improve its flaking quality. Silcrete responds to heat treatment with significant improvements in its workability, and it has a greater tolerance to high temperatures than materials such as chert or flint. The researchers found that such improvements were also seen when the Mossel Bay silcrete was heat-treated[124].

Three independent methods for recognising heat treatment were applied to silcrete artefacts from the caves: archaeomagnetism, thermoluminescence (TL), and maximum gloss (MG). The first of these methods measures thermoremnant magnetisation (see above). TL entails heating a sample to release electrons that have become trapped in it after originating from background radiation. The quantity of electrons that were trapped is determined by measuring the luminescence produced by their release. Geological material will eventually become saturated, but material subjected to heat treatment will lose its trapped electrons. An artefact made from heat-treated material will subsequently re-accumulate trapped electrons, but these will be fewer than those in untreated material. MG measures surface gloss. An increased gloss on the flaked surface of a silcrete artefact is an indication of heat treatment, but it is only visible on surfaces that are flaked after heat treatment.

All three tests showed that the Pinnacle Point silcrete artefacts had been made from silcrete that had previously been heat treated. The thermoremnant magnetisation indicated heating to 300 – 400° Celsius; TL results were consistent with this finding. MG results showed that the flaked surfaces of heated experimental samples have a significantly higher gloss than those of unheated control samples. When the surface gloss of the Pinnacle Point artefacts was measured, it was found to be more similar to that of the heated experimental samples[124]. Heat treatment was once thought to have been a much later development: previously, the earliest evidence for its use was from the European Solutrean period, around 20,000 years ago[125,126].

Heat treatment was also used in conjunction with another Middle Stone Age innovation: pressure flaking. This is a technique used for finishing a stone artefact by exerting pressure with the sharp end of a tool close to the unfinished edges of the piece. As the technique requires the prior use of heat treatment to improve flaking properties, it was likewise thought to have been a much later development. However, experimentation and microscopic study have shown that it was used during the final shaping of projectile points made on heat-treated silcrete at the sites of Blombos Cave on the Southern Cape coast roughly 75,000 years ago[127] and Sibudu Cave, KwaZulu-Natal, more than 77,000 years ago[128].

The Sibudu Cave projectile points and other stone tools were hafted using compound adhesives. A compound adhesive is one in which two or more components are mixed before use and dried by fire after application. Traces of such an adhesive, consisting of red ochre and plant gum, have been found on points and cutting tools at the site. The points show micro-fractures consistent with having been hafted for use as spear tips. Experiments have shown that the ochre/gum adhesive forms a tough bond, preventing the projectile point from breaking away from its haft when used. Considerable experimentation would have been required by the Sibudu Cave people to find a satisfactory combination of ingredients[62].

Shedding a light on prehistoric cave art

The first Upper Palaeolithic cave art was discovered in 1879 at Altamira, a system of caves near the town of Santillana del Mar in northern Spain. Amateur geologist and archaeologist

Marcelino de Sautuola, whose daughter Maria first noticed the polychrome images of bison on the ceiling of one of the caves, was widely ridiculed for his claims that the cave art was ancient. However, more discoveries of cave art followed and in 1902, longstanding critic Émile Cartailhac conceded that he was wrong. Unfortunately, this vindication came too late for de Sautuola, who died in 1888[129].

One implication of the recognition that this cave art was prehistoric is that the cave artists must have had some means of producing light to illuminate cave walls often situated hundreds of meters from natural daylight. These would have been of three types: fixed fireplaces, torches, and lamps. In the same year that Cartailhac recanted his views, archaeologists exploring the cave site of La Mouthe, Dordogne, found a heavily burned sandstone lamp, depicting an ibis on its underside. Subsequently, almost any more or less hollow object with some semblance of a receptacle was identified as a lamp. It was assumed that like the stone lamps used by Inuit people, they used animal fat as fuel, but no systematic studies had been carried out. In the 1980s, researchers tried to address these issues, starting with the need to sift through the 547 artefacts listed as 'lamps' in scientific literature and museum collections[130,131].

Of the 547 possible lamps mentioned in literature and catalogues, 245 were ruled out as having clearly served other purposes, such as mortars or ochre receptacles. Of the remaining 302, 133 were either doubtful or simply unavailable for study, leaving 169 as certain, probable, or possible. Only 85 came into the 'certain' category. The 302 artefacts included 285 of known provenance, which came from 105 different sites, mainly in southwestern France. Evidence for use as a lamp includes traces of soot and charcoal and rubefaction (reddening due to heating) of the lamp itself. Thermal reddening occurs after only a few uses of a lamp and is a helpful indicator as to which of the artefacts under consideration served as lamps.

The lamps were classed into three categories: open-circuit, closed-circuit, and closed-circuit with a carved handle. The simplest type, the open-circuit lamp, is a flat or slightly concave slab, up to 200 mm (8 inches) across, with natural cavities through which excess fuel can drain away as the animal fat melts. They typically show no sign of carving or shaping and many may have gone unnoticed in past excavations. Hence, this type is probably underrepresented in the literature and catalogues. Any slab can be used as an open-circuit lamp, so little effort is required to make one. The disadvantage is that they are very wasteful of fuel. They were likely makeshift, single-use devices, used when no convenient alternative was at hand.

Closed-circuit bowl lamps have a shallow circular or oval depression to retain the fuel. They range from crude, unmodified or only slightly modified natural objects to entirely fabricated on both inside and exterior. They consist of oval or circular pieces of limestone or sandstone, with a sloping-sided bowl 15 to 20 mm (0.6 – 0.8 inches) deep but several centimetres in width, capable of holding up to 10 cc of fuel. The most intricate type has a carved handle. These lamps were finely shaped, finished, and decorated with engravings, and tended to be more recent than the other types. They do not occur until before the Solutrean period (22,000 – 18,000 years ago), although most of the 'certain' lamps in the sample were only slightly earlier. The most common type of lamp in the sample was a closed-circuit lamp with a sloping-sided rather than a vertical-sided depression. The sloping sides facilitate emptying the lamp to prevent the wick from becoming swamped in melting fat without dislodging it.

Both limestone and sandstone are reasonably abundant, but limestone often occurs naturally in slabs that require little modification. It also has the advantage of having a much lower thermal conductivity than sandstone. Limestone lamps do not heat up when in use, whereas sandstone lamps rapidly become too hot to handle. However, sandstone is an attractive material, and Upper Palaeolithic people got around its limitations by carving sandstone lamps with a handle.

The next stage of the study was to identify the materials used as fuels and for making wicks. The best animal fats are those that melt quickly and at a low temperature. Experiments showed that the most effective fats were those from seals, horses, and bovids. To determine whether these were the fuels favoured by Upper Palaeolithic people, researchers used vapour phase chromatography and mass spectrometry to determine the stable carbon isotopic ratios of residues obtained from several lamps in the sample. The ratios were consistent with the animal fats of modern herbivores, including pigs, horses, and cattle. They were quite different to the ratios that would be seen for vegetable fats, proving that animal fat had – as long suspected – been the fuel used in Upper Palaeolithic lamps. A good wick must be able to draw up fuel by capillary action and convey it to the burning end without itself burning up. Experiments showed that the most efficient wick materials were lichen, moss, and juniper. Residue analysis detected traces of all of these materials, and also conifers and grass.

The final stage of the investigation was to determine how much illumination could be provided by an Upper Palaeolithic lamp. The researchers measured the light output of modern replicas in the metrology labs of Kodak Pathé in France. The lamps provided distinctly less light than a modern candle, but sufficient to guide a person through a cave or illuminate artwork when held nearby. These limitations suggested that Upper Palaeolithic artists never saw their work as we now see it in photographs. Human colour perception becomes less effective at levels of illumination below 150 lux. For comparison, the illumination in a well-lit room is around 1,000 lux. It has been estimated that to provide this level of illumination along a 5 m (16.5 ft) panel would require 150 lamps placed at a distance of 0.5 m (1.6 ft) from the cave wall. Ten to fifteen lamps would provide an illumination of 20 lux. The dim, flickering light provided by a single lamp would allow only a small portion of an artwork to be viewed at a time – but this may have been the intended effect, as animals would have appeared to suddenly materialise out of the dark.

Inside the caves, lamps have been at strategic points, such as intersections between two galleries, where they were presumably left where they could easily be found and used. At some sites, caches of up to 70 lamps have been found, implying that they were stored at particular locations when not in use. Lamps are also frequently found near fireplaces, possibly to preheat them and make the fat easier to light, but more likely because the fires were places people returned to after venturing deeper into the caves. Many of these were found upside-down, suggesting that they were turned over to extinguish them when people returned. The use of lamps was not restricted to providing illumination inside caves, as many have been found at open-air sites. The average number of lamps found does not differ significantly between cave sites, rock shelters, and open-air sites, suggesting that they were standard items, used to provide night-time illumination at a campsite.

Since the 1980s, further studies have been conducted. In 2019, a team of researchers led by archaeologist María Ángeles Medina Alcaide investigated Cueva de Nerja, Málaga, one of the largest decorated cave sites in southern Spain. Inside the cave, several hollows formed by naturally occurring corrosive processes were interpreted as having been used as 'fixed lamps', with evidence for possible combustion including charcoal and smoke marks. To confirm this interpretation, one of the hollows was selected for study because it includes different types of combustion residue: charcoal, smoke, and possibly ash. The wood charcoal was identified as having originated from Scots pine or Black pine (*Pinus sylvestris* or *nigra*) and formed at combustion temperatures of 700 – 800 °C. These pines were probably chosen because they contain resin, which makes them excellent fuels. Radiocarbon dating suggested that the charcoal was 22,500 years old, corresponding to the Solutrean period. These results confirmed that this natural formation had been used as a fixed light source and that not all Upper Palaeolithic lamps were handheld portables[132].

In 2021, in an attempt to replicate the artificial lighting used by Upper Palaeolithic cave artists, Medina Alcaide and her colleagues conducted a series of experiments at Isuntza I, a cave in the Basque region of northern Spain[133]. The experimental lighting included five torches, two stone lamps, and one hearth fireplace. The torches were all made from branches of dry juniper wood 12 mm (½ inch) thick, joined together. Birch bark was added to the juniper branches as tinder, and pine resin and/or animal fat were added in various combinations to assess the effectiveness of the torches with those fuel types. The stone lamps were replicas of an example from La Mouthe Cave, Dordogne. The original was made from sandstone, 170 mm (6.7 inches) long by 120 mm (4.7 inches) wide, with a 150 cc capacity. Bovid marrow was used as the main fuel with three wicks arranged in a tepee shape, made from dried and crushed juniper wood. Pine resin was added in one experiment to test the effectiveness of this vegetable fuel. The fireplace was 230 mm (9 inches) in diameter by 7 cm (2 ¾ inches) long. It used a wood fuel of thin branches of dry juniper and oak wood, arranged in a tepee shape. Birch bark placed inside the combustion was used to start the fire.

The results suggested that the different lighting systems all had their particular advantages, suggesting their likely use in different contexts. The torches were most effective for exploring caves or crossing wide spaces. They projected light in all directions up to almost 6 m (20 ft), were easy to transport, and did not dazzle the user despite having a light intensity almost five times greater than a double-wicked grease lamp. They remained alight for periods ranging from 20 minutes to an hour. They did function erratically and required constant supervision when burning, although they were easy to relight by quickly moving from side to side to increase the flow of oxygen. The main disadvantage was the amount of smoke they emitted.

By contrast, the lamps were most effective for lighting small spaces over a long period. The light intensity was similar to a candle, with an effective range of up to 3 m (10 ft). Though they were not ideal for moving around due to their poor ground illumination, they burned consistently and without emitting much smoke for well over an hour, hence complementing the use of torches. The fireplace produced better illumination over a wider area, as might be expected. However, it was very smoky and had to be put out after half an hour. It had not been appropriately located regarding the air currents that are necessary to evacuate smoke and gas from the cave.

In summary, the experiments demonstrated that Upper Palaeolithic people had a range of lighting systems with diverse features. The selection of a particular system would have depended on the activity to be carried out, its duration, the distance to be traversed underground, and the available ventilation. The experiments indicated planning in the human use of caves during the Upper Palaeolithic and underlined the importance of lighting studies to understanding the activities carried out by our ancestors in the deep areas of caves.

Epilogue

The end of the last Ice Age and the beginning of the Holocene brought a warm, stable climate, and a transition from hunter-gathering to agriculture in many parts of the world. On the back of this, the first urban societies emerged, beginning around 3200 BCE in Mesopotamia and Egypt. Control of fire now unlocked another secret: metallurgy. Bronze had many advantages over stone. It was easier to work, more durable, and when damaged or worn out, bronze implements could be recycled by melting them down. Longer, thinner knives could be made from bronze, giving rise to a new class of bladed weapons: daggers and swords. Bronze was also used for making prestige goods, which were traded between elites in many parts of the world, especially in China.

The Urban Revolution was driven by the earlier Neolithic Revolution, or the transition to agriculture. Metallurgy, and hence fire, played only a supporting role. Large-scale metallurgy never emerged at all in the New World, and the great civilisations of the Inca, Maya, and Aztec remained essentially Stone Age. Fire's next Great Leap Forward came in the second half of the eighteenth century. The use of fossil fuels to augment wood and other biomass goes back to Roman times and earlier, but large-scale usage began with the Industrial Revolution. Fire, produced by the burning of coal, powered the furnaces and steam engines of the industrialising nation, beginning with Britain and soon followed by Belgium, France, Germany, Sweden, Japan, and the United States.

But from quite early on in the history of urban society, fire had demonstrated the capacity to get out of control. Many Bronze Age urban settlements contain ash layers, testifying to destruction by fire. Much of Rome was destroyed by fire in 64 CE. The 1666 Great Fire of London was certainly not the first major fire in the city. Roman Londinium was destroyed by fire during Boudicca's revolt in 60 CE, and this was followed by fires in 122 CE, 675 CE, and 1087 CE. Medieval London was devastated by fires in 1133 and 1212. Other cities experiencing devastating fires include Lübeck (1157, 1251, and 1276), Amsterdam (1421 and 1452), Utrecht (1253), Munich (1327), Moscow (1547 and 1571), Oslo (1624), Stockholm (1625), and Glasgow (1652). Despite improved firefighting measures, the nineteenth and early twentieth centuries saw many notable fires: New York City (1835 and 1845), Bucharest (1847), Toronto (1849 and 1904), San Francisco (1841 and 1906), Krakow (1850), Montreal (1852), Chicago (1871 and 1874), Vancouver (1886), and Thessaloniki (1917).

The twenty-first century has seen deadly bushfires and forest fires make the news with alarming regularity. That these fires are more frequent, more intense, and far harder to bring under control is no mystery. Anthropogenic climate change has increased the frequency of drought events, which leads to increases in both tree mortality and 'fuel aridity' (the extent to which vegetation has been dried out). These factors, inevitably, result in more frequent, more intense forest fires in seasonally dry fire-prone ecosystems[134]. Climate change is also responsible for epidemics of insects harmful to trees. The mountain pine beetle (*Dendroctonus ponderosae*) is native to western North America and is the most significant cause of insect-induced tree mortality in mature forests in the region. The warmer climate is now enabling it to thrive at higher elevations and latitudes. Worse, it is speeding the beetles' development, increasing their life cycle from one to two generations per year[135]. The consequence of this increased tree mortality is, of course, even more forest fires.

During the period from 2000 to 2015, it is estimated that global warming contributed to 75 per cent more forested areas in the western United States experiencing high fire-season fuel aridity and an average of nine extra days of high fire risk per year. Between 1984 and 2015, global warming is estimated to have been responsible for an additional 4.2 million ha (10.4 million acres) of forest being affected by fires, or almost double the area that might have been expected in its absence. Alarmingly, around three-quarters of these additional hectares of forest fires occurred during the second half of the period, from 2000 to 2015, highlighting an accelerating trend[136].

By making unrestricted use of fossil fuels, humans were squandering energy resources that had taken hundreds of millions of years to accumulate. That these resources are finite has long been appreciated: in his 1930 novel *Last and First Men*, the British author Olaf Stapledon anticipated a global societal collapse around the year 4000 CE following the exhaustion of the last coal fields[137]. Stapledon did not anticipate the deleterious effects that two millennia of CO_2 emissions would have on Earth's climate – but perhaps he should have because others were already aware of the issue.

That atmospheric CO_2 levels could affect the climate was first suggested as long ago as the mid-nineteenth century by American amateur scientist and women's rights campaigner Eunice Foote in 1856 [138] and independently by Irish physicist John Tyndall in 1861[139]. In 1896, the Swedish chemist Svante Arrhenius noted that the burning of coal could have a significant effect on atmospheric CO_2 levels[140]. At the time, few believed that human activities could significantly affect the climate. It was not until 1938 that British engineer Guy Callendar estimated that over the previous fifty years, human activities had added 150 billion tons of CO_2 to the atmosphere and that three-quarters of this had remained. He noted that CO_2 levels measured at Kew from 1898 to 1901 had averaged 274 PPM but levels measured from 1930 to 1936 in the eastern United States had averaged 310 PPM. His calculations suggested that this would lead to global temperatures increasing by 0.003 °C per year. However, based on data from 200 meteorological stations in Europe and the United States, he estimated that the actual rate of increase was 0.005 °C per year, or a total increase of 0.25 °C over half a century[141]. Despite subsequent work by Callendar[142,143] and Canadian physicist Gilbert Plass[144], the scientific community remained unconvinced that a significant increase in atmospheric CO_2 levels had been demonstrated and called for further evidence[145,146].

In 1956, two scientists at the Scripps Institution of Oceanography at La Jolla, CA, Roger Revelle and Hans Suess warned that although the increase in atmospheric CO2 levels was still small, "*it may become significant during future decades if industrial fuel combustion continues to rise exponentially*". Revelle and Suess noted that there was still a lack of accurate data and suggested that the upcoming 1957-58 International Geophysical Year presented an opportunity to obtain much of the necessary information[147]. Shortly after, postdoctoral researcher Charles Keeling joined the Scripps Institution of Oceanography. Keeling had spent the earlier part of the decade researching methods for accurately measuring atmospheric CO2 levels, and he obtained IGY funding to begin making regular measurements of atmospheric CO_2 levels in Antarctica and on Mauna Loa, Hawaii. Keeling found that there were seasonal variations in CO_2 levels due to the growth cycles of plants, but that year on year, they were increasing.

The observed increase was close to what could be expected if most, if not all, the CO_2 emissions from the combustion of fossil fuels remained in the atmosphere[148,149]. Though Keeling had to at times fight to secure funding CO_2 monitoring at Mauna Loa has continued to the present day. The oscillating curve that results when this data is plotted on a graph is now known as the Keeling Curve[149].

As the 1950s drew to a close, physicist Edward Teller addressed a symposium entitled *Energy and Man* at Columbia University attended by over three hundred government officials, economists, historians, scientists, and executives from a broad range of industries. He warned the attendees that increasing atmospheric CO_2 levels would result in the polar ice caps melting and coastal cities such as New York being inundated. Teller, known for his involvement with the Manhattan Project and his subsequent work on thermonuclear weapons, used the rest of his speech to advocate for the peaceful use of nuclear energy[150]. Further warnings soon followed: climate scientists Syukuro Manabe and Richard Wetherald estimated that a doubling of CO_2 levels would cause an increase of 2 °C in global temperatures[151] and glaciologist John Mercer echoed Teller's warning that the polar ice caps could melt[152]. Such forecasts sound eerily percipient now, more than half a century later.

It has been claimed that the risks of climate change were known in the oil industry in the 1970s or even the 1950s[153,154]. Regardless, as we have seen, there has been concern among the broader scientific community for at least that long. Even the late 1980s, when the words 'greenhouse effect' entered widespread public consciousness, now lie almost four decades in the past. We have had plenty of time to stop the gift of Prometheus from getting dangerously out of control, and we must act now before it is too late.

07: Neanderthals

Introduction

In March 2021, the United States was beginning to emerge from the worst of the COVID-19 pandemic. In response to what he thought was the premature easing of mask-wearing requirements in Texas and Mississippi, newly elected President Joe Biden said, *"The last thing we need is Neanderthal thinking that in the meantime everything's fine, take off your mask, forget it. It still matters"*.

The Neanderthal Museum, located in the Neander Valley that gave the species its name, took to Twitter and retorted "#Neanderthals were smarter than you think!" Back in the United States, Sen. Marco Rubio, R-Fla. said on Twitter that the President's comments were an insult to the populations of Asia, Europe, and America, who *"inherit about two per cent of their genes"* from Neanderthals and suggested that he apologise and take *"unconscious bias training"*. Fellow Republican Sen. Marsha Blackburn, R-Tenn., speaking on Fox News, weighed in with, *"…because Neanderthals are hunter-gatherers, they're protectors of their family, they are resilient, they're resourceful, they tend to their own, So, I think Joe Biden needs to rethink what he is saying about the states that are choosing to move away from these mask mandates"*. Albeit the timing was a little suspicious, the GOP's sudden concern for the public image of Neanderthals was certainly welcome.

A quick search on Google will show just how widespread the use of the word 'Neanderthal' is as a slur. In September 2010, British politician Simon Hughes (Lib-Dem) used it to describe opposition to voting reform ahead of a referendum on replacing the United Kingdom's First Past the Post voting system. *"I think it is an entirely winnable campaign but only if we are really clear that people defending first past the post are Neanderthal"*, he said. In March 2015, complaining about sexual harassment in the House of Commons, Emily Thornbury (Lab) said, *"Some of the comments you get are just, you think, Neanderthal really"*. Two years earlier, Nicholas Watt, then the chief political correspondent for *The Guardian*, reported that *"Many women at Westminster – MPs, aides, ministers, lobbyists, and journalists – complain of encountering neanderthal* [sic] *behaviour among prominent parliamentarians"*.

Why would three liberal-minded politicians and a highly respected journalist make casual use of the word 'Neanderthal' as a slur? Why would the many other equally respectable people brought up by my search do so? The Merriam-Webster online thesaurus gives a clue. It lists words including 'clodhopper', 'hulk', 'lout', 'lump', and 'oaf' as synonyms of 'Neanderthal'. It has long been clear that such comparisons are entirely inappropriate, but how did they come about and why are they so persistent? It is a story that goes back to the discovery of the first Neanderthal remains in the mid-nineteenth century, at a time when Darwin and Wallace were working on the theory of natural selection, and archaeologists were seeking proof that humans had existed for far longer than was allowed for by Biblical timescales.

There is a darker side to the story: how for decades, Neanderthal remains were studied in the context of views about 'race' that most would now associate with the Nazis and the far right. Furthermore, many anthropologists expressed views about living populations that were overtly racist and used terminology that is now considered to be derogatory. While it is dismaying that some European and American scholars once held such views, it is important to recognise that they do not have the slightest validity and are not held by anybody in the scientific community today.

Discovery at Neander Valley

Neanderthals take their name from Neander Tal ('Neander Valley', then spelt Neander Thal), an undistinguished limestone valley located 13 km (7.5 miles) to the east of Düsseldorf. Until the middle of the nineteenth century, the valley was delineated by limestone walls that rose as high as 50 m (165 ft) above the river and extended for slightly less than 1 km (0.64 miles) in an east-west direction[1]. The Neander Valley in turn is named for Joachim Neander (1650-1680), a local Calvinist theologian and hymnist, who composed around sixty hymns during a life cut short by tuberculosis. His best-known work is the popular hymn *Lobe den Herren, den mächtigen* (*Praise to the Lord, the Almighty*). The name 'Neander' is a Greek translation of his original family name Neumann (corresponding to the English surname Newman), which was adopted by his grandfather following the fashion of the time for 'classical-sounding' names. Thus, the literal meaning of Neanderthal is (ironically) New Man's Valley.

Early nineteenth-century descriptions of the Neander Valley note that there were many caves and rock shelters of various sizes along the valley walls on both sides of the river. One of the smaller caves on the south side of the river was known as the Kleine Feldhofer Grotte, taking its name from a nearby farm[1]. The cave was "…*high enough to admit a man, and about 15 feet deep from the entrance, which is 7 or 8 feet* [2.0 – 2.5 m] *wide, exists in the southern wall of the gorge of the Neanderthal, as it is termed, at a distance of about 100 feet* [30 m] *from the Düssel, and about 60 feet* [18 m] *above the bottom of the valley*"[2]. Originally, the cave "…*opened upon a narrow plateau lying in front of it, and from which the rocky wall descended almost perpendicularly into the river. It could be reached, though with difficulty, from above*"[2].

It was in the Kleine Feldhofer Grotte that the first Neanderthal remains to be recognised as such were discovered in August 1856. By the middle of the nineteenth century, the Industrial Revolution had transformed Düsseldorf into a boom town, and limestone was much in demand for the steel and construction industries. Two years before the discovery, businessmen Wilhelm Beckershoff and Friedrich Wilhelm Pieper had established the Aktiengesellschaft für Marmorindustrie Neanderthal ("Neander Valley Joint-stock company for marble industry") and commenced extensive quarrying operations in the Neander Valley. These operations would eventually remove the whole of the south wall and much of the north wall of the valley, together with the caves therein. Whenever the quarriers encountered a cave, it was necessary to remove deposits on the cave floors to avoid contamination of the limestone during the quarrying operations. Accordingly, two workmen emptied Kleine Feldhofer Grotte of its deposits, dumping the material onto the valley floor 60 feet [18 m] below[1].

The circumstances of the discovery were chronicled by a local schoolteacher and amateur naturalist, Johann Carl Fuhlrott, who took possession of the remains. According to Fuhlrott, the remains were found about 2 feet [0.6 m] below the surface of the deposit, but they were covered in mineral deposits and had not been recognised as bones until after they were thrown out of the cave. It so happened that Beckershoff had been on-site, and he instructed the workers to look out for other bones. At the end of August, Pieper contacted Fuhlrott and invited him to visit the site. Fuhlrott noted that the bones were initially thought to be from a cave bear, and he suspected that this was probably the only reason that they had been saved. He also suspected that the quarry workers, unaware of the importance of the find, had saved only the larger bones. He pronounced the remains to be human and identified a skullcap, two thigh bones, three bones from the right arm, two from the left arm, part of the pelvis, fragments of a shoulder blade, and ribs. Fuhlrott noted that the remains were unlike those of modern humans. The braincase was long and low, quite different to the globular cranium of present-day people. The browridges were massive in comparison to those of a modern human, and they were completely fused together[3].

Newspaper reports of the discovery soon attracted the interest of anatomists Hermann Schaaffhausen and August Franz Mayer at the University of Bonn. Schaaffhausen was only able to procure a plaster cast of the skullcap, but this was sufficient to convince him that the remains were worthy of further investigation. On 4 February 1857, he presented his initial findings at a meeting of the Lower Rhine Medical and Natural History Society in Bonn[4]. Subsequently, Fuhlrott brought the remains to Bonn for a more accurate anatomical examination. He found Mayer bedridden with illness, but Schaaffhausen took over the examination of the bones "*with willing zeal*"[3].

With access to several important collections of human skulls, Schaaffhausen made a comparative study of the Feldhofer skull. He measured its cranial volume by filling it first with water, then with millet seed. He noted, as had Fuhlrott, that the skull was long and low rather than globular, with massive browridges that coalesced in the middle. Nothing comparable could be found among the other skulls he examined. The cranial volume of 1,033.24 cc, on the other hand, suggested that the brain size was within the range of modern populations. The postcranial remains were unusually robust, with large muscle attachments, suggesting that the Feldhofer individual had been very powerfully built. The skull was consistent with this supposition: the prominent browridges were no more than a side effect of the expanded frontal sinuses required to cater for the enhanced oxygen needs of such an individual[2].

Schaaffhausen believed that regardless of the skull's other peculiarities, its cranial volume suggested that the Feldhofer individual was human. Certainly, the brain size was well above the 750 cc that Scottish anatomist Sir Arthur Keith later described as "*the mental Rubicon which has to be crossed before the term 'human' can be claimed or admitted*". Keith chose this figure as being the midpoint between the largest known brain size for a gorilla (650 cc) and the smallest known adult brain size for a modern human (855 cc)[5]. Although Schaaffhausen did not compare the Feldhofer remains to those of other primates, he did note that such "*crania exist among living savages, which, though not exhibiting such a remarkable conformation of the forehead, which gives the skull somewhat the aspect of that of the large apes*"[2].

Schaaffhausen noted that the massive browridges were also characteristic of the large apes, albeit in their case not a side effect of the expansion of the frontal sinuses. Again, though, he argued that this feature was not diagnostic of an ape and that the Feldhofer individual had been human. He noted that "*traces of which can be perceived even at the present time, occurs most frequently in the crania of barbarous, and especially of northern races, to some of which a high antiquity must be assigned, it may fairly be supposed that a conformation of this kind represents the faint vestiges of a primitive type, which is manifested in the most remarkable manner in the Neanderthal cranium, and which must have given the human visage an unusually savage aspect*"[2].

Fuhlrott and Schaaffhausen subsequently reported their findings at the General Meeting of the Natural History Society of Prussian Rhineland and Westphalia on 2 June 1857. Fuhlrott spoke first, presenting an account of the discovery. He was followed by Schaaffhausen, who presented a report of the results of his anatomical examination. Schaaffhausen's main conclusions were, firstly, that the skull's unusual shape was due to "*a natural conformation hitherto not known to exist, even in the most barbarous races*", secondly, that the Feldhofer individual had belonged to "*one of the wild races of Northwestern Europe*" that predated the early Germanic and Celtic peoples, thirdly, that the remains dated to a period when "*the latest animals of the diluvium still existed*"[2]. 'Diluvium' literally means 'the flood', originally the Biblical Flood, but now taken broadly to be the Pleistocene. We now know that the Feldhofer remains are 42,000 years old[1]. In his concluding remarks, Schaaffhausen said that "*the human bones and cranium from the Neanderthal exceed all the rest in those peculiarities of conformation which lead to the conclusion of their belonging to a barbarous and savage race*"[2]. Although aspects of the Feldhofer individual's anatomy were outside the range of living populations, Schaaffhausen believed that it was no more than an ancient representative of our own species, albeit "*barbarous and savage*".

A most brutal assessment

Not everybody was convinced. The notable German pathologist Rudolf Virchow, known as the "father of modern pathology", was sceptical. He did not examine the remains until 1872, but he believed that they had belonged to an individual who had suffered from rickets in childhood and age-related osteoarthritis. The unusual skull shape he attributed to a combination of senile atrophy, age-related hyperostosis, craniosynostosis, and head injury[9]. British anthropologist Charles Carter Blake suggested that the skull "*belonged to some poor idiotic hermit whose remains were found in the cave where he died*"[10,11]. August Franz Mayer claimed that the Feldhofer remains belonged to a Mongolian Cossack suffering from rickets, who had deserted from the Russian army prior to the Battle of Paris in 1814, and sought refuge in the cave[12].

The problem for German scholars was a lack of convincing evidence for the supposedly great antiquity of the Feldhofer remains. Human antiquity was one of the hot topics of the day, but it did not become widely accepted until the end of the 1850s. Evidence was accumulating that humans had once lived alongside mammoths and other extinct animals, and the case was finally proven by the British scholars Joseph Prestwich and John Evans in 1859. The pair visited French archaeologist Jacques Boucher de Perthes at Abbeville in northern France, and they were convinced by his claims to have found human-made stone artefacts accompanying the remains of elephants and rhinoceros, which had long been extinct in France. Prestwich and Evans were supported by Sir Charles Lyell, the leading

British geologist of the time, and previously a sceptic of the 'Antiquity of Man'[13].

Were the Feldhofer remains genuinely fossilised? Fuhlrott believed that they were. Mayer had noticed dendritic deposits (small branching crystals) on the surfaces of the remains, which Fuhlrott took as evidence for fossilisation[3]. But, according to Schaaffhausen, Mayer himself did not regard the presence or absence of dendritic deposits as indicative of the great antiquity or recent age of the objects upon which they occur. Mayer was also sceptical of the efficacy of the so-called 'tongue test'. This involved licking a bone to see if it stuck to the tongue. If it did, it was likely to be fossilised; if not, then it was probably recent. But Mayer possessed the skull of a dog from a Roman site, which likewise stuck to the tongue despite being less than two thousand years old[2].

Another issue was the lack of geological context for the remains: vital geological information had been lost because the bones and deposits in which they lay had been dumped out of the Feldhofer cave without any *in situ* examination being conducted. In 1858, Fuhlrott questioned the two workers who had made the find in the hope that they could recall additional details that could be important. It was a long shot after so much time had passed, and in the event, Fuhlrott learned very little. The two men also appear to have been intimidated by the lawyer Fuhlrott brought with him[14].

Unable to gain acceptance for the fossils in Germany, Fuhlrott and Schaaffhausen contacted Sir Charles Lyell, who duly visited the Neander Valley in 1860. He found that the original cave "*…had been almost entirely quarried away… its complete destruction seemed near at hand*", although he was able to make a rudimentary assessment of its likely stratigraphy. While noting the caveats attached to these diagnostics, Lyell concluded that the "*profusion of dendritic crystallisations*" covering the remains and application of the 'tongue test' to them suggested that they were probably "*about the same age as those found by Schmerling in the Liège caverns*"[15]. The latter were human remains discovered in 1829 by Dutch palaeontologist Philippe-Charles Schmerling (1791-1836) at Engis Cave, near the village of Awirs, Belgium. They included the partial skull of an elderly individual (Engis 1), the skull of a juvenile (Engis 2), a fragmentary upper jawbone with two badly worn molar teeth, and miscellaneous postcranial bones including vertebrae, metatarsals, and phalanges. The juvenile skull, though initially intact, was so fragile that fell to pieces during extraction, and attempts to reconstruct it had been unsuccessful. Unlike the Feldhofer remains, the Engis Cave remains were found in association with the remains of woolly mammoths and woolly rhinoceros[16], meaning that they were undoubtedly very ancient.

Lyell had learned little new, but his generally sympathetic conclusions added authority to the claims of great antiquity for the remains. He also brought back a plaster cast of the skull, which on returning to England, he showed to Thomas Henry Huxley and George Busk. Both men were prominent figures in the Victorian scientific establishment. Huxley was the Professor of Natural History at the Royal School of Mines (now part of Imperial College) and the Fullerian Professor of Physiology at the Royal Institution of Great Britain. He had originally been a sceptic, and in 1862 in a lecture at the Royal Institution of Great Britain, he had maintained that the Engis and Neanderthal skulls were little different in configuration and development from those of Aboriginal Australians. At this point, however, he had relied solely on the rather inadequate descriptions and illustrations published by Schaaffhausen[17]. Busk was the Hunterian Professor of Comparative Anatomy and Physiology at the Royal College of Surgeons.

The Feldhofer skull and its cast occupied Huxley and Busk for the next few years. Busk[2] translated Schaaffhausen's 1857 report to the Natural History Society of Prussian Rhineland and Westphalia[18]. Huxley[16], for his part, partially translated Schmerling's 1833 report[19] of his discovery at Engis Cave. Busk and Huxley compared the skull cast with skulls from the large collection in the Hunterian Museum at the Royal College of Surgeons, using anatomical landmarks and systematic measurements. They exchanged correspondence with Schaaffhausen and Fuhlrott, and the latter provided photographs of the original skull from various angles[20,21]. Unlike Schaaffhausen, they considered the skulls of non-human primates as well as those of humans. What they failed to do at any stage was to consider the postcranial remains. In Germany, the skull had been considered in the context of the postcranial material, whereas in Britain Lyell's plaster cast had shifted the focus solely to the skull[21].

Huxley and Busk agreed with Schaaffhausen that the skull was human but of great antiquity. However, they differed from Schaaffhausen's interpretation of the skull's massive browridges. Busk showed that there was no correlation in other groups between such a large browridge and the extension of the sinuses. Instead of attributing them to frontal sinus enlargement, he viewed them as an apelike feature, similar to those of chimpanzees and gorillas[17].

Their definitive conclusions were published firstly in February 1863 as a section in Lyell's *The Geological Evidences of the Antiquity of Man*[15]. Lyell quoted "*Observations by Professor Huxley on the human skulls of Engis and Neanderthal*". Huxley noted that the Feldhofer skull was "*extremely different in appearance from the Engis cranium*". However, he was unable to study the broken fragments of the juvenile Engis 2 skull. It would eventually turn out that Engis 2 was a Neanderthal, but it was not identified as such until 1936[20]. The elderly Engis 1 skull is now thought to have been a modern human[22]. Lyell's work described the Feldhofer skull as "*the most brutal of all known human skulls*", bearing numerous resemblances to those of the apes including the massive browridges and the long and low shape of the braincase.

Huxley's more detailed conclusions followed in *Evidence as to Man's Place in Nature*[23], which was published two weeks later. Huxley also emphasised the apelike nature of the skull, describing it as the "*most pithecoid* [apelike] *of human crania yet discovered*". Nevertheless, the fact that the cranial volume fell within the human range qualified the Feldhofer individual as human. Huxley went on to say that the skull "*is by no means so isolated as it appears to be at first, but forms, in reality, the extreme term of a series leading gradually from it to the highest and best developed of human crania*". Apelike characteristics, while very pronounced in the Feldhofer skull, were not unique to it, but could also be seen to "*prevail universally among the lower races of mankind*".

Huxley's underlying methodology was to argue that skull growth in mammals followed a general pattern. He concluded that in a progression from 'lower' to 'higher' mammalian crania, the basicranial axis became shorter relative to the skull length; as the face became increasingly flexed downward relative to the braincase, so the angle of the face to the braincase became more acute and the braincase became increasingly more vaulted or globular, with a concomitant heightening and backward extension of the cerebrum. Having established a supposed hierarchy of mammalian skulls from the lowest species (rodents) to the highest (humans), Huxley extended the scheme to 'races' within *Homo sapiens*. He made comparisons between the skulls of Aboriginal Australians, Blacks, and Caucasoids, and tried to accommodate the Feldhofer skull within this paradigm[22]. Thus, Huxley regarded the Feldhofer skull as lying on the extreme end of a human continuum ranging from the 'best developed' (i.e., European) to the 'lower races'.

A new human species

At this stage, there had been no suggestion that the Feldhofer individual, if human, belonged to a species other than *Homo sapiens*. It fell to Anglo-Irish geologist William King to raise the possibility that it might. King was the first Professor of Mineralogy and Geology at Queen's College Galway (now Ollscoil na Gaillimhe – University of Galway), having moved to Ireland from the northeast of England in 1849. In 1882, he was appointed Professor of Natural History at Queen's. He was nevertheless something of an outsider in the Victorian paleoanthropological community. Both geographically and socially, he was located on the periphery of the London-based intellectual elite. Despite his undoubted contributions to the field of geology, he never became a Fellow of the Geological Society of London or the Geological Society of London[24].

King had little experience with primates or human variation prior to taking an interest in the Feldhofer remains. His interest might have been sparked by reading Lyell's *The Geological Evidences of the Antiquity of Man*. By August 1863, he had acquired a cast of the Feldhofer skull from a Mr. Gregory, a fossil and mineral dealer in London. He also began familiarising himself with skulls belonging to the major 'races' of humans in the various collections he had access to, and in September 1863, he attended the Thirty-Third Meeting of the British Association for the Advancement of Science (BAAS) in Newcastle[24].

King gave a presentation at the meeting, which is described briefly in the BAAS report of the meeting, and where King is referred to in the third person[25]. Another account, also in the third person, appeared in The Anthropological Review[26]. King's later, more detailed article in the *Quarterly Journal of Science*[27] may be the only actual writing on the matter[24].

King's presentation began by stating that the mental abilities of *Homo sapiens* place the existing human races above the highest anthropoid apes, albeit to different degrees. Although it is widely believed that these abilities are generic, there is no reason to suppose there have in the past been species within the genus *Homo* that lacked them. King went on to note that Andamaners (Andaman Islanders) possess only *"the dimmest conception"* of God or moral obligations and that *"Psychical gifts of a lower grade than those characterising the Andamaner cannot be conceived to exist: they stand next to brute benightedness"*. Yet, he argued, Andaman Islanders are *"essentially human"* and their braincases *"conform to the highest cranial type of our species"*. The Neanderthal skull, on the other hand, *"offers only approximate resemblances to that of Man, that it more closely agrees with the cranial type of the Chimpanzee"*. King noted that the mental faculties of the latter are *"unimprovable - incapable of moral and theositic conceptions"* and that he saw *"no reason to believe otherwise than that similar darkness characterized the being to which the fossil belonged"*. He concluded, *"that the thoughts and desires which once dwelt* [within the Feldhofer skull] *never soared beyond that of the brute"*. Accordingly, he proposed to distinguish the Neanderthal species from *Homo sapiens* by giving it the name *Homo neanderthalensis*.

In a footnote to his more detailed description of the Feldhofer skull, published in January 1864, King rejected Huxley's view that the Feldhofer skull was merely an extreme on a human continuum. But he also retracted his suggestion that the Feldhofer skull should be described as *Homo neanderthalensis* and now felt that it should not be included in *Homo* at all[27].

He gave no reason for this, proposed no alternative designation, and never commented on the matter again[20]. Despite the retraction, the name *Homo neanderthalensis* stood, thereby ensuring a second claim to fame for Joachim Neander. But it could easily have been very different.

Homo calpicus

The Feldhofer discovery was not the first Neanderthal fossil to be found. The Gibraltar skull, an adult female now known as Gibraltar 1, was discovered in 1848 at a site known locally as Forbes' Quarry. Unlike the Feldhofer remains, it was largely ignored until it was sent to London in 1864 and came to the attention of British palaeontologists Hugh Falconer and George Busk. In sharp contrast to the Feldhofer remains, very little is known about the early post-discovery history of the Forbes' skull.

Decades later, in 1910, Sir Arthur Keith obtained some of the missing detail from Col. Edward Kenyon, Commandant of the Royal Engineers at Gibraltar. According to Kenyon, the Forbes' cranium was first mentioned by Lieut. Edmund Flint, Secretary of the Gibraltar Scientific Society, in the minutes of a meeting held on 3 March 1848, where there is an entry reading "*Presented a human skull from Forbes' Quarry, North Front, by the Secretary*". Kenyon noted that "*old plans have been examined, and no place named 'Forbes* [without the apostrophe] *Quarry' can be found*", but he had no doubt that it was a disused limestone quarry south-east of "*the ancient 'Forbes Barrier'. The obsolete batteries there near there are the 'Forbes Batteries', and these are the only sites to which the name 'Forbes' is attached*". Kenyon also noted that the last recorded meeting of the Society was held in May 1853 and that Flint died in Mauritius on 12 January 1857, having attained the rank of captain[28].

More recently, researcher Alex Menez has carried out extensive research in an attempt to fill in some of the gaps[29]. Menez is an Honorary Fellow of the Gibraltar National Museum and is President of the Gibraltar Scientific Society. The latter was re-established in 2015, more than 150 years after it disbanded. The Society was originally founded on 19 October 1835 with Dr Edward John Burrow as president. In 1840, it was renamed the Gibraltar Museum Society, reflecting the membership's interest in collecting natural history specimens, coins, antiquities, and other items. In June 1844, Edmund Flint was placed in charge of the collection. He was aged 19 at the time, so must only have been in his early thirties when he died.

Flint presented the Forbes' skull to the Society on 3 March 1848, but no further mention of it is made in the minutes, and nothing is known about any discussion of it that might have ensued. The skull was covered with a limestone matrix, which to some extent hid its shape and features; possibly this was why it was not initially seen as anything out of the ordinary. Only after the matrix had been partially removed (with some difficulty) by Busk did its unusual characteristics become apparent.

Even the skull's finder is unknown, although it is generally supposed to have been Flint. British anatomist Bernard Wood[30,31] has suggested that it was an Army officer by the name of Capt. Frederick Brome, Governor of the Gibraltar garrison's Military Prison on Windmill Hill. Brome was a keen fossil collector who undertook the excavation of many caves in Gibraltar, most notably the nearby Genista Cave beneath Windmill Hill. To assist with these endeavours, he employed some of the prisoners in his charge. Unfortunately, his scientific enthusiasm was not shared by his superiors, and he was sacked from his post and dismissed from the Army[28].

Menez suggests that if Brome had been the finder, he would have made this known to Falconer and Busk when they visited Gibraltar. Two months after Flint presented the skull, Brome himself became a member of the Society, and he would surely have discussed its discovery with Flint. If the latter had been the finder, that information would likewise have been passed on.

Although it is often claimed that the Forbes' skull was left to gather dust following its presentation to the Society, Menez disputes this. The minutes of the Society refer to the purchasing and cataloguing of items for its collection. Scientific apparatus were displayed and their workings were explained. All of this points to a well-curated collection. However, Menez notes that in 1851, the Society's museum was subsumed by the Gibraltar Garrison Library. Bereft of its collection, the Society reverted to its original name, and two years later it was disbanded. Following the demise of the Society, the collection was neglected. By 1861, it had been moved to the Soldiers' Home, which was an institution set up to provide NCOs and privates with "*some means of improving their minds and of rationally and innocently employing their leisure hours*"[32]. Busk[33] noted the skull "*was originally deposited in a museum of natural curiosities, which at some time existed at Gibraltar, but which has been allowed to fall into a state of confusion and neglect*".

Menez confirmed that the name 'Forbes' Quarry' was not used on any official map and only appeared on those in scientific journals or books concerned with palaeoanthropology. The name might have been used by Flint and by others for the area around Forbes' Barrier, North Front, where quarrying was then taking place. Menez notes that George Forbes (1685–1765) was a naval officer who took part in the capture of Gibraltar in 1704. The skull's findspot remains unknown and the jawbone has never been found. Such matrix that remains attached to the skull might be of assistance in determining its provenance, but quarrying has long since removed breccias that could be matched against it.

To recap, a decade after the Gibraltar Scientific Society disbanded, the fossil that would become its major claim to fame languished as part of a now-neglected collection at a 'home' intended to help bored soldiers stay on the straight and narrow. Menez[29] notes that late in 1863, British physician Thomas Hodgkin (1798-1866) made a short visit to Gibraltar before travelling on to Morocco. Best known for his work with lymphoma, Hodgkin was treasurer of the Newcastle branch of the BAAS and would almost certainly have attended the meeting where King had described the Feldhofer skull. While in Gibraltar, he was introduced to Brome and viewed material from Genista Cave. We know that he saw the Forbes' skull because Busk[34] noted that the "*extraordinary peculiarities* [of the cranium] *fortunately struck the notice of Dr. Hodgkin in a visit paid by that ethnologist to Gibraltar in the course of last year*". Hodgkin himself never mentioned the cranium in any of his writings.

Even before Hodgkin's visit, material from Genista Cave and other sites in Gibraltar was being sent to Busk by Brome and others. Busk[34] mentions the receipt of several consignments before Brome sent the Forbes' skull. Menez[29] notes that for Hodgkin to have seen the cranium while viewing the Genista Cave material and Brome to have sent it to London implies that the latter must have taken possession of it at some stage after the Gibraltar Scientific Society disbanded.

On receiving the cranium, Busk immediately recognised that it *"resembles in all essential particulars, including its great thickness, the far-famed Neanderthal skull"*. He noted that the Forbes' skull was better preserved than the Feldhofer skull; unlike the latter, almost the entire face was intact. However, the real importance of the find was the confirmation that the Feldhofer skull was not a one-off peculiarity. The two fossils were possibly representatives of *"a race extending from the Rhine to the Pillars of Hercules"*. Busk set down his conclusions in a note entitled *Pithecoid Priscan Man from Gibraltar* ('apelike ancient man from Gibraltar'), published in *The Reader* on 23 July 1864, with the promise of a full description to follow[34]. We now know that the Forbes' skull belonged to a female[35], and Busk's bold assessment of the Neanderthal range was a huge underestimate.

In a letter obtained by Sir Arthur Keith dated 27 August (the year is missing, but was certainly 1864), Falconer wrote to Busk proposing the name *Homo calpicus*, derived from the Roman name for Gibraltar, Mons Calpe, and suggesting that it was less of a mouthful than 'Pithecoid Priscan Man'[28]. Falconer's humorous suggestion was never taken up. In September 1864, Busk gave a presentation at the Thirty-Fourth Meeting of the BAAS in Bath, where he noted that there were similarities between the Gibraltar and Feldhofer specimens[36], but apparently, neither he nor Falconer claimed that the Forbes' skull represented a human species distinct from *Homo sapiens*. Unfortunately, the contents of Falconer's presentation are not known as it appears not to have been printed and the BAAS report consists only of the title[24]. With no written record of the name having been proposed, it would not have been valid even if it had had priority[17].

Technically, it was already too late by almost a year to secure priority *Homo calpicus*. But, given King's retraction of *Homo neanderthalensis*, it might still have been adopted had it been formally proposed. In the event, it never was, and Falconer died early in 1865, having been in poor health for some years. The full description of the Forbes' skull that Busk had promised was never completed[37]. In a 1913 report to the Smithsonian, Czech anthropologist Aleš Hrdlička noted that the *"semihuman, apish"* skull was presented the skull to the Hunterian Museum at the Royal College of Surgeons by Busk in 1868. It was a *"highly valuable but comparatively little known specimen"* that was now *"universally recognised as a representative, possibly a very early one, of Homo neanderthalensis"*[38]. The Forbes' skull now resides in the collection of the Natural History Museum, London. The Museum's website notes that the skull is thought to be about 50,000 years old, but the dating is not very precise.

Naming Neanderthal

King died in 1886 without seeing his proposed *Homo neanderthalensis* become widely accepted. Neanderthals were widely regarded as no more than representatives of an earlier phase of what American anthropologist Lewis H. Morgan termed the 'Period of Savagery'[39]. It has been suggested that the fuller description given in his January 1864 paper would meet the standards of the International Commission on Zoological Nomenclature[17], even though he retracted the name in the same paper. The International Commission was not founded until 1895 but the BAAS had its own set of rules, established in 1842 by a committee appointed for that purpose. The committee's report[40] was the earliest to codify rules of priority for naming species[24].

In the same year that King died, more Neanderthal remains were recovered. The discovery was made at Spy d'Orneau, a cave under a limestone promontory near the small village of Spy in central Belgium. The cave was discovered at the start of the decade, and soon yielded fossils and stone tools. In 1885, the cave was investigated by archaeologist Marcel de Puydt and Max Lohest, a geologist from the University of Liège. Much of the cave had been disturbed by amateurs, but they found an undisturbed terrace at the mouth of the case. In July 1886, in one of the lowest levels of this terrace, they found the exceptionally well-preserved skeletons of two Neanderthals with skeletal elements from almost the entire body. They were found in association with stone tools of a type known as Mousterian, known for the site of Le Moustier, in the Dordogne region of southern France. This tool type would become virtually synonymous with Neanderthals. Puydt and Lohest had no practical knowledge of anatomy, so they enlisted the help of University of Liège anatomist Julien Fraipont. Lohest and Fraipont published a monograph on the find in 1887. Their report was of a very high standard, with excellent documentation of the geological context, precise measurements, and detailed descriptions of the find[20].

Any lingering doubts about what the Feldhofer and Forbes' remains represented were now banished. With the Spy remains, the anatomy of Neanderthals was becoming better understood, and the case for recognising them as a group distinct from *Homo sapiens* was not unreasonable[41]. Irish journalist Augustus Keane, writing in *Nature*, noted that *"The canines and incisors of cranium, trunk, and limbs are distinctly human, while the cranial capacity alone would suffice to justify the claim of Homo neanderthalensis to membership with the human rather than with the simian family. However great the distance separating him even from the lowest of modern races, far greater, undoubtedly, is the interval between him and the highest of the modern anthropoids"*[42].

However, the designation *Homo neanderthalensis* was not immediately adopted, and other suggestions were being made. German zoologist Ernst Haeckel had previously made two suggestions, *Protanthropus atavus* ('forefather') and *Homo primigenius* ('primitive man'), for a Pleistocene early human, and in 1895 he declared that the Feldhofer and Spy remains fell into this category[41]. Another suggestion was that Neanderthals were a regional variety of *Pithecanthropus*[41]. This designation was originally created by Haeckel for a hypothetical human ancestor *Pithecanthropus alalus* ('speechless ape-man'). It was adopted late in 1892 by the Dutch physician and anthropologist Eugène Dubois for the skull and thigh bone he had discovered at Trinil, Java while serving as a medic with the Dutch army.

Dubois believed that his discovery was an intermediate between humans and apes and named it *Pithecanthropus erectus* ('erect ape-man'). He published his conclusions in 1894 and gave presentations on his return to Europe the following year, but he met with considerable scepticism. The skull was widely dismissed as belonging to a gibbon and its claimed association with the thighbone was disputed (the latter is now thought to be modern). Support for *Pithecanthropus* eventually came from German anthropologist Gustav Schwalbe, after viewing the remains Dubois had brought back from Java. Beginning in 1899, he published extensively on the skull, in far greater detail than Dubois and his work was far better received. Dubois subsequently withdrew all access to his fossils, though this may have had more to do with protecting his intellectual property rights than pique at having his thunder stolen[20,43].

Along with American zoologist Edward Drinker Cope, Schwalbe used King's *Homo neanderthalensis*, but in 1902 Schwalbe proposed reorganising the genus *Homo*, replacing *Homo sapiens* with *Homo hodiernus* ('today's man'), and adopting *Homo primigenius* for Neanderthals. He proposed two phylogenies: one postulated that *Pithecanthropus* was the direct ancestor of modern humans, and Neanderthals were an extinct side branch on the other. The second postulated a line of evolution from *Pithecanthropus* to Neanderthal (*Homo primigenius*) to modern humans (*Homo hodiernus*) without branching[20,41,44].

Pithecanthropus erectus was reclassified as *Homo erectus* by German biologist Ernst Mayr. *Homo primigenius* was widely used by German anthropologists until well into the twentieth century and was frequently seen in journal articles as late as the mid-century. By this time, however, *Homo neanderthalensis* King 1864 was internationally recognised as being the correct name[41]. This remained the case despite a change in the German spelling of Neander Valley in 1901. Neander Thal became Neander Tal, hence the informal term 'Neanderthal' is often spelled 'Neandertal'. There was no change in pronunciation: the 'h' had been silent, as in the name 'Thompson'.

Boule's error

During the first decade of the twentieth century, several important Neanderthal finds were made, which regularly feature in anthropological literature to this day. These include Le Moustier, Krapina (Croatia), and La Chapelle-aux-Saints. The latter is a small cave site in central France. On 3 August 1908, two brothers, recently ordained Catholic priests Amédée Bouyssonie and Jean Bouyssonie were excavating the cave when they found what was the near-complete skeleton of an elderly male Neanderthal, the most complete remains found to date. The two brothers contacted archaeologist Abbé Henri Breuil, also a Catholic priest, who recommended that they send the remains to anthropologist Marcellin Boule, Professor of Palaeontology at the Muséum National d'Histoire Naturelle, Paris. For Boule, this was an opportunity to demonstrate that human fossils could be studied in the same rigorous manner as any other fossil, using the same methodologies[20,45].

Boule published a preliminary assessment of the Vieillard (Old Man) of La Chapelle-aux-Saints in 1908[46], followed by a highly detailed monograph that appeared in three instalments between 1911 and 1913[47–49]. The work was methodologically sound, closely following the same procedures that he had used in earlier studies of fossilised mammals. The remains were described systematically and compared with other Neanderthals, modern humans, and apes[20]. All in all, it could have been held up as a textbook example of how to do palaeontology[45]. But Boule had made a glaring error.

Throughout his analysis, Boule emphasised the physical similarities between Neanderthals and apes, and he distanced them from modern humans. He reconstructed the vertebral column as straight rather than the s-shape characterising modern humans, giving the Old Man a stooping posture and a slouching gait. The head was thrust forward, the knees were bent, and the big toe was opposable like that of an ape[20].

To Boule, the remarkable posture meant that Neanderthals could not be ancestral to modern humans. The evolutionary change to the modern condition was too great to have occurred in the relatively short timeframe thought to exist between it and the first modern humans. Furthermore, the ancestral status of *Pithecanthropus erectus*, which shared many features with *Homo neanderthalensis* in a more primitive form, was also placed in doubt. Both could be seen as part of the same evolutionary dead end, and humanity's true ancestors were still undiscovered[45].

Boule estimated that the Old Man was over fifty at death, based on the extent to which the bones of his braincase had fused together. He noted that the remains showed signs of age-related degeneration, but he mentioned them only briefly and failed to appreciate their significance. In fact, most of the Old Man's molar teeth were missing. He had severe arthritis of the lower neck, back, and shoulders, a healed broken rib, and a badly deteriorated left hip[50]. Recent estimates suggest that the Old Man was about 62 years old at death[51]. Ironically, it is now thought that despite suffering from widespread age-related osteoarthritis, he would have been able to maintain a fully upright axial posture[51].

'Boule's error', as it later became known, soon made an impact. In February 1909, the Parisian weekly *L'Illustration* published an illustration by the Czech painter František Kupka, in which the Old Man is portrayed as a brutish apelike creature brandishing a club. The same illustration appeared in the *London Illustrated News* later that month. There is a striking contrast between Kupka's illustration and one that appeared in *Harper's Weekly* in July 1873, in which the Feldhofer individual is depicted as a primitive but clearly human cave dweller, who is accompanied by a dog. Kupka's insistence that his illustration was based specifically on the La Chapelle-aux-Saints individual lent further authority to it[52]. Skeletal reproductions and dioramas featuring the Old Man were widely produced[52]. There was even a stone statue outside the Musée National de Préhistoire, Les Eyzies-de-Tayac, sculpted by French sculptor Paul Dardé in 1931[20]. "*The Grisly Folk and Their War With Men*" is a 1921 short story by HG Wells[53]. The story describes an encounter between Neanderthals and "*true men*" from the south, and it was illustrated by American wildlife illustrator Charles Livingston Bull with a depiction of a Neanderthal clearly inspired by Kupka's work.

Australian anatomist Sir Grafton Elliot Smith offered this singularly negative assessment of Neanderthals, "*…in particular the skeleton 1 found in 1908 in a grotto near La Chapelle-aux-Saints by the Abbes A. and J. Bouyssonnie* [sic]*, affords a clear-cut picture of the uncouth and repellent Neanderthal Man. His short, thick-set, and coarsely built body was carried in a half-stooping slouch upon short, powerful, and half-flexed legs of a peculiarly ungraceful form…. heavy overhanging eyebrow-ridges and retreating forehead, the great coarse face with its large eye- sockets, broad nose, and receding chin, combined to complete the picture of unattractiveness, which it is more probable than not was still further emphasized by a shaggy covering of hair over most of the body*"[54].

Removing *Homo neanderthalensis* and *Pithecanthropus erectus* from human ancestry was consistent with the 'brains first' view favoured by British anthropologists such as Sir Arthur Keith. This model supposed that the evolution of larger brains preceded that of upright walking and that human evolution went through a stage of intelligent but still arboreal apes. The rationale behind this view was that the most important difference between apes and humans is the large brain of the latter. Consequently, it was argued that large brains must have been a very early development, arising in the Miocene (23.03 to 5.33 Ma), Oligocene (33.9 to 23.03 Ma), or possibly even the Eocene (55.8 to 33.9 Ma)[55].

When, in 1912, a skull with a modern domed cranium and apelike jaw was found near the hamlet of Piltdown in East Sussex, the 'brains first' view was seemingly vindicated. That Piltdown Man seemingly predated pre-dated *Homo neanderthalensis* was confirmation that the latter was no more than a failed offshoot in human evolution[39,44]. Less than a year later, Scottish anatomist David Waterston, Professor of Anatomy at King's College London suggested that the lower jawbone of now-notorious Piltdown forgery was from a chimpanzee[56]. Such was the enthusiasm, in Britain at any rate, for the 'brains first' model, that Waterston was largely ignored. Piltdown Man was formally named *Eoanthropus dawsoni* ('Dawson's Dawn Man') after its supposed discoverer, Charles Dawson, and for the next forty years, it would feature prominently in textbooks about human evolution. During that period, Neanderthals were largely ignored. Boule's work was not re-examined in detail in his lifetime. New Neanderthal finds were not fully reconstructed, nor were they reported upon in any detail[45].

Who is to blame?

Marcellin Boule's 'error' is often blamed for the brutish, dumb image of Neanderthals. For more than forty years, these visual reconstructions of Old Man of La Chapelle-aux-Saints stood as the unchallenged avatars of *Homo neanderthalensis*. As we have seen, there is to this day a tendency to denigrate Neanderthals. But is this entirely Boule's fault? Consideration of the earliest descriptions of Neanderthals outlined above shows that negative perceptions go back to the Feldhofer discovery itself. Publications in the decade from 1856 devote almost as much time to the Feldhofer individual's supposed low intelligence and lack of cultural attainment as they do to anatomical considerations. Language abounds that would be unthinkable in a scientific journal today: "*barbarous and savage*" (Schaaffhausen), "*the most brutal of all known human skulls*" (Lyell/Huxley), and intelligence that "*never soared beyond that of the brute*" (King). Schaaffhausen refers to "*living savages*", Huxley to "*lower races of mankind*", and King notes that "*Psychical gifts of a lower grade than those characterising the Andamaner cannot be conceived to exist*". Schaaffhausen and Huxley both sought to align Neanderthals with these supposedly lesser races, and King only classified them as a separate species because he considered them to be even 'lower' than Andaman Islanders and closer to apes.

The question is, how could claims be made about the intelligence and even the morality of Neanderthals based on no more than fossil evidence? The answer is linked to the then prevalent views about human 'races' and how living races were studied. It goes without saying that nobody should entertain such views now, but how and why were they current in the mid-nineteenth century, and indeed much later?

At the time, it was widely believed that present-day human populations were made up of distinct 'races'. There were two schools of thought: monogenism and polygenism. Monogenists believed that the various races shared a common ancestor while polygenists believed that their origins were entirely separate. As evolution became accepted, the polygenists argued for a pre-*sapiens* common origin (*Homo erectus*) for the distinct races[57,58]. In both cases – monogenism and polygenism – it was assumed that some races were more developed than others[59].

Studies of human races were based around two main disciplines: craniometry and ethnography. The origins of craniometry (systematic measurement of differences in skull shape and size) and ethnography (the study of individual cultures) can be traced to the eighteenth century, but they had grown in popularity during the mid-nineteenth century. Much effort was devoted to measuring, categorising, and understanding human physical variations, chiefly through craniometry. Anatomists studied human skulls from all over the world, trying to categorise and understand differences. At the same time, European scientists were exploring the world and encountering diverse human cultures. Ethnographers investigated these cultures, intending to learn about the behaviours and cultures of non-European peoples. These two lines of enquiry – craniometry and ethnography – formed the basis of a framework for understanding human variation[60].

From around 1750, it was widely assumed that there was a link between biology and culture and that it was the biological limitations of 'primitive' people around the world that had prevented them from progressing to 'civilisation'. This allowed anthropologists to build a view of living human 'races' around the notion of 'progress'. European anthropologists ordered human groups into a hierarchy with higher and lower levels of physical development and cultural attainment[61]. Europeans were placed at the top of this hierarchy and geographically distant peoples like Aboriginal Australians, Tasmanians, and Hottentots [Khoekhoe] at the bottom, based upon their supposedly smaller brains, more apelike features, and intellectual inferiority[62].

British archaeologist Robin Dennell has described the period from 1870 to 1930 as "*the Age of Prejudice*"[55]. Dennell cites the views of British politician and science writer Samuel Laing as an early instance of the prejudices that were in place in Britain and the United States during this period. In his 1892 work *Human Origins*[63], Laing paid much attention to the origins of modern races, maintaining that "*if there is any truth in evolutions, then the Negro* [Black] *type must be one of the oldest, as nearest to the animal ancestor, and this ancestor must be placed very far back before the Quaternary period, to allow sufficient time for the development of such entirely different and improved races*". Laing continues with assertions including: "*civilised races have larger brains than inferior and savage ones*", "*the negro and lower races generally have chins weak and receding*", and "*the inferior races are short*". He concludes that the differences between orangutans, chimpanzees, and gorillas are less significant than those between Blacks and Europeans.

It was within this framework that European scholars began to study prehistoric people. It could easily be adapted to accommodate people separated by great temporal distances as well as geographical distances. The concept of a hierarchy or 'chain' of human 'races' was extended to a chain that connected humanity to other primates. On this extended model, geographically distant present-day 'lower races' were used to fill gaps in the fossil record. They were slotted in by use of the so-called 'comparative method', whereby modern 'lower races' were seen as analogous to prehistoric people. Hence, the 'lower races' were not just 'savage', they were biologically primitive. Savagery was interpreted as a relic of the primitive state of humanity from which some races had progressed further than others[60,62,64].

Views about European superiority continued into the twentieth century. British anthropologist William Sollas argued on craniometric grounds that Neanderthals were closely related to Aboriginal Australians. He claimed that "*The Neandertal race, the most remote from us in time of which we have any anatomical knowledge, and the Australian, the most remote from us in space, probably represent divergent branches of the same original stock. In that most important of all characters, the cranial capacity, the two races are almost identical*"[65]. Sollas is best known for his 1911 work "*Ancient Hunters and Their Modern Representatives*"[66] in which he proposed that the various 'races' of Palaeolithic times are represented today by various 'primitive' people around the world including Tasmanians, Aboriginal Australians, Bushmen [San people], and Eskimos [Inuit]. According to Sollas, these people were the descendants of less developed races who had been driven from their original homelands by more highly evolved races. The Mousterian people (Neanderthals) had been driven from Europe by the more highly evolved Aurignacian people (San people) and had migrated to Australia. The Aurignacian people were, in turn, driven out by the Magdalenian people (Inuit and Cro-Magnon) and migrated to South Africa. Finally, the Magdalenian people were driven out by Neolithic farmers and migrated to North America, with the Inuit settling in the north and the Cro-Magnon the interior of the continent. These people had been displaced from much of their territory in historical times by the 'highly civilised' Europeans[44].

Sollas wrote "*...the dispossession by a new comer* [sic] *of a race already in occupation of the soil has marked an upward step in the intellectual progress of mankind. It is not priority of occupation, but the power to utilise, which establishes a claim to the land. Hence it is a duty which every race owes to itself, and to the human family as well, to cultivate by every possible means its own strength: directly it falls behind in the regard it pays to this duty, whether in art or science, in breeding or organisation for self-defence, it incurs a penalty which Natural Selection, the stern but beneficent tyrant of the organic world, will assuredly exact, and that speedily, to the full*"[66]. Thus, in the Sollas picture of prehistory, 'higher races' must inevitably replace 'lower races', especially in geographically advantageous regions such as Europe. He argued that the successive cultures observed in the European archaeological record were the product not of indigenous evolution, but were the result of waves of higher types invading from the east. Racial violence and imperialism were seen as the key drivers of progress[44,62].

Robin Dennell[55] notes that Sir Grafton Elliot Smith expresses similar views in his 1930 work *Human History*[67]. Like Laing and Keith, Elliot Smith argued for the great antiquity of human races, and his tree of human evolution shows Aboriginal Australians branching off first, followed by Blacks, and finally, Nordics. He notes that "*the aboriginal Australian is regarded as the most primitive of existing peoples. He is to be regarded as the survivor of one of the lowest forms of the species Homo sapiens. The negro comes next, but he is not nearly as primitive as the Australian*". He suggests that "*anatomical peculiarities* [of Blacks] *suggesting affinities with the apes are commoner than they are in most other peoples*" and concludes that "*Critically studying the achievements of the Negro Race, the same conclusion is forced upon us as the study of the aboriginal Australians has already revealed. Neither in Africa nor in Melanesia can any significant element of culture be attributed to Negro invention. Many of them, like the African Pygmies and the Indonesian and Papuan Pygmies, seem to be almost wholly devoid of any culture. As regards the other Negroes in Africa ... the few arts and crafts that are scattered sporadically through the vast continent are all alien in origin. No more striking testimony is needed to emphasize the lack of enterprise and initiative in the Negro Race*".

Boule's error was no more than the tip of an iceberg of Neanderthal denigration that had begun more or less with the Feldhofer discovery. It must further be placed in the context of then-prevalent views about race that can only be described as abhorrent. Nine decades after Hitler rose to power, there will be many who naively assume that such views were largely confined to the Nazis and the far right. This was not the case: they were widely held in academia. But, as Dennell[55] points out, we must not tar everybody with the same brush. He notes that such views are not evident in the biogeographical writings of the likes of William King Gregory or Davidson Black, or the palaeontology of Ralph Von Koenigswald, Louis Leakey, and Franz Weidenreich. The latter, who was Jewish, had to flee Germany in 1933, and would certainly have been sensitive to such views.

So why did Boule get the blame? It might seem to be a nice, neat explanation, one that conveniently obscures the uncomfortable truth about pre-World War II racism. However, a more likely explanation is the extent to which the error circulated. Boule's negative assessment of the Old Man of La Chapelle-aux-Saints was repeated in both academic works and the popular press in a manner inconceivable a few decades earlier. Illustrations, dioramas, and statues of Neanderthals appeared worldwide. Many of these were based on Boule's descriptions[20,60,68].

The Renaissance of Neanderthals

It was not until the approach of the centenary of the Feldhofer discovery that anybody saw the necessity to revisit the La Chapelle-aux-Saints remains[45]. This belated reassessment took place against a scientific and social background very different to the one a few decades earlier. Piltdown Man, increasingly seen as an anomaly, had finally been exposed as a hoax in November 1953. The middle of the century had seen the emergence of the New Evolutionary Synthesis, which combined Darwinian natural selection with Mendelian genetic inheritance – a new paradigm within which established views on species and populations were examined and extensively revised[69]. Most importantly, eugenics and 'scientific' racism had been entirely discredited by the Nazis and the horrors of the Holocaust. Between 1950 and 1964, UNESCO issued three Statements on Race, affirming that *Homo sapiens* is one species made up of populations that differ from one another by far less than what they share in common[70].

In July 1955, anatomists William L. Straus, Jr and Alexander Cave visited the Muséum National d'Histoire Naturelle and examined the Old Man. At a symposium in New York late in 1956 held to mark the centenary, they announced that Boule's analysis had been incorrect. Straus and Cave were "*wholly unprepared for the severity and extent of the osteoarthritis deformans in the La Chapelle skeleton*" that Boule had so downplayed in his monograph. It was this that accounted for the Old Man's supposedly stooped posture. Although his limbs and skull were distinct from modern humans, there was nothing in the overall morphology to justify the "*common assumption*" that Neanderthals were other than fully erect bipeds. Even if the arthritic Old Man had stood and walked with a stoop, this would have been no different to the posture of a modern man similarly afflicted with spinal osteoarthritis. He could not be viewed as representative of a healthy Neanderthal. Noting that other researchers had reached similar conclusions at around the same time, Straus and Cave concurred that "*there exists no valid reason for Boule's assumption that the man of La Chapelle-aux-Saints differed fundamentally from modern man in his cervical curvature and the carriage of his head*". However, they declined to criticise Boule, arguing that the negative perception of Neanderthals "*undoubtedly goes back to the discovery of the holotype Neanderthal specimen near Düsseldorf, Germany, just 100 years ago, in 1856*". Referencing a 1939 illustration by Carleton Coon of a heavy-jawed Neanderthal businessman dressed for work in a hat, coat, and tie, they famously noted that if the Old Man could be "*reincarnated and placed in a New York subway – provided that he were bathed, shaved, and dressed in modern clothing - it is doubtful whether he would attract any more attention than some of its other denizens*"[71].

From this point onward, both academic and public perceptions of Neanderthals improved. It was the beginning of a Neanderthal renaissance, a rebirth of Neanderthals as humans[20]. Coon's image became the new symbol of Neanderthal humanity. *The Inheritors* (1955), by William Golding, was a sympathetic portrayal in which a Neanderthal group encounter Upper Palaeolithic *Homo sapiens*. Golding's Neanderthals were no longer subhuman brutes but were instead gentle and childlike[68]. Other literary portrayals included Jean M. Auel's *Clan of the Cave Bear* series. Portrayals in science fiction were also sympathetic. *The Ugly Little Boy* is a 1958 short story by Isaac Asimov in which a Neanderthal child is brought into the present. The *Neanderthal Parallax* is an award-winning trilogy by Canadian author Robert J. Sawyer where scientists make contact with a parallel universe in which *Homo sapiens* rather than Neanderthals became extinct. The contrast between Boule's Neanderthals and these portrayals could not have been greater.

Flower Power Neanderthals

Shanidar Cave is a Neanderthal site in the Baradost Mountains (part of the Zagros mountain chain) in Iraqi Kurdistan. The limestone cave is 760 m (2,500 ft) above sea level, with a ceiling that is up to 15 m (45 ft) above the floor. The site overlooks the Great Zab River, a tributary of the Tigris. Between 1951 and 1960, the site was excavated by American archaeologist Ralph Solecki. During the excavations, the remains of nine Neanderthal individuals (Shanidar 1-9) were recovered, comprising groups found on two different levels of the excavation. Shanidar 1, 3, and 5 were found in the upper level and the others in the lower level[39,72]. Some of the remains were transferred to the Smithsonian in Washington, DC, and the incomplete left leg and foot of a tenth Shanidar individual, an infant, were identified from this material in 2006[73]. Recent work suggests that Shanidar 1, 3, and 5 are 55,000 – 45,000 years old, and the lower level remains are 70,000 – 60,000 years old[74].

Solecki's team documented nine different rockfalls in the cave, which accounted for the deaths of four of the Neanderthals. The others are thought to have been intentionally buried[75]. Shanidar 1, a male aged 40 – 50 years old, had been in poor physical condition before his death. The crushing fracture he had sustained to his left orbit had probably left him blind in one eye. Exostoses (bone spurs) in the external auditory canals of both his ears suggest that he was probably deaf in at least one ear. He had also suffered a massive injury to the right side of his body that had caused arthritic degeneration of the right knee and ankle. In addition, there were fractures and the possible loss of part of the right forearm. That these injuries had subsequently healed implies that Shanidar 1 had been cared for by other group members during and indeed for years after his periods of convalescence[39,76].

Soil samples from another grave, that of Shanidar 4, were later analysed for pollen, in an attempt to reconstruct the climatic and vegetation history of the site. In addition to the usual pollen found throughout the site, some samples yielded whole clumps of pollen. This led Solecki to suggest that entire flowering plants had been placed in the grave, presumably by grieving relatives[75]. The possibility of floral tributes in the Shanidar 4 grave chimed with the 'flower power' counterculture of the time, but it posed the question as to why they were absent from the other Neanderthal burials. More recently, it has been suggested that the pollen had a natural origin. One suspect is the Persian Jird (*Meriones persicus*), a gerbil-like rodent known to store large numbers of seeds and flowers in their burrows[77]. Another possibility is that the pollen originated from a nearby bees nest[78].

Neanderthals were now seen as having compassion and humanity. The emphasis of Neanderthal studies shifted from pre-*sapiens* behaviour to pre-*sapiens* anatomy. This view saw modern humans descended from anatomically primitive ancestors that nevertheless shared with us the attributes that make us human[68].

Were they really dimwits?

Despite these findings, the idea that Neanderthals lacked the full range of behaviours attributed to modern humans has proved to be remarkably persistent. The behavioural package anthropologists refer to as 'modern human behaviour' relies on our ability to use symbols to organise our thoughts and behaviour. Symbols can take the form of sounds, images, or objects. They may refer directly to an object or idea (representational images), or they may be abstract (spoken or written words). For example, a cat may be referred to by either a drawing, the sound 'cat', or the written letters 'c-a-t'. Syntactic language is a system of communication that enables an effectively infinite range of meanings to be conveyed, but it is only one component of our ability to use symbols. We use symbols all the time – whenever we read a book, check the time, consult a map, or admire a painting or sculpture. All these activities involve symbolic behaviour, and our society could not function without it.

Long after 'Boule's error' had been addressed, the view persisted that symbolic behaviour was absent from Neanderthals, or at best it was severely reduced in comparison to modern humans. At the end of the last century, American anthropologist Richard Klein wrote, "*It is not difficult to understand why the Neanderthals failed to survive after behaviourally modern humans appeared. The archaeological record shows that in virtually every detectable aspect—artefacts, site modification, ability to adapt to extreme environments, subsistence, and so forth – the Neanderthals were behaviourally inferior to their modern successors, and to judge from their distinctive morphology, this behavioural inferiority may have been rooted in their biological makeup*"[79]. A few years later, British geneticist and science writer Stephen Oppenheimer complained that "*…we still all regard Neanderthals as lesser folk, and experts continue to emphasise perceived cultural differences*"[80].

Importantly, however, it was commonly believed at the time that even *Homo sapiens* had lacked behavioural modernity until around 70,000 – 50,000 years ago[81,82], and Klein[83] was one of the proponents of what was referred to as a "*human revolution*" or "*Great Leap Forward*"[84]. The latter was a reference to the disastrous economic and social plan implemented in China between 1958 and 1961 by Mao Zedong. This viewpoint was based on a perceived lack of archaeological evidence for advanced behaviours prior to this time. Such behaviours included increased intensification in resource use, greater planning depth, seasonal scheduling of hunting and fishing, exploitation of aquatic resources, long-distance trade networks, structured use of space for different activities within habitation sites, and evidence for symbolic behaviour including special treatment of the dead, beads and ornaments, and acquisition, processing, and use of pigment[85].

One theory proposed that the revolution occurred when a serendipitous 'smartness mutation' led to a rewiring of the human brain that enabled it to work more efficiently. This mutation would have been highly advantageous, and consequently, it spread rapidly through human populations worldwide[83]. More plausibly, archaeologist Steven Mithen[81] argued that the revolution occurred when humans attained what he termed 'cognitive fluidity'. Mithen proposed that the human mind is made up of several 'cognitive domains' or specialist intelligences that are dedicated to various tasks: a 'linguistic intelligence' for language, a 'social intelligence' for managing social interactions, a 'natural history intelligence' for dealing with such matters as animal behaviour, weather, and local geography, and a 'technical intelligence' for toolmaking. Underlying these specialist intelligences is a core of 'general intelligence'. In the behaviourally modern mind, the various intelligences are linked by 'cognitive fluidity', but Mithen argued that this was not always the case and that earlier humans were literally incapable of joined-up thinking. These included *Homo erectus*, Neanderthals, and even *Homo sapiens* prior to around 50,000 years ago.

Mithen believes that early human vocalisations were 'holistic and manipulative', similar to those of other primates: for example, the vervet monkey alarm calls manipulate emotions by inducing fear of a specific predator (leopards, snakes, or eagles), in turn triggering the appropriate survival response. The group living of early humans, coupled with the increased use of gestural communications, led to an extension of this communication mode into what Mithen called 'Hmmmmm' (five 'm's). This stands for Holistic, manipulative, multi-modal, musical, and mimetic', with dance and mime being added to the repertoire. As with vervet monkey vocalisations, Hmmmmm manipulated the actions of others. It was more complex than the vocalisations of non-human primates but less so than that of present-day humans. Mithen suggests that Hmmmmm emerged with *Homo erectus*. Later, as cognitive fluidity emerged in *Homo sapiens*, it gradually transformed into modern syntactic language. Neanderthals never attained cognitive fluidity, and Hmmmmm persisted, albeit it was more complex than that of *Homo erectus*[86].

Before considering the archaeological evidence, let us ask why the brains of people living today are cognitively fluid, but not the similarly sized brains of Neanderthals and earlier *Homo sapiens*. As we have seen, the globular braincase of *Homo sapiens* differs from the long, low braincase of Neanderthals and earlier humans such as *Homo erectus*. It is generally assumed that these differences relate to differences in the actual proportions of the brain. Although the cranial capacities of Middle Pleistocene *Homo* and Neanderthals were larger than that of *Homo erectus*, the braincase – and by implication, the brain itself – was simply a scaled-up version of that of the earlier species[87,88]. One factor responsible for the changes in *Homo sapiens* could be the expansion of the parietal lobes (located at the top and on each side of the brain)[89,90], the temporal lobes (located behind and below the frontal lobes, below the parietal lobes, and in front of the occipital lobes)[91], and the cerebellum[92].

Expansion of the parietal lobes and cerebellum could have enabled a small but significant increase in what is termed the 'working memory' of the brain[88,93]. Working memory is the ability to consciously hold and manipulate information – basically the ability to think about complex ideas[94]. The globular shape of the modern brain resulting from the expansion might also have increased neural connectivity by shortening the distance between the various regions. Even a small increase in data transfer rates could confer considerable advantages[90]. Recently, researchers have found differences between the Neanderthal and modern human versions of the protein TKTL1. It was suggested that these differences increase the number of basal radial glia – neocortex progenitor cells – in the modern human brain, resulting in an increased size of the neocortex, or its neuron density, or both, relative to the Neanderthal brain[95]. A larger neocortex – more 'grey matter' – could also be reflected in the change of shape from long and low to globular. If these differences were responsible for the emergence of cognitive fluidity, it would mean that modern human behaviour did not emerge until the transition from the elongated to the globular cranial shape was complete, and it was confined to fully modern *Homo sapiens*.

The earliest examples of our species, informally referred to as 'archaic' *Homo sapiens*[96], lived around 300,000 years ago[97]. Although the face is modern[98], the braincase is long and low, resembling the archaic condition[99]. Only later did the characteristic globular form emerge, first seen in the 233,000-year-old Omo 1 skull from southwestern Ethiopia[100,101]. However, it has been suggested that the *Homo sapiens* braincase did not reach the present-day range of variation until between 100,000 and 35,000 years ago. Researchers claimed that the transition from long and low to globular happened in two stages. In the first stage, the cerebellum, parietal, and temporal areas increased in size, loading to the Omo 1 skull shape. This was followed by a second stage in which the cerebellum continued to increase in size, and was accompanied by size increases in the occipital lobes[102].

The timing of the endpoint of this process is consistent with a late emergence of modern human behaviour in *Homo sapiens* around 50,000 years ago, although the start-to-finish timescale of around 250,000 years is more suggestive of a Long March than a Great Leap Forward. But the conclusions have been challenged by researchers who claim that the brain shape of *Homo sapiens* has not changed significantly in the last 200,000 years and that subsequent changes in the shape of the braincase reflect changes in facial anatomy rather than the shape of the brain[103].

The archaeological record, as it is now understood, does not support a late emergence of modern human behaviour. In a landmark paper published in 2000, American anthropologists Sally McBrearty and Alison Brooks argued that the 'human revolution' view stemmed from "*a profound Eurocentric bias and a failure to appreciate the depth and breadth of the African archaeological record*". The pair noted that many components of the 'human revolution' claimed not to occur until 50,000 years ago could be found in the African Middle Stone Age, dating to tens of thousands of years earlier. These include blade and microlithic technology, bone tools, increased geographic range, specialized hunting, the use of aquatic resources, long-distance trade, systematic processing and use of pigment, and art and decoration. They do not occur suddenly together, as would be expected on the 'human revolution' picture, but instead are found at sites widely separated in space and time. Thus, a package of modern human behaviours was gradually assembled in Africa and was subsequently exported to other regions of the Old World[85].

What of Neanderthals, if they did not receive the same 'working memory' or neocortex upgrades as *Homo sapiens*, never attained cognitive fluidity, and continued to communicate with 'Hmmmmm'? We can only judge them on an archaeological record that increasingly challenges the 'dumb Neanderthal' view. Surveys have found that Neanderthals enjoyed a diet as diverse as that of modern humans and that Neanderthal hunting techniques and capacity for innovation were not obviously inferior. Technologies associated with Neanderthals included manufacturing pitch for hafting spear points and making specialised bone tools for working animal hides. The ability to grind and polish bone in such a manner is thought to be indicative of behavioural modernity. Also disputed is the common view that modern humans had larger social networks than Neanderthals. Evidence for long-distance movement of raw materials, indicative of social networking, appears to have been very similar for Neanderthals in Europe and modern humans in Africa[104,105].

Evidence for Neanderthal symbolic behaviour now includes the ornamental use of shells[106–108], bird feathers[109–111], and the talons of birds of prey[112,113]. In 2018, hand stencils and abstract cave art were reported from three Spanish sites. Although no fossil remains were found at any of these cave sites, the artwork predates the earliest known arrival of modern humans in Spain by at least 20,000 years[114].

All of this adds up to a good case for Neanderthals having syntactic language. Even if they did not, the fact that they interbred with modern people[115] and that interbreeding was not uncommon[116] suggests that the two species could communicate. Neanderthals must have had some form of language, possibly resembling Mithen's Hmmmmm. The archaeological record that Neanderthals were just as effective as *Homo sapiens* at getting things done, which suggests that they were not disadvantaged by a lack, if any, of a syntactic language. Why, then, did they become extinct?

Demise

Although modern humans appear to have made sporadic incursions into Europe from as early as 56,800 years ago[117], and possibly much earlier[118], there is no evidence for a large-scale, long-term presence until around 46,000 years ago. Radiocarbon dating of Neanderthal Mousterian sites over a wide area from the Black Sea and Southwest Asia to the Atlantic coast suggests that stone tool industries thought to be associated with modern humans started to replace Mousterian industries around 45,000 years ago, and the Mousterian had ended across the whole of its range by 41,030 – 39,260 years ago. Thus, by just 2,600 - 5,400 years after their first significant contact with modern humans, Neanderthals had disappeared from the archaeological record[119].

Was their demise due to the 'behavioural inferiority' suggested by Klein? Archaeological evidence suggests that modern humans were better able to adapt to the unstable climate of Marine Isotope Stage 3 (57,000 – 24,000 years ago), which was mild overall but punctuated by cold, arid 'stadials', some of which were particularly harsh[120]. During these periods, woodlands were replaced by steppe landscapes. The archaeological record indicates that the expansion of the steppes caused a depopulation of Neanderthals and a subsequent repopulation by modern humans, suggesting that the latter were better adapted to this environment[121].

Dental microwear studies suggest the Neanderthal diet was heavily influenced by changes in the local environment, which in turn were driven by climate change. In warmer, wooded environments, their diet included more seeds and nuts, whereas in colder steppe environments there was a shift to greater dependence on animal protein. By contrast, modern humans of the European Upper Palaeolithic show much less dietary variation with the environment. Even in environments with equivalent tree cover, Neanderthals were far more opportunistic than modern humans, exploiting only the resources that were most abundant and accessible in their local habitat: almost exclusively animal protein in open conditions but substantial amounts of plant food in wooded conditions. By contrast, modern humans seem to have made more of an effort to exploit all available resources in their environment, such as more plant food in open environments than Neanderthals. This suggests that while modern humans were able to maintain the same diet by adapting their technology, Neanderthals had to adapt their diet to the local conditions. This might not have been a problem while all other groups were equally constrained, but the arrival of groups who were not subject to this limitation might have tipped the scales against Neanderthal populations[122].

Does this mean that 'dumb' Neanderthals were outcompeted by 'smart' *Homo sapiens*? The Upper Palaeolithic stone tool technology of modern humans was superior to the Mousterian technology of the Neanderthals. It was based on striking long thin blades from prismatic stone cores, enabling more tools to be produced from a given volume of raw material. Certain tool types made an appearance in Europe for the first time: 'carinate' (keel-shaped) and 'nosed' scrapers, small bladelets known as Dufour and Font-Yves forms that probably served as the tips and barbs of composite spears or arrowheads, and spearhead points carved from bone and antler, split at the base to permit hafting[123–125].

Their technology might have given modern humans the edge, but it does not mean that they were necessarily any 'smarter' than Neanderthals any more than the superior technology of the Spanish Conquistadores meant that they were 'smarter' than the Aztec or Inca. Neanderthal technology was highly conservative whereas that of modern humans was innovative. The Mousterian technology of the Neanderthals had served them well for around 200,000 years and there was little need to innovate. Neanderthal populations were also very low[126,127], which meant that it would have been difficult for any innovations to spread.

Ultimately, basic demographics rather probably lie at the root of the Neanderthal demise. The sheer weight of numbers might have enabled modern humans to expand their overall territory at the expense of Neanderthals. Consideration of site numbers suggests that the ratio might have been as high as 10:1 in favour of the modern human population[128]. Factors such as inbreeding[129] and/or a slightly reduced fertility among younger Neanderthal women could have further exacerbated the demographic situation. The latter could have come about through food stress resulting either from climate change or competition with modern humans[130].

At the peripheries of Europe, Neanderthals might have persisted after their extinction elsewhere. Possible late survival is documented from two quite different settings: Gorham's Cave, Gibraltar, and Byzovaya, in the western foothills of the northernmost Urals. Gorham's Cave seems to have been a favoured location that was visited repeatedly over many thousands of years. Natural light penetrates deep into the cave, and a high ceiling permits ventilation of smoke from the hearths that were repeatedly made there. Neanderthal occupation of the cave continued until around 32,000 years ago, and possibly until as recently as 28,000 years ago. The site was later used by modern humans until Phoenician and Carthaginian times, although there was a 5,000-year hiatus after the last Neanderthal occupation before the first modern humans took up residence there[131,132]. No human remains have been recovered at Byzovaya, so we cannot be certain that the toolmakers were Neanderthals. However, a total of 313 stone artefacts have been collected over the years, ranging in age from 34,000 to 31,000 years old. All were produced with typical Middle Palaeolithic tool production techniques characteristic of Neanderthal Mousterian industries[133].

However, the exact circumstances of the Neanderthal extinction remain uncertain, as does how the populations interacted with each other. That Neanderthals and *Homo sapiens* interbred shows that there must have been some interaction between them, and it is in any case difficult to believe that these populations shunned each other completely. But, once they were gone from their southern Iberian refugium, the long Neanderthal story was at an end. Or was it?

E pluribus unum

The announcement, in 2010, that modern humans and Neanderthals had interbred made headlines around the world. Four years earlier, a project to sequence the Neanderthal genome had been launched at the Max Planck Institute for Evolutionary Anthropology[134,135], and in May 2010, researchers published a first draft[115]. It was reported that one to four per cent of the genome of modern Eurasians was derived from Neanderthals. In other words, interbreeding had taken place – but not in Africa. This latter detail was unsurprising, because Neanderthals are not known to have lived in Africa.

At first, it was suggested that there had only been a single episode of interbreeding of interbreeding[136], possibly in the Levant[137], or that interbreeding was very rare, possibly occurring only once every 70 or 80 generations[138,139]. As more ancient DNA was recovered from Upper Palaeolithic human remains, this suggestion was disproved. Ancient DNA from modern humans who lived in Eastern Europe 40,000 years ago has revealed Neanderthal ancestors from no more than 4 to 7 generations back[116,140]. Had interbreeding not been a reasonably common occurrence, the chances of discovering the remains of people with such recent Neanderthal ancestry would be vanishingly small.

The scientific and lay communities alike had barely six months to digest the news that modern humans had interbred with Neanderthals before geneticists discovered that our ancestors had encountered and interbred with a second archaic human species. Unlike Neanderthals, the existence of Denisovans had been entirely unsuspected prior to March 2010. Ancient DNA was recovered from a small finger bone found in Denisova Cave in the Altai Krai, a krai (federal subject) within the Russian Federation. It was expected that the fingerbone had belonged to either a Neanderthal or a modern human, but it turned out to be from a hitherto unknown human species[141]. Late in 2010, further work showed that this new species, now informally known as 'Denisovan', had also interbred with modern humans[142]. Denisovans remain unrecognised as a formal species. The only physical remains confirmed as Denisovan are bone fragments and teeth from Denisova Cave and a 160,000-year-old partial lower jawbone from Xiahe on the Tibetan Plateau[143]. Other fossil remains, most notably a skull from Harbin, northeastern China, are suspected to be Denisovan, but this has yet to be confirmed by recovery of ancient DNA.

An estimated 35 to 70 per cent of the Neanderthal genome survives in the present-day population, albeit no one individual possesses more than a small fraction of this amount[144]. Interbreeding with both species was clearly beneficial to our ancestors. High frequencies of Neanderthal alleles are found in genes involved in the production of keratin, a protein that is used in skin, hair, and nails[145]. In East Asian populations, the HYAL region, a cluster of genes associated with protection from the Sun's UV rays, is rich in Neanderthal alleles[146] and genes associated with the ability to detect subtle scents are enriched with Denisovan alleles[147]. Tibetans have several genetic variants of Denisovan origin that are associated with adaption to the low oxygen levels on the Tibetan plateau[148]. In this sense, neither Neanderthals nor Denisovans are extinct. They are still here, still a part of us.

Conclusion

Anthropology has long since moved on from the 'Age of Prejudice'. Yet, despite this and all the evidence to the contrary, the popular perception of Neanderthals as dimwits has persisted. Is it a case of people using 'Neanderthal' because other slurs have become socially unacceptable? I would argue not and would suggest that in the main, 'Neanderthal', like 'dinosaur', has become a placeholder for 'blundering stupidity', 'outdated', etc. That was certainly the context intended by the politicians I named at the start of this text, and I suspect also by most of the people in the other instances brought up by my Google search.

So how do we move on and retire this wholly inappropriate slur? The Neanderthal Museum in Germany has made a commendable effort with dioramas depicting a Neanderthal woman mourning the death of her partner and the dialogue between an old woman and a child. The women are depicted wearing leather trousers rather than loincloths, suggesting a greater degree of sophistication[68]. In reality, it is not thought that Neanderthals made tailored clothing[149,150]. Nevertheless, the intention is good.

Neanderthals are always considered newsworthy, and newly announced discoveries tend to be widely reported. Reports in the popular press feature descriptions of Neanderthals as 'primitive' and 'apelike'. Science writers really need to educate themselves; this is bad science. Neanderthals and *Homo sapiens* shared a common ancestor less than a million years ago. Neither species is any more apelike than the other. Occasionally, I even come across the expression 'humans and Neanderthals' in scientific journals, where 'human' has been left unqualified. Please, don't do so. Use 'modern human', 'AMH' (anatomically modern human), or *Homo sapiens*.

A 'human' is any species included in the genus *Homo*, not just us. We could debate forever about what it means to be human, but that does not mean that we should deny the humanity of Neanderthals. How Neanderthals perceived and interacted with the world might well have differed from ourselves in many ways, but that does not mean that we should assume that they were any less intelligent, or that we have any reason to suppose that their extinction was due to the innate superiority of *Homo sapiens*.

08: Early funerary practices

Hadar, East Africa: 3,200,000 years ago

A short distance to the north of what would one day be named the Awash River was a relatively featureless, seasonally dry, grassy plain where a slight depression caused by a dying channel hosted bushes and trees that bushes and trees that were able to grow under conditions of more stable soil moisture. Hominins and other animals traversed the linear depressions left by old channels when they ventured into the more open grassland environments or used such areas as places to shelter. Within one such channel was a large collection of bones: mainly hominins, but also fish, a crocodile tooth, a bovid horn, and the lower jawbone of an elephant. In time, the bones were buried beneath layers of clay-rich soil, where they would remain for more than three million years.

In 1975, what was now known as Afar Locality 333 was investigated by the International Afar Research Expedition, a multidisciplinary team that carried out extensive paleoanthropological fieldwork at Hadar, Ethiopia, between 1973 and 1981. The team is best known for the discovery of the fossil hominin AL 288-1, better known as 'Lucy', in November 1973. During the 1975 excavation season, the team found over two hundred separate fossil bone fragments at the 3.2 million-year-old fossil bed designated AL 333. The fossil remains represented at least thirteen individuals, all belonging to the same species as Lucy: *Australopithecus afarensis*. They included adult males and females accompanied by four or more infants and were thought to represent a single, relatively large social group, which became known as the First Family. It was at first suggested that they had fallen victim to a single catastrophic event. There were no signs that any of the group had been attacked by predators[1], and one suggestion was that they had been overwhelmed by a flash flood[2]. However, later work also ruled out this possibility. A study of sediments at the site confirmed the channel in which they were found had indeed flooded at one stage, but the flow of water had been too gentle to have imperilled a group of hominins. It was not clear if the remains had been transported by the flow of water from upstream[3].

This left unresolved the question of how the remains had reached the site. British archaeologist Paul Pettitt[4] has suggested that the corpses of the group's dead were intentionally left in a field of tall grass by other group members. He believes that this was an example of what he terms 'structured abandonment', which he argues was a stage in the development of mortuary practices that preceded later rituals such as formal burials. He defines structured abandonment as deliberately placing a corpse in a particular place for reasons such as to protect it from scavengers. Pettitt's suggestion poses an obvious question. The brain size of *Australopithecus afarensis* averaged 445 cc[5], no greater than the upper end of the 280 – 450 cc range for chimpanzees, and about a third of the size of present-day humans[6]. Could such small-brained hominins have been capable of such advanced behaviours?

The answer appears to be 'yes'.

In November 2009, the *National Geographic* ran a photograph of a newly deceased female chimpanzee named Dorothy being wheeled past a wire fence, behind which stood sixteen of her former chimpanzee companions in two rows. The photograph was taken on 23 September 2008 at the Sanaga-Yong Chimpanzee Rescue Centre, Cameroon, following Dorothy's death from congestive heart failure. She was in her late 40s. According to photographer Monica Szczupider, who took the picture, the centre's management decided to let the other members of Dorothy's community witness her burial so that they would realise that she was gone and would not be returning. The chimpanzees, for the most part, remained uncharacteristically silent throughout the proceedings[7].

The picture went viral, and the scene was invariably described as a chimpanzee funeral. Given that our divergence from our closest living ape relatives is estimated to have occurred 6.6 million years ago[8], the AL-333 remains at Afar could represent a pattern of behaviour with roots that already lay millions of years in the past.

The ancient primate roots of mortuary activity

The Sanaga-Yong 'funeral' renewed interest in death awareness in non-human primates and other animals. There were reports of chimpanzee mothers continuing to carry the bodies of deceased infants after their deaths for several weeks, until mummification occurred[9,10]. Similar behaviours were reported for gelada monkeys[11]. One study reported behaviours including the pre-death care of an elderly female chimpanzee, close inspection and testing for signs of life following her death, all-night attendance by the deceased's adult daughter, and cleaning the body. The study concluded that chimpanzees show several behaviours that recall human responses to the death of a close relative[12], although the suggestion that group members had attempted to resuscitate the deceased met with a degree of scepticism[13]. Paul Pettitt[4] notes that among the chimpanzee community at Gombe National Park, Tanzania, symptoms consistent with depression were observed in individuals aged between 14 months and 8.5 years following the deaths of their mothers. These included lethargy, loss of appetite, decreased play, anxiety, and whimpering when left behind during travel.

Guarding a body has been observed with a range of primate species. Barbary macaques will respond defensively to humans (or feral dogs) in proximity to one of their deceased conspecifics, Phayre's langurs (*Trachypithecus phayrei*) reportedly formed a protective circle around a deceased female in response to vultures, a rhesus macaque attacked crows that gathered around the body of her dead infant, and alpha female bonobo was recorded opposing the removal of the body of a young male by a caretaker. Higher-ranking individuals in primate communities have been seen to deny access to a body by younger or lower-ranking individuals. For example, a female chimpanzee who had been killed by a leopard was guarded by three males and a high-ranking female for six hours, during which lower-ranking individuals were chased away, with the exception of the deceased's younger brother[4,13].

A wide range of unusual behaviours were noted following the death of a 10-year-old juvenile female named Tina, who was killed by a leopard. These included individuals gathering around the body and making unusual calls not heard in other contexts, others sitting in silence around the body, inspections of the body, grooming the body, swatting away insects and removing eggs they had laid on the body, and denying low-ranking individuals access to the body[4].

Paul Pettitt[4] believes that these behaviours are examples of the "*core mortuary phase*" of mortuary behaviour, which has its origins millions of years before humans diverged from chimpanzees. Although chimpanzees have continued to evolve since the split, he believes that studying them is informative of behaviours that were associated with the core mortuary phase. He notes similarities between the social organisation of present-day humans and chimpanzees, in particular, an apparent 'cultural' variation in tool use and other behaviours. The behaviours noted above Pettitt categorised as manifestations of the following:

- *Morbidity*: inspecting and grooming the bodies of the deceased. Pettitt defined morbidity as "*An enquiring concern with the injured, diseased or dead body, whether or not this derives from a desire to understand the nature or cause of death of an individual*". Chimpanzees treat a dead body differently from a gravely ill individual, suggesting that they are aware that death has occurred, for example, they will examine but never lick the wounds of dead conspecifics.
- *Mourning*: signs of depression and uttering calls not heard in other contexts. The carrying of the bodies of deceased infants Pettitt interpreted as an act of detachment – a gradual process of weakening the bonds between the living and the dead. Pettitt also notes signs of depression and uttering calls not heard in other contexts.
- *Social theatre*: Gatherings taking place around corpses and the restriction of access to high-ranking individuals; behaviours not witnessed in other contexts. Pettitt termed these as 'funerary gatherings'.

Pettitt argues that elements of these behaviours can be traced back to the Late Miocene (11.63 to 5.333 million years ago), and they evolved into the rule-regulated, formal mourning seen with humans.

To serve man

Pettitt also notes two behaviours which, from a contemporary point of view, might be seen as less sympathetic: infanticide and cannibalism. He refers to these as Cronos compulsions, after the Greek Titan Cronos (Saturn in Roman mythology), who swallowed his children Demeter, Hestia, Hera, Hades, and Poseidon alive (they were later rescued by a sixth child, Zeus). Infanticide is widespread in the animal kingdom, albeit individual occurrences within groups are relatively rare. Among primates, it happens for a variety of reasons, but the most important is thought to be sexual selection: females whose offspring have been killed will rapidly return to fertility. It may also serve to reduce inbreeding and population size to levels within the carrying capacity of the local environment[4].

Among humans, the practice of 'exposing' unwanted newborn children was common in the ancient world[14]. Nineteenth-century prehistorian Sir John Lubbock (Lord Avebury) cited several instances of infanticide among the various traditional peoples around the world whom he described as "*modern savages*" in his 1865 work *Pre-Historic Times*. Of the indigenous Khoikhoi of South Africa (referred to by the now unacceptable term 'Hottentots'), for example, Lubbock noted that "*Infanticide, again, was very common among them, and was not regarded as a crime. Girls were generally the victims; and, if a woman had twins, the ugliest of them was almost always exposed or buried alive. This was done with the consent of the whole kraal, which generally allows it without taking much pains to look into it. The poverty and the hardships which they had to undergo may perhaps plead as some excuse…"*[15].

Cannibalism also has a long tradition in human societies, and it takes many forms. These include *survival cannibalism*, where individuals resort to eating the bodies of others in the absence of other means of sustenance. One well-known example involved members of a Uruguayan rugby team whose plane crashed in the Andes in 1972 and who ate the bodies of some of those killed in the crash while two of their number went to seek help. *Psychopathic cannibalism*, such as that practised by the fictional character Hannibal Lecter, is well documented in criminology. Exocannibalism is the eating of individuals from outside a group. It often occurs in the context of warfare, and it has been reported from South America, Africa, and the South Pacific. Endocannibalism is the eating of individuals from within a group. It usually occurs in the form of funerary or mortuary consumption, in which all or part of the body is ingested as an act of affection[16].

Kuru

Among the groups practising mortuary cannibalism were the Fore people, who live in the Eastern Highlands province of Papua New Guinea. Gold prospectors, Protestant missionaries, and government officials became aware of the practice in the late 1930s. At that time Papua New Guinea was administered by Australia. When a body was considered for human consumption, only the bitter gall bladder was discarded. The corpse would be dismembered by maternal kin, who first removed the hands and feet, and then cut open the arms and legs to strip the muscles. The head was cut off, and the skull was broken open to remove the brain. Meat, viscera, and brain were all eaten. Marrow was sucked from cracked bones, and sometimes the bones were pulverised and cooked and eaten with green vegetables. By the 1950s, under pressure from missionaries and the Australian authorities, cannibalism had ceased among the North Fore, though it continued surreptitiously by the South Fore throughout that decade[17–19].

In the Fore region, the bodies of the deceased could be disposed of by burial or placing on a platform, or by being eaten. The latter was by far the most prevalent: if the body was buried, it would be eaten by worms, and if it was placed on a platform, it would be eaten by maggots. The Fore believed it was much better that the body was eaten by people who loved the deceased than by worms and insects. By eating the dead body, they could show their love and express their grief. The ritual allowed the *aona* (the deceased's abilities) and *yesegi* (the deceased's occult power that in the past made him a great warrior and powerful sorcerer) to be recycled within the family and for the loved ones to receive blessings from the *ama* (a simulacrum of the *auma* (soul) but more powerful, and remaining in the land of the living until all the funeral rites have been carried out correctly), which would strengthen their *aona*. By performing the funeral rites correctly, the relatives ensured that the souls of the deceased departed to *kwelanandamundi* (home of the ancestors) and the deceased was reborn as an ancestor[20].

The Fore people were afflicted by a disease they referred to as kuru, which means, in the native language, "*to tremble from fever or cold*". The clinical description of kuru is "*an invariably fatal cerebellar ataxia accompanied by tremor, choreiform and athetoid movements. In contrast to the neuropathological picture, neurological signs and symptoms are highly uniform. Dementia typical for most subtypes of sporadic CJD, is barely noticeable, and if it is present, then only late during the evolution of the illness. In contrast, kuru patients often displayed emotional alterations, including inappropriate euphoria and compulsive laughter (the journalistic notorious 'laughing death' or 'laughing disease'), or apprehension and depression. Kuru is divided into three clinical stages: ambulant, sedentary and terminal (the Pidgin expressions, wokabaut yet; i.e., is still walking, sindaun pinis; i.e., is able only to sit and slip pinis; i.e., is unable to sit up). The duration of kuru, as measured from the onset of prodromal signs and symptoms until death was about 12 months (3 – 23 months)*" Among the Fore people, more women were affected than men[19].

Anthropologists first learned about kuru in the early 1950s, although a gold prospector had witnessed it in 1936. It was first mentioned in the reports of patrol officers in 1953. The outbreak had begun within living memory but had now become an increasingly serious problem. Its incidence had increased throughout the 1940s and 1950s, with a mortality rate of 35 deaths per 1,000 in some villages. The greater incidence among women began to distort male/female ratios, with men eventually outnumbering women by three to one in the worst-affected South Fore[18]. In the early 1960s, based on the detailed accounts of the Fore, Australian anthropologists Robert Glasse and Shirley Lindenbaum established that the disease had first appeared in a single village in the northwest around 1900, reaching the North Fore around 1920 and the South Fore by 1930. Some regions in the southeast and southwest were not affected until the 1940s[17].

Kuru was thought to be an infectious neurodegenerative disease, but patients had no signs or symptoms of meningoencephalitis (fever, confusion, convulsions, or coma), no cerebrospinal fluid pleocytosis or elevated protein level. Autopsies revealed no signs of inflammatory brain pathology. All attempts to isolate a causative bacterium or virus were unsuccessful, and wide-ranging investigations failed to reveal nutritional deficiencies or environmental toxins that could provide an explanation. The most striking neuropathologic feature of kuru was the presence of numerous round or oval amyloid plaques found in the brains of many of the victims, most commonly in the granular cell layer of the cerebellum, basal ganglia, thalamus, and cerebral cortex[19].

In 1955, the disease came to the attention of Vincent Zigas, a medical officer based in the Kainantu Sub-District of the Eastern Highlands, who began investigating after a typical case was sent to Kainantu for medical observation. In 1957, Zagas was joined by American physician Daniel Carleton Gajdusek. In July 1959, Gajdusek received a letter from the American veterinary pathologist William Hadlow, who had noticed similarities between the kuru plaques and those associated with scrapie, a slow neurodegenerative disease of sheep and goats that had been endemic in Britain since the eighteenth century. At the start of the 1960s, it became apparent that there was an almost total absence of cases in South Fore among children born after 1954. The rising age of kuru cases year by year suggested that transmission of kuru to children had stopped in the 1950s – which was when the Fore people had ceased to cannibalise their deceased relatives. Deaths between 1961-1963 and 1957-1959 showed a 23 per cent reduction overall and a 57 per cent reduction among children. Mortality rates dropped from 7.64 to 5.58 deaths per thousand. Reductions were greater in the North Fore than in the South Fore; the latter accounted for 60 per cent of the total kuru deaths.

This trend would continue until the end of the epidemic[18,19].

That there might be a connection between the cessation of mortuary cannibalism and the easing of the kuru epidemic was first suggested by Glasse and Lindenbaum. They noted that cannibalism among adult men occurred more frequently in the North Fore than the South Fore. In the south, those who did practise cannibalism said that they avoided eating the bodies of women, which would diminish their strength. Small children, living with their mothers, ate what their mothers gave them. But young males left their mothers at the approximate age of ten to live in a communal 'men's house'. They did not partake in funerary cannibalism, which was thus largely limited to women, children, and only a few men. This pattern matched the epidemiology of kuru in the early 1960s[17].

In the early 1960s, Gajdusek demonstrated that kuru could be transmitted to chimpanzees by inoculation with brain material from kuru patients, and from the affected chimpanzees to other chimpanzees[21]. This work earned Gajdusek the 1976 Nobel Prize in Physiology or Medicine. The discovery opened a window into 'prion' diseases or transmissible spongiform encephalopathies (TSEs) including Creutzfeldt-Jakob disease (CJD). Prions are abnormal, pathogenic agents that are transmissible and can induce abnormal folding of specific normal proteins that are found in the brain known as prion proteins. The abnormal folding of these proteins leads to brain damage and the characteristic signs and symptoms of the disease. Prion diseases are invariably fatal. It is now thought that kuru first arose in a single individual from a spontaneous change that created such a pathogenic, infectious agent in the brain, just as sporadic CJD does. The recycling of the infectious agent through eating deceased relatives amplified the agent and the disease in the community, leading to the epidemic[19].

Prehistoric outbreaks of kuru-like diseases

Research in the early twenty-first century has shown that for the human prion protein gene (PRNP), a coding polymorphism at codon 129 is a strong susceptibility factor for human prion diseases. The site can code for either methionine (M) or valine (V), resulting in 3 possible genotypes: M129M, M129V, and V129V. Heterozygosity (i.e., M129V) for this polymorphism has been found to confer relative resistance to prion diseases. Elderly survivors of the kuru epidemic, who had multiple exposures to pathogenic agents at the mortuary feasts, are predominantly heterozygous for PRNP 129. This is in marked contrast to younger Fore, who were never exposed. The kuru epidemic imposed a strong balancing selection[39] on the Fore and essentially eliminated PRNP 129 methionine and valine homozygotes (i.e., M129M and V129V)[22].

PRNP does not evolve rapidly, and there are only four noncoding and two coding changes between the human version and the chimpanzee version. The human version has around a dozen haplotypes worldwide, divided into two deeply diverging lineages: 129M (the ancestral version, coding for M at codon 129 in common with the chimpanzee version) and 129V. The divergence between the two lineages is approximately 10 per cent of that observed

---

[39] Balancing selection occurs when multiple alleles are maintained in a population, which can result in their preservation over long evolutionary periods. In this case, both the M and V-coding alleles are required to confer resistance.

between the human and chimpanzee versions. Assuming a minimum figure of 5 million years for the divergence of humans from chimpanzees, it implies that the two PRNP lineages separated at least 500,000 years ago. While this is only a very rough estimate, it does suggest that the separation was very ancient. This is consistent with strong balancing selection having occurred at PRNP 129 during the evolution of modern humans, and possibly predating their appearance. In turn, this is consistent with kuru-type epidemics having occurred throughout prehistory[22].

This result has been taken to imply an ancient tradition of cannibalism, but this view does need to be subject to a critical examination. Between 1995 and 2016, a total of 178 people in the United Kingdom died from variant CJD (vCJD) as a result of eating beef infected with Bovine Spongiform Encephalitis (BSE). There have also been cases arising from blood transfusions and the use of infected human growth hormones[23]. Could prehistoric hunter-gatherers not have contracted vCDJ from bovids affected by BSE? There is no reason why not, but the incidence would surely have been low. The vCJD outbreak in the United Kingdom was blamed on the use of infected meat and bone meal in cattle feeds. Industrial-scale rendering dates back no further than the nineteenth century. Even at the height of the outbreak at the turn of the century, it affected only a minute percentage of the population. Indeed, there were more than twice as many cases of sporadic CJD as there were vCJD. There were fears that onward transmission through blood transfusions and the use of inadequately decontaminated surgical instruments could lead to the outbreak becoming self-sustaining[24], but these have not been realised. These routes were, of course, unavailable in prehistoric times. While we cannot rule out some means other than cannibalism for the onward transmission of a prehistoric kuru-like disease, there are no records of such outbreaks during the historical period – but even if an ancient, widespread tradition of cannibalism is accepted, it does not necessarily follow that it occurred in the context of mortuary rituals as was the case with the Fore.

However, Paul Pettit[4] argues for a much earlier origin for mortuary cannibalism. He notes that all observed cases of chimpanzee cannibalism arose from infanticide and that the bodies were not treated in the same manner as other prey. At Gombe, only a few individuals present participated. Bodies were poked and prodded and were abandoned after relatively little of them had been eaten. Other 'abnormal' behaviours were observed, such as repeatedly charging at the body and flailing it. These behaviours typically occur during the capture and killing of other prey, but not afterwards. Pettitt thus sees cannibalism as part of the same 'package' of chimpanzee mortuary activity noted above, and sharing its Late Miocene origins.

Early hominin cannibalism

There is very little evidence for possible mortuary cannibalism in the fossil and archaeological records of the Lower Palaeolithic. One exception is STW 53, a 2.0 – 1.5 million-year-old fossil hominin skull that was discovered in 1976 at Sterkfontein, South Africa. Its taxonomic affinities are uncertain; it could be early *Homo* or late *Australopithecus*[25]. In 2000, cutmarks inflicted by a stone tool were reported on the fossil's upper jawbone. The report's authors noted that the location of the cutmarks on the lateral aspect of the zygomatic process of the upper jawbone was consistent with that expected from slicing through the masseter muscle, presumably to remove the lower jawbone from the cranium. The cutmark pattern has been demonstrated across a wide range of butchered species of mammal and was best explained as damage caused by disarticulation. The excavation methods used to recover STW 53 eliminated the possibility that the cutmarks were the result of excavation damage, and carnivore damage was also ruled out. The report concluded that *"Reasonable hypotheses include cannibalism, curation, mutilation, and/or funerary procedures"*[26].

Pettitt[4] concedes that it is not possible to distinguish between any of these hypotheses, but dietary cannibalism is probably the simplest explanation when considered alongside more recent evidence from northern Spain. *Homo antecessor* is a human species[27] known from fossil remains excavated from level TD6 at Gran Dolina ('Great Depression'), part of a large system of caves in the Sierra de Atapuerca, near the city of Burgos, northern Spain. The fossils are 770,000 – 950,000 years old[28,29] and could represent a species closely related to the common ancestor of Neanderthals and *Homo sapiens*[30]. Fossils of *Homo antecessor* have not been found elsewhere, but analysis of footprints uncovered at Happisburgh, Norfolk[31], suggests that they reached England, which was then joined to mainland Europe.

Around 25 per cent of the bones found at Gran Dolina show signs of damage including chopping, cutmarks, peeling where bones have been broken and bent, and marks where bones have been splintered to extract marrow. It is difficult to argue that this damage was not the result of cannibalism – but the extent and pattern of the damage marks suggest butchery for food purposes rather than mortuary cannibalism, as it does not differ from that seen with non-human remains also found in level TD6[32]. Interestingly, though, the pollen record and mammal community for level TD6 do not suggest that the cannibalism occurred at a time of climate stress or a shortage of prey animals[33]. The hominin-bearing level TD6 comprises at least six layers[34], suggesting that the cannibalism was not a one-off event. Pettitt[4] views the TD6 hominins as evidence that Cronos compulsions *"seem to have been deeply and perhaps routinely embedded in the subsistence behaviour of at least one hominin group at this time"*. What is absent is any evidence that cannibalism at Gran Dolina was related to mortuary behaviour.

The Pit of Bones

Only a short distance from the Gran Dolina is Sima de los Huesos ('Pit of Bones'), a small muddy chamber located at the bottom of a 13 m (42.5 ft) chimney deep within the Cueva Mayor cave system. The cramped site lies more than 500 m (⅓ mile) from the mouth of the cave system and is hard to access, necessitating at times crawling on the stomach. The first hominin remains were found there in 1976, but the challenging conditions meant full-scale excavations did not commence until 1984. Currently, over 6,500 fragmentary hominin fossils have been found, representing at least 28 individuals. A solitary hand axe has also been recovered from the site. A variety of dates for the remains have been proposed over the years, but the hominin-bearing layers LU-6 and LU-7 are now thought to be 430,000 years old[35,36]. The Sima hominins show a mixture of *Homo heidelbergensis* and Neanderthal characteristics[36], though it is not clear whether they are very early Neanderthals or a sister lineage that was closely related to Neanderthals[37].

The Sima hominins are crucial to our understanding of human evolution during the Middle Pleistocene, but what concerns us here is how and why the remains reached the site.

Physically, the only means of delivery was via the deep vertical chimney, which is only accessible via the narrow corridors of the Cueva Mayor[38]. The obvious conclusion is that the individuals either fell or their bodies were dropped down the chimney into the chamber[39], but this might not have been the case. Most of the fossilised bones in the chamber are broken, whereas experimental work suggests that fewer than 20 per cent of bones would be broken by the fall into the chamber[40]. Furthermore, smaller bones (ribs, vertebrae, bones of the hands and feet, etc.) are underrepresented in the assemblage, occurring in far smaller quantities than would be expected if whole bodies had been thrown intact into the pit[41].

Over half the bones have carnivore toothmarks. The size distribution is similar to that observed for sheep bones scavenged by foxes, which would account for the absence of the smaller skeletal elements. However, the accumulation itself is unlikely to have been due to carnivore activity by lions or bears: had it been so, it would be expected that the Sima fossil assemblage would include herbivores as well as hominins, but herbivores are entirely absent. Anthropogenic selection of the corpses is consistent with the lack of herbivore remains in the chamber, with the carnivores having entered the chamber independently[40]. However, it cannot be ruled out that natural processes contributed to the ultimate condition of the fossil assemblage[42]. One possibility is that fluvial/mudflow processes relocated the remains from elsewhere in the cave system[43].

Unlike the Gran Dolina remains, there are no signs of cannibalism and barring one individual who had been assaulted with a blunt instrument, there is no reason to suppose that the individuals were deliberately killed[39]. Many of the remains are of adolescents and young adults: either a marked underrepresentation of the individuals aged 5–14 years or an overrepresentation of those aged 15–24 years, along with an underrepresentation of the younger (below five years) and older individuals (25 years and above). It has been suggested that the mortality distribution is not consistent with either food shortages and drought or an epidemic and is indicative of an unspecified catastrophic event that resulted in the Sima hominins all dying together at the same time, possibly after taking shelter in the cave exhausted[44]. However, a similar pattern of mortality is also seen at later Neanderthal sites, suggesting that it was not abnormal[45]. Pettitt[46] suggests that a mortality peak in adolescence/early adulthood could reflect hunting accidents and childbirth complications. Hunting accidents were probably common with inexperienced hunters, and women likely fell pregnant soon after commencing menstruation.

The assumption that all the hominins died at the same time is questionable. There is a roughly even split between transverse and spiral fractures in the assemblage of predominantly broken bones. It is assumed that the transverse fractures occurred a while after death when bones were partially mineralised, and the spiral fractures occurred at or soon after death[40]. A mixture of mineralised and fresh bones is incompatible with the simultaneous deaths of all the individuals[41].

Paul Pettitt[4] has argued for what he terms 'funerary caching': the deliberate placing of corpses in caves, fissures, or other naturally occurring features in the landscape. He regards this as a more advanced behaviour than structured abandonment because the site is given greater meaning than somewhere the corpse will be protected from scavengers, and concepts such as 'places of the dead' may arise from such practices. Pettitt believes varying degrees of weathering of the remains suggest that they could have accumulated over thousands of years. Given this, the significant fracturing of all remains, the indications of light carnivore damage, and an absence of evidence for serious carnivore activity, the simplest interpretation is that the hominin bodies were brought to the cave or its exterior and exposed in or near the shaft. Scavenging by foxes and lions would begin the process of carcass disarticulation, and it would continue as remains were dragged or fell further into the cave system. The process would have been intensified by mudflows within the cave, resulting in the jumble of remains now seen. However, Pettitt rejects the idea that the site was a proto-cemetery. He also dismisses suggestions[35] that the solitary hand axe represents some form of mortuary symbolism and believes that it was a chance loss by somebody who brought the corpses to the site, or it was in a pouch belonging to one of the dead.

The Sima de le Huesos remains could represent multiple isolated funerary caching events over a long period of time, motivated in part by a need for the hygienic disposal of the corpses. The site might have been known as an appropriate place to dispose of dead bodies because the Sima people periodically came across the remains of dead cave bears there. It became a place where the dead could be removed from the ordinary places of the living, so the landscape took on a dichotomy between places of life and places of the dead.

Neanderthal burial of the dead

It is commonly asserted that Neanderthals intentionally buried their dead, and there is evidence for Neanderthal burials at many sites in Europe and Western Asia. However, Paul Pettitt[4] notes that the total amounts to fewer than 100 individuals. Even some of these are better classed as funereal caching rather than true burials. The latter he defines as the intentional creation of a space in which to deposit and cover a body. Pettitt argues, therefore, that the conclusion that Neanderthals habitually buried their dead may be premature, and when they did, it might have been the exception rather than the rule.

One of the best-known Neanderthal burial sites is La Ferrassie, near the town of Les Eyzies in the Dordogne Valley. The 65,000 – 70,000-year-old rock shelter site was discovered by two local men in September 1909. The site held the remains of eight Neanderthals in seven graves: two adults, three neonates, and three infants. All the graves were aligned in an east-west direction. They fell into four groups, all of which were sited in a rich occupation horizon. The first and westmost of these groups, located close to the rear wall of the shelter, contains the graves of the two adults: a male and a female. The male, aged 40 – 55, was found lying flexed in a depression (LF1) that was probably deliberately excavated and associated with three large stone slabs – one underneath his head and the other two flanking the torso. Just 0.5 m (1.5 ft) away is the grave of the female (LF2), which does not contain any slabs. Strictly speaking, it is not a double burial, because the pair are not interred in the same cutting. However, the close association of the two cannot be interpreted as anything other than intentional. The second group lay 2 m (6 ft 6 in) to the east of the two adults. It contained two graves (LF3 and LF4), side by side, each measuring 0.7 × 0.3 m (2 ft 4 in × 1 ft). LF3 contained a 3 – 10-year-old child, and LF4 contained two neonates. The third group contained two more graves (LF5 and LF8). LF5 contained a neonate, and LF8 a 2-year-old child. Finally, the fourth group contained a single grave (LF6), where a 3-year-old child was interred in a depression and covered by a large triangular limestone slab. A feature originally designated LF7 was later found not to be a burial. There is some dispute over whether stone tools found in some of the graves represent grave goods or whether cup-like depressions on the LF6 limestone slab were intentionally carved or were simply natural features. However, the eight individuals were spatially associated, and their graves share general characteristics and the same orientation. They were organised with the adults in the west and children and neonates in the centre and east of the site. It is difficult to interpret La Ferrassie as anything other than an intentionally planned, multiple burial site[4].

Another well-known Neanderthal burial site is Shanidar, a cave site in Iraqi Kurdistan, which was excavated by American archaeologist Ralph Solecki between 1951 and 1960. Situated in mountainous terrain, the limestone cave is 760 m (2,500 ft) above sea level and overlooks the Great Zab River, a tributary of the Tigris. The remains of nine Neanderthals designated Shanidar 1 to 9 were recovered during Solecki's excavations. They comprise groups found on two different levels of the excavation. Shanidar 1, 3, and 5 were found in the upper level and the others in the lower level[1]. Shanidar 1, 3, and 5 are 55,000 – 45,000 years old, and the lower level remains are 70,000 – 60,000 years old[47].

When Shanidar 4, a male aged 30 to 45, was found, Solecki's team decided to transport the entire sediment block containing the remains to the Baghdad Museum to complete the excavation of the remains. This revealed the remains of three further individuals – two more adults (Shanidar 6 and 8) and an infant (Shanidar 9). Rather unwisely, the block had been driven to Baghdad on the roof of a taxi, and inevitably, it was disturbed during the journey. Although Shanidar 4 was the uppermost, the exact stratigraphic relationships between the individuals are unknown. Either the individuals all died and/or were interred at the spot, or there were multiple burials at the same spot over an extended interval[47]. Shanidar 4 and some other remains were transferred to the Smithsonian in Washington, DC, although most of the finds remained in Iraq. In 2006, archaeologist Melinda Zeder identified incomplete lower left leg bones and foot bones of a one or two-year-old infant in the Smithsonian material. This new find was designated Shanidar 10[48].

Shanidar 1, 3, and 5 were found in the upper level immediately below rock-fall debris, and Solecki believed that they were killed by a cave-in. One of the victims was Shanidar 1, an elderly male who had been in poor health before his death. He had suffered numerous injuries to both the upper and lower body, leaving him badly disabled and probably blind in one eye. His injuries had healed, implying that he had been cared for by other group members during his convalescence. In death, Shanidar 1 was found lying on his back, legs fully extended, and arms folded across his chest, covered with small pieces of limestone. It suggests that others – possibly survivors of the cave-in – had later returned to the cave to bury him[1,49].

The individuals in the lower level of the excavation appeared to have been intentionally buried. In an attempt to reconstruct the climatic and vegetation history of the site, soil samples gathered from around the body of Shanidar 4 (an adult male) were later analysed for pollen. In addition to the usual pollen found throughout the site, some samples yielded whole clumps of pollen. Solecki[50] suggested that this could represent floral tributes placed in the grave by grieving relatives. In the event, claims of 'flower power Neanderthals' turned out to be premature. One problem was the lack of similar ritual treatment of other remains in the cave. The pollen was almost certainly introduced into the cave by either the Persian Jird (a gerbil-like rodent known to store large numbers of seeds and flowers at certain points in their burrows)[51] or by ground-nesting bees[52,53].

The debate over the supposed floral burial of Shanidar 4 was a distraction from the other remains: along with Shanidar 6 – 8, Shanidar 4 is part of a tight spatial cluster that respects the position of its members and appears to form an intentional sequential burial group. None of them appears to have been killed by a rockfall or deposited by natural agents. Shanidar 8 (a child) was the first to be buried, followed by Shanidar 6 and 7 (both adult females), and finally Shanidar 4. Shanidar 6 lay only 0.1 m (4 in) below Shanidar 4, and Shanidar 4 and 7 were adjacent, suggesting that all four were interred within a relatively short timescale[4].

In 2014, the Kurdish Regional Government invited a British team of archaeologists to conduct the first excavations at Shanidar since Solecki's work, although the fieldwork had to be delayed for a year because of the threat of terrorist activity. The intention was to conduct detailed work at the original trench margins to place Solecki's findings into a robust chronological, climatic, ecological, and cultural framework, taking advantage of archaeological techniques that were unavailable in the 1950s. Between 2015 and 2017, further Neanderthal remains were found, including a partial articulated leg attributed to Shanidar 5 and the remains of the upper body of a completely new individual in the lower layer, just to the east of the supposed 'flower power' burial of Shanidar 4[47]. Temporarily designated Shanidar Z, the newly found individual appears to have been intentionally buried. The sediments containing the remains are paler than layers above and below, and they are capped on their northern side by two horizontally oriented stones. To the south is a vertical slab from a rockfall that occurred before the burial. To date, Shanidar Z has only been partially excavated, but he/she was probably placed on their back, with their shoulders and head raised, and their head resting on its left side on top of the left hand. The lower limbs have not yet been found, but the presence of the vertical slab to the south suggests that they were probably flexed for burial[47].

Periodically, there have been claims of grave goods from several Neanderthal sites in the form of artefacts and once-meaty bones (presumably intended to ensure that the deceased did not get too peckish *en route* to the next world) found in burial infill. However, it is just as likely that these items were accidentally introduced when the graves were filled in. Grotta Guattari is a cave site at Monte Circeo, an isolated promontory on the southwest coast of Italy, 100 km (60 miles) from Rome. The site was discovered in 1939 by construction workers, having been sealed by rock debris for around 50,000 years. On the cave floor was found an irregular ring of rocks surrounding a Neanderthal skull, implying ceremonial treatment of a kind. Unfortunately, the skull was moved and then replaced before it could be photographed or witnessed by archaeologists, so its initial position inside the ring is open to question. It is now thought that hyenas damaged the skull and were also responsible for it ending up inside the ring. Similarly, the skull of a young male Neanderthal found at Teshik-Tash, Uzbekistan, was surrounded by five or six pairs of ibis horns – but such horns also occurred throughout the deposit associated with the site, so there is no reason to suppose those found with the skull had been deliberately placed there[1,6,54].

Overall, the view that the burials do represent deliberate interment is supported by the survival of largely intact, articulated skeletons, the relatively large number of individuals recovered at certain sites, including young children whose bones are particularly delicate, and combined with stratigraphic observations[54]. However, there is an issue in that most of the supposed burial sites were discovered and excavated long before modern excavation methods came into use, and there are some who remain sceptical[55]. In an attempt to allay such doubts, researchers conducted a twelve-year fieldwork project at La Chapelle aux Saints, central France, where the burial of a 40-year-old Neanderthal male was discovered in 1908. They concluded that the depression in which the body was found had been intentionally created, and the absence of scavenger damage to the bones indicated that the body had been protected by burial soon after death [56]. These findings confirmed that, in this case at least, a recently deceased Neanderthal had been intentionally buried by other members of his group. If La Chapelle aux Saints does represent an intentional burial, it is difficult to argue that La Ferrassie, the lower-level group at Shanidar, and other similar sites across Europe and Western Asia do not. It is unlikely that Neanderthals simply dug graves to remove corpses from habitation areas, as there are far easier ways of accomplishing this. However, the graves are not proof of Neanderthal spirituality or religion, and such claims must be regarded as unproven[54]. The consideration of these matters takes place against the broader question of Neanderthal symbolic behaviour and how closely their behavioural patterns resembled the modern condition. Regardless of such considerations, there is no reason to suppose that Neanderthals felt the loss of kin or friends any less keenly than modern people.

Funerary traditions of early *Homo sapiens*

Our own species, *Homo sapiens*, first enters the fossil and archaeological record around 300,000 years ago at Jebel Irhoud, a cave site located about 100 km (60 miles) west of Marrakech, Morocco[57]. Though retaining primitive features such as prominent browridges, robust lower jawbones, and a long, low rather than globular cranial vault, the Irhoud people were morphologically closer to modern people than to *Homo erectus*, *Homo heidelbergensis*, or Neanderthals[1,49,57,58]. However, the earliest tentative evidence for mortuary rituals involving *Homo sapiens* is rather more recent. The Herto people, whose remains were discovered in 1997 at Middle Awash, Ethiopia, lived around 155,000 years ago[59]. The find comprised three well-preserved crania: two adult males and a six-year-old child. There were also some fragmentary remains. Like the Irhoud people, the Herto people were not entirely modern and were initially described as a new subspecies, remains, *Homo sapiens idaltu*. The word *idaltu* means 'elder' or 'first-born' in the local Afar language[60].

The better-preserved of the two adult crania was found to bear cutmarks, which had been made with stone tools. Some of these are deep marks typical of those made by de-fleshing, but most are more superficial and suggest repetitive scraping. Such marks are not seen on animal remains processed for food, which suggests an explanation other than cannibalism. The juvenile cranium also exhibits cutmarks, which were made by a very sharp stone flake deep in its base. The rear of the base was broken away, and its edges polished. The sides of this cranium also show a deep polish, which could have been the result of repeated handling. The second adult cranium was also 'modified', but only with two cutmarks. There are ethnographic parallels in several cultures where skulls have been similarly treated, with cutmarks, decoration, and polishing, and preserved in mortuary rituals. Such parallels raise the possibility that the Herto people might have had similar rituals[59].

Levantine burials

The next evidence for mortuary activity involving early representatives of our species comes from two sites in Israel, Mugharet es-Skhul at Mount Carmel and Jebel Qafzeh near Nazareth. The Skhul people are dated to 100,000 – 135,000 years ago[61], and the Qafzeh people to 100,000 – 130,000 years ago[62]. Until recently, they were thought to represent the earliest presence of *Homo sapiens* outside Africa. Though essentially modern, with globular crania and pronounced chins, the Skhul and Qafzeh people still retained some archaic characteristics, such as their greater robustness than living populations[46].

Mugharet es-Skhul ('Cave of the Kids') is a cave site on the western slopes of Mount Carmel, 3 km (2 miles) south of Haifa. It was discovered by chance by British engineers planning a road to Haifa, and between 1929 and 1934, they were excavated by British archaeologist Dorothy Garrod[63]. The cave contains three main layers; Garrod's team recovered the remains of nine individuals (Skhul I – IX) from the second layer, Layer B. Subsequently, the lower jawbone of a tenth individual, a child (Skhul X), was found in the same sediment block as Skhul VII. These individuals appear to have been intentionally buried. Enclosed in the arms of Skhul V was the lower jawbone of a large boar[61]. Two dog whelk shells (*Nassarius gibbosulus*), perforated for use as beads, have been identified as probably originating from the layer containing the fossils by an analysis of material still adhering to them[64], though whether they were grave goods directly associated with the Skhul V burial cannot be confirmed from the original description of the burials and their archaeological context[65]. The jawbone has likewise been interpreted as possible grave goods, as has a flint scraper found between the hands of the Skhul IV individual. However, these items could have just happened to be in the grave infill, heaped on top of the bodies at burial[66].

Paul Pettitt[4] notes that not all of the Skhul burials can be regarded as formal inhumations, although at least four can be. The Skhul I, IV, V, and IX individuals were placed in intentionally excavated grave cuttings, but the Skhul VIII individual seems to have been placed in a natural channel, probably water-worn. He regards the latter as an example of funerary caching. Pettitt believes that the stratigraphic position of the burials and the close spatial association of some of them suggests that they all date to a relatively discrete time period, except Skhul IX, which could be older. He views them as simple inhumations, though a demonstration beyond reasonable doubt of grave goods in the Skhul V burial or the association of Skhul VII and X in an adult and child burial would represent a significant advance in funerary behaviour.

The second site, Jebel Qafzeh ('Mount of the Leap'), is a cave located near Mount Precipice, south of Nazareth. It was first excavated between 1933 and 1934 and then again between 1965 and 1979[65]. Five partial skeletons and fragments of as many as ten other individuals have been recovered at the site[6]. Pettitt suggests that at least six Qafzeh individuals received formal burials: Qafzeh 8 – 11, 13, and 15. An adult female (Qafzeh 9) and a child (Qafzeh 10) were apparently buried together in a distinct rectangular grave cutting measuring 1.4×0.5 m (4.5×1.5 ft) with the child at the woman's feet. The fragmentary remains of Qafzeh 6, 7, and possibly 3 may also represent a multiple burial. There is also good evidence for grave goods. A large ochre block with signs of scraping and two worked flints was found with Qafzeh 8, and Pettitt notes that such an association is unlikely to be the result of chance. Ochre fragments were also found in several other graves. Further ochre, together with ochre-stained artefacts, was found close to the grave area, suggesting that possibly ochre was processed for activities relating to the burials[4].

Qafzeh 11, an adolescent, was found with an antler lying on their chest[65], together with an abundance of ochre fragments, which Pettitt believes were deliberate grave inclusions[4]. The grave was large for the body size at 1 × 0.5 m (3 × 1.5 ft) and was lined and/or marked with stone blocks[4]. The Qafzeh 11 individual was aged 12 – 13 years old at death and had suffered a traumatic brain injury earlier in life. The injury resulted in delayed brain growth and probably caused personality and neurological troubles. Although this is speculation, there could be a connection between Qafzeh 11's condition and the funerary treatment they received[67].

The first cremation

Archaeological evidence suggests that humans reached Australia, which was then joined to New Guinea, around 65,000 years ago[68]. However, the earliest fossil human remains to be found in Australia are rather more recent. Lake Mungo is one of a series of dried-up lakes making up the Willandra Lakes system. The Willandra Lakes Region is a World Heritage Site that covers 2,400 sq km (925 sq miles) in the southwest of New South Wales, about 1,000 km (620 miles) west of Sydney.

The remains of two individuals, WLH 1 and WLH2, were discovered in 1969 by archaeologist Jim Bowler and reconstructed in the lab by anthropologist Alan Thorne. They were found to comprise around 25 per cent of a lightly built skeleton representing a woman aged around 25 and a few fragments of a second individual. The remains had been partly cremated before being intentionally fragmented and placed in a small, shallow pit. The female became known as 'Mungo Woman'. These finds were followed, in 1974, by the discovery of a full skeleton within the same geological stratum as the original cremation site and only 450 m (1,500 ft) from it. Bowler and Thorne then excavated the remains, which turned out to represent an older adult male. He had been laid out in a shallow grave and liberally sprinkled with ochre before burial. Officially known as WLH 3, he became known, inevitably, as Mungo Man[6,63,69,70].

Mungo Woman and Mungo Man are thought to be around 42,000 years old[70], though Thorne[71] suggested that they were as old as 62,000 years. Regardless, they are far older than the 30,000 years suggested at the time of their discovery. The finds represent the earliest-known cremation and the earliest-known ritual ochre burial. Paul Pettitt[4] notes that the young Mungo Woman was probably cremated on the foreshore, and then her remains were smashed up and deposited in the pit. This took place in an area in which hearths and earth ovens are abundant, and Pettitt suggests the possibility of cannibalism. Mungo Man may have been wrapped in an ochre-stained shroud or dressed in ochre-stained clothing in the wider context of the use of ochre as a pigment for painting. He suggests that the Mungo Man burial does not differ significantly from the Skhul and Qafzeh, although he concedes the significance of Mungo Woman as the earliest-known cremation.

In 1992, Mungo Woman's remains were returned to local Aboriginal groups, though in practice her remains were kept under lock and key at the Mungo National Park museum.

Mungo Man was retained by the Australian National University and later the National Museum of Australia, but he was eventually repatriated in a solemn three-day-long ceremony in 2017, at which Jim Bowler, now 88, was present. Both Mungo Woman and Mungo Man have since been reburied, although the decision to do so without a public memorial or keeping place has divided opinion.

Early and mid-Upper Palaeolithic mortuary traditions in Europe

Homo sapiens began dispersing into Europe as early as 56,800 years ago[72], though it was not until around 46,000 years ago that they began arriving in large numbers[73]. Paul Pettitt notes that human remains are generally rare during the earlier part of the Upper Palaeolithic in Europe. Caves in the Czech Republic and Romania have yielded a relatively large number of human remains, which are sufficient to suggest funerary caching by the earliest *Homo sapiens* in Europe. At the Mladeč cave system in Moravia, for example, over 100 fossil *Homo sapiens* remains have been recovered, associated with the Aurignacian culture. The remains include adults of both sexes and juveniles. The presence of multiple specimens of both cranial and postcranial remains suggests that entire bodies were deposited at the site. During this period, the archaeological record of Europe also reveals for the first time the use of human remains for ornamentation. Several sites in France have yielded human teeth perforated through the root for use as ornaments. French sites have also yielded head parts (frontal bones, lower jawbones, etc.) with cutmarks indicating defleshing. While the teeth could, in principle, have been saved after falling out, the defleshed head parts are consistent with the teeth having been intentionally removed. Pettitt views these finds as indicative of a strongly regionalised mortuary picture: the curation of human body parts in some places and funerary caching in others. In turn, this could indicate that underlying belief systems were likewise regionalised[4].

It is not until the mid-Upper Palaeolithic that the first burials of *Homo sapiens* in Europe occur, associated with the Gravettian and other contemporary cultures. The Gravettian culture, which followed the Aurignacian, began around 38,000 – 34,000 years ago[74,75], probably in the Danubian region[76]. The Gravettian spread across Europe, replacing the Aurignacian, though estimates of the timescale vary considerably. They range from as long as 7,500 years (suggesting that the Gravettian spread by population movements)[77] to as little as a few hundred years (suggesting cultural transmission)[78]. Probably, both demic and cultural factors were involved.

The earliest unequivocal burial is at Sungir, 200 km (125 miles) east of Moscow. The remains of a boy and girl, both aged around 11 to 13 years old, were buried in a long, narrow grave, covered with red ochre, and accompanied by an impressive collection of grave goods. These included thousands of ivory beads, hundreds of fox teeth, ivory pins, pendants, animal carvings, and spears made from mammoth tusks. The largest of these was 2.4 m (7 ft 11 in) long[79]. The Sungir remains are 34,600 years old and the Streletskian artefact assemblage at the site places it at the transition between the early and mid-Upper Palaeolithic[80]. Elaborate burials such as this probably reflect increasingly complex societies and the emergence of high-status individuals[81]. The wealth accorded to the burial of these children, who could not have accrued it in their lifetimes, suggests that such status could have been inherited[82]. A

Prehistoric Investigations 2

rather more sinister possibility is human sacrifice[79].

Another site where there is evidence for the variable treatment of human remains is Grotte de Cussac, a 25,000-year-old Gravettian cave site at Le Buisson-de-Cadouin in the Dordogne. The cave complex comprises two branches, which extend 1,000 m (3,280 ft) to the southeast and 600 m (1,970 ft) to the northwest of the entrance. The site is unusual in that the human remains occur in conjunction with extensive artwork of more than 800 engravings on the walls of the cave complex. The artwork comprises representations of bison, mammoths, bovids, and horses, as well as human representations including stylistic female silhouettes and male and female genitalia. The human remains have been found in two groups in the northwest branch of the cave, located 150 m (490 ft) and 230 m (755 ft) from the entrance. They suggest three distinct forms of mortuary treatment. In the first group, the intact body of a young male was deposited in a shallow bear hibernation nest. Three further bear nests were used for secondary burials of collections of postcranial bones from individuals whose bodies presumably were initially buried elsewhere to decompose before their remains were exhumed for reburial. The second group comprises postcranial body parts of two adults and one adolescent in shallow depressions high along the cave wall. These differing mortuary practices were presumably of significance to the Grotte de Cussac people, as was the association of the burial sites with cave art, but the ultimate significance remains unknown[83].

Just over fifty burials are known for the mid-Upper Palaeolithic, many associated with repeated burials at the same location. They include double and triple interments. Most of the burials include grave goods and ornamentation with ochre. During the Gravettian, there is evidence for both primary inhumation, *i.e.*, the immediate burial of an intact body – but also, for the first time in Europe, the secondary burial of human body parts from a body buried some time previously. Pettitt suggests that a tradition of ritual burial emerged at the start of the mid-Upper Palaeolithic alongside regional variations of the continent-wide Gravettian culture. Accordingly, though these mortuary traditions had much in common, there were regional variations. Burial may not even have been ubiquitous. Many Gravettian sites, for instance in southern Germany, have been excavated where there is no evidence for mortuary rituals. Human teeth continued to be perforated for use as personal ornaments in France, where funerary caching may have continued[4,46].

The Magdalenian culture appeared towards the end of the last Ice Age, around 18,000 years ago, and reached Britain in the guise of the Creswellian around 14,000 years ago[46]. Gough's Cave, Cheddar Gorge, is a Creswellian site that has yielded an extensive assemblage of human remains, thought to represent at least six individuals. Their cranial vaults are relatively intact, but their postcranial remains are highly fragmented, and all six show clear signs of butchery. However, some notches are not associated with de-fleshing and appear to be deliberate incisions rather than unintentional cutmarks. They were made on regions of the bone where there are no muscle attachments. The cranial vaults had been made into cuplike artefacts, possibly to be used as ritual drinking vessels. Taken together, the cranial and postcranial material from Gough's Cave has been interpreted as evidence for mortuary practices involving ritual cannibalism of the deceased[84,85]. Possible ritual/mortuary cannibalism has also been reported from 13 Magdalenian sites in France, Spain, Germany, and Poland[86,87].

The first cemeteries

The Epipalaeolithic was once thought to be a relatively brief episode towards the end of the Upper Palaeolithic in Southwest Asia. It is now known to have extended back to around 24,000 years ago, a time when the Last Glacial Maximum (LGM)[40] was at its height. It lasted until 11,700 years ago, when the last Ice Age ended, and the world emerged into the present Holocene epoch. In the Levant, it is divided between Early (24,000 – 18,000 years ago), Middle (18,000 – 14,900 years ago), and Late (14,900 – 11,700 years ago), with the emergence of the Natufian culture around 14,900 years ago being taken as the boundary between the latter two[88].

The Levant is a long way from the ice sheets that covered much of Europe and northern Asia, but during the LGM it experienced a cold, arid climate. Pollen records suggest that the Mediterranean coastal region was woodland and forest steppe and the rest of the region was steppe and desert-steppe. The woodland and forest steppe would have offered an abundance of acorns, almonds, cereals, tubers, and edible seeds[89], and herbivores including sheep, goats, aurochs, wild boar, gazelle, and deer[90]. Some groups appear to have adopted an at least semi-sedentary lifestyle[91], and burials[92], grave goods[93], and cremations have been found at various sites[94].

The earliest-known cemetery in the Levant – and possibly in the world - has been found at the site of 'Uyun al-Hammam in northern Jordan. The site is associated with the Geometric Kebaran culture, which was current from 18,000 to 16,250 years ago[95]. The cemetery holds the remains of at least eleven individuals, interred in eight graves. In two adjacent graves, human remains were accompanied by those of foxes, suggesting increasingly complex mortuary rituals. Other grave goods from these two graves included red ochre, worked bone implements, chipped and ground stone tools, and the remains of deer, gazelle, aurochs, and tortoise[96].

The Early Natufian culture was current from 14,900 to 13,700 years ago[95]. It flourished during the Bølling-Allerød interstadial, a warm period towards the end of the last Ice Age. It is associated with increasing sedentism, and many Early Natufian villages were probably occupied throughout the year[97]. The burial practices of the Early Natufian people are certainly consistent with sedentism. Many of their semi-buried circular houses were associated with graves, located either under floors or in fills[98]. In addition to these under-floor burials, cemeteries now became widespread and some contained far larger numbers of burials than 'Uyun al-Hammam. At the site of Wadi-en-Natuf, the remains of almost 100 individuals were found. At the sites of 'Ain Mallaha and Hayonim, many graves were dug in abandoned dwellings and outside of houses, although not in houses that were still in use. Shelter 131, a possibly purpose-built semi-circular building at 'Ain Mallaha, contained twelve burials[99].

Although some Natufian burials were single graves, around 80 per cent were multiple inhumations. In the latter case, individuals of both sexes and all ages were typically buried together. Such burials could reflect nuclear or extended families. Many individuals were buried wearing items of personal ornamentation, mostly made from tooth-shaped dentalium shells[100]. The increase in the number of cemetery burials could reflect an increasing sense

---

[40]The coldest stage of the last Ice Age, usually abbreviated to LGM.

that people belonged to a distinct village community, as well as to a family or extended family[95]. Cemeteries could also reflect a need by villagers to mark their territory by establishing an ancestor presence there[101].

Dentalium shells have often been found at sites far from the coast, which must have been obtained through long-distance trade networks[88,95]. Although the trade in dentalium shells predated the Natufian period, there is a significant increase in their numbers compared to Early Epipalaeolithic cultures[102,103]. British archaeologist Steven Mithen[97] has suggested that dentalium jewellery represented a form of social identity. Certain individuals took advantage of sedentism to acquire surpluses of food and goods and gain control of trading relationships. One way to do this was to limit the number of shells in circulation at any given time by burying large quantities of them with the dead. Those remaining in circulation would thus confer greater prestige on their owners. Ethnographic evidence suggests that present-day sedentary hunter-gatherer groups tend to be socially stratified, whereas more mobile groups are egalitarian. An increase in both social complexity and long-distance exchange during the Natufian would have created a need for powerful individuals to assert and display their status within their own group and possibly among members of neighbouring groups[88]. The dentalium shells could have held the same status in Early Natufian society as a Rolex or a Patek Philippe today. A problem with this view is that Natufian mortuary practices do not appear to highlight social hierarchies or the existence of any form of elite. Anthropologists Brian Byrd and Christopher Monahan[100] conducted a comprehensive survey of Natufian burials, in which they considered grave goods and burial site complexity. They found that there was a lack of any standardised Natufian regional burial tradition and did not find any correlations that could identify high-status individuals or kin groups.

The climatic amelioration of the Bølling-Allerød interstadial ended around 12,900 years ago[104,105], and the Earth was plunged back into the renewed cold and aridity of the Younger Dryas stadial. It was once thought that the Natufian people were forced to abandon their villages as foraging returns declined, and returned to a more mobile lifestyle[97]. More recently, it has been found that the transition from Early to Late Natufian slightly preceded the Younger Dryas[106]. The impact of the Younger Dryas in the Levant was not as pronounced as once believed, and at least some of the populations retained the sedentary way of life[107–109]. Factors other than the climate downturn could have been involved in the transition, such as food shortages arising from the over-exploitation of game animals and plants[97]. Regardless of these considerations, many sites were abandoned, and their inhabitants returned to a more mobile way of life. At 'Ain Mallaha, there was no longer a permanent settlement. The large houses gave way to far less substantial structures, occupied only seasonally. The site continued to be used for burials, possibly now regarded as a sacred place where the dead were united with their ancestors[97,99,110].

The Late Natufian saw a significant change in mortuary practices. Graves were always in dug pits and there were no more burials under the floors of houses. People were now very rarely buried with grave goods. There was also a widespread though not universal shift from group burials to single interments and secondary burial of skulls and long bones was now practised[98,100]. The changed circumstances of many Natufian groups almost certainly led to changes in their worldview and belief systems, in turn leading to changes in their mortuary practices. However, the latter are open to conflicting interpretations. Steven Mithen[97] believes that the abandonment of village living meant the end of the power base for the elite who controlled the distribution of the dentalium shells, and without this control over their availability, the shells became worthless – as gold or diamonds would if they became freely available. As a consequence, Late Natufian society was more egalitarian than that of the Early Natufian period. The shift from kin-based group burials reflected the reduced importance of lineage. Instead, people were judged on what they had achieved in life and their personal qualities. Mithen also suggests that the increase in secondary burial could have come about because the majority of people died away from their ancestral homes, and the now-nomadic groups periodically returned to these places to rebury the remains of the recently deceased. Bryan Byrd and Christopher Monahan[100] also see single interments as reflecting a growing emphasis on the importance of the individual over the group, although as previously noted, they have raised doubts about the existence of high-status kin groups during the Early Natufian.

Anthropologist Ian Kuijt[111] takes a rather different view. He suggests that secondary burials, single interments, and the lack of grave goods reflect the development of community-based mortuary rituals intended to cut across household and kin group lines and to emphasise the importance of group membership over the status of individuals. Any differences within a community were minimised by ensuring similar mortuary treatment for all its members. These new practices arose from a desire to maintain solidarity and stability during a period of significant economic change. The problem with this model is that it is a 'functionalist' explanation. Structural functionalism views society as composed of institutions that function for the common good, but its critics argue that it downplays conflict and inequality. It is also argued that such models are more descriptive than explanatory, and could be formulated as 'the purpose of X is to do what it does'[112]. Despite these criticisms, functionalist models positing ritual as a means of promoting social cohesion are widely accepted.

Social complexity and cemeteries of the Mesolithic

The Mesolithic is the period lying between the Upper Palaeolithic and Neolithic, now defined as the period between the end of the last Ice Age and the transition to agriculture. In Europe, agriculture first appeared in Greece between 6500 and 6000 BCE and spread westwards, reaching Britain and Ireland soon after 4000 BCE[113]. A significant feature of the Mesolithic in Europe is the appearance for the first time of dedicated cemeteries. The oldest-known Mesolithic cemeteries in Europe are El Collado, on the Mediterranean coast of Spain south of Valencia, which dates to around 7500 BCE and others on Portugal's Atlantic coast, which range from around 6500 to 5110 BCE[114]. Cemeteries are usually found in regions capable of supporting large populations, such as in coastal areas, or near lakes and rivers. They vary considerably in size: some are very large, such as Oleneostrovski Mogilnik in the Republic of Karelia (part of Russia) with 170 burials and Cabeço da Arruda, Portugal with 150 burials. However, most are far smaller and do not exceed 20 to 60 burials. Often, it is difficult to determine if the larger cemeteries served a large local population, or were simply in use for longer[101].

Knowledge of the social complexity and diversity of Mesolithic societies may be inferred from the relationship between the age and sex of those interred in cemeteries, the accompanying grave goods, and variations in burial rituals. In most cases, these suggest egalitarian societies where status reflected individual personal achievement. Tooth pendants and antlers are very common grave offerings, which probably reflect the success individuals enjoyed as hunters. However, in some cases, there is evidence for ranked societies with hereditary status. One sign of such societies is child burials with extensive grave goods. Children are unlikely to have acquired high status on merit in a short lifetime, so it is inferred that it was inherited from high-status parents[101]. Examples of child burials with extensive grave goods have been found at the cemeteries on the islands of Hoëdic and Téviec in the Bay of Quiberon, Brittany[82] and at the cave site of Arma Veirana in the Neva River Valley, northwestern Italy[115].

Oleneostrovski Mogilnik ('Red Deer Island') is an extensively studied island site at Lake Onega, Karelia, with evidence for even greater social complexity[116]. A total of 170 burials have been excavated in two burial clusters, one northern and one southern. The original number might have been as high as 500 but unfortunately, many graves are thought to have been lost at what was once a quarry. The graves are typically rectangular, aligned east-west, with bodies facing east. The site was first excavated in the 1950s, and over 7,000 artefacts were recovered from the burials, including pendants, sculptured effigies, hunting implements, and other tools. The pendants were made from the pierced teeth of bears, beavers, and elks. The absence of pendants made from the teeth of any other animal suggests that this troika was of particular symbolic importance to the Oleneostrovski Mogilnik people.

There is a considerable variation in grave goods, which leaves little doubt that the Oleneostrovski Mogilnik people lived in a large, socially complex society. Some graves contained over 400 items of grave goods, but around 20 per cent contained no grave goods at all. Some grave goods were gender-specific: bone points, pins, harpoons, and stone adzes were regularly associated with male burials, whereas ornaments made from carved beaver teeth were found in female burials. A small number of graves contained slate knives and daggers, which were probably high-prestige items. The main raw material used by the Oleneostrovski Mogilnik was flint, and slate must have been obtained by trade with slate-producing regions. The knives and daggers could have reflected the role of the deceased as middlemen in a trade network. The pierced-tooth pendants could have been an indication of an individual's 'wealth'. The bear tooth pendants were only found with the prestigious slate knives and daggers, suggesting that they were worth more than those made from beaver and elk teeth. Individuals in the prime of life were found to be 'better off' in terms of the number of pendants than were the young and the old. The system could have reflected success in hunters as well as trading. As hunting abilities declined with age, individuals were less able to hold on to their wealth. Oleneostrovski Mogilnik appears to have been a meritocracy, but there was no way to save for your retirement.

In addition to the individuals who were ranked by teeth pendants, there were three small groups of individuals who seem to have had a special status within Oleneostrovski Mogilnik society. The first group, consisting of two men and two women, were interred in vertical funnel-shaped shafts with extensive grave goods. These graves have been interpreted as belonging to shamans. The second group consists of nine individuals – two interred in the southern cluster and seven in the northern cluster. Their graves contained sculptured stone, wood, or bone effigies. Those in the northern cluster graves are carvings of elks, but those in the southern cluster graves are carvings of snakes and humans. One possibility is that the two burial clusters might have represented a division of the Oleneostrovski Mogilnik society, such as a moiety. The third group comprised eleven individuals who had no grave goods apart from bone projectile points. All were male, and around half were middle-aged or elderly. Possibly, this group represented a specialised male role that barred them from accumulating personal wealth. Since the bone points were hunting implements and there was a close association of the wealth symbols with food procurement, these individuals may have held special responsibilities connected with hunting that prohibited any activities connected with the acquisition of wealth.

Early Neolithic burials in Southwest Asia and Europe

The warm, wet, and stable climate of the Holocene was a key factor in what influential Australian archaeologist Vere Gordon Childe[117] described as the Neolithic Revolution, drawing an analogy with the Industrial Revolution of the late eighteenth and early nineteenth centuries. Agriculture arose independently and at different times in parts of the world where local animal and plant species were suitable for domestication. For example, in Southwest Asia, suitable animals were sheep, goats, pigs, and cattle, and suitable plants were barley, wheat, lentils, and peas. In China, there were rice, millet, and pigs, and in the New World, there were the 'Three Sisters' of maize, beans, and squashes. Unlike hunter-gathering, subsistence agriculture could support large, sedentary populations. As these populations grew, farming groups spread out to found new settlements. Farming settlements appeared across Europe, Africa, Asia, the Pacific, and the New World. Unsurprisingly, we have far more burials from Neolithic settlements around the world than we do from earlier times and a great diversity of funerary practices: far more than could be covered even in a far longer work than this.

Studies of ancient DNA suggest that there was genetic continuity between the Epipalaeolithic Natufian people and the early Pre-Pottery Neolithic (PPNA) farmers who followed them around 9700 BCE[118]. Many elements of Late Natufian technology and culture persisted into the PPNA, including mortuary practices. Graves were simple and grave goods were largely absent. Secondary burial also continued, with the majority of adults having their skulls removed for subsequent reburial elsewhere in their home settlement. However, skull removal was rare for children. Primary burials generally took place under the floors of houses, or in courtyards between buildings[111]. During the later Pre-Pottery Neolithic (PPNB) from around 8500 BCE, skull removal and secondary burial continued, but the practice now arose of modelling facial features on the skull in plaster. Plastered skulls have been found at many sites. There are subtle differences between those at each site, though all conform to the same basic design. Sometimes, only part of the skull was plastered, but in other cases, natural features such as ears, nose, eyes, and mouth were modelled with clay. With some skulls, clay was used to represent eyes, and with others, marine shells were used. The plastered skulls were probably not intended to accurately portray the deceased. With many skulls, features such as the ears or the lower jaw are missing, or there are anatomical impossibilities such as the nose superimposed over the mouth. The range of variation of facial types in skulls from any one site is far smaller than what is seen in living populations. They seem to reflect a system of idealised representation rather than an attempt to represent actual individuals. Fewer than five per cent of skulls were plastered, so it can be assumed that only certain individuals were so treated. Probably, they were tribal elders or other people of importance[119].

As agriculture spread westwards into Europe, cemeteries began to reflect differing traditions between indigenous Mesolithic hunter-gatherers and the incoming Neolithic farmers. By around 6200 BCE, Neolithic communities were established along the Iron Gates, a series of gorges situated on the Danube between the Carpathian Mountains and the Dinaric Alps. Settlements comprised several semi-subterranean trapezoidal, flat-roofed dwellings[120], many of which contained burials, although burials were also placed outside houses[121]. For the first two hundred years, the newcomers were buried in an extended supine position characteristic of the indigenous Mesolithic mortuary tradition, although they were buried with Neolithic-style beads as grave goods. However, by around 6000 BCE, Neolithic crouched burials, with the legs drawn up, had begun to predominate. This would seem to indicate that there was a period of coexistence between the hunter-gathering and farming communities before the former was completely absorbed into the latter[122].

From the Balkans, farming spread into Central Europe. In time, there arose a cultural phenomenon known as the Linearbandkeramik (Linear Pottery) Culture, or LBK. The LBK is named for its incised banded decorated pottery, and it was characterised by settlements of massive timber-built longhouses, sometimes up to 70 m (230 ft) in length[123]. It first appeared in the Carpathian region about 5600 BCE, spreading east to Ukraine and west to the Rhineland by 5400 BCE, and the Paris Basin by 5050 BCE. It had ended by around 4900 BCE[124,125]. In many cases, indigenous hunter-gatherer populations were assimilated into the LBK farming communities. Strontium isotope analysis of dental enamel of skeletons from LBK cemeteries at the German sites of Flomborn, Schwetzingen, and Dillingen has indicated that some of those interred did not originate locally. The burial orientation and grave goods of the farmers frequently differed from those of local people, suggesting social differentiation. Notably, most of these outsiders were women, suggesting that men from the LBK farming communities were taking wives from local hunter-gatherer groups. This would be consistent with ethnographically recorded cases of exogamy[41], where women from hunter-gatherer groups marry into farming communities[126]. A slightly different picture was found at Vaihingen near Stuttgart. Here, some burials were made in a ditch near the site rather than within the settlement itself. Although there were no gender distinctions between the two burial sites, strontium isotope analysis showed that significantly more of these buried in the ditch were non-local[127].

Similar scenarios played out throughout Europe and other parts of the world as agriculture transformed human society. The European Upper Palaeolithic lasted for more than 35,000 years. Less than a third of that length of time separates the first farmers from the first Moon landing.

Megalithic tombs and social complexity

The Neolithic and Early Bronze Age saw the appearance in Western Europe of megalithic monuments including stone circles, stone rows, and standing stones. They include sites such

---

[41] Marrying outside one's own social group.

as Stonehenge, Avebury, and Carnac. Predating these world-famous sites are large numbers of funerary monuments known as megalithic tombs, which began appearing around 4500 BCE in Britain, Ireland, and Atlantic Europe. They include chambered long barrows such as Hazleton North in the Cotswolds, West Kennet Long Barrow, near Avebury, Wiltshire, and Wayland's Smithy, near Ashbury, Oxfordshire.

Studies of ancient DNA recovered from those interred in megalithic tombs are informative about who was buried where, revealing in turn a picture of increasing social complexity. Results from megalithic tombs in Ireland, the Orkneys, and the island of Gotland in the Baltic dating from 4500 to 3000 BCE show that there were close kin relationships among those interred. It was also found that the same Y chromosomal haplogroups reoccurred, indicating that there was paternal continuity through time. The implication is that the tombs were associated with patrilineal[42] kin groups and that there was a degree of social stratification among Neolithic farming communities[128].

Studies revealed a similar but more complex picture at Hazleton North around 3700 BCE. Hazleton North is one of two barrows located in Barrow Ground Field to the north of the Cotswolds village of Hazleton. The barrow was excavated between 1979 and 1982. The trapezoidal barrow comprises two separate chambered areas consisting of cellular units on an east-west alignment, one of which is accessed via a northern entrance and the other via a southern entrance. At the wider (west) end of the barrow is a forecourt area consisting of a drystone wall framed between two projections or 'horns', thought to be where ceremonies took place[129].

Ancient DNA obtained from 35 individuals interred in the barrow has shown that 27 of them were biological relatives representing five generations of a single extended family. Fifteen intergenerational transmissions were identified, all through the male line. This suggests that it was patrilineal descent that determined who was interred in the tomb. The presence of women who had had children with male lineage members and the absence of adult lineage member daughters suggest patrilocal[43] interment and female exogamy. Four women all had children with the same man, and the descendants of two of those women were buried in the same half of the tomb. This suggests a relationship between maternal sub-lineages and the layout of the tomb. Four men had fathers who were not lineage members, but their mothers also had children with men who were lineage members. In these cases, apparently, some men adopted their partner's children by other men into their lineage grouping. Finally, there were eight individuals who were unrelated to the main lineage. Here, it seems, kinship encompassed social bonds outside of biological relatedness[130].

Hazleton North, West Kennet Long Barrow, and Wayland's Smithy belong to a well-defined class of megalithic tombs found across south Wales and the Cotswolds, known as the Cotswold-Severn group. Archaeologist Francis Pryor[131] notes that evidence from other Cotswold-Severn tombs suggests that bones might commonly have been moved between different chambers and, on occasions, between different tombs. He suggests that the bones might have served as a symbolic 'currency' for sealing and endorsing family ties and obligations, ranging from marriage alliances to land and hunting deals. Thus, the dead continued to play an active role in the lives of the living. At Hazleton North, the forecourt

---

[42] Descent through the father's line.

[43] When women move to the man's place of residence upon marriage.

would have provided a theatrical setting for ceremonies related to death and the next world, while the chambers remained open to people who needed to move bones within or between tombs.

Pryor[131] notes that after around 3500 BCE, there is less evidence for the practice of moving bones, and bodies were buried or cremated intact. Single graves become the norm, with communal burials occurring less frequently. Pryor believes that this represents a shift in beliefs: instead of retaining a role in the land of the living as generalised symbolic beings, they retained their identities on death and continued to exist as individuals in a parallel realm of ancestors. Cremation might have been seen as a way of preventing body parts from being manipulated after death. Such changes were setting the scene for complex ritual landscapes such as Stonehenge and Avebury.

Of wood and stone

Stonehenge has long been the centre of astronomical speculations. In the 1960s, it was described as a 'Neolithic computer' for predicting eclipses[132]. Such speculations surely stem in part from the well-known alignment of the Heel Stone at Stonehenge on the summer solstice was noted by the antiquarian William Stukeley in 1721[133]. We now know that Stonehenge was sited near a pair of naturally occurring parallel ridges flanking a deep, corrugated fissure, 30 m (100 ft) wide, that was formed as the glaciers retreated at the end of the last Ice Age. By pure chance, this feature aligned on the summer solstitial sunrise in one direction and the winter solstitial sunset in the other. Postholes have been found that date to Mesolithic times, suggesting that this natural alignment had been noticed in Mesolithic times, long before the erection of the Heel Stone. By the time the first phase of Stonehenge began to take shape around 3000 BCE, the site had probably been regarded as auspicious for almost five thousand years[134].

The imposing but surprisingly compact monument that comes into view as visitor drives westwards along the A303 from nearby Amesbury did not form part of the original structure, which was the result of around 1,500 years of construction and modification continuing off and on until around 1500 BCE. The major phase of construction was from around 2620 to 2480 BCE[135]. Stonehenge is now thought to have been only part of a much larger ritual landscape that included the sites of Durrington Walls and Woodhenge, located 3 km (1.8 miles) northeast of Stonehenge. These two sites are broadly contemporary with the major phase of construction at Stonehenge. They were once large circular monuments comparable in size to Stonehenge, but they were constructed of wood rather than stone. They each comprise six concentric rings, which is the same number as Stonehenge (if all the postholes that once held stones are counted, i.e., the X, Z, and Aubrey holes)[136].

In 2020, a geophysical survey identified 20 massive, circular pits each measuring 20 m (66 ft) in diameter and 5 m (16 ft) deep. Lithics and bones were recovered from silts at the base of one of the pits, and radiocarbon dating suggests that they are contemporary with the timber henges. The similarity between the pits suggests that they could have formed part of a circle of similar structures around Durrington Walls, which exceeded 2 km (1.25 miles) in diameter and was larger than anything else in Neolithic Britain[137].

Extensive remains of pigs and cattle have been found at Durrington Walls[138]. The wear of the pigs' teeth suggests that many were slaughtered in their first autumn or winter[139]. Strontium, sulphur, carbon, oxygen, and nitrogen isotope analysis of remains have revealed that the animals were brought to Durrington Walls from many different locations 30 to 100 km (18 to 60 miles) and possibly further away, and only a few were raised locally. Durrington Walls was probably the site of major 'please bring a pig or cow' feasts, which could have been associated with midwinter rituals and attended by people who would have travelled long distances with their animals to reach the site[140–142].

In the 1990s, archaeologists Mike Parker-Pearson and Ramilisonina proposed an interpretation of the complex based on ethnographic evidence from Madagascar, where houses in the central highlands are traditionally built of wood and other perishable materials, but stone is never used. Stone is associated with ancestors, and its use is reserved for commemorating the dead. This tradition reflects the durability of stone as opposed to the ephemeral nature of wood. Thus, Durrington Walls, with its timber henges and where there are no burials, is interpreted as a place of the living, while Stonehenge is interpreted as a place of the dead[136,143].

The Varna Necropolis

The Bronze Age was preceded by a period when stone and unalloyed copper artefacts were both in use. This period is known as the Chalcolithic, meaning 'copper stone'. The practicalities of day-to-day living were largely unchanged from Neolithic times, but metal objects became desirable status symbols and were often traded over long distances. The Chalcolithic cemetery at Varna on the Black Sea coast of Bulgaria was discovered in 1972. It covers 7.5 ha (18.5 acres) and holds 294 graves including 43 that lack any human remains. These cenotaphs ('empty tombs') are usually interpreted as the symbolic graves of members of the community who died far away. Unfortunately, around a third of the graves had been damaged by animal holes, tree roots, later graves, and agricultural activity before excavation began. The cemetery was only in use for just over a century between 4560 and 4450 BCE. Over this relatively brief period, there is no linear or zonal spread of graves, suggesting that several different communities used the cemetery to bury their dead in different areas[144,145].

The cemetery is noted for its large quantity of gold grave goods. There are more than three thousand items, weighing over 6 kg (13.2 lb), which represent the world's earliest-known example of gold-working. Gold was not the only grave goods found at Varna: there are also items made from copper and flint, polished stone and bone and antler tools, ceramics, various minerals, over 12,200 dentalium shells, and around 1,100 imported *Spondylus* shell ornaments including bracelets, necklaces, and appliqués[145]. The gold artefacts include beads, gold rings, bracelets, bangles, pendants, hammered sheet breastplates, appliqués with perforated edges for sewing to clothing, and decorations added to the shafts of axes, hammers, and sceptres. Many of these items were probably made specifically for burial[123].

The distribution of gold in the graves is very unequal. Only 62 of the graves contained any gold at all, and 5 kg (11 lb) or around 85 per cent of the gold was found in just four graves, three of which were cenotaphs. The one grave holding a body, Grave 43, contained a man aged between 40 and 50. He had been buried wearing clothes trimmed with gold and carnelian beads and circular gold appliqués. The grave goods consisted of gold items including rings, bracelets, beads, and a penis sheath weighing a total of 1.5 kg (3.3 lb). Overall, the grave held over a thousand items of grave goods[145]. The cenotaphs contained clay masks with gold placed on the eyes, mouth, nose, and ears. Only around fifteen graves held significant assemblages of grave goods[146]. Most of the graves contained ten or fewer items, and some held no grave goods at all[123].

The obvious conclusion that Varna society was stratified needs to be examined critically. Can we be certain that gold was as prized then as highly as it is today? It could be argued that there is no reason to suppose that it was any more valued than dentalium shells or copper. The latter is in any case far more useful than gold, which is too soft to have many practical applications. However, if we can look past gold that is currently trading at more than $2,000/oz (more than double the value of platinum) and consider wealth simply in terms of the range of goods, then the prominence of gold in these graves suggests that it did indeed hold a special significance to the Varna people[147].

The exact structure of Bulgarian Chalcolithic societies is disputed, but they are probably best interpreted as chiefdoms[147]. The radiocarbon dates for Varna indicate not just a brief period of usage but also show that the most lavish burials all occurred within the first 50 or 60 years of the cemetery's use. This would suggest that a small number of paramount chiefs were buried at the cemetery during the early period, but only lower-ranking individuals were buried there subsequently until it was abandoned for good[144]. It is not clear why the cemetery so rapidly declined and was abandoned, but it could have been the result of tensions arising within an increasingly stratified society[146].

Social complexity continued to increase in Bronze Age societies. By around 3200 BCE, the first state-level societies were emerging in Mesopotamia and Egypt. These, and later developments in India, China, and the New World, were described by Vere Gordon Childe as the Urban Revolution, following on from his Neolithic Revolution. Mortuary practices reached new levels of elaboration, some of which survive today as monuments such as the Pyramids and the tomb of Qin Shi Huangi with its Terracotta Army. Other examples include the now-ruined Tomb of King Mausolus in Bodrum, Turkey, one of the Seven Wonders of the Ancient World, and the source of the term 'mausoleum'.

Epilogue

At 15:10 BST on 8 September 2022, Queen Elizabeth II died at Balmoral Castle aged 96. Her death was announced by the BBC at 18:31, closely followed by news channels around the world. The announcement triggered Operation London Bridge, a set of plans for the death and funeral of the Queen that had originally been drawn up early on in her record-breaking 70-year reign. The Queen's coffin lay at rest in St Giles' Cathedral in Edinburgh from 12 to 13 September, after which it was flown to London to lie in state in Westminster Hall from 14 to 19 September. Around 33,000 people filed past the coffin in Edinburgh, followed by an estimated 250,000 people in London. Queues of up to 16 km (10 miles) were reported in London, with wait times of up to 24 hours. The United Kingdom observed a national mourning period of 10 days.

The Queen's funeral in Westminster Abbey took place on 19 September and was the first state funeral held in Britain since that of Sir Winston Churchill in 1965. Among the 2,000 attendees in the Abbey were six of her former prime ministers and around five hundred foreign dignitaries representing 168 countries, including 18 monarchs, 55 presidents, and 25 prime ministers. Around a million people lined the route of the funeral procession, and an estimated four billion viewers – more than half the world's population – watched on television. A total of 5,949 military personnel were deployed throughout these events including 4,416 from the Army, 847 from the Royal Navy, 686 from the Royal Air Force, and 175 armed forces personnel from Commonwealth nations. The gun carriage bearing the Queen's coffin was drawn by 138 Royal Navy sailors.

Most funerals are, of course, far smaller in scale. In 2022, there were 577,160 deaths registered in England and Wales. Many were reported in local and sometimes national newspapers, and on social media, but most of the ensuing funerals would have been attended by no more than a few tens of mourners. Nevertheless, each would have been a deeply personal experience for families and friends of the deceased. We all die and are mourned by those we leave behind. Mourning and remembering the dead is a very ancient part of the human condition, but as we have seen, it may not be confined to modern or even archaic humans.

09: The origins of *Homo sapiens*

The Great Chain of Being

How do we as humans view ourselves? We tend to think we are very different to anything else living on the planet Earth, even if we concede that we are part of the animal kingdom. Evolutionary biologists, supported by genetic evidence, tell us that humans (*Homo sapiens*) are closely related to African apes. Our full place in nature is Domain Eukaryota (organisms with nucleated cells), Kingdom Animalia (the animal kingdom), Phylum Chordata (animals with a notochord, or stiffening rod at some stage in their lifecycle), Subphylum Vertebrata (animals with a backbone), Class Mammalia (mammals), Order Primates (lemurs, lorises, tarsiers, simians), Suborder Haplorhini (tarsiers, simians), Infraorder Simiiformes (apes, monkeys), Parvorder Catarrhini (apes, Old World monkeys), Superfamily Hominoidae (gibbons, great apes), Family Hominidae (great apes, humans, and close relatives), Subfamily Homininae (African apes, humans and close relatives), Tribe Hominini (hominins, i.e., humans and close relatives), Genus *Homo* (humans), Species *sapiens*. In other words, humans are just another species in the animal kingdom. Or, as biologist and author Jared Diamond put it, "*just another species of big mammal*"[1]. The story of how we came to recognise that there is nothing special about our place in nature has been a long one.

The *Scala Naturae*, or Great Chain of Being, was the Theory of Everything of the Middle Ages, envisaging a grand hierarchy of all things divine, living, and inorganic. The concept was first systematised by the Neoplatonist philosopher Plotinus (AD 204-270), though the basic ideas go back to Plato and Aristotle. It was further developed during the European Renaissance. At the top of the hierarchy was God, followed in order by the angels, humanity, animals, plants, and finally, minerals. In the human world, not unexpectedly, kings and princes outranked peasants. This hierarchical system was also applied to the other subdivisions: the animal kingdom was ruled by lions, the plant kingdom by oak trees, and the mineral kingdom by gold, diamonds, and marble. Animals were divided into three categories: those living on land, those living in water, and those living in the air. They were further categorised as those 'with' and those 'without' blood (broadly speaking, what we would now term vertebrates and invertebrates). It was a system that assigned everything to an appointed place – but there was just one problem. Where did apes and monkeys fit into the picture?

There is no getting away from the fact that apes and monkeys look very similar to people. I remember being struck by the similarities as a young child at London Zoo. The similarities are real but unremarkable. They reflect nothing more than the close evolutionary relationship between humans and other primates. But from the perspective of the Great Chain of Being, they represent a category error. How could apes and monkeys – members of the animal kingdom – resemble humans? Aristotle's view was that apes and monkeys represented a category situated between humans and quadrupedal animals. Aristotle was on the right lines, but later authorities suggested that apes and monkeys were God's final efforts before making Adam, and He left this 'deformed image of man' as an example. The Italian philosopher Lucilio Vanini suggested that humans and apes must have a common ancestor. He was correct, of course, but the idea was not well received in an era when few doubted that God had created humankind in His own image. After numerous run-ins with the Catholic Church, Vanini was burned at the stake in 1619. Not for two and a half centuries would he be vindicated.

Although creationism remained largely unchallenged, knowledge of the natural world began to reach a point where Aristotle's system was no longer adequate. The number of species known to science increased dramatically during the Age of Discovery, as European seafarers brought back exotic animal and plant specimens from their travels all over the world. Unfortunately, there was very little consensus on how biological organisms should be classified. As new species continued to be found, so the problem became steadily worse.

Linnaeus

Onto the scene came Carl Linné, usually known by the Latinised version of his name, Carolus Linnaeus. The son of a Lutheran curate, he was born in 1707 in the village of Råshult, in southern Sweden. Although not the most promising of scholars, he became interested in botany from an early age. In 1727, he enrolled at Lund University to study medicine, but soon transferred to Uppsala University, where there were better opportunities for him to combine his medical studies with his interest in botany. His mentors included botanist Olof Celsius, whose nephew Anders Celsius invented the Celsius ('centigrade') temperature scale. Anders' scale was originally calibrated with the freezing point of water at one hundred degrees and the boiling point at zero degrees; it was Linnaeus who later reversed the convention to produce the scale now in use.

In 1735, Linnaeus published the first edition of *Systema Naturae*, the work for which he is now largely remembered. In it, he adopted binomial nomenclature, whereby a species is assigned a generic name and a specific name. The generic name refers to the genus, a group of species more closely related to one another than to any other group of species. The specific name represents the species itself. For example, lions (*Panthera leo*) and tigers (*Panthera tigris*) are different species, but they are similar enough to both be assigned to the Genus *Panthera*. Linnaeus did not invent this system: it had been proposed by the Swiss botanist Gaspard Bauhin over a century earlier, but it had failed to catch on. What he did do was to extend the system to humans, giving us what is one of the most familiar of all pieces of scientific 'jargon': *Homo sapiens* – our name for ourselves.

In *Systema Naturae*, Linnaeus also put forward his taxonomic scheme for the natural world. A taxonomy is a classification for any given set of objects and is typically hierarchical. A taxon (plural taxa) is any item within such a scheme, and all objects within a particular taxon will be united by one or more defining features: 'mammal', 'primate', 'insect' and 'beetle' are all examples of taxa. Linnaeus subdivided the three Kingdoms of the Great Chain of Being (Animals, Plants and Minerals) by Class, Order, Genus, and Species. Each taxonomic category is nested within the next category up; for example, lions and tigers are two species within the Genus *Panthera*. This forms part of Order Carnivora (a group that also includes other cats, along with dogs and bears), which in turn forms part of Class Mammalia (mammals). In 1758, in the tenth edition of *Systema Naturae*, Linnaeus classified humans as *Homo sapiens*, a species within Order Primates. Note that by convention, only Genus and Species are italicised, and the latter is not capitalised; thus, our species is written *Homo sapiens* and not *Homo Sapiens*. Along with humans, Linnaeus included the Simians (apes and monkeys) and lemurs. For some reason, he also included bats, although these were soon given their own order, the Chiroptera. 'Primate' means 'of first rank', reflecting Linnaeus's view that this group ranked first in God's grand scheme of things. He saw no reason to abandon the orthodox view of creationism and – never the most modest of men – he claimed that *"Deus Creavit, Linnaeus Disposuit"* ("God created, Linnaeus arranged"). He was nevertheless criticised for daring to suggest any connection between humans and mere animals.

Other critics objected to the bizarre sexual imagery he used when categorising plants. For example, *"The flowers' leaves… serve as bridal beds which the Creator has so gloriously arranged, adorned with such noble bed curtains, and perfumed with so many soft scents that the bridegroom with his bride might there celebrate their nuptials with so much the greater solemnity…"*. The botanist Johann Siegesbeck denounced this *"loathsome harlotry"*, but Linnaeus had the last word and named a weed he considered to be insignificant *Siegesbeckia orientalis*. It retains this name to this day.

Linnaeus was elevated to the nobility in 1761, taking the name Carl von Linné. He continued his work until the early 1770s, when he became afflicted by strokes, memory loss, and general ill health until his death in 1778. In his publications, Linnaeus provided a concise, usable survey of all the world's then-known plants and animals, comprising about 7,700 species of plants and 4,400 species of animals. The works helped to establish and standardise consistent binomial nomenclature for these many species. The Mineral Kingdom has long since been abandoned, as has the 'loathsome harlotry', but the classification system in use today is very similar to that introduced by Linnaeus.

The Linnaean system assigns humanity a place in the animal kingdom, but it has nothing to tell us about how we got there. It is based on similarities between species and higher-level taxa, not on evolutionary relationships between them. It does not tell us that humans are closely related to apes and monkeys, only that we share many features with them. Creationism holds that species are immutable and, by definition, does not allow the concept that one species can evolve into another. Had Linnaeus believed in evolution, he might well have devised a different system.

Darwin

In Linnaeus' time, most people believed that the Bible and the works of Classical scholars contained everything there was to know about human origins. Few doubted that the Earth and every living thing upon it had been created, by God, out of nothing. It was widely believed that this had happened in 4004 BC, a date computed by Archbishop James Ussher of Armagh in 1650 from purely Biblical sources. This viewpoint was first challenged during the latter part of the eighteenth century when geologists began to understand the processes that had shaped the surface of the Earth. Scottish geologist James Hutton argued that geological principles do not change with time and have remained constant throughout

Earth's history. He suggested that changes in the Earth's geology occurred gradually, and were driven by volcanic action, deposition of sediment, and erosion by wind and rain, rather than by floods and other biblical catastrophes. Hutton recognised that these processes would have required far longer than 6,000 years to shape the Earth as we know it. It also became clear that the fossil record contained evidence for life forms that no longer existed, implying a sequence of events more complex than could be explained by the Biblical account of a single great flood.

It was not until 1859 that the first edition of Charles Darwin's *The Origin of Species* was published. Darwin was not the first to propose a theory of evolution: even while Linnaeus was still alive, evolutionists were beginning to propose alternatives to creationist orthodoxy, most notably the French biologist Jean-Baptiste Lamarck. Indeed, in early editions of *The Origin of Species*, Darwin avoided the word 'evolution' altogether, preferring the term 'descent with modification'.

What Darwin proposed was 'natural selection', whereby differences between individuals of the same species mean that some are more successful than others at evading predators or competing for limited resources. Accordingly, such individuals will stand more chance of reproducing and passing on their advantageous traits to their offspring. One of the best-known examples of natural selection is the Peppered moth, of which there are speckled light grey and all-black (melanic) varieties. Before the Industrial Revolution, the speckled light grey form was the most common variety, but the smoke and soot from the factories blackened many of the trees on which the moths rested. The previously rare all-black moths were now better camouflaged against predators and were more likely to reproduce and pass their dark colour scheme on to their offspring. During the mid-nineteenth century, numbers of the all-black moths increased steadily, accounting for 98 per cent of Peppered moths in the Manchester area by 1895.

Darwin developed the theory of natural selection between 1844 and 1858, but the Welsh naturalist and explorer Alfred Russel Wallace was thinking along the same lines, and he wrote to Darwin with a short description of the same evolutionary mechanism. Darwin, whose infant son had just died from scarlet fever, was unable to give the matter much thought. He was persuaded to publish a synopsis of his work, which was jointly presented with Wallace's paper to the Linnaean Society of London. To the credit of both men, neither wished to take sole credit for their work, and there were none of the unseemly squabbles over priority that have bedevilled many joint discoveries over the centuries. *The Origin of Species*[2] was published a year later, and the first edition promptly sold out.

Nevertheless, the theory remained unpopular in clerical circles and controversial elsewhere. Darwin was even portrayed as an ape in some satirical publications. He was not the first to propose that humans evolved from apes, and *The Origin of Species* only hints that the theory may cast light on human origins. It was his friend and self-styled 'bulldog' Thomas Henry Huxley, who first publicised the anatomical similarities between humans and apes and presented anatomical and other evidence for the evolution of humans and apes from a common ancestor in his 1863 work *Evidence as to Man's Place in Nature*, which was the first book ever to be devoted to human evolution[3]. It would be another eight years before Darwin proposed that humans were most closely related to African apes in his 1871 work *The Descent of Man*[4]. During the last quarter of the nineteenth century, the close connection between apes and humans became widely accepted. The search for our origins had begun, but first, it had to escape from the dark cloud of what British archaeologist Robin Dennell has described as the "*Age of Prejudice*"[5].

Apartheid

Apartheid ('separateness') was the system of racial segregation practised in South Africa during the period of White minority rule, and a similar notion of separate development underpinned early models of human evolution. From around the middle of the eighteenth century, there was a widespread view that there is a link between biology and culture. The biological limitations of 'primitive' people around the world prevented them from progressing to 'civilisation'. Hence, human 'races' could be ranked into a hierarchy with higher and lower levels of physical development and cultural attainment[6]. Europeans were placed at the top of this hierarchy and geographically distant peoples like Aboriginal Australians, Tasmanians, and Khoikhoi were placed at the bottom, based upon their supposedly smaller brains, more apelike features, and intellectual inferiority[7].

There were two schools of thought within this 'race' paradigm: monogenism and polygenism. The monogenist view was that the various races shared a common ancestor, while the polygenist view was that their origins were entirely separate. However, both models viewed each race as evolving separately into *Homo sapiens*, and some completed the transition before others. Hence, it was assumed that some races were more developed than others[8].

Linked to these models was the view that the split between apes and humans was very ancient. Some placed it at the start of the Miocene (20.03 – 5.33 million years ago)[9,10], others in the Oligocene (33.9 – 23.03 million years ago)[11], or even the Eocene (55.8 – 33.9 million years ago)[12]. The 'early origins' view remained dominant until the 1960s, with various models relying on embryological evidence, comparative anatomy, or dental evidence[13]. But there was also a darker, racist element to this thinking in that the differences between the various races were thought to be so significant as to imply a great time depth. Even the whole length of the Pleistocene was thought to be insufficient to account for the differences between Europeans and Africans[14,15]. In the 1920s, phylogenetic trees depicting human origins typically depicted a very long history of the modern human 'races'[11,16].

Multiregional continuity

Race-based models had largely fallen out of favour by the end of World War II, the whole concept having been totally discredited by the horrors of Nazism. German anatomist and palaeontologist Franz Weidenreich suggested that humans of the Middle Pleistocene around the world could all be described as *Homo erectus*. This was a single, evolving lineage which gradually evolved into *Homo sapiens*[17]. Weidenreich's theory was an elementary form of what later became known as the Multiregional continuity model. It was controversial, but it was accepted by some, including American anthropologist Carleton Coon[18] and Ukrainian geneticist Theodosius Dobzhansky[19].

Coon proposed a variant of the model, but with important differences. Whereas Weidenreich had stressed the generic unity of *Homo erectus* during its evolution into *Homo sapiens*, Coon revived the race model, albeit in a watered-down form. In a 1962 work entitled

The Origin of Races, he divided living *Homo sapiens* into five races, or 'subspecies': Australoids, Mongoloids, Caucasoids, Congoids (Blacks) and Capoids (Khoekhoe). Each, he argued, had evolved separately in its own part of the world from *Homo erectus* and had independently passed a critical threshold from a more brutal to a more sapient state. The threshold was passed at different times, with the Caucasoid race the first to make the transition to *Homo sapiens* 250,000 years ago. The Congoids did not make the transition until 50,000 years ago[18,20]. Coon followed up this work with *The Living Races of Man* in 1965[20].

Dobzhansky was critical and said that possibility that *Homo erectus* could evolve into *Homo sapiens* twice, let alone five times, was "*vanishingly small*". He noted that Coon had claimed that the ancestors of the Capoid race lived in Africa to the north of the ancestors of the Congoid race, whereas they now live to the south of the Congoids. But they could not have migrated south and remained a separate race unless "*these peoples practised racial segregation during their wanderings*". Dobzhansky went on to note that Coon's claim that Blacks were 200,000 years behind Whites in their evolutionary development was being used by organisations opposed to desegregation in the United States[19].

British-American anthropologist Montague Francis Ashley Montagu described Coon's model as "*very far-fetched*" and felt that *The Origin of Races* read like it had been published in 1862, not 1962. He noted that brain size in modern people varies considerably without any correlation to intelligence. Coon had cited an Aboriginal Australian woman's smaller brain as proof of her low intelligence but failed to mention that according to his model, Mongoloids, having larger brains than Caucasoids, should also be more intelligent[21].

Weidenreich's original multiregional theory was further developed by American palaeoanthropologist Milford Wolpoff and Australian anthropologist Alan Thorne in the 1980s. The underlying concept of the developed model was 'centre and edge' evolution. The model proposed that Africa was the most significant source of genetic variation throughout the course of human evolution. The predominant direction of gene flow was from the more densely populated centre in Africa to less densely populated edges in Europe, Asia, and Australia[22]. *Homo erectus* was viewed as a polytypic species with several distinct geographical variants that showed some continuity with later geographical variants of *Homo sapiens*. There was no distinct boundary between *Homo erectus* and *Homo sapiens*, either in time or geographically; no speciation event where *Homo sapiens* emerged as a distinct species from a population of *Homo erectus*. Hence, *Homo erectus* was no more than the earlier form of a single, evolving lineage for which the correct name, by virtue of taxonomic priority, is *Homo sapiens*[23].

Out of Africa

The Replacement model, commonly referred to as Out of Africa, emerged as a rival to the Multiregional continuity model. The common name is taken from the Latin phrase *ex Africa semper aliquid novi* ('out of Africa there is always something new'), usually attributed to the Roman author Pliny the Elder but likely originating with Aristotle. The model proposed that *Homo sapiens* evolved in Africa and migrated to Eurasia, replacing the archaic populations there. The 'strong' version of this model supposed that the latter died out completely, contributing nothing little or nothing to the ancestry of present-day populations. 'Weak' versions allowed varying degrees of interbreeding between the modern and archaic populations. We do now know that there was significant interbreeding with Neanderthals[24] and Denisovans[25].

The current thinking of an African origin for modern humans can be traced to a 1975 paper by the German anthropologist Reiner Protsch. He claimed that fossils resembling modern humans are found in Africa before they appear elsewhere, and must therefore have originated there[26]. Although some of Protsch's later work was discredited, the dates in this paper have withstood the test of time[27]. The Multiregional continuity and Replacement models make differing predictions, which in theory can be tested against the fossil record[28].

Predictions of the Multiregional continuity model:

- Interpopulation differences are high, greatest between each peripheral area.
- Intrapopulation variations are greatest at the centre of the human range.
- Transitional fossils are widespread.
- Modern regional characters of great antiquity are seen at the peripheries.
- No consistent temporal pattern of the appearance of *Homo sapiens* characters between areas.
- Selective and behavioural factors involved in the origin of *Homo sapiens* varied and widespread, perhaps related to technology; local behavioural continuity is expected.

Predictions of the Replacement model:

- Interpopulation differences are relatively low, greatest between African and non-African populations.
- Intrapopulation variation is greatest in African populations.
- Transitional fossils are restricted to Africa.
- Modern regional characters of low antiquity are seen at the peripheries (except in Africa).
- The *Homo sapiens* suite of characters appears first in Africa, then in Southwest Asia, and finally, in other areas.
- Selective and behavioural factors involved in the origin of *Homo sapiens* are special and localised in Africa, with behavioural discontinuities expected outside Africa.

In the 1980s, far less fossil evidence was known than now, and much of that was poorly dated. Unable to distinguish between the two models with the available evidence, researchers turned to genetics.

Mitochondrial Eve

The Out of Africa model was brought to the fore by a 1987 study focusing on mitochondrial DNA (mtDNA), conducted by geneticist Allan Wilson and postdoctoral researchers Rebecca Cann and Mark Stoneking at the University of California, Berkeley. Unlike nuclear DNA, mtDNA is not found in the nuclei of cells of living organisms. Instead, it resides in small quantities in small, membrane-enclosed bodies known as mitochondria. These are also found in the cells of living organisms, but they are separate from the nucleus. Their main function is to generate a substance known as ATP, which is used to provide energy for various cellular processes. Mitochondria are often described as the cell's 'batteries'. They were probably once free-living bacteria that took up residence inside cells about two billion years ago and established a symbiotic relationship with them. Although they are no longer capable of independent existence, mitochondria have retained a small amount of their own DNA. This is known as mitochondrial DNA to distinguish it from nuclear DNA.

All mammals, including humans, inherit mitochondrial DNA solely from their mothers. The mitochondria in a sperm cell are located in the whiplash tail, which is discarded after fertilisation, and never becomes part of the fertilised ovum. Because the maternal mtDNA does not recombine with that from the father, it is useful for tracing maternal lineages. Given the limitations of genetic sequencing techniques in the 1980s, it was far easier to track mitochondrial than nuclear lineages over many generations.

Wilson and his team studied patterns of mitochondrial DNA variation in people from five geographic populations around the world: Africa, Asia, Australia, Europe, and New Guinea. In January 1987, they published their mitochondrial results in the journal *Nature*. They had discovered that the entire human population of the world could be arranged into one family tree with 133 different maternal lineages. There was a split between the African and non-African populations, with the former showing a far greater number of lineages. This implied that the African population had been established for longer than any other population, in turn implying that modern humans had originated there[29].

By invoking a principle known as the genetic clock, it was also possible to estimate the extent to which the various mitochondrial lineages had diverged from one another since the time of their common ancestor, taken to be the mitochondria of one woman. In all biological entities, from coronaviruses to humans, genetic material undergoes occasional mutations. These occur at a roughly constant rate; hence, the 'genetic distance' between two species (the differences between equivalent genetic sequences) will be related to the divergence time, or time since these species last shared a common ancestor. To obtain the divergence time in calendar years, it is necessary to determine the rate at which genetic distances increase with time. The most common approach is to look at genetic distances for species where actual divergence times are known from the fossil record, from which divergence times are calculated for other species.

Wilson, Cann, and Stoneking estimated that the divergence time was about 200,000 (140,000 – 290,000) years ago and that the world's population today can trace their mitochondrial DNA to one African woman who lived at that time[29]. The story made the front cover of *Newsweek*, under the headline "*The Search for Adam and Eve*". In 1991, the date range for when she lived was refined to 166,000 – 249,000 years ago by a follow-up study[30]. Inevitably, this one woman became known as 'Mitochondrial Eve', although the term is a little misleading. If it had been possible to use another part of the human genome, it would have yielded lineages that led back to a different ancestor. Nor was Mitochondrial Eve the only woman alive at the time, but the mitochondrial lineages of all her contemporaries ended at some point with women who did not have any daughters[31].

Mitochondrial Eve is really no more than an example of genetic drift – the random intergenerational changes in the frequency with which alleles[44] occur in a population. Even if none of the resulting characteristics (hair colour, blood group, etc.) confers any particular survival advantage, these changes will occur because some individuals will have more children than others. In a small population, this can result in some characteristics becoming very common, while others disappear altogether. An analogy for genetic drift is a small, isolated village where everybody ends up with the same surname. If Mr. and Mrs. Smith are the only Smiths living in the village and they have only daughters, then the surname Smith will disappear from the village's next generation. Over enough generations, the villagers will 'drift' to just one surname. Similarly, the various mitochondrial lineages drifted down to just the one of Mitochondrial Eve.

A date of 200,000 years ago fitted the fossil record as it was then understood, which suggested that the first appearance of anatomically modern forms of *Homo sapiens* dated to 140,000 – 100,000 years ago, in Africa. An African origin for *Homo sapiens* also fitted the archaeological record. Blades – defined as a long, narrow stone flake at least twice as long as it is wide, and then assumed to be predominantly a *Homo sapiens* technology – were in widespread use in Africa 90,000 – 80,000 years ago, long before they first appeared in Europe. But at the time, there was much uncertainty about the ages of many fossil remains. Also, the mtDNA data is not informative about the genetic contribution to early *Homo sapiens* of individuals whose mitochondrial lineages later went extinct.

A family tree for the world's population

Wilson's conclusions were challenged on statistical grounds, and it was also noted that his team had examined only a small portion of the mtDNA genome[32,33]. Nevertheless, researchers were quick to recognise the utility of mitochondrial DNA in the study of prehistoric human migrations. A common naming convention was adopted, where mitochondrial groups were named for letters of the alphabet in the order of discovery[34]. In 1995, the most ancient continent-specific haplogroup had been identified as having originated in Africa 98,000 – 130,000 years ago and given the designation haplogroup L. The age of the total African mitochondrial variation was estimated to be 101,000 - 133,000 years. These dates greatly exceeded any Eurasian values, consistent with an African origin for modern humans[35]. More extensive regions of the mtDNA genome were then studied, showing that the mitochondrial genetic diversity of Africans is far greater than that of non-Africans, as would be expected if modern humans had originated there[36–38].

During the 'noughties', the African mitochondrial picture became clearer, and what was in effect a mitochondrial family tree for the world's population could be plotted. Mitochondrial Eve was estimated to have lived just over 200,000 years ago[38]. Present-day African populations could be assigned to two daughter branches of Eve's mitochondrial haplogroup L: L0 and L1-6. L0 and its daughters remained largely confined to sub-Saharan African populations, notably the Khoe-San (Khoekhoe and San people). L1-6, as the name suggests, gave rise to the daughter haplogroups L1, L2, L3, L4, L5, and L6. In turn, L3 gave rise to L3(M) and L3(N), from which the entire non-African population of the world

---

[44] Variant forms of the same gene.

subsequently descended[39].

L3 is thought to have originated in East Africa[40] 86,000 – 61,000 years ago[41]. Its appearance and expansion coincided with the end of a prolonged period of extreme drought[42,43], which reduced African populations to small, isolated groups[39]. The improving climate likely played a part in the L3 expansion[44], but this leaves unexplained why East African populations carrying other haplogroups[45] failed to expand as well. Possibly, an initially small L3-carrying group gained a technological advantage over others, allowing it to out-compete rival groups[41,46]. One possibility is the invention of tailored clothing. Researchers assumed that its invention would coincide with when the body louse (*Pediculus humanus corporis*) diverged from the head louse (*Pediculus humanus capitis*) and took advantage of the new niche that had opened. The researchers used data from mitochondrial and nuclear DNA to show that the body louse originated in Africa 72,000 years ago, which is in good agreement with the date of the L3 expansion[47]. Another possibility is microlith technology. Microliths are small blades with a width of less than 10 mm (0.375 in). Although usually thought to have originated in South Africa, an East African or Central African origin cannot be ruled out, with a subsequent spread to South Africa[46,48].

The subsequent split between L3 and all non-African haplogroups could have occurred any time after the emergence of the former. Typical estimates for M and N suggest that both emerged in the region of 65,000 – 50,000 years ago[49–52]. Haplogroup R diverged from N very early on and is regarded as a third non-African founding haplogroup. All three were conventionally supposed to have originated somewhere between East Africa and the Persian Gulf[53].

The mitochondrial picture suggested that *Homo sapiens* had emerged in Africa 200,000 years ago and stayed put until 65,000 years ago, at which point a single group had left and gone on to populate the entire non-African world. A single migration was inferred from the three mitochondrial haplogroups M, N, and R all being about the same age. Had the ages all been different, it would have implied multiple migrations at different times. The founding group was not large. Estimates based on mitochondrial data suggested that it included no more than 500 to 2000 reproductively active women[50,54]. Of course, the total number of men, women, and children taking part in the migration would have been greater, and a total founding population of around 3,000 was suggested[55].

And nobody else followed, for tens of thousands of years.

To leave Africa

To leave Africa, there are four routes into Eurasia: by sea from Morocco across the Straits of Gibraltar, by sea from Tunisia to Sicily and thence to Italy, overland from Egypt across the Sinai desert into the Levant and Arabia, and by sea across the Bab el-Mandeb Strait between the Red Sea and the Gulf of Aden[56]. There is no archaeological or fossil evidence that early modern populations ever reached Europe from North Africa[57], leaving just the last two routes.

The Sahara and Sinai can only be crossed during warm, wet climatic interglacial periods, during which vegetation flourishes in these normally inhospitable regions, and the Levant becomes a northeasterly extension of Africa[58,59]. Three periods have been identified in the last 200,000 years when the central Sahara and Sahel contained trees, indicating substantially wetter conditions than at present. The presence of trees was inferred by stable isotope analysis of carbon from individual plant leaf waxes, which were recovered from a marine sediment core containing windblown dust from the Sahara. The isotope ^{13}C occurs at lower levels in trees and bushes than in other vegetation. The first wet phase occurred from 120,000 to 110,000 years ago during the warm Eemian Interglacial period, and the second occurred from 50,000 to 45,000 years ago during MIS[45] 3, a period of recurring mild intervals. The third warm, wet phase occurred during the early part of the current Holocene period[60]. Satellite radar images have revealed networks of now-buried river channels that extend across the Sahara Desert to the Mediterranean coast. Geochemical data has shown that water in these systems originated from the south during warm, wet episodes. During the period from 120,000 to 110,000 years ago, the channel network penetrated all the way to the Mediterranean, providing an uninterrupted freshwater corridor across what is now an arid desert. By travelling along this humid, life-sustaining corridor, it was possible to leave Africa[61,62].

Around 120,000 years ago, anatomically modern people took advantage of the then-open humid corridor through the Sahara to reach the Levant. Fossil evidence for a human presence comes from two sites in Israel, Mugharet es-Skhul at Mount Carmel and Jebel Qafzeh near Nazareth. ('Cave of the Kids') is a cave site on the western slopes of Mount Carmel, 3 km (2 miles) south of Haifa. Mugharet es-Skhul is one of several caves at Mount Carmel excavated between 1929 and 1934 by British archaeologist Dorothy Garrod, accompanied by palaeontologist Dorothea Bate from the Natural History Museum in London. Garrod and Bate recovered the remains of nine individuals (Skhul I-IX), most of whom had been intentionally buried. The date of the remains has long been an issue, but it has been estimated that the burials took place 100,000 – 135,000 years ago[63]. This is consistent with an arrival in the Levant at a time when the Saharan humid corridor was open.

Jebel Qafzeh is a cave near Mount Precipice, south of Nazareth. It was first excavated between 1933 and 1934, and then later between 1965 and 1979[64]. Five partial skeletons and fragments of as many as ten other individuals were recovered[65], who again had been intentionally buried[64]. Once again, there is uncertainty about the age of this site, although an estimate of 115,000 years old has been obtained[66] and is again consistent with the time when the Saharan humid corridor was open. Though robust[46] by today's standards, the Skhul and Qafzeh people were essentially modern, with high and well-rounded skulls and pronounced chins[67].

As colder conditions returned, the modern populations either died out or returned to Africa, and the region was reoccupied by Neanderthals. It was believed this Eemian Interglacial excursion was the full extent of the wanderings of *Homo sapiens* beyond Africa until 65,000 years ago, as there was no evidence to suggest that they had gone any further into Asia despite the favourable climatic conditions. There are significant geographical

---

[45] Marine Isotope Stages (MIS) are alternating cold (glacial) and warm (interglacial) climatic episodes, determined by the ratios of the two principal isotopes of oxygen ^{18}O and ^{16}O in ancient ice core samples, plankton, or marine sediments. They are numbered back in time from the present day (MIS 1). Even-numbered stages correspond to glacial periods and odd-numbered stages (including the present) to interglacial periods.

[46] Big-boned, heavily-built.

barriers to movement between the Levant and the rest of Asia: to the north lies the Taurus mountain chain in southern Turkey, running along a curve from Lake Eğirdir in the west to the upper reaches of the Tigris and Euphrates in the east, and to the east the Zagros mountain chain runs some 1,800 km (1,100 miles) southeast along the western border of Iran from the southeastern Turkish border to the Straits of Hormuz. During cold, arid periods, these combine with the Syrian desert to prevent northwards or eastern migration and the Arabian Desert blocks access to the south. To the west of the Syrian Desert and to the north and east of the Tigris and Euphrates valleys is the hilly arc known as the Fertile Crescent. It offers a way to reach the southern Asian coast, but again is completely inhospitable during cold, arid periods[68,69].

The Sinai route is nevertheless the most obvious way out of Africa, as it does not involve any form of water crossing. During warm, wet interglacial periods, the Levant serves as a staging point for onward dispersals into Europe and Asia, and it is by this route that earlier human species are assumed to have left Africa[57]. However, the migration time indicated by the mitochondrial data, 65,000 years ago, corresponds to MIS 4, a period of cold, arid conditions[70]. For this reason, the view was that the migrants had left Africa via the southern route.

The Bab el-Mandeb Strait – meaning 'The Gate of Tears' – is a narrow waterway at the southern end of the Red Sea, separating Djibouti from Yemen. At times of cold, dry conditions, such as those prevailing at the time in question, it is just 11 km (6.8 miles) across. Even when sea levels are high, as presently, the strait is only 18 km (11 miles) across at its narrowest point, about half the width of the Strait of Dover. On a clear day, Yemen is clearly visible from the shores of Djibouti. The crossing is nevertheless treacherous, with swift-running currents that could have swept African Middle Stone Age watercraft out into the Indian Ocean. It is known as the Gate of Tears for good reason. To cross it is hazardous, though unlikely to have been beyond the abilities of African seafarers of that time[71].

To people able to make the crossing, the southern route offers an attractive lifestyle of beachcombing. Seafood provides a good quality diet and is far easier to obtain than savannah game. Having crossed the Red Sea, migrants would have found such a food supply available to them all the way along the Indian Ocean Rim. They could have moved along the southern Asian coast through Yemen and Oman, and then onwards to the Indian subcontinent and Southeast Asia[68,69].

Express train to Australia

The fossil evidence of the time was consistent with the mitochondrial evidence for a single migration from Africa via the southern route 65,000 years ago. Human remains at Lake Mungo in New South Wales were dated to 42,000 years ago, with artefacts found there suggesting a human presence as early as 46,000 – 50,000 years ago[72]. Humans were implied to have reached northern Australia much earlier, and this has since been confirmed with a date of 65,000 years ago for the site of the Madjedbebe in the Northern Territory[73]. By contrast, there was no evidence that modern humans had reached Europe prior to 46,000 years ago[74]. These dates suggested a migration south towards Australia rather than north towards Europe and were consistent with a departure from Africa around 65,000 years ago.

Having left Africa, the migrants then dispersed along the southern Asian coast. Throughout Southeast Asia, scattered along the route of the projected beachcomber migration, are isolated populations long thought to be aboriginal because their culture and appearance mark them out from surrounding people. They closely resemble Khoe-San Africans, being short in stature with tightly curled hair and an epicanthic fold. They include the inhabitants of the Andaman Islands in the Bay of Bengal, the Semang from the Malay Peninsula, the Mani people of Thailand, and several indigenous groups in the Philippines[59].

Mitochondrial DNA studies found that the Andaman Islanders, the Semang, Papuans, and Aboriginal Australians all possess localised but very ancient branches of the three founder haplogroups M, N, and R. Two branches of M, M31 and M32, were thought to be ancient lineages that had evolved *in situ* in the Andaman Islands. Accordingly, it was suggested that these groups must have settled along the coastline of the Indian Ocean a long time ago and had remained largely in the same place ever since. Researchers applied a statistical technique known as founder analysis to the genetic data to identify and date the migrations, and the results suggested that the settlement took place at least 60,000 years ago. Accordingly, these peoples were assumed to be relict populations left over from the original migration out of Africa[50,75].

The physical logistics of the southern migration have been described as the coastal 'express train' scenario. This model proposes that migrants from Africa moved swiftly along the coast of Arabia and the Indian Ocean Rim to Southeast Asia and Australia. Having adapted to the beachcombing lifestyle and migrating at up to 4 km (2.5 miles) per year along the shorelines, the low sea levels would have enabled them to progress all the way to Indonesia. The process would have taken no more than 15,000 years, and probably less than 10,000 years[76]. A date of 65,000 years ago for reaching Australia implies a departure from Africa around 75,000 years ago, which roughly corresponds to the onset of the cold, arid period[70]. As beachcombers, the migrants could also have largely avoided the climate change-related problems faced by inland populations during the rapid climatic fluctuations of the Late Pleistocene. Archaeological evidence in support of this hypothesis is lacking, but it would probably be lost as a result of rises in sea levels after the last Ice Age. The model would conveniently explain the early dates for the first human presence in Australia, and the presence of the relict populations discussed above[50,54,76,77].

A problem with the scenario, as initially proposed, is that it lacked a convincing rationale for the ever-eastwards movement of the migrants. Australian archaeologist David Bulbeck suggested that the migrants adapted to living in river estuaries. Estuarine habitats along the rim of the Indian Ocean provided the migrants with access to drinking water, food, and timber. These resources supported healthy population growth and eventually led to crowded conditions, even if the surrounding stretches of land remained uninhabited. In time, though, settlements became overcrowded, and a need to seek out new estuarine habitats further along the coast provided the main impetus for the ongoing migratory movement. Dispersals were aided by watercraft that could transport colonists together with sufficient food, water, and other supplies needed to negotiate long stretches of inhospitable coast. Watercraft also enabled onward migrants to keep in touch with their parent communities, resulting in a chain of interlinked settlements. Bulbeck suggested that the migrants initially became familiar with watercraft through the need to exploit niches such as reefs and marine shallows[78].

Migrants might also have followed rivers inland from time to time. Computer simulations suggest that they could have followed several routes, both coastal and inland. Both the coasts and the interior of the Indian subcontinent would have been attractive to mobile human groups, who could have moved inland via the river corridors of the Indus, Narmada, and Ganges-Brahmaputra Delta. Indeed, large river deltas would have represented significant barriers, forcing migratory groups far inland[56,79].

It was supposed that Europe was settled by a side branch of the Out of Africa migration moving west from South Asia, with the earliest evidence for the presence of modern humans there dating to around 46,000 years ago[74]. Between 50,000 and 40,000 years ago, groups moved inland from the Indo-Pacific coastline in a pincer movement to Central and East Asia, and then northwards to adapt to the extreme conditions of the Russian Arctic by around 30,000 years ago[68]. The final stage of the global expansion was the peopling of the New World: settlers are thought to have lived for thousands of years in Beringia – the 'land bridge' that connected Siberia to Alaska during the last Ice Age – before moving eastwards into North America. They then moved south, possibly along the Pacific Coast, reaching Monte Verde in Chile perhaps as early as 18,500 years ago[80].

This, then, was the model of how modern humans came to populate the world that became an orthodoxy during the 'noughties'[46,68,69]. It had the benefit of being an elegant theory that fitted the facts as they were then known. A criticism is that it relied principally on mitochondrial data, which does not give the full genetic picture. In particular, it assumed that the age of the L3 haplogroup puts an upper boundary on an exit from Africa, but this assumption neglects the possibility of gene flow between African and non-African populations. When this is taken into account, there are possible scenarios involving earlier dispersals, or even of a non-African origin for L3[81]. The main problem, though, is that it was difficult to believe that for at least 100,000 years, no groups of modern humans ever went any further afield than the Levant, and after this single migration from Africa 65,000 years ago, no further groups followed.

Eemian migrations to Arabia

If humans were able to cross the Bab el-Mandeb Strait during the period of low sea level 65,000 years ago, could they not have done so during an earlier such period, possibly just before the start of the Eemian Interglacial? During warm, wet climate phases, the Arabian Peninsula was a fertile, habitable ecosystem, very different to the largely desert region that it now is[71]. Even during cold, arid climate phases, there are refugia that would remain habitable and continue to provide reliable sources of food and water[82].

The orthodox view was that humans, at least *Homo sapiens*, had not reached the Arabian Peninsula prior to 65,000 years ago. There was plenty of evidence for human presence, but it was poorly dated. Several Middle Palaeolithic prepared-core stone tool industries had been documented, and associations between them and industries in the Levant, the Indian subcontinent, and East Africa have been proposed on the grounds of tool typology. But without secure dating, these associations were tentative. Also, as no human fossils had ever been found, even the toolmakers were unknown. The level of technology was consistent with Neanderthals and other archaic humans as well as early *Homo sapiens*[71,83].

More definite information began to emerge from the region after 2010. Secure dates were obtained for Middle Palaeolithic artefacts from Jebel Faya in the United Arab Emirates[84] and the Dhofar region of southwestern Oman[85]. Jebel Faya is a limestone escarpment lying due south of the Straits of Hormuz. The finds were made in a rock shelter 180 m (600 ft) above sea level. Archaeological layers have been found ranging in age from the Iron and Bronze Ages to the Middle Palaeolithic. The oldest stone artefacts range from 127,000 to 95,000 years old, and it was suggested that the manufacturing techniques indicate a connection with East Africa, although they could not be associated with any specific industry.

Modern humans could have crossed the Bab el-Mandeb Strait just before the start of the Eemian Interglacial, while sea levels were still low. Having occupied the southern Yemeni coast, groups were able to spread out both along the coast and inland. The warm, wet conditions transformed the now-arid Nejd Plateau into a region of abundant vegetation and readily available water, enabling the migrants to expand all the way to Jebel Faya. However, during the subsequent cooler, arid periods that followed the Eemian Interglacial, the Nejd Plateau reverted to an arid highland, cutting off the Jebel Faya people from groups living further south[84]. But in the absence of any fossil remains, the African connection was far from secure. British archaeologist Sir Paul Mellars expressed doubts that the tool style was explicitly African, or that the tools were even made by modern humans. He noted that the Jebel Faya bifaces are stouter than those that were common in Africa at the time[86].

Unlike the Jebel Faya tools, those found at Dhofar have been firmly associated with the Nubian Complex, a prepared-core Middle Stone Age industry from the Middle and Lower Nile Valley, which was thought to be associated exclusively with modern humans. It was first reported from northern Sudan in the 1960s. In Africa, Nubian artefacts have been found from Sinai to the Horn of Africa, with dates ranging from roughly 120,000 to 100,000 years ago. Following tentative reports of Nubian artefacts in Yemen, the Dhofar Archaeological Project (DAP) was initiated in 2010 to explore the Late Pleistocene archaeological record of the Dhofar region. Two seasons of fieldwork were conducted over the winters of 2010 and 2011, and over a hundred finds of artefacts were made, ranging from isolated cores to high-density scatters. Based on similarities in both tool typology and manufacturing techniques, the tools were classified as belonging to the Late Nubian Complex. A date of 106,600 years ago was obtained from the open-air site of Aybut Al Auwal, consistent with Nubian dates from Africa[85].

The Dhofar findings were hailed as providing clear evidence for cultural exchange between Africa and Arabia by modern humans some 40,000 years before they were supposed to have crossed the Bab el-Mandeb Strait. Even if an African origin for the Jebel Faya artefacts was rejected, the Dhofar evidence could not be so readily dismissed. Given the range of the Nubian Complex in Africa, migrants could have reached Arabia from the north, the south, or both.

Again, though, no fossil remains were associated with any of the finds. Problems emerged as the assumption that Nubian technology was exclusive to modern humans was shown to be false. Shuqbah Cave, located to the north of Jerusalem, was excavated by Dorothy Garrod in 1928. Findings included a large collection of Middle Palaeolithic artefacts, and a small number of fossil remains, but they were largely overlooked for decades having been housed in the private collection of Scottish anatomist Sir Arthur Keith. An investigation in 2021 revealed Nubian-type artefacts – and a Neanderthal molar tooth. The site has not been directly dated, but faunal records collected by Dorothea Bate are consistent with the period after 70,000 years ago, by which time the Levant had been reoccupied by Neanderthals following the departure of the Skhul and Qafzeh people[87].

Direct evidence for *Homo sapiens* in the Arabian Peninsula during the Eemian finally emerged from the southwest of the Nefud Desert in 2020. The site, Alathar, is an ancient, dried-up lake, but during the Eemian Interglacial, the area was a well-watered semi-arid grassland. Footprints in the lacustrine deposits suggest that the lake served as a focal point for large mammals, but it was also visited by humans. Analysis of the human footprints suggests that they were made by *Homo sapiens* rather than Neanderthals in a group of at least two individuals. The footprints are 121,000 – 112,000 years old. The lack of stone tools or evidence for butchery suggests that the visit was only brief and that the lake might have served as a stopping point and place to drink and forage during long-distance travel[88].

Actual human remains were finally discovered at the site of Al Wusta, also in the Nefud Desert. Here, an assemblage of typical Middle Palaeolithic tools has been found in association with a finger bone, which is in the *Homo sapiens* range. The site dates to 95,000 – 86,000 years ago, and faunal remains suggest that at the time of human occupation the region comprised lakes and temperate to semi-arid grasslands, lakes[89]. Though well after the Eemian Interglacial, Al Wusta provides incontrovertible evidence that modern humans were in the Arabian Peninsula well before the canonical date for the migration from Africa of 65,000 years ago.

Pre-Eemian excursions

Until recently, the oldest *Homo sapiens* remains were thought to be no more than 200,000 years old. Two fossil crania, Omo 1 and Omo 2, were discovered in 1967 at the Omo Kibish Formation in Lower Omo Valley of southwestern Ethiopia and were at first thought to be 130,000 years old[90]. In 2005, following a re-evaluation of the site, a revised estimate of 195,000 years old was published[91]. Even this turned out to be an underestimate: the crania are now thought to be at least 233,000 years old[92].

By this time, though, they had been comfortably surpassed in age by fossil human remains from Jebel Irhoud, a cave site about 100 km (60 miles) west of Marrakech, Morocco. Discovered in 1961, the remains, which included two partial crania, two lower jawbones, and some postcranial bones, were originally thought to be no more than 40,000 years old[93]. In 2007, an age of 160,000 years was obtained for a tooth fragment from one of the lower jawbones[94]. As with the Omo remains, this turned out to be a considerable underestimate: the Jebel Irhoud remains are now thought to be 286,000 years old[95].

These new dates have pushed the origins of *Homo sapiens* back into the MIS 7 period of warm, wet conditions lasting from 243,000 to 191,000 years ago[70]. Conditions would have been comparable to those of the Eemian, raising the possibility of earlier excursions from Africa to the Levant, or even beyond. In 2018, the left half of an adult upper jawbone and associated dentition were found at Misliya Cave on Mount Carmel. They were reported to be 194,000 – 177,000 years old, with affinities to *Homo sapiens*. In reality, the age must be at the upper end of that range, since it would not have been possible to reach the Levant during the subsequent cold, arid period. Therefore, the Misliya Cave jawbone and teeth predate the remains from Mughairet es-Skhul and Jebel Qafzeh by around 70,000 years[96].

With modern humans having existed during this warm, wet period, it was perhaps unsurprising that they reached the Levant, but could they have gone any further? Two fossilised partial crania, known as Apidima 1 and Apidima 2, from Apidima Cave in southern Greece, were discovered in 1978. Apidima 1 is 210,000 years old, and Apidima 2 is 170,000 years old, but the two crania remained poorly understood due to being incomplete and distorted. However, virtual reconstruction has now shown that Apidima 1 belongs to an early *Homo sapiens* population with some archaic features, and Apidima 2 is a Neanderthal[97]. Apidima 1 is thus the earliest-known example of *Homo sapiens* anywhere outside Africa. That the later Apidima 2 is a Neanderthal suggests that this excursion of early *Homo sapiens* into Europe was terminated by the onset of colder, more arid conditions.

Onwards to China?

Could early *Homo sapiens* have also moved east from the Levant before the cold of MIS 4 set in 71,000 years ago, or even before MIS 6 191,000 years ago? Although unequivocal fossil evidence for such an early migration is lacking, there is tentative evidence from sites in southern China. An age of up to 139,000 years old[98] has been reported for the Liujiang Skull, discovered in 1958 in Liujiang District, Guangxi Zhuang Autonomous Region, close to the border with Vietnam, but the exact geological position of the find was not documented, and the skull could actually be as little as 30,000 years old[99].

A lower jawbone and two molar teeth from Zhirendong ('*Homo sapiens* cave') in Guizhou Province have been securely dated to 106,000 years old, but it is not certain that these are from a modern human. The jawbone exhibits a mixture of archaic and modern features: its robustness suggests that it is from an archaic human, but it has a chin characteristic of a modern human[100]. The Zhirendong remains could simply represent a late *Homo erectus* population whose lower jaw had over time become more like that of a modern human[101].

What was initially thought to be definite evidence emerged in 2015, when 47 teeth were discovered at the newly excavated site of Fuyan Cave in Daoxian, Hunan Province and thought to be 80,000 – 120,000 years old. When compared with those of Late Pleistocene humans from Europe, Asia, and Africa, they were found to fall consistently within the *Homo sapiens* size range. They are generally smaller than other Late Pleistocene samples from Asia and Africa, and they are closer to European Late Pleistocene samples and to the teeth of present-day people[102]. However, later work suggested that the teeth are no more than 40,000 years old[103]. It remains an open question as to whether modern humans reached China at this early stage.

Surviving Toba

The eruption of a supervolcano beneath Lake Toba in northern Sumatra, 75,000 years ago[104], was the largest volcanic event of the last two million years. The eruption was of Volcanic Explosivity Index intensity of 8 ('Ultra-Plinian'), ejecting 2,500 to 3,000 cubic km (600 to 720 cubic miles) of magma[105]. The historical eruptions of Krakatau, Tambora, and Pinatubo were feeble in comparison. The largest of these, Tambora in 1815, ejected just 50 cubic km (12 cubic miles) of magma. Even the last eruption of the Yellowstone Caldera, 640,000 years ago, ejected far less material[105].

Around 800 cubic km (190 cubic miles) of ejected magma fell as ash[106], blanketing much of the Indian subcontinent to a depth of 100 to 150 mm (4 to 6 in). In places, drifting caused the ash to pile up to depths of up to 6 m (19 ft 8 in). Ash also fell on the Malay Peninsula, in the Indian Ocean, the Arabian Sea, and the East China Sea. The resulting deposits are now known as Youngest Toba Tuff (YTT)[107,108]. The dispersal of ash in both western and eastern directions from Sumatra indicates two contrasting wind directions, and it suggests that the Toba eruption probably happened during the Southeast Asian summer monsoon season[109].

The plume from the eruption was 27 to 37 km (16 to 23 miles) high, creating dense stratospheric dust and aerosol clouds. The increase in atmospheric opacity might have produced a brief pronounced volcanic winter regionally or possibly even globally. Sulphuric acid aerosols corresponding to the eruption have been detected in Greenland ice core samples. The aerosols remained present in the atmosphere for at least six years, suggesting the eruption might have involved multiple phases over several years. Subsequently, temperatures might have fallen by 3 to 5 degrees Celsius, accelerating the shift to colder conditions already underway at that time[110,111].

The Indian subcontinent would certainly not have been the healthiest of places to be. Nevertheless, there is evidence that modern humans were present and that they survived the catastrophe. This further complication for the standard model emerged in 2007, when artefacts were reported from India dating to the time of the eruption. Thus, they predate the canonical African exodus date of 65,000 years ago by at least eight millennia, and the date of the exodus itself would, of course, have to have been earlier still.

Stone artefacts were recovered from both above and below a 2.55 m (8 ft 0 in) thick YTT deposit near Jwalapuram, in the Jurreru River valley of Andhra Pradesh, southern India. Given the known date of the eruption, the age of the artefacts is reasonably secure. The two sets of artefacts are sufficiently similar to suggest that their makers survived the catastrophe. The tools and toolmaking technology were said to bear a closer resemblance to African Middle Stone Age modern human industries than to the prepared-core industries typical of the Eurasian Middle Palaeolithic. This, together with the behavioural flexibility needed to survive the eruption and its aftermath, suggested that modern humans were already in India at the time of the eruption – and that at least some of them lived through it[112,113]. As with most of the Arabian artefacts, no associated human remains have been found, and some have expressed scepticism that modern humans were responsible for the Jwalapuram artefacts[48].

A pre-Toba exit from Africa can be just about accommodated within the standard model, albeit the range of the genetic dates for leaving Africa lies at the upper end. A number of estimates have also been obtained for the dates of the earliest Indian-specific branches of the mitochondrial haplogroup M: the Toba eruption does lie within the range of some of these[114–116], but others are more recent[44,117].

New genetic data further challenges the standard model

In recent years, we have learned that *Homo sapiens* was in Greece 210,000 years ago, the Levant 190,000 years ago, both the Levant and the Arabian Peninsula during the Eemian interglacial, and almost certainly in India before the Toba eruption. Is it really possible that all of these early modern human migrants died out, contributing nothing to the genetic heritage of present-day populations? Can this archaeological and fossil data be squared with a non-African world populated by solely the descendants of a single group of migrants who left Africa 65,000 years ago, albeit they interbred with Neanderthals and Denisovans? It is becoming increasingly apparent that it cannot.

One of the main pillars of the coastal migration theory is the view that the Andaman Islanders are relict populations that have inhabited the region for the last 60,000 years. However, the mitochondrial haplogroup M31, originally thought to occur only in the Andaman Islands, was later found in West Bengal[118]. Follow-up work showed that the Andaman-specific branch of M31, now designated M31a1, is a comparatively recent branch of the M31 haplogroup and that the true origins of M31 are to be found in northeastern India. Other branches of M31 have been found in Nepal and Myanmar. Humans probably first reached the Andaman Islands just 25,000 years ago, during the Last Glacial Maximum, when sea levels were low, and the archipelago was part of the mainland[119].

In a further blow to the coastal migration theory, more recent studies suggest that the oldest branches of mitochondrial haplogroups N, M, and R are located in East Asia and Southeast Asia rather than in India. The simplest explanation for these findings is that migrants took a northern route through the Levant into Central Asia, then on to Southeast Asia and Australia. India was then settled by secondary migrations from Central and Southeast Asia[120–122].

Since the standard model was first proposed, high-coverage whole genomic studies have become available, and these also point to multiple migrations. They show that Aboriginal Australians and Papuans diverged from Africans before Eurasian populations diverged from Africans. This result is not compatible with a single dispersal from Africa. It also cannot be explained by the effects of either interbreeding with archaic humans or a back migration into Africa from Europe. The best explanation is that Aboriginal Australian and Papuan populations retained the genetic signature of an earlier migration from Africa[123]. This is borne out by the discovery that at least 2 per cent of the genome of present-day Papuans suggests that at least 2 per cent of their genome originates from a largely extinct expansion of modern humans from Africa that occurred approximately 120,000 years ago[124].

Studies involving skull shape variations have reached similar conclusions. Results suggest that there were multiple dispersals via both the northern and the southern routes, beginning around 130,000 years ago[125]. They have demonstrated an affinity between the early Australians and the Skhul and Qafzeh people[126], implying that a population related to the Levantine groups reached Australia. While there is no evidence that humans reached Australia during the Eemian, the ancestors of present-day Papuans and Aboriginal Australians could have encountered and interbred with the descendants of the earlier expansion while still within Eurasia.

These new findings are far more consistent with the latest Eurasian archaeological and fossil evidence. They suggest that the early Levantine and Arabian excursions were not 'failed migrations'. Archaeologists Robin Dennell and Michael Petraglia[127] note that when proposed, the single Out of Africa coastal migration model was useful for interpreting a very small amount of data. The data, though still sparse, is now much improved, and Dennell and Petraglia suggest widening the range of possible hypotheses. The archaeological, fossil, and genetic evidence now available suggests a far more complex scenario involving multiple exits and multiple routes out of Africa, and several episodes of interbreeding with archaic humans.

A pan-African phenomenon?

The existence of a Mitochondrial Eve 200,000 years ago suggests that *Homo sapiens* emerged in a small population in a small population in a specific part of Africa. However, this is contradicted by the fossil evidence, which suggests that the true picture was a pan-African phenomenon, spanning more than 100,000 years. Rather than a single founder population, there were morphologically and geographically diverse populations pertaining to the *Homo sapiens* clade living throughout Africa. These populations periodically became geographically isolated from one another and subsequently reconnected as a result of ecological and climatic changes.

The emergence of *Homo sapiens* in Africa was set against a background of recurring episodes of extreme drought. There were three glacial episodes: MIS 8 (300,000 – 243,000 years ago), MIS 6 (191,000 – 126,000 years ago), and the Würm Glacial ('the last Ice Age') (110,000 – 11,700 years ago). There were also three warmer periods: MIS 9 (337,000 – 300,000 years ago), MIS 7 (243,000 – 190,000 years ago), and the Eemian Interglacial (126,000 – 110,000 years ago). Tropical Africa additionally suffered recurring episodes of extreme drought, occurring during three main periods: from 132,000 to 127,000 years ago, from 111,000 to 108,000 years ago, and from 105,000 to 95,000 years ago. Lesser episodes of aridity occurred thereafter and continued until around 60,000 years ago[42]. The climate during MIS 3 (57,000 – 24,000 years ago) was generally milder, but it was nevertheless punctuated by millennial-scale pulses of aridity. The most severe of these occurred around 37,250 years ago, broadly coinciding with the cold Heinrich Event H4[128]. A final episode of acute aridity occurred towards the end of the Last Glacial Maximum and is associated with the cold Heinrich Event H1 (17,000 to 16,000 years ago)[129].

The aridity is documented by core samples from the Great Lakes of the Rift Valley. The data from Lake Malawi from these periods reveals that pollen levels dropped, and that there was a lack of charcoal particles of the type that would result from flash fires. It is implied that the region around the lake had become a near-desert, with vegetation too sparse to sustain flash fires. Between 135,000 and 85,000 years ago, the lake itself became shallow and saline as its water level, currently 706 m (2,316 ft) deep, dropped to just 125 m (410 ft), and the volume was reduced by 95 per cent. Data from nearby Lake Tanganyika and also Lake Bosumtwi in Ghana reveals a similar picture[42,43,130].

Genetic studies suggest that human populations in Africa experienced extended periods of isolation from one another[39,131,132]. They indicate that rather than originating from a single population, modern humans are descended from multiple subpopulations that periodically came into contact and interbred[133–135]. An estimate of 350,000 to 260,000 years ago has been obtained for the deepest split among modern human populations. This range is in good agreement with the revised dates for Jebel Irhoud[132].

The anatomical and behavioural features now associated with modern humans might have appeared at different times. Isolated human populations, each possessing some modern characteristics, periodically encountered one another and interbred. Over time, more of these characteristics began to accumulate in single populations, until what we see today emerged[136].

The fossil evidence suggests that humans in Africa were only gradually 'modernised' after splitting from the archaic Eurasian populations. If the Jebel Irhoud dates are correct, modern facial and near-modern jawbone characteristics emerged around 300,000 years ago, and the modern globular cranial vault had emerged by 233,000 years ago (Omo 1), though (assuming it is the same age) the Omo 2 skull suggests that populations with the archaic cranial vault form still existed then. At this stage, populations represented by the fossil remains were still more robust than any living people, and it is only after 35,000 years ago that people with the more gracile, fully modern skeletal form make their appearance[93,137,138].

The question, perhaps, is at what point could humans first be described as 'modern'? Is it with the Jebel Irhoud hominins, as Hublin believes, or is it not until later? Although the Jebel Irhoud remains are quite distinct from *Homo heidelbergensis* or *Homo rhodesiensis*, the braincases of Irhoud 1 and Irhoud 2 lie outside the modern range. Should they be classified as a separate species? British palaeoanthropologist Chris Stringer[136] has argued that since there are already difficulties in differentiating *Homo heidelbergensis* and *Homo rhodesiensis* from the earlier stages of evolution towards Neanderthals and modern humans, introducing another species would be unhelpful. Stringer's preferred option is to revive the informal term 'archaic *Homo sapiens*' for early members of the modern human lineage. This option would recognise that the Jebel Irhoud and other hominins from this period are part of the *Homo sapiens* clade, even though there are significant differences between them and later *Homo sapiens*. It would also imply that 'modern human' and *Homo sapiens* are not necessarily synonymous[139]. It could be argued that even the term 'modern human' is problematic, given that the genomes of present-day populations contain significant components from Neanderthals, Denisovans, and probably other archaic human species.

A northern dispersal into Central Asia

Any new model for the peopling of the world must consider that one element of the coastal migration theory has remained unchallenged. That is the expansion of the mitochondrial haplogroup L3, which was clearly associated with major demographic changes both inside and outside Africa. These changes must have been on a sufficient scale to erase the mitochondrial signature of all earlier, and possibly concurrent migrations from Africa. Only a faint echo of these remains in the nuclear genomes of Papuans and Aboriginal Australians. Other early migrations probably occurred but did not contribute detectably to the genetic makeup of present-day populations[140].

A major reason for favouring the southern coastal route is that the expansion of L3 began in East Africa. However, proximity to Arabia is not the only factor. As noted above, the L3 expansion occurred around 86,000 – 61,000 years ago. While the cold climatic conditions 65,000 years ago would have favoured a southern exit, the warmer, wetter conditions prior to 71,000 years ago would have favoured the northern route. The favourable climate, believed to have enabled the L3 expansion within Africa, could also have triggered the migration out of Africa. The discovery that the oldest branches of N, M, and R have been found in East Asia and Southeast Asia explains why earlier mitochondrial studies failed to identify early, indigenous lineages of these haplogroups in the Arabian Peninsula[141].

The initial dispersal is likely to have occurred during the warm, wet period from 84,000 to 71,000 years ago, or possibly during the latter part of that from 103,000 to 93,000 years ago. The migrants moved through the Sinai Desert into the Levant, then up to the Caucasus. From there, some groups proceeded through southern Siberia, where 73,000 years ago, a period of cold, arid conditions drove some groups to move south to Southeast Asia, and from there – aided by low sea levels - to Australia.

During the subsequent climatic amelioration from 57,000 years until the Last Glacial Maximum, there was a series of secondary migrations. From Central Asia, groups moved south into the Indian subcontinent, northeast into East Asia, and west towards the Levant and North Africa, and from the Levant into Europe; from Southeast Asia, groups moved west into the Indian subcontinent and northeast into China[120,121]. Mitochondrial genetic diversity data suggests that by 52,000 years ago, the populations of southern and Southeast Asia had increased fivefold[51]. Therefore, population pressures likely also played a part in triggering these secondary migrations.

Conclusion

By 18,500 years ago, the L3 expansion had reached every continent on Earth, barring Antarctica. During their travels, descendants of the original migrants encountered and interbred not only with Neanderthals and Denisovans, but the descendants of earlier migrations of *Homo sapiens*. Our genetic makeup today represents the reconnecting of lineages that had been separated for periods ranging from a few tens of thousands of years to as much as three-quarters of a million years. Thus, we can see that the true picture of our origins is neither Out of Africa nor multiregional continuity, but somewhere between the two.

We were neither created in 4004 BC nor are we Conquistadores who overcame Neanderthals, Denisovans, and other archaic people who lived in Eurasia before us. Our interbreeding with these supposedly primitive people is no more than another example of reproductive behaviour common among primates. Currently, natural hybridisation has been reported for around 10 per cent of existent Old World primate species and 7 per cent of New World species, including species that diverged as long ago as four million years[142].

Even the term 'primate' is a conceit: a term introduced by somebody who never disputed the idea that humans ranked first in God's grand scheme. In reality, had it not been for an asteroid impact 66 million years ago, the world would quite possibly still be ruled by dinosaurs. For all our technological advances, the recent COVID-19 pandemic was a timely warning of just how vulnerable we are to the forces of Nature. In the late 1960s, American biologist Paul Ehrlich, in reference to then-current fears about environmental pollution and exponential growth in world population, warned that "*Nature bats last*". As world leaders try to reach agreements that would limit global warming to 1.5 degrees Celsius, Ehrlich's warning is as relevant as ever.

10: Prehistoric Art

What is art?

Art is a form of human expression that can take many forms, including visual art, music, literature, theatre, and dance. But what is art, what purpose does it serve, if any, and when was the first art made? The definition of art has been debated for centuries, and it is safe to say that there is no agreement. The *Stamford Encyclopaedia of Philosophy* notes that *"The definition of art is controversial in contemporary philosophy. Whether art can be defined has also been a matter of controversy. The philosophical usefulness of a definition of art has also been debated"*[1]. Some would say, 'We know art when we see it', but that is purely subjective. Nobody would dispute that Botticelli's 1480 *The Birth of Venus*, Michelangelo's 1512 *The Creation of Adam*, and da Vinci's 1498 *The Last Supper* are art. But what of Marcel Duchamp's 1917 *Fountain* (a porcelain urinal signed 'R. Mutt'), Carl Andre's 1966 *Equivalent VII* (120 bricks arranged in a rectangle), and Tracey Emin's 1998 *My Bed* (an unmade bed)? These are just three works from the last century that people have argued are not art. The latter sold at auction at Christie's in July 2014 for more than £2.5 million.

Equally, the purpose of art is contentious. There is no doubt that as a means of communication, art can be put to many practical uses ranging from advertising to conveying political or social messages. Are these no more than spinoffs from something that originally came about for no other reason than to be enjoyed or appreciated for its aesthetic or intellectual qualities? Or is it the other way around, and *art pour l'art* is a spinoff from something that originally served a more significant purpose?

There are no definitive answers. We do know that the origins of art are very ancient, though just how ancient is also uncertain. We begin our journey into the prehistory of art at the cave site of Lascaux in the South of France, sometimes described as the Sistine Chapel of Prehistory.

A discovery in unhappy times

In September 1940, a year after the outbreak of World War II, and less than three months after the fall of France, four teenage boys and a dog made one of the most important archaeological discoveries of the last century, although there is no definitive account of the sequence of events. According to one version, on 12 September, the boys – Marcel Ravidat, Jacques Marsal, Georges Agnel, and Simon Coencas, accompanied by Ravidat's dog Robot – were walking through the woods at Lascaux Manor, near the town of Montignac on the River Vézère in the Dordogne region, outside the zone occupied by the Nazis. The boys were investigating a local legend about an old tunnel, which supposedly connected Lascaux Manor to the ruined Château de Montignac on the other side of the river. The dog Robot was running on ahead and was attracted to a deep hole in the ground. Covered with overgrowth, it had been exposed by the falling of a tree[2,3].

The boys enlarged the hole with their penknives and estimated its depth by dropping stones down it. In another version of the story, Ravidat discovered the hole on his own some days earlier. He and his friends returned on 12 September equipped with picks, shovels, and lighting to investigate further. This version seems rather more likely, but whichever version is correct, Ravidat and his friends enlarged the hole until they were able to slide through it feet-first, one by one, along a stalagmite-embedded, semi-vertical shaft, eventually reaching a dark underground chamber. There, in the flickering glow of their oil lamp, they saw polychrome images of horses, cattle, and herds of deer, unseen by human eyes for at least 18,000 years[2,3].

The boys began showing the cave paintings to villagers for a small fee, and they also told retired schoolteacher and amateur archaeologist Léon Laval about their discovery. Laval at once recognised the great importance of the discovery and stressed the need to protect the cave from vandalism. The cave paintings soon came to the attention of the Catholic priest and archaeologist Abbé Henri Breuil, who visited the caves on 21 September and attested to the great antiquity of the artwork. The caves soon became known as 'The Sistine Chapel of Prehistory'[2]. An oft-repeated (and almost certainly apocryphal) story is that Pablo Picasso was an early visitor to the site, claiming – in reference to modern art that – "*We have invented nothing*". Another version suggests that Picasso made his remarks after visiting Altamira, not Lascaux[4].

After the war, Comte de la Rochefoucauld, the landowner of the site, carried out significant work to facilitate access to the caves with the intention of opening them as a tourist attraction. The works included the provision of a monumental entrance, and while it now sounds unthinkable, the entire project was carried out without any proper archaeological considerations. In July 1948, the caves were opened to the public, and soon they were attracting as many as 1,800 visitors a day. Unfortunately, they quite literally became a victim of their own success. By 1955, the CO_2 exhaled by such large numbers of people was promoting the growth of algae, causing significant damage to the paintings. In April 1963, after several unsuccessful attempts to alleviate the problem, André Malraux, Minister of State for Cultural Affairs, ordered the caves to be closed to the general public. Only five people a day are now admitted, five days a week, and scholars wishing to visit the caves for research purposes face a lengthy wait for a 35-minute slot. For the benefit of ordinary visitors, a replica of the two main halls known as Lascaux II was opened in 1983. In 2016, the Centre International d'Art Pariétal opened at Lascaux, featuring a complete replica of all the painted areas of the cave[5].

The Lascaux cave paintings include 915 animals, mainly horses, deer, aurochs (wild cattle), and bison – animals that at that time roamed wild on the steppe of Ice Age Europe. The paintings are now believed to be around 18,000 – 19,000 years old, or four times older than the Pyramids[6]. Yet they are actually among the more recent European Upper Palaeolithic cave paintings: the oldest artworks in the Altamira and El Castillo caves in northern Spain are at least twice as old at 36,000 and 40,800 years old, respectively[7].

The cave paintings at these and many other sites are perhaps the most spectacular examples of Ice Age art; art that proclaims the arrival of modern humans in Europe. The archaeological record of Europe is marked by a dramatic discontinuity that first appeared in the Balkans about 46,000 years ago and spread across the continent over the next 5,000 years[8]. Below the transition point are the largely utilitarian artefacts of the Middle Palaeolithic, but above it we begin to see artworks that are indisputably the work of behaviourally modern minds[9,10]. They are executed *"with great skill and a sense of aesthetics still worthy of our admiration today"*, to quote eminent French prehistorian Jean Clottes[6].

Altamira

The first examples of European Upper Palaeolithic cave art were discovered in the nineteenth century at Altamira, a cave complex near the town of Santillana del Mar in northern Spain. The complex comprises a series of chambers and passages, meandering into the hillside for around 270 m (885 ft). The height varies between 2 and 12 m (6.5 and 39 ft), and the width between 6 and 20 m (19.5 to 65.5 ft). The cave culminates in a narrow, twisting passage, 50 m (164 ft) in length and no more than 1.5 m (5 ft) wide, known as the Horse's tail. The cave complex was discovered in 1876 when a local man found a crack through which he could gain access[11] and was subsequently investigated by Marcelino de Sautuola, an amateur geologist and archaeologist. De Sautuola's finds included stone tools and animal bones, but in 1879, his young daughter Maria noticed polychrome images of bison on the ceiling of a side chamber located 30 m (100 ft) from the entrance. A year earlier, De Sautuola had seen similar images engraved on Palaeolithic stone blocks at the Paris Exposition Universelle 1878, where he had also met the French archaeologist Édouard Piette. He concluded that the Altamira ceiling paintings must date to the same period[12].

The Altamira paintings attracted considerable interest, and visitors included King Alfonso XII. In 1880, de Sautuola published his conclusions in a booklet in which he linked the bison paintings to the portable art he had seen in Paris. However, by that time, the initial interest had begun to wane. Juan Vilanova y Piera, Professor of Palaeontology at the University of Madrid, was supportive, as was Piette, but the majority of the archaeological community was highly sceptical. The fine artwork did not fit with the then-current notions that the people of the Palaeolithic period were primitive savages. French archaeologists Louis Laurent Gabriel de Mortillet and Émile Cartailhac were particularly critical. Another French scholar, Édouard Harlé, went even further and claimed that the images were forgeries, produced between 1875 and 1879. He suggested that de Sautuola must have been duped or, worse still, forged them himself. Over the next two decades, more cave sites with paintings were discovered, and their Palaeolithic association was gradually accepted. Eventually, in 1902, Cartailhac conceded that he had been wrong about the cave paintings of Altamira. Sadly, this came too late for de Sautuola, who had died in 1888 with his reputation destroyed[12].

The main archaeological phases of occupation at Altamira occurred during the Gravettian, Solutrean, and Magdalenian periods. The earliest phase is from the Gravettian period (21,900 years old)[13]. These are followed by two phases from Solutrean (17,200 to 19,630 years old) and five from the Magdalenian (14,070 to 15,580 years old). The prehistoric occupation of Altamira ended when the entrance collapsed around 13,000 years ago[14]. However, human activity in the cave complex considerably predates the Gravettian period. Though much of the art is dated from the Late Gravettian to the Magdalenian, the earliest work is a large red claviform symbol forming part of the *Techo de los polícromos* ('Polychrome ceiling'). Researchers used the uranium-series method on overlying calcite deposits to obtain a minimum age of 36,160 years, placing it in the preceding Aurignacian period[7]. Claviform ('club-shaped') symbols, resembling the letter P, are common in Upper Palaeolithic cave art. It has been suggested that they are stylised female figures[15].

Even the Altamira claviform is not the earliest-known example of European Upper Palaeolithic cave art. The current record-holder is a red stippled disc, which has been uranium-series dated and is at least 41,400 years old. The disc forms part of the *Panel de las Manos* (Panel of hands) in El Castillo, a cave site 25 km (15 miles) from Altamira. At the same site, there is also a red hand stencil, which is 37,630 years old, produced by spraying pigment over hands pressed against rock surfaces[7].

Lion-men of the Swabian Jura

The European Upper Palaeolithic is characterised not just by cave art but by ivory sculptures, engraved stone blocks, and bas-reliefs. Portable art objects include statuettes of animals, human and anthropomorphic figures, representations of both male and female sex organs, and so-called Venus figurines[9,10]. The Löwenmensch (Lion-man) of Hohlenstein-Stadel is one of the earliest-known examples of what is unequivocally figurative art. The 300 mm (11.8 in) high figurine is carved from mammoth ivory and is a therianthropic (part human, part animal) figurine of a human figure with a lion's head. The figurine's gender is uncertain: it lacks male genitalia, but the body proportions and lack of breasts suggest that it is male. Slanting marks on its left arm have been interpreted as tattoos. Regardless of gender, the figure is clearly both human and feline at the same time[6]. The Löwenmensch is around 36,000 years old[16]. It was discovered in fragments in 1939 in the Aurignacian levels of Hohlenstein-Stadel, a cave site located in the Lone Valley in the Swabian Jura mountains. With the outbreak of World War II shortly afterwards, it was put aside and then forgotten. It was thirty years before reconstruction began in 1969, and it was not completed until 1988[6].

More recently, in 2003, a second Löwenmensch was discovered at Hohle Fels in the Ach Valley, only a short distance from Lone Valley. Like the original Löwenmensch, the Hohle Fels figurine depicts a mixture of feline and human traits, and again no sexual characteristics can be discerned. However, it is considerably smaller, measuring only 25.5 mm (1 in). It is slightly older than its Hohlenstein-Stadel counterpart at around 36,500 years old. It was found with a bird-like figurine that probably represents a cormorant or a duck and a slightly more recent figurine of a horse's head[16].

The Löwenmensch figurines could represent shamans partially transformed into lions, or possibly mythical beings or spirits. The people of the Ach and Lone Valleys apparently shared a belief system connected with therianthropic images of felines and humans, and possibly one in which the borders separating humans from animals were easy to cross[6].

Ice Age flutes

dOCUMENTA (13) was a contemporary art exhibition held in Kassel, Germany, in 2012, but one of the works shown featured an object that was very ancient indeed. *Raptor's Rapture* was a video installation displayed in the labyrinthine tunnels beneath the town's Weinberg

Park. Originally used to store ice and beer in the early nineteenth century, the complex served as an air-raid shelter during World War II. The work featured flautist Bernadette Käfer playing in the presence of a griffon vulture. The dark, ice-cold cavernous space was perhaps an appropriate setting for the video, in which Käfer played the world's oldest-known musical instrument – a flute made by the Swabian Jura people more than 40,000 years ago.

The flute is one of eight flutes that have been found in the caves of Geißenklösterle, Hohle Fels, and Vogelherd since 1995. They were originally all thought to be around 36,000 years old, but a revised date of 43,000 – 42,000 years old has since been obtained for the Geißenklösterle flutes. The ages of the other artefacts from the region have possibly also been underestimated[17].

Four of the flutes were carved from hollow bird bones and the other four were from mammoth ivory. The mammoth ivory flutes would have been more difficult to make. Manufacture would entail shaping the flute from a piece of mammoth ivory, then splitting it in half, hollowing it out and carving holes, and finally re-joining the halves with air-tight seals. One of the ivory flutes from Geißenklösterle has a large number of finely carved notches along the edges of the two halves to facilitate binding and sealing. A bird bone flute, also from Geißenklösterle, has three holes and produces four basic notes and three overtones, comparable to many modern flutes. The Swabian Jura flutes have a range of diameters, to produce different tones[18].

Music clearly played a part in the lives of the Swabian Jura people, though whether it was for ritual purposes or simply for entertainment is not known. Most of the flutes were found with stone tools and animal remains, suggesting that they were played in a wide range of social and cultural settings[18]. One interpretation is that the flutes and the Löwenmensch figurines were used in ritual performances combining song, dance, and music, acting out a corpus of mythology and ancestral tales. Such rituals have been documented among recent and present-day hunter-gatherer societies, serving to pass tribal lore down from generation to generation in the absence of written texts[19].

Venus figurines

Also found at Hohle Fels was the earliest-yet-known example of a so-called 'Venus' figurine. The mammoth ivory piece is at least 35,000 years old and was discovered in six fragments along with one of the flutes[20]. Similar female carvings are known throughout the European Upper Palaeolithic, although they are primarily associated with the later Gravettian period. They are known as Venus figurines, although they predate the Roman goddess by tens of millennia. Typically lozenge-shaped, they are characterised by exaggerated sexual characteristics, very large breasts, accentuated hips, thighs, buttocks, and large, explicit vulvas. Other anatomical details, such as arms and feet, tend to be neglected, and the heads generally lack facial detail[21]. They bear very little resemblance to the classical portrayal of Venus.

The figurines were carved from a variety of materials including mammoth ivory, serpentine, steatite, or limestone, and were often coloured with ochre. Others were made from fired clay, making them among the earliest-known ceramics[22]. In total, around two hundred are known, ranging in size from 25 to 240 mm (1 to 9 ½ in) high[21]. Most are from the Gravettian period, and it was widely believed that the 'Venus' tradition originated then, but the Hohle Fels discovery confirms an Aurignacian origin and suggests that there was at least a degree of cultural continuity between the Aurignacian and Gravettian.

The first examples were discovered in the nineteenth century, and many have since attained iconic status. These include the Venus of Willendorf, which is 111 mm (4.4 in) high and carved from oolitic limestone. It was discovered in 1908 by archaeologist Josef Szombathy near the village of Willendorf in Austria, and is now exhibited in the Natural History Museum, Vienna. The limestone from which it was made is now believed to have originated from Lake Garda in northern Italy, which is 650 km (400 miles) from where the figurine was found[23]. Other Venus figurines include the ceramic Black Venus of Dolní Věstonice in the Czech Republic, the serpentine Venus of Galgenberg, Austria, and the ivory Venus of Lespugue from the Pyrenees.

Venus figurines are predominantly a European phenomenon, but they occur as far east as Siberia, where examples have been found at Mal'ta, in the Lake Baikal region. Ancient DNA has been obtained from the remains of a boy who lived 24,000 years ago at Mal'ta[24], and this shows that his people, known as Ancient north Eurasians, did not contribute to the European genome until Late Neolithic times[25,26]. If there is a connection between the Siberian and European Venus figurines, it must represent cultural diffusion rather than population movements[26].

The Venus figurines are commonly interpreted as fertility figures or mother goddesses, but their real function is unknown. It could be that rather than a single function, they had a variety of meanings in different places at different times within an overall theme[27]. One suggestion, by anthropologists Leroy McDermott and Catherine Hodge McCoid[28,29], was that they are self-portrayals of pregnant women. McDermott and Hodge noted likenesses between a photograph of a 'Venus' figurine viewed from above and one of a pregnant woman standing with her feet together, viewed from her own perspective looking down on her breasts and abdomen. This 'paleo-selfie' theory met with a certain amount of scepticism, but McDermott and McCoid argued that it explains the features found in representations of the female form from the Upper Palaeolithic.

Archaeologist Sir Paul Mellars has noted that explicit sexual imagery was not limited to the female form. Some sites have yielded equally explicit phallic representations carved out of bone, ivory, or, in one case, the horn core of a bison. While their function is also uncertain, Mellars refused to rule out the possibility that some of these could have been Upper Palaeolithic sex toys[10].

Other portable art

The earliest-known portable art object is an oval mammoth ivory pendant from the Aurignacian cave site of Stajnia, Poland, which was found during excavations in 2010. The pendant is around 41,500 years old, or around 5,000 years older than the Swabian Jura artefacts. The pendant measures 45 by 15 mm (1.8 by 0.6 in) and is 3.9 – 3.6 mm (0.15 – 0.14 in) thick. It was probably worn around the neck: there is one drilled hole and a partly preserved second hole, where part of the pendant is missing. On one side, the pendant is decorated with a pattern of fifty puncture marks in a looping curve. These may represent hunting kills, although it has also been suggested that it is a lunar calendar (see below)[30].

However, the greatest range of portable art is to be found in the latter part of the Upper Palaeolithic, with dates from 15,000 to 12,000 years ago. Many items have been found at Magdalenian sites in the Franco-Cantabrian region of northern Spain and southwestern France, and also in southern Germany. Animals depicted include reindeer, horses, ibex, mammoths, fish, birds, and seals. The images are highly naturalistic and are engraved on bone or stone, or carved from fragments of bone or stone[31].

Such finds include an engraved deer shoulder blade from the cave site of El Mirón in northern Spain. On the flat surface is an engraved image of the head, neck, and part of the dorsal line of a red deer hind, including such details as a nostril, an eye, and the base of an ear. A small slate plaque pendant, engraved with the image of a horse, was also found at this site[32]. Human subjects have also been depicted, though these are generally more stylised[27,31]. These include a bone plaque from the Laugerie-Basse rock shelter in the Dordogne, which depicts a pregnant woman apparently lying at the feet of a reindeer[6]. Even functional objects, such as atlatls, harpoons, and spatulas, were sometimes beautifully carved and engraved with both naturalistic and geometric designs that bely their utilitarian nature[6,31].

Lunar calendars

Could some portable art objects have served a calendrical function, and if so, what was being recorded? In 1972, the American researcher Alexander Marshack examined a large number of prehistoric artefacts and looked for possible calendrical notches. He published his findings in a book entitled *The Roots of Civilization*[33] in which he claimed that Upper Palaeolithic people in Europe were making records of the phases of the Moon. At a first glance, this seems highly plausible. We can be certain that Upper Palaeolithic people were aware that the appearance of the Moon changes from night to night in a predictable manner. One of the objects studied by Marshack was an engraved oval bone plaque from Abri Blanchard. The plaque measures 110 mm (4.33 in) in length. At one end is engraved a looping pattern of small crescent or kidney-shaped marks, aligned in gradually changing directions. Marshack interpreted these as representing the phases of the Moon recorded over two-and-a-quarter months.

Two problems arise, though. The first, albeit from a numerate perspective, is that it seems unnecessary to record, say, the days since the last full Moon when one can simply look at the Moon, note the current phase, and work forward to when the next full Moon will occur. If, for example, a waxing half-Moon was seen in the evening sky, then Upper Palaeolithic people would have been aware that it would be full in another seven days – or at least in a period of time that we would recognise as seven days. The second problem is the tallies vary in the number of days by more than can be explained by the small seasonal variations in the length of the lunar cycle, or by observational error, or due to the weather preventing the Moon from being seen. However, there is another cycle with an average length almost identical to that of the lunar cycle that does show a certain amount of variation – the human menstrual cycle. Possibly, this is what was being recorded, although Marshack[34] rejected the idea. That the human menstrual cycle is almost exactly one lunar month in duration is pure coincidence (other primates have similar but slightly differing cycles), but it is one that was noticed many thousands of years ago. The words 'moon', 'month', 'menstruate', and 'measure' (time) all have the same ancient etymological root.

Others have noted that the pattern on the Abri Blanchard plaque resembles a lunar analemma. This is an apparent figure-of-eight pattern traced in the sky if the Moon is photographed on successive nights 52 minutes later than the night before. This is the average time by which the Moon rises later each day. Interestingly, the Abri Blanchard pattern resembles that on the Stajnia pendant, raising the possibility that the Aurignacian people might have been aware of the phenomenon and that the analemma was of ritual significance to them. This is, of course, pure speculation, but the Ancient Greeks were familiar with analemmas[35], and we cannot rule out that the Aurignacian people were also.

Hunting magic and 'crowding stress'

Understanding the context in which cave art was produced might give an indication as to whether such traditions arose only once or on multiple occasions. As might be expected, such questions have been asked ever since an Upper Palaeolithic origin for the European cave art became widely accepted.

An early suggestion was that the caves were Upper Palaeolithic art galleries, with paintings created and appreciated by people with time on their hands for leisure pursuits outside the daily round of hunting, gathering, and toolmaking. An objection to this theory is that much of the art is located in the depths of caves rather than places where it could easily be appreciated[12]. For example, the Shaft of the Dead Man at Lascaux is, as its name implies, a deep shaft. Present-day art critics often complain that contemporary art can be inaccessible, but for Upper Palaeolithic cave art, this was literally true.

Totemism and hunting magic were popular explanations during the first half of the last century. Totemism is a belief system in which a group or clan identifies itself by a species of animal or plant, for example, 'Eagle People', 'Bear People', etc. The word 'totem' originates from the North American Indian Ojibwe 'odoodem', meaning 'clan' or 'kinship group'. The problem is that if the totemic explanation was correct, it would be expected that the artwork in a particular cave would depict a single species, for example, the Bear People's cave would depict only bears. Instead, the caves invariably depict multiple species[12].

Abbé Henri Breuil and others proposed hunting magic as an explanation. Hunting magic is the belief that an image of an animal or person can influence it. Such beliefs are common in traditional societies to this day. The hunting magic explanation supposed that if people went deep underground to make images that could not readily be seen by others, it could only be for magical purposes. The important action was making the images, rather than viewing them subsequently. The purpose was to ensure successful hunting, and images of dangerous predators could be explained in terms of the artists hoping to acquire the strength and hunting skills of these animals. Abstract images represented traps, weapons, or hunters' hides[6,12,31].

Structuralism is a philosophical movement that originated early in the twentieth century with the work of the Swiss linguist Ferdinand de Saussure. It was subsequently applied to anthropology by the French anthropologist Claude Levi-Strauss, who proposed that the language, kinship systems, and mythology of any human culture can be explained in terms of 'binary opposites' (for example, up/down, life/death, and male/female), and the relationships between them. This view was applied to cave art by the French archaeologists Andre Leroi-Gourhan and Annette Laming-Emperaire, who interpreted the images of animals and the abstract designs as either male or female symbols. For example, horses and stags symbolise males, whereas bison and aurochs represent females. Similarly, line or arrow-like figures are male, and broader triangular designs are female, in both cases representing genitalia[12].

Some have suggested that rather than trying to interpret the art itself, the emphasis should be on seeking to explain its distribution geographically and over time, and the social and environmental contexts in which it was produced[31,36]. Cave art is highly localised both in space and time: 90 per cent of it is concentrated in the Franco-Cantabrian region of southwestern France and Northern Spain, despite other regions of Europe having limestone caves suitable for cave art[6,31]. The cave art is also concentrated in time, reaching a peak from 26,500 to 17,000 years ago during the Last Glacial Maximum of the last Ice Age, when northern and central Europe was uninhabitable[36].

It was proposed that the high concentration of art in the Franco-Cantabrian region can be explained in terms of a high population density leading to 'crowding stress' and a need for distinct territories. The Franco-Cantabrian region lies at what was the southernmost part of the open tundra and steppe environment in Ice Age Europe, and supported migratory herd animals that could readily be exploited by human groups. As more people were forced south by the deteriorating climate, the problem of overcrowding grew. This created a need for ritual and ceremonial activities to maintain social cohesion and enforce territorial boundaries. On this view, cave art is seen as an integral part of the ideology of Ice Age hunter-gatherers, a social and cultural adaptation to extreme conditions. Lascaux and Altamira could have served as major ritualistic or ceremonial centres during annual gatherings by various groups. Possibly, the production of the art was controlled by chiefs or religious leaders who used its creation and associated ceremony to reinforce their roles of power and authority within Upper Palaeolithic societies. After conditions improved, populations began to spread out again, and northern and central Europe was repopulated. With the ending of the 'crowding stress', there was no longer any need for tightly demarcated territories, and after 20,000 years, the era of cave art came to an end[31,36,37].

The Mind in the Cave

The problem with this view is that it is what is known as a 'functionalist' explanation. In sociology, structural functionalism is a model that sees society as composed of institutions that function for the common good. Critics of functionalism argue that it not only downplays conflict and inequality but is also logically flawed and begins by assuming the very thing it sets out to prove. Religion and ritual do indeed create social cohesion – but this, critics argue, is more a description rather than an explanation. It could be formulated as 'the purpose of X is to do what it does'. It does not tell us why religion and ritual exist unless you suppose that people consciously invented them for that purpose. It is difficult to argue that the elders of Upper Palaeolithic groups sat down to discuss introducing rituals that would bind their society together to deal with 'crowd stress' or other issues[38].

An alternative explanation has been put forward by South African anthropologist David Lewis-Williams[12]. In a book titled *The Mind in the Cave*, he drew on ethnographic studies of present-day South African and North American rock art and traditions, he proposes that Upper Palaeolithic cave art is associated with shamanistic belief systems, a suggestion that as we saw has also been made for the Löwenmensch of Hohlenstein-Stadel and Hohle Fels. Lewis-Williams suggests that the universal belief in a multi-tiered cosmos is rooted in the actual structure of the human brain, and that in altered states of consciousness, people can experience journeys to realms other than that of our everyday existence. Such altered states are commonly induced with psychotropic substances, but other means include intense concentration, chanting, clapping, drumming, prolonged rhythmic movement, and hyperventilation. Sensory deprivation, of the type that may be experienced in the depths of the cave networks, also induces hallucinations.

The high incidence of shamanistic belief systems in traditional societies worldwide suggests that shamanism is very ancient, originating from a common source. However, another possibility is that the universality of these shamanistic traditions arises from the ability of the human neural system to generate entoptic images (images originating anywhere between the eye itself and the cortex of the brain) while in altered states of consciousness. While unlikely to have been identical to any ethnographically recorded shamanistic tradition, Upper Palaeolithic belief systems probably shared core features. They would inevitably have varied from place to place, and over time, but would have remained essentially shamanistic.

Lewis-Williams believes that cave art represents visions experienced by people in altered states of consciousness. Upper Palaeolithic shamans saw both images of animals and geometrical patterns apparently 'projected' onto the walls of the caves. By painting what they saw, the shamans 'fixed' the images. They might have believed that the images were entities that were released or coaxed from a living membrane between the image maker and the spirit world. Even the paint used to make the images could have had its own significance as a solvent to dissolve rock and allow the entities of the spirit world to pass through. Interestingly, the cave images lack a naturalistic setting of trees, rivers, or grassy plains, suggesting that they are mental images, unconstrained by the natural world. The images could have been painted while the artist remained in an altered state of consciousness. Handprints, too, might have been more than just the individual marks of particular artists or the Upper Palaeolithic equivalent of 'Kilroy was here'. When a hand is put against the wall of a cave and sprayed with paint, it seemingly merges into the rock and disappears. Paint could also have been significant in this context, facilitating intimate contact with the realm behind the cave wall.

In altered states of consciousness, all the senses rather than just sight hallucinate, so shamanistic visions are not silent, and they communicate with shamans with speech or animal sounds. Sounds would also have been made by the participants to accompany the rituals. Lighting, too, might have played a ritual as well as a purely functional role. Unlike electric lighting, the light of oil lamps and torches only illuminates portions of a cave wall, and the images of animals would have seemingly materialised out of the darkness. Lamps have been found in the caves engraved with animal motifs or geometric designs similar to those found on the walls of caves, suggesting that they were more than just a means of illumination.

People living in Europe during the Upper Palaeolithic might have seen the subterranean passages and chambers of the caves as the entrails of the spirit world. By entering them, they were physically entering a nether realm where they could see the 'fixed' visions of the spirit animals that empowered the shamans, and they could experience the same visions for themselves. Lewis-Williams suggests that the origins of social stratification and inequality could also be found in Upper Palaeolithic belief systems. Those who could master the techniques necessary to enter the altered states of consciousness and access the spirit world were set apart from those who could not. Indeed, the cramped nature of the caves suggests such a social structure.

At Lascaux, for example, only the Hall of the Bulls is large enough to have accommodated communal ritual activity. The carefully composed images there must have been the result of a communal effort involving highly skilled people and the use of scaffolding. Notably, this hall is the nearest part of the complex to the surface, and it might have served as an antechamber into deeper parts of the subterranean realm. By contrast, the Shaft of the Dead Man at Lascaux is accessible only by ropes and ladders, and the floor space is so limited that only a few people could have occupied it at a time. The imagery there includes a highly stylised man, who has the head of a bird, four-fingered birdlike hands, and a prominent phallus. He is confronting a partially eviscerated bison. Below him, a bird is perched atop a post. With its back to this scene and its tail raised is a rhinoceros, and on the opposite side is a black horse. These images have been interpreted as shamanistic: the death of the bison parallels the metaphorical 'death' of a shaman as he enters the spirit world and his fusion with his spirit helper, a bird. The chamber is characterised by high levels of naturally occurring CO_2, which might have induced altered states if people stayed down there long enough.

However, in other lower levels at Lascaux, individual images do not appear to form parts of larger compositions, and they are often superimposed upon each other. Lewis-Williams interprets these images as uncoordinated participation by different isolated individuals at different times over a long period. It is in these regions of the cave complex that the entoptic images were 'fixed'. By moving through the narrow passages, people might have felt that they were passing through the vortex experienced when in altered states of consciousness.

Only a few select individuals might have been permitted to enter the cramped lower levels of Lascaux and other caves. Lewis-Williams suggests that the use of inaccessible regions of the caves that could only accommodate a few people at a time was deliberate. Access to even areas where communal rituals took place might have been prohibited to most members of the community. Art and religion might have been born in a process of incipient social stratification.

Palaeolithic planetariums

Shamanistic interpretations do not preclude a suggestion put forward by several researchers that the cave paintings are ancient star maps depicting actual star groups as they appeared in the skies of Ice Age Europe. Shamanistic travel to specific constellations or stars to contact the spirit world is part of the belief systems of many present-day hunter-gatherer groups[39].

The Hall of the Bulls is a large, vaulted rotunda-like chamber near the entrance of the Lascaux cave complex, containing a panoramic mural depicting aurochs, horses, and stags. Several researchers including Luz Antequera Congregado[40], Frank Edge[41], and Michael

Rappenglück[42,43] have noted that a pattern of six dots above the mural's Bull No. 18, resembles the Pleiades. A V-shaped set of dots on its face can be associated with the Hyades open star cluster, and the bull's eye with the bright star Aldebaran (α Tauri). These are all constituents of the present-day zodiacal constellation of Taurus (the Bull), and if the correlations are intentional, then the association of Taurus with a bull is very ancient indeed.

The Taurus theory is certainly feasible, and indeed, it could be argued that the accurate placement of the dots resembling the Pleiades, Hyades, and Aldebaran would be a remarkable coincidence if not intentional. Taurus is one of the most distinctive in the night sky and the Pleiades feature in many present-day traditions. The identification of the Hyades with a bull is attested 4,000 years ago in ancient Mesopotamia, so it is entirely possible that the tradition originated in the Upper Palaeolithic.

American astronomer Frank Edge[41] suggested that many other constellations were also represented in the Hall of the Bulls mural. He associated the constellations of Orion (the Hunter) and Gemini (the Twins) with a second aurochs, Bull No. 13, and that of Leo (the Lion) with a third, Bull No. 9. Unlike the other bulls in the mural, these two animals stand head-to-head. Other animals are associated with Canis Minor (the Lesser Dog), Virgo (the Virgin), Libra (the Scales), Scorpius (the Scorpion), and Sagittarius (the Archer). The last three are represented by the mural's Figure No. 2, which is known as the 'Unicorn' despite having two horns. The Unicorn lies on the opposite side of the gallery to the 'Taurus' Bull, just as in the skies, Scorpius lies opposite Taurus.

If Edge is correct, then the mural represents just over half the prominent constellations lying along or close to the zodiac. Today, Taurus, Orion, and Gemini are prominent in the winter skies. However, due to the precession of the equinoxes[47] when Lascaux was in use, they would have been prominent in spring. As summer approached, they would have begun to sink towards the western horizon, and at the summer solstice, they would have stood low down on the horizon just after sunset.

The two bulls, Nos. 18 and 13, which we now see as Taurus, Orion, and Gemini, would have, in Edge's words, "*seemed to walk on the horizon*", and the other constellations depicted would have been visible between sunset and sunrise. Edge believed that they were used in conjunction with the phases of the Moon to predict and keep track of the time of the summer solstice. Like Alexander Marshack, he believed that Upper Palaeolithic people were observing the phases of the Moon, and would have been doing so thousands of years before the Lascaux cave complex was painted. He noted that at the time the Hall of the Bulls mural was painted, the summer solstitial full Moon would have appeared low in the sky between Taurus and Gemini. The theory does sound plausible, even though it goes rather beyond the 'standard' Taurus interpretations. One problem is that there is no evidence in the ethnographic record for hunter-gatherer societies for any particular interest in the zodiac[39].

Origins of Upper Palaeolithic cave art

In addition to the debate over why Upper Palaeolithic cave art was created, there are also

---

[47]A slow, cyclical change in the Earth's orientation in space, similar to the wobbling of a spinning top. Each cycle takes just under 26,000 years.

two rival viewpoints concerning its origins in Europe. Did it develop gradually over thousands of years, or did it first appear in Europe as a mature, fully developed tradition? The first possibility, which has long been the mainstream viewpoint[44], draws support from the dates for the earliest at Altamira and El Castillo, which are abstract and monochrome (red). Only later, during the Late Gravettian, do polychrome images of animals appear there. The dates from these two sites suggest that the earliest expressions of art in Europe were characterised by monochrome red dots, discs, lines, and hand stencils rather than polychrome depictions of animals. Over time, there was a gradual increase in technological and graphic complexity and a gradual increase in figurative images[7,45].

Against this, there is the Aurignacian Löwenmensch at of Hohlenstein-Stadel and Hohle Fels. Aurignacian dates have also been claimed for the earliest cave art at Chauvet-Pont-d'Arc in southern France, which was discovered by a group of cavers in 1994. As with Altamira, the entrance had eventually been blocked by a collapse in prehistoric times, in this case around 21,000 years ago[46]. When UNESCO granted the site World Heritage status, they noted that it "*contains the earliest and best-preserved expressions of artistic creation of the Aurignacian people, which are also the earliest known figurative drawings in the world*". The Chauvet cave art was originally attributed to the Solutrean and Magdalenian periods on stylistic grounds, but then radiocarbon dates from charcoal samples suggested that it dated to the Aurignacian period[47]. The dates were criticised because the charcoal samples were mostly obtained from the floor of the cave rather than from the pigments used in the artwork[48], but later work, using material removed from the artwork, confirmed the original conclusion. Other radiocarbon dates showed two main phases of occupation: one from 34,000 to 30,000 years ago and another from 25,000 to 21,000 years ago. Animal paintings, hand stencils, and various marks were made during both these phases, and also during the intermediate period between them[49].

Critics note that other than Jura Mountains examples, portable figurative art objects from the Aurignacian are few and far between. Many are crudely executed engravings on stone blocks with ambiguous depictions that are not necessarily figurative[48,50]. While the Löwenmensch figurines and Chauvet cave art demonstrate the existence of an Aurignacian figurative art tradition, the fact remains that the 41,400-year-old red stippled disc at El Castillo predates the Löwenmensch figurines by nearly five millennia and the earliest figurative images at Chauvet by nearly seven and a half millennia. To put these dates in a modern context, 5,000 years ago corresponds to the earliest phase of construction at Stonehenge and 7,500 years ago predates the earliest civilisations in Mesopotamia and Egypt.

An early art tradition in Sulawesi and Borneo

Until recently, the cave and portable art of Upper Palaeolithic Europe was the earliest-known figurative art in the world. The debate over its origins took a new turn when revised dates started to emerge for cave art from sites in Southeast Asia, thousands of miles from Europe. The rock art of the Maros-Pangkep limestone caves of Sulawesi has been known since the 1950s, and more than ninety rock art sites are known. They have been extensively studied by Indonesian scholars and are thought to belong to two distinct periods. The earlier period artwork consists mainly of hand stencils, but there are also a smaller number of large, naturalistic paintings of large Sulawesi mammals. These include the anoa (a dwarf buffalo), the Celebes warty pig, and the babirusa (a member of the pig family). The later period artwork is believed on stylistic grounds to have been produced by Austronesian migrants, and it is thought to be no more than a few thousand years old. It consists mainly of small anthropomorphic depictions and a wide range of geometric signs, typically drawn using a black pigment.

Though the earlier artwork was thought to be much older than the Austronesian artwork, it was still not believed to be any older than 10,000 years. Then, in 2014, researchers used the uranium-series method to date a hand stencil at Leang Timpuseng, a cave forming part of the karst complex, and discovered that it was at least 39,500 years old. A minimum age of 35,400 years was also obtained for a painting of a female babirusa at the same site[44].

Even older paintings were soon identified. These included a 4.5 m (14 ft 9 in) rock art panel with monochrome paintings on the rear cave wall of Leang Bulu' Sipong 4, a high-level limestone cave. The panel was initially dated 43,900 years B2K, later revised to 50,200 years B2K. The paintings have been interpreted as therianthropic (part human, part animal) figures equipped with spears and ropes, hunting animals including pigs and anoa[51,52].

The oldest artwork so far identified is a cave painting of three humanlike figures interacting with a pig in Leang Karampuang, a cave located at the base of the karst complex. With a minimum date of 53,500 ± 2,300 years B2K, it is the earliest known example of figurative art anywhere in the world[52]. It is at least 5,700 years older than the previous record holder: a cave painting of a warty pig in Leang Tedongnge, a cave located in a secluded valley on the border of the karst district, with a minimum date of 45,500 years B2K[53]. It is more than 10,000 years older than the artwork at Altamira and El Castillo. Other Maros-Pangkep cave paintings range from 39,900 to 27,200 years old[44,53].

Early cave art has also been discovered on the neighbouring island of Borneo. Since the 1990s, a large number of rock art images have been found in the limestone caves of the Sangkulirang-Mangkalihat Karst in the Indonesian province of East Kalimantan. In 2018, a large reddish-orange animal painting at the cave site of Lubang Jeriji Saléh was dated by the uranium-series method, to give a minimum age of 40,000 years. Three reddish-orange hand stencils were also dated. The oldest of these is at least 51,800 years old, and the others are at 37,200 years. The range of dates from Sulawesi and Borneo suggests an art tradition that endured for almost 30,000 years, which is at least as long as the duration of the European Upper Palaeolithic cave painting era[54].

The existence of separate traditions of Upper Palaeolithic cave art in two regions as far apart as Europe and Indonesia implies either independent developments or a common origin dating much further back in time. But which of the two possibilities is correct – and if the two traditions do share a common origin, could even earlier examples of cave art still await discovery?

Technical interlude: the Great Leap Forward

Innovation – indeed all art, literature and science are consequences of a behavioural package anthropologists refer to as 'modern human behaviour'. People living today all possess the ability to use symbols to convey information, ranging from the spoken and written word to figurative art. A symbol is anything that refers to an object or an idea, and it can take the form of sound, an image, or an object. Symbols can refer directly to an object or concept, for example, a figurative image, or they can be totally abstract, such as spoken or written words.

As recently as the 1990s and early 2000s, some anthropologists argued that behavioural modernity was a relatively late development, emerging around 50,000 years ago – well after the emergence of anatomically modern *Homo sapiens*[55-57]. Proponents of this view pointed to the late appearance of cave art and portable art in Europe as the most dramatic manifestation of what science author Jared Diamond described as the Great Leap Forward[58]. It was argued that art and other supposed innovations reflected a fundamental shift in cognition and the emergence of modern syntactical language. But others claimed that evidence for behavioural modernity – albeit less clear-cut – is to be found much earlier. In a landmark paper entitled *The revolution that never was*, published in 2000, anthropologists Sally McBrearty and Alison Brooks argued that there was no Great Leap Forward, and the elements of modern human behaviour emerged only very gradually over tens and possibly hundreds of millennia[59].

Blombos Cave

Soon after the publication of McBrearty and Brooks' paper, evidence began to emerge suggesting that modern human behaviour had emerged well before 50,000 years ago. Blombos Cave, on the Southern Cape coast of South Africa, is one of the most extensively studied of all African Middle Stone Age sites. The cave has yielded many artefacts, most notably two 73,000-year-old engraved pieces of ochre, which were described as the oldest examples of abstract art anywhere in the world. Located on a limestone cliff 35 m (115 ft) above sea level, it was discovered by archaeologist Christopher Henshilwood in 1991, and archaeological work has continued there ever since[60].

Three major phases of occupation have been identified, known as M1, M2, and M3. The M1 phase is 73,000 years old, M2 has an upper phase that is 77,000 years old and a lower phase that is 80,000 years old, and M3 spanned a period from 143,000 to 90,000 years ago. All of these dates are subject to considerable uncertainty. Each phase contains several occupation layers, and these are mostly quite shallow. The cave appears to have been occupied only sporadically, and for relatively short periods[61-66].

Ochre-processing toolkits and coloured beads

Blombos Cave has provided what Henshilwood and his team claimed was strong evidence for symbolic behaviour. Finds include several thousand pieces of ochre, coloured beads, and two 'toolkits' for processing ochre. The 'toolkits', which are over 100,000 years old, consist of abalone shells containing a mixture of ochre, charcoal, and crushed bone. One of the kits was found with a quartzite cobble, which was stained with red ochre and showed signs of having been used for pounding and grinding. An animal bone, found with the ochre residues, was probably used as a stirrer and for transferring some of the mixture from the shells. It is not known for certain what the mixture was used for – it could have been used for decorative purposes[62], but there are other possibilities, as ochre is an effective sunscreen or insect repellent[67,68].

The two 'toolkits' were found close together, suggesting that they were used at the same time. There were few other archaeological remains in the same layer, suggesting that at this point in its long history, Blombos Cave was being used as a workshop. It was abandoned shortly after the compounds were made. Long before the cave was next occupied, sand blew in from outside and buried the toolkits for the next 100,000 years[62].

Finds at Blombos Cave also include 41 beads, mostly originating from the M1 phase. They were made from perforated shells of the marine snail *Nassarius kraussianus* ('tick shell'), which occurs only in estuaries. The shells probably originated from the Duiwenhoks River and the Goukou River, which are 20 km (12 miles) from the cave and are too far away for the shells to have been deposited there by non-human predators. The edible content is too small for it to have been worthwhile collecting the shells as food. The shells are all adults, suggesting that they were chosen for size, and they were perforated by artificial means rather than by some natural process – most likely a sharp tool with an elliptical cross-section. The beads show signs of wear from having rubbed against thread or human skin, suggesting they were worn as bracelets or necklaces. Traces of ochre found on the shells could indicate that they had been coloured, although it could also have come from body paint. The beads were found in several groups with similar sizes, colours, perforation types, and patterns of use-wear, suggesting that each group represented a single beadwork item. Henshilwood claimed that the wearing of such personal ornaments implies the existence of modern fully syntactical language[65,69,70].

But do beads or pigment use imply modern language and behavioural modernity, as Henshilwood believes? Not necessarily, according to psychologist Frederick Coolidge and archaeologist Thomas Wynn[71]. Instead, they could simply be markers of an individual's status within a group. Users could be aware of how they were perceived by others, but not necessarily behaviourally modern. Another point is that ochre and possible pigment use appears in the archaeological record well before the earliest use of beads, with the earliest use being attested 400,000 – 266,000 years ago[72]. At the site of Pinnacle Point, near the coastal town of Mossel Bay, Western Cape Province, South Africa, ochre use is attested 164,000 years ago[73]. Even if the beads are accepted as evidence for modern human behaviour, could it be that the earliest pigment users, including those at Pinnacle Point, were not yet fully behaviourally modern?

Archaeologist Larry Barham[74] cited ethnographic research[75] and has noted that among present-day hunter-gatherers in New Guinea, there are pronounced social differences between groups that rely on hunting unpredictable land and tree-based animals and those dependent on fish and other aquatic foods. The former are highly mobile, egalitarian, and have few forms of physical expression other than body painting, dancing, and singing, whereas the latter are densely packed, sedentary, and socially stratified. There is often a pronounced hierarchy, with some villages even exhibiting hereditary rankings. Such groups have complex rituals, involving elaborate visual arts. Barham suggested that long-standing ochre use without any other material culture would be consistent with small, widely scattered groups that have little need to engage in elaborate social signalling.

Anthropologists Steven Kuhn and Mary Stiner[76] have noted that beads have several advantages over pigments for social signalling. They are more durable than body painting, they are expensive in terms of materials and time needed for their manufacture and hence are more prestigious, and they can be used as part of a social exchange network. Kuhn and Stiner suggested that beads are more likely to indicate increased social complexity than increased cognitive abilities. They might have appeared in response to increased levels of intra-group competition as populations grew.

Engraved ochres at Blombos Cave

Thought-provoking discoveries at Blombos Cave were announced in 2001 and 2002. The first discovery, announced in June 2001, was a pattern of abstract engravings on a bone fragment originally recovered from the 73,000-year-old M1 phase in 1992. The engravings consisted of nine parallel, subparallel, or diverging lines of various lengths, crossed at an oblique angle by a tenth line[77]. As notable as this was, it was overshadowed early in 2002, when Henshilwood reported the two pieces of engraved ochre, also from the M1 phase. The two pieces of engraved ochre, designated AA 8937 and AA 8938, were both engraved with cross-hatched patterns. In addition, on AA 8938 the pattern was bounded top and bottom by parallel lines, with a third parallel line running through the middle. The similarities suggest a deliberate intent, rather than somebody absent-mindedly scratching away at the pieces with a sharp object. Somebody who knew just what they were doing must have sat down and intentionally engraved the patterns on the two pieces[61]. Other engraved ochres were later discovered in all three phases of the site, some of which were over 100,000 years old. Four basic categories of pattern have been identified: 1) cross-hatched designs, 2) dendritic shapes, 3) parallel lines, and 4) right-angled juxtapositions. The first category has been found in phases M1 and M3, the second in all three phases, the third in M1 only, and the fourth in M3 only[78].

Henshilwood argued that like the beads, the ochres AA 8937 and AA 8938 provide evidence for modern fully syntactical language[61,65]. He dismissed other possible explanations for the engravings. For example, he noted that only a few lines would be required to test the quality of powder from the ochres, so the marks could not be the by product of such testing. He noted that great care was taken in completing the patterns and ensuring the incisions matched up, making it unlikely that the marks were the result of absent-minded doodling. Furthermore, engraving lines on hard pieces of ochre requires full concentration to apply the right pressure and keep the depth of the incision constant. Henshilwood argued that not only were the marks on the ochres made with deliberate intent, but recurring motifs on ochres found in all three of the Middle Stone Age phases are evidence for a tradition of engraved geometric patterns that began more than 100,000 years ago and persisted for more than 25,000 years[62].

More recently, the world's earliest-known drawing has been found in the M1 phase: a 73,000-year-old silcrete flake on which a cross-hatched pattern had been drawn with a red ochre crayon. The pattern consists of six straight near-parallel lines crossed obliquely by three slightly curved lines. The lines all terminate abruptly at the edges of the flake, and it is likely that the pattern originally extended over a larger area. The flake is quite small, measuring 38.6 mm (1.52 in) by 12.8 mm (0.50 in), with a thickness of 15.4 mm (0.60 in). Its discovery puts an end to arguments about powder quality testing and strongly supports Henshilwood's view that the similar engraved patterns on the ochres were made with deliberate intent[79].

A graphic tradition at Diepkloof Rock Shelter

Diepkloof Rock Shelter, Western Cape Province, has provided evidence for the existence of another multi-generational African Middle Stone Age graphic tradition[80,81]. Like Blombos Cave, Diepkloof Rock Shelter was repeatedly occupied over tens of millennia, in this case, from prior to 130,000 years ago to about 45,000 years ago. Archaeologists have recovered over four hundred engraved fragments of ostrich eggshells, mainly from layers dating from 85,000 to 52,000 years ago, with a few from layers dating to 109,000 years ago and 90,000 years ago. The decorated eggshells were probably used as water flasks, a purpose for which indigenous Kalahari people use them to this day. A 12 mm (½ in) diameter hole was punched in one piece that came from the apex of the eggshell. Ostrich eggs are ideal for this purpose, being larger than the eggs of any other living bird species. They are by necessity sturdy, as they have to endure being sat on by a 100 kg (220 lb) female ostrich.

Eight main styles have been identified: 1) hatched bands consisting of two long parallel lines, intersected at roughly right angles by shorter, regularly spaced lines, 2) hatched bands with oblique intersecting spaced lines, 3) crosshatched grids, 4) converging groups of subparallel lines, 5) curved and subparallel lines, 6) lines with reversed curvature, 7) distantly spaced straight or curved subparallel lines, and 8) isolated or irregular striations. The engravings appear to be standardised, with repetitive patterns made in accordance with a set of rules, albeit with scope for individual expression within these rules. However, the assemblage was dominated by the hatched band styles and the converging groups of subparallel lines. Within the hatched band styles, craftspeople exercised a certain amount of variation in both the width of the bands and the spacing of the hatching.

Where is the figurative art?

As we saw, the earliest unequivocal figurative art is a 45,500-year-old cave painting of a pig in the Leang Tedongnge cave site, Sulawesi, which is more than 50,000 years after the appearance of the first abstract engravings at Blombos Cave. Why is there such a long delay? Could figurative depictions be associated with fully modern human behaviour and the abstract depictions at Blombos Cave with symbolic behaviour that was not yet fully modern? Henshilwood did not dismiss this view, but suggested that there are problems with it. He noted that there are present-day traditional peoples who do not make representational art, and many others who do so only on perishable materials that would not survive for tens of thousands of years. Furthermore, the Blombos patterns might only appear abstract from the point of view of an outsider. He cited the Christian cross as an example of something that would appear abstract to somebody unfamiliar with religious iconography[78]. He suggests that the Blombos Cave markings could be such an expression of group identity[77], although this is a functionalist explanation.

However, this does not really address the question. While it is entirely possible that we could yet find unequivocal figurative cave art associated with the Middle Stone Age, we have not yet done so, and it could be that it simply does not exist. British archaeologist Derek Hodgson[82] criticises the group identity model as circular reasoning, in that it assumes that which it seeks to explain. It leaves the precise mechanism for the production of the marks still to be established – a common criticism of functionalist explanations, as we have seen. Rather than markers of modern human behaviour, the Blombos marks could be analogous to the scent-marking of territory by wolves. But, he argues, this is still a description rather than an explanation. Hodgson has proposed a model he terms the Neurovisual Resonance Theory (NRT). He notes that what he terms 'geometric primitives' are often made by infants when they first begin to draw and suggests that they derive pleasure from viewing such patterns. This, in turn, derives from a bias towards parallel or crossed lines in the visual cortex of the brain[82]. Accordingly, the Blombos and Diepkloof engravings could be manifestations of an intrinsic attraction to such patterns, and symbolic intent cannot be assumed[83]. Hodgson suggests that the production of geometric primitives could have been a precursor and a prerequisite for the production of figurative images[82].

That there was symbolic intent behind the Blombos and Diepkloof engravings and other non-figurative Palaeolithic images is nevertheless suggested by neurological studies using functional magnetic resonance imaging (fMRI) to identify areas of the brain activated by the abstract prehistoric images. Results were compared with those obtained from showing subjects images of landscapes, objects, words in alphabetic writing, and fragments of the ancient Cretan Linear B script, as well as computer-scrambled versions of every image presented. All the unscrambled images, including the abstract prehistoric patterns, triggered the same patterns of brain activation, suggesting that they are processed as organised visual representations. By contrast, the computer-scrambled versions were processed in the primary visual cortex, indicating simple visual perception without further processing by the brain. The implication is that the abstract engravings were processed as meaningful representations, to which symbolic meaning could be attached[84]. As to how early humans started making engraved patterns, one suggestion is that they noticed that the cutmarks inadvertently made on animal bones during butchery often took the form of juxtaposed or intersecting incisions, and began experimenting with making similar marks on other materials[85].

It has been claimed that the compositions of Blombos engraved ochres and the Diepkloof engraved ostrich eggs evolved over time to become more memorable and easier to reproduce, evolving from simple patterns of parallel lines to complex cross-hatched patterns characterised by greater symmetry and cardinal and diagonal lines[86]. However, it is for the most part difficult to discern a chronological trend to greater complexity in the styles, albeit there are considerable uncertainties in the dating. There is one obvious exception in that the engravings of the Blombos pieces AA 8937 and AA 8938 are markedly more complex than the other Blombos engravings.

A further possible issue with making comparisons between the Blombos and Diepkloof engravings is that the Blombos patterns are mostly complete, whereas the Diepkloof patterns are fragments of what were originally larger compositions. Some of the ostrich eggshell fragments have indeed been reassembled, allowing larger portions of the original compositions to be seen. Another possible factor is that the engravings were made on two quite different classes of objects. The ostrich eggshells are thought to have been used as water flasks – functional objects – whereas blocks of ochre would have had no immediate function and merely served as sources of material. Can we assume that similar motives applied for engraving patterns on the two? Can we assume that there was cultural continuity at the two sites over the lengthy period in question, especially at Blombos Cave, where there was a history of short-term occupations? In short, there is considerable uncertainty surrounding these early graphic traditions and the implications for later figurative art traditions.

Neanderthal cave paintings

The Aurignacian people were among the first modern humans in Europe, but the continent had long been inhabited by Neanderthals. In 2018, there was a major development in the long-running debate over the extent of Neanderthal symbolic behaviour and whether they were capable of artistic expression.

The Spanish sites of Cueva de La Pasiega in Cantabria, Cueva de Maltravieso in Extremadura, and Cueva de Ardales in Andalucía have a lengthy archaeological record of human occupation beginning at a time when Neanderthals were the sole human inhabitants of Europe. However, the cave paintings at these sites have long been assumed to be the work of modern humans. La Pasiega is part of Monte Castillo, a cave complex that also includes El Castillo and the sites of Las Chimeneas and Las Monedas. The complex has been occupied by humans throughout the past 100,000 years. The paintings there consist of mainly red and black paintings, including groups of animals, linear and club-shaped signs, dots, and possible anthropomorphic figures. Maltravieso has a longer but sporadic history of human occupation, extending over the past 180,000 years and the artwork there includes red hand stencils, geometric designs, and painted and engraved figures. Ardales was occupied by Neanderthals during the Middle and by modern humans during Upper Palaeolithic. There are over one thousand paintings and engravings, including hand stencils and prints, dots, discs, lines, and other geometric shapes, and representations of animals, including horses, deer, and birds[87].

Researchers used uranium-series dating to obtain dates for calcite crusts overlaying cave paintings. As this was laid down after the paintings were completed, it would give the minimum age of the latter. A red ladder-like abstract painting at La Pasiega was thus found to be at least 64,800 years old. Animals and other symbols accompanied the ladder, but no dates for these have been obtained, so they could have been later additions by modern humans. Similarly, a minimum age of 66,700 years was obtained for a red hand stencil at Maltravieso. At Ardales, dates were obtained for multiple layers of carbonate curtains from areas of the cave that had been painted red. In some cases, the researchers were able to obtain both maximum and minimum ages by dating carbonate samples lying immediately underneath the pigment and the carbonate layer that had subsequently formed above. These showed that there had been episodes of painting between 48,700 and 45,300 years ago, between 45,500 and 38,600 years ago, and between 63,700 and 32,100 years ago. Other samples revealed an earlier painting episode at least 65,500 years ago and one at least 45,900 years ago. At all three cave sites, the earliest paintings preceded the widespread arrival of modern human groups in Europe by almost twenty millennia[87].

Neanderthals disappeared from the archaeological record of Europe around 41,000 – 39,250 years ago[88] and may have persisted rather longer in Spain[89,90]. It certainly cannot be ruled out that they were responsible for the earliest paintings at Altamira and El Castillo[7].

The Berekhat Ram pebble

The Berekhat Ram pebble is a small lump of volcanic lava that some have claimed is a representation of a woman. It was discovered in 1981 at the site of Berekhat Ram in the Israeli-occupied Golan Heights, in a layer of archaeological deposits sealed between two basalt flows. The dates of these are known, and are 800,000 and 233,000 years, respectively. Based on the pebble's position in the intervening layer, a date range of 250,000 – 280,000 years ago has been estimated. The pebble has been incised, probably with a sharp-edged flake tool. It has been claimed that the intention was to represent the female form, with indications of head, neck, arms, shoulders, and breasts[91,92].

Sceptics point out that the resemblance to a woman is poor[93], and it certainly bears little resemblance to the finely crafted Venus figurines of the European Upper Palaeolithic. Nevertheless, the pebble appears to be a human-modified object that possesses no obvious utilitarian function, and it might have held symbolic meaning for its maker[94]. The maker is unknown, but could have been an early Neanderthal.

The earliest use of ochre

Twin Rivers is a complex of caves near Lusaka in southern Zambia. The site was studied as far back as the 1950s, but in 1999, Larry Barham led an excavation and recovered over 300 pieces of haematite, limonite, and specularite, ranging in age from 266,000 to 400,000 years old. These minerals are all types of ochre and can be used to produce a range of colours including red, yellow, brown, and purple. However, none of them is found naturally anywhere near the site, so they must have been brought to the site from elsewhere. Some of the specularite pieces showed signs of grinding, and a quartzite cobble, which had been recovered in 1954, was found to be stained with traces of specularite. Specularite is harder than other types of ochre, and more effort is required to obtain powder for pigments[72].

A date of 266,000 years ago brings us into the era of the earliest forms of our own species, sometimes referred to as archaic *Homo sapiens*. The African humans of 400,000 years ago were of an archaic type commonly referred to as *Homo heidelbergensis* or *Homo rhodesiensis*. To what extent these early humans were capable of symbolic behaviour is uncertain.

We cannot be certain that the Twin Rivers ochres were used as pigments. There are other, more utilitarian possibilities, such as medicinal purposes or use in hide processing. However, Barham noted the range of colours seen at Twin Rivers, the effort put into obtaining the different materials and in particular, the grinding of the specularite, and he suggested that such functional explanations are inadequate. He believes that the ochres were used primarily for ritual body painting and possibly even for cave painting. Barham suggested that pigment use, even at this early stage, implies language. Rituals are group activities, and their meaning and significance are most effectively communicated by using language[72]. There is no possibility of finding evidence for body painting from this far back, but should 400,000-year-old cave paintings ever be found, it would be one of that year's great news stories.

The earliest evidence for symbolic behaviour

The earliest tantalising evidence for symbolic behaviour by humans is 500,000 years old and associated with *Homo erectus*. Archaeologists studying freshwater mussel shells excavated by Dutch anthropologist Eugène Dubois at Trinil, Java, in 1891 discovered a geometric pattern of grooves engraved into one of the shells. The pattern appears to have been made intentionally, probably with a shark's tooth. It consists of a zigzag line with three sharp turns producing an 'M' shape, a set of lighter parallel lines, and a zigzag with two turns producing a back-to-front 'N'. The shell is part of the Dubois Collection in the Naturalis Biodiversity Centre in Leiden. The engraved geometric pattern suggests that at least some capacity for symbolic thought was already present in early humans 500,000 years ago[95].

Conclusion

Having travelled back in time half a million years, are we in a position to say when and why humans first started creating art? The answer seems to be 'no'. At one end, we have the Trinil engraved mussel shell, and at the other, the Leang Tedongnge pig. It seems entirely plausible that archaic humans sought to reproduce the pleasing geometric patterns they sometimes saw in butchery cutmarks on animal bones. Was there an intrinsic attraction to such patterns, as Hodgson suggests? Neurological fMRI studies have suggested otherwise and that humans process the patterns just as they would process organised visual representations. The caveat is that these studies, by necessity, involved present-day people and we cannot be certain that the same results would be obtained with the people who originally made the patterns.

What can be said is that complex cognitive processes were surely required to conceive and execute the reproduction of a cutmark pattern onto a new and unrelated medium. But this leads to further questions. While it is hard to believe that the Trinil engraved mussel shell was a one-off and that other, similar pieces must have been made, was each conceived and executed independently, or did their production ever become a tradition, passed from one individual to another, from one generation to another?

The engraved ochres at Blombos Cave and the engraved eggshells at Diepkloof Rockshelter do appear to represent a tradition, and possibly one that evolved over time. It could be that these traditions arose from what might be better described as the earlier practice of engraving simple geometric designs on organic objects.

How did we get from abstract, geometrical patterns to figurative art? Were geometric primitives a precursor to figurative art, as Hodgson believes? It could be that abstract and figurative art were two entirely separate developments. If the cutmark theory is correct, then the Trinil engraved mussel shell represents the transfer of a 2D pattern to a 2D medium. However, the Leang Tedongnge pig represents the transfer of a 3D pig to a 2D medium. Possibly, the earliest figurative art was three-dimensional. It is worth noting that the Löwenmensch figurines of Hohlenstein-Stadel and Hohle Fels predate the earliest figurative cave art in Europe by around 2,500 years. The antecedents of figurative art might be objects such as the Berekhat Ram pebble rather than the Blombos ochres or Diepkloof eggshells. Crude as it is, the Berekhat Ram pebble could represent the earliest glimmerings of a sculptural tradition that would one day lead to the Venus de Milo, Michelangelo's *David*, and Rodin's *The Thinker*.

11: Early seafarers

Introduction

More than two-thirds of the Earth's surface is covered with water. Away from the oceans, in non-desert regions of the world, the landscape is dotted by lakes and traversed by rivers and streams. Very early on, people must have realised that waterways could be used for transportation or that fishing could be carried out more effectively inshore rather than onshore or on a lake or river than from the lakeside or riverbank. In terms of human prehistory, the earliest direct evidence for watercraft is comparatively recent. This is unsurprising – the first iron-hulled ships did not appear until the early nineteenth century, and vessels constructed from wood and other organic materials are far less likely to be preserved. The oldest-known boat is the Pesse canoe, a Mesolithic-era dugout canoe that was discovered at Pesse in the Netherlands in the 1950s and has been dated to 8040 – 7510 BCE[1]. The Pesse canoe is predated by an Early Mesolithic petroglyph of a boat at Valle, on the Efjorden fjord, northern Norway, which is believed to date to around 9,140 – 8,840 BCE. The life-sized outline depiction is 4.05 m (13 ft 3 ½ inch) long, although one end has been eroded, and either the bow or stern is missing. The boat resembles an Arctic skin boat or umiak of the type used by the Inuit[2]. Such craft consist of animal hides stretched over a wooden frame.

Despite this, we can say with reasonable certainty that humans have been building and sailing watercraft for far longer than 12,000 years. The first Australians are now believed to have reached the island continent at least 65,000 years ago, and they could only have arrived by sea. Even this date is quite late in the history of seafaring, which predates the emergence of modern humans.

Seafaring or unexpected journeying?

Seafaring – albeit probably involuntary – considerably predates the emergence of anatomically modern *Homo sapiens*. The island of Flores, Indonesia, is associated with the so-called 'hobbits' (*Homo floresiensis*), a species of diminutive, small-brained hominins that made headline news with their discovery at the cave site of Liang Bua in 2003. The common view is that they were descended from larger hominins who underwent what is known as insular dwarfism: in an environment where food was relatively scarce but predators absent, they 'downsized' over many generations, as smaller, more 'fuel-efficient' individuals had a survival advantage[3,4]. A similar phenomenon also affected *Stegodon*, an extinct elephant species and one of the few large animals on Flores[5].

Exactly which the ancestral species from which *Homo floresiensis* downsized is disputed[6].

Homo erectus was in Java at least 1.3 million years ago[7], which would fit the timescale. Fossil evidence suggests that *Homo floresiensis* had already downsized 700,000 years ago[8], and stone tools from the sites of Mata Menge and Wolo Sege suggest that their ancestors had arrived no later than 880,000 – 1 million years ago[9,10].

Although there have been periods when sea levels were much lower than the present day and much of the Indonesian archipelago was connected to the mainland, this was never the case for Flores. It, along with Sulawesi, Lombok, Sumbawa, Sumba, Timor, Halmahera, Buru, Seram, and many smaller islands, make up the Wallacea islands, located in deep-water straits between the Asian (Sunda) and Australian (Sahul) continental shelves. Wallacea is named for the British naturalist and explorer Alfred Russel Wallace, who proposed the theory of evolution by natural selection independently of Darwin and is jointly credited with him.

Even at the times of lowest sea levels, three deep-water straits occur between Flores and the mainland, and crossings of at least 19 km (12 miles) would have been required. Accordingly, it has been suggested *Homo erectus* (or whatever the ancestral species was) was capable of repeated water crossings using boats[11]. The cranial capacity of *Homo erectus* averaged just over 1,000 cc, far smaller than the modern average of 1,350 cc[12]. Could such small-brained hominins have built and sailed primitive watercraft, possibly logs lashed together to make rafts? The same question arises with *Homo luzonensis*, discovered in 2007 at Callao Cave, Luzon, Philippines, although not named until some years later. The 67,000-year-old remains included teeth, finger bones, toe bones, and a partial juvenile thighbone[13,14]. They did not attract as much attention as the Flores 'hobbits', but like them could have evolved from *Homo erectus*, and their ancestors must have reached Luzon by sea. A subsequent discovery of stone tools and a butchered rhinoceros in the nearby Cagayan Valley suggests these ancestors were on Luzon at least 700,000 years ago[15].

We should never underestimate the abilities of archaic humans[16], but we should be open to other explanations. The anthropoids are the primate group that includes Old World monkeys, New World monkeys, apes, and humans. The Old World monkeys (Catarrhini) are found in tropical and equatorial Africa and South and Southeast Asia, and the New World monkeys (Platyrrhini) are found in the tropical regions of Mexico, Central, and South America. The two groups are closely related and diverged from one another an estimated 35 – 43 million years ago, during the Middle to Late Eocene epoch[17–19]. The divergence is thought to have happened in Africa, with the Platyrrhini subsequently dispersing to South America[20]. The Platyrrhini were not the only primate group to find its way to the New World from Africa: the parapithecids, primitive anthropoids known from sites in Egypt and Libya[21–23] have recently been identified in Peru and probably arrived in South America 35.0 – 31.7 million years ago(Seiffert *et al.*, 2020).

How did these early primates, who were accompanied by the ancestors of the caviomorph rodents (guinea pigs, chinchillas, coypus, etc), cross the Atlantic to reach South America? We can safely assume that they did not build boats. Could they have gone overland across Asia and across the Bering Strait before migrating south through North America? Asia and North America are periodically conjoined by a land bridge across the Bering Strait, but the Isthmus of Panama formed only 2.8 million years ago[24]. However, the strongest argument against this route is the complete lack of fossil anthropoids in North America[25]. A migration across the supercontinent of Gondwanaland (comprising India, Africa, Australia, Antarctica, and South America) can be ruled out because South America separated from Africa 100 million years ago, well before either primates or rodents evolved[26]. Overall, there has been no time within the period under consideration where there was an unbroken land connection between Africa and South America. The anthropoids and caviomorphs must have reached South America by crossing the Atlantic, but how?

Africa and South America were closer together 35 million years ago, but they were still 1,500 – 2,000 km (900 – 1,200 miles) apart. One possibility is 'island hopping'. This model proposes that animals migrate through chains of volcanic islands stretching across the Atlantic. The islands did not all persist throughout the entire migration between Africa and South America, but adjacent islands were successively connected over geological time. Drilling studies have shown that such islands existed as late as 25 million years ago, but it is not known if their distribution in time and space was sufficient to enable an island-hopping migration[25].

A second possibility is that the anthropoids and caviomorphs reached South America on floating islands of vegetation. Such islands are found in locations such as floodplain lakes and form initially from the agglomeration of aquatic vegetation. Over time, they can accumulate a substrate of organic matter sufficient to grow forest patches of several hectares in area and up to 12 m (40 ft) in height[27]. They have been reported on the Brazilian coast, having drifted from the Niger and Congo Rivers on the west coast of Africa[28]. Should a genetically viable primate group have been trapped on such an island when it became detached from the mainland, it could have been the means by which anthropoids reached South America[28,29].

The question is, how long would such an ocean crossing take, and would any of the group members still be alive at the end? In addition to hazards such as storms, there would be a complete lack of fresh water. Survival would depend on the island's vegetation providing enough food and moisture for the duration of the crossing. However, studies based on winds and oceanic currents prevalent at the time in question suggest that a floating island would take 5 – 15 days to cross the Atlantic. Larger animals, with a greater resistance to water deprivation, could survive such a crossing. The odds would be stacked against the survival of any group drifting out onto the Atlantic in such circumstances – but it would only need to happen once. Platyrrhini and parapithecid anthropoids, caviomorph rodents, accompanied by spiders, insects, and other invertebrates, could all have made the transatlantic voyage on the same floating island and reached the New World on the same day[28,29].

The distances involved in reaching Flores or Luzon from the Southeast Asian mainland are far less than those involved in an Atlantic crossing, especially at times of low sea levels. A flash flood or a tsunami could have swept a group of hominins out to sea, and they could have survived on a floating island and reached Flores or Luzon. There are many instances of people who have survived for long periods on vegetation rafts after being swept out to sea by retreating tsunamis. Studies suggest that the unintentional arrival of a group of individuals on an island is about half as likely to lead to a flourishing population as a planned colonisation effort – but this difference could be entirely counteracted by further unintentional arrivals of small groups of individuals in the centuries following the initial colonisation. While the entire scenario may sound unlikely, it must be remembered that we are considering timescales of hundreds of thousands of years, that there are 6,000 – 10,000 inhabited islands in the Pacific, and that the entire region lies within the so-called 'ring of fire' where earthquakes and tsunami are common[30].

Then again, this view could be entirely wrong, and *Homo erectus* was, after all, capable of building boats.

Did Neanderthals build boats?

Even if we reject the idea that *Homo erectus* could build boats, that does not mean that later, larger-brained archaic hominins could not have done so. By 600,000 years ago, hominins with larger brains had emerged in Africa and Eurasia[12]. Commonly referred to as *Homo heidelbergensis*, these archaic humans had brains closer in size to those of modern people. By 400,000 – 300,000 years ago, three major hominin lineages had emerged: Neanderthals in Europe, Denisovans in Asia, and archaic *Homo sapiens* in Africa. At the same time, the venerable Acheulean stone tool industries began to give way to the more sophisticated prepared-core industries[31].

In recent years, it has become clear that Neanderthals were far from being the dimwits of popular perception: surveys of the archaeological record suggest that in terms of diet diversity, hunting techniques, capacity for innovation, and social networking, Neanderthals in Europe were not obviously inferior to contemporary *Homo sapiens* in Africa[32,33]. Could their innovations have included boat-building, and if so, is there any possibility that we might one day discover a Neanderthal boat? The answer to the first question, I would argue, is 'why not?' and the same answer could be given to the second question. By now, wooden artefacts are starting to appear in the archaeological record. The earliest-known are four wooden spears, which were found at a mine near the town of Schöningen in Germany in 1995. The spears are 337,000 – 300,000 years old[34].

If wooden spears can survive for 300,000 years or more, then could we hope to find dugout canoes of comparable age? The Schöningen spears owe their preservation to having been embedded in wet, anaerobic sediment and remaining below the water table until their discovery[35]. Dugout canoes and other watercraft would have been constructed and used in exactly the type of environment that favours their preservation. Yet, as noted, the oldest-known boat is no more than 10,000 years old. The European Upper Palaeolithic (46,000 – 15,000 years ago) is ten times more recent than Schöningen. Despite a rich archaeological record that has been extensively studied since the nineteenth century, the European Upper Palaeolithic has never yielded so much as a single boat. The European Upper Palaeolithic is associated with modern humans, who, given the much earlier presence of modern humans in Australia, must surely have been capable of constructing boats.

Can we infer the existence of Neanderthal boats from evidence for Neanderthals in places they could not have easily reached without them? While many of what are now the Greek islands have been joined to the Greek mainland at various times during the Middle and Upper Palaeolithic, some islands, such as Crete, have remained insular throughout[36,37]. No Neanderthal remains have been found on any of the Greek islands, but island sites have yielded tools dating to the Middle Palaeolithic, and others said to resemble Neanderthal Mousterian industries in mainland Greece[36–39]. Given dense concentrations of Middle Palaeolithic assemblages in northwestern Greece and the Ionian Islands, it is feasible to suppose that some Neanderthal groups could have crossed from the Epirus coast to the islands, which would have, at times, been separated by narrow straits of sea. However, investigation of possible seafaring among the Greek islands by Neanderthals and by other pre-modern hominins such as *Homo erectus* and *Homo heidelbergensis* remains hampered by a lack of chronostratigraphic data, the lack of a comprehensive reference collection of stone tools, and the fact that much data remains unpublished[40]. Overall, it remains unproven that Neanderthals constructed and used watercraft, but given their considerable expertise in other areas, it seems highly likely that they did.

Along the Indian Ocean Rim

The earliest fossil examples of our species *Homo sapiens* are those from Irhoud Jebel, a cave site located about 100 km (60 miles) west of Marrakech, Morocco. Now thought to be around 286,000 years old[41], they retain primitive features such as a long, low cranial vault rather than the globular shape associated with present-day people[42]. Along with other hominins anatomically closer to present-day people than to any archaic species, they are sometimes described informally as 'archaic *Homo sapiens*'[43]. Hominins closer to the fully modern cranial vault condition first appeared around 233,000 years ago[44].

Although *Homo sapiens* was in Greece 210,000 years ago[45], the Levant 194,000 years ago[46], and the Arabian Peninsula no later than around 115,000 years ago[47], genetic studies suggest that the world's present-day non-African population is largely descended from migrants who left Africa 86,000 – 61,000 years BP, as identified by the expansion of the L3 mitochondrial DNA haplogroup[48]. Its subsequent differentiation into the supposed 'founder' haplogroups M, N, and R was thought to have occurred in India soon after the dispersal[49].

Under what became known as the Single Out of Africa model, it was supposed that a single group had left Africa, either taking an overland route via Sinai and the Levant or a southern route across the narrow Bab el-Mandeb Strait between Djibouti and Yemen. The southern route was more consistent with the differentiation of L3 into M, N, and R in India, and there were other reasons to favour this option. At times of cold, arid conditions such as those 65,000 years ago, the strait is just 11 km (6.8 miles) across. Even at the present time, it is only 18 km (11 miles) across at its narrowest point, about half the width of the Strait of Dover, and on a clear day, it is easy to see all the way across from the shores of Djibouti. Crossing it is nevertheless hazardous, with swift-running currents that have earned it the nickname 'the Gate of Tears'. These currents could have swept early watercraft out into the Indian Ocean[50], but once across the Red Sea, a very attractive lifestyle would be available to the migrants – beachcombing. Seafood provides a good quality diet, is far easier to obtain than large herbivores, and would have been available to them all the way along the rim of the Indian Ocean. Migrating groups could have moved along the southern Asian coast through Yemen and Oman, and then onwards to the Indian subcontinent and Southeast Asia[49,51]. It was believed that Andaman Islanders possess localised but very ancient mitochondrial lineages that had evolved *in situ* in the Andaman Islands, suggesting that they must have settled there a long time ago. Genetically obtained settlement dates of 60,000 years ago were taken to imply that the Andaman Islanders are relict populations left over from this coastal migration from Africa[52,53].

A problem with the scenario as proposed was that it lacked any obvious rationale for the ever-eastwards movement of the migrants. Australian archaeologist David Bulbeck[54] suggested that the motive was overcrowding as the migrants adapted to living in river estuaries. Such habitats provided easy access to food, drinking water, and timber, and supported healthy population growth. Inevitably, these settlements became overcrowded, despite the surrounding stretches of land remaining uninhabited. It was this overcrowding that motivated the search for new estuarine habitats further along the coast. Such onward migrations were aided by watercraft that could transport settlers and their food, water, and other supplies on potentially long voyages along an inhospitable coast. The watercraft also enabled the onward migrants to keep in touch with their parent communities, resulting in a chain of interlinked settlements. Bulbeck argues that the migrants had long been familiar with watercraft, which had originally been used to exploit niches such as reefs and marine shallows.

The Single Out of Africa and southern coastal migration models were the dominant paradigms of the early 2000s, but then cracks began to appear. At the time these models were proposed, *Homo sapiens* was not thought to have left Africa prior to around 65,000 years ago, apart from a short-lived excursion into the Levant during the warm Eemian interglacial period 126,000 years ago at a time when the Levant was to all intents and purposes a northeastern extension of North Africa[55]. The model had never addressed the very obvious question as to why a species that has existed in its essentially present-day form for at least 233,000 years should wait so long before leaving Africa. Some argued that the first anatomically modern humans were still not behaviourally modern[12,56], although this view was largely refuted in 2000[57]. In any case, if *Homo erectus* was capable of leaving Africa, the earliest *Homo sapiens* should also have been. It should have been no surprise when non-African fossils began turning up that were far older than 65,000 years. Advances in whole genomic sequencing began to reveal multiple migrations rather than just one. They showed that Aboriginal Australians and Papuans diverged from Africans before the divergence between Eurasian and African populations. This was best explained by Aboriginal Australian and Papuan populations retaining the genetic signature of an earlier migration from Africa around 120,000 years ago[58,59]. Cranial shape variation analysis yielded similar results and suggested that there had been multiple dispersals by both the northern and southern routes from around 130,000 years ago[60].

One of the main pillars of the coastal migration model was that the Andaman Islanders are a 60,000-year-old relict population from the original Out of Africa migration. However, in 2006, the mitochondrial haplogroup M31, originally thought to occur only in the Andaman Islands, was also found in West Bengal[61]. Follow-up work showed that the Andaman-specific variant of M31 is a comparatively recent branch of the M31 haplogroup, and the true origins of M31 are found in northeastern India. Other branches of M31 have been found in Nepal and Myanmar. It was suggested the Andaman archipelago was settled just 25,000 years ago, when sea levels were low, and it was part of the mainland[62]. In a further blow to the coastal migration model, later work suggested that the oldest branches of mitochondrial haplogroups N, M, and R are found in East Asia and Southeast Asia rather than in India. This was best explained by migrants having taken a northern route through the Levant into Central Asia, then on to Southeast Asia and Australia. India would have been settled later, by secondary migrations from Central and Southeast Asia[63–65].

Of course, this does not rule out the possibility that some groups did cross the Bab el-

Mandeb Strait at a time of low sea level and migrated along the Indian Ocean rim, using watercraft as suggested by David Bulbeck. Unfortunately, there is no chance of any evidence for his settlement chains ever being found. Sea levels now are much higher than they were 65,000 years ago, and such evidence – assuming it existed at all – has long since been submerged.

Australia

The demise of the Single Out of Africa and coastal migration models notwithstanding, there is absolutely no doubt that humans reached Australia by boat. The earliest evidence for humans in Australia comes from the Madjedbebe (formerly Malakunanja II) rock shelter in Kakadu National Park, located on the western edge of the Arnhem Land plateau in the Northern Territory. The site was first occupied around 65,000 years ago, with evidence for occupation that includes grinding stones, ground ochres, and hatchet heads[66]. The timing corresponds to a period of minimum sea levels[67], during which the Sunda and Sahul continental shelves were above water. Australia, New Guinea, and Tasmania formed a single continental landmass known as Sahul, with only the Wallacea archipelago remaining insular.

The first humans to reach the Sahul continent probably only did so after settlers had been island-hopping across the Wallacean archipelago for some time, probably establishing a chain of settlements stretching back to the Asian/Sunda mainland. Settlements would have required not only a founding population but also continued contact with their parent communities and other outside groups to avoid the problems of inbreeding and unbalanced sex ratios. In turn, the settlers would have required an effective boat-building technology to build, provision, and navigate vessels capable of making frequent voyages between the various islands[68].

Indeed, without such technology, it is unlikely that a viable colony could have been established in the first place. It has been estimated that a minimum founding population of 1,300 – 1,550 individuals would have been required to avoid the eventual extinction of a Sahul colony. These people could have arrived at once or in groups of at least 130 individuals over 700 – 900 years, but either scenario suggests a substantial and pre-planned operation rather than various groups arriving at random[69,70]. The first Europeans to reach Australia recorded Aboriginal Australians as using only simple, short-ranged watercraft such as rafts and canoes made of logs or sewn bark, bark, or reed bundles. An intentional colonisation effort would have required more sophisticated vessels, and constructing them would have required woodworking, cordage, and twisted-fibre technologies[71].

It has long been recognised that there are two main routes by which it is possible to island-hop from the Sunda mainland to Sahul: a northern route via Sulawesi, the Banda islands, and Maluku east into western New Guinea, and a southern route via the Lesser Sunda islands into northwest Australia[72]. Early studies suggested that either route would require at least eight to seventeen separate crossings, including at least three of 30 km (18 miles) or more and one of 70 km (44 miles) or more[68]. At the mid-point of such a voyage, the land in both directions would be below the horizon, which would be daunting enough for these early seafarers even if they knew that there was land in the direction they were heading.

More recent work has been aided by establishing the time of colonisation at 65,000 years ago and a better understanding of the sea levels at that time. A study featuring a least-cost path analysis came down on the side of the northern route[73]. This option would have required only three sea crossings after Sulawesi, and each crossing could have been completed in 2 to 3 days under favourable conditions. For each of these crossings, the destination island was visible throughout the voyage, which greatly simplified navigation. By contrast, the southern route would have required generally longer crossing times. Furthermore, while the now-submerged destination islands of the Sahul Banks would have been visible from high points within 10 km (6.2 miles) of the coast of Timor and Roti, they would not have been visible from the coast itself, and would have been out of sight during the voyage[69]. Despite these issues, the southern route was viable, and quite possibly settlers reached Sahul via both routes[74,75].

Mesolithic boats and offshore fishing

The last Ice Age ended around 9700 BCE, and the unstable, often cold and arid climate of the Pleistocene was replaced by the stable, warm, and wet climate of the Holocene. In these very favourable conditions, a fundamentally new way of life emerged – agriculture. In parts of the world where there were animals suitable for herding and plants that could be grown as crops, farming began to replace hunter-gathering as a means of subsistence. These 'agricultural packages' could support far greater numbers than hunting and gathering, and consequently, Neolithic farming populations grew and farmers began spreading out into unfarmed regions, where they often encountered pre-existing populations.

The European Mesolithic is the period of European prehistory that followed the end of the last Ice Age and preceded the arrival of the first Neolithic farmers from Southwest Asia. Mesolithic people, like their Upper Palaeolithic forbears, lived as hunter-gatherers, but they benefitted from the very favourable climate of the Early Holocene. Mesolithic sites have been found on many offshore islands including the Hebrides, Gotland, Corsica, Sardinia, and Corfu, implying that the Mesolithic people could build boats capable of deep-sea navigation[76]. For the first time, there is direct evidence for boats in the form of the Valle petroglyph of a skin boat and the Pesse dugout canoe.

Dugout canoes are the first watercraft we have actual examples of. They are made by hollowing out and shaping a log of suitable size. Canoe-making is both an important skill in present-day traditional societies and an important part of their cultural heritage. They are an invaluable means of transportation of people and goods and play an important role in the subsistence of small-scale fishers[77]. It is not hard to imagine that they would have been equally important in Mesolithic societies.

Despite this, such findings remain rare. Aside from the two examples noted, Mesolithic watercraft have mostly been found in Scandinavia and the eastern Baltic regions[76]. These include the dugout canoes of Tybrind Vig, a Late Mesolithic site on the west coast of Fyn, Denmark. The site was in use from around 5500 to 4000 BCE, but it is now submerged in shallow water due to subsequent rises in sea levels. The two boats and their accompanying paddles date to around 4200 BCE. The more intact of the two boats is 9.5 m (31 ft) long with a beam of 0.65 m (2 ft), with a cut-off stern to which a transom board would have been attached. The ten paddles are each carved in one piece from ash trunks and comprise a heart-shaped blade on a 1m (3ft 3 inch) shaft. The blades of two of the paddles were decorated with elaborate patterns carved into the wood and filled with brown colouring matter. Near the sterns of the boats were fireplaces, which were possibly used for attracting eels. These could have been caught by spearing with fishing leisters, examples of which were also found at the site[78].

A question arising from this is, could Mesolithic people have been regular deep-water fishers? Traditional societies use four main types of fishing gear: hooks and lines, nets, fish spears and harpoons, and weirs and traps. All four types have been found at Mesolithic sites. Although the first three types can be used for both inshore and offshore fishing, ethnographic parallels suggest that nets and long-line fishing (a long line with multiple hooks) were more likely to have been used offshore. The next question is, would Mesolithic boats have been suitable for deep-water fishing? Long, narrow dugout canoes are unsuitable for use away from lakes, rivers, and sheltered coastal waters. Skin or bark-covered watercraft like the Valle umiak, which are more flexible and hence more able to absorb wave action, would have been more suited to rough offshore waters than a dugout canoe. Although ethnographically known watercraft such as the umiak and the currach are capable of open-sea voyaging, they were normally used only for transport and inshore fishing. Only when there was a limited availability of alternatives on dry land was fishing extended to deep waters. Examples include the Māori following the extinction of the giant moa and the people of the Aleutian Islands. Consistent with this observation, the remains of deep-water species have only been found at Mesolithic sites in regions where deep water, defined as water with a depth of 30 m (100 ft), occurs close to the shore. There would have been a considerable cost in terms of time and raw materials for maintaining boats and fishing gear suitable for deep-water fishing. Furthermore, fishing in the often-stormy North Sea, especially at night, would have been a hazardous undertaking. In the generally bountiful environment of Early Holocene Europe, there was probably little need to take the risk[76].

Currachs and Neolithic farmers

By around 6500 BCE, Neolithic farmers had begun moving into Europe from Anatolia. An 'agricultural package' of sheep, goats, pigs, cattle, wheat, barley, and pulses had gradually taken shape in Southwest Asia and Cyprus during the early millennia of the Holocene, and groups were now moving further afield in search of fresh farming land. Early Neolithic farmers could reach mainland Greece by travelling overland from the Anatolian plateau, but many groups are thought to have arrived by sea. Genetic studies involving both ancient DNA and present-day populations suggest that they took a maritime route into southeastern Europe, settling the Dodecanese and Crete *en route*[79,80]. The earliest evidence for human activity in Cyprus has been dated to around 10,700 BCE[81], and seafaring in the Aegean probably dates back at least as far as the later stages of the Upper Palaeolithic. Obsidian found in Mesolithic levels at Franchthi Cave on the southern Greek coast has been shown to have originated from the volcanic island of Melos[82], and dates obtained for obsidian finds from a number of other Greek mainland and island sites range back to as far as 12,500 years BCE[83]. Therefore, there seems to have been a mature seafaring tradition in the eastern Mediterranean well before 6500 BCE.

Farming groups travelling to Crete would probably have had to be at least forty strong to establish a viable colony. They would have required 5 – 10 breeding pairs each of pigs, sheep or goats, and cattle and 250 kg of grain per person to establish an agricultural economy. The total weight of humans, livestock, and grain would be around 15,000 – 20,000 kg (15 – 20 tons), requiring a flotilla of 10 – 15 vessels for the voyage[84]. Either dugout canoes or skin boats could have been used, but the latter would have been the better option: they have a greater capacity, but they are light enough to be carried and launched by their crew[85]. The present-day Irish currach demonstrates just how effective such vessels are for transporting cargo[86].

From Greece, farming spread north into the Balkans, but it also spread west along the Mediterranean Basin, reaching southern Italy around 6000 BC. The earliest Italian Neolithic sites are nearly all situated in the south of the country, suggesting that the farmers arrived by sea[87,88]. There are hundreds of Neolithic sites on the Tavoliere delle Puglie plain on the Adriatic coast of northern Apulia. The topography and potential for farming are similar to those of Thessaly, and Neolithic groups on the other side of the Adriatic must have been aware of the excellent prospects there[89].

By around 5400 BCE, farming had spread north to central Italy, and subsequently to the south of France, Spain, and Portugal. This westward spread was exceptionally rapid and took no more than 100 to 200 years[87]. It was marked by the appearance of an unpainted style of pottery known as Cardial Ware, which was decorated by impressing cockle shells into the wet clay prior to firing. The Cardial Ware farming settlements were set up as enclaves in favourable locations around the French and Iberian coastline[89,90]. The sheer speed of this dispersal suggests that the colonist farmers travelled by sea[86,87], making voyages of around 350 km (220 miles)[91]. The logistics of such pioneer voyaging were probably similar to those envisaged for the Neolithic colonisation of Crete: a group of around forty individuals with livestock and grain in a flotilla of 10 – 15 currach-type boats with a payload of one to two tons each[86].

While the Cardial people were moving along the Mediterranean, other groups were spreading inland. The Linear Bandkeramik Kultur (LBK) is named for its distinctive pottery with incised banded decoration and characterised by settlements of massive timber-built longhouses[89]. The LBK first appeared in the Carpathian region about 5600 BCE, spreading east to Ukraine and west to the Rhineland by 5400 BCE, and the Paris Basin by 5050 BCE[92]. Again, this dispersal was extremely rapid, and it would also have entailed the farmers driving their herds through a challenging landscape of woodlands and mires. An attractive alternative would have been to use the rivers of Central Europe as highways. In most cases, only short overland crossings would have been required to move from one river to another. A 10 m (33 ft) skin boat could carry several people, two dogs, two cows, two calves, and their bedding[86].

One of the remotest parts of the European agricultural expansion was Orkney, where the earliest Neolithic settlements date from around 3400 BCE[93]. The archipelago was unquestionably reached by sea, but from where? The Orkney vole is a subspecies of the common vole (*Microtus arvalis*), which is found in continental Europe but does not occur in mainland Britain. The oldest remains suggest that it has been present in Orkney since at least 3150 BCE, and it must have been brought to Orkney by Neolithic settlers, either unintentionally as stowaways in boats or intentionally for food or as pets[94].

Early genetic studies suggested that the Orkney vole is most similar to common voles in the Bay of Biscay region and that voyagers had made the lengthy trip from Brittany, through the Irish Sea, to Orkney. It was suggested that the voyage – longer than any proposed for a curragh – would have taken around two weeks[86]. However, later work suggested that the progenitor voles lived on the Belgian coast and that the first Orcadians must have made a still-demanding voyage from Belgium[94].

Oceania

The dispersal of Austronesian language-speaking Neolithic farmers from Taiwan was driven by the same economic considerations as other Neolithic dispersals: a need for farming land to feed a growing population. Also in common with many other agricultural dispersals, it did not take place in a vacuum: many of the areas they moved into were already inhabited: Late Pleistocene human remains are known from Sulawesi, Borneo, Java, Palawan, and Alor[95–97]. There is archaeological evidence that human populations had spread through the region to as far to the east as the Solomon Islands more than 30,000 years ago[98]. There were Austroasiatic farmers in Sumatra, Java, Borneo, Sulawesi, and the Maluku Islands[99,100], and Papuan farmers in New Guinea[101].

Where it differed and was indeed unique is that it took place entirely by sea. Oceania is a region of the Pacific defined as the islands from New Guinea eastwards. In turn, it is divided into three regions: Melanesia, Micronesia, and Polynesia. Melanesia comprises the archipelago to the north and northeast of Australia, from New Guinea to Fiji. To the north of this is Micronesia, a region containing Palau, the Mariana Islands, the Caroline Islands, the Marshall Islands, and Kiribati. To the east of Melanesia and Micronesia lies Polynesia, a triangular region bounded by Hawaii, Rapa Nui (Easter Island), and New Zealand. In addition, the term Near Oceania is often used for islands lying as far to the east as the Solomon Islands, with Remote Oceania referring to those lying beyond.

The Austronesians were originally rice farmers who moved to Taiwan from the Chinese mainland around 3000 BCE. Their Proto-Austronesian language broke up into ten subgroups, of which nine were never spoken outside Taiwan. The tenth, known as Malayo-Polynesian, was carried further afield when its speakers moved onwards to the northern Philippines[102,103]. This did not happen until at least a millennium after the initial settlement of Taiwan, suggesting that the first settlers there lacked the boat-building technology to make the 350 km (215 miles) sea crossing to Luzon. Proto-Austronesian contains words pertaining to boats, such as sails and paddles, but not for outrigger canoes or their associated paraphernalia. It is not known for certain whether this is because such technologies, hallmarks of later Polynesian culture, were later lost or had simply yet to be invented. By contrast, Proto-Malayo-Polynesian does contain words for outrigger canoes. Some words for canoe parts are missing from the reconstructed vocabulary, such as for 'outrigger float', but the presence of other words, such as for 'outrigger boom', implies that these parts must have existed[103,104].

From the northern coast of Luzon, the Austronesian farmers began to spread out across the rest of the Philippines, Borneo, Sumatra, Java, Bali, and the smaller islands of the Island Southeast Asia (ISEA) archipelagos lying east and southeast of the Southeast Asian mainland.

As they settled islands east of the Philippines and Borneo, rice gradually gave way to tree crops, yams, and taro, all of which are better suited to the climate in which the farmers now found themselves[101,105,106].

Soon, the Austronesian expansion would take boatloads of settlers into Remote Oceania. The Lapita culture appeared in the Bismarck Archipelago around 1350 BCE[107], characterised by its distinctive red-slipped pottery decorated with incised and dentate-stamped rectilinear or curvilinear designs. The Lapita economy was based on pigs, chickens, dogs, the new roster of crops, and seafood. The pigs seem to have originated from the Moluccas, and the pottery has possible antecedents in the Marianas Islands. This suggests that the Lapita culture was a fusion of two closely related groups speaking virtually the same Malayo-Polynesian language with only small dialect variations[98,108]. Proto-Oceanic – the reconstructed Malayo-Polynesian branch associated with the expansion into Remote Oceania – hints that Lapita fishing technology contained several innovations. There are words for draglines, fish weirs, and pronged spears, but these are not found in Proto-Malayo-Polynesian[104].

By 1300 BCE[107], Early Lapita communities were established over a wide area of the Bismarck Archipelago and by around 1200 to 1100 BCE, they had moved beyond the Bismarck Archipelago and settled parts of Remote Oceania[104]. In just 700 years, the Lapita people spread through Melanesia to the central Pacific, reaching Vanuatu by 3250 – 3100 cal. years BP, Fiji by 130 – 3010 cal. years BP, and Samoa by 2,700 years BP[107,109].

Having reached Samoa, the migration paused after covering some 5,500 km (3,400 miles) in one of the fastest movements of a prehistoric colonising population on record[101]. The pause suggests that sailing technology might not yet have been sufficient to make the lengthy voyages that would have been necessary to go further. For example, from Samoa to the Cook Islands is 1,200 km (750 miles), and to the Society Islands is 2,000 km (1,250 miles). In addition, around 3,000 years BP, sea levels in the mid-Pacific were higher than those of today, and many present-day atolls were then submerged[98]. It was probably the invention of the twin-hulled double canoe and possibly advances in hull form that ended the hiatus and enabled the colonists to travel long distances, together with their crops and animals[98,110].

Migration into the archipelagos of Eastern Polynesia did not begin until around 1025 CE, although it might have been preceded by a period of eastward exploration lasting a century or more[111]. There were two phases of migration: to the Society Islands between 1025 and 1120 CE, to the remote islands and New Zealand around 1200 to 1290 CE[112], and to Rapa Nui at around the same time[113]. Sweet potato has been reported from the Cook Islands and Hawai'i from about 1200 CE, implying that there was contact between Polynesians and native South Americans by this date[112].

In geographical scope, the Austronesian expansion dwarfed any other agricultural expansion, eventually encompassing Island Southeast Asia, Madagascar, Melanesia, Micronesia, and Polynesia. We have inferred much about the sailing technologies involved by studying the languages of the Austronesian-speaking peoples – but there are also the accounts of early European explorers of the Pacific and ethnographic work going up to the present day. The Austronesians used three main types of multi-hulled watercraft: the double canoe (two hulls), the single outrigger (primary hull plus outrigger on one side), and the double outrigger (primary hull plus outriggers on both sides). The first two types were the most common, though the sailing rigs used varied. In Eastern Polynesia including Tahiti and

Hawai'i, single outriggers or double canoes were both in use, with a spritsail[48] stepped well forward of amidships. In Western Polynesia and Fiji, the watercraft used were mainly double canoes with lateen sails[49]. In Micronesia, watercraft were mostly plank-built single outriggers with lateen sails, and in Melanesia, they were mostly single outriggers with rectangular lugsails. The differences reflected available construction materials and wind, sea, and coastal conditions. Double canoes were used more frequently than single outriggers for long-distance voyaging. Although it is slower and more difficult to handle bad weather, the double canoe is more seaworthy and has a far greater carrying capacity than a single outrigger. Polynesian double canoes ranged in size from 9 m (30 ft) to more than 18 m (60 ft), with some being as large as 27 m (90 ft)[114–116]. All the components of a boat were lashed or stitched together. Sewn joints between planks were sealed with resin or the pounded nuts of the putty-nut tree (*Parinarium glaberrimum*), which forms a strong and rigid joint and ensures that the planks do not move relative to each other after it has set[117].

These watercraft could not sail closer to the wind than about 75 degrees[110] and, when sailing upwind (in common with other sailboats), would have to sail in a series of zigzags known as tacks. To maintain their overall heading, they would have to periodically come about, or switch from one tack to the next. Tacking, the method most familiar to Western sailors, entails swinging the bow across the wind and onto the new course. This method is employed by craft ranging from Laser yachts to the *Cutty Sark*. However, there is a second method, known as shunting. This entails reversing the direction of the sailing rig and steering oar and alternating which end of the boat is the bow, and the wind continues to come from the same side. When tacking, sailors must avoid losing steerage way, but shunting requires the boat to come to a full stop. In a single outrigger, shunting enables the outrigger float to be kept on the windward side, where it counterbalances wind pressures. On the leeward side, the outrigger float is forced downwards into the water, where it increases the overall drag on the craft. A craft designed for shunting is said to be reversible, but the constant windward orientation of the outrigger places increased demands on the rigging and was probably responsible for the adoption of the 'Oceanic lateen' sail in Oceania. Single outriggers and double-hulled canoes may be either tacked or shunted, but double outriggers are always tacked. In Eastern Polynesia, watercraft were tacked to come about, whereas in Fiji, Western Polynesia, Micronesia, and Melanesia, they were shunted[115,116,118].

Austronesian navigators found their way by the Sun, wind, and waves by day and used guiding stars and zenith stars by night. A voyage began by lining up the canoe with sighting stones, which were set up on the shore as direction markers to known destinations. Departure would be at first light, with the markers and the brightest stars both visible. A guiding star over the bow and another over the stern were then aligned on the shore markers. During the day, the course was maintained by waves, wind, and the Sun and by night, stars with the same azimuth[50] as those that had been selected at first light were used. As these

---

[48] A four-sided, fore-and-aft sail supported at its highest points by the mast and a diagonally running spar known as the sprit.

[49] A triangular sail set on a long yard mounted at an angle on the mast and running fore-and-aft.

[50] The direction of a celestial object from the observer, expressed as the angular distance from the north or south point of the horizon to the point at which a vertical circle passing

stars rose higher above the horizon, they were replaced by those that were just becoming visible. Zenith stars were used to determine latitude. They were associated with particular islands: the zenith star of any island is one that passes directly overhead as seen from that island, so when a voyager observes that it is overhead, they will be at the latitude of the island in question. Zenith stars can give the latitude to within 30 arcmin. The Austronesians were familiar with the solstices and sometimes the equinoxes, the celestial equator, the zenith, the distinction between stars and planets, the precise azimuths of all navigationally useful stars, and the approximate dates of their appearance in the night sky. To make the final approach to an island or archipelago, navigators used signs indicating the proximity of land including the character of swell, the types of birds and their direction of flight, standing clouds over high land, the reflection of lagoons in the sky over atolls to produce a greenish or turquoise colour, and 'sea marks'. The latter include types of seaweed and fish, swell refraction, and the colour of water[119–121].

Rigorous and prolonged training was required to learn navigation. It included instruction ashore and at sea, as well as memorising the vast body of navigational knowledge – all in the absence of writing. The navigational knowledge was organised in a systematic and schematic manner and taught and learned in this form. Standard drills and exercises were used to build in redundancy and continually rehearsed. The organised data takes the figure of a compass and recalls the 'method of loci' or 'memory palace' used in Classical antiquity to memorise items in a precise order. These mnemonic techniques rely on spatial relationships. The subject memorises the layout of a building or structure, which may be imaginary (in this case, a compass) and comprise several discrete loci (bearings and compass points). To remember a set of items, an individual 'walks' through the loci (or, in this case, 'sails' along these bearings) and commits an item to each locus by associating forming an image (or a verse in a chant) between the item and that locus[122].

For a long time, many Western anthropologists argued that drift voyaging was an important factor in the dispersal of Polynesian people. In this scenario, watercraft were blown off course and made unintentional landfall far from their intended destination, although as far back as the 1930s, there was strong evidence against it. American anthropologist Roland B. Dixon noted that many drift voyages had been reported over the years, but most had covered distances of less than 800 km (500 miles; 435 nautical miles), and the majority had been from east to west, or north to south, with only one from west to east. In this case, during a 950 km (600 miles; 520 nautical miles) drift voyage from Tahiti to the Tuamotus archipelago, a third of the 48 people on board died[114].

Nevertheless, proponents continued to argue the case for drift voyaging into the 1950s and 1960s. One notable sceptic of intentional voyaging by the Polynesians was New Zealand historian Andrew Sharp, who claimed that intentionally voyaging to Hawaii and New Zealand from Tahiti was "*impossible*" without instruments. Sharp noted that three voyages would be required to establish a new colony: the initial voyage of discovery, a navigated return voyage to report the discovery, and a navigated voyage with settlers. Sharp believed that winds and oceanic currents were too unpredictable to navigate purely by the stars and rely on seabirds and cloud formations as indicators of land beyond the horizon[123].

The case for intentional voyaging was conclusively made by the voyages of the *Hōkūle'a*,

---

through the object intersects the horizon.

a large, double-hulled canoe, built in 1975. *Hōkūle'a* means 'star of gladness', referring to Arcturus, the zenith star of Hawai'i. Between 1975 and 1987, the *Hōkūle'a* made three return voyages between Hawai'i and Tahiti, a round trip of over 8,000 km (5,000 miles; 4,350 nautical miles) and also sailed to Aotearoa (New Zealand), Tonga, and Samoa, the Tuamotu archipelago, Leeward, Societies, and Cook Islands. All in all, the *Hōkūle'a* sailed over 45,000 km (27,500 miles; 24,000 nautical miles) during these twelve years, mostly navigated by non-instrumental means. The *Hōkūle'a's* two navigators, Mau Piailug and his apprentice Nainoa Thompson, relied on naked eye observations of stars, the Sun and Moon, and ocean swells to orientate themselves and set course. They tracked progress through the acute perception of the distance and course sailed, and used bird sightings to detect land while it was still below the horizon. For the Aotearoa voyage, they used sailing instructions from Māori tradition and found that they were accurate not only as to directions but also the time of year to make the voyage[124].

The Ferriby boats

North Ferriby is a village on the outskirts of Hull, located on the banks of the Humber estuary. The 2011 Census listed a population of 3,893. In 1937, two local boys, Edward Wright, aged 19, and his brother William found the projecting ends of three planks on the Humber shore east of the village. After "*rather destructive cleaning*" and the planks traced by prodding with a walking stick, they were found to extend over 12 m (40 ft) at a depth of about 1 m (3 ft), and it was obvious that it was the remains of "*a boat of some sort*". At first, they thought they had found a Viking longship, but temporary excavations suggested that the boat was older, possibly dating to early in the Roman occupation of Britain and associated with British Celtic groups living in East Yorkshire before the Romans advanced north. The boat suggested parallels with large sewn plank boats of the type used in the Pacific (see above) and Ceylon (now Sri Lanka). Ethnographer James Hornell noted that boats used on Lake Victoria, East Africa, were very similar in their construction to the Ferriby boat. The East African boats were made from large strakes on a broad dugout base, with seams caulked with plantain fibre, covered with a strip of wood, and sewn with twine passing through holes in the edges of the planks[125].

It was clear that recovery of the boat would be difficult as it was submerged for all but five hours of the day, so it was left *in situ* with plans to fully excavate it in 1940[125]. The outbreak of war ruled out such an excavation, and with fears that the boat would be entirely lost to the river, the decision was taken to recover three sections from the lower end. Around half of the recovered pieces were kept in the Hull Municipal Museum and were lost when the museum was bombed in 1942. Other pieces remained in North Ferriby and survived despite a lack of conservation treatment. Despite the Wright brothers' best endeavours, about a third of the remaining part of the boat had been swept away by the river by 1946. In the meantime, in 1941, they found the remains of a second boat, which they examined between 1941 and 1942 while on leave from wartime service in the army. About 1 m (3 ft) of this second boat was washed away between 1942 and the end of the war. With the war over and erosion threatening further losses, the boats were finally excavated after the intervention of archaeologist Charles Phillips, who had led the pre-war excavation of the Sutton Hoo Viking burial ship[126].

The first boat, now known as Ferriby 1, is represented by most of the bottom planks and a short length of the lowest strake on one side. The bottom was built up of three oak planks: a keel and two outer planks, which had been shaped with an adze. The two outer planks were about 10.5 m (35 ft) long, 0.65 m (2 ft) wide, and 75 to 125 mm (3 to 5 in) thick. The keel was longer at 13.3 m (43 ft 6 in), projecting beyond the ends of the two outer planks. The planks were joined together by separate stitches of wicker-like cracked and twisted yew, spaced from 180 to 360 mm (7 to 14 in) apart, and countersunk to avoid wear. All holes were plugged with pounded wood, and seams were caulked with woodland moss. The structure was stiffened by eight transverse bars made of ash passing through holes in large ridges on the upper surfaces of the planks, and secured with wedges. The second boat, Ferriby 2, was less well-preserved. All that survived was the keel plank, which was similar to that of Ferriby 1, though slightly smaller at 11.25 m (37 ft), and with eighteen transverse bars instead of only eight. When complete, it is estimated that Ferriby 1 would have been 15.35 m (51 ft 7 in) in length[126,127].

Early attempts to radiocarbon date the Ferriby boats were hampered by contamination produced by the conservation treatments and had to rely on other dateable material associated with the finds. In 1953, a sample of oak sealing strip found 10 m from Ferriby 1 was dated at the British Museum, and a rather uncertain date of 1260 – 400 BCE was obtained, suggesting that the boats dated to the Late Bronze Age or Early Iron Age[128,129].

In 1963, Edward Wright and his son Roderick discovered a third boat, consisting of two oak planks. The largest of these was an outer bottom plank measuring 8.69 m (28 ft 6 in), attached to a piece of the lowest strake on the side. The boat is likely to have been similar in size to the first two. It was now apparent that the find site had once been a settlement where the boats had been built and operated from. Ferriby 2 and Ferriby 3 were thought to be discarded portions of boats that had been dismantled [127]. Finds continued: Ferriby 4, found in 1984, comprises a fragment of a sheer strake[130] and Ferriby 5, found in 1989, is the detached top of a cleat from a boat[131]. At Kilnsea, at the mouth of the Humber, an oak plank thought to be either the keel or an outer bottom strake of a plank-built boat was found in 1996[132].

By the end of the 1980s, more reliable radiocarbon dates were available. Ferriby 1, 2 and 3 were dated to around 1300 BCE, placing them in the Middle Bronze Age[133]. However, the Ferriby 4 and Ferriby 5 fragments were more recent, dating to around 400 BC. They suggested a tradition of boat-building at the site that continued for a millennium into the Early Iron Age[131,133]. The Kilnsea plank dates to 1870 – 1670 BCE[132]. In 2001, using better methods to remove contaminating preservatives, fresh radiocarbon dates were obtained for Ferriby 1, 2, and 3. The results - 1880 – 1680 BCE (Ferriby 1), 1940 – 1720 BCE (Ferriby 2), and 2030 – 1780 BCE (Ferriby 3) – suggested that the boats date to the Early Bronze Age[129]. This makes them the earliest-known sewn plank bouts outside Ancient Egypt[134].

It is not known for certain whether the Ferriby boats were sea-going vessels or restricted to use as estuary ferries. There have been various attempts to reconstruct what the boats would have looked like, but only two of these are now thought to have been likely: a flat-bottomed boat, or a boat with a rocker bottom (curved from fore to aft). Of the two, the rocker design, being more seaworthy, is more likely to have been used for a sea-going vessel.

A boat with a rocker bottom will have a deeper hull and can cope better with waves. Also, as with a round-bottomed boat, a rocker prevents the large loss of stability that occurs in a flat-bottomed vessel, even if quite small amounts of bilge water from either leakage or waves slopping over the gunwale are allowed to move about freely[135]. The debate over seaworthiness is arguably of limited value. Cultural exchanges between Britain and continental Europe are archaeologically well attested by the Early Bronze Age, so seaworthy boats must have existed. It is very unlikely that the Ferriby boats would be less capable than the skin boats that had existed for millennia, and it is probable that they were sea-going vessels capable of reaching continental Europe and carrying small cargoes[132].

The *Morgawr* is a full-scale plank-built boat constructed between 2012 and 2013 at Falmouth, Cornwall, using tools and materials that would have been available to Bronze Age boatbuilders. Oak planks were shaped using bronze tools and stitched together with yew. Giving the boat rocker by carving the required shape using bronze axes and adzes was straightforward. Named after the sea serpent that supposedly inhabits Falmouth Bay, the 15 m (50 ft) craft made its maiden voyage in March 2013 with a crew of 18. The craft was not intended to be a replica of Ferriby 1 but was described as a "*floating hypothesis of a Bronze Age-type sewn-plank boat based on the Ferriby boats*". The *Morgawr* proved to be an awkward boat to handle, being extremely heavy and unwieldy, but improving as the crew gained more experience with the craft's sailing characteristics. Accurate steering would have been less important in the Early Bronze Age, as beaches and salt marshes rather than jetties would have served as harbours, and tidal movements could have been used to launch or beach a boat[136].

There were probably a range of factors behind the choice of North Ferriby for maritime activities during the Early Bronze Age and the longevity of the site's use. One of these was likely the proximity to raw materials for boat-building, but a key factor was probably ease of pilotage (wayfinding in and out of port). The red-coloured cliffs near Ferriby and Kilnsea would have been major landmarks within an otherwise uniform landscape. Notably, they are only visible from the water, and they could have formed the basis for wayfinding from the North Sea to Ferriby. As such, they would have been particularly useful for seafarers who had not previously visited the area[134].

The Uluburun ship

The boatbuilders of North Ferriby lived at a time when urban societies had existed in the eastern Mediterranean for around 1,500 years. These included the Sumerian city-states of Mesopotamia, the Egyptian Old Kingdom, the Minoan civilisation of Crete, and the Mycenaean civilisation of mainland Greece. From 2500 BCE, there were substantial contacts between the Minoans and the civilisations of Mesopotamia and Egypt. Import included Egyptian scarabs and stone vessels, faience, ivory, lapis lazuli, Levantine seals, and semi-precious stones[137]. The scarabs reached Crete very soon after their introduction in Egypt, and the Minoans subsequently began producing them for themselves. Spirals, a popular motif on Minoan seals, became popular with the Egyptians and was a very common design on Egyptian scarabs. Despite the close trading relationship with Egypt, goods from there probably reached the Aegean via the Levant, Türkiye, and Cyprus. The prevailing winds and currents in the eastern Mediterranean meant that ships had to sail in an anticlockwise direction. Although it was straightforward to sail from Crete to Egypt, it was much more difficult to return there directly[138]. Plank-built sailing ships with masts first appeared in the Aegean around 2300 – 1850 BCE and are depicted in Minoan seal stones of that period[139]. Ships are also depicted on a fresco at West House, a private residence at Akrotiri, Thera[140]. Minoan ships were probably around 15 m (50 ft) in length and were propelled by a single square sail with 15 rowers on each side[141]. They were thus probably similar in size and construction to the Ferriby boats.

The Minoan civilisation went into eclipse around 1425 BCE, and Crete came under the control of the Mycenaeans of mainland Greece[137,138]. The reasons for the collapse are not known with any certainty, but the emerging urban societies on the mainland were geographically better placed to trade directly with their counterparts in Egypt and Southwest Asia. They probably took advantage of the situation to cut out the Minoan intermediaries[142], which would have been disastrous for a civilisation based primarily on peaceful trade rather than military conquest[143].

The presence of Baltic amber necklaces and other imported items in the shaft graves of the Mycenaean elite suggests an emphasis on trade beyond Greece. Lacking gold, precious stones, and other prestigious materials, the Mycenaeans relied upon commercial enterprise. Their major export was probably wool, for which the cold winter climate of Central Europe guaranteed a strong market there. Fine ceramics were exported to Italy, Sicily, Egypt, and throughout the eastern Mediterranean and domestically produced unguents were exported to Egypt and the Levant. Imports included tin from Britain, Baltic amber and gold from Northern Europe, seal stones from Anatolia, copper, tin, and lapis lazuli from Central Asia, copper, ivory, cylinder seals, and glass beads from Southwest Asia, and gold, ivory, amethyst, ostrich eggs, scarab seals, and stone vases from Egypt[144].

Mycenaean ships are depicted on pottery and were similar to Minoan ships. They were propelled by a single square sail and rowers. Depictions include those on a cup from Bademgediği Tepe, Ionia, a sherd from the Philistine city of Ashkelon, and a vase from Tragana, Messenia, all dating to around 1200 BCE. The Tragana depiction, which was the most complete, represents what was probably a typical large Mycenaean ship. At the prow of the ship was an elaborate forecastle linked to the stern by a raised gangway. At the stern was a square stern cabin, from which the ship was steered by a large steering oar. The stern also featured a high stern post decorated with a fishtail[145].

One of the most important archaeological discoveries from this period is the Uluburun shipwreck, which was discovered near Kaş on the Turkish coast by a sponge diver in 1982. Investigations began in 1984 and continued until 1994. The 13 m (42 ft) ship has been dated by dendrochronology (tree-ring dating) to 1305 BCE, or shortly thereafter[146]. It was carrying 354 slab ingots of copper from Cyprus, with an average weight of 24 kg (53 lb) totalling 8.5 tonnes (9.4 tons), just under one tonne of tin (though an unknown amount of tin had turned into powdery, non-metallic α-tin and was lost during the excavation), and 175 ingots of coloured glass ingots. These were mostly cobalt blue or turquoise, though a few were purple or amber. Chemical analyses of the alkalis and the colouring agents used in the manufacture of the glass suggest origins from both Egypt and Southwest Asia. The ship's cargo also included Canaanite jars holding an estimated 450 kg (0.5 tons) of holding terebinth resin intended for dyeing cloth, spices, fruits, olives, 18 ebony logs, elephant and hippopotamus ivory, Cypriot pottery, and a small gold Egyptian scarab bearing the name of Nefertiti, wife of the Egyptian pharaoh Akhenaten. There was approximately 0.53 kg (117 troy oz) of gold bullion aboard, including a large chalice, ingots, and scrap jewellery, as well as silver bar ingots. Two sets of writing boards were also found. They were intended to hold wax upon which inscriptions could be made and indicated the language used by the ship's crew. Unfortunately, if there was any wax there at the time of the sinking, it failed to survive. Assuming the ship was following the standard anticlockwise trade route, it would have been *en route* from Cyprus to the Aegean when it foundered[147].

It has been estimated that the Uluburun ship and its cargo would have had a value of 12,000 Ugarit shekels of silver. One Ugarit shekel was 9.4 gm (0.30 troy oz) of silver, so the total value was 40,000 troy oz of silver, worth around £790,000 ($1,000,000) at present-day rates. Wages at the time ranged from three to five shekels per month, which were paid in silver and/or grain, and 12,000 shekels would have paid a thousand workers for a year. The ship is likely to have been operated by private entrepreneurs, and its loss could have been catastrophic unless they had previously taken steps to spread the risk. We have no way of knowing whether or not they actually did so[148].

A spherical Earth

It is a popular misconception that Christopher Columbus' plan to reach the East Indies by crossing the Atlantic was repeatedly rejected because people thought that the Earth was flat. The Ancient Greeks were aware of the sphericity of the Earth, and around 240 BCE, the polymath Eratosthenes of Cyrene (274-194 BCE) obtained a reasonably accurate estimate of its circumference. However, only a few centuries earlier, the prevalent view was that the Earth is flat. Early Egyptian, Mesopotamian, Hebrew, and Homeric Greek cosmologies are all based around a flat Earth. The ancient Hebrews believed that the Earth is a disc supported by pillars and surrounded by a primal Ocean. Below it is an underworld known as Sheol, and above it, again supported by pillars, is the Firmament of Heaven, a solid dome separating the Sun, Moon, stars, and planets from the Ocean of Heaven[149,150]. The notion of a spherical Earth only became generally accepted around the end of the fifth century BCE. The discovery has been attributed to Parmenides (512-400 BC) or even Hesiod (c.650 BC). More plausibly, it was Pythagoras (c.570-495 BC) or the Pythagorean school that first put forward the idea, but when Socrates (470-399 BC) was in his youth, the matter was still apparently being debated[151,152].

Socrates was born early in the Greek Classical period, less than a decade after the end of the Persian Wars. More than 800 years had passed since the Uluburun shipwreck, and the eastern Mediterranean was now firmly within the historical period. Ships had become far larger than those of the Late Bronze Age: the merchant ship that sank off the coast of the Aegean island of Alonnisos in the last quarter of the fifth century BCE measured at least 25 m (82 ft) in length and 10 m (32 ft) in beam. The cargo of amphora containing wine is estimated to have weighed around 125 tonnes[153]. In this context, it is difficult to believe that a spherical Earth was not already a well-established fact.

The classic proof that the Earth must be round is the appearance or disappearance of a ship over the horizon. As it sails away from the land, it will gradually disappear. First, the hull, then the superstructure, and finally, for a sailing ship, the masts and sails will sink below the horizon. Conversely, the upper parts of an incoming vessel will be seen before the hull comes into view. The same effect can be seen for the tall buildings of the Chicago skyline viewed from across Lake Michigan or Malmo's 190 m (623 ft) Turning Torso building viewed from across the Øresund. The effect can clearly be seen with a telescope or a pair of binoculars, and the internet abounds with photographs and videos taken with high-zoom cameras. Why, then, did nobody notice the gradual disappearance of Minoan ships below the horizon as they sailed from Crete *en route* to Egypt? Or did they, and the knowledge was lost during the general disruption at the end of the Late Bronze Age?

Apart from the obvious lack of telescopes and binoculars in the Bronze Age, there is another reason why following the disappearance or reappearance of a ship might have been harder than is customarily assumed. Bronze Age ships were far smaller than even coastal merchant vessels of the present day. The Uluburun ship, which was probably representative of a Bronze Age merchant vessel, was no larger than a present-day Moody 54 sailing yacht. Would even a keen-eyed observer have been able to see that the hull of such a ship, when outward-bound, vanished while its sails remained visible? Even if they could do so, would they have been able to do so with enough consistency to realise that it was a genuine phenomenon and not just an artefact of sea, weather, or lighting conditions?

Consider an individual of average height (eye level 1.7 m or 5ft 7 in) standing on the shore, watching a ship of comparable size to the Uluburun merchant vessel standing out to sea:

Length of hull:	15 m approx. (50 ft).
Height of hull above waterline:	2 m approx. (6 ft 6 in).
Hoist of mainsail:	15 m approx. (50 ft).
Width of mainsail:	15 m approx. (50 ft).

Using a computer program that the hidden height of a target from the eye height of an observer and their distance from the target, we find that the hull will have just disappeared as the ship reaches 10 km (6.2 miles) from the shore. A second observer, sited on a clifftop at a height of 10 m (32 ft), would still be able to see the whole of the ship. At a distance of 10 km, the sail would subtend $15/10,000 = 0.0015$ radians or 5 arcmin. This is about the same apparent size as a UK five-pence coin or a US or Canadian dime viewed from 12 metres (40 ft). The hull, on the other hand, would subtend an angle of just $2/10,000 = 0.0002$ radians or 0.7 arcmin above the waterline, or less than the maximum apparent diameter of Venus. The theoretical maximum resolving power of the human eye is about 0.4 arcmin, but most people cannot resolve better than about 1.0 arcmin. Venus, like the Moon, exhibits phases, but only people with exceptional eyesight can discern them with the naked eye. There is the additional complication that even if our Bronze Age observers possessed sufficient visual acuity, it would have been very difficult for them to distinguish the hull from the sea except under the most favourable conditions of clarity and calmness.

By the time the ship was 15 km (9.3 miles) out, roughly half the sail would have disappeared as viewed from shore level, although it and the top half of the hull would still be visible from the clifftop. At this point, the sail would be subtending only $15/15,000 = 0.0010$ radians or 3.3 arcmin. Would the shore-level observer have been able to pick out enough detail against the background of an open sea to realise that the sail was disappearing below the horizon? Would they have thought that the ship was doing anything other than vanishing into the distance? The converse of a ship dropping below the horizon as seen from the land is the disappearance of the land as seen by those on board the ship. Again, though, would Bronze Age mariners conclude other than that the land was simply too far away to be seen? On a clear day, the Taurus Mountains of southern Turkey can be seen from far out to sea – but with the naked eye, it is difficult to see that the shore is no longer visible. Not until the fifth century BCE did ships like the Alonnisos merchantman become large enough to be visibly 'hull down' on the horizon. Possibly, this is the clue that led to the realisation that the Earth could not be flat.

Let us now consider the more thought-provoking possibility that well before the time of Socrates, as far back as the Bronze Age, there was some knowledge, if not widely shared, that the Earth was spherical. Could people have seen the actual curvature with their own eyes, giving them a clue that they were not living on a large plateau? It is often claimed that the curvature of the Earth can be seen from an aircraft, a mountain, or even a tall building. There are even claims that you can see a curved horizon by looking out to sea from a clifftop. This latter claim is easily disposed of. By viewing the horizon over a level straight edge such as a ruler, you would be able to see a perceptible convex meniscus, but – and I have tried this – the edge of the ruler and the horizon line up perfectly. There are many photographs on the internet purporting to show a clear curvature from aircraft and even from vantage points such as the Blackpool Tower, but they are invariably artefacts of barrel distortion by the camera lens.

Nevertheless, the curvature is clearly visible at 60,000 feet from high-altitude aircraft. Passengers on Concorde could see it, and astronomer David Lynch[154] has claimed that it is just discernible from an ordinary airliner at 35,000 feet under ideal conditions. He speculated that it might also be visible from very high mountains, although he was unable to see it from Mauna Kea (elevation 13,796 ft; 4205 m) and Haleakala (elevation 10,223 ft; 3116 m), despite a relatively unobstructed horizon in several directions. Lynch suggested that a measurable curvature might be seen in photographs taken from as low as 20,000 ft (6,000 m), roughly the height of Denali, Alaska (formerly Mount McKinley) and comfortably exceeded by at least 150 mountains worldwide. The problem is that at these altitudes, the air is too thin to breathe unaided. Accordingly, we can rule out any possibility that Bronze Age people could have seen the Earth's curvature for themselves.

However, there is another way by which people living during the European Bronze Age could have deduced that the Earth must be spherical. During that period, there was an increase in long-distance trade[155], and as noted above, Baltic amber reached Greece[156]. The night skies in Athens at 38° N are significantly different from those in Riga on the Baltic at 57° N. As seen from Athens, the pole star Polaris is much closer to the horizon than it appears from Riga, and the constellation of Ursa Major (the Great Bear), ever-present in the Baltic skies, scrapes along the northern horizon at lower culmination. There are also more subtle differences, which will be apparent to an experienced skywatcher. For example, the Belt of Orion, as it rises in Riga, is inclined at around twenty degrees from the vertical, but in Athens, it is very nearly perpendicular to the horizon. It is difficult to believe that traders would not have been aware of the changes in the night sky as they travelled along the Amber Road between the Baltic and the Mediterranean. At the same time, the Egyptians had trading contacts with Punt, believed to be in southern Sudan or Eritrea[157], and, as noted above, with the Minoans. Eritrea lies at 15° N, some 16 degrees of latitude south of the Nile Delta, and 20 degrees of latitude south of southern Crete. Again, traders would have seen significant changes in the night skies.

One consideration is that the night skies of the Bronze Age were different to those of the present day. Due to the precession of the equinoxes[51], there was no bright star at the north celestial pole from 2400 to 1500 BCE. Around 1400 BCE, Ursa Major remained circumpolar[52] as far south as Luxor. However, the bright stars Arcturus and Vega, and the conspicuous constellations of Cassiopeia and Corona Borealis, were circumpolar from Riga but not from Athens. Meanwhile, the Southern Cross, which had all but disappeared from the Mediterranean skies, remained clearly visible from Luxor. The differences, though not the same as those that may be observed today, were nevertheless clearly there to be seen.

Bronze Age traders making these long journeys and recognising that the night skies at their destinations looked different to those of their homelands might have asked themselves how these differences might be explained. If they did, they might have begun to query the orthodox cosmological model and consider a revised version in which the Earth is a hemisphere rather than a disc, located inside the Firmament of Heaven dome. This model would still not explain why the stars do not begin to 'run out', even as far south as the land of Punt, and that previously unseen stars come into view. However, it would have been a relatively straightforward mental leap to go from a hemisphere to a complete sphere, with Sheol presumably relocated to the centre of the spherical Earth. By 1400 BCE, it seems entirely plausible that observant traders and travellers were aware or at least had begun to suspect that Heaven and the Earth were not as they had been led to believe.

If so, why did it take another millennium for their suspicions to become mainstream knowledge? The problem is that long-distance traders were unlikely to have been ritual or religious specialists, or part of the urban intellectual elite. As they travelled mostly overland, their knowledge was of no practical significance. Mediterranean sailors, who would have been very likely to notice differences in the night skies on their voyages, were navigating a sea whose principal axis lies east-west rather than north-south. Their long-distance voyaging took place around the 36th parallel. Even a voyage from Crete to Egypt spans only four degrees of latitude. Any long-distance trader deducing the true nature of the Earth would probably have found that their insight was at best of passing interest. Indeed, their views could well have attracted the ridicule and disbelief of their peers. Worse still, if these were to come to the attention of priests or ritual specialists, they could have faced a reaction of the type faced thousands of years later by Galileo in response to his 'heretical' ideas. All in all, they might have felt it prudent to keep their suspicions to themselves or family and friends.

Epilogue

On 17 June 2017, the *Hōkūle'a*, by now more than forty years old, arrived in Honolulu at the end of a 3 ½ year voyage around the world. The circumnavigation had covered 75,000 km (47,000 miles; 40,000 nautical miles) and had been completed entirely under sail and without

---

[51] A slow, cyclical change in the Earth's orientation in space, similar to the wobbling of a spinning top. Each cycle takes just under 26,000 years.

[52] A star or constellation is said to be circumpolar at a particular latitude if it never sets at that latitude. For example, in Britain, Ursa Major is always above the horizon.

the use of charts, sextants, compasses, global positioning system, or other devices used by modern navigators. An estimated crowd of 50,000 greeted the *Hōkūle'a*'s homecoming.

12: Early metallurgy

The Seven Metals of the Ancient World

The use of stone for toolmaking predates the emergence of the earliest humans, but the use of metal for toolmaking is far more recent. The reason for this is straightforward: although there are 76 naturally occurring metallic elements, only a few are commonly found in the native state. In antiquity – and indeed for centuries after – only seven metals were known: gold, silver, copper, lead, tin, iron, and mercury. Of these, only gold, silver, and copper occur in significant quantities in the native state. Of these, only copper is suitable for toolmaking, though all three could be used for making ornaments. Unlike gold and silver, copper is reasonably abundant. Arsenic, antimony, nickel, and zinc alloys were known in antiquity, but the elemental metals were not widely recognised as distinct.

Seven was a highly significant number in the ancient world. The ancients knew of certain heavenly bodies that behaved differently from the fixed stars. Unlike the latter, which never move relative to one another, these changed their relative positions at varying rates. The Ancient Greeks named them *planetes*, meaning 'wanderer'[53], although their behaviour had been noticed much earlier. They are the five naked-eye planets and the Moon. It was also recognised – possibly during total solar eclipses, though it could be inferred from the positions of the stars visible at dusk or dawn – that the Sun exhibits the same behaviour. Hence, there were seven wanderers and the number seven came to be viewed as auspicious. It has been suggested that this was why the Mesopotamian ruler Sargon of Akkad (reigned 2288 – 2235 BCE) introduced a seven-day week[1]. Seven planets, seven days of the week, seven metals.

Is it a coincidence that the ancients recognised seven distinct metals? Could others have been isolated on occasion but ignored because seven was regarded as a 'full house'? It is certainly possible. There were the supposed Seven Wonders of the Ancient World, but the Hanging Gardens of Babylon probably never existed at all and could have been invented to make up the numbers. Similarly, the Greek historian Theopompus (c. 380 – 325 BCE) was reportedly familiar with metallic zinc. In this case, eight metals might have been one too many, and zinc was dismissed as 'false silver' even though Theopompus was aware that alloying copper with it gave 'mountain copper' (i.e., brass)[2].

---

[53] Hence also, Earth was not originally regarded as a planet, though the Sun and Moon were. The debate about what is and is not a planet has continued ever since; until around the 1850s the four then-known asteroids were considered to be planets, and Pluto officially ceased to be a planet in 2006.

Early use of native metals

Although people of the Upper Palaeolithic period in Eurasia produced beautifully worked art objects in stone, bone, and shells, there is no evidence that they ever made any ornaments from native metals. This might seem surprising, but it is rare for non-agricultural societies to produce metal artefacts. For example, Aboriginal Australians have a tradition of rock art going back at least 28,000 years[3] but they did not develop a metal culture and had no exposure to metals until the arrival of the Europeans[4]. However, there are exceptions, as we shall see.

The earliest known use of metals occurs in Southwest Asia, where by around 8000 BCE early Neolithic people were hammering native copper to make beads and other small objects at sites in locations stretching from Anatolia to Iran. The most prolific of these is Çayönü Tepesi in eastern Anatolia, where over 100 small copper artefacts including beads and pins with a total weight of 139 gm (4.9 oz) have been found. Metallographic analyses of these artefacts have shown evidence for annealing of native copper, indicating the early application of heat to the production process[5-7]. However, longstanding claims that copper was being smelted by 6500 BCE have been refuted. Alleged metallurgical slag from the large Neolithic site of Çatalhöyük site in central Anatolia has now been interpreted as green cuprous minerals that were ground up for use as pigment and subsequently caught up in a fire in the building in which they were found[8].

Rather earlier, during the transition to agriculture in the region around 9600 – 8200 BCE, there was an increase in the use of green minerals such as malachite for making beads and pendants. It has been suggested that early Neolithic farmers associated the colour green with plants and agriculture, and they regarded it as auspicious[9]. Cuprous minerals such as malachite were regularly collected and used alongside the native copper from the same deposits. Thus, there was an early association between copper ore and the metal itself[5]. It was possibly this interest in green cuprous minerals for bead-making that drew attention to the native metal itself, and why no copper beads from the Upper Palaeolithic have been found.

From annealing to smelting

Smelting copper ore (sulphides and/or oxides) to produce metallic copper is far more complex than working with native copper. The process entails heating the ore with charcoal in the presence of an air supply. The charcoal combines with oxygen to produce carbon monoxide, which in turn reduces the heated ore to metallic copper. The chemistry underlying this process is elementary, but the practicalities of regulating the temperature and air supply are far from straightforward.

It has often been suggested that the discovery of copper smelting was a spinoff from the kiln technology developed for the firing of painted ceramics. However, this is unlikely as the temperatures achieved in pottery kilns are significantly lower than those required to smelt metals, and the earliest-surviving smelting furnaces do not resemble pottery kilns. The use of charcoal for reducing copper ore might have been a multi-step discovery. Annealing of copper causes the surface to discolour due to oxidation, and it could have been noticed that the use of charcoal limited this unwanted effect. Gradually, it would become standard

12: Early metallurgy

practice to cover native copper with charcoal before annealing. The next step would have been the development of crucibles in which native copper was melted down and cast. As with annealing, the metal would have been covered with charcoal to prevent oxidation. On occasions, incompletely separated mixtures of native copper and cuprous ore would have been melted down, and the charcoal would have been reduced to metal. It would soon be realised that when such mixtures were melted down, there was more copper metal at the end of the process than there had been at the start. It can be envisaged that once experimentation had shown that the metal could be obtained from ore alone, the process would have been refined until a practical smelting technology was developed[5].

Where, when, and on how many occasions copper smelting was invented has long been debated. In the 1960s, British archaeologist Colin Renfrew suggested that there had been multiple independent inventions throughout Eurasia, but the American historian Theodore Wertime believed that the process was too complex to have been invented more than once. At that time, and indeed for some time thereafter, there was insufficient data from field and laboratory work to provide definitive answers. If the appearance of copper smelting was synchronous throughout Southwest Asia and Southeast Europe before spreading across the rest of Eurasia, it would suggest that there was a single invention in Southwest Asia or Southeast Europe, and there was no independent invention elsewhere in Eurasia[6]. However, recent discoveries have revived the possibility of multiple independent discoveries[10].

Chalcolithic developments in the Balkans

Copper ore was mined in 20 m (66 ft) deep trenches at Ai Bunar, southern Bulgaria, from around 5100 BCE and in galleries at Rudna Glava, Serbia, from around 5000 BCE [11]. The presence of cast copper tools in the Balkans from 5000 BCE was thought to imply an indigenous Balkan copper industry. It was estimated that around 4,300 copper tools were circulating in the region throughout the period, whereas no more than 300 were present in Southwest Asia at this time. Therefore, it seemed unlikely that the Balkan implements had been imported. Subsequently, geological provenance analysis of trace elements and lead isotope ratios demonstrated that the Balkan tools had been made from ore deposits originating in Bulgaria and Serbia[10].

One problem was the lack of any evidence for copper smelting and a disagreement as to how this may be recognised in the archaeological record. It was questioned whether or not early extraction processes would have left vitrified slag. Reduction of copper ore to metallic copper occurs at the relatively low temperature of around 700°C, but the melting point of copper is much higher, at 1,080°C. One suggestion was a two-step process in which the metal was first extracted from ore at low temperatures and subsequently melted at higher temperatures for casting into ingots or artefacts. This would leave little vitrified slag and hence would be difficult to detect archaeologically. However, it was also suggested that a one-step process at higher temperatures would be easier to control, and the reduction process would be more efficient. It was argued that such a process, which would have produced slag as a waste product, was more likely to have been used. Slag can result simply from melting metallic copper, so its presence alone is not conclusive proof of smelting technology and chemical analysis is required to distinguish between the two cases. Smelting produces a slag that is rich in metals such as iron and manganese, whereas slag resulting from melting consists mainly of fused ceramic material with ash and varying amounts of metallic copper and copper oxides[10].

Evidence finally emerged from the site of Belovode, Serbia, which was discovered in 1993. The site is associated with the Vinča culture, a Balkan culture that lasted from 5300 to 4600 BCE and is named for the type site of Vinča near Belgrade. The Vinča culture is associated with large copper implements such as hammer axes, chisels, and armbands. Radiocarbon dating shows that the site was occupied throughout the Vinča cultural period and during mining activities at Rudna Glava. Excavations yielded copper smelting slag, copper minerals and ores, and a droplet of copper metal. This is found from 5000 BCE and continues for the remainder of the Vinča occupation of the site. Geological provenance studies found that manganese-rich ores were used for smelting and malachite (copper carbonate hydroxide) was used for making beads. The smelting slag predates by 500 years any similar evidence currently known in the Balkans or Southwest Asia, suggesting that it was independent of these later developments[10].

British author Sir Arthur C. Clarke once observed that any sufficiently advanced technology is indistinguishable from magic, and copper metallurgy would have been seen that way by people not involved with the process. While it is obvious that the raw material for making pottery is clay, the manufacture of shiny copper artefacts from greenish rock would have appeared magical. Copper metallurgy would have been viewed as a new and entirely different kind of craft from ceramics. It would have set those involved apart from other craftspeople and stimulated demand for copper goods. Prospecting, mining, and long-distance trade both for ore and manufactured copper goods would in turn have intensified interregional trade networks[12]. At the same time, differing access to these trade networks would have resulted in growing social inequality, and the emergence of elites[13]. However, metallurgy did not bring about any immediate great change in the practicalities of day-to-day life, and the character of society remained predominantly Neolithic. Stone tools remained in use alongside the new copper tools, and this period is consequently known as the Chalcolithic or Æneolithic, meaning 'copper-stone'[14].

Bronze and the rise of the tin trade

While serviceable tools can be made from pure copper, it is still a relatively soft metal, and its mechanical properties are considerably improved by alloying it with other metals or metalloids. Artefacts made from naturally occurring tin-copper alloys include a heavily corroded bead from the site of Aruchlo I in Georgia, dating to 5800 – 5300 BCE and a corroded remains of an awl from the site of Tel Tsaf in the Jordan Valley, dating to 5100 – 4600 BCE. The latter is believed to have reached the southern Levant via long-distance exchange networks, probably from the Caucasus[15]. The discovery that such alloys could be created artificially was probably an accident. At some stage, it might have been noticed that the hardness of copper was improved when certain ores or combinations of ores were smelted[16,17].

The earliest-known tin bronze artefact is a foil from the Vinča culture site of Pločnik in southern Serbia. The foil dates to 4650 BCE and may have been used for wrapping a ceramic vessel. Other Vinča tin bronze artefacts are known, including a ring from the site of Gomolava, but they are not securely dated. The foil and the ring were carefully made artefacts, which were smelted from complex tin and copper ores. The foil was left in a soft annealed state so that it could be wrapped around a ceramic vessel, whereas the ring was left in a hardened state. The annealing temperatures used were much higher than those required for annealing native copper, indicating an understanding of the particular properties and requirements of tin bronzes[18].

The tin bronze at Vinča sites, like the copper smelting, appears to have been a precocious development that was not immediately seen elsewhere. It was several centuries before bronze production appeared elsewhere, and when it did, it was not tin bronze. During the late fifth millennium BCE, copper smelters in Anatolia and the Iranian Plateau began smelting copper ores chosen for their natural impurities. Copper-based alloys were produced containing amounts of lead, antimony, arsenic, tin, and iron that varied depending on the ore used, with mechanical properties and physical appearance that also varied. During the fourth millennium BCE, arsenical bronzes came to predominate. At the site of Tepe Yahya, Iran, arsenical bronze replaced copper between 3600 and 3400 BCE[17,19,20].

Tin bronze reappeared in Anatolia and northern Syria around 3000 BCE[20], but its use still did not immediately become widespread. During the period from 2200 to 1600 BCE, arsenical bronze remained the more commonly used type across Europe and Southwest Asia, and it was not until around 1500 BCE that it was completely replaced by tin bronze. The properties of tin bronze are only slightly superior to those of arsenical bronze, but it must have gradually been realised that the use of tin avoided the deleterious effects of long-term exposure to arsenic[17,21,22].

The advent of tin bronze metallurgy did not have any immediate technological impact on day-to-day living, but the social impact was considerable. Tin is far less abundant in the Earth's crust than copper, and the only major European sources were northern Bohemia, Brittany, Cornwall, and Galicia. The demand for tin from these distant sources led to the establishment of exchange networks across Europe through which other valuable materials such as Baltic amber also circulated[11]. A combination of tin and lead isotope analysis together with trace element analysis suggests that Cornish tin was traded as far as the Levant[23].

Brass[54] – copper alloyed with zinc – was not intentionally produced until the first millennium BCE, with production probably commencing in Anatolia. By the first century BCE, the Romans were producing brass by the cementation process: metallic copper was heated with calamine (zinc carbonate). Though earlier brass artefacts are known, they are rare. Zinc boils at 905°C, 175°C below the melting point of copper, so when zinc-bearing copper ores were smelted, the zinc would tend to oxidise and be lost before it could dissolve in the copper[24].

---

[54] The origins of the terms brass and bronze are obscure, but until the Renaissance, all copper alloys were referred to as 'brass'. The Latin for both bronze and brass is *aereus*. During the Renaissance in Italy, the term *bronzo* was applied to copper-tin alloys, but in England until the nineteenth century the terms 'bronze' and 'brass' were used more or less interchangeably.

From bullion to coinage

The association of gold and silver with wealth is something we are all familiar with from childhood. Stories for young children about pirates and treasure are unlikely to ever go out of fashion. In addition to jewellery, luxury goods, and a wide range of industrial uses, these metals are to this day used as a store of wealth. Countries including Britain, the United States, Canada, and South Africa issue 1oz legal tender bullion coins. In recent years, gold has regained its status as the king of metals, shrugging off the century-long challenge of platinum.

Prestige items made from gold first appeared during the Chalcolithic period. The cemetery at Varna on the Black Sea coast of Bulgaria was in use from 4560 to 4450 BCE. It is known for its exceptional quantity of finely worked gold grave goods: more than three thousand items, weighing over 6 kg (13.2 lb). These items, which represent the world's earliest-known example of gold-working, are not equally distributed among the site's just under 300 graves. Instead, 85 per cent of the gold came from just four graves, and most held no gold at all[25,26]. Such a lopsided distribution suggests that the Varna people lived in a socially stratified society where gold was prized as highly as it is today[27], despite being far less useful than copper for toolmaking. Soon thereafter, gold artefacts appeared in the Levant[28].

Silver, too, became a valuable commodity. Silver occurs as a native metal in only limited amounts, and silver ores such as argentite (silver sulphide) are not abundant. Most silver is found as a minor component in the ores of other metals, especially lead ores such as galena. The silver may be extracted by cupellation, where argentiferous lead ore is smelted to a lead/silver alloy, which is then heated to high temperatures in the presence of oxygen in a hearth. The molten lead is oxidised to lead monoxide, which is absorbed into the hearth lining to leave the metallic silver[29].

It might be asked how the small quantities of silver were ever noticed in the first place. In the 1920s, British chemist and Egyptologist Albert Lucas suggested a plausible scenario: *"When lead was produced from galena it was highly probable that it was not always removed at once from the fire and since the metal oxidizes when strongly heated and the molten oxide is absorbed by any porous material, such as ashes, on which it may rest, leaving behind the silver it contains in the form of a tiny metallic bead, it is reasonable to suppose that sooner or later a quantity of lead was oxidized and that the oxide disappeared, leaving the silver. The amount of silver, however, produced from a small quantity of lead would have been so minute that its presence would not ordinarily have been noticed and it would not have been until a considerable amount of lead rich in silver was oxidized that the residue of silver would have been sufficient in amount to have attracted attention"*[30].

The process was known in the Ancient Near East by the fourth millennium BCE and used to extract small quantities of silver. Lead monoxide has been found at smelting sites in northern Syria and eastern Anatolia[29]. Silver artefacts have been found in elite Chalcolithic burials in Byblos, Lebanon, and the metal was also an element in trade between Byblos and the Naqada I culture of predynastic Egypt[31]. Mine workings dating from around 3000 BCE have been found in Anatolia, and Early Bronze Age silver artefacts have been found at many Anatolian sites[32].

The use of coinage instead of bullion as a medium of trade was a much later development. The first coins were issued by the kingdom of Lydia in western Anatolia in the seventh century BCE, though there is no consensus as to when. Arguments have been advanced for mid-century, third quarter, or last quarter[33,34]. A date of 630 BCE is commonly accepted[35].

12: Early metallurgy

The coins, commonly referred to as 1/3 staters or trits[55], were struck from an alloy of gold and silver known as electrum. Natural electrum contains 65 to 85 per cent gold by weight. Scholars were perplexed by why coins should be issued with variable gold content, but we now know that the gold content of the Lydian coins was debased by the addition of silver and copper. Analysis of seven Lydian coins shows that the average content was 55.3 per cent gold, 43.2 per cent silver, and 1.4 per cent copper[36]. This would have provided the consistency required for the coins to be accepted as currency. Not until 550 BCE, during the reign of Croesus, were separate gold and silver coins issued. The technology to separate gold from silver in natural electrum either did not exist or was too expensive prior to then[35].

Before the introduction of coinage, bullion in the form of nuggets, dust, ingots, bars, and broken jewellery had served as a medium of trade in the Near East since the Middle Bronze Age. In western Anatolia, a relative abundance of natural electrum resulted at some point in its adoption as a medium of trade in Lydia and neighbouring Ionia. It must have occurred to somebody that the weakness of such a system could be addressed by alloying to a consistent fineness and producing pieces of a consistent weight, with marks identifying the maker and the gold content. If the issuer was sufficiently well-connected and respected, trading with such an issue would give the issuer a competitive advantage that would outweigh the cost of production. The next step would be for a state to make such an issue and declare them legal tender for all taxes and debts. Many private Lydian issues have been identified, though we cannot be certain that they preceded the government issues[35].

For governments, seigniorage[56] could have made the issuing of coins a profitable activity. However, seigniorage was not the only benefit of coinage to the state and might not even have been the main motive. Rather, it was probably the convenience coinage brought to dealing with large numbers of payments and receipts of relatively small amounts. Coins were not issued outside Lydia until around 550 BCE when Greek city-states on the mainland and offshore islands began to issue silver coinage, the use of which became widespread within 30 to 50 years[35].

Gold and silver did not enjoy high status everywhere. In India, gold mining began around 3900 BCE[37]. Gold working was practised by craft workers of the Harappan civilisation[38], but it has been suggested that the Harappan people did not regard gold and silver as luxury materials. British anthropologist Daniel Miller[39] noted that there are quantities of beads at all Harappan sites and a certain amount of gold and silver, but they seem to be in general use as ornaments rather than select items for the elite. Concentrations are only found in hoards, which could have been intended for trading rather than personal use. There is nothing to suggest that gold was regarded as anything more than just another substance from which ornaments could be made. Similarly, in China, gold and silver were valued primarily for their colour to enhance artefacts made of other materials, such as bronze and lacquer[40]. Coinage was an independent development in China, where coins were predominantly copper and

---

[55] The term 'stater' is commonly used by numismatists and is of Greek origin. In ancient Greece, it meant 'that which balances the scales'. The stater was the standard unit on which smaller denominations were based, and it could refer to coins struck in electrum, gold, or silver. 'Trit' was a term used by the Greeks for one-third of an electrum stater.

[56] Seigniorage is the profit made from coinage by the issuing state where the face value of a coin is more than the bullion value plus the cost of minting it.

bronze, and were cast rather than struck. Higher-value transactions were typically conducted in silks of set sizes and qualities rather than gold, though there were exceptions, such as the Zhou Dynasty state Chu[35].

The Old Assyrian *karum* at Kanesh

The Early Bronze Age in Southwest Asia saw the rise of the world's first urban state-level societies, and by 3200 BCE, many people were living in large, complex societies that could be described as urban[14,41]. The economies of these early city-states were rigidly state-controlled, but by the start of the Middle Bronze Age around 2000 BCE, there was a shift to an economy in which private enterprise played an increasingly important role[42]. An early example of just how lucrative the tin trade could be to this new breed of entrepreneurs was the *karum* or trade centre at Kültepe in central Anatolia, then known as Kanesh or Nesha. Taking advantage of the high prices that could be obtained for tin in Anatolia, Old Assyrian traders began operating there from around 1920 BCE.

The Assyrians take their name from their capital, Assur, located on the Tigris, 100 km (64 miles) west of present-day Kirkuk. In Biblical times, they were feared as ruthless empire-builders, but this was not always the case. In the early Middle Bronze Age, Assur was politically unimportant, but it became the centre of a mercantile empire as its traders began to operate on a large scale at the *karum* Kanesh. The word 'karum' means 'quay' or 'port', although Kanesh was not located near the sea or a river. The Kanesh trade centre was given this name by the Old Assyrian traders who operated there ('Old Assyrian' distinguishes them from the later, more militaristic Neo-Assyrians). At the time the *karum* was operating, Anatolia was a network of small kingdoms that were frequently in conflict with one another. Their populations spoke a variety of languages, including Hittite, Luwian, Palaic, and Hattic[42]. Business with the Assyrians was controlled by Hittite speakers, and most of the local names recorded by the traders at the *karum* were Hittite. The traders became so accustomed to dealing with Hittite speakers that they adopted Hittite words for 'contract' and 'lodgings' even in private correspondence[12].

The activities of the Assyrian traders operating at the *karum* are recorded in around 22,500 cuneiform tablets[42] found at Kültepe. The site has four main phases of occupation. Around 19,000 of the tablets are from Level II, and the remainder are from Level Ib. None have been found in the earlier Levels III and IV. The tablets from Level II have been dated to a period from approximately 1920 to 1835 BCE based on stratigraphy and the references they contain to Old Assyrian rulers. At the end of this period, the trade was interrupted when Kanesh was sacked, possibly by the king of Zalpa, a still-undiscovered Bronze Age Anatolian city. It resumed again five years later, only to eventually decline after around 1740 BCE[43].

The Assyrians traded tin and textiles for Anatolian gold and silver. They acted principally as middlemen: the textiles were both locally produced in Assyria and imported from Babylonia, but the latter were considered to be of superior quality[14,44]. The source of the tin is uncertain, but it is thought to have come from the east, probably Iran. Afghanistan was once thought to be a possible source, but has been ruled out by lead isotope and elemental analysis[22]. The goods were transported by donkey caravans from Assur, with groups of traders sharing expenses. A donkey could carry around 70 kg (150 lb) of tin and 30 items of textiles. The 1,200 km (745 miles) journey took at least 50 days and included passage through the Taurus Mountains. The gold and silver the traders received in exchange were far smaller in bulk, so they probably sold most of their donkeys in Kanesh before making the journey back to Assur. An estimated 150 donkey loads per year reached Kanesh. This trade was extremely lucrative: tin fetched twice as much in Anatolia than in Assur, and the textiles were worth three times as much. A consignment could return a 50 to 100 per cent profit. However, it was not risk-free. Caravans had to travel through the territories of many independent rulers, and not all of them were friendly. Fortunately, Assur was able to negotiate trade agreements that protected its monopoly, provided fair judgment for its traders when they ran into legal difficulties, and protected their property[42].

Although the *karum* trade was a private venture, strict controls were exercised by both the Anatolian and Assyrian authorities. Traders were taxed on each consignment leaving Assur, and had to pay a further levy upon arrival at Kanesh to meet the running costs of the *karum*. There were further taxes to pay on the imported goods. Within Anatolia, the Assyrians were not permitted to trade in local Anatolian textiles, presumably to protect the interests of the local traders. The Assyrian authorities exercised a monopoly on trade in certain luxury items, and smugglers were jailed if caught[44]. Luxuries included iron, which was a very valuable commodity. Native iron is almost unknown on Earth and in the Middle Bronze Age, iron smelting was in its infancy (see below). The source of metallic iron traded at Kanesh was extraterrestrial in the form of meteorites. The Kültepe tablets suggest that iron was worth up to 40 times its weight in silver[44,45].

Many Assyrian traders lived in the *karum* full-time, working as part of the trade network that operated throughout Anatolia. Their wives often remained at home to take charge of the textiles used in the exchange, remaining in contact by letter. These arrangements seem to have frequently led to friction over the quality of textiles sent to Anatolia and the lack of gold and silver coming back. The wives were also unhappy about the long periods of absence, during which the men did not always remain faithful[42].

Early bronzeworking in China

In ancient China, gold and silver were less valued than bronze and jade. Their primary use was for their colour to enhance artefacts made of other materials, such as bronze and lacquer. Only later did gold and silver become valued in the same way, and even then, it did not completely replace jade and bronze for the manufacture of the most prestigious artefacts[40]. The earliest-known bronze artefact found in China is a knife discovered at Majiayao in Gansu Province. It is thought to date to around 3000 BCE but appears to be an isolated and probably imported item. More recent bronzes from the sites of Ganggangwa and Huoshiliang, both in Gansu Province, along with slag and charcoal, suggest that bronze production began possibly around 2135 BCE. This is much later than its appearance in Southwest Asia, suggesting that bronzemaking technology was imported into China. That no arsenical bronze has ever been reported in China also argues against an indigenous origin. Despite these considerations, most Chinese archaeologists insist that bronzemaking technology was developed independently in China[46,47].

The transition from this relatively small-scale bronze metallurgy to something far more ambitious and large-scale is first seen at the large site of Erlitou in Henan Province[48], which is the type site of the Erlitou period. There are earlier occupations at Erlitou, but the Erlitou period occupation began around 1900 BCE and followed an occupational hiatus of 600 years. At its maximum extent, Erlitou covered an area of around 300 ha (740 acres). The Erlitou period occupation spanned four phases, ending around 1520 BCE[49,50]. The Erlitou period has been associated with the Xia Dynasty, once thought to be no more than a legend[51].

An important feature of Chinese bronzeworking is the use of casting. Elsewhere in the ancient work, vessels and other simple artefacts were made by hammering, a technique which is far more economical with its use of metal. The geological abundance of metal ores and the labour resources required to mine them made such economies unnecessary. The Erlitou bronzeworkers constructed a clay mould around a model of the article to be cast, then removed the clay in sections, and finally reassembled the sections around a core. Before reassembling the mould, they carved decoration into the inner faces of the mould sections. The decoration was simply transferred to the bronze during the casting operation rather than having to be subsequently cut into the cold bronze. It also meant that each section of the mould had to be decorated individually, with the consequence that the close relationship between the sectioning of the mould and the finished artefact was reflected in the decoration. Bronze vessels are nevertheless rare at Erlitou and unknown at other Erlitou culture sites. Not until the subsequent Erligang period do they become more abundant. The Erligang period is associated with the historical Shang Dynasty[48].

The Erlitou bronzeworkers had made even their most ambitious products, such as tripod cups, with a single 'pour' of molten bronze, requiring a mould of six or so sections. The more complicated shapes now being produced made it difficult to remove sections from the initial model and to fill the finished mould without trapping air pockets. Erligang bronzeworkers adopted the solution of casting in a sequence of pours. A part cast in one pour would then be embedded in the mould for the next pour. For example, handles could be cast in one step and then embedded in the mould for casting the main body of the vessel. This method enabled complex artefacts to be made in pieces without the necessity to solder or rivet them together[48]. The ability of the molten metal alloy to flow and fill a mould was significantly improved by adding lead to tin bronze to form a copper-tin-lead ternary alloy. This enabled the casting of large, complex, and detailed bronzes[52].

Sky metal

Ahnighito (Inuit 'the Tent') is a 30.8-tonne meteorite found near Cape York, Greenland. It is one of three fragments from the same asteroid impact residing at the American Museum of Natural History (AMNH) in New York, having been brought back from Greenland in the late nineteenth century by American naval officer and explorer Robert Peary. Ahnighito is one of the largest meteorites known and the largest on display in a museum. It is the centrepiece of the Arthur Ross Hall of Meteorites and is so massive that the steel supports for the display go straight down to the Manhattan bedrock beneath the museum. The other two fragments are smaller and known by the English translations of their Inuit names: 'the Woman' (3,000 kg) and 'the Dog' (407 kg)[53,54]. The estimated minimum mass of the asteroid was around 1,000 tonnes, and it is thought to have entered Earth's atmosphere at a speed of

20 – 25 km sec[-1] (12.5 – 15 miles/sec). At this speed, it would have begun breaking up at around 100 km (62 miles) above the surface, and fragments would have been scattered over a large area. A few smaller pieces have been found around Thule Air Base, 110 km (68 miles) northwest of the main impact site[55]. Eight large specimens totalling 58 tonnes in weight are now known, including the 20-tonne Agpalilik ('Man') discovered by Danish planetary scientist Vagn Buchwald in 1963 and now in the collection of the University of Copenhagen Geological Museum[53]. The date of the Cape York impact is not accurately known, but it has been estimated at 2,000 – 10,000 years ago[56]. The AMNH website claims that the asteroid "*slammed into Earth some 10,000 years ago*".

The Cape York meteorite is the most notable exception to the lack of use of native metals by non-agricultural people. In 1818, Scottish polar explorer John Ross was leading an expedition to find the supposed Northwest Passage when he encountered a previously unknown Inuit people in Melville Bay, on the northwestern coast of Greenland. Ross named them 'Arctic Highlanders'. He saw that some of the tools used by the Arctic Highlanders people had metal blades, although they had no obvious source of metal. Ross's crew included a Southern Greenland Inuit interpreter named Sacheuse, who was able to communicate with the Arctic Highlanders, albeit with some initial difficulty due to differences in dialect. The Inughuit, as they are now named, had been isolated for centuries from Innuit groups living further south, and indeed now had no knowledge of the southern groups. Through Sacheuse, Ross learned that the Inughuit obtained their metal from an 'iron mountain', from which they broke off pieces of iron with hard stone hammers. These pieces were subsequently cold-hammered into the desired shape. Ross correctly reasoned that the 'iron mountain' must be a meteorite. Weather and ice conditions prevented Ross from investigating further, but he procured two dog sledges and several tools from the Inughuit. On his return, he donated these items to the British Museum[54,55]. Analysis by the chemist William Thomas Brande confirmed the meteoric origin of the metal used[57].

In the decades that followed the Ross expedition, there were several unsuccessful attempts to locate the meteorite. The Inughuit were understandably reluctant to lead European explorers to the source of the iron upon which they depended. Eventually, in 1886, the American naval officer and explorer Robert Peary made the first of several expeditions to northwestern Greenland as the starting point for his plans to reach the North Pole. By this time, there was an established trade between explorers and the Inughuit, who sought wood, knives, nails, needles, and guns. They became less reliant on the 'iron mountain', and there was less of a need to keep its location secret. Peary traded extensively with the Inughuit, and in May 1894, he persuaded them to lead him to the three meteorites now known as 'the Woman' and 'the Dog' (located near Melville Bay, 50 m (150 ft) apart), and Ahnighito (located on the eastern side of the island subsequently known as Meteorite Island). Accompanying the meteorites were large quantities of basalt stones, which had been used as hammerstones to extract iron flakes for toolmaking[54,55].

A year later, Peary brought 'the Woman' and 'the Dog' back to New York (having floated them out to his ship SS *Kite* on ice-flows) and loaned them to the AMNH, but removing the much larger Ahnighito proved to be more of a challenge. Peary's first attempt, in 1896, was unsuccessful. Aided by a team of Inuit and a 100-tonne jack, he succeeded in moving the huge meteorite to the coastline, but bad weather forced the project to be abandoned. However, Peary persisted and returned in 1897 aboard SS *Hope*. A bridge was constructed from the shore to the ship, and the meteorite was lifted onto a trolley with jacks. When the tide was right, the trolley was run on rails out to the ship, and the meteorite was lifted into the hold. The *Hope* then sailed for New York via Boston, arriving at Brooklyn Naval Yard on 2 October 1897. Ahnighito remained at the Brooklyn Naval Yard until 1909, when it was sold to the AMNH for $40,000 and drawn through the streets of New York with much fanfare by 28 horses[54]. A rather less meritorious aspect of the 1897 expedition was that Peary persuaded six Inughuit to return with him to the United States. They were enticed by the possibility of seeing new places, but the real purpose was so that they could be studied by the anthropologists at the AMNH. The entire group soon contracted tuberculosis, and four of them subsequently died.

The present-day Inughuit population is around 750. The name 'Inughuit' is of recent origin, and is not widely used by the people themselves[58]. The Inughuit are believed to have migrated into the Avanersuaq (Thule) region of northwestern Greenland around 1050 – 1100 CE, but the Cape York meteorite had previously been exploited by earlier groups associated with the Dorset culture[54]. Work with ancient DNA has shown that present-day Native Americans descend from at least three streams of ancient migration into the New World from Asia. The initial migrants were the First Peoples, who crossed the Beringia land bridge that then connected Siberia to Alaska during the last Ice Age. The First Peoples were followed by two more recent migrations. The first occurred around 3000 BCE and spread throughout northern Alaska, northern Canada, and Greenland, and was associated with the prehistoric Dorset and Saqqaq cultures. These people, who are sometimes referred to as 'Paleo-Eskimos', were replaced by the Thule people or 'Neo-Eskimos', ancestors of the present-day Inuit and Yupik, who had spread throughout the Arctic region by around 1200 CE. It should be noted that the term 'Eskimo' is considered to be offensive by Indigenous groups in Canada and the United States. However, the terms 'Eskimo-Aleut', 'Paleo-Eskimo', and 'Neo-Eskimo' are still used in scientific literature[59].

The Dorset culture people settled the eastern High Arctic including Cape York in the seventh and eighth century CE. They are referenced in Inuit legend as the Tunit. The Dorset/Tunit people established long-distance interaction networks between the regions they settled. Evidence for these networks is seen in the distribution of exotic raw materials, including not just meteoric iron, but also telluric (native) iron and copper. These were used to produce blades for tools and weapons, but all could have been substituted by other locally available raw materials if necessary. That they are distributed so widely highlights their importance. Iron from the Cape York meteorite fragments, identifiable by its trace element signature, has been found at Late Dorset culture sites across much of the Arctic Archipelago, including Smith Sound, Axel Heiberg Island, Devon Island, Little Cornwallis Island, Somerset Island, and the Igloolik area in Foxe Basin. Telluric iron occurs only in small globules, and its use was by necessity restricted to the manufacture of small tool components. Such artefacts have been found only in the Disko Bay area of western Greenland. The distribution of native copper is similar to that of the meteoric iron, but it is also found at sites on Victoria Island, at the westernmost limit of the Late Dorset culture area. This probably reflects the presence of major copper sources in the Coronation Gulf region. Most copper blades have survived only as verdigris in the blade slots of knife handles[55,57].

All these metal artefacts were made by cold hammering into objects of suitable size and shape and then finished by grinding. No evidence has been found of forge welding, annealing, soldering, or riveting[57]. As primitive as this metalworking technology was, it enabled the Dorset culture people and later the Inuit to make use of the Cape York meteorite and other sources of native metal to manufacture tools that were far superior to tools made from stone or bone and made hunting and skinning animals far easier[54].

From bronze to iron in the Ancient Near East

The iron so prized at the *karum* Kanesh was not the earliest use of meteoric iron in the Ancient Near East. In Egypt, beads made from meteoric iron have been found at the Naqada period site of Gerzeh, dating to around 3400 – 3100 BCE. Later examples, which underline the great value of meteoric iron, include iron studs associated with gold and lapis lazuli on an ivory box found at the Anatolian site of Acemhöyük, dating to the eighteenth century BCE. A well-known example is the gold and iron dagger found in the tomb of King Tutankhamun, dating to 1324 BCE[45]. It is almost certain that knowledge of meteoric iron preceded the technology to smelt iron from iron ore.

Iron smelting is a far more complex process than making bronze. Early iron production involved the bloomer process, where ore is heated with charcoal in a clay furnace. Air enters a furnace through openings near the bottom, either via a natural updraft or with bellows. The incomplete oxidation of charcoal produces carbon monoxide, which in turn reduces iron ore to native iron. The process requires high temperatures of 1,150 – 1,200°C, and the amount of air passing through is critical to ensure the correct balance between burning the charcoal fuel to reach the required temperatures and reducing the iron ore. Too much oxygen will halt or reverse the reduction of the ore, turning it back into iron oxide. These high temperatures are still well below the melting point of iron (1,538°C) and result in a spongy mass of iron known as a bloom, which must be forged into the desired shape.

To identify smelted iron in the archaeological record, it is obviously necessary to distinguish between it and meteoric iron. Fortunately, there are several analytic methods available. A high nickel content in the range of 6 – 20 per cent is typically regarded as indicative of an extraterrestrial origin. This is not infallible, as some terrestrial iron ores also contain nickel, though generally less than 3 per cent. Traces of other elements, such as germanium and a nickel/cobalt ratio of 18:1, are also considered to be diagnostic of meteoric iron. Some iron meteorites also exhibit Widmanstätten patterns, consisting of alternating bands of nickel-rich alloys of kamacite and taenite. However, not all iron meteorites have this structure, and it can be eliminated by forging at high temperatures[45].

While most early iron has now been confirmed as meteoric, there are exceptions. Analysis of iron artefacts from the Anatolian site of Kaman-Kalehöyük 100 km (62 miles) southeast of Ankara has revealed slag inclusions in material from the Old Assyrian Colony period dating to between the twentieth and eighteenth centuries BCE. Unfortunately, it is not possible to determine whether the slag came from a smelting or a smithing operation. There is an even earlier possibility from the same site in a heavily corroded object from the Early Bronze Age dating to between the twenty-second and twentieth centuries BCE. Though the supposed slag inclusion is suspiciously regular in shape and the heavy corrosion necessitates caution, the nickel/cobalt and nickel/iron ratios are outside the normal ranges for meteoritic iron[45].

There is no substantial evidence such as furnaces or significant quantities of slag until after 1000 BCE, but there is textual evidence from Anatolia. Texts from 2000 BCE onwards use several different terms to refer to iron. Scholars have attempted to equate these to modern categories of metallic iron and iron ore, but the ancient and modern terminologies might not necessarily match[45]. Much debate has centred around the Hittites (Hatti), who enjoyed two periods of ascendancy: the Old Kingdom, which flourished briefly in the seventeenth century BCE and the New Kingdom, which was powerful between 1400 and 1200 BCE[42]. They were once thought to owe their success to being early adopters of iron, but are now known to have been primarily a Bronze Age society[14]. By the Iron Age, the Neo-Hittites, who feature prominently in the Bible, had splintered into several minor kingdoms[60].

Hittite texts nevertheless provide tantalising hints of iron smelting. The Hittite word for iron – *hapalki* – is usually written with the Sumerian logogram AN.BAR. The logogram GUNNI is normally used in Hittite texts with the meaning of 'hearth'. Therefore, a reference to 22 AN.BAR ŠA GUNNI could be interpreted as meaning '22 iron (blooms) of the furnace'. The best-known Bronze Age reference to iron is the so-called 'Iron Letter' from the New Kingdom Hittite King Hattušili III (reigned 1267-1237 BCE) to an Assyrian king: "*As for the good iron about which you wrote to me, there is no good iron in my storehouse in Kizzuwatna. The iron (ore) is (of) too low (a grade) for smelting. I have given orders and they are (now) smelting good iron ore but up until now they have not finished (the iron). When they have finished, I shall send (it) to you. Meanwhile, I am sending to you a blade of iron for a dagger*" (translation by J. D. Muhly). This suggests that the Hittites were known for making iron but they did not have sufficient knowledge of ores to be able to produce good-quality iron to order[61].

Both textual and analytical evidence from Anatolia suggest that small quantities of iron were smelted in the early second millennium BC. There was a noticeable increase in references to iron in texts of the late Hittite Empire period (especially during and after the 13th century BCE[45]. However, this could reflect differences in the types of written records that are preserved at different times during the Hittite period. Overall, written sources do not provide conclusive evidence for a progressively developing iron industry. Rather than a progressively increasing production and use of iron, the picture is one of continuity. Terms related to iron quality and technology do not seem to have changed over the centuries: advances in technology would be expected to drive the progressive development of the iron industry. Use appears to have been largely restricted to making statues, jewellery, and objects for ritual purposes[62].

If we accept that extractive iron metallurgy did emerge in Anatolia soon after 2000 BCE, why was it not until a millennium later that smelted iron was widely adopted? One suggestion is that early smelted iron was an unintended by-product of copper smelting[63], although this is unlikely. A fused mass of iron with a high percentage of copper would have been difficult to process into usable iron. Iron is a far more reactive metal than copper, so it is far easier to remove it from copper by oxidation than it is to remove the copper to leave metallic iron[45,64]. A more likely possibility lies with the limitations of early iron-smelting technology in the Ancient Near East. Early iron-smelting technology might only have been able to produce small blooms that then had to be forged together. Technological limitations on consistent quality could also have been an issue. Such small-scale production could explain why iron was so highly prized and why its use was so restricted[45].

Another factor is that pure iron is softer than bronze and inferior to it for making tools or weapons. Only when it is alloyed with carbon to make steel and quenched (rapidly cooled from high temperatures to form a crystalline structure) and tempered (heat-treating to reduce brittleness) does it become significantly harder than bronze. Although steel artefacts have been found, there is only weak evidence that they resulted from the intentional carburisation of iron with charcoal. There is as yet no convincing evidence that quenching or tempering were widespread practices, although surface corrosion poses problems for identifying microstructures resulting from quenching, and the issue remains unresolved[45].

The eventual widespread adoption of iron is certainly connected with the Late Bronze Age collapse of the Great Powers of the eastern Mediterranean, though as a consequence rather than a cause[45]. At the start of the twelfth century BCE, the political situation in that region had changed very little in centuries. The Great Powers included Ahhiyawa (the Mycenaeans), the Hittite New Kingdom, Assyria, the Kassite Dynasty of Babylon, and the Egyptian New Kingdom. In addition, there were many smaller states on the Syrian and Lebanese coasts. Within a short period, these states, great and small alike, suffered varying degrees of disruption. The upheaval was at its greatest in the Aegean and Anatolia, although it diminished in intensity further east. In the Aegean, the Mycenaean Bronze Age palace culture disappeared early in the twelfth century BCE. Overseas trade ended, the elite were no longer buried with elaborate grave goods, and fortresses were destroyed, although the decline and destruction were spread across several decades. The subsequent culture retained its Mycenaean identity, but it was impoverished. The Hittite New Kingdom disintegrated around 1190 BCE, and there was widespread disruption in the Levant. The Great Powers of Assyria and Babylon survived, but their influence was drastically reduced. Babylon declined after the death of Nebuchadnezzar I in 1104 BCE and Assyria had been reduced to a rump by 1050 BCE. Egypt was attacked in 1207 BCE and 1177 BCE. Although it escaped the worst of the troubles, the New Kingdom had collapsed by 1069 BCE. Although many regions experienced continuity and only gradual change, overall, the Ancient Near East of 1050 BCE bore little resemblance to that of 1250 BCE[42].

The collapse has been blamed on marauding 'Sea People', internal rebellions, a series of devastating earthquakes, disruption of international trade routes, and climate change leading to drought and famine[65]. The international system of the Middle Bronze Age onwards was arguably fragile and overly dependent upon international trade. Tin was of great strategic importance and has been likened to oil in the present day. It is far scarcer than copper, and without it the production of 'weapons-grade' bronze was impossible. Aside from its military applications, it was used for making tools that were widely used in all manner of trades. Tin was essential to Late Bronze Age societies. Ugarit, on the coast of present-day Lebanon, owed its wealth to its role as the major hub for the international tin trade, and its commodity merchants have been likened to the oligarchs of the present day[66]. While it is clear that international trade routes were disrupted for a while, it is unlikely that this on its own would have brought about a collapse on this scale. The disruption is more likely to have been an effect rather than a cause of the collapse. Letters found at Ugarit show that international connections continued right up until the final sacking of the city, suggesting that there was no gradual decline in trade before the collapse[65].

Overall, the collapse is best interpreted as somewhere between what American archaeologist Eric Cline has termed a *"perfect storm of calamities"*[65] and a model viewing climate change as the primary cause. The inherent weaknesses of the international system of the Late

Bronze Age were probably sufficient to preclude survival of a long, debilitating period of cold, arid climate. In addition to an overdependence on international trade, these weaknesses included huge differences in wealth between ruling elites and the agricultural communities they controlled, leading to migrations, labour shortages, and revolts[42].

Following the collapse, the Ancient Near East entered a dark age during which few written records were kept, and there was little building activity. The first state to recover was Assyria but even there, written texts are very rare from around 1050 to 935 BCE. The most significant consequence of the collapse was the replacement of bronze with iron. Without international trade, many parts of the eastern Mediterranean were cut off from supplies of copper and tin, and people turned to ironworking. The wide availability of iron ore meant that an elaborate trade network was unnecessary[42]. Probably, the need for a replacement for bronze drove innovation in smelting technologies to produce larger, more consistent iron yields. Methods for hardening iron such as intentional carburisation, quenching, and tempering might have been a consequence of the widespread use of iron, rather than its initial impetus[45].

From stone to iron in Africa

The adoption of ironworking in Africa followed a very different trajectory than elsewhere. Most of the continent bypassed the Bronze Age, progressing from stone tools straight to ironworking. Bronze metallurgy was largely confined to Egypt. Small numbers of copper artefacts have been found in Nubia, dating to around 4000 BCE. These were probably imported from Egypt. Copper smelting technology reached Nubia from Upper Egypt during the early Old Kingdom period (2686 to 2160 BCE). Elsewhere in sub-Saharan Africa, there is no evidence for metallurgy until early in the first millennium BCE. Copper mines and a smelting site dating from the ninth to the third centuries BCE have been excavated at Akjoujt, Mauretania. The origin of this technology, which was very small in scale, was probably Punic North Africa. The remains of copper smelting furnaces have been discovered in the region west of Agadez, Niger, though there is no definite evidence for copper metallurgy in Niger before the early first millennium BCE. There were also early developments in Ethiopia, which are still obscure. A mature bronze and ironworking industry with strong stylistic affinities to southern Arabia had emerged by the fifth century BCE. Elsewhere in sub-Saharan Africa, the first metal to appear in the archaeological record is iron[67].

The origins of iron metallurgy in Africa are uncertain. It is disputed as to whether it diffused from Southwest Asia or Mediterranean Europe, or whether it was a purely indigenous African development. The conventional view is that only people with experience of copper smelting would be able to master the more complex technologies associated with ironworking. It is argued, therefore, that they must have diffused to sub-Saharan Africa via the Nile or the North African coast[67,68].

The Royal City of Meroë, on the east bank of the Middle Nile in Sudan, was the capital of the Kingdom of Kush between 300 BCE and 400 CE. The Kushite rulers owed much of their power to their control over large-scale iron production. Archaeological evidence suggests that iron was produced on a significant scale from at least the seventh century BCE and continued for over a millennium, making Meroë the longest-lived centre of ancient ironmaking in Africa. Experimental iron smelting in a replica Meroitic furnace has been used to provide an understanding of the construction of furnaces, types of iron ore used, air supplies required, and charcoal sizes used[69]. The importance of iron to the Kushite rulers has led to Meroë being dubbed 'the Birmingham of Africa'[70], and it has often been suggested that the city was a staging point for a postulated spread of ironworking into sub-Saharan Africa[68].

However, there is evidence that iron smelting was developed independently at several locations in sub-Saharan Africa. In Gabon, sites associated with clay-lined furnace pits date to around the middle of the first millennium BCE[71]. The Nok culture of Central Nigeria is named for the village of Nok in Kaduna State and spans the period from 900 BCE to 200 CE. Furnace remains have been excavated at several Nok sites, with dates that suggest that iron production began around the seventh century BCE[72,73]. A total of 19 kg (42 lb) of smelting slag has been recovered at the site of Walaldé, Senegal, dating to around 800 – 550 BCE[74]. A furnace base at Do Dimmi, Niger, has been dated to as early as 1300 – 985 BCE[71], and the sites of Opi, Lejja, and Aku in the Nsukka region of Nigeria suggest even earlier ironworking in the late third or early second millennium BCE[71]. All these dates are earlier than the evidence for ironworking at Meroë. Sites in Rwanda, Burundi, and the Central African Republic have produced evidence for ironworking technology that could be as early as 3600 BCE, though the radiocarbon dates are suspect as they could be based on wood far older than the ironworking evidence[68,70].

By around 200 CE, there is evidence for ironworking among farming communities of the eastern highlands and coastal regions of Kenya and the northeastern highlands of Tanzania. However, widespread evidence for ironworking among the largely herding communities of the Central Rift Valley is lacking until around 700 CE. These sites are associated with the Pastoral Iron Age of East Africa[75,76]. Ancient DNA studies have demonstrated affinities between Pastoral Iron Age individuals and present-day Nilotic language speakers, suggesting that they might represent a later expansion of an ironworking tradition from Sudan into the Central Rift Valley[77].

Iron metallurgy is believed to have played a major part in the success of the Bantu farmers, who spread across much of sub-equatorial Africa between 3000 BCE and 500 CE. Similarities between languages spoken in widely separated regions of sub-equatorial Africa were first noticed by early Portuguese navigators and recognised by South African colonists in the early nineteenth century. That they represented a single language family was recognised by the German linguist Wilhelm Bleek in the 1860s. Bleek coined the term 'Bantu' from a word meaning 'people' or 'humans' in many Bantu languages. Bantu is a subgroup of the Niger-Congo linguistic family, which comprises 1,436 reported languages and 300 million speakers[78]. Bantu is one of the largest subgroups of the Niger-Congo family, with around 500 languages[79]. It is generally assumed that the Bantu family arose from a single language, known as Proto-Bantu. Linguists believe that it arose in the Grasslands of western Cameroon to the north of the tropical rainforests[80,81]. Bantu is traditionally divided into West and East Bantu branches, although this is no more than a convenient approximation and is not the whole picture[82].

Proto-Bantu has words for oil palm, yams, beans, groundnuts, dogs, goats, pigs, and pottery, suggesting that the early Bantu farmers were already familiar with them when the expansion began. The archaeological record suggests that root crop agriculture and pottery appeared in the western Cameroon Grasslands around 3000 years BCE, which implies that the Bantu expansion began after that date[81]. The expansion was probably triggered by an increased demand for farmland[83]. It was once believed that the dispersing farmers were equipped with a package that included ironworking and cereal agriculture, but it is now recognised that these were acquired after the initial dispersal[76].

The migrants initially proceeded in two directions from their homeland. Some moved southwards into the West African rainforest, eventually reaching the savannahs of Angola around 500 BCE. In the meantime, other groups began to move eastwards along the northern fringes of the equatorial rainforests, reaching the Great Lakes region of East Africa around 1000 – 500 BCE[83]. Based on linguistic data, it is now believed that the eastward migrants acquired sorghum and pearl millet and possibly ironworking technology from Nilotic-speaking groups in the northern Great Lakes and southern Sudan region. They acquired domesticated cattle and sheep, probably by trading yam flour for livestock[84-86].

Regardless of how the East Bantu farmers acquired ironworking technology, it was a potent addition to their repertoire that would have greatly facilitated forest clearance for agriculture. Pollen evidence from the lake sediments at Lake Victoria suggests a significant reduction in forest vegetation in the region around 500 BCE, which was probably the result of agricultural activity[68]. Among ethnographically documented Bantu people, ironworking is strongly associated with ritual. The ability to use fire to transform a naturally occurring substance like iron ore into metallic tools confers status upon master ironworkers comparable to chiefs or shamans. Furnaces were often given female anthropomorphic attributes, and ritual and symbolic reasons as much as practical considerations dictated their siting. We cannot be certain that this was the case during the Bantu expansion, but it seems highly likely[87].

It is no coincidence that the acquisition of ironworking technology by the East Bantu farmers was followed by one of the most rapid agricultural expansions on record. Although there is no complete agreement on the number of migrant streams involved or their sources, the overall picture is reasonably clear[83,86].

Pottery styles in East Africa are sufficiently similar to be grouped as the Chifumbaze complex, beginning west of Lake Victoria in the period from 500 BCE to 1 CE. Pottery styles further south demonstrate the subsequent speed of the expansion. Kwale ware dates to around 1 CE and is named for a site in the coastal region of southeastern Kenya. Broadly contemporary with the Kwale are the Nkope of Malawi and Zambia, and the Matola of Mozambique. Other traditions include the Gokomere/Ziwa of Zimbabwe and the Kalundu and Dambwa of Zambia. By 500 CE, Chifumbaze pottery had reached KwaZulu-Natal, having covered the distance of 3,500 km (2,175 miles) from Lake Victoria in just a few centuries[68,83,86].

By 500 CE, the Bantu expansion had reached the limits of the summer-rainfall belt of KwaZulu-Natal. Further south, the climate is Mediterranean rather than monsoonal, and the Bantu summer-rainfall crops could spread no further. By 1652, when the Dutch settlers arrived, they found the southernmost limits of the expansion represented by the Xhosa, on the northern side of the Great Fish River in Eastern Cape Province[83,88].

12: Early metallurgy

Lead and the Romans

Lead is occasionally found as a native metal but is usually found as sulphides. Galena (lead sulphide) is the most common source and smelting with charcoal to extract the native metal is straightforward. Lead melts at 327.5 °C, so in principle, even a campfire will suffice. Hence, the use of lead seems to have been both early and geographically widespread. Crucibles found at the Romanian sites of Pietrele and Blejeşti show that galena was being smelted in the Lower Danube region around 4400 - 4300 BCE[89]. In the Levant, the earliest-known lead artefact is a possible spindle whorl dating to 4300 – 4000 BCE, found at Ashalim Cave on the northern outskirts of the Negev Desert. Isotopic data suggests an Anatolian origin for either the artefact or the lead from which it was made[90]. In China, as noted above, lead was added to bronze alloys to improve their casting properties. Analysis of furnace slag suggests that lead was added during copper melting, and lead-bearing smelting slag dating to the Erlitou cultural period has also been found. The discovery of lead ingots in a storage pit at the site of Liujiazhuang Locus North, Yinxu Province, has provided further evidence that it was an intentional additive[52].

In the Classical world, the use of lead is mostly associated with the Romans, who gave us the words 'plumbing' and 'plumber', as well as the chemical symbol Pb for lead. All are derived from the Latin word *plumbum*. Originally, however, it was a generic term for any soft metal. Lead was known as *plumbum candidum* or *album* ('bright lead') as opposed to *plumbum nigrum* ('black lead'), although the term *stannum* (from which we get the chemical Sn for tin) was also used.

The Romans made extensive use of lead. At the peak of the Roman Empire, the annual production of lead was around 80,000 tonnes. This was around two-thirds of the annual production of lead in the United States in the 1970s and amounted to approximately 4 kg (9 lb) of lead per capita annually. Lead was used for piping, roofing, guttering, the building and shipping industries, ornaments, and coins. Copper and bronze cookware were lined with lead to prevent the formation of verdigris and the leeching of copper, which would otherwise spoil the taste of the food being cooked. In addition to smelting ores such as galena, the Romans made use of other lead-based minerals including yellow lead or litharge (lead oxide) in the building trade, white lead or cerusa (lead carbonate) was used in facial powders, ointments, eye medicine, and white paint, and lead acetate was commonly used as a sweetener, and for preserving food and wine. Lead preparations are also said to have been used as contraceptives and prescribed for skin ailments[91,92].

There does seem to have been some contemporary awareness of the deleterious effects of lead exposure. Pedanius Dioscorides (40 – 90 CE) wrote that ingesting cerusa was potentially fatal and that certain sweet wines adversely affected the abdomen and nerves. Pliny the Elder (23/4 – 79 CE) noted the poisonous nature of lead fumes, the toxicity of certain lead preparations, and the adverse effects of wines sweetened with *sapa* (a grape concentrate prepared in lead-lined copper pots). Aulus Cornelius Celsus (*c.* 25 BCE – 50 CE) referred to the toxicity of white lead, and Vitruvius (*c.* 80 – 70 – after 15 BCE) wrote that lead pipes caused illness. However, these descriptions are too vague to suggest that there was a wider appreciation of lead poisoning. The first full classical description of chronic lead poisoning was by Paul of Aegina (*c.* 625 – 690 CE)[92].

There have been many suggestions that lead contamination could have hastened the decline and fall of the Roman Empire. Speculation centred around poisoning that specifically affected the aristocracy, diminishing their fertility and reproduction, and so weakening Roman leadership. It was argued that the use of lead-contaminated water supplies, cooking procedures, and wine production made the elite particularly susceptible to lead poisoning. However, studies suggest that the average lead load in the Roman population was less than half of that in present-day Europeans[92]. Lead levels in tap water in Rome were around 100 times higher than in local spring water, but they were unlikely to be truly harmful[93].

Mercury madness

Another notoriously toxic metal known to the ancients is mercury. It was known to the Romans as *hydrargyrum* ('water-silver'), giving rise to the chemical symbol Hg (and the lamentable chemistry student joke that it is obtained from HG Wells). Mercury is one of only two elements that are liquid at room temperature (the other is bromine) and the only metal. Its melting point is -38.9°C and boils at 357°C. It is readily obtained from cinnabar (mercuric sulphide) by heating in air, which oxidises the ore to mercury vapour and sulphur dioxide. The vapour is then condensed back to liquid. Mercury readily forms alloys known as amalgams with other metals, a property which has several applications including dentistry, silvering and gilding, and the extraction of gold and silver from sand, gravel, and sediments. In the latter case, the precious metals are recovered from the amalgam by heating to boil off the mercury, which is distilled for reuse.

Cinnabar, also known as vermillion, is a red crystalline solid. It was commonly used in mortuary rituals by the Maya and other pre-Columbian Mesoamerican civilisations; the colour red was associated with the underworld. At the seventh-century CE Maya site of Palenque, the remains of an elite woman known as the 'Red Queen' were covered by a thick layer of red pigment. Burials covered by red pigment have also been reported at the Zapotec site of Monte Albán, Oaxaca and the ancient city of Teotihuacán in the Valley of Mexico[94]. A similar burial has been reported from pre Inca Peru, dating to 900 – 1000 CE, but the earliest-known example is La Velilla, a Neolithic burial site in Osorno, northwestern Spain, dating to around 3000 BCE. Up to 100 individuals were interred and so treated, and hundreds of kilograms of cinnabar were reported at the site. There are no sources of cinnabar within 160 km (100 miles) of Osorno[95].

In Ancient Greece, cinnabar has been found on limestone statues dating to the sixth century BCE and mixtures probably used for painting date to the fifth century BCE. Although native mercury does occur with cinnabar, there is no archaeological or literary evidence that the Ancient Greeks knew about the metal itself before the fourth century BCE. Theophrastus (*c.* 371 – 287 BCE), a follower of Aristotle, describes its preparation from cinnabar by mixing the ore with vinegar and grinding it in a copper vessel with a copper pestle. The copper would have displaced the mercury from the sulphide to form copper sulphide. However, the newly liberated mercury would have formed an amalgam with some of the unchanged copper and it would have been further necessary to distil the mercury from the amalgam. Theophrastus does not seem to have been aware of this additional requirement, but it was later described by both Dioscorides and Pliny. Vitruvius was the first ancient author to note a practical use for mercury, noting its use for gilding[96].

12: Early metallurgy

The mausoleum of Emperor Qin Shi Huangi (reigned 221 – 210 BCE) at Lintong (a district of Xi'an, Shaanxi Province) is famous for its Terracotta Army of life-sized soldiers. The Emperor's tomb itself has never been excavated, but it is said to contain Qin Shi Huangi's personal belongings, with pearls displaying the heavens and rivers of metallic mercury depicting the waterways and rivers of the empire. The inner sanctum is supposed to have been booby-trapped, *Raiders of the Lost Ark*-style, to deter tomb robbers[97–99]. In pursuit of eternal life, Qin Shi Huangi is said to have drunk mercury-based elixirs[57]. He died aged 49.

Metallurgy in the New World

Metallurgy in the ancient New World followed a different path from Eurasia. There were no reasonably well-defined Chalcolithic or Bronze Ages. Meteoric iron was highly prized by the Aztec, who were even aware of its extraterrestrial origin[100]. However, technologies for smelting iron from ore were never developed at all[101]. The first native metal to be worked in the New World was gold. In 2007, a necklace of cold-hammered gold and turquoise beads was found in a burial at Jiskairumoko, a small site occupied by hunter-gatherers in the Lake Titicaca basin of southeastern Peru. Huts and storage facilities at the site suggest long-term residence for at least part of the year. The necklace dates to around 2155 – 1935 BCE (Late Archaic Period/Early Initial Period), and its presence in a society undergoing a transition to a more sedentary life is a possible indicator that social inequalities were already emerging[102].

The next examples of Andean metalworking do not emerge for another 600 years, by which time more complex societies had emerged: sedentary farmers capable of generating economic surpluses and constructing impressive ceremonial architecture[102]. Several pieces of copper foil and two pieces of gold foil have been recovered from Initial Period (2000 – 900 BCE) contexts at the site of Mina Perdida in Lurin Valley, Peru, dating from 1410 to 1090 BCE. The thin copper foils were made by cold-hammering native copper, in one case with intermediate annealing. The gold foils were found adhering to copper foil substrates, which would have been used for gilding. The copper is thought to be native because it contains traces of arsenic and silver but lacks traces of iron. The former two are commonly found in native copper; the latter is present in smelted copper. The artefacts show that fundamental elements of the Andean metallurgical tradition were in place before the start of the Early Horizon (900 to 200 BCE), though copper smelting was still some centuries off[103].

The first tentative evidence for smelting is copper slag dating to 900 – 700 BCE, from the site of Wankarani in the highlands of Bolivia. Unfortunately, although this discovery was made in the 1970s, very little research has been conducted on the metallurgy at Wankarani, and little is currently known about the type of metal artefacts that were being produced there. To the southwest of Wankarani, in northern Chile, excavations at the site of Ramaditas in the Valley of Guatacondo have revealed slag and sheet copper dating to around 50 BCE. This finding confirmed that Andean metallurgy dates back more than 2,000 years. It also

---

[57] As horrific as a mercury-based elixir sounds, it is surely topped by the radium-based patent medicines that were marketed during the first third of the last century and led to the death of American golfer Eben Byers.

showed that a state-level society or an empire was not a prerequisite for the development of copper smelting technology: Ramaditas is one of several agricultural villages in the Valley of Guatacondo that represent the earliest occupation of the Atacama Desert, but it predates the rise of Tiwanaku in the south Central Andean altiplano[104–106]. Tiwanaku (older spelling Tiahuanaco) was first settled around 400 BCE but did not become a regional power until around 700 CE[107].

Despite these discoveries, our knowledge of pre-Columbian South American metallurgy is limited. The looting of archaeological sites is a pervasive problem[105]. The Conquistadores did document their looting of Inca palaces and exploitation of their mines for gold and silver. Though these records are useful, they contain very little information about the Inca use of copper and its alloys and no information at all about the Andean civilisations that preceded the Inca. Their records do note that between 1545 and 1572 CE, Inca silversmiths used three different types of furnaces: simple pits dug into the ground that reduced ores rich in silver, small charcoal-fired, wind-drafted, and clay-lined reduction furnaces known as *huayrachinas* and a third type known as *tocochimpus*, which were used to refine silver in combination with silver-bearing galena ores[105,108].

A technique that has proved valuable is the geochemical analysis of ice core samples, lake sediments, etc, to look for traces of pollution caused by metal smelting. Results show that smelting technology was well established long before the rise of the Inca. A study based on ice-core records from the Illimani glacier in Bolivia obtained a 6,500-year copper emission record for the Andean altiplano. The earliest pollution caused by copper smelting was associated with the Early Horizon Chavín culture, between 700 and 50 BCE. This was followed by a second peak between 500 and 850 CE, coinciding with the later Moche civilisation, the Tiwanaku empire in the south, and the Wari empire in the north. The latter two have left archaeological evidence for sophisticated copper metallurgy including the use of both arsenical and tin bronze and copper-arsenic-nickel bronze to manufacture needles, knives, tupu pins, broaches, and rings. At Tiwanaku, copper-arsenic-nickel bronze was also used to make architectural I-cramps[109].

These three alloys were the most commonly used bronzes, though bismuth bronze has also been reported from the fifteenth-century CE Inca site of Machu Picchu. A small knife with a handle in the shape of a llama head was recovered at the site in 1912. X-ray spectrophotometry has shown that the average composition of the llama head handle is 73 per cent copper, 18 per cent bismuth, and 9 per cent tin. Bismuth bronze is whiter than tin bronze, which suggests it was chosen for aesthetic reasons[110].

Geochemical analysis has also shown that silver smelting was also practised in pre-Inca times. Cerro Rico de Potosí is a major silver mine supposedly discovered by the Inca emperor Huayna Capac (reigned 1493 – 1527). Analysis of sediment samples taken from a lake 6 km (4 miles) east of Cerro Rico de Potosí revealed a much earlier history of silver smelting activity, beginning shortly after 1000 CE[111].

Metallurgy was a much later development in Mesoamerica. Metal artefacts were first introduced into western Mexico from South America by a maritime route around 650 CE. For 900 years, Mexican metalworkers primarily made ritual and sacred objects. Before 1200 CE, they used copper, mainly for making bells, but also small cold-worked implements. From 1200 to 1300 CE, they made arsenical bronze, tin bronze, and copper-silver alloys, not only for the gold and silver colours that could be produced but also for the improvements these

12: Early metallurgy

alloys offered over copper. Bells, elaborate tweezers, needles, awls, and other tools from this time appear at Mesoamerican sites. Lead isotope data suggests that many of these artefacts were produced in western Mexico[112]. Metal objects were appreciated for their colour and the sounds that could be made with them. Only rarely were metals used to make weapons or heavy-duty tools, and to all intents and purposes the technology of pre-Columbian Mesoamerica remained Stone Age[113].

Epilogue

All the seven metals of antiquity remain important to this day, though to varying degrees. In 2023, worldwide production figures ranged from 18.82 billion tonnes for steel to 1,200 tonnes for mercury. Despite its toxicity and the phasing out of many of its traditional uses (such as in thermometers and fluorescent lighting), mercury continues to find use in instruments where there are no alternatives to its unique set of properties. These include mercury sphygmomanometers (blood pressure meters), which are more accurate than electronic home-use monitors, and do not require periodic recalibration. Another use is in mercury tilt switches.

Though dwarfed by the figures for steel, copper production in 2023 totalled 22 million tonnes. The electrical conductivity of copper is bettered only by silver, and 60 per cent of worldwide production finds its way into wiring. Another 20 per cent is used in plumbing, where it is replacing legacy lead piping. Perhaps surprisingly, lead production still came in at 4.7 million tonnes. The chief use for lead is in lead acid batteries, which remain significantly cheaper than lithium-ion batteries. Lead continues to be used as a roofing material, cladding, flashing, gutters, and gutter joints, and on roof parapets. Tin production, in comparison, was modest at 380,000 tonnes. Tin still finds use in bronzemaking, but the main uses are in solder and the canning industry.

Gold and silver remain the two most important jewellery and monetary metals, but they also have many other uses. Around ten per cent of the 3,100 tonnes of gold mined in 2023 will be used in the electronics industry – but less than half of the 26,000 tonnes of silver mined in 2023 will become jewellery. Silver has innumerable uses in the electronics industry, in engineering, and in medicine. Possibly the most important application for silver now is its use in solar panels as the world faces a race against time to transition to net zero.

References

01: The first hominins

1. Dart, R. Recollections of a reluctant anthropologist. *J. Hum. Evol.* **2**, 417–427 (1973).
2. Keith, A. *An Autobiography*. (Watts and Co., London, 1950).
3. Wheelhouse, F. *Raymond Arthur Dart: A Pictorial Profile*. (Transpareon Press, Hornsby, NSW, 1983).
4. Dart, R. *Adventures with the Missing Link*. (Harper, New York, NY, 1959).
5. Dart, R. Australopithecus africanus: The Man-Ape of South Africa. *Nature* **115**, 195–199 (1925).
6. Tobias, P. The discovery of the Taung skull of Australopithecus africanus Dart and the neglected role of Professor R.B. Young. *Trans. R. Soc. South Afr.* **61**, 131–138 (2006).
7. Keith, A. The Taungs Skull. *Nature* **116**, 11 (1925).
8. Lacruz, R., Rozzi, F. & Bromage, T. Dental enamel hypoplasia, age at death, and weaning in the Taung child : research letter. *South Afr. J. Sci.* **101**, 567–569 (2005).
9. Keith, A. The Fossil Anthropoid Ape from Taungs. *Nature* **115**, 234–236 (1925).
10. Keith, A. The New Missing Link. *Br. Med. J.* **1**, 325–326 (1925).
11. Madison, P. All things bleak and bare beneath a brazen sky: practice and place in the analysis of Australopithecus. *Hist. Philos. Life Sci.* **41**, 19 (2019).
12. Dawson, C. & Woodward, A. On the Discovery of a Palæolithic Human Skull and Mandible in a Flint-bearing Gravel overlying the Wealden (Hastings Beds) at Piltdown, Fletching (Sussex). *Q. J. Geol. Soc.* **69**, 117–123 (1913).
13. Weiner, J., Oakley, K. & Le Gros Clark, W. The Solution of the Piltdown Problem. *Bull. Br. Mus. Nat. Hist. Geol.* **2**, 141–146 (1953).
14. Keith, A. *The Antiquity of Man*. vol. 2 (Williams and Norgate, London, 1925).
15. Gregory, W. Dawn-Man or Ape? *Sci. Am.* **137**, 230–232 (1927).
16. Osborn, H. Recent Discoveries Relating to the Origin and Antiquity of Man. *Science* **65**, 481–488 (1927).
17. Darwin, C. *The Descent of Man, and Selection in Relation to Sex*. (John Murray, London, 1871).
18. Dennell, R. East Asia and human evolution: from cradle of mankind to cul-de-sac. in *East of Africa: Southern Asia, Australia and Modern Human Origins* (eds Dennell, R. & Porr, M.) 8–20 (2014). doi:10.1017/CBO9781139084741.002.
19. Richmond, J. Design and Dissent: Religion, Authority, and the Scientific Spirit of Robert Broom. *Isis* **100**, 485–504 (2009).
20. Gibbard, P. & Head, M. The newly-ratified definition of the Quaternary System/Period and redefinition of the Pleistocene Series/Epoch, and comparison of proposals advanced prior to formal ratification. *Episodes* **33**, 152 (2010).
21. Emiliani, C. *et al.* The Pleistocene Epoch and the Evolution of Man [and Comments and Reply]. *Curr. Anthropol.* **9**, 27–47 (1968).
22. Cita, M. *et al.* The Calabrian Stage redefined. *Episodes* **31**, 408–419 (2008).
23. Broom, R. Some Notes on the Taungs Skull. *Nature* **115**, 569–571 (1925).
24. Keith, A. [Letters to Editor]. *Nature* **116**, 462–463 (1925).
25. Colbert, E. & Morales, M. *Evolution of the Vertebrates: A History of the Backboned Animals Through Time*. (Wiley-Liss, New York, NY, 1991).
26. Hrdlička, A. The Taungs ape. *Am. J. Phys. Anthropol.* **8**, 379–392 (1925).
27. Broom, R. Note on the Milk Dentition of Australopithecus. *Proc. Zool. Soc. Lond.* **99**, 85–88 (1929).
28. Zuckerman, S. Age-changes in the chimpanzee, with special reference to growth of brain, eruption of teeth, and estimation of age; with a note on the Taungs ape. *J. Zool.* **98**, 1–42 (1928).
29. Broom, R. New Fossil Anthropoid Skull from South Africa. *Nature* **138**, 486–488 (1936).
30. Broom, R. The Dentition of Australopithecus. *Nature* **138**, 719–719 (1936).
31. Broom, R. The Pleistocene Anthropoid Apes of South Africa. *Nature* **142**, 377–379 (1938).
32. Gregory, W. & Hellman, M. Fossil Man-Apes of South Africa. *Nature* **143**, 25–26 (1939).
33. Broom, R. & Schepers, G. *The South African Fossil Ape-Man the Australopithecinae*. (Transvaal Museum, Pretoria, 1946).
34. Le Gros Clark, W. Significance of the Australopithecinae. *Nature* **157**, 863–865 (1946).
35. Anonymous. Pan-African Congress on Prehistory. *Nature* **159**, 216–218 (1947).
36. Keith, A. Australopithecinae or Dartians. *Nature* **377** (1947).

37.   Broom, R. Discovery of a New Skull of the South African Ape-man, Plesianthropus. *Nature* **159**, 672–672 (1947).
38.   Broom, R. The Upper Milk Molars of the Ape-man, Plesianthropus. *Nature* **159**, 602–602 (1947).
39.   Broom, R. & Robinson, J. Two Features of the Plesianthropus Skull. *Nature* **159**, 809–810 (1947).
40.   Broom, R. & Robinson, J. Size of the Brain in the Ape-Man, Plesianthropus. *Nature* **161**, 438–438 (1948).
41.   Broom, R. & Robinson, J. Jaw of the Male Sterkfontein Ape-man. *Nature* **160**, 153–153 (1947).
42.   Broom, R. & Robinson, J. Further Remains of the Sterkfontein Ape-man, Plesianthropus. *Nature* **160**, 430–431 (1947).
43.   Broom, R. Jaw of the Ape-Man Paranthropus crassidens. *Nature* **163**, 903–903 (1949).
44.   Broom, R. & Robinson, J. T. Note on the skull of the Swartkrans ape-man Paranthropus crassidens. *Am. J. Phys. Anthropol.* **8**, 295–304 (1950).
45.   Broom, R. & Robinson, J. A New Type of Fossil Man. *Nature* **164**, 322–323 (1949).
46.   Robinson, J. The Nature of Telanthropus capensis. *Nature* **171**, 33–33 (1953).
47.   Klein, R. *The Human Career*. (University of Chicago Press, Chicago, IL, 1999).
48.   Broom, R. The genera and species of the South African fossil ape-men. *Am. J. Phys. Anthropol.* **8**, 1–14 (1950).
49.   Washburn, S. & Patterson, B. Evolutionary Importance of the South African 'Man-apes'. *Nature* **167**, 650–651 (1951).
50.   Watson, D. Robert Broom. 1866-1951. *Obit. Not. Fellows R. Soc.* **8**, 37–70 (1952).
51.   Tobias, P. In memory of Raymond Arthur Dart, FRSSAf. *Trans. R. Soc. South Afr.* **48**, 183–185 (1992).
52.   Leakey, L. A New Fossil Skull From Olduvai. *Nature* **184**, 491–493 (1959).
53.   Robinson, J. The Affinities of the New Olduvai Australopithecine. *Nature* **186**, 456–458 (1960).
54.   Leakey, L., Tobias, P. & Napier, J. A new species of the genus Homo from Olduvai Gorge. *Nature* **202**, 7–9 (1964).
55.   Tobias, P. Homo habilis—A Premature Discovery: Remembered by One of Its Founding Fathers, 42 Years Later. in *The First Humans – Origin and Early Evolution of the Genus Homo: Contributions from the Third Stony Brook Human Evolution Symposium and Workshop October 3 – October 7, 2006* (eds Grine, F., Fleagle, J. & Leakey, R.) 7–15 (Springer Netherlands, Dordrecht, 2009). doi:10.1007/978-1-4020-9980-9_2.
56.   Dennell, R. & Roebroeks, W. An Asian perspective on early human dispersal from Africa. *Nature* **438**, 1099–1104 (2005).
57.   Lieberman, D. Homing in on early Homo. *Nature* **449**, 291–292 (2007).
58.   Spoor, F. *et al.* Reconstructed Homo habilis type OH 7 suggests deep-rooted species diversity in early Homo. *Nature* **519**, 83–86 (2015).
59.   Johanson, D. The paleoanthropology of Hadar, Ethiopia. *Hum. Palaeontol. Prehistory* **16**, 140–154 (2017).
60.   Pattison, K. *Fossil Men*. (William Morrow, New York, NY, 2020).
61.   Johanson, D. & Edey, M. *Lucy, the Beginnings of Humankind*. (Simon & Schuster, London, 1990).
62.   Patterson, C. Age of meteorites and the earth. *Geochim. Cosmochim. Acta* **10**, 230–237 (1956).
63.   Gilbert, W. Garniss Curtis (1919–2012): Dating Our Past. *PLOS Biol.* **11**, e1001650 (2013).
64.   Leakey, L., Evernden, J. & Curtis, G. Age of Bed I, Olduvai Gorge, Tanganyika. *Nature* **191**, 478–479 (1961).
65.   Curtis, G. & Evernden, J. Age of Basalt underlying Bed I, Olduvai. *Nature* **194**, 611–612 (1962).
66.   Leakey, L. Age of Basalt underlying Bed I, Olduvai. *Nature* **194**, 610–611 (1962).
67.   Evernden, J. *et al.* The Potassium-Argon Dating of Late Cenozoic Rocks in East Africa and Italy [and Comments and Reply]. *Curr. Anthropol.* **6**, 342–385 (1965).
68.   Herries, A. *et al.* A Multi-Disciplinary Perspective on the Age of Australopithecus in Southern Africa. in *The Paleobiology of Australopithecus* (eds Reed, K., Fleagle, G. & Leakey, R.) 21–40 (Springer Netherlands, Dordrecht, 2013). doi:10.1007/978-94-007-5919-0_3.
69.   Granger, D. *et al.* New cosmogenic burial ages for Sterkfontein Member 2 Australopithecus and Member 5 Oldowan. *Nature* **522**, 85–88 (2015).
70.   Granger, D. *et al.* Cosmogenic nuclide dating of Australopithecus at Sterkfontein, South Africa. *PNAS* **119**, e2123516119 (2022).
71.   Johanson, D. & Coppens, Y. A preliminary anatomical diagnosis of the first Plio/Pleistocene hominid discoveries in the central Afar, Ethiopia. *Am. J. Phys. Anthropol.* **45**, 217–233 (1976).
72.   Johanson, D. & Taieb, M. Plio—Pleistocene hominid discoveries in Hadar, Ethiopia. *Nature* **260**, 293–297 (1976).
73.   Conroy, G. *Reconstructing Human Origins: A Modern Synthesis*. (W. W. Norton & Company, Inc., New York, NY, 1997).
74.   Johanson, D., White, T. & Coppens, Y. A new species of the genus Australopithecus (Primates: Hominidae) from the Pliocene of eastern Africa. *Kirtlandia* **28**, 1–14 (1978).
75.   Kappelman, J. *et al.* Perimortem fractures in Lucy suggest mortality from fall out of tall tree. *Nature* **537**, 503–507 (2016).
76.   Behrensmeyer, A. Paleoenvironmental context of the Pliocene A.L. 333 "First Family" hominin locality, Hadar Formation, Ethiopia. in *The Geology of Early Humans in the Horn of Africa: Geological Society of America Special Paper 446* (eds Quade, J. & Wynn, J.) 203–214 (The Geological Society of America, Boulder, CO, 2008).
77.   Cameron, D. & Groves, C. *Bones, Stones and Molecules: "Out of Africa" and Human Origins*. (Elsevier Academic Press, London, 2004).
78.   Pettitt, P. *The Palaeolithic Origins of Human Burial*. (Routledge, Abingdon, 2011).

79. Gonçalves, A. & Carvalho, S. Death among primates: a critical review of non-human primate interactions towards their dead and dying. *Biol. Rev.* **94**, 1502–1529 (2019).
80. Simons, E. Ramapithecus. *Sci. Am.* **236**, 28–35 (1977).
81. Pilbeam, D. The Earliest Hominids. *Nature* **219**, 1335–1338 (1968).
82. Sarich, V. & Wilson, A. Immunological time scale for hominid evolution. *Science* **158**, 1200–1203 (1967).
83. Wilson, A. & Sarich, V. A molecular time scale for human evolution. *PNAS* **63**, 1088–1093 (1969).
84. Takahata, N. & Satta, Y. Evolution of the primate lineage leading to modern humans: Phylogenetic and demographic inferences from DNA sequences. *PNAS* **94**, 4811–4815 (1997).
85. Besenbacher, S., Hvilsom, C., Marques-Bonet, T., Mailund, T. & Schierup, M. Direct estimation of mutations in great apes reconciles phylogenetic dating. *Nat. Ecol. Evol.* **3**, 286–292 (2019).
86. Crompton, T. *et al.* Human-like external function of the foot, and fully upright gait, confirmed in the 3.66 million year old Laetoli hominin footprints by topographic statistics, experimental footprint formation and computer simulation. *J. R. Soc. Interface* **9**, 707–719 (2012).
87. Zaitsev, A. *et al.* Was Sadiman volcano a source for the Laetoli Footprint Tuff? *J. Hum. Evol.* **61**, 121–124 (2011).
88. Ward, C., Kimbel, W. & Johanson, D. Complete Fourth Metatarsal and Arches in the Foot of Australopithecus afarensis. *Science* **331**, 750–753 (2011).
89. Raichlen, D., Gordon, A., Harcourt-Smith, W., Foster, A. & Haas, W. Laetoli Footprints Preserve Earliest Direct Evidence of Human-Like Bipedal Biomechanics. *PLOS ONE* **5**, e9769 (2010).
90. Leakey, M., Feibel, C., McDougall, I. & Walker, A. New four-million-year-old hominid species from Kanapoi and Allia Bay, Kenya. *Nature* **376**, 565–571 (1995).
91. Asfaw, B. *et al.* Australopithecus garhi: A New Species of Early Hominid from Ethiopia. *Science* **284**, 629–635 (1999).
92. Haile-Selassie, Y. *et al.* New species from Ethiopia further expands Middle Pliocene hominin diversity. *Nature* **521**, 483–488 (2015).
93. Brunet, M. *et al.* The first australopithecine 2,500 kilometres west of the Rift Valley (Chad). *Nature* **378**, 273–275 (1995).
94. Berger, L. *et al.* Australopithecus sediba: A New Species of Homo-Like Australopith from South Africa. *Science* **328**, 195–204 (2010).
95. Haile-Selassie, Y. Phylogeny of early Australopithecus: New fossil evidence from the Woranso-Mille (central Afar, Ethiopia). *Philos. Trans. R. Soc. Lond. B. Biol. Sci.* **365**, 3323–31 (2010).
96. Pickering, R. *et al.* Australopithecus sediba at 1.977 Ma and Implications for the Origins of the Genus Homo. *Science* **333**, 1421–1423 (2011).
97. White, T., Suwa, G. & Asfaw, B. Australopithecus ramidus, a new species of early hominid from Aramis, Ethiopia. *Nature* **371**, 306–312 (1994).
98. Haile-Selassie, Y. Late Miocene hominids from the Middle Awash, Ethiopia. *Nature* **412**, 178–181 (2001).
99. Diamond, J. *The Third Chimpanzee*. (Random, London, 1991).
100. De Waal, F. & Lanting, F. *Bonobo: The Forgotten Ape*. (University of California Press, Berkley & Los Angeles, CA, 1997).
101. Isbell, A. & Young, T. The evolution of bipedalism in hominids and reduced group size in chimpanzees: alternative responses to decreasing resource availability. *J. Hum. Evol.* **30**, 389–397 (1996).
102. McHenry, H. How Big Were Early Hominids? *Evol. Anthropol.* **1**, 15–20 (1992).
103. Pickford, M. & Senut, B. The geological and faunal context of Late Miocene hominid remains from Lukeino, Kenya. *Comptes Rendus L'Académie Sci.* **332**, 145–152 (2001).
104. Senut, B. *et al.* First hominid from the Miocene (Lukeino Formation, Kenya). *Comptes Rendus L'Académie Sci.* **332**, 137–144 (2001).
105. Galik, K. *et al.* External and Internal Morphology of the BAR 1002'00 Orrorin tugenensis Femur. *Science* **305**, 1450–1453 (2004).
106. Strait, D., Grine, F. & Moniz, M. A reappraisal of early hominid phylogeny. *J. Hum. Evol.* **32**, 17–82 (1997).
107. Strait, D. Integration, phylogeny, and the hominid cranial base. *Am. J. Phys. Anthropol.* **114**, 273–297 (2001).
108. Strait, D. & Grine, F. Inferring hominoid and early hominid phylogeny using craniodental characters: the role of fossil taxa. *J. Hum. Evol.* **47**, 399–452 (2004).
109. Gibbons, A. Oldest Human Femur Wades into Controversy. *Science* **305**, 1885 (2004).
110. Ohman, J., Lovejoy, O. & White, T. Questions about Orrorin femur. *Science* **307**, 845 (2005).
111. Richmond, B. & Jungers, W. Orrorin tugenensis Femoral Morphology and the Evolution of Hominin Bipedalism. *Science* **319**, 1662–1665 (2008).
112. Mongle, C., Strait, D. & Grine, F. Expanded character sampling underscores phylogenetic stability of Ardipithecus ramidus as a basal hominin. *J. Hum. Evol.* **131**, 28–39 (2019).
113. Brunet, M. *et al.* A new hominid from the Upper Miocene of Chad, Central Africa. *Nature* **418**, 145–151 (2002).
114. Vignaud, P. *et al.* Geology and palaeontology of the Upper Miocene Toros-Menalla hominid locality, Chad. *Nature* **418**, 152–155 (2002).
115. Brunet, M. *et al.* New material of the earliest hominid from the Upper Miocene of Chad. *Nature* **434**, 752–755 (2005).
116. Lebatard, A. *et al.* Cosmogenic nuclide dating of Sahelanthropus tchadensis and Australopithecus bahrelghazali: Mio-Pliocene hominids from Chad. *PNAS* **105**, 3226–3231 (2008).

117. Beauvilain, A. The contexts of discovery of Australopithecus bahrelghazali (Abel) and of Sahelanthropus tchadensis (Toumaï): unearthed, embedded in sandstone, or surface collected?: commentary. *South Afr. J. Sci.* **104**, 165–168 (2008).

118. Patterson, N., Richter, D., Gnerre, S., Lander, E. & Reich, D. Genetic evidence for complex speciation of humans and chimpanzees. *Nature* **441**, 1103–1108 (2006).

119. Zollikofer, C. *et al.* Virtual cranial reconstruction of Sahelanthropus tchadensis. *Nature* **434**, 755–758 (2005).

120. Guy, F. *et al.* Morphological affinities of the Sahelanthropus tchadensis (Late Miocene hominid from Chad) cranium. *PNAS* **102**, 18836–18841 (2005).

121. Wolpoff, M., Hawks, J., Senut, B., Pickford, M. & Ahern, J. An Ape or the Ape: Is the Toumaï Cranium TM 266 a Hominid? *PaleoAnthropology* 36–50 (2006).

122. Macchiarelli, R., Bergeret-Medina, A., Marchi, D. & Wood, B. Nature and relationships of Sahelanthropus tchadensis. *J. Hum. Evol.* **149**, 102898 (2020).

123. Daver, G. *et al.* Postcranial evidence of late Miocene hominin bipedalism in Chad. *Nature* **609**, 94–100 (2022).

124. Aiello, L. & Collard, M. Our Newest Oldest Ancestor. *Nature* **410**, 526–527 (2001).

125. Wood, B. & Harrison, T. The evolutionary context of the first hominins. *Nature* **470**, 347–352 (2011).

126. Haile-Selassie, Y., Suwa, G. & White, T. Late Miocene Teeth from Middle Awash, Ethiopia, and Early Hominid Dental Evolution. *Science* **303**, 1503–1505 (2004).

127. France-Lanord, C. & Derry, L. France-Lanord, C. & Derry, L. A. Organic carbon burial forcing of the carbon cycle from Himalayan erosion. Nature 390, 65-67. *Nature* **390**, 65–67 (1997).

128. Wilson, R., Drury, S. & Chapman, J. *The Great Ice Age.* (Routledge, London, 2000).

129. Kürschner, W., Kvaček, Z. & Dilcher, D. The impact of Miocene atmospheric carbon dioxide fluctuations on climate and the evolution of terrestrial ecosystems. *PNAS* **105**, 449–453 (2008).

130. Lewin, R. & Foley, R. *Principles of Human Evolution.* (Blackwell Publishing, Oxford, 2004).

131. Sepulchre, P. *et al.* Tectonic Uplift and Eastern Africa Aridification. *Science* **313**, 1419–1423 (2006).

132. Maslin, M. *et al.* East African climate pulses and early human evolution. *Quat. Sci. Rev.* **101**, 1–17 (2014).

133. Richmond, B. & Strait, D. Evidence that humans evolved from a knuckle-walking ancestor. *Nature* **404**, 382–385 (2000).

134. Wheeler, P. The Evolution of Bipedality and Loss of Functional Body Hair in Hominoids. *J. Hum. Evol.* **13**, 91–98 (1984).

135. White, T. *et al.* Macrovertebrate Paleontology and the Pliocene Habitat of Ardipithecus ramidus. *Science* **326**, 87–93 (2009).

136. White, T. *et al.* Ardipithecus ramidus and the Paleobiology of Early Hominids. *Science* **326**, 75–86 (2009).

137. Richmond, B., Begin, D. & Strait, D. Origin of Human Bipedalism: The Knuckle-Walking Hypothesis Revisited. *Yearb. Phys. Anthropol.* **116**, 70–105 (2001).

138. Rodman, P. & McHenry, H. Biogenetics and the Origin of Hominid Bipedalism. *Am. J. Phys. Anthropol.* **52**, 103–106 (1980).

139. Steudel, K. Limb morphology, bipedal gait, and the energetics of hominid locomotion. *Am. J. Phys. Anthropol.* **99**, 345–355 (1996).

140. Lovejoy, O. The Origins of Man. *Science* **211**, 341–350 (1981).

141. Suwa, G. *et al.* The Ardipithecus ramidus Skull and Its Implications for Hominid Origins. *Science* **326**, 68 (2009).

142. Lovejoy, O., Latimer, B., Suwa, G., Asfaw, B. & White, T. Combining Prehension and Propulsion: The Foot of Ardipithecus ramidus. *Science* **326**, 72e1-72e8 (2009).

143. Lovejoy, O., Suwa, G., Simpson, S., Matternes, J. & White, T. The Great Divides: Ardipithecus ramidus Reveals the Postcrania of Our Last Common Ancestors with African Apes. *Science* **326**, 100–106 (2009).

144. Lovejoy, O., Suwa, G., Spurlock, L., Asfaw, B. & White, T. The Pelvis and Femur of Ardipithecus ramidus: The Emergence of Upright Walking. *Science* **326**, 71 (2009).

145. Lovejoy, O., Simpson, S., White, T., Asfaw, B. & Suwa, G. Careful Climbing in the Miocene: The Forelimbs of Ardipithecus ramidus and Humans Are Primitive. *Science* **326**, 70e1-70e8 (2009).

146. White, T., Lovejoy, O., Asfaw, B., Carlson, J. & Suwa, G. Neither chimpanzee nor human, Ardipithecus reveals the surprising ancestry of both. *PNAS* **112**, 4877–4884 (2015).

147. Suwa, G. *et al.* Paleobiological Implications of the Ardipithecus ramidus Dentition. *Science* **326**, 94–99 (2009).

148. Reno, P., Meindl, R., McCollum, M. & Lovejoy, O. Sexual dimorphism in Australopithecus afarensis was similar to that of modern humans. *PNAS* **500**, 9404–9409 (2003).

149. Tavaré, S., Marshall, C., Will, O., Soligo, C. & Martin, R. Using the fossil record to estimate the age of the last common ancestor of extant primates. *Nature* **416**, 726–729 (2002).

150. Hughes, J. *et al.* Conservation of Y-linked genes during human evolution revealed by comparative sequencing in chimpanzee. *Nature* **437**, 101–104 (2005).

151. Hughes, J. *et al.* Chimpanzee and human Y chromosomes are remarkably divergent in structure and gene content. *Nature* **463**, 536–539 (2010).

02: *Homo erectus*

1. Hrdlička, A. Dr. Eugene Dubois, 1858-1940. *Sci. Mon.* **52**, 578–580 (1941).
2. Keith, A. Dr. Eugene Dubois. *Nature* **147**, 473–474 (1941).
3. Keith, A. The creeds of two anthropologists. in *The Rationalist Annual* (C. A. Watts & Co. Ltd., London, 1942).
4. Shipman, P. *The Man Who Found the Missing Link: The Extraordinary Life of Eugene Dubois: The Life and Times of Eugene Dubois.* (Simon & Schuster, New York, NY, 2001).
5. Curtis, G., Swisher, C. & Lewin, R. *Java Man.* (Little, Brown and Company, New York, NY, 2000).
6. Shipman, P. & Storm, P. Missing Links: Eugène Dubois and the Origins of Paleoanthropology. *Evol. Anthropol. Issues News Rev.* **11**, 108–116 (2002).
7. Darwin, C. *The Descent of Man, and Selection in Relation to Sex.* (John Murray, London, 1871).
8. Haeckel, E. *The History of Creation (English Translation).* vol. 2 (D. Appleton & Co, New York, NY, 1880).
9. Wilson, A. & Sarich, V. A molecular time scale for human evolution. *PNAS* **63**, 1088–1093 (1969).
10. White, T. *et al.* Ardipithecus ramidus and the Paleobiology of Early Hominids. *Science* **326**, 75–86 (2009).
11. Klein, R. *The Human Career.* (University of Chicago Press, Chicago, IL, 1999).
12. Dennell, R. East Asia and human evolution: from cradle of mankind to cul-de-sac. in *East of Africa: Southern Asia, Australia and Modern Human Origins* (eds Dennell, R. & Porr, M.) 8–20 (2014). doi:10.1017/CBO9781139084741.002.
13. Dubois, E. *Pithecanthropus Erectus. Eine Menschenaehnliche Uebergangsform Aus Java.* (G.E. Stechert (Alfred Hafner), New York, 1894).
14. Lydekker, R. Pithecanthropus Erectus, eine Menschenaehnliche Uebergangsform aus Java. *Nature* **51**, 291–291 (1895).
15. Jacob, T. *et al.* Pygmoid Australomelanesian Homo sapiens skeletal remains from Liang Bua, Flores: Population affinities and pathological abnormalities. *PNAS* **103**, 13421–13426 (2006).
16. Cunningham, D. Dr. Dubois' So-Called Missing Link. *Nature* **51**, 428–429 (1895).
17. Keith, A. Pithecanthropus erectus- a brief review of human fossil remains. *Sci. Prog. 1894-1898* **3**, 348–369 (1895).
18. Turner, W. On M. Dubois' Description of remains recently found in Java, named by him Pithecanthropus erectus. With Remarks on so-called Transitional Forms between Apes and Man. *Proc. R. Soc. Edinb.* **20**, 422–436 (1895).
19. Haeckel, E. On our present knowledge of the origin of man. Translation of a discourse given at the Fourth International Congress of Zoologists at Cambridge, England, August 26, 1898. *Annu. Rep. Smithson. Inst. 1898* 460–481 (1899).
20. Manouvrier, L. Discussion sur le 'pithecanthropus erectus' comme précurseur présumé de l'homme. *Bull. Mém. Société Anthropol. Paris* **6**, 12–47 (1895).
21. Marsh, O. Pithecanthropus erectus, from the Tertiary of Java. *Am. J. Sci.* **s4-1**, 475 (1896).
22. Dubois, E. On Pithecanthropus Erectus: A Transitional form Between Man and the Apes. *J. Anthropol. Inst. G. B. Irel.* **25**, 240–255 (1896).
23. Schwalbe, G. Studien über Pithecanthropus erectus Dubois. *Z. Für Morphol. Anthropol.* **1**, 16–240 (1899).
24. Schwalbe, G. Ziele und Wege einer vergleichenden physischen Anthropologie. *Z. Für Morphol. Anthropol.* **1**, 1–15 (1899).
25. Hrdlička, A. New Casts of the Pithecanthropus Remains. *Science* **60**, 200–200 (1924).
26. Black, D. Tertiary Man in Asia--The Chou Kou Tien Discovery. *Science* **64**, 586–587 (1926).
27. Elliot Smith, G. Sinanthropus--Peking Man its Discovery and Significance. *Sci. Mon.* **33**, 193–211 (1931).
28. Black, D. On a lower molar hominid tooth from the Chou Kou Tien deposit. *Palaeontol. Sin. Ser. D* **7**, 1–28 (1927).
29. Zuckerman, S. Sinanthropus and other fossil men: Their relations to each other and to modern types. *Eugen. Rev.* **24**, 273–284 (1933).
30. Black, D. Discovery of Further Hominid Remains of Lower Quaternary Age from the Chou Kou Tien Deposit. *Science* **67**, 135–136 (1928).
31. Black, D. Discovery of Skull of Adult Sinanthropus at Chou Kou Tien. *Anthropol. Anz.* **6**, 358–359 (1930).
32. Weidenreich, F. The Sinanthropus Population of Choukoutien (Locality 1) with a Preliminary Report on New Discoveries. *Bull. Geol. Soc. China* **14**, 427–468 (1935).
33. Weidenreich, F. The New Discoveries of Sinanthropus pekinensis and Their Bearing on the Sinanthropus and Pithecanthropus Problems. *Bull. Geol. Soc. China* **16**, 439–470 (1937).
34. De Chardin, T. Sinanthropus Pekinensis. *Primit. Man* **3**, 46–48 (1930).
35. Dubois, E. On the gibbon-like appearance of Pithecanthropus erectus. *Verh. Koninklikje Akad. Van Wet. Te Amst.* **38**, 578–585 (1935).
36. Dubois, E. On the Fossil Human Skulls Recently Discovered in Java and Pithecanthropus Erectus. *Man* **37**, 1–7 (1937).
37. Coqueugniot, H., Hublin, J., Veillon, F., Houet, F. & Jacob, T. Early brain growth in Homo erectus and implications for cognitive ability. *Nature* **431**, 299–302 (2004).
38. Von Koenigswald, R., Bandoeng & Weidenreich, F. The Relationship between Pithecanthropus and Sinanthropus. *Nature* **144**, 926–929 (1939).
39. Dubois, E. The fossil human remains discovered in Java by Dr. G. H. R. von Koenigswald and attributed by him to Pithecanthropus erectus, in reality remains of Homo wadjakensis. *Proc K. Akad Wet.* **43**, 494–496 (1940).

40. Dubois, E. The fossil human remains discovered in Java by Dr. G. H. R. von Koenigswald and attributed by him to Pithecanthropus erectus, in reality remains of Homo soloensis, continuation. *Proc K. Akad Wet.* **43**, 842–851 (1940).

41. Dubois, E. The fossil human remains discovered in Java by Dr. G. H. R. von Koenigswald and attributed by him to Pithecanthropus erectus, in reality remains of Homo sapiens soloensis, conclusion. *Proc K. Akad Wet.* **43**, 1268–1275 (1940).

42. Xing, S. *et al.* Middle Pleistocene Hominin Teeth from Longtan Cave, Hexian, China. *PLOS ONE* **9**, e114265 (2014).

43. Chang, C. *et al.* The first archaic Homo from Taiwan. *Nat. Commun.* **6**, 6037 (2015).

44. Berger, L., Liu, W. & Wu, X. Investigation of a credible report by a US Marine on the location of the missing Peking Man fossils. *South Afr. J. Sci.* **108**, 6–8 (2012).

45. Dennell, R., Corbey, R. & Roebroeks, W. From Sangiran to Olduvai, 1937-1960: The quest for 'centres' of hominid origins in Asia and Africa. in *Studying Human Origins: Disciplinary History and Epistemology* 45–66 (Amsterdam University Press, Amsterdam, 2001).

46. Dart, R. Australopithecus africanus: The Man-Ape of South Africa. *Nature* **115**, 195–199 (1925).

47. Broom, R. & Schepers, G. *The South African Fossil Ape-Man the Australopithecinae.* (Transvaal Museum, Pretoria, 1946).

48. Keith, A. Australopithecinae or Dartians. *Nature* 377 (1947).

49. Weiner, J., Oakley, K. & Le Gros Clark, W. The Solution of the Piltdown Problem. *Bull. Br. Mus. Nat. Hist. Geol.* **2**, 141–146 (1953).

50. Leakey, L. A New Fossil Skull From Olduvai. *Nature* **184**, 491–493 (1959).

51. Leakey, L., Tobias, P. & Napier, J. A new species of the genus Homo from Olduvai Gorge. *Nature* **202**, 7–9 (1964).

52. Tobias, P. Homo habilis—A Premature Discovery: Remembered by One of Its Founding Fathers, 42 Years Later. in *The First Humans – Origin and Early Evolution of the Genus Homo: Contributions from the Third Stony Brook Human Evolution Symposium and Workshop October 3 – October 7, 2006* (eds Grine, F., Fleagle, J. & Leakey, R.) 7–15 (Springer Netherlands, Dordrecht, 2009). doi:10.1007/978-1-4020-9980-9_2.

53. Swisher, C. *et al.* Age of the earliest known hominids in Java, Indonesia. *Science* **263**, 1118–1121 (1994).

54. Morwood, M., O'Sullivan, P., Susanto, E. & Aziz, F. Revised age for Mojokerto 1, an early Homo erectus cranium from East Java, Indonesia. *Aust. Archaeol.* **57**, 1–4 (2003).

55. Larick, R. *et al.* Early Pleistocene 40Ar-39Ar ages for Bapang Formation hominins, Central Java, Indonesia. *PNAS* **98**, 4866–4871 (2001).

56. Matsu'ura, S. *et al.* Age control of the first appearance datum for Javanese Homo erectus in the Sangiran area. *Science* **367**, 210–214 (2020).

57. Broom, R. & Robinson, J. A New Type of Fossil Man. *Nature* **164**, 322–323 (1949).

58. Robinson, J. The Nature of Telanthropus capensis. *Nature* **171**, 33–33 (1953).

59. Arambourg, C. A recent discovery in human paleontology: Atlanthropus of ternifine (Algeria). *Am. J. Phys. Anthropol.* **13**, 191–201 (1955).

60. Geraads, D. *et al.* The Pleistocene hominid site of Ternifine, Algeria: New results on the environment, age, and human industries. *Quat. Res.* **25**, 380–386 (1986).

61. Bermúdez de Castro, J., Martinón-Torres, M., Gómez-Robles, A. & Prado et S. Sarmiento, L. Comparative analysis of the Gran Dolina-TD6 (Spain) and Tighennif (Algeria) hominin mandibles. *Bull. Mém. Société D'Anthropologie Paris* **19**, 150–167 (2007).

62. Ni, X. *et al.* Massive cranium from Harbin in northeastern China establishes a new Middle Pleistocene human lineage. *The Innovation* **2**, 100130 (2021).

63. Arambourg, C. & Biberson, P. The fossil human remains from the Paleolithic site of Sidi Abderrahman (Morocco). *Am. J. Phys. Anthropol.* **14**, 467–489 (1956).

64. Leakey, L. New Finds at Olduvai Gorge. *Nature* **189**, 649–650 (1961).

65. Groves, C. *A Theory of Human and Primate Evolution.* (Oxford University Press, Oxford, 1989).

66. Larick, R. & Ciochon, R. The African Emergence and Early Asian Dispersals of the Genus Homo. *Am. Sci. - AMER SCI* **84**, 538–551 (1996).

67. Cameron, D. & Groves, C. *Bones, Stones and Molecules: "Out of Africa" and Human Origins.* (Elsevier Academic Press, London, 2004).

68. Wood, B. Reconstructing human evolution: Achievements, challenges, and opportunities. *PNAS* **107**, 8902–8909 (2010).

69. Spoor, F. *et al.* Implications of new early Homo fossils from Ileret, east of Lake Turkana, Kenya. *Nature* **448**, 688–691 (2007).

70. Rightmire, P. Human Evolution in the Middle Pleistocene: The Role of Homo heidelbergensis. *Evol. Anthropol.* **6**, 218–227 (1998).

71. Klein, R. Hominin Dispersals in the Old World. in *The human past* (ed. Scarre, C.) 84–123 (Thames & Hudson, London, 2013).

72. Brown, F., Harris, J., Leakey, R. & Walker, A. Early Homo erectus skeleton from west Lake Turkana, Kenya. *Nature* **316**, 788–792 (1985).

73. Bennett, M. *et al.* Early Hominin Foot Morphology Based on 1.5-Million-Year-Old Footprints from Ileret, Kenya. *Science* **323**, 1197–1201 (2009).

74. Hatala, K. *et al.* Footprints reveal direct evidence of group behavior and locomotion in Homo erectus. *Sci. Rep.* **6**, 28766 (2016).

75. Smith, H. Dental development as a Measure of Life History in Primates. *Evolution* **43**, 683–688 (1989).

76. Risnes, S. Growth tracks in dental enamel. *J. Hum. Evol.* **35**, 331–350 (1998).

77. Smith, T. Experimental determination of the periodicity of incremental features in enamel. *J. Anat.* **208**, 99–113 (2006).

78. Smith, T. *et al.* Earliest evidence of modern human life history in North African early Homo sapiens. *PNAS* **104**, 6128–6133 (2007).

79. Dean, C. *et al.* Growth processes in teeth distinguish modern humans from Homo erectus and earlier hominins. *Nature* **414**, 628–631 (2001).

80. Ruff, C. & Walker, A. Body size and body shape. in *The Nariokotome Homo erectus Skeleton* (eds Walker, A. & Leakey, R.) 234–265 (Harvard University Press, Cambridge, MA, 1993).

81. Graves, R., Lupo, A., McCarthy, R., Wescott, D. & Cunningham, D. Just how strapping was KNM-WT 15000? *J. Hum. Evol.* **59**, 542–554 (2010).

82. Ruff, C. & Burgess, L. How much more would KNM-WT 15000 have grown? *J. Hum. Evol.* **80**, 74–82 (2015).

83. Gabunia, L. *et al.* Earliest Pleistocene Hominid Cranial Remains from Dmanisi,Republic of Georgia: Taxonomy, Geological Setting, and Age. *Science* **228**, 1019–1025 (2000).

84. Gabunia, L. & Vekua, A. A Plio-Pleistocene hominid from Dmanisi, East Georgia, Caucasus. *Nature* **373**, 509–512 (1995).

85. Vekua, A. *et al.* A New Skull of Early Homo from Dmanisi, Georgia. *Science* **297**, 85–89 (2002).

86. Lordkipanidze, D. *et al.* Postcranial evidence from early Homo from Dmanisi, Georgia. *Nature* **449**, 305–310 (2007).

87. Lordkipanidze, D. *et al.* A Fourth Hominin Skull From Dmanisi, Georgia. *Anat. Rec. A. Discov. Mol. Cell. Evol. Biol.* **288A**, 1146–1157 (2006).

88. Lordkipanidze, D. *et al.* A Complete Skull from Dmanisi, Georgia, and the Evolutionary Biology of Early Homo. *Science* **342**, 326–331 (2013).

89. Lordkipanidze, D. *et al.* The earliest toothless hominin skull. *Nature* **434**, 717–718 (2005).

90. Ferring, R. *et al.* Earliest human occupations at Dmanisi (Georgian Caucasus) dated to 1.85–1.78 Ma. *PNAS* **108**, 10432–10436 (2011).

91. Gabunia, L., de Lumley, M., Vekua, A., Lordkipanidze, D. & de Lumley, H. Découverte d'un nouvel hominidé à Dmanissi (Transcaucasie, Géorgie). *CR Palévol* **1**, 243–253 (2002).

92. Lieberman, D. Homing in on early Homo. *Nature* **449**, 291–292 (2007).

93. Zhu, Z. *et al.* New dating of the Homo erectus cranium from Lantian (Gongwangling), China. *J. Hum. Evol.* **78**, 144–157 (2015).

94. Zhu, R. *et al.* Earliest presence of humans in northeast Asia. *Nature* **413**, 413–417 (2001).

95. Zhu, R. *et al.* New evidence on the earliest human presence at high northern latitudes in northeast Asia. *Nature* **431**, 559–562 (2004).

96. Zhu, Z. *et al.* Hominin occupation of the Chinese Loess Plateau since about 2.1 million years ago. *Nature* **559**, 608–612 (2018).

97. Harmand, S. *et al.* 3.3-million-year-old stone tools from Lomekwi 3, West Turkana, Kenya. *Nature* **521**, 310–315 (2015).

98. Dennell, R. & Roebroeks, W. An Asian perspective on early human dispersal from Africa. *Nature* **438**, 1099–1104 (2005).

99. Asfaw, B. *et al.* Remains of Homo erectus from Bouri, Middle Awash, Ethiopia. *Nature* **416**, 317–320 (2002).

100. Swisher, C. *et al.* Latest Homo erectus of Java: Potential Contemporaneity with Homo sapiens in Southeast Asia. *Science* **274**, 1870–1874 (1996).

101. Indriati, E. *et al.* The Age of the 20 Meter Solo River Terrace, Java, Indonesia and the Survival of Homo erectus in Asia. *PLOS ONE* **6**, e21562 (2011).

102. Rizal, Y. *et al.* Last appearance of Homo erectus at Ngandong, Java, 117,000–108,000 years ago. *Nature* **577**, 381–385 (2020).

103. Curnoe, D. *et al.* Human Remains from the Pleistocene-Holocene Transition of Southwest China Suggest a Complex Evolutionary History for East Asians. *PLOS ONE* **7**, e31918 (2012).

104. Curnoe, D., Ji, X., Taçon, P. & Yaozheng, G. Possible Signatures of Hominin Hybridization from the Early Holocene of Southwest China. *Sci. Rep.* **5**, 12408 (2015).

105. Slon, V. *et al.* The genome of the offspring of a Neanderthal mother and a Denisovan father. *Nature* **561**, 113–116 (2018).

106. Curnoe, D. *et al.* A Hominin Femur with Archaic Affinities from the Late Pleistocene of Southwest China. *PLOS ONE* **10**, e0143332 (2015).

107. Liao, W. *et al.* Mosaic dental morphology in a terminal Pleistocene hominin from Dushan Cave in southern China. *Sci. Rep.* **9**, 2347 (2019).

108. Aiello, L. & Collard, M. Our Newest Oldest Ancestor. *Nature* **410**, 526–527 (2001).

109. Keith, A. *A New Theory of Human Evolution*. (Watts and Co., London, 1948).

110. Johanson, D. *et al.* New partial skeleton of Homo habilis from Olduvai Gorge, Tanzania. *Nature* **327**, 205–209 (1987).
111. Ruff, C. Relative Limb Strength and Locomotion in Homo habilis. *Am. J. Phys. Anthropol.* **138**, 90–100 (2009).
112. Richmond, B., Aiello, L. & Wood, B. Early hominin limb proportions. *J. Hum. Evol.* **43**, 529–548 (2002).
113. Haeusler, M. & McHenry, H. Body proportions of Homo habilis reviewed. *J. Hum. Evol.* **46**, 433–465 (2004).
114. Conroy, G. *Reconstructing Human Origins: A Modern Synthesis.* (W. W. Norton & Company, Inc., New York, NY, 1997).
115. Strait, D. & Grine, F. Inferring hominoid and early hominid phylogeny using craniodental characters: the role of fossil taxa. *J. Hum. Evol.* **47**, 399–452 (2004).
116. Gonzalez-Jose, R., Escapa, I., Neves, W., Cuneo, R. & Pucciarelli, H. Cladistic analysis of continuous modularized traits provides phylogenetic signals in Homo evolution. *Nature* **453**, 775–779 (2008).
117. Tobias, P. Hominid Evolution in Africa. *Can. J. Anthropol.* **3**, 163–190 (1983).
118. McHenry, H. How Big Were Early Hominids? *Evol. Anthropol.* **1**, 15–20 (1992).
119. McDougall, I. *et al.* New single crystal 40Ar/39Ar ages improve time scale for deposition of the Omo Group, Omo–Turkana Basin, East Africa. *J. Geol. Soc.* **169**, 213–226 (2012).
120. Antón, S., Potts, R. & Aiello, L. Evolution of early Homo: An integrated biological perspective. *Science* **345**, 45 (2014).
121. Leakey, M. *et al.* New fossils from Koobi Fora in northern Kenya confirm taxonomic diversity in early Homo. *Nature* **488**, 201–204 (2012).
122. Spoor, F. *et al.* Reconstructed Homo habilis type OH 7 suggests deep-rooted species diversity in early Homo. *Nature* **519**, 83–86 (2015).
123. Kimbel, W., Johanson, D. & Rak, Y. Systematic Assessment of a Maxilla of Homo From Hadar, Ethiopia. *Am. J. Phys. Anthropol.* **103**, 235–262 (1997).
124. Gathago, P. & Brown, F. Revised stratigraphy of Area 123, Koobi Fora, Kenya, and new age estimates of its fossil mammals, including hominins. *J. Hum. Evol.* **51**, 471–479 (2006).
125. Herries, A., Martin, J., Leece, A., Adams, J. & Boschian, G. Contemporaneity of Australopithecus, Paranthropus, and early Homo erectus in South Africa. *Science* **368**, 47, eaaw7293 (2020).
126. Spoor, F. Small-brained and big-mouthed. *Nature* **502**, 452–453 (2013).
127. Sanchez-Yustos, P. *et al.* The origin of the Acheulean. Technofunctional study of the FLKWlithic record (Olduvai, Tanzania). *PLOS ONE* **12**, e0179212 (2017).
128. Mithen, S. *The Prehistory of the Mind.* (Thames & Hudson, London, 1996).
129. Joordens, J. *et al.* Homo erectus at Trinil on Java used shells for tool production and engraving. *Nature* **518**, 228–231 (2015).
130. MacLarnon, A. & Hewitt, G. The Evolution of Human Speech: The Role of Enhanced Breathing Control. *Am. J. Phys. Anthropol.* **109**, 341–363 (1999).
131. Wrangham, R. *Catching Fire: How Cooking Made Us Human.* (Basic Books, New York, NY, 2009).
132. Pickering, T. What's new is old: Comments on (more) archaeological evidence of one-million-year-old fire from South Africa. *South Afr. J. Sci.* **108**, 1–2 (2012).
133. Brain, C. & Sillen, A. Evidence from the Swartkrans cave for the earliest use of fire. *Nature* **336**, 464–466 (1988).
134. Berna, F. *et al.* Microstratigraphic evidence of in situ fire in the Acheulean strata of Wonderwerk Cave, Northern Cape province, South Africa. *PNAS* **109**, E1215–E1220 (2012).
135. Roebroeks, W. & Villa, P. On the earliest evidence for habitual use of fire in Europe. *PNAS* **108**, 5209–5214 (2011).
136. Weiner, S., Xu, Q., Goldberg, P., Liu, J. & Bar-Yosef, O. Evidence for the Use of Fire at Zhoukoudian, China. *Science* **281**, 251–253 (1998).
137. Goren-Inbar, N. *et al.* Evidence of Hominin Control of Fire at Gesher Benot Ya'aqov, Israel. *Science* **304**, 725–727 (2004).
138. Brittingham, A. *et al.* Geochemical Evidence for the Control of Fire by Middle Palaeolithic Hominins. *Sci. Rep.* **9**, 15368 (2019).
139. Zink, K. & Lieberman, D. Impact of meat and Lower Palaeolithic food processing techniques on chewing in humans. *Nature* **531**, 500–503 (2016).
140. Wood, B. Fifty years after Homo habilis. *Nature* **508**, 31–33 (2014).
141. DiMaggio, E. *et al.* Late Pliocene fossiliferous sedimentary record and the environmental context of early Homo from Afar, Ethiopia. *Science* **347**, 1355–1359 (2015).
142. Villmoare, B. *et al.* Early Homo at 2.8 Ma from Ledi-Geraru, Afar, Ethiopia. *Science* **347**, 1352–1355 (2015).
143. Langbroek, M. My Asteroid Discoveries. *Dr Marco Langbroek - Spy satellites, Archaeology, Asteroids, Meteorites* https://langbrom.home.xs4all.nl/asteroid.html (2015).
144. Anonymous. *Minor Planet Circ.* (2009).

03: The Acheulean hand axe

1. Lepre, C. *et al.* An earlier origin for the Acheulian. *Nature* **477**, 82–85 (2011).
2. Key, A., Jarić, I. & Roberts, D. Modelling the end of the Acheulean at global and continental levels suggests widespread persistence into the Middle Palaeolithic. *Humanit. Soc. Sci. Commun.* **8**, 55 (2021).
3. Frere, J. Account of Flint Weapons discovered at Hoxne in Suffolk. *Archaeologia* **13**, 204–205 (1800).
4. Wylmer, J. The Lower Palaeolithic site at Hoxne. *Suffolk Inst. Archaeol. Hist.* **25/3**, 169–189 (1983).
5. Turner, R. & Wymer, J. J. An Assemblage of Palaeolithic Hand-Axes from the Roman Religious Complex at Ivy Chimneys, Witham, Essex. *Antiqu. J.* **67**, 43–60 (1987).
6. Proctor, R. Three Roots of Human Recency: Molecular Anthropology, the Refigured Acheulean, and the UNESCO Response to Auschwitz. *Curr. Anthropol.* **44**, 213–239 (2003).
7. Cockburn, J., King, H. & McDonnell, K. *A History of the County of Middlesex.* vol. 1 (Victoria County History, London, 1969).
8. Heizer, R. The Background of Thomsen's Three-Age System. *Technol. Cult.* **3**, 259–266 (1962).
9. Eskildsen, K. The Language of Objects: Christian Jürgensen Thomsen's Science of the Past. *Isis* **103**, 24–53 (2012).
10. Pope, M. & Roberts, M. Clenching Authority: Joseph Prestwich and the proofs of the Antiquity of Man. in *Great Prehistorians: 150 Years of Palaeolithic Research, 1859–2009* (eds Hosfield, R., F. Wenban-Smith & Pope, M.) 34–44 (Lithic Studies Society, London, 2009).
11. Sackett, J. Boucher de Perthes and the Discovery of Human Antiquity. *Bull. Hist. Archaeol.* **24**, 1–11 (2014).
12. Gamble, C. Breaking the Time Barrier. *Geoscientist* **18**, 11–19 (2008).
13. Beyene, Y. *et al.* The characteristics and chronology of the earliest Acheulean at Konso, Ethiopia. *PNAS* **110**, 1584–1591 (2013).
14. Klein, R. Hominin Dispersals in the Old World. in *The human past* (ed. Scarre, C.) 84–123 (Thames & Hudson, London, 2013).
15. Corbey, R., Jagich, A., Vaesen, K. & Collard, M. The Acheulean handaxe: More like a bird's song than a beatles' tune? *Evol. Anthropol.* **25**, 6–19 (2016).
16. Coolidge, F. & Wynn, T. *The Rise of Homo Sapiens.* (Wiley-Blackwell, Hoboken, NJ, 2009).
17. Herzlinger, G., Wynn, T. & Goren-Inbar, N. Expert cognition in the production sequence of Acheulian cleavers at Gesher Benot Ya'aqov, Israel: A lithic and cognitive analysis. *PLOS ONE* **12**, e0188337 (2017).
18. Sanchez-Yustos, P. *et al.* The origin of the Acheulean. Technofunctional study of the FLKWlithic record (Olduvai, Tanzania). *PLOS ONE* **12**, e0179212 (2017).
19. Solodenko, N. *et al.* Fat Residue and Use-Wear Found on Acheulian Biface and Scraper Associated with Butchered Elephant Remains at the Site of Revadim, Israel. *PLOS ONE* **10**, e0118572 (2015).
20. Binneman, J. & Beaumont, P. Use-Wear Analysis of Two Acheulean Handaxes from. Wonderwerk Cave, Northern Cape. *South Afr. Field Archaeol.* **1**, 92–97 (1992).
21. O'Brien, E. The Projectile Capabilities of an Acheulian Handaxe From Olorgesailie. *Curr. Anthropol.* **22**, 76–79 (1981).
22. Whittaker, J. & McCall, G. Handaxe-Hurling Hominids: An Unlikely Story. *Curr. Anthropol.* **42**, 566–572 (2001).
23. Klein, R. *The Human Career.* (University of Chicago Press, Chicago, IL, 1999).
24. Toth, N. The Oldowan reassessed: a close look at early stone artefacts. *J. Archaeol. Sci.* **12**, 101–120 (1985).
25. Assaf, E. *et al.* Shaped stone balls were used for bone marrow extraction at Lower Paleolithic Qesem Cave, Israel. *PLOS ONE* **15**, e0230972 (2020).
26. Tennie, C., Premo, L., Braun, D. & McPherron, S. Early Stone Tools and Cultural Transmission: Resetting the Null Hypothesis. *Curr. Anthropol.* **58**, 652–672 (2017).
27. De la Torre, I. Searching for the emergence of stone tool making in eastern Africa. *PNAS* **116**, 11567–11569 (2019).
28. Semaw, S., Rogers, M. & Stout, D. The Oldowan-Acheulian Transition: Is there a "Developed Oldowan" Artifact Tradition? in *Sourcebook of Paleolithic Transitions: Methods, Theories, and Interpretations* (eds Camps, M. & Chauhan, P.) 173–193 (Springer New York, New York, NY, 2009). doi:10.1007/978-0-387-76487-0_10.
29. Isaac, G. Studies of Early Culture in East Africa. *World Archaeol.* **1**, 1–28 (1969).
30. Stout, D. & Chaminade, T. The evolutionary neuroscience of tool making. *Neuropsychologia* **45**, 1091–1100 (2007).
31. Stout, D., Toth, N., Schick, K. & Chaminade, T. Neural correlates of Early Stone Age toolmaking: technology, language and cognition in human evolution. *Philos. Trans. R. Soc. B* **363**, 1939–1949 (2008).
32. Stout, D., Hecht, E., Khreisheh, N., Bradley, B. & Chaminade, T. Cognitive Demands of Lower Paleolithic Toolmaking. *PLOS ONE* **10**, e0121804 (2015).
33. Faisal, A., Stout, D., Apel, J. & Bradley, B. The Manipulative Complexity of Lower Paleolithic Stone Toolmaking. *PLOS ONE* **5**, e13718 (2010).
34. DiMaggio, E. *et al.* Late Pliocene fossiliferous sedimentary record and the environmental context of early Homo from Afar, Ethiopia. *Science* **347**, 1355–1359 (2015).
35. Villmoare, B. *et al.* Early Homo at 2.8 Ma from Ledi-Geraru, Afar, Ethiopia. *Science* **347**, 1352–1355 (2015).
36. Herries, A., Martin, J., Leece, A., Adams, J. & Boschian, G. Contemporaneity of Australopithecus, Paranthropus, and early Homo erectus in South Africa. *Science* **368**, 47, eaaw7293 (2020).

37. Spoor, F. *et al.* Reconstructed Homo habilis type OH 7 suggests deep-rooted species diversity in early Homo. *Nature* **519**, 83–86 (2015).

38. Wood, B. Fifty years after Homo habilis. *Nature* **508**, 31–33 (2014).

39. Ponce de León, M. *et al.* The primitive brain of early Homo. *Science* **372**, 165–171 (2021).

40. Carlson, K. *et al.* The Endocast of MH1, Australopithecus sediba. *Science* **333**, 1402–1407 (2011).

41. Tobias, P. The brain of Homo habilis: a new level of organization in cerebral evolution. *J. Hum. Evol.* **16**, 741–761 (1987).

42. Semaw, S. *et al.* Co-occurrence of Acheulian and Oldowan artifacts with Homo erectus cranial fossils from Gona, Afar, Ethiopia. *Sci. Adv.* **6**, eaaw4694 (2020).

43. Geribàs, N., Mosquera, M. & Vergès, J. M. What novice knappers have to learn to become expert stone toolmakers. *J. Archaeol. Sci.* **37**, 2857–2870 (2010).

44. Shipton, C. The Unity of Acheulean Culture. in *Culture History and Convergent Evolution: Can We Detect Populations in Prehistory?* (ed. Groucutt, H.) 13–28 (Springer Nature Switzerland AG, Cham, 2020).

45. Diez-Martín, F. *et al.* The Origin of The Acheulean: The 1.7 Million-Year-Old Site of FLK West, Olduvai Gorge (Tanzania). *Sci. Rep.* **5**, 17839 (2015).

46. Chazan, M. *et al.* Radiometric dating of the Earlier Stone Age sequence in Excavation I at Wonderwerk Cave, South Africa: preliminary results. *J. Hum. Evol.* **55**, 1–11 (2008).

47. Gibbon, R., Granger, D., Kuman, K. & Partridge, T. Early Acheulean technology in the Rietputs Formation, South Africa, dated with cosmogenic nuclides. *J. Hum. Evol.* **56**, 152–160 (2009).

48. Pappu, S. *et al.* Early Pleistocene Presence of Acheulian Hominins in South India. *Science* **331**, 1596–1598 (2011).

49. Scott, G. & Gibert, L. The oldest hand-axes in Europe. *Nature* **461**, 82–85 (2009).

50. Vallverdu, J. *et al.* Age and Date for Early Arrival of the Acheulian in Europe (Barranc de la Boella, la Canonja, Spain). *PLOS ONE* **9**, e103634 (2014).

51. Antoine, P. *et al.* The earliest evidence of Acheulean occupation in Northwest Europe and the rediscovery of the Moulin Quignon site, Somme valley, France. *Sci. Rep.* **9**, 13091 (2019).

52. Key, A. *et al.* On the earliest Acheulean in Britain: first dates and in-situ artefacts from the MIS 15 site of Fordwich (Kent, UK). *R. Soc. Open Sci.* **9**, 211904 (2022).

53. Clark, J. *et al.* African Homo erectus: Old Radiometric Ages and Young Oldowan Assemblages in the Middle Awash Valley, Ethiopia. *Science* **264**, 1907–1910 (1994).

54. Wagner, G. *et al.* Radiometric dating of the type-site for Homo heidelbergensis at Mauer, Germany. *PNAS* **107**, 19726–19730 (2010).

55. Clark, P. *et al.* The Middle Pleistocene transition: characteristics, mechanisms, and implications for long-term changes in atmospheric pCO2. *Quat. Sci. Rev.* **25**, 3150–3184 (2006).

56. Ruddiman, W. F., Raymo, M. & McIntyre, A. Matuyama 41,000-year cycles: North Atlantic Ocean and northern hemisphere ice sheets. *Earth Planet. Sci. Lett.* **80**, 117–129 (1986).

57. Ruddiman, W. & Raymo, M. Northern Hemisphere climate regimes during the past 3 Ma: possible tectonic connections. *Philos. Trans. R. Soc. Lond. B* **318**, 411–430 (1988).

58. Dennell, R. Dispersal and colonisation, long and short chronologies: how continuous is the Early Pleistocene record for hominids outside East Africa? *J. Hum. Evol.* **45**, 421–440 (2003).

59. Tattersall, I. The Case for Saltational Events in Human Evolution. in *The Speciation of Modern Homo sapiens* (ed. Crow, T.) 49–59 (Oxford University Press, Oxford, 2002).

60. Berger, L., Hawks, J., de Ruiter, D. & Churchill, S. Homo naledi, a new species of the genus Homo from the Dinaledi Chamber, South Africa. *eLife* **4**, e09560 (2015).

61. Brown, P. *et al.* A new small-bodied hominin from the Late Pleistocene of Flores, Indonesia. *Nature* **431**, 1055–1061 (2004).

62. Détroit, F. *et al.* A new species of Homo from the Late Pleistocene of the Philippines. *Nature* **568**, 181–186 (2019).

63. Rizal, Y. *et al.* Last appearance of Homo erectus at Ngandong, Java, 117,000–108,000 years ago. *Nature* **577**, 381–385 (2020).

64. Saragusti, I., Sharon, I., Katzenelson, O. & Avnir, D. Quantitative Analysis of the Symmetry of Artefacts: Lower Paleolithic Handaxes. *J. Archaeol. Sci.* **25**, 817–825 (1998).

65. Potts, R. *et al.* Environmental dynamics during the onset of the Middle Stone Age in eastern Africa. *Science* **360**, 86–90 (2018).

66. McNabb, J. & Cole, J. The mirror cracked: Symmetry and refinement in the Acheulean handaxe. *J. Archaeol. Sci. Rep.* **3**, 100–111 (2015).

67. Li, H., Kuman, K., Leader, G. M. & Couzens, R. Handaxes in South Africa: Two case studies in the early and later Acheulean. *New Perspect. Acheulean Acheulean-Adapt.* **480**, 29–42 (2018).

68. Deino, A. *et al.* Chronology of the Acheulean to Middle Stone Age transition in eastern Africa. *Science* **360**, 95–98 (2018).

69. Isaac, G. *Olorgesailie.* (University of Chicago Press, Chicago, IL, 1977).

70. Moore, M. & Perston, Y. Experimental Insights into the Cognitive Significance of Early Stone Tools. *PLOS ONE* **11**, e0158803 (2016).

71. Iovita, R. *et al.* High handaxe symmetry at the beginning of the European Acheulian: The data from la Noira (France) in context. *PLOS ONE* **12**, e0177063 (2017).

72. Rightmire, P. Homo erectus and Middle Pleistocene hominins: Brain size, skull form, and species recognition. *J. Hum. Evol.* **65**, 223–252 (2013).

73. Falguères, C. *et al.* Earliest humans in Europe: the age of TD6 Gran Dolina, Atapuerca, Spain. *J. Hum. Evol.* **37**, 343–352 (1999).

74. Duval, M. *et al.* The first direct ESR analysis of a hominin tooth from Atapuerca Gran Dolina TD-6 (Spain) supports the antiquity of Homo antecessor. *Quat. Geochronol.* **47**, 120–137 (2018).

75. Bermúdez de Castro, J. *et al.* A Hominid from the Lower Pleistocene of Atapuerca, Spain: Possible Ancestor to Neandertals and Modern Humans. *Science* **276**, 1392–1395 (1997).

76. Bermúdez de Castro, J. *et al.* A new early Pleistocene hominin mandible from Atapuerca-TD6, Spain. *J. Hum. Evol.* **55**, 729–735 (2008).

77. Carbonell, E. *et al.* Lower Pleistocene Hominids and Artifacts from Atapuerca-TD6 (Spain). *Science* **269**, 826–830 (1995).

78. Bermúdez de Castro, J. & Martinón-Torres, M. Evolutionary interpretation of the modern human-like facial morphology of the Atapuerca Gran Dolina-TD6 hominins. *Anthropol. Sci.* **122**, 149–155 (2014).

79. Somel, M., Liu, X. & Khaitovich, P. Human brain evolution: Transcripts, metabolites and their regulators. *Nat. Rev. Neurosci.* **14**, 112–127 (2013).

80. Pinker, S. *The Language Instinct.* (Penguin, London, 1994).

81. Villa, P. & Roebroeks, W. Neandertal Demise: An Archaeological Analysis of the Modern Human Superiority Complex. *PLOS ONE* **9**, e96424 (2014).

82. Mithen, S. *The Prehistory of the Mind.* (Thames & Hudson, London, 1996).

83. Klein, R. & Edgar, B. *The Dawn of Human Culture.* (John Wiley & Sons, Inc., New York, NY, 2002).

84. McBrearty, S. & Brooks, A. The revolution that wasn't: a new interpretation of the origin of modern human behaviour. *J. Hum. Evol.* **39**, 453–563 (2000).

85. Barham, L. Systematic Pigment Use in the Middle Pleistocene of South-Central Africa. *Curr. Anthropol.* **43**, 181–190 (2002).

86. Joordens, J. *et al.* Homo erectus at Trinil on Java used shells for tool production and engraving. *Nature* **518**, 228–231 (2015).

87. Finkel, M. & Barkai, R. The Acheulean Handaxe Technological Persistence: A Case of Preferred Cultural Conservatism? *Proc. Prehist. Soc.* **84**, 1–19 (2018).

88. Hosfield, R., Cole, J. & McNabb, J. Less of a bird's song than a hard rock ensemble. *Evol. Anthropol. Issues News Rev.* **27**, 9–20 (2018).

89. Movius, H. The Lower Palaeolithic Cultures of Southern and Eastern Asia. *Trans. Am. Philos. Soc.* **38**, 329–420 (1948).

90. Coon, C. *The Living Races of Man.* (Jonathon Cape, London, 1965).

91. Dennell, R. *The Palaeolithic Settlement of Asia.* (Cambridge University Press, Cambridge, 2009).

92. Caspari, R. From Types to Populations: A Century of Race, Physical Anthropology, and the American Anthropological Association. *Am. Anthropol.* **105**, 65–76 (2003).

93. Athreya, S. & Ackermann, R. Colonialism and narratives of human origins in Asia and Africa. in *Interrogating Human Origins* 72–95 (2019). doi:10.4324/9780203731659-4.

94. Groves, C. *A Theory of Human and Primate Evolution.* (Oxford University Press, Oxford, 1989).

95. Lycett, S. & Bae, C. The Movius Line controversy: the state of the debate. *World Archaeol.* **42**, 521–544 (2010).

96. Brumm, A. The Movius Line and the bamboo hypothesis: early hominin stone technology in Southeast Asia. *Lithic Technol.* **35**, 7–24 (2010).

97. Dennell, R. East Asia and human evolution: from cradle of mankind to cul-de-sac. in *East of Africa: Southern Asia, Australia and Modern Human Origins* (eds Dennell, R. & Porr, M.) 8–20 (2014). doi:10.1017/CBO9781139084741.002.

98. Swisher, C. *et al.* Age of the earliest known hominids in Java, Indonesia. *Science* **263**, 1118–1121 (1994).

99. Gabunia, L. *et al.* Earliest Pleistocene Hominid Cranial Remains from Dmanisi,Republic of Georgia: Taxonomy, Geological Setting, and Age. *Science* **228**, 1019–1025 (2000).

100. Larick, R. *et al.* Early Pleistocene 40Ar-39Ar ages for Bapang Formation hominins, Central Java, Indonesia. *PNAS* **98**, 4866–4871 (2001).

101. Matsu'ura, S. *et al.* Age control of the first appearance datum for Javanese Homo erectus in the Sangiran area. *Science* **367**, 210–214 (2020).

102. Zhu, Z. *et al.* New dating of the Homo erectus cranium from Lantian (Gongwangling), China. *J. Hum. Evol.* **78**, 144–157 (2015).

103. Ferring, R. *et al.* Earliest human occupations at Dmanisi (Georgian Caucasus) dated to 1.85–1.78 Ma. *PNAS* **108**, 10432–10436 (2011).

104. Zhu, Z. *et al.* Hominin occupation of the Chinese Loess Plateau since about 2.1 million years ago. *Nature* **559**, 608–612 (2018).

105. Scardia, G. *et al.* Chronologic constraints on hominin dispersal outside Africa since 2.48 Ma from the Zarqa Valley, Jordan. *Quat. Sci. Rev.* **219**, 1–19 (2019).

106. Lahr, M. & Foley, R. Towards a Theory of Modern Human Origins: Geography, Demography, and Diversity in Recent Human Evolution. *Yearb. Phys. Anthropol.* **107**, 137–176 (1998).

107. Wells, S. *The Journey of Man.* (Penguin Books Ltd, London, 2002).

108. Goren-Inbar, N. *et al.* Pleistocene Milestones on the Out-of-Africa Corridor at Gesher Benot Ya'aqov, Israel. *Science* **289**, 944–947 (2000).

109. Lycett, S. & von Cramon-Taubadel, N. Acheulean variability and hominin dispersals: a model-bound approach. *J. Archaeol. Sci.* **35**, 553–562 (2008).

110. Toth, N. & Schick, K. *The Cutting Edge: New Approaches to the Archaeology of Human Origins.* (The University of Chicago Press, Chicago, IL, 2009).

111. Boriskovskii, P. Vietnam in Primeval Times [Part I]. *Sov. Anthropol. Archeol.* **7**, 14–32 (1968).

112. Watanabe, H. The chopper-chopping tool complex of eastern asia: An ethnoarchaeological-ecological reexamination. *J. Anthropol. Archaeol.* **4**, 1–18 (1985).

113. West, J. & Louys, J. Differentiating bamboo from stone tool cut marks in the zooarchaeological record, with a discussion on the use of bamboo knives. *J. Archaeol. Sci.* **34**, 512–518 (2007).

114. Heaney, L. "A Synopsis of Climatic and Vegetational Change in Southeast Asia. *Clim. Change* **19**, 53–61 (1991).

115. Brandon-Jones, D. The Asian Colobinae (Mammalia: Cercopithecidae) as indicators of Quaternary climatic change. *Biol. J. Linn. Soc.* **59**, 327–350 (1996).

116. Hope, G. *et al.* History of vegetation and habitat change in the Austral-Asian region. *Clim. Hum. Nat. Syst. PEPII Transect* **118–119**, 103–126 (2004).

117. Lycett, S. & Norton, C. A demographic model for Palaeolithic technological evolution: The case of East Asia and the Movius Line. *Hominin Morphol. Behav. Var. East. Asia Australas. Curr. Perspect.* **211**, 55–65 (2010).

118. Dennell, R. Hallum Movius, Helmut de Terra and the Line than Never Was: Burma, 1038. in *Living in the Landscape: Essays in honour of Graeme Barker* (eds Boyle, K., Rabett, R. & Hunt, C.) 11–34 (McDonald Institute for Archaeological Research, Cambridge, 2014).

119. Dennell, R. Life without the Movius Line: The structure of the East and Southeast Asian Early Palaeolithic. *Peking Man Relat. Stud.* **400**, 14–22 (2016).

120. Yang, S. *et al.* The lithic assemblages of Donggutuo, Nihewan basin: Knapping skills of early pleistocene hominins in North China. *PLOS ONE* **12**, e0185101 (2017).

121. White, M. The Clactonian Question: On the Interpretation of Core-and-Flake Assemblages in the British Lower Paleolithic. *J. World Prehistory* **14**, 1–63 (2000).

122. McNabb, J. Problems and Pitfalls in Understanding the Clactonian. in *Culture History and Convergent Evolution: Can We Detect Populations in Prehistory?* (ed. Groucutt, H. S.) 29–53 (Springer International Publishing, Cham, 2020). doi:10.1007/978-3-030-46126-3_3.

123. Lisiecki, L. & Raymo, M. A Pliocene-Pleistocene stack of 57 globally distributed benthic δ18 O records. *Paleoceanography* **20**, PA1003 (2005).

124. Ashton, N., McNabb, J., Irving, B., Lewis, S. & Parfitt, S. Contemporaneity of Clactonian and Acheulian flint industries at Barnham, Suffolk. *Antiquity* **68**, (1994).

125. Roberts, M. *et al.* Boxgrove, West Sussex: Rescue Excavations of a Lower Palaeolithic Landsurface (Boxgrove Project B, 1989–91). *Proc. Prehist. Soc.* **63**, 303–358 (1997).

126. Kohn, M. & Mithen, S. Handaxes: products of sexual selection? *Antiquity* **73**, 518–526 (1999).

127. Mithen, S. *The Singing Neanderthal.* (Weidenfeld & Nicholson, London, 2005).

128. Darwin, C. *On the Origin of Species by Means of Natural Selection, or the Preservation of Favoured Races in the Struggle for Life.* (John Murray, London, 1859).

129. Darwin, C. *The Descent of Man, and Selection in Relation to Sex.* (John Murray, London, 1871).

130. Nowell, A. & Chang, M. L. The Case Against Sexual Selection as an Explanation of Handaxe Morphology. *Paleoanthropology* **2009**, 77–88 (2009).

131. Hodgson, D. The First Appearance of Symmetry in the Human Lineage: Where Perception Meets Art. *Symmetry* **3**, 37–53 (2011).

132. Shimelmitz, R., Kuhn, S., Ronen, A. & Weinstein-Evron, M. Predetermined Flake Production at the Lower/Middle Paleolithic Boundary: Yabrudian Scraper-Blank Technology. *PLOS ONE* **9**, e106293 (2014).

133. Mellars, P. *The Neanderthal Legacy.* (Princeton University Press, Princeton, NJ, USA, 1996).

134. Stout, D. Stone toolmaking and the evolution of human culture and cognition. *Philos. Trans. R. Soc. B* **366**, 1050–1059 (2011).

135. Villa, P. *et al.* The Acheulian and Early Middle Paleolithic in Latium (Italy): Stability and Innovation. *PLOS ONE* **11**, e0160516 (2016).

04: Piltdown Man

1. Weiner, J. *The Piltdown Forgery.* (Oxford University Press, Oxford, 1955).

2. Dawson, C. & Woodward, A. On the Discovery of a Palæolithic Human Skull and Mandible in a Flint-bearing Gravel overlying the Wealden (Hastings Beds) at Piltdown, Fletching (Sussex). *Q. J. Geol. Soc.* **69**, 117–123 (1913).

3. Straus, W. The Great Piltdown Hoax. *Science* **119**, 265–269 (1954).

4. Tobias, P. *et al.* Piltdown: An Appraisal of the Case against Sir Arthur Keith [and Comments and Reply]. *Curr. Anthropol.* **33**, 243–293 (1992).

5. Russell, M. *Piltdown Man : The Secret Life of Charles Dawson & the World's Greatest Archaeological Hoax.* (Tempus Publishing Ltd, Stroud, 2003).

6. De Groote, I. *et al.* New genetic and morphological evidence suggests a single hoaxer created 'Piltdown man'. *R. Soc. Open Sci.* **3**, 160328 (2016).

7. Woodward, A. *The Earliest Englishman.* (Watts and Co., London, 1948).

8. Cooper, C. F. Arthur Smith Woodward. 1864-1944. *Obit. Not. Fellows R. Soc.* **5**, 79–112 (1945).

9. Millar, R. *The Piltdown Man : A Case of Archaeological Fraud.* (Victor Gollancz, London, 1972).

10. Dawson, C. & Woodward, A. Supplementary Note on the Discovery of a Palæolithic Human Skull and Mandible at Piltdown (Sussex). *Q. J. Geol. Soc.* **70**, 82–93 (1914).

11. Dawson, C. & Woodward, A. On a Bone Implement from Piltdown (Sussex). *Q. J. Geol. Soc. Lond.* **71**, 144–149 (1915).

12. Anonymous. The Discoverer Of The Piltdown Skull. *Br. Med. J.* **2**, 265–265 (1916).

13. Woodward, A. Fourth Note on the Piltdown Gravel, with Evidence of a Second Skull of Eoanthropus dawsoni. *Q. J. Geol. Soc. Lond.* **73**, 1–11 (1917).

14. Keith, A. The Significance of the Discovery at Piltdown. *Bedrock* **2**, 435–453 (1914).

15. Keith, A. *A New Theory of Human Evolution.* (Watts and Co., London, 1948).

16. Waterston, D. The Piltdown mandible. *Nature* **92**, 319 (1913).

17. Miller, G. Smithsonian Miscellaneous Collections. **65**, (1915).

18. Gregory, W. Note on the Molar Teeth of the Piltdown Mandible. *Am. Anthropol.* **18**, 384–387 (1916).

19. Gregory, W. The dawn man of Piltdown. *Am. Mus. J.* **14**, 189–200 (1914).

20. Keith, A. Men of the Old Stone Age: Their Environment, Life, and Art. by Henry Fairfield Osborn Review by: A. Keith. *Man* **17**, 82–85 (1917).

21. Pycraft, W. P. The Jaw of the Piltdown Man: a reply to Mr. Gerrit S. Miller. *Sci. Prog. 1916-1919* **11**, 389–409 (1917).

22. Miller, G. The Piltdown jaw. *Am. J. Phys. Anthropol.* **1**, 25–52 (1918).

23. Dixon, A. Note on the fragment of the lower jaw from Piltdown. *Nature* **99**, 399 (1917).

24. Thomson, K. S. Marginalia: Piltdown Man: The Great English Mystery Story. *Am. Sci.* **79**, 194–201 (1991).

25. Keith, A. *The Antiquity of Man.* (Williams and Norgate, London, 1915).

26. Sollas, W. *Ancient Hunters and Their Modern Representatives.* (Macmillan, London, 1915).

27. Lankester, R. *Diversions of a Naturalist.* (Methuen, London, 1915).

28. Keith, A. *An Autobiography.* (Watts and Co., London, 1950).

29. Keith, A. *The Antiquity of Man.* vol. 2 (Williams and Norgate, London, 1925).

30. Besenbacher, S., Hvilsom, C., Marques-Bonet, T., Mailund, T. & Schierup, M. Direct estimation of mutations in great apes reconciles phylogenetic dating. *Nat. Ecol. Evol.* **3**, 286–292 (2019).

31. DiMaggio, E. *et al.* Late Pliocene fossiliferous sedimentary record and the environmental context of early Homo from Afar, Ethiopia. *Science* **347**, 1355–1359 (2015).

32. Villmoare, B. *et al.* Early Homo at 2.8 Ma from Ledi-Geraru, Afar, Ethiopia. *Science* **347**, 1352–1355 (2015).

33. Huxley, T. *Evidence as to Man's Place in Nature.* (Williams and Norgate, London, 1863).

34. Darwin, C. *The Descent of Man, and Selection in Relation to Sex.* (John Murray, London, 1871).

35. Dart, R. Australopithecus africanus: The Man-Ape of South Africa. *Nature* **115**, 195–199 (1925).

36. Madison, P. All things bleak and bare beneath a brazen sky: practice and place in the analysis of Australopithecus. *Hist. Philos. Life Sci.* **41**, 19 (2019).

37. Dennell, R. East Asia and human evolution: from cradle of mankind to cul-de-sac. in *East of Africa: Southern Asia, Australia and Modern Human Origins* (eds Dennell, R. & Porr, M.) 8–20 (2014). doi:10.1017/CBO9781139084741.002.

38. Elliot Smith, G. *Evolution of Man: Essays.* (Oxford University Press, Oxford, 1924).

39. Osborn, H. Recent Discoveries Relating to the Origin and Antiquity of Man. *Science* **65**, 481–488 (1927).

40. Gregory, W. Dawn-Man or Ape? *Sci. Am.* **137**, 230–232 (1927).

41. Wood Jones, F. *The Problem of Man's Ancestry.* (Society for Promoting Christian Knowledge, London, 1918).

42. Lewin, R. & Foley, R. *Principles of Human Evolution.* (Blackwell Publishing, Oxford, 2004).

43. Laing, S. *Human Origins.* (Chapman and Hall, London, 1892).

44. Selcer, P. Beyond the Cephalic Index: Negotiating Politics to Produce UNESCO's Scientific Statements on Race. *Curr. Anthropol.* **53**, S173–S184 (2012).

45. UNESCO. *Four Statements on the Race Question.* (UNESCO, Paris, 1969).

46. Dennell, R. The Far West from the Far East. in *Interrogating Human Origins* (eds Porr, M. & Matthews, J.) 211–238 (Routledge, Abingdon-on-Thames, 2019). doi:10.4324/9780203731659-10.

47. Straus, W. The Riddle of Man's Ancestry. *Q. Rev. Biol.* **24**, 200–223 (1949).

48. Keith, A. Australopithecinae or Dartians. *Nature* **377** (1947).

49. Goodrum, M. R. & Olson, C. The Quest for an Absolute Chronology in Human Prehistory: Anthropologists, Chemists and the Fluorine Dating Method in Palaeoanthropology. *Br. J. Hist. Sci.* **42**, 95–114 (2009).

50. Oakley, K. Some Applications of the Fluorine Test. *Archaeol. News Lett.* 1–3 (1949).

51. Weiner, J., Oakley, K. & Le Gros Clark, W. The Solution of the Piltdown Problem. *Bull. Br. Mus. Nat. Hist. Geol.* **2**, 141–146 (1953).

52. Washburn, S. L. The Piltdown Hoax. *Am. Anthropol.* **55**, 759–762 (1953).

53. Hooton, E. A. Comments on the Piltdown Affair. *Am. Anthropol.* **56**, 287–289 (1954).
54. Heizer, R. & Cook, S. Comments on the Piltdown Remains. *Am. Anthropol.* **56**, 92–94 (1954).
55. Weiner, J. *et al.* Further contributions to the solution of the Piltdown problem. *Bull. Br. Mus. Nat. Hist. Geol.* **2**, 225–288 (1955).
56. De Vries, H. & Oakley, K. Radiocarbon Dating of the Piltdown Skull and Jaw. *Nature* **184**, 224–226 (1959).
57. Hedges, R., Housley, R., Law, I. & Bronk Ramsey, C. Radiocarbon dates from the Oxford AMS system: Archaeometry Datelist 9. *Archaeometry* **31**, 207–234 (1989).
58. Lowenstein, J., Molleson, T. & Washburn, S. Piltdown jaw confirmed as orang. *Nature* **299**, 294–294 (1982).
59. Russell, M. *The Piltdown Man Hoax Case Closed.* (The History Press, Stroud, Gloucs., 2012).
60. Clemens, W. Wealden mammalian fossils. *Palaeontology* **6**, 55–69 (1963).
61. Gould, S. Piltdown revisited. *Nat. Hist.* **88**, 86–97 (1979).
62. Gould, S. The Piltdown Conspiracy. *Nat. Hist.* **89**, 121–124 (1980).
63. Weiner, J. Grafton Elliot Smith and Piltdown. in *The concepts of human evolution* (ed. Zuckerman, S.) 23–26 (Academic Press/Zoological Society of London (Symposia of the Zoological Society of London, no. 33), 1973).
64. Weiner, J. Piltdown Hoax: new light. *Nature* **277**, 10 (1979).
65. Winslow, J. & Meyer, A. The perpetrator at Piltdown. *Sci. 83* **4**, 32–34 (1983).
66. Langham, I. Sherlock Holmes, Circumstantial Evidence and Piltdown Man. *Phys. Anthropol. News* **3**, 1–5 (1984).

05: Muddle in the Middle

1. Trinkaus, E. & Shipman, P. *Neandertals: Changing the Image of Mankind.* (Jonathan Cape, London, 1993).
2. Neubauer, S., Gunz, P., Weber, G. & Hublin, J. Endocranial volume of Australopithecus africanus: New CT-based estimates and the effects of missing data and small sample size. *J. Hum. Evol.* **62**, 498–510 (2012).
3. Gunz, P. *et al.* Australopithecus afarensis endocasts suggest ape-like brain organization and prolonged brain growth. *Sci. Adv.* **6**, eaaz4729 (2020).
4. Rightmire, P. Brain size and encephalization in early to Mid-Pleistocene Homo. *Am. J. Phys. Anthropol.* **124**, 109–123 (2004).
5. Klein, R. *The Human Career.* (University of Chicago Press, Chicago, IL, 1999).
6. Clark, P. *et al.* The Middle Pleistocene transition: characteristics, mechanisms, and implications for long-term changes in atmospheric pCO2. *Quat. Sci. Rev.* **25**, 3150–3184 (2006).
7. Schoetensack, O. *Der Unterkiefer Des Homo Heidelbergensis.* (Verlag Wilhelm Engelmann, Leipzig, 1908).
8. Rosas, A. & Bermúdez De Castro, J. M. The Mauer mandible and the evolutionary significance of Homo heidelbergensis. *Geobios* **31**, 687–697 (1998).
9. Mounier, A., Marchal, F. & Condemi, S. Is Homo heidelbergensis a distinct species? New insight on the Mauer mandible. *J. Hum. Evol.* **56**, 219–246 (2009).
10. Mounier, A. & Caparrós, M. The phylogenetic status of Homo heidelbergensis – a cladistic study of Middle Pleistocene hominins. *Bull. Mém. Société Anthropol. Paris* **27**, 110–134 (2015).
11. Wagner, G. *et al.* Radiometric dating of the type-site for Homo heidelbergensis at Mauer, Germany. *PNAS* **107**, 19726–19730 (2010).
12. Hrdlička, A. The Rhodesian Man. *Am. J. Phys. Anthropol.* **9**, 173–204 (1926).
13. Woodward, A. A New Cave Man from Rhodesia, South Africa. *Nature* **108**, 371–372 (1921).
14. Brauer, G. The Origin of Modern Anatomy: By Speciation or Intraspecific Evolution? *Evol. Anthropol.* **17**, 22–37 (2008).
15. Grün, R. *et al.* Dating the skull from Broken Hill, Zambia, and its position in human evolution. *Nature* **580**, 372–375 (2020).
16. Musonda, F. Decolonising the Broken Hill Skull: Cultural Loss and a Pathway to Zambian Archaeological Sovereignty. *Afr. Archaeol. Rev.* **30**, (2013).
17. Clark, J. African Homo erectus: Old Radiometric Ages and Young Oldowan Assemblages in the Middle Awash Valley, Ethiopia. *Science* **264**, 1907–1910 (1994).
18. Bae, C. The Late Middle Pleistocene Hominin Fossil Record of Eastern Asia: Synthesis and Review. *Yearb. Phys. Anthropol.* **143**, 75–93 (2010).
19. Ao, H., Liu, C., Roberts, A., Zhang, P. & Xu, X. An updated age for the Xujiayao hominin from the Nihewan Basin, North China: Implications for Middle Pleistocene human evolution in East Asia. *J. Hum. Evol.* **106**, 54–65 (2017).
20. Sun, X., Yi, S., Lu, H. & Zhang, W. TT-OSL and post-IR IRSL dating of the Dali Man site in central China. *Quat. Int.* **343**, 99–106 (2017).
21. Cameron, D. & Groves, C. *Bones, Stones and Molecules: "Out of Africa" and Human Origins.* (Elsevier Academic Press, London, 2004).
22. Manzi, G. Human Evolution at the Matuyama-Brunhes Boundary. *Evol. Anthropol.* **13**, 11–24 (2004).
23. Rightmire, P. Human Evolution in the Middle Pleistocene: The Role of Homo heidelbergensis. *Evol. Anthropol.* **6**, 218–227 (1998).

24. Stringer, C. The Status of Homo heidelbergensis (Schoetensack 1908). *Evol. Anthropol.* **21**, 101–107 (2012).
25. Harvati, K. 100 years of Homo heidelbergensis - life and times of a controversial taxon. *Mitteilungen Ges. Für Urgesch.* **16**, 85–94 (2007).
26. Klein, R. Hominin Dispersals in the Old World. in *The human past* (ed. Scarre, C.) 84–123 (Thames & Hudson, London, 2013).
27. Arsuaga, J. *et al.* Neandertal roots: Cranial and chronological evidence from Sima de los Huesos. *Science* **344**, 1358–1363 (2014).
28. Carbonell, E. & Mosquera, M. The emergence of a symbolic behaviour: the sepulchral pit of Sima de los Huesos, Sierra de Atapuerca, Burgos, Spain. *Comptes Rendus Palevol* **5**, 155–160 (2006).
29. Aranburu, J., Arsuagab, J. & Sala, N. The stratigraphy of the Sima de los Huesos (Atapuerca, Spain) and implications for the origin of the fossil hominin accumulation. *Quat. Int.* **443**, 5–21 (2017).
30. Sala, N. *et al.* Lethal Interpersonal Violence in the Middle Pleistocene. *PLOS ONE* **10**, e0126589 (2015).
31. Bocquet-Appel, J. & Arsuaga, L. Age Distributions of Hominid Samples at Atapuerca (SH) and Krapina Could Indicate Accumulation by Catastrophe. *J. Archaeol. Sci.* **26**, 327–338 (1999).
32. Wolpoff, M. & Caspari, R. Does Krapina Reflect Early Neandertal Paleodemography? *Period. Biol.* **108**, 425–432 (2006).
33. Pettitt, P. The Rise of Modern Humans. in *The human past* (ed. Scarre, C.) 124–173 (Thames & Hudson, London, 2013).
34. Bischoff, J. *et al.* The Sima de los Huesos Hominids Date to Beyond U/Th Equilibrium (>350 kyr) and Perhaps to 400–500 kyr: New Radiometric Dates. *J. Archaeol. Sci.* **30**, 275–280 (2003).
35. Bischoff, J. *et al.* High-resolution U-series dates from the Sima de los Huesos hominids yields 600 +/-66 kyrs: implications for the evolution of the early Neanderthal lineage. *J. Archaeol. Sci.* **34**, 763–770 (2007).
36. Carbonell, E. *et al.* The Pleistocene site of Gran Dolina, Sierra de Atapuerca, Spain: a history of the archaeological investigations. *J. Hum. Evol.* **37**, 313–324 (1999).
37. Carbonell, E. *et al.* Lower Pleistocene Hominids and Artifacts from Atapuerca-TD6 (Spain). *Science* **269**, 826–830 (1995).
38. Bermúdez de Castro, J. *et al.* A new early Pleistocene hominin mandible from Atapuerca-TD6, Spain. *J. Hum. Evol.* **55**, 729–735 (2008).
39. Carbonell, E. *et al.* The TD6 level lithic industry from Gran Dolina, Atapuerca (Burgos, Spain): production and use. *J. Hum. Evol.* **37**, 653–693 (1999).
40. Falguères, C. *et al.* Earliest humans in Europe: the age of TD6 Gran Dolina, Atapuerca, Spain. *J. Hum. Evol.* **37**, 343–352 (1999).
41. Duval, M. *et al.* The first direct ESR analysis of a hominin tooth from Atapuerca Gran Dolina TD-6 (Spain) supports the antiquity of Homo antecessor. *Quat. Geochronol.* **47**, 120–137 (2018).
42. Bermúdez de Castro, J. *et al.* A Hominid from the Lower Pleistocene of Atapuerca, Spain: Possible Ancestor to Neandertals and Modern Humans. *Science* **276**, 1392–1395 (1997).
43. Martinón-Torres, M. *et al.* New permanent teeth from Gran Dolina-TD6 (Sierra de Atapuerca). The bearing of Homo antecessor on the evolutionary scenario of Early and Middle Pleistocene Europe. *J. Hum. Evol.* **127**, 93–117 (2019).
44. Bermúdez de Castro, J., Martinón-Torres, M., Arsuaga, J. & Carbonell, E. Twentieth anniversary of Homo antecessor (1997-2017): a review. *Evol. Anthropol.* **26**, 57–171 (2017).
45. Carbonell, E. *et al.* The first hominin of Europe. *Nature* **452**, 465–470 (2008).
46. Bermúdez de Castro, J. *et al.* Early Pleistocene human mandible from Sima del Elefante (TE) cave site in Sierra de Atapuerca (Spain): A comparative morphological study. *J. Hum. Evol.* **61**, 15–25 (2011).
47. Bermúdez de Castro, J., Martinón-Torres, M., Blasco, R., Rosell, J. & Carbonell, E. Continuity or discontinuity in the European Early Pleistocene human settlement: the Atapuerca evidence. *Quat. Sci. Rev.* **76**, 53–63 (2013).
48. Ashton, N. *et al.* Hominin Footprints from Early Pleistocene Deposits at Happisburgh, UK. *PLOS ONE* **9**, e88329 (2014).
49. Parfitt, S. *et al.* Early Pleistocene human occupation at the edge of the boreal zone in northwest Europe. *Nature* **466**, 229–233 (2010).
50. Dennell, R. Dispersal and colonisation, long and short chronologies: how continuous is the Early Pleistocene record for hominids outside East Africa? *J. Hum. Evol.* **45**, 421–440 (2003).
51. Fernandez-Jalvo, Y., Diez, J., Caceres, I. & Rosell, J. Human cannibalism in the Early Pleistocene of Europe (Gran Dolina, Sierra de Aterpuerca, Burgos, Spain). *J. Hum. Evol.* **37**, 591–622 (1999).
52. Rightmire, P. Homo in the Middle Pleistocene: Hypodigms, Variation, and Species Recognition. *Evol. Anthropol.* **17**, 8–21 (2008).
53. Endicott, P., Ho, S. & Stringer, C. Using genetic evidence to evaluate four palaeoanthropological hypotheses for the timing of Neanderthal and modern human origins. *J. Hum. Evol.* **59**, 87–95 (2010).
54. Stewart, J. & Stringer, C. Human Evolution Out of Africa: The Role of Refugia and Climate Change. *Science* **335**, 1317–1321 (2012).
55. Lahr, M. & Foley, R. Towards a Theory of Modern Human Origins: Geography, Demography, and Diversity in Recent Human Evolution. *Yearb. Phys. Anthropol.* **107**, 137–176 (1998).
56. Stringer, C. Modern human origins: progress and prospects. *Philos. Trans. R. Soc. B* **357**, 563–579 (2002).

57. Roksandic, M., Radovic, P., Wu, X. & Bae, C. Resolving the "muddle in the middle": The case for Homo bodoensis sp. nov. *Evol. Anthropol.* **31**, 20–29 (2022).

58. Delson, E. & Stringer, C. The naming of Homo bodoensis by Roksandic and colleagues does not resolve issues surrounding Middle Pleistocene human evolution. *Evol. Anthropol. Issues News Rev.* **31**, 233–236 (2022).

59. Prüfer, K. *et al.* The complete genome sequence of a Neanderthal from the Altai Mountains. *Nature* **505**, 43–49 (2014).

60. Reich, D. *et al.* Genetic history of an archaic hominin group from Denisova Cave in Siberia. *Nature* **468**, 1053–1060 (2010).

61. Rogers, A., Harris, N. & Achenbach, A. Neanderthal-Denisovan ancestors interbred with a distantly related hominin. *Sci. Adv.* **6**, eaay5483 (2020).

62. Gómez-Robles, A. Dental evolutionary rates and its implications for the Neanderthal–modern human divergence. *Sci. Adv.* **5**, eaaw1268 (2019).

63. Welker, F., Ramos-Madrigal, J., Gutenbrunner, P., Mackie, M. & Tiwary, S. The dental proteome of Homo antecessor. *Nature* **580**, 235–238 (2020).

64. Stringer, C. The origin and evolution of Homo sapiens. *Philos. Trans. R. Soc. B* **371**, 20150237 (2016).

65. Lacruz, R. *et al.* The evolutionary history of the human face. *Nat. Ecol. Evol.* **3**, 726–736 (2019).

66. Ni, X. *et al.* Massive cranium from Harbin in northeastern China establishes a new Middle Pleistocene human lineage. *The Innovation* **2**, 100130 (2021).

67. Hublin, J. Accretion of the Neanderthal features: a shift in frequency. in *Neandertals and Modern Humans in Western Asia* (eds Akazawa, T., Aoki, K. & Bar-Yosef, O.) 295–310 (Plenum Press, New York, NY, 1998).

68. Hublin, J. The origin of Neandertals. *PNAS* **106**, 16022–16027 (2009).

69. Daura, J. *et al.* New Middle Pleistocene hominin cranium from Gruta da Aroeira (Portugal). *PNAS* **114**, 3397–3402 (2017).

70. Marra, F. *et al.* The Aggradational Successions of the Aniene River Valley in Rome: Age Constraints to Early Neanderthal Presence in Europe. *PLOS ONE* **12**, e0170434 (2017).

71. Weaver, T. The meaning of Neandertal skeletal morphology. *PNAS* **106**, 16028–16033 (2009).

72. Dennell, R., Martinón-Torres, M. & Bermúdez de Castro, J. Hominin variability, climatic instability and population demography in Middle Pleistocene Europe. *Quat. Sci. Rev.* **30**, 1511–1524 (2011).

73. Tattersall, I. The Case for Saltational Events in Human Evolution. in *The Speciation of Modern Homo sapiens* (ed. Crow, T.) 49–59 (Oxford University Press, Oxford, 2002).

74. Mounier, A., Condemi, S. & Manzi, G. The Stem Species of Our Species: A Place for the Archaic Human Cranium from Ceprano, Italy. *PLOS ONE* **6**, e18821 (2011).

75. Muttoni, G., Scardia, G., Kent, D., Swisher, C. & Manzi, G. Pleistocene magnetochronology of early hominin sites at Ceprano and Fontana Ranuccio, Italy. *Earth Planet. Sci. Lett.* **286**, 255–268 (2009).

76. Manzi, G. *et al.* The new chronology of the Ceprano calvarium (Italy). *J. Hum. Evol.* **59**, 580–585 (2010).

77. Rink, W. *et al.* New Radiometric Ages for the BH-1 Hominin from Balanica (Serbia): Implications for Understanding the Role of the Balkans in Middle Pleistocene Human Evolution. *PLOS ONE* **8**, e54608 (2013).

78. Conroy, G. *Reconstructing Human Origins: A Modern Synthesis*. (W. W. Norton & Company, Inc., New York, NY, 1997).

79. Bruner, E. & Pearson, O. Neurocranial evolution in modern humans: the case of Jebel Irhoud 1. *Anthropol. Sci.* **121**, 31–41 (2013).

80. Hublin, J. *et al.* New fossils from Jebel Irhoud, Morocco and the pan-African origin of Homo sapiens. *Nature* **546**, 289–291 (2017).

81. Smith, T. *et al.* Earliest evidence of modern human life history in North African early Homo sapiens. *PNAS* **104**, 6128–6133 (2007).

82. White, T. *et al.* Pleistocene Homo sapiens from Middle Awash, Ethiopia. *Nature* **423**, 742–747 (2003).

83. Clark, J. *et al.* Stratigraphic, chronological and behavioural contexts of Pleistocene Homo sapiens from Middle Awash, Ethiopia. *Nature* **423**, 747–752 (2003).

84. McDougall, I., Brown, F. & Fleagle, J. Stratigraphic placement and age of modern humans from Kibish, Ethiopia. *Nature* **433**, 733–736 (2005).

85. Day, M. Early Homo sapiens Remains from the Omo River Region of South-west Ethiopia: Omo Human Skeletal Remain. *Nature* **222**, 1135–1138 (1969).

86. Rightmire, P. Middle and later Pleistocene hominins in Africa and Southwest Asia. *PNAS* **106**, 16046–16050 (2009).

87. Vidal, C. *et al.* Age of the oldest known Homo sapiens from eastern Africa. *Nature* **601**, 579–583 (2022).

88. Richter, D. *et al.* The age of the hominin fossils from Jebel Irhoud, Morocco, and the origins of the Middle Stone Age. *Nature* **546**, 293–296 (2017).

89. Henderson, Z. Florisbad, South Africa: Over 120,000 years of human activity. *Nyame Akuma* **56**, 53–56 (1995).

90. Scott, L. & Rossouw, L. Reassessment of Botanical Evidence for Palaeoenvironments at Florisbad, South Africa. *South Afr. Archaeol. Bull.* **60**, 96–102 (2005).

91. Broom, R. Man contemporary with extinct animals in South Africa. *Ann. South Afr. Mus.* **12**, 13–16 (1913).

92. Henderson, Z. Captain R. Edgerton Helme - a benefactor of research. *CULNA* 28–24 (1994).

93. Grün, R. *et al.* Direct dating of the Florisbad hominid. *Nature* **382**, 500–501 (1996).

94. Dreyer, T. A human skull from Florisbad, Orange Free State, with a note on the endocranial cast, by CU Ariens Kappers. *Proc K. Akad Wet. Te Amst.* **38**, 3–12 (1935).

95. Bräuer, G. The origin of modern anatomy: By speciation or intraspecific evolution? *Evol. Anthropol. Issues News Rev.* **17**, 22–37 (2008).

96. Bräuer, G., Yokoyama, Y., Falguères, C. & Mbua, E. Modern human origins backdated. *Nature* **386**, 337–338 (1997).

97. Bräuer, G. & Leakey, R. E. The ES-11693 cranium from Eliye Springs, West Turkana, Kenya. *J. Hum. Evol.* **15**, 289–312 (1986).

98. Bräuer, G. The Origin of Modern Anatomy: By Speciation or Intraspecific Evolution? *Evol. Anthropol.* **17**, 22–37 (2008).

99. Neubauer, S., Hublin, J. & Gunz, P. The evolution of modern human brain shape. *Sci. Adv.* **4**, eaao5961 (2018).

100. Henn, B., Steele, T. & Weaver, T. Clarifying distinct models of modern human origins in Africa. *Curr. Opin. Genet. Dev.* **53**, 148–156 (2018).

101. Krause, J. *et al.* The complete mitochondrial DNA genome of an unknown hominin from southern Siberia. *Nature* **464**, 894–897 (2010).

102. Reich, D. *et al.* Denisova Admixture and the First Modern Human Dispersals into Southeast Asia and Oceania. *Am. J. Hum. Genet.* **89**, 516–528 (2011).

103. Browning, S., Browning, R., Zhou, Y., Tocci, S. & Akey, J. Analysis of Human Sequence Data Reveals Two Pulses of Archaic Denisovan Admixture. *Cell* **173**, 53–61 (2018).

104. Jacobs, G. *et al.* Multiple Deeply Divergent Denisovan Ancestries in Papuans. *Cell* **177**, 1010–1021 (2019).

105. Slon, V. *et al.* The genome of the offspring of a Neanderthal mother and a Denisovan father. *Nature* **561**, 113–116 (2018).

106. Sawyer, S. *et al.* Nuclear and mitochondrial DNA sequences from two Denisovan individuals. *PNAS* **112**, 15696–15700 (2015).

107. Bennett, A. *et al.* Morphology of the Denisovan phalanx closer to modern humans than to Neanderthals. *Sci. Adv.* **5**, eaaw3950 (2019).

108. Chen, F. *et al.* A late Middle Pleistocene Denisovan mandible from the Tibetan Plateau. *Nature* **569**, 409–412 (2019).

109. Cooper, A. & Stringer, C. Did the Denisovans Cross Wallace's Line? *Science* **342**, 321–323 (2013).

110. Li, Z. *et al.* Late Pleistocene archaic human crania from Xuchang, China. *Science* **355**, 969–972 (2017).

111. Ji, Q., Wu, W., Ji, Y., Li, Q. & Ni, X. Late Middle Pleistocene Harbin cranium represents a new Homo species. *The Innovation* **2**, 100132 (2021).

112. Shao, Q. *et al.* Geochemical provenancing and direct dating of the Harbin archaic human cranium. *The Innovation* **2**, 100131 (2021).

113. Wheeler, Q., Assis, L. & Rieppe, O. Heed the father of cladistics. *Nature* **496**, 295–296 (2013).

114. Brown, P. *et al.* A new small-bodied hominin from the Late Pleistocene of Flores, Indonesia. *Nature* **431**, 1055–1061 (2004).

115. Kubo, D., Kono, R. & Kaifu, Y. Brain size of Homo floresiensis and its evolutionary implications. *Proc. R. Soc. B* **280**, 20130338 (2013).

116. Morwood, M. *et al.* Archaeology and age of a new hominin from Flores in eastern Indonesia. *Nature* **431**, 1087–1091 (2004).

117. Morwood, M. *et al.* Further evidence for small-bodied hominins from the Late Pleistocene of Flores, Indonesia. *Nature* **437**, 1012–1017 (2005).

118. Sutikna, T. *et al.* Revised stratigraphy and chronology for Homo floresiensis at Liang Bua in Indonesia. *Nature* **532**, 366–369 (2016).

119. Diniz-Filho, J. *et al.* Quantitative genetics of body size evolution on islands: an individual-based simulation approach. *Biol. Lett.* **15**, 0481 (2019).

120. Jacob, T. *et al.* Pygmoid Australomelanesian Homo sapiens skeletal remains from Liang Bua, Flores: Population affinities and pathological abnormalities. *PNAS* **103**, 13421–13426 (2006).

121. Martin, R. *et al.* Comment on "The Brain of LB1, Homo floresiensis". *Science* **312**, 999 (2006).

122. Eckhardt, R., Henneberg, M., Weller, A. & Hsüc, K. Rare events in earth history include the LB1 human skeleton from Flores, Indonesia, as a developmental singularity, not a unique taxon. *PNAS* **111**, 11961–11966 (2014).

123. Henneberg, M., Eckhardt, R., Chavanaves, S. & Hsüc, K. Evolved developmental homeostasis disturbed in LB1 from Flores, Indonesia, denotes Down syndrome and not diagnostic traits of the invalid species Homo floresiensis. *PNAS* **111**, 11967–11972 (2014).

124. Falk, D. *et al.* The Brain of LB1, Homo floresiensis. *Science* **308**, 624–628 (2005).

125. Falk, D. *et al.* Brain shape in human microcephalics and Homo floresiensis. *PNAS* **104**, 2513–2518 (2007).

126. Argue, D., Donlon, D., Groves, C. & Wright, R. Homo floresiensis: Microcephalic, pygmoid, Australopithecus, or Homo? *J. Hum. Evol.* **51**, 360–374 (2006).

127. Kaifu, Y. *et al.* Unique Dental Morphology of Homo floresiensis and Its Evolutionary Implications. *PLOS ONE* **10**, e0141614 (2015).

128. Lyras, G., Dermitzakis, M., Van der Geer, A., Van der Geer, S. & De Vos, J. The origin of Homo floresiensis and its relation to evolutionary processes under isolation. *Anthropol. Sci.* **117**, 33–43 (2008).

129. Tocheri, M. *et al*. The Primitive Wrist of Homo floresiensis and Its Implications for Hominin Evolution. *Science* **317**, 1743–1745 (2007).

130. Baab, K. *et al*. A Critical Evaluation of the Down Syndrome Diagnosis for LB1, Type Specimen of Homo floresiensis. *PLOS ONE* **11**, e0155731 (2016).

131. Baab, K., McNulty, K. & Harvati, K. Samples, Homo floresiensis Contextualized: A Geometric Morphometric Comparative Analysis of Fossil and Pathological Human. *PLOS ONE* **8**, e69119 (2013).

132. Balzeau, A. & Charlier, P. What do cranial bones of LB1 tell us about Homo floresiensis? *J. Hum. Evol.* **93**, 12–24 (2016).

133. Montgomery, S., Capellini, I., Barton, R. & Mundy, N. Reconstructing the ups and downs of primate brain evolution: implications for adaptive hypotheses and Homo floresiensis. *BMC Biol.* **8**, 1–19 (2010).

134. Diniz-Filho, A. & Raia, P. Island Rule, quantitative genetics and brain–body size evolution in Homo floresiensis. *Proc. R. Soc. B* **284**, 1065 (2017).

135. Jungers, W. *et al*. The foot of Homo floresiensis. *Nature* **459**, 81–84 (2009).

136. Lieberman, D. Homo floresiensis from head to toe. *Nature* **459**, 41–42 (2009).

137. Argue, D., Groves, C., Lee, M. & Jungers, W. The affinities of Homo floresiensis based on phylogenetic analyses of cranial, dental, and postcranial characters. *J. Hum. Evol.* **107**, 107–133 (2017).

138. Morwood, M., O'Sullivan, P., Aziz, F. & Raza, A. Fission-track ages of stone tools and fossils on the east Indonesian island of Flores. *Nature* **392**, 173–176 (1998).

139. Gibbons, A. Ancient Island Tools Suggest Homo erectus Was a Seafarer. *Science* **279**, 1635–1637 (1998).

140. Brumm, A. *et al*. Age and context of the oldest known hominin fossils from Flores. *Nature* **534**, 249–254 (2016).

141. Van den Bergh, G. *et al*. Homo floresiensis-like fossils from the early Middle Pleistocene of Flores. *Nature* **534**, 245–248 (2016).

142. Brumm, A. *et al*. Early stone technology on Flores and its implications for Homo floresiensis. *Nature* **441**, 624–628 (2006).

143. Brumm, A. *et al*. Hominins on Flores, Indonesia, by one million years ago. *Nature* **464**, 748–753 (2010).

144. Morley, M. *et al*. Initial micromorphological results from Liang Bua, Flores (Indonesia): Site formation processes and hominin activities at the type locality of Homo floresiensis. *J. Archaeol. Sci.* **77**, 125–142 (2017).

145. Mijares, A. *et al*. New evidence for a 62000-year-old human presence at Callao Cave, Luzon, Philippines. *J. Hum. Evol.* **59**, 123–132 (2010).

146. Détroit, F. *et al*. A new species of Homo from the Late Pleistocene of the Philippines. *Nature* **568**, 181–186 (2019).

147. Ingicco, T. *et al*. Earliest known hominin activity in the Philippines by 709 thousand years ago. *Nature* **557**, 233–237 (2018).

148. Bolter, D., Elliott, M., Hawks, J. & Berger, L. Immature remains and the first partial skeleton of a juvenile Homo naledi, a late Middle Pleistocene hominin from South Africa. *PLOS ONE* **15**, e0230440 (2020).

149. Berger, L., Hawks, J., de Ruiter, D. & Churchill, S. Homo naledi, a new species of the genus Homo from the Dinaledi Chamber, South Africa. *eLife* **4**, e09560 (2015).

150. Dirks, P., Berger, L., Roberts, E., Kramers, J. & Hawks, J. Geological and taphonomic context for the new hominin species Homo naledi from the Dinaledi Chamber, South Africa. *eLife* **4**, e09561 (2015).

151. Feuerriegel, E. *et al*. The upper limb of Homo naledi. *J. Hum. Evol.* **104**, 155–173 (2017).

152. Kivell, T. *et al*. The hand of Homo naledi. *Nat. Commun.* **6**, 8431 (2015).

153. Harcourt-Smith, W. *et al*. The foot of Homo naledi. *Nat. Commun.* **6**, 8432 (2015).

154. Berger, L., Hawks, J., Dirks, P., Elliott, M. & Roberts, E. Homo naledi and Pleistocene hominin evolution in subequatorial Africa. *eLife* **6**, e24234 (2017).

155. Schroeder, L. *et al*. Skull diversity in the Homo lineage and the relative position of Homo naledi. *J. Hum. Evol.* **104**, 124–135 (2017).

156. Hawks, J. *et al*. New fossil remains of Homo naledi from the Lesedi Chamber, South Africa. *eLife* **6**, e24232 (2017).

157. Brophy, J. *et al*. Immature Hominin Craniodental Remains From a New Locality in the Rising Star Cave System, South Africa. *PaleoAnthropology* **1**, 1–13 (2021).

158. Thackeray, J. Estimating the age and affinities of Homo naledi. *South Afr. J. Sci.* **111**, 1–2 (2015).

159. Dembo, M. *et al*. The evolutionary relationships and age of Homo naledi: An assessment using dated Bayesian phylogenetic methods. *J. Hum. Evol.* **97**, 17–26 (2016).

160. Dirks, P. *et al*. The age of Homo naledi and associated sediments in the Rising Star Cave, South Africa. *eLife* **6**, e24231 (2017).

161. Robbins, J. *et al*. Providing context to the Homo naledi fossils: Constraints from flowstones on the age of sediment deposits in Rising Star Cave, South Africa. *Chem. Geol.* **567**, 120108 (2021).

162. Dirks, P. *et al*. Comment on 'Deliberate body disposal by hominins in the Dinaledi Chamber, Cradle of Humankind, South Africa?'. *J. Hum. Evol.* **96**, 145–148 (2016).

163. Egeland, C., Domínguez-Rodrigo, M., Pickering, T., Menter, C. & Heaton, J. Hominin skeletal part abundances and claims of deliberate disposal of corpses in the Middle Pleistocene. *PNAS* **115**, 4601–4606 (2018).

164. Elliot, M. *et al*. Expanded Explorations of the Dinaledi Subsystem, Rising Star Cave System, South Africa. *PaleoAnthropology* **1**, 15–22 (2021).

165. Pettitt, P. *The Palaeolithic Origins of Human Burial*. (Routledge, Abingdon, 2011).

166. Pettitt, P. Did Homo naledi dispose of their dead in the Rising Star Cave system? *South Afr. J. Sci.* **118**, (2022).
167. Aiello, L. & Collard, M. Our Newest Oldest Ancestor. *Nature* **410**, 526–527 (2001).
168. Zhang, X. *et al.* The earliest human occupation of the high-altitude Tibetan Plateau 40 thousand to 30 thousand years ago. *Science* **362**, 1049–1051 (2018).
169. Kuhlwilm, M., Han, S., Sousa, V., Excoffier, L. & Marques-Bonet, T. Ancient admixture from an extinct ape lineage into bonobos. *Nat. Ecol. Evol.* **3**, 957–965 (2019).
170. Ackermann, R. Phenotypic Traits of Primate Hybrids: Recognizing Admixture in the Fossil Record. *Evol. Anthropol.* **19**, 258–270 (2010).

06: First use of fire

1. Darwin, C. The Descent of Man, and Selection in Relation to Sex. (John Murray, London, 1871).
2. Scott, A. The Pre-Quaternary history of fire. Fire Palaeoenvironment **164**, 281–329 (2000).
3. Scott, A. C. Charcoal recognition, taphonomy and uses in palaeoenvironmental analysis. Charcoal Its Use Palaeoenvironmental Anal. **291**, 11–39 (2010).
4. Glasspool, I. J., Edwards, D. & Axe, L. Charcoal in the Silurian as evidence for the earliest wildfire. Geology **32**, 381–383 (2004).
5. Rimmer, S., Hawkins, S., Scott, A. & Cressler, W. The rise of fire: Fossil charcoal in late Devonian marine shales as an indicator of expanding terrestrial ecosystems, fire, and atmospheric change. Am. J. Sci. **315**, 713–733 (2015).
6. Scott, A. C. & Glasspool, I. J. The diversification of Paleozoic fire systems and fluctuations in atmospheric oxygen concentration. PNAS **103**, 10861–10865 (2006).
7. Glasspool, I. & Scott, A. Phanerozoic atmospheric oxygen concentrations reconstructed from sedimentary charcoal. Nat. Geosci. **3**, 627–630 (2010).
8. Glasspool, I., Scott, A., Waltham, D., Pronina, N. & Shao, L. The impact of fire on the Late Paleozoic Earth System. Front. Plant Sci. **6**, 756 (2015).
9. Pruetz, J. D. & Herzog, N. M. Savanna Chimpanzees at Fongoli, Senegal, Navigate a Fire Landscape. Curr. Anthropol. **58**, S337–S350 (2017).
10. Wrangham, R. Catching Fire: How Cooking Made Us Human. (Basic Books, New York, NY, 2009).
11. Organ, C., Nunn, C. L., Machanda, Z. & Wrangham, R. W. Phylogenetic rate shifts in feeding time during the evolution of Homo. PNAS **108**, 14555–14559 (2011).
12. Aiello, L. & Wheeler, P. The expensive tissue hypothesis: the brain and the digestive system in human and primate evolution. Curr. Anthropol. **36**, 199–221 (1995).
13. Byrne, R. & Whiten, A. Machiavellian Intelligence. (Oxford University Press, Oxford, 1988).
14. Dunbar, R. The Social Brain Hypothesis. Evol. Anthropol. **6**, 178–190 (1998).
15. Dunbar, R. The Human Story. (Faber and Faber Ltd., London, 2004).
16. Dunbar, R. The Social Brain and the Cultural Explosion of the Human Revolution. in Rethinking the human revolution (eds Mellars, P., Boyle, K., Bar-Yosef, O. & Stringer, C.) 91–105 (McDonald Institute, Cambridge, 2007).
17. DiMaggio, E. et al. Late Pliocene fossiliferous sedimentary record and the environmental context of early Homo from Afar, Ethiopia. Science **347**, 1355–1359 (2015).
18. Villmoare, B. et al. Early Homo at 2.8 Ma from Ledi-Geraru, Afar, Ethiopia. Science **347**, 1352–1355 (2015).
19. Kimbel, W., Johanson, D. & Rak, Y. Systematic Assessment of a Maxilla of Homo From Hadar, Ethiopia. Am. J. Phys. Anthropol. **103**, 235–262 (1997).
20. Lordkipanidze, D. et al. A Complete Skull from Dmanisi, Georgia, and the Evolutionary Biology of Early Homo. Science **342**, 326–331 (2013).
21. Spoor, F. et al. Reconstructed Homo habilis type OH 7 suggests deep-rooted species diversity in early Homo. Nature **519**, 83–86 (2015).
22. Trauth, M., Maslin, M., Deino, A. & Strecker, M. Late Cenozoic Moisture History of East Africa. Science **309**, 2051–2053 (2005).
23. Pickering, T. What's new is old: Comments on (more) archaeological evidence of one-million-year-old fire from South Africa. South Afr. J. Sci. **108**, 1–2 (2012).
24. Hlubik, S. et al. Hominin fire use in the Okote member at Koobi Fora, Kenya: New evidence for the old debate. J. Hum. Evol. **133**, 214–229 (2019).
25. Gowlett, J. A. J., Harris, J. W. K., Walton, D. & Wood, B. A. Early archaeological sites, hominid remains and traces of fire from Chesowanja, Kenya. Nature **294**, 125–129 (1981).
26. Barbetti, M., Clark, J., Williams, F. & Williams, M. Palaeomagnetism and the search for very ancient fireplaces in Africa. Anthropol. 1962- **18**, 299–304 (1980).
27. Barbetti, M. Traces of fire in the archaeological record, before one million years ago? J. Hum. Evol. **15**, 771–781 (1986).
28. Brain, C. & Sillen, A. Evidence from the Swartkrans cave for the earliest use of fire. Nature **336**, 464–466 (1988).

29. Berna, F. et al. Microstratigraphic evidence of in situ fire in the Acheulean strata of Wonderwerk Cave, Northern Cape province, South Africa. PNAS **109**, E1215–E1220 (2012).
30. Roebroeks, W. & Villa, P. On the earliest evidence for habitual use of fire in Europe. PNAS **108**, 5209–5214 (2011).
31. Gao, X., Zhang, S., Zhang, Y. & Chen, F. Evidence of Hominin Use and Maintenance of Fire at Zhoukoudian. Curr. Anthropol. **58**, S267–S277 (2017).
32. Weiner, S., Xu, Q., Goldberg, P., Liu, J. & Bar-Yosef, O. Evidence for the Use of Fire at Zhoukoudian, China. Science **281**, 251–253 (1998).
33. Goren-Inbar, N. et al. Evidence of Hominin Control of Fire at Gesher Benot Ya'aqov, Israel. Science **304**, 725–727 (2004).
34. Stepka, Z., Azuri, I., Horwitz, L. K., Chazan, M. & Natalio, F. Hidden signatures of early fire at Evron Quarry (1.0 to 0.8 Mya). PNAS **119**, e2123439119 (2022).
35. Cohen, K., Harper, D. & Gibbard, P. ICS International Chronostratigraphic Chart v 2023/09. (2023).
36. Gowlett, J. A. J. The early settlement of northern Europe: Fire history in the context of climate change and the social brain. Clim.-Cult.-Soc. Aux Temps Préhistoriques Apparit. Hominidés Jusquau Néolothique **5**, 299–310 (2006).
37. Gowlett, J. & Wrangham, R. Earliest fire in Africa: Towards the convergence of archaeological evidence and the cooking hypothesis. Azania Archaeol. Res. Afr. **48**, 5–30 (2013).
38. Twomey, T. The Cognitive Implications of Controlled Fire Use by Early Humans. Camb. Archaeol. J. **23**, 113–128 (2013).
39. Chazan, M. Toward a Long Prehistory of Fire. Curr. Anthropol. **58**, S351–S359 (2017).
40. Gowlett, J. The discovery of fire by humans: a long and convoluted process. Philos. Trans. Biol. Sci. **371**, 1–12 (2016).
41. Gowlett, J., Brink, J., Caris, A., Hoare, S. & Rucina, S. Evidence of Burning from Bushfires in Southern and East Africa and Its Relevance to Hominin Evolution. Curr. Anthropol. **58**, S206–S216 (2017).
42. Zink, K. & Lieberman, D. Impact of meat and Lower Palaeolithic food processing techniques on chewing in humans. Nature **531**, 500–503 (2016).
43. Wrangham, R. Control of Fire in the Paleolithic: Evaluating the Cooking Hypothesis. Curr. Anthropol. **58**, S303–S313 (2017).
44. Sankararaman, S. et al. The genomic landscape of Neanderthal ancestry in present-day humans. Nature **507**, 354–357 (2014).
45. Simonti, C. et al. The phenotypic legacy of admixture between modern humans and Neandertals. Science **351**, 737–741 (2016).
46. Prüfer, K. et al. A high-coverage Neandertal genome from Vindija Cave in Croatia. Science **358**, 655–658 (2017).
47. Wichlinski, L. J. Adaptive Solutions to the Problem of Vulnerability During Sleep. Evol. Psychol. Sci. **8**, 442–477 (2022).
48. Aiello, L. & Dunbar, R. Neocortex Size, Group Size and the Evolution of Language. Curr. Anthropol. **34**, 184–193 (1993).
49. Bramble, D. & Lieberman, D. Endurance running and the evolution of Homo. Nature **432**, 345–352 (2004).
50. Reed, D. L., Light, J. E., Allen, J. M. & Kirchman, J. J. Pair of lice lost or parasites regained: the evolutionary history of anthropoid primate lice. BMC Biol. **5**, 7 (2007).
51. Perry, G. H. Parasites and human evolution. Evol. Anthropol. Issues News Rev. **23**, 218–228 (2014).
52. Sørensen, B. Energy use by Eem Neanderthals. J. Archaeol. Sci. **36**, 2201–2005 (2009).
53. Kittler, R., Kayser, M. & Stoneking, M. Molecular Evolution of Pediculus humanus and the Origin of Clothing. Curr. Biol. **13**, 1414–1417 (2003).
54. Toups, M., Kitchen, A., Light, J. & Reed, D. Origin of Clothing Lice Indicates Early Clothing Use by Anatomically Modern Humans in Africa. Mol. Biol. Evol. **28**, 29–32 (2011).
55. Collard, M., Tarle, L., Sandgathe, D. & Allan, A. Faunal evidence for a difference in clothing use between Neanderthals and early modern humans in Europe. J. Anthropol. Archaeol. **44**, 235–246 (2016).
56. Dennell, R. Dispersal and colonisation, long and short chronologies: how continuous is the Early Pleistocene record for hominids outside East Africa? J. Hum. Evol. **45**, 421–440 (2003).
57. Parker, C. H., Keefe, E. R., Herzog, N. M., O'connell, J. F. & Hawkes, K. The pyrophilic primate hypothesis. Evol. Anthropol. Issues News Rev. **25**, 54–63 (2016).
58. Bird, R., Bird, D., Codding, B., Parker, C. & Jones, J. The fire stick farming hypothesis: Australian Aboriginal foraging strategies, biodiversity, and anthropogenic fire mosaics. PNAS **105**, 14796–14801 (2008).
59. Scherjon, F., Bakels, C., MacDonald, K. & Roebroeks, W. Burning the Land: An Ethnographic Study of Off-Site Fire Use by Current and Historically Documented Foragers and Implications for the Interpretation of Past Fire Practices in the Landscape. Curr. Anthropol. **56**, 299–326 (2015).
60. Innes, J. & Blackford, J. The Ecology of Late Mesolithic Woodland Disturbances: Model Testing with Fungal Spore Assemblage Data. J. Archaeol. Sci. **30**, 185–194 (2003).
61. Miller, G. et al. Ecosystem Collapse in Pleistocene Australia and a Human Role in Megafaunal Extinction. Science **309**, 297–290 (2005).
62. Wadley, L., Hodgskiss, T. & Grant, M. Implications for complex cognition from the hafting of tools with compound adhesives in the Middle Stone Age, South Africa. PNAS **106**, 9590–9594 (2009).

63. Degano, I. et al. Hafting of Middle Paleolithic tools in Latium (central Italy): New data from Fossellone and Sant'Agostino caves. PLOS ONE **14**, e0213473 (2019).

64. Niekus, M. et al. Middle Paleolithic complex technology and a Neandertal tar-backed tool from the Dutch North Sea. PNAS **116**, 22081–22087 (2019).

65. Wilkins, J., Schoville, B., Brown, K. & Chazan, M. Evidence for Early Hafted Hunting Technology. Science **338**, 942–946 (2012).

66. Mellars, P. The Neanderthal Legacy. (Princeton University Press, Princeton, NJ, USA, 1996).

67. Klein, R. The Human Career. (University of Chicago Press, Chicago, IL, 1999).

68. Rosell, J. & Blasco, R. The early use of fire among Neanderthals from a zooarchaeological perspective. Neanderthals Ecol. Evol. **217**, 268–283 (2019).

69. Sanz, M. et al. Early evidence of fire in south-western Europe: the Acheulean site of Gruta da Aroeira (Torres Novas, Portugal). Sci. Rep. **10**, 12053 (2020).

70. Stancampiano, L. et al. Organic geochemical evidence of human-controlled fires at Acheulean site of Valdocarros II (Spain, 245 kya). Sci. Rep. **13**, 7119 (2023).

71. Aranguren, B. et al. Wooden tools and fire technology in the early Neanderthal site of Poggetti Vecchi (Italy). PNAS **115**, 2054–2059 (2018).

72. Koller, J., Baumer, U. & Mania, D. High-tech in the middle Palaeolithic: Neandertal-manufactured pitch identified. Eur. J. Archaeol. **4**, 385–397 (2001).

73. Grünberg, J. Middle Palaeolithic birch-bark pitch. Antiquity **76**, 15–16 (2002).

74. Pawlik, A. F. & Thissen, J. P. Hafted armatures and multi-component tool design at the Micoquian site of Inden-Altdorf, Germany. J. Archaeol. Sci. **38**, 1699–1708 (2011).

75. Schmidt, P., Rageot, M., Blessing, M. & Tennie, C. The Zandmotor data do not resolve the question whether Middle Paleolithic birch tar making was complex or not. PNAS **117**, 4456–4457 (2020).

76. Schmidt, P. et al. Birch tar production does not prove Neanderthal behavioral complexity. PNAS **116**, 17707–17711 (2019).

77. Roebroeks, W. et al. Landscape modification by Last Interglacial Neanderthals. Sci. Adv. **7**, eabj5567 (2021).

78. Richter, D. & Krbetschek, M. The age of the Lower Paleolithic occupation at Schöningen. J. Hum. Evol. **89**, 46–56 (2015).

79. Sorensen, A., Claud, E. & Soressi, M. Neandertal fire-making technology inferred from microwear analysis. Sci. Rep. **8**, 10065 (2018).

80. Heyes, P. et al. Selection and Use of Manganese Dioxide by Neanderthals. Sci. Rep. **6**, 22159 (2016).

81. Slimak, L. et al. Modern human incursion into Neanderthal territories 54,000 years ago at Mandrin, France. Sci. Adv. **8**, eabj9496 (2022).

82. Mellars, P. The Impossible Coincidence. A Single-Species Model for the Origins of Modern Human Behavior in Europe. Evol. Anthropol. **14**, 12–27 (2005).

83. Angelucci, D., Nabais, M. & Zilhão, J. Formation processes, fire use, and patterns of human occupation across the Middle Palaeolithic (MIS 5a-5b) of Gruta da Oliveira (Almonda karst system, Torres Novas, Portugal). PLOS ONE **18**, e0292075 (2023).

84. Brittingham, A. et al. Geochemical Evidence for the Control of Fire by Middle Palaeolithic Hominins. Sci. Rep. **9**, 15368 (2019).

85. Sandgathe, D. et al. On the Role of Fire in Neandertal Adaptations in Western Europe: Evidence from Pech de l'Azé IV and Roc de Marsal, France. PaleoAnthropology **2011**, 216–242 (2011).

86. Duveau, J., Berillon, G., Verna, C., Laisné, G. & Cliquet, D. The composition of a Neandertal social group revealed by the hominin footprints at Le Rozel (Normandy, France). PNAS **116**, 19409–19414 (2019).

87. Rosas, A. et al. Paleobiology and comparative morphology of a late Neandertal sample from El Sidron, Asturias, Spain. PNAS **103**, 19266–19271 (2006).

88. Dalén, L. et al. Partial genetic turnover in neandertals: continuity in the east and population replacement in the west. Mol. Biol. Evol. **29**, 1893–1897 (2012).

89. Kubo, D., Kono, R. & Kaifu, Y. Brain size of Homo floresiensis and its evolutionary implications. Proc. R. Soc. B **280**, 20130338 (2013).

90. Morwood, M. et al. Archaeology and age of a new hominin from Flores in eastern Indonesia. Nature **431**, 1087–1091 (2004).

91. Morwood, M. et al. Further evidence for small-bodied hominins from the Late Pleistocene of Flores, Indonesia. Nature **437**, 1012–1017 (2005).

92. Argue, D., Donlon, D., Groves, C. & Wright, R. Homo floresiensis: Microcephalic, pygmoid, Australopithecus, or Homo? J. Hum. Evol. **51**, 360–374 (2006).

93. Sutikna, T. et al. Revised stratigraphy and chronology for Homo floresiensis at Liang Bua in Indonesia. Nature **532**, 366–369 (2016).

94. Morley, M. et al. Initial micromorphological results from Liang Bua, Flores (Indonesia): Site formation processes and hominin activities at the type locality of Homo floresiensis. J. Archaeol. Sci. **77**, 125–142 (2017).

95. Dirks, P., Berger, L., Roberts, E., Kramers, J. & Hawks, J. Geological and taphonomic context for the new hominin species Homo naledi from the Dinaledi Chamber, South Africa. eLife **4**, e09561 (2015).

96. Berger, L. & Hawks, J. Cave of Bones. (National Geographic Partners, Washington, DC, 2023).

97. Berger, L., Hawks, J., de Ruiter, D. & Churchill, S. Homo naledi, a new species of the genus Homo from the Dinaledi Chamber, South Africa. eLife **4**, e09560 (2015).
98. Garvin, H. et al. Body size, brain size, and sexual dimorphism in Homo naledi from the Dinaledi Chamber. J. Hum. Evol. **111**, 119–138 (2017).
99. Thackeray, J. Estimating the age and affinities of Homo naledi. South Afr. J. Sci. **111**, 1–2 (2015).
100. Dembo, M. et al. The evolutionary relationships and age of Homo naledi: An assessment using dated Bayesian phylogenetic methods. J. Hum. Evol. **97**, 17–26 (2016).
101. Dirks, P. et al. The age of Homo naledi and associated sediments in the Rising Star Cave, South Africa. eLife **6**, e24231 (2017).
102. Robbins, J. et al. Providing context to the Homo naledi fossils: Constraints from flowstones on the age of sediment deposits in Rising Star Cave, South Africa. Chem. Geol. **567**, 120108 (2021).
103. Elliott, M. et al. Description and analysis of three Homo naledi incudes from the Dinaledi Chamber, Rising Star cave (South Africa). J. Hum. Evol. **122**, 146–155 (2018).
104. Dirks, P. et al. Geological Setting and Age of Australopithecus sediba from Southern Africa. Science **328**, 205–208 (2010).
105. Val, A., Dirks, P., Backwell, L., d'Errico, F. & Berger, L. Taphonomic Analysis of the Faunal Assemblage Associated with the Hominins (Australopithecus sediba) from the Early Pleistocene Cave Deposits of Malapa, South Africa. PLOS ONE **10**, e0126904 (2016).
106. Elliot, M. et al. Expanded Explorations of the Dinaledi Subsystem, Rising Star Cave System, South Africa. PaleoAnthropology **1**, 15–22 (2021).
107. Dirks, P. et al. Comment on 'Deliberate body disposal by hominins in the Dinaledi Chamber, Cradle of Humankind, South Africa?' J. Hum. Evol. **96**, 145–148 (2016).
108. Berger, L. et al. Evidence for deliberate burial of the dead by Homo naledi. eLife **12**, RP89106 (2023).
109. Berger, L. et al. 241,000 to 335,000 Years Old Rock Engravings Made by Homo naledi in the Rising Star Cave system, South Africa. eLife **12**, RP89102 (2023).
110. Fuentes, A. et al. Burials and engravings in a small-brained hominin, Homo naledi, from the late Pleistocene: contexts and evolutionary implications. bioRxiv 2023.06.01.543135 (2023) doi:10.1101/2023.06.01.543135.
111. Martinón-Torres, M., Garate, D., Herries, A. & Petraglia, M. No scientific evidence that Homo naledi buried their dead and produced rock art. J. Hum. Evol. **195**, 103464 (2023).
112. Brown, P. et al. A new small-bodied hominin from the Late Pleistocene of Flores, Indonesia. Nature **431**, 1055–1061 (2004).
113. Richter, D. et al. The age of the hominin fossils from Jebel Irhoud, Morocco, and the origins of the Middle Stone Age. Nature **546**, 293–296 (2017).
114. Stringer, C. The origin and evolution of Homo sapiens. Philos. Trans. R. Soc. B **371**, 20150237 (2016).
115. Stringer, C. & Crété, C. Mapping Interactions of Homo neanderthalensis and Homo sapiens From the Fossil and Genetic Record. PaleoAnthropology **2022**, 401−412 (2022).
116. Day, M. Early Homo sapiens Remains from the Omo River Region of South-west Ethiopia: Omo Human Skeletal Remain. Nature **222**, 1135–1138 (1969).
117. Vidal, C. et al. Age of the oldest known Homo sapiens from eastern Africa. Nature **601**, 579–583 (2022).
118. Harvati, K. et al. Apidima Cave fossils provide earliest evidence of Homo sapiens in Eurasia. Nature **571**, 500–504 (2019).
119. Abbas, M. et al. Human dispersals out of Africa via the Levant. Sci. Adv. **9**, eadi6838 (2023).
120. Mackay, A. Nature and significance of the Howiesons Poort to post-Howiesons Poort transition at Klein Kliphuis rockshelter, South Africa. J. Archaeol. Sci. **38**, 1430–1440 (2011).
121. Marean, C. et al. Early human use of marine resources and pigment in South Africa during the Middle Pleistocene. Nature **449**, 905–909 (2007).
122. McBrearty, S. & Stringer, C. The coast in colour. Nature **449**, 793–794 (2007).
123. Mithen, S. After the Ice: A Global Human History 20,000 - 5,000 BC. (Weidenfield & Nicholson, London, 2003).
124. Brown, K. et al. Fire As an Engineering Tool of Early Modern Humans. Science **325**, 859–862 (2009).
125. Tiffagom, M. Témoignages d'un traitement thermique des feuilles de laurier dans le Solutréen supérieur de la grotte du Parpalló (Gandia, Espagne)/Testimonios de un tratamiento térmico de las ojas de Laurel en el Solutrense superior de la cueva del Parpalló/Evidence for thermal treatment of Laurel Leaf points in the Upper Solutrean of the grotte du Parpalló. Paléo Rev. Archéologie Préhistorique **10**, 147–161 (1998).
126. Inizan, M. & Tixier, J. L'émergence des arts du feu : le traitement thermique des roches siliceuses. Paléorient **26**, 23–36 (2000).
127. Mourre, V., Villa, P. & Henshilwood, C. Early Use of Pressure Flaking on Lithic Artifacts at Blombos Cave, South Africa. Science **330**, 659–662 (2010).
128. Rots, V., Lentfer, C., Schmid, V., Porraz, G. & Conard, N. Pressure flaking to serrate bifacial points for the hunt during the MIS5 at Sibudu Cave (South Africa). PLOS ONE **12**, e0175151 (2017).
129. Lewis-Williams, D. The Mind in the Cave: Consciousness And The Origins Of Art. (Thames & Hudson, London, 2002).
130. de Beaune, S. A. Palaeolithic Lamps and Their Specialization: A Hypothesis. Curr. Anthropol. **28**, 569–577 (1987).

131. de Beaune, S. A. & White, R. Ice Age Lamps. Sci. Am. **268**, 108–113 (1993).
132. Medina-Alcaide, M. Á. et al. Multianalytical and multiproxy approach to the characterization of a Paleolithic lamp. An example in Nerja cave (Southern Iberian Peninsula). J. Archaeol. Sci. Rep. **28**, 102021 (2019).
133. Medina-Alcaide, M. Á. et al. The conquest of the dark spaces: An experimental approach to lighting systems in Paleolithic caves. PLOS ONE **16**, e0250497 (2021).
134. Goodwin, M. J., Zald, H. S. J., North, M. P. & Hurteau, M. D. Climate-Driven Tree Mortality and Fuel Aridity Increase Wildfire's Potential Heat Flux. Geophys. Res. Lett. **48**, e2021GL094954 (2021).
135. Mitton, J. B., Ferrenberg, S. & Benkman, C. Mountain Pine Beetle Develops an Unprecedented Summer Generation in Response to Climate Warming. Am. Nat. **179**, E163–E171 (2012).
136. Abatzoglou, J. & Williams, P. Impact of anthropogenic climate change on wildfire across western US forests. PNAS **113**, 11770–11775 (2016).
137. Stapledon, O. Last and First Men. (Methuen, London, 1930).
138. Foote, E. Circumstances Affecting the Heat of Sun's Rays. Am. J. Art Sci. **2nd Series XXII**, 382–383 (1856).
139. Tyndall, J. The Bakerian Lecture: On the Absorption and Radiation of Heat by Gases and Vapours, and on the Physical Connexion of Radiation, Absorption, and Conduction. Philos. Trans. R. Soc. Lond. **151**, 1–36 (1861).
140. Arrhenius, S. XXXI. On the influence of carbonic acid in the air upon the temperature of the ground. Lond. Edinb. Dublin Philos. Mag. J. Sci. **41**, 237–276 (1896).
141. Callendar, G. S. The artificial production of carbon dioxide and its influence on temperature. Q. J. R. Meteorol. Soc. **64**, 223–240 (1938).
142. Callendar, G. S. Infra-red absorption by carbon dioxide, with special reference to atmospheric radiation. Q. J. R. Meteorol. Soc. **67**, 263–275 (1941).
143. Callendar, G. S. Can carbon dioxide influence climate? Weather **4**, 310–314 (1949).
144. Plass, G. The Carbon Dioxide Theory of Climatic Change. Tellus **8**, 140–154 (1956).
145. Slocum, G. Has the amount of carbon dioxide in the atmosphere changed significantly since the beginning of the twentieth century? Mon. Weather Rev. **83**, 225–231 (1955).
146. Fonselius, S., Koroleff, F. & Warme, K. Carbon Dioxide Variations in the Atmosphere. Tellus **8**, 176–183 (2010).
147. Revelle, R. & Suess, H. Carbon Dioxide Exchange Between Atmosphere and Ocean and the Question of an Increase of Atmospheric CO2 during the Past Decades. Tellus **9**, 18–27 (1957).
148. Keeling, C. D. The Concentration and Isotopic Abundances of Carbon Dioxide in the Atmosphere. Tellus **12**, 200–203 (1960).
149. Keeling, C. D. Rewards and Penalties of Monitoring the Earth. Annu. Rev. Energy Environ. **23**, 25–82 (1998).
150. Teller, E. Energy patterns of the future. in Energy and Man: A Symposium (ed. Nevins, A.) 53–72 (Appleton-Century-Crofts,Inc, New York, NY, 1960).
151. Manabe, S. & Wetherald, R. T. Thermal Equilibrium of the Atmosphere with a Given Distribution of Relative Humidity. J. Atmospheric Sci. **24**, 241–259 (1967).
152. Mercer, J. Antarctic ice and Sangamon sea level. in vol. 79 217–225 (1968).
153. Franta, B. Early oil industry knowledge of CO2 and global warming. Nat. Clim. Change **8**, 1024–1025 (2018).
154. Supran, G., Rahmstorf, S. & Oreskes, N. Assessing ExxonMobil's global warming projections. Science **379**, eabk0063 (2023).

07: Neanderthals

1. Schmitz, R. *et al.* The Neandertal type site revisited: Interdisciplinary investigations of skeletal remains from the Neander Valley, Germany. *PNAS* **99**, 13342–13347 (2002).
2. Busk, G. On the Crania of the Most Ancient Races of Man. By Professor D. Schaaffhausen, of Bonn. (From Müller's Archive 1858, pp 453). With Remarks, and original Figures, taken from a Cast of the Neanderthal Cranium. *Nat. Hist. Rev. Q. J. Biol. Sci.* 155–76 (1861).
3. Fuhlrott, J. Menschliche Ueberreste aus einer Felsengrotte des Düsselthals. Ein Beitrag zur Frage tiber die Existenz fossiler Menschen. *Verh Naturhist Ver Preuss Rheinl* **16**, 131–153 (1859).
4. Schaaffhausen, H. in *Sitzungsberichte der Niederrlieinisclien Gesellschaft für Naturund Heilkunde zu Bonn.* 38–52 (Bonn, 1857).
5. Keith, A. *A New Theory of Human Evolution.* (Watts and Co., London, 1948).
6. Rosen, G. Rudolf Virchow and Neanderthal man. *Am. J. Surg. Pathol.* **1**, 183–7 (1977).
7. Blake, C. On the occurrence of human remains contemporaneous with those of extinct animals. *The Geologist* **4**, 395–399 (1861).
8. Blake, C. On the Alleged Peculiar Characters, and Assumed Antiquity of the Human Cranium from the Neanderthal. *J. Anthropol. Soc. Lond.* **2**, 139–157 (1864).
9. Mayer, A. Ueber die fossilen Ueberreste eines menschlichen Schädels und Skeletes in einer Felsenhöhle des Dussel-oder Neander- Thaies. in *Archiv für Anatomie, Physiologie und wissenschaftliche Medicin.* (eds Reichert, C. & Du Bois-Reymond, E.) 1–26 (Müller's Archiv, Leipzig, 1864).

10. Gamble, C. Breaking the Time Barrier. *Geoscientist* **18**, 11–19 (2008).
11. Schmitz, R. & Thissen, J. *Neandertal: Die Geschichte Geht Weiter*. (Spektrum Akademischer Verlag, Heidelberg, 2000).
12. Lyell, C. *The Geological Evidences of the Antiquity of Man: With Remarks on Theories of the Origin of Species by Variation*. (John Murray, London, 1863).
13. Huxley, T. On Some Fossil Remains of Man. *Proc. R. Inst. G. B.* **3**, 420–422 (1862).
14. Campbell, B. The Centenary of Neandertal Man: Part I. *Man* **56**, 156–158 (1956).
15. Schaaffhausen, H. Zui Kenntniss der ältesten Rassenschädel. in *Archiv für Anatomie, Physiologie und wissenschaftliche Medicin* 453 (Müller's Archiv, Leipzig, 1858).
16. Schmerling, P. *Recherches Sur Les Ossemens Fossiles Découverts Dans Les Cavernes de La Province de Liège*. vol. 1 (P.-J. Collardin, Liège, 1833).
17. Trinkaus, E. & Shipman, P. *Neandertals: Changing the Image of Mankind*. (Jonathan Cape, London, 1993).
18. Madison, P. The most brutal of human skulls: measuring and knowing the first Neanderthal. *Br. J. Hist. Sci.* **49**, 411–432 (2016).
19. Schwartz, J. Race and the odd history of human paleontology. *Anat. Rec. B. New Anat.* **289B**, 225–240 (2006).
20. Huxley, T. *Evidence as to Man's Place in Nature*. (Williams and Norgate, London, 1863).
21. Walker, J., Clinnick, D. & White, M. We Are Not Alone: William King and the Naming of the Neanderthals. *Am. Anthropol.* **123**, 805–818 (2021).
22. Anonymous. On the Neanderthal Skull; or Reasons for Believing It to Belong to the Clydian Period, and to a Species Different from That Represented by Man. in *Report of the Thirty-Third Meeting of the British Association for the Advancement of Science held in Newcastle upon Tyne in August and September 1863* 81–82 (John Murray, London, 1864).
23. Anonymous. Anthropology at the British Association. *Anthropol. Rev.* **1**, 379–464 (1863).
24. King, W. The Reputed Fossil Man of the Neanderthal. *Q. J. Sci.* **1**, 88–97 (1864).
25. Keith, A. The early history of the Gibraltar cranium. *Nature* **87**, 314 (1911).
26. Menez, A. The Gibraltar Skull: Early history, 1848–1868. *Arch. Nat. Hist.* **45**, 92–110 (2018).
27. Wood, B. Reconstructing human evolution: Achievements, challenges, and opportunities. *PNAS* **107**, 8902–8909 (2010).
28. Wood, B. The Neanderthals of the College of Surgeons. *Ann. R. Coll. Surg. Engl.* **61**, (1979).
29. Anonymous. Report upon the Soldiers' Home Gibraltar. (1861).
30. Busk, G. Ancient human cranium from Gibraltar. *The Bath chronicle* 3 (1864).
31. Busk, G. Pithecoid Priscan Man from Gibraltar. *The Reader* **4**, 129–130 (1864).
32. Rose, E. & Stringer, C. Gibraltar woman and Neanderthal Man. *Geol. Today* **13**, 179–184 (1997).
33. Busk, G. On a Very Ancient Human Cranium from Gibraltar. in *Report of the Thirty-Fourth Meeting of the British Association for the Advancement of Science: Held at Bath in September 1864* 91–92 (John Murray, London, 1865).
34. Madison, P. A forgotten fossil: The wild Homo calpicus of Gibraltar. *Endeavour* **40**, 268–70 (2016).
35. Hrdlička, A. The Most Ancient Skeletal Remains of Man. in *Annual Report Smithsonian Institution, 1913* 491–552 (Government Printing Office, Washington, D.C., 1914).
36. Trinkaus, E. & Shipman, P. Neandertals: Images of ourselves. *Evol. Anthropol. Issues News Rev.* **1**, 194–201 (1993).
37. Strickland, H. Report of a Committee Consisting of Mr. C. Darwin, Prof. Henslow, Rev. L. Jenyns, Mr.W. Ogilby,Mr. J. Philips ,Dr.Richardson, Mr.W.E. Strickland (Reporter) & Mr. J. O.Westwood, Appointed 'to Consider If the Rules by Which the Nomenclature of Zoology May Be Established on a Uniform and Permanent Basis. in *Report of the Twelfth Meeting of the British Association for the Advancement of Science, Manchester June 1842* (John Murray, London, 1842).
38. Campbell, B. The Centenary of Neandertal Man: Part II. *Man* **56**, 171–173 (1956).
39. Keane, A. H. The European Prehistoric Races. *Nature* **35**, 564–565 (1887).
40. Curtis, G., Swisher, C. & Lewin, R. *Java Man*. (Little, Brown and Company, New York, NY, 2000).
41. Sommer, M. Ancient Hunters and Their Modern Representatives: William Sollas's (1849-1936) Anthropology from Disappointed Bridge to Trunkless Tree and the Instrumentalisation of Racial Conflict. *J. Hist. Biol.* **38**, 327–365 (2005).
42. Hammond, M. The Expulsion of the Neanderthals from Human Ancestry: Marcellin Boule and the Social Context of Scientific Research. *Soc. Stud. Sci.* **12**, 1–36 (1982).
43. Boule, M. L'homme fossile de La Chapelle-aux-Saints (1908). *L'Anthropologie* **19**, 512–525 (1908).
44. Boule, M. L'homme fossile de La Chapelle-aux-Saints (1911). *Ann. Paléontol.* **6**, 1–64 (1911).
45. Boule, M. L'homme fossile de La Chapelle-aux-Saints (1912). *Ann. Paléontol.* **7**, 65–208 (1912).
46. Boule, M. L'homme fossile de La Chapelle-aux-Saints (1913). *Ann. Paléontol.* **8**, 209–279 (1913).
47. Trinkaus, E. Pathology and the posture of the La Chapelle-aux-Saints Neandertal. *Am. J. Phys. Anthropol.* **67**, 19–41 (1985).
48. Haeusler, M. *et al.* Morphology, pathology, and the vertebral posture of the La Chapelle-aux-Saints Neandertal. *PNAS* **116**, 4923–4927 (2019).
49. Sommer, M. Mirror, Mirror on the Wall: Neanderthal as Image and 'Distortion' in Early 20th-Century French Science and Press. *Soc. Stud. Sci.* **36**, 207–240 (2006).
50. Wells, H. G. The Grisly Folk and Their War With Men. *Story Teller Magazine* (1921).
51. Elliot Smith, G. *Evolution of Man: Essays*. (Oxford University Press, Oxford, 1924).

52. Dennell, R. East Asia and human evolution: from cradle of mankind to cul-de-sac. in *East of Africa: Southern Asia, Australia and Modern Human Origins* (eds Dennell, R. & Porr, M.) 8–20 (2014). doi:10.1017/CBO9781139084741.002.

53. Waterston, D. The Piltdown mandible. *Nature* **92**, 319 (1913).

54. Coon, C. *The Origin of Races.* (Alfred A. Knopf, New York, NY, 1962).

55. Coon, C. *The Living Races of Man.* (Jonathon Cape, London, 1965).

56. Athreya, S. & Ackermann, R. Colonialism and narratives of human origins in Asia and Africa. in *Interrogating Human Origins* 72–95 (2019). doi:10.4324/9780203731659-4.

57. Madison, P. Characterized by Darkness: Reconsidering the Origins of the Brutish Neanderthal. *J. Hist. Biol.* **53**, 493–519 (2020).

58. Delisle, R. The biology/culture link in human evolution, 1750–1950: the problem of integration in science. *Stud. Hist. Philos. Sci. Part C Stud. Hist. Philos. Biol. Biomed. Sci.* **31**, 531–556 (2000).

59. Bowler, P. From 'savage' to 'primitive': Victorian evolutionism and the interpretation of marginalized peoples. *Antiquity* **66**, 721–729 (1992).

60. Laing, S. *Human Origins.* (Chapman and Hall, London, 1892).

61. Manias, C. The problematic construction of 'Palaeolithic Man': The Old Stone Age and the difficulties of the comparative method, 1859–1914. *Stud. Hist. Philos. Sci. Part C Stud. Hist. Philos. Biol. Biomed. Sci.* **51**, 32–43 (2015).

62. Sollas, W. On the Cranial and Facial Characters of the Neandertal Race. *Philos. Trans. R. Soc. Lond. Ser. B Contain. Pap. Biol. Character* **199**, 281–339 (1908).

63. Sollas, W. *Ancient Hunters and Their Modern Representatives.* (Macmillan, London, 1911).

64. Elliot Smith, G. *Human History.* (Jonathon Cape, London, 1934).

65. Drell, J. Neanderthals: A History of Interpretation. *Oxf. J. Archaeol.* **19**, 1–24 (2000).

66. Selcer, P. Beyond the Cephalic Index: Negotiating Politics to Produce UNESCO's Scientific Statements on Race. *Curr. Anthropol.* **53**, S173–S184 (2012).

67. UNESCO. *Four Statements on the Race Question.* (UNESCO, Paris, 1969).

68. Straus, W. & Cave, A. Pathology and the Posture of Neandertal Man. *Q. Rev. Biol.* **32**, 348–363 (1957).

69. Cameron, D. & Groves, C. *Bones, Stones and Molecules: "Out of Africa" and Human Origins.* (Elsevier Academic Press, London, 2004).

70. Cowgill, L., Trinkaus, E. & Zeder, M. Shanidar 10: A Middle Paleolithic immature distal lower limb from Shanidar Cave, Iraqi Kurdistan. *J. Hum. Evol.* **53**, 213–223 (2007).

71. Pomeroy, E. *et al.* New Neanderthal remains associated with the 'flower burial' at Shanidar Cave. *Antiquity* **94**, 11–26 (2020).

72. Solecki, R. Shanidar IV, a Neanderthal flower burial in northern Iraq. *Science* **190**, 880–881 (1975).

73. Trinkaus, E. & Villotte, S. External auditory exostoses and hearing loss in the Shanidar 1 Neandertal. *PLOS ONE* **12**, e0186684 (2017).

74. Sommer, J. The Shanidar IV 'flower burial': A reevaluation of Neanderthal burial ritual. *Camb. Archæological J.* **9**, 127–129 (1999).

75. Fiacconi, M. & Hunt, C. Pollen taphonomy at Shanidar Cave (Kurdish Iraq): An initial evaluation. *Rev. Palaeobot. Palynol.* **223**, 87–93 (2015).

76. Klein, R. *The Human Career.* (University of Chicago Press, Chicago, IL, 1999).

77. Oppenheimer, S. *Out of Eden.* (Constable & Robinson Ltd, London, 2003).

78. Mithen, S. *The Prehistory of the Mind.* (Thames & Hudson, London, 1996).

79. Mellars, P. Why did modern human populations disperse from Africa ca. 60,000 years ago? A new model. *PNAS* **103**, 9381–9386 (2006).

80. Klein, R. & Edgar, B. *The Dawn of Human Culture.* (John Wiley & Sons, Inc., New York, NY, 2002).

81. Diamond, J. *The Third Chimpanzee.* (Random, London, 1991).

82. McBrearty, S. & Brooks, A. The revolution that wasn't: a new interpretation of the origin of modern human behaviour. *J. Hum. Evol.* **39**, 453–563 (2000).

83. Mithen, S. *The Singing Neanderthal.* (Weidenfeld & Nicholson, London, 2005).

84. Lieberman, D. Speculations About the Selective Basis for Modern Human Craniofacial Form. *Evol. Anthropol.* **17**, 55–68 (2008).

85. Coolidge, F. & Wynn, T. *The Rise of Homo Sapiens.* (Wiley-Blackwell, Hoboken, NJ, 2009).

86. Bruner, E., Manzi, G. & Arsuaga, J. Encephalization and allometric trajectories in the genus Homo: Evidence from the Neandertal and modern lineages. *PNAS* **100**, 15335–15340 (2003).

87. Bruner, E. Geometric morphometrics and paleoneurology: brain shape evolution in the genus Homo. *J. Hum. Evol.* **47**, 279–303 (2004).

88. Bastir, M. *et al.* Evolution of the base of the brain in highly encephalized human species. *Nat. Commun.* **2**, 588 (2011).

89. Kochiyama, T. *et al.* Reconstructing the Neanderthal brain using computational anatomy. *Sci. Rep.* **8**, 6296 (2018).

90. Wynn, T. & Coolidge, F. Did a Small but Significant Enhancement in Working Memory Capacity Power the Evolution of Modern Thinking. in *Rethinking the human revolution* (eds Mellars, P., Boyle, K., Bar-Yosef, O. & Stringer, C.) 79–90 (McDonald Institute, Cambridge, 2007).

91. Baddeley, A. & Hitch, G. Working Memory. in *Recent Advances in Learning and Motivation* (ed. Bower, G.) 47–90 (Academic Press, New York, NY, 1974).

92. Pinson, A. *et al.* Human TKTL1 implies greater neurogenesis in frontal neocortex of modern humans than Neanderthals. *Science* **377**, eabl6422 (2022).

93. Stringer, C. The origin and evolution of Homo sapiens. *Philos. Trans. R. Soc. B* **371**, 20150237 (2016).

94. Richter, D. *et al.* The age of the hominin fossils from Jebel Irhoud, Morocco, and the origins of the Middle Stone Age. *Nature* **546**, 293–296 (2017).

95. Hublin, J. *et al.* New fossils from Jebel Irhoud, Morocco and the pan-African origin of Homo sapiens. *Nature* **546**, 289–291 (2017).

96. Bruner, E. & Pearson, O. Neurocranial evolution in modern humans: the case of Jebel Irhoud 1. *Anthropol. Sci.* **121**, 31–41 (2013).

97. Day, M. Early Homo sapiens Remains from the Omo River Region of South-west Ethiopia: Omo Human Skeletal Remain. *Nature* **222**, 1135–1138 (1969).

98. Vidal, C. *et al.* Age of the oldest known Homo sapiens from eastern Africa. *Nature* **601**, 579–583 (2022).

99. Neubauer, S., Hublin, J. & Gunz, P. The evolution of modern human brain shape. *Sci. Adv.* **4**, eaao5961 (2018).

100. Zollikofer, C. *et al.* Endocranial ontogeny and evolution in early Homo sapiens: The evidence from Herto, Ethiopia. *PNAS* **119**, e2123553119 (2022).

101. Villa, P. & Roebroeks, W. Neandertal Demise: An Archaeological Analysis of the Modern Human Superiority Complex. *PLOS ONE* **9**, e96424 (2014).

102. Roebroeks, W. & Soressi, M. Neandertals revised. *PNAS* **113**, 6372–6379 (2016).

103. Zilhão, J. *et al.* Symbolic use of marine shells and mineral pigments by Iberian Neandertals. *PNAS* **107**, 1023–1028 (2010).

104. Peresani, M., Vanhaeren, M., Quaggiotto, E., Queffelec, A. & d'Errico, F. An Ochered Fossil Marine Shell From the Mousterian of Fumane Cave, Italy. *PLOS ONE* **8**, e68572 (2013).

105. Hoffmann, D., Angelucci, D., Villaverde, V., Zapata, J. & Zilhão, J. Symbolic use of marine shells and mineral pigments by Iberian Neandertals 115,000 years ago. *Sci. Adv.* **4**, eaar5255 (2018).

106. Peresani, M., Fiore, I., Gala, M., Romandini, M. & Tagliacozzo, A. Late Neandertals and the intentional removal of feathers as evidenced from bird bone taphonomy at Fumane Cave 44 ky B.P., Italy. *PNAS* **108**, 3888–3893 (2011).

107. Finlayson, C. *et al.* Birds of a Feather: Neanderthal Exploitation of Raptors and Corvids. *PLOS ONE* **7**, e45927 (2012).

108. Finlayson, S., Finlayson, G., Guzman, F. & Finlayson, C. Neanderthals and the cult of the Sun Bird. *Quat. Sci. Rev.* **217**, 217–224 (2019).

109. Morin, E. & Laroulandie, V. Presumed Symbolic Use of Diurnal Raptors by Neanderthals. *PLOS ONE* **7**, e32856 (2012).

110. Radovčić, D., Sršen, A., Radovčić, J. & Frayer, D. Evidence for Neandertal Jewelry: Modified White-Tailed Eagle Claws at Krapina. *PLOS ONE* **10**, e0119802 (2015).

111. Hoffmann, D. *et al.* U-Th dating of carbonate crusts reveals Neandertal origin of Iberian cave art. *Science* **359**, 912–915 (2018).

112. Green, R. *et al.* A Draft Sequence of the Neandertal Genome. *Science* **328**, 710–722 (2010).

113. Hajdinjak, M. *et al.* Initial Upper Palaeolithic humans in Europe had recent Neanderthal ancestry. *Nature* **592**, 253–257 (2021).

114. Slimak, L. *et al.* Modern human incursion into Neanderthal territories 54,000 years ago at Mandrin, France. *Sci. Adv.* **8**, eabj9496 (2022).

115. Harvati, K. *et al.* Apidima Cave fossils provide earliest evidence of Homo sapiens in Eurasia. *Nature* **571**, 500–504 (2019).

116. Higham, T. *et al.* The timing and spatiotemporal patterning of Neanderthal disappearance. *Nature* **512**, 306–309 (2014).

117. Rasmussen, S. *et al.* A stratigraphic framework for abrupt climatic changes during the Last Glacial period based on three synchronized Greenland ice-core records: refining and extending the INTIMATE event stratigraphy. *Quat. Sci. Rev.* **106**, 14–28 (2014).

118. Staubwasser, M. *et al.* Impact of climate change on the transition of Neanderthals to modern humans in Europe. *PNAS* **115**, 9116–9121 (2018).

119. El Zaatari, S., Grine, F., Ungar, P. & Hublin, J. Neandertal versus Modern Human Dietary Responses to Climatic Fluctuations. *PLOS ONE* **11**, e0153277 (2016).

120. Mellars, P. The Upper Palaeolithic Revolution. in *The Oxford Illustrated History of Prehistoric Europe* (ed. Cunliffe, B.) 42–78 (Oxford University Press, Oxford, 1994).

121. Mellars, P. Neanderthals and the modern human colonization of Europe. *Nature* **432**, 461–465 (2004).

122. Kuhn, S. & Zwyns, N. Rethinking the initial Upper Paleolithic. *Quat. Int.* **347**, 29–38 (2014).

123. Briggs, A. *et al.* Targeted Retrieval and Analysis of Five Neandertal mtDNA Genomes. *Science* **325**, 318–321 (2009).

124. Prüfer, K. *et al.* The complete genome sequence of a Neanderthal from the Altai Mountains. *Nature* **505**, 43–49 (2014).

125. Mellars, P. & French, J. Tenfold Population Increase in Western Europe at the Neandertal–to–Modern Human Transition. *Science* **333**, 623–627 (2011).

126. Vaesen, K., Scherjon, F., Hemerik, L. & Verpoorte, A. Inbreeding, Allele effects and stochasticity might be sufficient to account for Neanderthal extinction. *PLOS ONE* **14**, e0225117 (2019).

127. Degioanni, A., Bonenfant, C., Cabut, S. & Condemi, S. Living on the edge: Was demographic weakness the cause of Neanderthal demise? *PLOS ONE* **14**, e0216742 (2019).

128. Finlayson, C. *et al.* Late survival of Neanderthals at the southernmost extreme of Europe. *Nature* **443**, 850–853 (2006).

129. Finlayson, C. *et al.* Gorham's Cave, Gibraltar - The persistence of a Neanderthal population. *Quat. Int.* **181**, 74–71 (2008).

130. Slimak, L. *et al.* Late Mousterian Persistence near the Arctic Circle. *Science* **332**, 841–845 (2011).

131. Green, R. *et al.* Analysis of one million base pairs of Neanderthal DNA. *Nature* **444**, 330–336 (2006).

132. Green, R. *et al.* A Complete Neandertal Mitochondrial Genome Sequence Determined by High-Throughput Sequencing. *Cell* **134**, 416–426 (2008).

133. Yotova, V. *et al.* An X-Linked Haplotype of Neandertal Origin Is Present Among All Non-African Populations. *Mol. Biol. Evol.* **28**, 1957–1962 (2011).

134. Sankararaman, S., Patterson, N., Li, H., Pääbo, S. & Reich, D. The Date of Interbreeding between Neandertals and Modern Humans. *PLOS Genet.* **8**, e1002947 (2012).

135. Currat, M. & Excoffier, L. Strong reproductive isolation between humans and Neanderthals inferred from observed patterns of introgression. *PNAS* **108**, 15129–15134 (2011).

136. Neves, A. & Serva, M. Extremely Rare Interbreeding Events Can Explain Neanderthal DNA in Living Humans. *PLOS ONE* **7**, e47076 (2012).

137. Fu, Q. *et al.* An early modern human from Romania with a recent Neanderthal ancestor. *Nature* **524**, 216–219 (2015).

138. Krause, J. *et al.* The complete mitochondrial DNA genome of an unknown hominin from southern Siberia. *Nature* **464**, 894–897 (2010).

139. Reich, D. *et al.* Genetic history of an archaic hominin group from Denisova Cave in Siberia. *Nature* **468**, 1053–1060 (2010).

140. Chen, F. *et al.* A late Middle Pleistocene Denisovan mandible from the Tibetan Plateau. *Nature* **569**, 409–412 (2019).

141. Vernot, B. & Akey, J. Resurrecting Surviving Neandertal Lineages from Modern Human Genomes. *Science* **343**, 1017–1021 (2014).

142. Sankararaman, S. *et al.* The genomic landscape of Neanderthal ancestry in present-day humans. *Nature* **507**, 354–357 (2014).

143. Ding, Q., Hu, Y., Xu, S., Wang, J. & Jin, L. Neanderthal Introgression at Chromosome 3p21.31 Was Under Positive Natural Selection in East Asians. *Mol. Biol. Evol.* **31**, 683–695 (2014).

144. Sankararaman, S., Mallick, S., Patterson, N. & Reich, D. The Combined Landscape of Denisovan and Neanderthal Ancestry in Present-Day Humans. *Curr. Biol.* **26**, 1241–1247 (2016).

145. Huerta-Sanchez, E. *et al.* Altitude adaptation in Tibetans caused by introgression of Denisovan-like DNA. *Nature* **512**, 194–197 (2014).

146. Hoffecker, J. Innovation and Technological Knowledge in the Upper Paleolithic of Northern Eurasia. *Evol. Anthropol.* **14**, 186–198 (2005).

147. Collard, M., Tarle, L., Sandgathe, D. & Allan, A. Faunal evidence for a difference in clothing use between Neanderthals and early modern humans in Europe. *J. Anthropol. Archaeol.* **44**, 235–246 (2016).

08: Early funerary practices

1. Cameron, D. & Groves, C. *Bones, Stones and Molecules: "Out of Africa" and Human Origins.* (Elsevier Academic Press, London, 2004).

2. Johanson, D. The paleoanthropology of Hadar, Ethiopia. *Hum. Palaeontol. Prehistory* **16**, 140–154 (2017).

3. Behrensmeyer, A. Paleoenvironmental context of the Pliocene A.L. 333 "First Family" hominin locality, Hadar Formation, Ethiopia. in *The Geology of Early Humans in the Horn of Africa: Geological Society of America Special Paper 446* (eds Quade, J. & Wynn, J.) 203–214 (The Geological Society of America, Boulder, CO, 2008).

4. Pettitt, P. *The Palaeolithic Origins of Human Burial.* (Routledge, Abingdon, 2011).

5. Gunz, P. *et al.* Australopithecus afarensis endocasts suggest ape-like brain organization and prolonged brain growth. *Sci. Adv.* **6**, eaaz4729 (2020).

6. Klein, R. *The Human Career.* (University of Chicago Press, Chicago, IL, 1999).

7. Berlin, J. The Story Behind National Geographic's Viral Chimp Funeral Photo. *Huffington Post* https://www.huffpost.com/entry/the-story-behind-national_n_338120 (2011).

8. Besenbacher, S., Hvilsom, C., Marques-Bonet, T., Mailund, T. & Schierup, M. Direct estimation of mutations in great apes reconciles phylogenetic dating. *Nat. Ecol. Evol.* **3**, 286–292 (2019).

9. Biro, D. *et al.* Chimpanzee mothers at Bossou, Guinea carry the mummified remains of their dead infants. *Curr. Biol.* **20**, R351-2 (2010).

10. Cronin, K. A., van Leeuwen, E. J. C., Mulenga, I. C. & Bodamer, M. D. Behavioral response of a chimpanzee mother toward her dead infant. *Am. J. Primatol.* **73**, 415–421 (2011).

11. Fashing, P. *et al.* Death Among Geladas (Theropithecus gelada): A Broader Perspective on Mummified Infants and Primate Thanatology. *Am. J. Primatol.* **73**, 405–9 (2011).

12. Anderson, J. R., Gillies, A. & Lock, L. C. Pan thanatology. *Curr. Biol.* **20**, R349–R351 (2010).

13. Gonçalves, A. & Carvalho, S. Death among primates: a critical review of non-human primate interactions towards their dead and dying. *Biol. Rev.* **94**, 1502–1529 (2019).

14. Boswell, J. E. Expositio and Oblatio: The Abandonment of Children and the Ancient and Medieval Family. *Am. Hist. Rev.* **89**, 10–33 (1984).

15. Lubbock, J. *Pre-Historic Times as Illustrated by Ancient Remains, and the Manners and Customs of Modern Savages.* (Williams and Norgate, London, 1865).

16. Lindenbaum, S. Thinking About Cannibalism. *Annu. Rev. Anthropol.* **33**, 475–498 (2004).

17. Lindenbaum, S. Cannibalism, kuru and anthropology. *Folia Neuropathol.* **47**, 138–44 (2009).

18. Liberski, P. Kuru: A Journey Back in Time from Papua New Guinea to the Neanderthals' Extinction. *Pathog. Basel Switz.* **2**, 472–505 (2013).

19. Liberski, P. P., Gajos, A., Sikorska, B. & Lindenbaum, S. Kuru, the First Human Prion Disease. *Viruses* **11**, 232 (2019).

20. Whitfield, J., Pako, W., Collinge, J. & Alpers, M. Mortuary rites of the South Fore and kuru. *Philos. Trans. R. Soc. Lond. B. Biol. Sci.* **363**, 3721–3724 (2008).

21. Gajdusek, D. C., Gibbs, C. J. & Alpers, M. Transmission and Passage of Experimental 'Kuru' to Chimpanzees. *Science* **155**, 212–214 (1967).

22. Mead, S. *et al.* Balancing Selection at the Prion Protein Gene Consistent with Prehistoric Kurulike Epidemics. *Science* **300**, 640–643 (2003).

23. Gill, O. *et al.* Prevalence in Britain of abnormal prion protein in human appendices before and after exposure to the cattle BSE epizootic. *Acta Neuropathol. (Berl.)* **139**, 965–976 (2020).

24. Garske, T., Ward, H. J. T., Clarke, P., Will, R. G. & Ghani, A. C. Factors determining the potential for onward transmission of variant Creutzfeldt–Jakob disease via surgical instruments. *J. R. Soc. Interface* **3**, 757–766 (2006).

25. Ferguson, W. W. Reappraisal of the taxonomic status of the cranium Stw 53 from the Plio/Pleistocene of Sterkfontein, in South Africa. *Primates* **30**, 103–109 (1989).

26. Pickering, T., White, T. & Toth, N. Brief communication: Cutmarks on a Plio-Pleistocene hominid from Sterkfontein, South Africa. *Am. J. Phys. Anthropol.* **111**, 579–84 (2000).

27. Bermúdez de Castro, J. *et al.* A Hominid from the Lower Pleistocene of Atapuerca, Spain: Possible Ancestor to Neandertals and Modern Humans. *Science* **276**, 1392–1395 (1997).

28. Falguères, C. *et al.* Earliest humans in Europe: the age of TD6 Gran Dolina, Atapuerca, Spain. *J. Hum. Evol.* **37**, 343–352 (1999).

29. Duval, M. *et al.* The first direct ESR analysis of a hominin tooth from Atapuerca Gran Dolina TD-6 (Spain) supports the antiquity of Homo antecessor. *Quat. Geochronol.* **47**, 120–137 (2018).

30. Martinón-Torres, M. *et al.* New permanent teeth from Gran Dolina-TD6 (Sierra de Atapuerca). The bearing of Homo antecessor on the evolutionary scenario of Early and Middle Pleistocene Europe. *J. Hum. Evol.* **127**, 93–117 (2019).

31. Ashton, N. *et al.* Hominin Footprints from Early Pleistocene Deposits at Happisburgh, UK. *PLOS ONE* **9**, e88329 (2014).

32. Fernandez-Jalvo, Y., Diez, J., Caceres, I. & Rosell, J. Human cannibalism in the Early Pleistocene of Europe (Gran Dolina, Sierra de Aterpuerca, Burgos, Spain). *J. Hum. Evol.* **37**, 591–622 (1999).

33. Bermúdez de Castro, J. M. *et al.* The Atapuerca sites and their contribution to the knowledge of human evolution in Europe. *Evol. Anthropol. Issues News Rev.* **13**, 25–41 (2004).

34. Bermúdez de Castro, J. *et al.* A new early Pleistocene hominin mandible from Atapuerca-TD6, Spain. *J. Hum. Evol.* **55**, 729–735 (2008).

35. Carbonell, E. & Mosquera, M. The emergence of a symbolic behaviour: the sepulchral pit of Sima de los Huesos, Sierra de Atapuerca, Burgos, Spain. *Comptes Rendus Palevol* **5**, 155–160 (2006).

36. Arsuaga, J. *et al.* Neandertal roots: Cranial and chronological evidence from Sima de los Huesos. *Science* **344**, 1358–1363 (2014).

37. Stringer, C. The Status of Homo heidelbergensis (Schoetensack 1908). *Evol. Anthropol.* **21**, 101–107 (2012).

38. Aranburu, J., Arsuagab, J. & Sala, N. The stratigraphy of the Sima de los Huesos (Atapuerca, Spain) and implications for the origin of the fossil hominin accumulation. *Quat. Int.* **443**, 5–21 (2017).

39. Sala, N. *et al.* Lethal Interpersonal Violence in the Middle Pleistocene. *PLOS ONE* **10**, e0126589 (2015).

40. Andrews, P. & Fernández-Jalvo, Y. Surface modifications of the Sima de los Huesos fossil humans. *J. Hum. Evol.* **33 2–3**, 191–217 (1997).

41. Fernández-Jalvo, Y. & Andrews, P. Atapuerca, le conte de deux sites. *L'Anthropologie* **105**, 223–236 (2001).

42. Egeland, C., Domínguez-Rodrigo, M., Pickering, T., Menter, C. & Heaton, J. Hominin skeletal part abundances and claims of deliberate disposal of corpses in the Middle Pleistocene. *PNAS* **115**, 4601–4606 (2018).

43. Endicott, P., Ho, S. & Stringer, C. Using genetic evidence to evaluate four palaeoanthropological hypotheses for the timing of Neanderthal and modern human origins. *J. Hum. Evol.* **59**, 87–95 (2010).

44. Bocquet-Appel, J. & Arsuaga, L. Age Distributions of Hominid Samples at Atapuerca (SH) and Krapina Could Indicate Accumulation by Catastrophe. *J. Archaeol. Sci.* **26**, 327–338 (1999).

45. Wolpoff, M. & Caspari, R. Does Krapina Reflect Early Neandertal Paleodemography? *Period. Biol.* **108**, 425–432 (2006).

46. Pettitt, P. The Rise of Modern Humans. in *The human past* (ed. Scarre, C.) 124–173 (Thames & Hudson, London, 2013).

47. Pomeroy, E. *et al.* New Neanderthal remains associated with the 'flower burial' at Shanidar Cave. *Antiquity* **94**, 11–26 (2020).

48. Cowgill, L., Trinkaus, E. & Zeder, M. Shanidar 10: A Middle Paleolithic immature distal lower limb from Shanidar Cave, Iraqi Kurdistan. *J. Hum. Evol.* **53**, 213–223 (2007).

49. Conroy, G. *Reconstructing Human Origins: A Modern Synthesis*. (W. W. Norton & Company, Inc., New York, NY, 1997).

50. Solecki, R. Shanidar IV, a Neanderthal flower burial in northern Iraq. *Science* **190**, 880–881 (1975).

51. Sommer, J. The Shanidar IV 'flower burial': A reevaluation of Neanderthal burial ritual. *Camb. Archæological J.* **9**, 127–129 (1999).

52. Fiacconi, M. & Hunt, C. Pollen taphonomy at Shanidar Cave (Kurdish Iraq): An initial evaluation. *Rev. Palaeobot. Palynol.* **223**, 87–93 (2015).

53. Hunt, C., Pomeroy, E., Reynolds, T., Tilby, E. & Barker, G. Shanidar et ses fleurs? Reflections on the palynology of the Neanderthal 'Flower Burial' hypothesis. *J. Archaeol. Sci.* **159**, 105822 (2023).

54. Mellars, P. *The Neanderthal Legacy*. (Princeton University Press, Princeton, NJ, USA, 1996).

55. Gargett, R. H. *et al.* Grave Shortcomings: The Evidence for Neandertal Burial [and Comments and Reply]. *Curr. Anthropol.* **30**, 157–190 (1989).

56. Rendu, W. *et al.* Evidence supporting an intentional Neandertal burial at La Chapelle-aux-Saints. *PNAS* **111**, 81–86 (2014).

57. Richter, D. *et al.* The age of the hominin fossils from Jebel Irhoud, Morocco, and the origins of the Middle Stone Age. *Nature* **546**, 293–296 (2017).

58. Bruner, E. & Pearson, O. Neurocranial evolution in modern humans: the case of Jebel Irhoud 1. *Anthropol. Sci.* **121**, 31–41 (2013).

59. Clark, J. *et al.* Stratigraphic, chronological and behavioural contexts of Pleistocene Homo sapiens from Middle Awash, Ethiopia. *Nature* **423**, 747–752 (2003).

60. White, T. *et al.* Pleistocene Homo sapiens from Middle Awash, Ethiopia. *Nature* **423**, 742–747 (2003).

61. Grün, R. *et al.* U-series and ESR analyses of bones and teeth relating to the human burials from Skhul. *J. Hum. Evol.* **49**, 316–334 (2005).

62. Schwarcz, H. *et al.* ESR dates for the hominid burial site of Qafzeh in Israel. *J. Hum. Evol.* **17**, 733–737 (1988).

63. Roberts, A. *The Incredible Human Journey*. (Bloomsbury, London, 2009).

64. Vanhaeren, M. *et al.* Middle Paleolithic Shell Beads in Israel and Algeria. *Science* **312**, 1785–1788 (2006).

65. Bar-Yosef Mayer, D., Vandermeersch, B. & Bar-Yosef, O. Shells and ochre in Middle Paleolithic Qafzeh Cave, Israel: indications for modern behavior. *J. Hum. Evol.* **56**, 307–314 (2009).

66. Smirnov, Y. Intentional Human Burial: Middle Paleolithic (Last Glaciation) Beginnings. *J. World Prehistory* **3**, 199–233 (1989).

67. Coqueugniot, H. *et al.* Earliest Cranio-Encephalic Trauma from the Levantine Middle Palaeolithic: 3D Reappraisal of the Qafzeh 11 Skull, Consequences of Pediatric Brain Damage on Individual Life Condition and Social Care. *PLOS ONE* **9**, e102822 (2014).

68. Clarkson, C. *et al.* Human occupation of northern Australia by 65,000 years ago. *Nature* **547**, 306–310 (2017).

69. Bowler, J., Jones, R., Allen, H. & Thorne, A. Pleistocene Human Remains from Australia: A Living Site and Human Cremation from Lake Mungo, Western New South Wales. *World Archaeol.* **2**, 39–60 (1970).

70. Bowler, J. *et al.* New ages for human occupation and climatic change at Lake Mungo, Australia. *Nature* **421**, 837–840 (2003).

71. Thorne, A. *et al.* Australia's oldest human remains: age of the Lake Mungo 3 skeleton. *J. Hum. Evol.* **36**, 591–612 (1999).

72. Slimak, L. *et al.* Modern human incursion into Neanderthal territories 54,000 years ago at Mandrin, France. *Sci. Adv.* **8**, eabj9496 (2022).

73. Mellars, P. A new radiocarbon revolution and the dispersal of modern humans in Eurasia. *Nature* **493**, 931–935 (2006).

74. Higham, T. *et al.* Testing models for the beginnings of the Aurignacian and the advent of figurative art and music: The radiocarbon chronology of Geißenklösterle. *J. Hum. Evol.* **62**, 664–676 (2012).

75. Taller, A. & Conard, N. Transition or Replacement? Radiocarbon Dates from Hohle Fels Cave (Alb-Donau-Kreis / D) and the Passage from Aurignacion to Gravettian. *Archaologisches Korresp.* **49**, 165–181 (2019).

76. Kozlowski, J. The origin of the Gravettian. *Quat. Int.* **359–360**, 3–18 (2015).

77. Bicho, N., Cascalheira, J. & Goncalves, C. Early Upper Paleolithic colonization across Europe: Time and mode of the Gravettian diffusion. *PLOS ONE* **12**, e0178506 (2017).

78. Reynolds, N. & Green, C. Spatiotemporal modelling of radiocarbon dates using linear regression does not indicate a vector of demic dispersal associated with the earliest Gravettian assemblages in Europe. *J. Archaeol. Sci. Rep.* **27**, 101958 (2019).

79. Formicola, V. From the Sunghir Children to the Romito Dwarf: Aspects of the Upper Paleolithic Funerary Landscape. *Curr. Anthropol.* **48**, 446–453 (2007).

80. Marom, A., McCullagh, J., Higham, T., Sinitsyn, A. & Hedges, R. Single amino acid radiocarbon dating of Upper Paleolithic modern humans. *PNAS* **109**, 6878–6881 (2012).

81. Mellars, P. The Upper Palaeolithic Revolution. in *The Oxford Illustrated History of Prehistoric Europe* (ed. Cunliffe, B.) 42–78 (Oxford University Press, Oxford, 1994).

82. Schulting, R. Antlers, bone pins and flint blades: the mesolithic cemeteries of Teviec and Hoedic, Brittany. *Antiquity* **70**, 335–350 (1996).

83. Kacki, S. *et al.* Complex mortuary dynamics in the Upper Paleolithic of the decorated Grotte de Cussac, France. *PNAS* **117**, 14851–14856 (2020).

84. Bello, S., Wallduck, R., Parfitt, S. & Stringer, C. An Upper Palaeolithic engraved human bone associated with ritualistic cannibalism. *PLOS ONE* **12**, e0182127 (2017).

85. Bello, S., Parfitt, S. & Stringer, C. Earliest Directly-Dated Human Skull-Cups. *PLOS ONE* **6**, e17026 (2011).

86. Marsh, W. A. & Bello, S. Cannibalism and burial in the late Upper Palaeolithic: Combining archaeological and genetic evidence. *Quat. Sci. Rev.* **319**, 108309 (2023).

87. Orschiedt, J. *et al.* Human Remains from Maszycka Cave (woj. małopolskie / PL): the Treatment of Human Bodies in the Magdalenian. *Archäol. Korresp.* **47**, 423–439 (2017).

88. Belfer-Cohen, A. & Goring-Morris, N. Becoming Farmers: The Inside Story. *Curr. Anthropol.* **52**, S209–S220 (2011).

89. Hillman, G. Late Pleistocene changes in wild plant-foods available to hunter-gatherers of the Fertile Crescent: possible preludes to cereal cultivation. in *The Origins and Spread of Agriculture and Pastoralism in Eurasia* (ed. Harris, D.) 159–201 (Routledge, London, 1996).

90. Barker, G. *The Agricultural Revolution in Prehistory: Why Did Foragers Become Farmers*. (Oxford University Press, Oxford, 2006).

91. Kislev, M., Nadel, D. & Carmi, I. Epipalaeolithic (19,000 BP) cereal and fruit diet at Ohalo II, Sea of Galilee, Israel. *Rev. Palaeobot. Palynol.* **73**, 161–166 (1992).

92. Hershkovitz, L. *et al.* Ohalo II H2: A 19,000-Year-Old Skeleton From a Water-Logged Site at the Sea of Galilee, Israel. *Am. J. Phys. Anthropol.* **96**, 215–234 (1995).

93. Watkins, T. From Foragers to Complex Societies in Southwest Asia. in *The human past* (ed. Scarre, C.) 200–233 (Thames & Hudson, London, 2013).

94. Maher, L., Macdonald, D., Pomeroy, E. & Stock, J. Life, death, and the destruction of architecture: Hunter-gatherer mortuary behaviors in prehistoric Jordan. *J. Anthropol. Archaeol.* **61**, 101262 (2021).

95. Goring-Morris, N. & Belfer-Cohen, A. Neolithization Processes in the Levant The Outer Envelope. *Curr. Anthropol.* **52**, S195–S208 (2011).

96. Maher, L. *et al.* A Unique Human-Fox Burial from a Pre-Natufian Cemetery in the Levant (Jordan). *PLOS ONE* **6**, e15815 (2011).

97. Mithen, S. *After the Ice: A Global Human History 20,000 - 5,000 BC*. (Weidenfield & Nicholson, London, 2003).

98. Valla, F. *et al.* Eynan (Ain Mallaha). in *Quaternary of the Levant* (eds Enzel, Y. & Bar-Yosef, O.) 337–346 (Cambridge University Press, Cambridge, 2017).

99. Bar-Yosef, O. The Natufian Culture in the Levant,Threshold to the Origins of Agriculture. *Evol. Anthropol.* **6**, 159–177 (1998).

100. Byrd, B. & Monahan, C. Death, Mortuary Ritual, and Natufian Social Structure. *J. Anthropol. Archaeol.* **14**, 251–287 (1995).

101. Mithen, S. The Mesolithic Age. in *The Oxford Illustrated History of Prehistoric Europe* (ed. Cunliffe, B.) 79–135 (Oxford University Press, Oxford, 1994).

102. Bar-Yosef, D. Changes in the Selection of Marine Shells from the Natufian to the Neolithic. in *The Natufian Culture in the Levant* (eds Bar-Yosef, O. & Valla, F.) 629–636 (International Monographs in Prehistory, Ann Arbor, MI, 1991).

103. Reese, D. Marine Shells in the Levant: Upper Palaeolithic, Epipalaeolithic and Neolithic. in *The Natufian Culture in the Levant* (eds Bar-Yosef, O. & Valla, F.) 613–628 (International Monographs in Prehistory, Ann Arbor, MI, 1991).

104. Severinghaus, J., Sowers, T., Brook, E., Alley, R. & Bender, M. Timing of abrupt climate change at the end of the Younger Dryas interval from thermally fractionated gases in polar ice. *Nature* **391**, 141–146 (1998).

105. Rasmussen, S. *et al.* A new Greenland ice core chronology for the last glacial. *J. Geophys. Res.* **111**, X1-15 (2006).

106. Maher, L., Banning, E. & Chazan, M. Oasis or Mirage? Assessing the Role of Abrupt Climate Change in the Prehistory of the Southern Levant. *Camb. Archaeol. J.* **21**, 1–29 (2011).

107. Torfstein, A., Goldstein, S., Stein, M. & Enzel, Y. Impacts of abrupt climate changes in the Levant from Last Glacial Dead Sea levels. *Quat. Sci. Rev.* **69**, 1–7 (2013).

108. Grosman, L. *et al.* Nahal Ein Gev II, a Late Natufian Community at the Sea of Galilee. *PLOS ONE* **11**, e0146647 (2016).

109. Hartman, G., Bar-Yosef, O., Brittingham, A., Grosman, L. & Munro, N. Hunted gazelles evidence cooling, but not drying, during the Younger Dryas in the southern Levant. *PNAS* **113**, 3997–4002 (2016).

110. Valla, F. Les Natoufiens de Mallaha et l'espace. in *The Natufian Culture in the Levant* (eds Bar-Yosef, O. & Valla, F.) 111–122 (University of Michigan, International Monographs in Prehistory, Ann Arbor, MI, 1991).

111. Kuijt, I. Negotiating Equality through Ritual: A Consideration of Late Natufian and Prepottery Neolithic A Period Mortuary Practices. *J. Anthropol. Archaeol.* **15**, 313–336 (1996).

112. Lewis-Williams, D. & Pearce, D. *Inside the Neolithic Mind.* (Thames & Hudson, London, 2005).

113. Gkiasta, M., Russell, T., Shennan, S. & Steele, J. Neolithic transition in Europe: the radiocarbon record revisited. *Antiquity* **77**, 45–62 (2003).

114. Gibaja, J. *et al.* The Emergence of Mesolithic Cemeteries in SW Europe: Insights from the El Collado (Oliva, Valencia, Spain) Radiocarbon Record. *PLOS ONE* **10**, e0115505 (2015).

115. Hodgkins, J. *et al.* An infant burial from Arma Veirana in northwestern Italy provides insights into funerary practices and female personhood in early Mesolithic Europe. *Sci. Rep.* **11**, 23735 (2021).

116. O'Shea, J. & Zvelebil, M. Oleneostrovski Mogilnik: Reconstructing the Social and Economic Organization of Prehistoric Foragers in Northern Russia. *J. Anthropol. Archaeol.* **3**, 1–40 (1984).

117. Childe, G. *Man Makes Himself.* (Watts and Co., London, 1936).

118. Lazaridis, I. *et al.* Genomic insights into the origin of farming in the ancient Near East. *Nature* **536**, 419–424 (2016).

119. Kuijt, I. The Regeneration of Life: Neolithic Structures of Symbolic Remembering and Forgetting. *Curr. Anthropol.* **49**, 171–197 (2008).

120. Borić, D. The Lepenski Vir conundrum: reinterpretation of the Mesolithic and Neolithic sequences in the Danube Gorges. *Antiquity* **76**, 1026–1039 (2002).

121. Radovanovic, I. Houses and burials at Lepenski Vir. *Eur. J. Archaeol.* **3**, 330–349 (2000).

122. Borić, D. & Price, D. Strontium isotopes document greater human mobility at the start of the Balkan Neolithic. *PNAS* **110**, 3298–3303 (2013).

123. Scarre, C. Holocene Europe. in *The human past* (ed. Scarre, C.) 392–431 (Thames & Hudson, London, 2013).

124. Crombé, P. & Vanmontfort, B. The neolithisation of the Scheldt basin in western Belgium. *Proc. Br. Acad. Press* **144**, 263–285 (2007).

125. Saqalli, M. *et al.* Revisiting and modelling the woodland farming system of the early Neolithic Linear Pottery Culture (LBK), 5600-4900 B.C. *Veg. Hist. Archaeobotany* **23**, S37–S50 (2014).

126. Bentley, A. *et al.* Prehistoric Migration in Europe: Strontium Isotope Analysis of Early Neolithic Skeletons. *Curr. Anthropol.* **43**, 799–804 (2002).

127. Bentley, R., Krause, R., Price, T. & Kaufmann, B. Human mobility at the Early Neolithic settlement of Vaihingen, Germany: evidence from strontium isotope analysis. *Archaeometry* **45**, 471–486 (2003).

128. Sánchez-Quinto, F. *et al.* Megalithic tombs in western and northern Neolithic Europe were linked to a kindred society. *PNAS* **116**, 9469–9474 (2019).

129. Saville, A. *Hazleton North: The Excavation of a Neolithic Long Cairn of the Cotswold-Severn Group.* (English Heritage, York, 1990).

130. Fowler, C. *et al.* A high-resolution picture of kinship practices in an Early Neolithic tomb. *Nature* **601**, 584–587 (2022).

131. Pryor, F. *Britain B.C.* (HarperCollins, London, 2003).

132. Hawkins, G. Stonehenge: a Neolithic computer. *Nature* **202**, 1258–1261 (1964).

133. Chippindale, C. *Stonehenge Complete.* (Thames & Hudson, London, 2001).

134. Parker Pearson, M. Researching Stonehenge: Theories Past and Present. *Archaeol. Int.* **16**, 72–83 (2013).

135. Darvill, T., Marshall, P., Parker Pearson, M. & Wainwright, G. Stonehenge remodelled. *Antiquity* **86**, 1021–1040 (2012).

136. Pearson, M. P. & Ramilisonina. Stonehenge for the ancestors: the stones pass on the message. *Antiquity* **72**, 308–326 (1998).

137. Gaffney, V. *et al.* A Massive, Late Neolithic Pit Structure associated with Durrington Walls Henge. *Internet Archaeol.* **5**, https://doi.org/10.11141/ia.55.4 (2020).

138. Craig, O. *et al.* Feeding Stonehenge: cuisine and consumption at the Late Neolithic site of Durrington Walls. *Antiquity* **89**, 1096–1109 (2015).

139. Wright, E., Viner-Daniels, S., Parker Pearson, M. & Albarella, A. Age and season of pig slaughter at Late Neolithic Durrington Walls (Wiltshire, UK) as detected through a new system for recording tooth wear. *J. Archaeol. Sci.* **52**, 497–514 (2014).

140. Viner, C., Evans, J., Albarella, U. & Parker Pearson, M. Cattle mobility in prehistoric Britain: strontium isotope analysis of cattle teeth from Durrington Walls (Wiltshire, Britain). *J. Archaeol. Sci.* **37**, 2812–2820 (2010).

141. Evans, J., Parker Pearson, M., Madgwick, R., Sloane, H. & Albarella, U. Strontium and oxygen isotope evidence for the origin and movement of cattle at Late Neolithic Durrington Walls, UK. *Archaeol. Anthropol. Sci.* **11**, 5181–5197 (2019).

142. Madgwick, R. *et al.* Multi-isotope analysis reveals that feasts in the Stonehenge environs and across Wessex drew people and animals from throughout Britain. *Sci. Adv.* **5**, eaau6078 (2019).

143. Parker Pearson, M. *et al.* Materializing Stonehenge: The Stonehenge Riverside Project and New Discoveries. *J. Mater. Cult.* **11**, 227–261 (2006).

144. Higham, T., Bronk Ramsey, C., Owen, D., Pike, A. & Hedges, R. Radiocarbon dates from the Oxford AMS system: Archaeometry datelist 32. *Archaeometry* **49**, S1-60 (2007).

145. Slavchev, V. The Varna Eneolithic Cemetery in the Context of the Late Copper Age in the East Balkans. in *The lost worlds of Old Europe: The Danube Valley 5300 - 5000 BC* (ed. Anthony, D.) 193–212 (Institute for the Study of the Ancient World, New York, NY, 2010).

146. Chapman, J., Higham, T., Gaydarska, B., Slavchev, V. & Honch, N. The social context of the emergence, development and abandonment of the Varna Cemetery, Bulgaria. *Eur. J. Archaeol.* **2–3**, 159–183 (2006).

147. Renfrew, C. Varna and the social context of early metallurgy. *Antiquity* **51**, 199–203 (1978).

09: *Homo sapiens*

1. Diamond, J. The Third Chimpanzee. (Random, London, 1991).

2. Darwin, C. On the Origin of Species by Means of Natural Selection, or the Preservation of Favoured Races in the Struggle for Life. (John Murray, London, 1859).

3. Huxley, T. Evidence as to Man's Place in Nature. (Williams and Norgate, London, 1863).

4. Darwin, C. The Descent of Man, and Selection in Relation to Sex. (John Murray, London, 1871).

5. Dennell, R. East Asia and human evolution: from cradle of mankind to cul-de-sac. in East of Africa: Southern Asia, Australia and Modern Human Origins (eds Dennell, R. & Porr, M.) 8–20 (2014). doi:10.1017/CBO9781139084741.002.

6. Delisle, R. The biology/culture link in human evolution, 1750–1950: the problem of integration in science. Stud. Hist. Philos. Sci. Part C Stud. Hist. Philos. Biol. Biomed. Sci. **31**, 531–556 (2000).

7. Bowler, P. From 'savage' to 'primitive': Victorian evolutionism and the interpretation of marginalized peoples. Antiquity **66**, 721–729 (1992).

8. Athreya, S. & Ackermann, R. Colonialism and narratives of human origins in Asia and Africa. in Interrogating Human Origins 72–95 (2019). doi:10.4324/9780203731659-4.

9. Keith, A. The Antiquity of Man. vol. 2 (Williams and Norgate, London, 1925).

10. Gregory, W. Dawn-Man or Ape? Sci. Am. **137**, 230–232 (1927).

11. Osborn, H. Recent Discoveries Relating to the Origin and Antiquity of Man. Science **65**, 481–488 (1927).

12. Wood Jones, F. The Problem of Man's Ancestry. (Society for Promoting Christian Knowledge, London, 1918).

13. Lewin, R. & Foley, R. Principles of Human Evolution. (Blackwell Publishing, Oxford, 2004).

14. Laing, S. Human Origins. (Chapman and Hall, London, 1892).

15. Keith, A. The Antiquity of Man. (Williams and Norgate, London, 1915).

16. Elliot Smith, G. Evolution of Man: Essays. (Oxford University Press, Oxford, 1924).

17. Weidenreich, F. Facts and Speculations concerning The Origin of Homo Sapiens. Am. Anthropol. **49**, 187–203 (1947).

18. Coon, C. The Origin of Races. (Alfred A. Knopf, New York, NY, 1962).

19. Dobzhansky, T. Two Views of Coon's Origin of Races with Comments by Coon and Replies. Curr. Anthropol. **4**, 360–367 (1963).

20. Coon, C. The Living Races of Man. (Jonathon Cape, London, 1965).

21. Montagu, A. Two Views of Coon's Origin of Races with Comments by Coon and Replies. Curr. Anthropol. **4**, 360–367 (1963).

22. Wolpoff, M., Xinzhi, W. & Thorne, A. Modern Homo sapiens origins : A general theory of hominid evolution involving the fossil evidence from East Asia. in The Origins of Modern Humans: A World Survey of the Fossil Evidence (eds Smith, F. & Spencer, F.) 411–483 (Alan R. Liss, New York, NY, 1984).

23. Wolpoff, M., Thorne, A., Jelinek, J. & Yinyun, Z. The case for sinking Homo erectus. 100 years of Pithecanthropus is enough! Cour. Forschungsinstitut Senckenberg **171**, 341–361 (1994).

24. Green, R. et al. A Draft Sequence of the Neandertal Genome. Science **328**, 710–722 (2010).

25. Reich, D. et al. Genetic history of an archaic hominin group from Denisova Cave in Siberia. Nature **468**, 1053–1060 (2010).

26. Protsch, R. The absolute dating of Upper Pleistocene sub-Saharan fossil hominids and their place in human evolution. J. Hum. Evol. **4**, 297–322 (1975).

27. Caspari, R. & Wolpoff, M. The Process of Modern Human Origins. in The Origins of Modern Humans: Biology Reconsidered (eds Smith, F. & Ahern, J.) 355–391 (John Wiley & Sons, Inc., New York, NY, 2013). doi:10.1002/9781118659991.ch11.

28. Stringer, C. & Andrews, P. Genetic and Fossil Evidence for the Origin of Modern Humans. Science **239**, 1263–1268 (1988).

29. Cann, R., Stoneking, M. & Wilson, A. Mitochondrial DNA and human evolution. Nature **325**, 31–36 (1987).

30. Vigilant, L., Stoneking, M., Harpending, H., Hawkes, K. & Wilson, A. African Populations and the Evolution of Human Mitochondrial DNA. Science **253**, 1503–1507 (1991).

31. Lewin, R. The Unmasking of Mitochondrial Eve. Science **238**, 24–26 (1987).

32. Maddison, D. African Origin of Human Mitochondrial DNA Reexamined. Syst. Zool. **40**, 355–363 (1991).

33. Maddison, D., Ruvolovo, M. & Swofford, D. Geographic Origins of Human Mitochondrial DNA: Phylogenetic Evidence from Control Region Sequences. Syst. Biol. **41**, 111–124 (1992).

34. Torroni, A. et al. Mitochondrial DNA analysis in Tibet: Implications for the origin of the Tibetan population and its adaptation to high altitude. Am. J. Phys. Anthropol. **93**, 189–199 (1994).

35. Chen, Y., Torroni, A., Excoffier, L., Santachiara-Benerecett, A. & Wallace, D. Analysis of mtDNA variation in African populations reveals the most ancient of all human continent-specific haplogroups. Am J Hum Genet **57**, 133–49 (1995).

36. Ingman, M., Kaessmann, H., Pääbo, S. & Gyllensten, U. Mitochondrial genome variation and the origin of modern humans. Nature **408**, 708–713 (2000).

37. Jorde, L. et al. The Distribution of Human Genetic Diversity: A Comparison of Mitochondrial, Autosomal, and Y-Chromosome Data. Am. J. Hum. Genet. **66**, 979–988 (2000).

38. Alexe, G. et al. PCA and Clustering Reveal Alternate mtDNA Phylogeny of N and M Clades. J. Mol. Evol. **67**, 465–487 (2008).

39. Behar, D. et al. The Dawn of Human Matrilineal Diversity. Am. J. Hum. Genet. **82**, 1130–1140 (2008).

40. Watson, E., Forster, P., Richards, M. & Bandelt, H. Mitochondrial Footprints of Human Expansions in Africa. Am. J. Hum. Genet. **61**, 691–704 (1997).

41. Atkinson, Q., Gray, R. & Drummond, A. Bayesian coalescent inference of major human mitochondrial DNA haplogroup expansions in Africa. Proc. R. Soc. B **276**, 367–373 (2009).

42. Cohen, A. et al. Ecological consequences of early Late Pleistocene megadroughts in tropical Africa. PNAS **107**, 16422–16427 (2007).

43. Scholz, C. et al. East African megadroughts between 135 and 75 thousand years ago and bearing on early-modern human origins. PNAS **104**, 16416–16421 (2007).

44. Soares, P. et al. Correcting for Purifying Selection: An Improved Human Mitochondrial Molecular Clock. Am. J. Hum. Genet. **84**, 740–759 (2009).

45. Salas, A. et al. The Making of the African mtDNA Landscape. Am. J. Hum. Genet. **71**, 1082–1111 (2002).

46. Mellars, P. Why did modern human populations disperse from Africa ca. 60,000 years ago? A new model. PNAS **103**, 9381–9386 (2006).

47. Kittler, R., Kayser, M. & Stoneking, M. Molecular Evolution of Pediculus humanus and the Origin of Clothing. Curr. Biol. **13**, 1414–1417 (2003).

48. Mellars, P., Gori, K., Carr, M., Soares, P. & Richards, M. Genetic and archaeological perspectives on the initial modern human colonization of southern Asia. PNAS **110**, 10699–10704 (2013).

49. Forster, P., Torroni, A., Renfrew, C. & Rohl, A. Phylogenetic Star Contraction Applied to Asian and Papuan mtDNA Evolution. Mol. Biol. Evol. **18**, 1864–1881 (2001).

50. Macaulay, V. et al. Single, Rapid Coastal Settlement of Asia Revealed by Analysis of Complete Mitochondrial Genomes. Science **308**, 1034–1036 (2005).

51. Atkinson, Q., Gray, R. & Drummond, A. mtDNA Variation Predicts Population Size in Humans and Reveals a Major Southern Asian Chapter in Human Prehistory. Mol. Biol. Evol. **25**, 468–474 (2008).

52. Behar, D. et al. A 'Copernican' Reassessment of the Human Mitochondrial DNA Tree from its Root. Am. J. Hum. Genet. **90**, 675–684 (2012).

53. Torroni, A., Achilli, A., Macaulay, V., Richards, M. & Bandelt, H. Harvesting the fruit of the human mtDNA tree. Trends Genet. **22**, 339–345 (2006).

54. Forster, P. & Matsumura, S. Did Early Humans Go North or South. Science **308**, 965–966 (2005).

55. Liu, H., Prugnolle, F., Manica, A. & Balloux, F. A Geographically Explicit Genetic Model of Worldwide Human-Settlement History. Am. J. Hum. Genet. **79**, 230–237 (2006).

56. Field, J. & Lahr, M. Assessment of the Southern Dispersal: GIS-Based Analyses of Potential Routes at Oxygen Isotopic Stage 4. J. World Prehistory **19**, 1–45 (2005).

57. Derricourt, R. Getting "Out of Africa": Sea Crossings, Land Crossings and Culture in the Hominin Migrations. J. World Prehistory **19**, 119–132 (2005).

58. Lahr, M. & Foley, R. Towards a Theory of Modern Human Origins: Geography, Demography, and Diversity in Recent Human Evolution. Yearb. Phys. Anthropol. **107**, 137–176 (1998).

59. Wells, S. The Journey of Man. (Penguin Books Ltd, London, 2002).

60. Castañeda, I. et al. Wet phases in the Sahara/Sahel region and human migration patterns in North Africa. PNAS **106**, 20159–20163 (2009).

61. Osborne, A. et al. A humid corridor across the Sahara for the migration of early modern humans out of Africa 120,000 years ago. PNAS **105**, 16444–16447 (2008).

62. Drake, N., Blench, R., Armitage, S., Bristow, C. & White, K. Ancient watercourses and biogeography of the Sahara explain the peopling of the desert. PNAS **108**, 458–462 (2011).

63. Grün, R. et al. U-series and ESR analyses of bones and teeth relating to the human burials from Skhul. J. Hum. Evol. **49**, 316–334 (2005).

64. Bar-Yosef Mayer, D., Vandermeersch, B. & Bar-Yosef, O. Shells and ochre in Middle Paleolithic Qafzeh Cave, Israel: indications for modern behavior. J. Hum. Evol. **56**, 307–314 (2009).

65. Klein, R. The Human Career. (University of Chicago Press, Chicago, IL, 1999).

66. Schwarcz, H. et al. ESR dates for the hominid burial site of Qafzeh in Israel. J. Hum. Evol. **17**, 733–737 (1988).

67. Pettitt, P. The Rise of Modern Humans. in The human past (ed. Scarre, C.) 124–173 (Thames & Hudson, London, 2013).

68. Oppenheimer, S. Out of Eden. (Constable & Robinson Ltd, London, 2003).

69. Oppenheimer, S. The great arc of dispersal of modern humans:Africa to Australia. Quat. Int. **202**, 2–13 (2008).

70. Lisiecki, L. & Raymo, M. A Pliocene-Pleistocene stack of 57 globally distributed benthic δ18 O records. Paleoceanography **20**, PA1003 (2005).

71. Rose, J. The Arabian Corridor Migration Model: archaeological evidence for hominin dispersals into Oman during the Middle and Upper Pleistocene. Proc. Semin. Arab. Stud. **37**, 219–237 (2007).

72. Bowler, J. et al. New ages for human occupation and climatic change at Lake Mungo, Australia. Nature **421**, 837–840 (2003).

73. Clarkson, C. et al. Human occupation of northern Australia by 65,000 years ago. Nature **547**, 306–310 (2017).

74. Mellars, P. A new radiocarbon revolution and the dispersal of modern humans in Eurasia. Nature **493**, 931–935 (2006).

75. Thangaraj, K. et al. Reconstructing the Origin of Andaman Islanders. Science **308**, 996 (2005).

76. Mellars, P. Going East: New Genetic and Archaeological Perspectives on the Modern Human Colonization of Eurasia. Science **313**, 796–800 (2006).

77. Stringer, C. Coasting out of Africa. Nature **405**, 24–27 (2000).

78. Bulbeck, D. Where River Meets Sea: A Parsimonious Model for Homo sapiens Colonization of the Indian Ocean Rim and Sahul. Curr. Anthropol. **48**, 315–321 (2007).

79. Field, J., Petraglia, M. & Lahr, M. The southern dispersal hypothesis and the South Asian archaeological record: Examination of dispersal routes through GIS analysis. J. Anthropol. Archaeol. **26**, 88–108 (2006).

80. Dillehay, T. et al. New Archaeological Evidence for an Early Human Presence at Monte Verde, Chile. PLOS ONE **10**, (2015).

81. Groucutt, H. et al. Rethinking the dispersal of Homo sapiens out of Africa. Evol. Anthropol. **24**, 149–164 (2015).

82. Rose, J. New Light on Human Prehistory in the Arabo-Persian Gulf Oasis. Curr. Anthropol. **51**, 849–883 (2010).

83. Petraglia, M. & Alsharekh, A. The Middle Palaeolithic of Arabia: Implications for modern human origins, behaviour and dispersals. Antiquity **77**, 671–684 (2003).

84. Armitage, S. et al. The Southern Route "Out of Africa": Evidence for an Early Expansion of Modern Humans into Arabia. Science **331**, 453–456 (2011).

85. Rose, J. et al. The Nubian Complex of Dhofar, Oman: An African Middle Stone Age Industry in Southern Arabia. PLOS ONE **6**, e28239 (2011).

86. Lawler, A. Did Modern Humans Travel Out of Africa Via Arabia? Science **331**, 387 (2011).

87. Blinkhorn, J. et al. Nubian Levallois technology associated with southernmost Neanderthals. Sci. Rep. **11**, 2869 (2021).

88. Stewart, M. et al. Human footprints provide snapshot of last interglacial ecology in the Arabian interior. Sci. Adv. **6**, eaba8940 (2020).

89. Groucutt, H. et al. Homo sapiens in Arabia by 85,000 years ago. Nat. Ecol. Evol. **2**, 800–809 (2018).

90. Butzer, K., Brown, F. & Tburber, D. Horizontal sediments of the lower Omo Valley: the Kibish Formation. Quaternaria **11**, 15–29 (1969).

91. McDougall, I., Brown, F. & Fleagle, J. Stratigraphic placement and age of modern humans from Kibish, Ethiopia. Nature **433**, 733–736 (2005).

92. Vidal, C. et al. Age of the oldest known Homo sapiens from eastern Africa. Nature **601**, 579–583 (2022).

93. Hublin, J. et al. New fossils from Jebel Irhoud, Morocco and the pan-African origin of Homo sapiens. Nature **546**, 289–291 (2017).

94. Smith, T. et al. Earliest evidence of modern human life history in North African early Homo sapiens. PNAS **104**, 6128–6133 (2007).

95. Richter, D. et al. The age of the hominin fossils from Jebel Irhoud, Morocco, and the origins of the Middle Stone Age. Nature **546**, 293–296 (2017).

96. Hershkovitz, I. et al. The earliest modern humans outside Africa. Science **359**, 456–459 (2018).

97. Harvati, K. et al. Apidima Cave fossils provide earliest evidence of Homo sapiens in Eurasia. Nature **571**, 500–504 (2019).

98. Shen, G. et al. U-Series dating of Liujiang hominid site in Guangxi, Southern China. J. Hum. Evol. **43**, 817–829 (2002).

99. Curnoe, D. et al. Human Remains from the Pleistocene-Holocene Transition of Southwest China Suggest a Complex Evolutionary History for East Asians. PLOS ONE **7**, e31918 (2012).

100. Liu, W. et al. Human remains from Zhirendong, South China,and modern human emergence in East Asia. PNAS **107**, 19201–1920 (2010).

101. Dennell, R. Early Homo sapiens in China. Nature **468**, 512–513 (2010).

102. Liu, W. et al. The earliest unequivocally modern humans in southern China. Nature **526**, 696–699 (2015).

103. Sun, X. et al. Ancient DNA and multimethod dating confirm the late arrival of anatomically modern humans in southern China. PNAS **118**, e2019158118 (2021).

104. Mark, D. et al. A high-precision 40Ar/39Ar age for the Young Toba Tuff and dating of ultra-distal tephra: Forcing of Quaternary climate and implications for hominin occupation of India. Quat. Geochronol. **21**, 90–103 (2014).

105. Chesner, C., Westgate, J., Rose, W., Drake, R. & Deino, A. Eruptive history of Earth's largest Quaternary caldera (Toba, Indonesia). Geology **19**, 200–203 (1991).

106. Rose, W. & Chesner, C. Dispersal of ash in the great Toba eruption, 75 ka. Geology **15**, 913–917 (1987).

107. Acharyya, S. & Basu, P. Toba ash on the Indian subcontinent and its implications for correlation of Late Pleistocene alluvium. Quat. Res. **40**, 10–19 (1993).
108. Williams, M. et al. Environmental impact of the 73 ka Toba super-eruption in South Asia. Palaeogeogr. Palaeoclimatol. Palaeoecol. **284**, 295–314 (2009).
109. Bühring, C., Sarnthein, M. & Party, L. 184 S. S. Toba ash layers in the South China Sea: Evidence of contrasting wind directions during eruption ca. 74 ka. Geology **28**, 275–278 (2000).
110. Rampino, M. & Self, S. Volcanic winter and accelerated glaciation following the Toba super-eruption. Nature **359**, 50–52 (1992).
111. Zielinski, G. et al. Potential atmospheric impact of Toba mega-eruption 71,000 years ago. Geophys. Res. Lett. **23**, 837–840 (1996).
112. Petraglia, M. et al. Middle Paleolithic Assemblages from the Indian Subcontinent Before and After the Toba Super-Eruption. Science **317**, 114–116 (2007).
113. Petraglia, M., Ditchfield, P., Jones, S., Korisettar, R. & Pal, J. The Toba volcanic super-eruption, environmental change, and hominin occupation history in India over the last 140,000 years. Quat. Int. **258**, 119–134 (2012).
114. Kivisild, T. et al. The Genetic Heritage of the Earliest Settlers Persists Both in Indian Tribal and Caste Populations. Am. J. Hum. Genet. **72**, 313–332 (2003).
115. Metspalu, M. et al. Most of the extant mtDNA boundaries in South and Southwest Asia were likely shaped during the initial settlement of Eurasia by anatomically modern humans. BMC Genet. **5**, 26 (2004).
116. Thangaraj, K. et al. In situ origin of deep rooting lineages of mitochondrial Macrohaplogroup 'M' in India. BMC Genomics **7**, 151 (2006).
117. Rajkumar, R., Banerjee, J., Gunturi, H., Trivedi, R. & Kashyap, V. Phylogeny and antiquity of M macrohaplogroup inferred from complete mt DNA sequence of Indian specific lineages. BMC Evol. Biol. **26**, 5 (2005).
118. Palanichamy, M. et al. Comment on 'Reconstructing the Origin of Andaman Islanders'. Science **311**, 470 (2006).
119. Wang, H. et al. Mitochondrial DNA evidence supports northeast Indian origin of the aboriginal Andamanese in the Late Paleolithic. J. Genet. Genomics **38**, 117–122 (2011).
120. Fregel, R., Cabrera, V., Larruga, J., Abu-Amero, K. & González, A. Carriers of Mitochondrial DNA Macrohaplogroup N Lineages Reached Australia around 50,000 Years Ago following a Northern Asian Route. PLOS ONE **10**, e0129839 (2015).
121. Marrero, P., Abu-Amero, K., Larruga, J. & Cabrerac, V. Carriers of human mitochondrial DNA macrohaplogroup M colonized India from southeastern Asia. BMC Evol. Biol. **16**, 246 (2016).
122. Larruga, J., Marrero, P., Abu-Amero, K., Golubenko, M. & Cabrera, V. Carriers of mitochondrial DNA macrohaplogroup R colonized Eurasia and Australasia from a southeast Asia core area. BMC Evol. Biol. **17**, 1–12 (2017).
123. Tassi, F. et al. Early modern human dispersal from Africa: genomic evidence for multiple waves of migration. Investig. Genet. **6**, 13 (2015).
124. Pagani, L. et al. Genomic analyses inform on migration events during the peopling of Eurasia. Nature **538**, 238–242 (2016).
125. Reyes-Centeno, H. et al. Genomic and cranial phenotype data support multiple modern human dispersals from Africa and a southern route into Asia. PNAS **111**, 7248–7253 (2014).
126. Schillaci, M. Human cranial diversity and evidence for an ancient lineage of modern humans. J. Hum. Evol. **54**, 814–826 (2008).
127. Dennell, R. & Petraglia, M. The dispersal of Homo sapiens across southern Asia: how early, how often, how complex? Quat. Sci. Rev. **47**, 15–22 (2012).
128. Tierney, J. et al. Northern Hemisphere Controls on Tropical Southeast African Climate During the Past 60,000 Years. Science **322**, 252–255 (2008).
129. Stager, C., Ryves, D., Chase, B. & Pausata, F. Catastrophic Drought in the Afro-Asian Monsoon Region During Heinrich Event 1. Science **331**, 1299–1302 (2011).
130. Lane, C., Chorn, B. & Johnson, T. Ash from the Toba supereruption in Lake Malawi shows no volcanic winter in East Africa at 75 ka. PNAS **110**, 8025–8029 (2013).
131. Quintana-Murci, L. et al. Maternal traces of deep common ancestry and asymmetric gene flow between Pygmy hunter–gatherers and Bantu-speaking farmers. PNAS **105**, 1596–1601 (2008).
132. Schlebusch, C. et al. Southern African ancient genomes estimate modern human divergence to 350,000 to 260,000 years ago. Science **358**, 652–655 (2017).
133. Garrigan, D., Mobasher, Z., Kingan, S., Wilder, J. & Hammer, M. Deep Haplotype Divergence and Long-Range Linkage Disequilibrium at Xp21.1 Provide Evidence That Humans Descend From a Structured Ancestral Population. Genetics **170**, 1849–1856 (2005).
134. Plagnol, V. & Wall, J. Possible Ancestral Structure in Human Populations. PLOS Genet. **2**, 972–979 (2006).
135. Li, H. & Durbin, R. Inference of human population history from individual whole-genome sequences. Nature **475**, 493–496 (2011).
136. Stringer, C. The origin and evolution of Homo sapiens. Philos. Trans. R. Soc. B **371**, 20150237 (2016).
137. Bräuer, G. The Origin of Modern Anatomy: By Speciation or Intraspecific Evolution? Evol. Anthropol. **17**, 22–37 (2008).

138. Rightmire, P. Middle and later Pleistocene hominins in Africa and Southwest Asia. PNAS **106**, 16046–16050 (2009).

139. Henn, B., Steele, T. & Weaver, T. Clarifying distinct models of modern human origins in Africa. Curr. Opin. Genet. Dev. **53**, 148–156 (2018).

140. Mallick, S. et al. The Simons Genome Diversity Project: 300 genomes from 142 diverse populations. Nature **538**, 201–206 (2016).

141. Abu-Amero, K., Larruga, J., Cabrera, V. & González, A. Mitochondrial DNA structure in the Arabian Peninsula. BMC Evol. Biol. **8**, (2008).

142. Ackermann, R. Phenotypic Traits of Primate Hybrids: Recognizing Admixture in the Fossil Record. Evol. Anthropol. **19**, 258–270 (2010).

10: Prehistoric Art

1. Adajian, T. The Definition of Art. *Stamford Encyclopedia of Philosophy* https://plato.stanford.edu/entries/art-definition/ (2018).

2. Cavendish, C. Discovery of the Lascaux Cave Paintings. *History Today* vol. 65 (2015).

3. Sewell, J. How Did A Dog Discover The Lascaux Cave Paintings? *The Collector* https://www.thecollector.com/how-did-a-dog-discover-the-lascaux-cave-paintings/ (2020).

4. Bahn, P. A Lot of Bull? Pablo Picasso and Ice Age cave art. *Munibe Antropol.-Arkeol.* **57**, 217–223 (2005).

5. Mauriac, M. Lascaux: The history of the discovery of an outstanding decorated cave. *Adoranten* 5–25 (2011).

6. Clottes, J. *Cave Art*. (Phaidon, New York, NY, 2008).

7. Pike, A. et al. U-Series Dating of Paleolithic Art in 11 Caves in Spain. *Science* **336**, 1409–1413 (2012).

8. Mellars, P. A new radiocarbon revolution and the dispersal of modern humans in Eurasia. *Nature* **493**, 931–935 (2006).

9. Mellars, P. Neanderthals and the modern human colonization of Europe. *Nature* **432**, 461–465 (2004).

10. Mellars, P. Origins of the female image. *Nature* **439**, 176–177 (2009).

11. Lasheras, J. The Caves of Altamira 22,000 years of history. *Adoranten* 5–33 (2009).

12. Lewis-Williams, D. *The Mind in the Cave: Consciousness And The Origins Of Art*. (Thames & Hudson, London, 2002).

13. De las Heras, C. & Lasheras, J. The Altamira Cave. in *Pleistocene and Holocene hunter-gatherers in Iberia and the Gibraltar Strait: the current archaeological record* (ed. Salla Ramos, R.) 615–627 (Universidad de Burgos & Fundación Atapuerca, Burgos, 2014).

14. Labonne, M., Hillaire-Marcel, C., Ghaleb, B. & Goy, J. Multi-isotopic age assessment of dirty speleothem calcite: an example from Altamira Cave, Spain. *Quat. Sci. Rev.* **21**, 1099–1110 (2002).

15. Leroi-Gourhan, A. *The Dawn of European Art: An Introduction to Palaeolithic Cave Painting*. (Cambridge University Press, Cambridge, 1982).

16. Conard, N. Palaeolithic ivory sculptures from southwestern Germany and the origins of figurative art. *Nature* **426**, 830–832 (2003).

17. Higham, T. et al. Testing models for the beginnings of the Aurignacian and the advent of figurative art and music: The radiocarbon chronology of Geißenklösterle. *J. Hum. Evol.* **62**, 664–676 (2012).

18. Conard, N., Malina, M. & Munzel, S. New flutes document the earliest musical tradition in southwestern Germany. *Nature* **460**, 738–740 (2009).

19. Flannery, K. & Marcus, J. *The Creation of Inequality*. (Harvard University Press, Cambridge, MA, 2012).

20. Conard, N. A female figurine from the basal Aurignacian of Hohle Fels Cave in southwestern Germany. *Nature* **459**, 248–252 (2009).

21. Liew, J. Venus figurines. *World History Encyclopedia* https://www.worldhistory.org/Venus_Figurine/ (2017).

22. Vandiver, P., Soffer, O., Klima, B. & Svoboda, J. The Origins of Ceramic Technology at Dolni Věstonice, Czechoslovakia. *Science* **246**, 1002–1008 (1989).

23. Weber, G. et al. The microstructure and the origin of the Venus from Willendorf. *Sci. Rep.* **12**, 2926 (2022).

24. Raghavan, M. et al. Upper Palaeolithic Siberian genome reveals dual ancestry of Native Americans. *Nature* **505**, 87–94 (2014).

25. Lazaridis, I. et al. Ancient human genomes suggest three ancestral populations for present-day Europeans. *Nature* **513**, 409–413 (2014).

26. Fu, Q. et al. The genetic history of Ice Age Europe. *Nature* **534**, 200–205 (2016).

27. Pettitt, P. The Rise of Modern Humans. in *The human past* (ed. Scarre, C.) 124–173 (Thames & Hudson, London, 2013).

28. McCoid, C. & McDermott, L. Towards Decolonizing Gender: Female Vision in the Upper Palaeolithic. *Am. Anthr.* **98**, 319–326 (1996).

29. McDermott, L. Self-Representation in female figurines. *Curr. Anthropol.* **37**, 227–275 (1996).

30. Talamo, S. et al. A 41,500 year-old decorated ivory pendant from Stajnia Cave (Poland). *Sci. Rep.* **11**, 22078 (2021).

31. Mellars, P. The Upper Palaeolithic Revolution. in *The Oxford Illustrated History of Prehistoric Europe* (ed. Cunliffe, B.) 42–78 (Oxford University Press, Oxford, 1994).

32. Morales, M. & Straus, L. Extraordinary Early Magdalenian finds from El Mirón Cave, Cantabria (Spain). *Antiquity* **3**, 267–281 (2009).

33. Marshack, A. *The Roots of Civilization*. (McGraw-Hill, New York, NY, 1972).

34. Marshack, A. The female image - a time-factored symbol. *Proc. Prehist. Soc.* **57**, 17–31 (1991).

35. Pingree, D. The recovery of early Greek astronomy from India. *J. Hist. Astron.* **7**, 109–123 (1976).

36. Barton, M., Clark, G. & Cohen, A. Art as information: explaining Upper Palaeolithic art in western Europe. *World Archaeol.* **26**, 185–207 (1994).

37. Straus, L. The Upper Palaeolithic of Europe: An Overview. *Evol. Anthropol.* **4**, 4–16 (1995).

38. Lewis-Williams, D. & Pearce, D. *Inside the Neolithic Mind*. (Thames & Hudson, London, 2005).

39. Hayden, B. & Villeneuve, S. Astronomy in the Upper Palaeolithic? *Camb. Archaeol. J.* **21**, 331–355 (2011).

40. Congregado, L. *Arte y Astronomía: Evolución de Los Dibujos de Las Constelaciones*. (1991).

41. Edge, F. *Aurochs in the Sky, Dancing with the Summer Moon*. (1995).

42. Rappenglück, M. A Palaeolithic planetarium underground - the caves of Lascaux Part 1. *Migr. Diffus.* **5**, 93–119 (2004).

43. Rappenglück, M. A Palaeolithic planetarium underground - the caves of Lascaux Part 2. *Migr. Diffus.* **5**, 6–46 (2004).

44. Aubert, M. *et al.* Pleistocene cave art from Sulawesi, Indonesia. *Nature* **514**, 223–227 (2014).

45. García-Diez, M. *et al.* Uranium series dating reveals a long sequence of rock art at Altamira Cave (Santillana del Mar, Cantabria). *J. Archaeol. Sci.* **40**, 4098–4106 (2013).

46. Sadier, B. *et al.* Further constraints on the Chauvet cave artwork elaboration. *PNAS* **109**, 8002–8006 (2012).

47. Cuzange, M. *et al.* Radiocarbon Intercomparison Program for Chauvet Cave. *Radiocarbon* **49**, 339–347 (2007).

48. Pettitt, P. Art and the Middle-to-Upper Paleolithic transition in Europe: Comments on the archaeological arguments for an early Upper Paleolithic antiquity of the Grotte Chauvet art. *J. Hum. Evol.* **55**, 908–917 (2008).

49. Valladas, H. *et al.* Radiocarbon Dating of the Decorated Cosquer Cave (France). *Radiocarbon* **59**, 1–13 (2017).

50. Rivero, O. *et al.* To be or not to be: reassessing the origins of portable art in the Cantabrian Region (Northern Spain). *Archaeol. Anthropol. Sci.* **14**, 18 (2022).

51. Aubert, M. *et al.* Earliest hunting scene in prehistoric art. *Nature* **576**, 442–445 (2019).

52. Oktaviana, A. *et al.* Narrative cave art in Indonesia by 51,200 years ago. *Nature* **631**, 814–818 (2024).

53. Brumm, A. *et al.* Oldest cave art found in Sulawesi. *Sci. Adv.* **7**, eabd4648 (2021).

54. Aubert, M. *et al.* Palaeolithic cave art in Borneo. *Nature* **564**, 254–257 (2018).

55. Mithen, S. *The Prehistory of the Mind*. (Thames & Hudson, London, 1996).

56. Klein, R. Archeology and the evolution of human behavior. *Evol. Anthropol. Issues News Rev.* **9**, 17–36 (2000).

57. Klein, R. & Edgar, B. *The Dawn of Human Culture*. (John Wiley & Sons, Inc., New York, NY, 2002).

58. Diamond, J. *The Third Chimpanzee*. (Random, London, 1991).

59. McBrearty, S. & Brooks, A. The revolution that wasn't: a new interpretation of the origin of modern human behaviour. *J. Hum. Evol.* **39**, 453–563 (2000).

60. Henshilwood, C. Stratigraphic Integrity of the Middle Stone Age Levels at Blombos Cave. in *From Tools to Symbols. From Early Hominids to Modern Humans* (eds d'Errico, F. & Backwell, L.) 441–458 (Witwatersrand University Press, Johannesburg, 2005).

61. Henshilwood, C. *et al.* Emergence of Modern Human Behavior: Middle Stone Age Engravings from South Africa. *Science* **295**, 1278–1280 (2002).

62. Henshilwood, C. *et al.* A 100,000-Year-Old Ochre-Processing Workshop at Blombos Cave, South Africa. *Science* **334**, 219–222 (2011).

63. Jacobs, Z., Duller, G., Wintle, A. & Henshilwood, C. Extending the chronology of deposits at Blombos Cave,South Africa, back to 140 ka using optical dating of single and multiple grains of quartz. *J. Hum. Evol.* **51**, 255–273 (2006).

64. Tribolo, C. *et al.* TL dating of burnt lithics from Blombos Cave (South Africa): further evidence for the antiquity of modern human behaviour. *Archaeometry* **48**, 341–357 (2006).

65. Henshilwood, C. Fully Symbolic Sapiens behaviour: Innovation in the Middle Stone Age at Blombos Cave, South Africa. in *Rethinking the human revolution* (eds Mellars, P., Boyle, K., Bar-Yosef, O. & Stringer, C.) 123–132 (McDonald Institute, Cambridge, 2007).

66. Douze, K., Wurz, S. & Henshilwood, C. Techno-Cultural Characterization of the MIS 5 (c. 105 – 90 Ka) Lithic Industries at Blombos Cave, Southern Cape, South Africa. *PLOS ONE* **10**, e0142151 (2015).

67. Rifkin, R. *et al.* Evaluating the Photoprotective Effects of Ochre on Human Skin by In Vivo SPF Assessment: Implications for Human Evolution, Adaptation and Dispersal. *PLOS ONE* **10**, e0136090 (2015).

68. Hodgskiss, T. & Wadley, L. How people used ochre at Rose Cottage Cave, South Africa: Sixty thousand years of evidence from the Middle Stone Age. *PLOS ONE* **12**, e0176317 (2017).

69. Henshilwood, C., d'Errico, F., Vanhaeren, M., van Niekerk, K. & Jacobs, Z. Middle Stone Age Shell Beads from South Africa. *Science* **304**, 404 (2004).

70. D'Errico, F., Henshilwood, C., Vanhaeren, M. & van Niekerke, K. Nassarius kraussianus shell beads from Blombos Cave: evidence for symbolic behaviour in the Middle Stone Age. *J. Hum. Evol.* **48**, 3–24 (2005).

71. Wynn, T. & Coolidge, F. Did a Small but Significant Enhancement in Working Memory Capacity Power the Evolution of Modern Thinking. in *Rethinking the human revolution* (eds Mellars, P., Boyle, K., Bar-Yosef, O. & Stringer, C.) 79–90 (McDonald Institute, Cambridge, 2007).

72. Barham, L. Systematic Pigment Use in the Middle Pleistocene of South-Central Africa. *Curr. Anthropol.* **43**, 181–190 (2002).

73. Marean, C. *et al.* Early human use of marine resources and pigment in South Africa during the Middle Pleistocene. *Nature* **449**, 905–909 (2007).

74. Barham, L. Modern Is as Modern Does? Technological Trends and Thresholds in the South-central African Record. in *Rethinking the human revolution* (eds Mellars, P., Boyle, K., Bar-Yosef, O. & Stringer, C.) 163–176 (McDonald Institute, Cambridge, 2007).

75. Roscoe, P. The hunters and gatherers of New Guinea. *Curr. Anthropol.* **43**, 153–162 (2002).

76. Kuhn, S. & Stiner, M. Body Ornamentation as Information Technology: Towards an Understanding of the Significance of Early Beads. in *Rethinking the human revolution* (eds Mellars, P., Boyle, K., Bar-Yosef, O. & Stringer, C.) 45–54 (McDonald Institute, Cambridge, 2007).

77. D'Errico, F., Henshilwood, C. & Nilssen, P. An engraved bone fragment from c. 70,000-year-old Middle Stone Age levels at Blombos Cave, South Africa: implications for the origin of symbolism and language. *Antiquity* **75**, 309–318 (2001).

78. Henshilwood, C., d'Errico, F. & Watts, I. Engraved ochres from the Middle Stone Age levels at Blombos Cave, South Africa. *J. Hum. Evol.* **57**, 27–47 (2009).

79. Henshilwood, C. S. *et al.* An abstract drawing from the 73,000-year-old levels at Blombos Cave, South Africa. *Nature* **562**, 115–118 (2018).

80. Texier, P. *et al.* A Howiesons Poort tradition of engraving ostrich eggshell containers dated to 60,000 years ago at Diepkloof Rock Shelter, South Africa. *PNAS* **107**, 6180–6185 (2010).

81. Texier, P. *et al.* The context, form and significance of the MSA engraved ostrich eggshell collection from Diepkloof Rock Shelter, Western Cape, South Africa. *J. Archaeol. Sci.* **40**, 3412–3421 (2013).

82. Hodgson, D. Understanding the Origins of Paleoart: The Neurovisual Resonance Theory and Brain Functioning. *PaleoAnthropology* 54–67 (2006).

83. Hodgson, D. Decoding the Blombos Engravings, Shell Beads and Diepkloof Ostrich Eggshell Patterns. *Camb. Archaeol. J.* **24**, 57–69 (2014).

84. Mellet, E. *et al.* Neuroimaging supports the representational nature of the earliest human engravings. *R. Soc. Open Sci.* **6**, 190086 (2019).

85. Mellet, E. *et al.* What processes sparked off symbolic representations? A reply to Hodgson and an alternative perspective. *J. Archaeol. Sci. Rep.* **28**, 102043 (2019).

86. Tylén, K. *et al.* The evolution of early symbolic behavior in Homo sapiens. *PNAS* **117**, 4578–4584 (2020).

87. Hoffmann, D. *et al.* U-Th dating of carbonate crusts reveals Neandertal origin of Iberian cave art. *Science* **359**, 912–915 (2018).

88. Higham, T. *et al.* The timing and spatiotemporal patterning of Neanderthal disappearance. *Nature* **512**, 306–309 (2014).

89. Finlayson, C. *et al.* Late survival of Neanderthals at the southernmost extreme of Europe. *Nature* **443**, 850–853 (2006).

90. Finlayson, C. *et al.* Gorham's Cave, Gibraltar - The persistence of a Neanderthal population. *Quat. Int.* **181**, 74–71 (2008).

91. Goren-Inbar, N. A Figurine from the Acheulian Site of Berekhat Ram. *Mitekufat Haeven J. Isr. Prehist. Soc.* **19**, 7–12 (1986).

92. Marshack, A. The Berekhat Ram figurine: a late Acheulian carving from the Middle East. *Antiquity* **71**, 327–333 (1997).

93. Coolidge, F. & Wynn, T. *The Rise of Homo Sapiens.* (Wiley-Blackwell, Hoboken, NJ, 2009).

94. D'Errico, F. & Nowell, A. A New Look at the Berekhat Ram Figurine: Implications for the Origins of Symbolism. *Camb. Archaeol. J.* **10**, 123–167 (2000).

95. Joordens, J. *et al.* Homo erectus at Trinil on Java used shells for tool production and engraving. *Nature* **518**, 228–231 (2015).

11: Early seafarers

1. Morrow, J. E. Early Paleoindian Mobility and Watercraft: An Assessment from the Mississippi River Valley. *Midcont. J. Archaeol.* **39**, 103–129 (2014).

2. Gjerde, J. The earliest boat depiction in Northern Europe: Newly discovered early Mesolithic rock art at Valle, northern Norway. *Oxf. J. Archaeol.* **40**, 136–152 (2021).

3. Brown, P. *et al.* A new small-bodied hominin from the Late Pleistocene of Flores, Indonesia. *Nature* **431**, 1055–1061 (2004).

4. Diniz-Filho, J. *et al.* Quantitative genetics of body size evolution on islands: an individual-based simulation approach. *Biol. Lett.* **15**, 0481 (2019).

5. van der Geer, A. *et al.* The effect of area and isolation on insular dwarf proboscideans. *J. Biogeogr.* **43**, 1656–1666 (2016).

6. Lieberman, D. Homo floresiensis from head to toe. *Nature* **459**, 41–42 (2009).
7. Matsu'ura, S. *et al.* Age control of the first appearance datum for Javanese Homo erectus in the Sangiran area. *Science* **367**, 210–214 (2020).
8. Van den Bergh, G. *et al.* Homo floresiensis-like fossils from the early Middle Pleistocene of Flores. *Nature* **534**, 245–248 (2016).
9. Brumm, A. *et al.* Early stone technology on Flores and its implications for Homo floresiensis. *Nature* **441**, 624–628 (2006).
10. Brumm, A. *et al.* Hominins on Flores, Indonesia, by one million years ago. *Nature* **464**, 748–753 (2010).
11. Morwood, M., O'Sullivan, P., Aziz, F. & Raza, A. Fission-track ages of stone tools and fossils on the east Indonesian island of Flores. *Nature* **392**, 173–176 (1998).
12. Klein, R. *The Human Career.* (University of Chicago Press, Chicago, IL, 1999).
13. Mijares, A. *et al.* New evidence for a 62000-year-old human presence at Callao Cave, Luzon, Philippines. *J. Hum. Evol.* **59**, 123–132 (2010).
14. Détroit, F. *et al.* A new species of Homo from the Late Pleistocene of the Philippines. *Nature* **568**, 181–186 (2019).
15. Ingicco, T. *et al.* Earliest known hominin activity in the Philippines by 709 thousand years ago. *Nature* **557**, 233–237 (2018).
16. Gibbons, A. Ancient Island Tools Suggest Homo erectus Was a Seafarer. *Science* **279**, 1635–1637 (1998).
17. Goodman, M. *et al.* Toward a Phylogenetic Classification of Primates Based on DNA Evidence Complemented by Fossil Evidence. *Mol. Phylogenet. Evol.* **9**, 585–598 (1998).
18. Schrago, C. G. & Russo, C. A. M. Timing the Origin of New World Monkeys. *Mol. Biol. Evol.* **20**, 1620–1625 (2003).
19. Seiffert, E. *et al.* A parapithecid stem anthropoid of African origin in the Paleogene of South America. *Science* **368**, 194–197 (2020).
20. Bond, M. *et al.* Eocene primates of South America and the African origins of New World monkeys. *Nature* **520**, 538–541 (2015).
21. Simons, E. The Cranium of Parapithecus grangeri, an Egyptian Oligocene Anthropoidean Primate. *PNAS* **98**, 7892–7 (2001).
22. Seiffert, E. *et al.* Basal Anthropoids from Egypt and the Antiquity of Africa's Higher Primate Radiation. *Science* **310**, 300–304 (2005).
23. Jaeger, J. *et al.* Late middle Eocene epoch of Libya yields earliest known radiation of African anthropoids. *Nature* **467**, 1095–1099 (2010).
24. O'Dea, A. *et al.* Formation of the Isthmus of Panama. *Sci. Adv.* **2**, e1600883 (2016).
25. De Oliveira, F., Molina, E. & Marroig, G. Paleogeography of the South Atlantic: a Route for Primates and Rodents into the New World? in *South American Primates* (eds Garber, P., Estrada, A., Bicca-Marques, J., Heymann, E. & Strier, K.) 55–68 (Springer, New York, NY, 2009).
26. Scotese, C. A Continental Drift Flipbook. *J. Geol.* **112**, 729–741 (2004).
27. de Freitas, C. T., Shepard, G. H., Jr & Piedade, M. T. F. The Floating Forest: Traditional Knowledge and Use of Matupá Vegetation Islands by Riverine Peoples of the Central Amazon. *PLOS ONE* **10**, e0122542 (2015).
28. Houle, A. Floating Islands: A Mode of Long-Distance Dispersal for Small and Medium- Sized Terrestrial Vertebrates. *Divers. Distrib.* **4**, 201–216 (1998).
29. Houle, A. The origin of platyrrhines: An evaluation of the Antarctic scenario and the floating island model. *Am. J. Phys. Anthropol.* **109**, 541–59 (1999).
30. Ruxton, G. D. & Wilkinson, D. M. Population trajectories for accidental versus planned colonisation of islands. *J. Hum. Evol.* **63**, 507–511 (2012).
31. Shimelmitz, R., Kuhn, S., Ronen, A. & Weinstein-Evron, M. Predetermined Flake Production at the Lower/Middle Paleolithic Boundary: Yabrudian Scraper-Blank Technology. *PLOS ONE* **9**, e106293 (2014).
32. Villa, P. & Roebroeks, W. Neandertal Demise: An Archaeological Analysis of the Modern Human Superiority Complex. *PLOS ONE* **9**, e96424 (2014).
33. Roebroeks, W. & Soressi, M. Neandertals revised. *PNAS* **113**, 6372–6379 (2016).
34. Richter, D. & Krbetschek, M. The age of the Lower Paleolithic occupation at Schöningen. *J. Hum. Evol.* **89**, 46–56 (2015).
35. Lang, J. *et al.* The Pleistocene of Schöningen, Germany: a complex tunnel valley fill revealed from 3D subsurface modelling and shear wave seismics. *Quat. Sci. Rev.* **39**, 86–105 (2012).
36. Strasser, T. F. *et al.* Dating Palaeolithic sites in southwestern Crete, Greece. *J. Quat. Sci.* **26**, 553–560 (2011).
37. Ferentinos, G., Gkioni, M., Geraga, M. & Papatheodorou, G. Early seafaring activity in the southern Ionian Islands, Mediterranean Sea. *J. Archaeol. Sci.* **39**, 2167–2176 (2012).
38. Kourtessi-Philippakis, G. The Lower and Middle Palaeolithic in the Ionian islands: new finds. *Br. Sch. Athens Stud.* **3**, 282–287 (1999).
39. Carter, T. *et al.* Earliest occupation of the Central Aegean (Naxos), Greece: Implications for hominin and Homo sapiens' behavior and dispersals. *Sci. Adv.* **5**, eaax0997 (2019).
40. Papoulia, C. Seaward dispersals to the NE Mediterranean islands in the Pleistocene. The lithic evidence in retrospect. *Quat. Int.* **431**, 64–87 (2017).

41. Richter, D. *et al.* The age of the hominin fossils from Jebel Irhoud, Morocco, and the origins of the Middle Stone Age. *Nature* **546**, 293–296 (2017).

42. Bruner, E. & Pearson, O. Neurocranial evolution in modern humans: the case of Jebel Irhoud 1. *Anthropol. Sci.* **121**, 31–41 (2013).

43. Stringer, C. The origin and evolution of Homo sapiens. *Philos. Trans. R. Soc. B* **371**, 20150237 (2016).

44. Vidal, C. *et al.* Age of the oldest known Homo sapiens from eastern Africa. *Nature* **601**, 579–583 (2022).

45. Harvati, K. *et al.* Apidima Cave fossils provide earliest evidence of Homo sapiens in Eurasia. *Nature* **571**, 500–504 (2019).

46. Hershkovitz, I. *et al.* The earliest modern humans outside Africa. *Science* **359**, 456–459 (2018).

47. Stewart, M. *et al.* Human footprints provide snapshot of last interglacial ecology in the Arabian interior. *Sci. Adv.* **6**, eaba8940 (2020).

48. Atkinson, Q., Gray, R. & Drummond, A. Bayesian coalescent inference of major human mitochondrial DNA haplogroup expansions in Africa. *Proc. R. Soc. B* **276**, 367–373 (2009).

49. Oppenheimer, S. *Out of Eden.* (Constable & Robinson Ltd, London, 2003).

50. Rose, J. The Arabian Corridor Migration Model: archaeological evidence for hominin dispersals into Oman during the Middle and Upper Pleistocene. *Proc. Semin. Arab. Stud.* **37**, 219–237 (2007).

51. Oppenheimer, S. The great arc of dispersal of modern humans:Africa to Australia. *Quat. Int.* **202**, 2–13 (2008).

52. Macaulay, V. *et al.* Single, Rapid Coastal Settlement of Asia Revealed by Analysis of Complete Mitochondrial Genomes. *Science* **308**, 1034–1036 (2005).

53. Thangaraj, K. *et al.* Reconstructing the Origin of Andaman Islanders. *Science* **308**, 996 (2005).

54. Bulbeck, D. Where River Meets Sea: A Parsimonious Model for Homo sapiens Colonization of the Indian Ocean Rim and Sahul. *Curr. Anthropol.* **48**, 315–321 (2007).

55. Wells, S. *The Journey of Man.* (Penguin Books Ltd, London, 2002).

56. Klein, R. & Edgar, B. *The Dawn of Human Culture.* (John Wiley & Sons, Inc., New York, NY, 2002).

57. McBrearty, S. & Brooks, A. The revolution that wasn't: a new interpretation of the origin of modern human behaviour. *J. Hum. Evol.* **39**, 453–563 (2000).

58. Tassi, F. *et al.* Early modern human dispersal from Africa: genomic evidence for multiple waves of migration. *Investig. Genet.* **6**, 13 (2015).

59. Pagani, L. *et al.* Genomic analyses inform on migration events during the peopling of Eurasia. *Nature* **538**, 238–242 (2016).

60. Reyes-Centeno, H. *et al.* Genomic and cranial phenotype data support multiple modern human dispersals from Africa and a southern route into Asia. *PNAS* **111**, 7248–7253 (2014).

61. Palanichamy, M. *et al.* Comment on 'Reconstructing the Origin of Andaman Islanders'. *Science* **311**, 470 (2006).

62. Wang, H. *et al.* Mitochondrial DNA evidence supports northeast Indian origin of the aboriginal Andamanese in the Late Paleolithic. *J. Genet. Genomics* **38**, 117–122 (2011).

63. Fregel, R., Cabrera, V., Larruga, J., Abu-Amero, K. & González, A. Carriers of Mitochondrial DNA Macrohaplogroup N Lineages Reached Australia around 50,000 Years Ago following a Northern Asian Route. *PLOS ONE* **10**, e0129839 (2015).

64. Marrero, P., Abu-Amero, K., Larruga, J. & Cabrerac, V. Carriers of human mitochondrial DNA macrohaplogroup M colonized India from southeastern Asia. *BMC Evol. Biol.* **16**, 246 (2016).

65. Larruga, J., Marrero, P., Abu-Amero, K., Golubenko, M. & Cabrera, V. Carriers of mitochondrial DNA macrohaplogroup R colonized Eurasia and Australasia from a southeast Asia core area. *BMC Evol. Biol.* **17**, 1–12 (2017).

66. Clarkson, C. *et al.* Human occupation of northern Australia by 65,000 years ago. *Nature* **547**, 306–310 (2017).

67. Lambeck, K., Esat, T. & Potter, E. Links between climate and sea levels for the past three million years. *Nature* **419**, 199–206 (2002).

68. O'Connell, J. & Allen, J. Pre-LGM Sahul (Pleistocene Australia-New Guinea) and the Archaeology of Early Modern Humans. in *Rethinking the human revolution* (eds Mellars, P., Boyle, K., Bar-Yosef, O. & Stringer, C.) 395–410 (McDonald Institute, Cambridge, 2007).

69. Bird, M. I. *et al.* Early human settlement of Sahul was not an accident. *Sci. Rep.* **9**, 8220 (2019).

70. Bradshaw, C. J. A. *et al.* Minimum founding populations for the first peopling of Sahul. *Nat. Ecol. Evol.* **3**, 1057–1063 (2019).

71. Balme, J. Of boats and string: The maritime colonisation of Australia. *Peopling Last New Worlds First Colon. Sahul Am.* **285**, 68–75 (2013).

72. Birdsell, J. The recalibration of a paradigm for the first peopling of greater Australia. in *Sunda and Sahul: Prehistoric Studies in Southeast Asia, Melanesia and Australia* (eds Allen, J., Golson, J. & Jones, R.) 113–167 (Academic Press, London, 1977).

73. Kealy, S., Louys, J. & O'Connor, S. Least-cost pathway models indicate northern human dispersal from Sunda to Sahul. *J. Hum. Evol.* **125**, 59–70 (2018).

74. Bird, M. I. *et al.* Palaeogeography and voyage modeling indicates early human colonization of Australia was likely from Timor-Roti. *Quat. Sci. Rev.* **191**, 431–439 (2018).

75. Norman, K. *et al.* An early colonisation pathway into northwest Australia 70-60,000 years ago. *Quat. Sci. Rev.* **180**, 229–239 (2018).

76. Pickard, C. & Bonsall, C. Deep sea fishing in the European Mesolithic: Fact or Fantasy? *Eur. J. Archaeol.* **7**, 273–290 (2004).

77. Peterson, D., Hanazaki, N. & Li, F. Understanding Canoe Making as a Process of Preserving Cultural Heritage. *Ethnobiol. Lett.* **10**, 59–68 (2019).

78. Andersen, S. Tybrind Vig. *J. Dan. Archaeol.* **4**, 52–69 (1985).

79. Fernández, E. *et al.* Ancient DNA Analysis of 8000 B.C. Near Eastern Farmers Supports an Early Neolithic Pioneer Maritime Colonization of Mainland Europe through Cyprus and the Aegean Islands. *PLOS Genet.* **10**, e1004401 (2014).

80. Paschou, P. *et al.* Maritime route of colonization of Europe. *PNAS* **111**, 9211–9216 (2014).

81. Vigne, J., Carrère, I., Briois, F. & Guilaine, J. The Early Process of Mammal Domestication in the Near East New Evidence from the Pre-Neolithic and Pre-Pottery Neolithic in Cyprus. *Curr. Anthropol.* **52**, S255–S271 (2011).

82. Durrani, S., Khan, H. & Renfrew, C. Obsidian Source Identification by Fission Track Analysis. *Nature* **233**, 242–245 (1971).

83. Laskaris, N., Sampson, A., Mavridis, F. & Liritzis, I. Late Pleistocene/Early Holocene seafaring in the Aegean: new obsidian hydration dates with the SIMS-SS method. *J. Archaeol. Sci.* **38**, 2475–2479 (2011).

84. Broodbank, C. & Strasser, T. F. Migrant farmers and the Neolithic colonization of Crete. *Antiquity* **65**, 233–245 (1991).

85. Case, H. Neolithic Explanations. *Antiquity* **43**, 176–186 (1969).

86. Rowley-Conwy, P. Westward ho! *Curr. Anthropol.* **52**, S431–S451 (2011).

87. Zilhão, J. Radiocarbon evidence for maritime pioneer colonization at the origins of farming in west Mediterranean Europe. *PNAS* **98**, 14180–14185 (2001).

88. Gkiasta, M., Russell, T., Shennan, S. & Steele, J. Neolithic transition in Europe: the radiocarbon record revisited. *Antiquity* **77**, 45–62 (2003).

89. Scarre, C. Holocene Europe. in *The human past* (ed. Scarre, C.) 392–431 (Thames & Hudson, London, 2013).

90. Zeder, M. Domestication and early agriculture in the Mediterranean Basin: Origins, diffusion, and impact. *PNAS* **105**, 11597–11604 (2008).

91. Isern, N., Zilhão, J., Fort, J. & Ammerman, A. Modeling the role of voyaging in the coastal spread of the Early Neolithic in the West Mediterranean. *PNAS* **114**, 897–902 (2017).

92. Saqalli, M. *et al.* Revisiting and modelling the woodland farming system of the early Neolithic Linear Pottery Culture (LBK), 5600-4900 B.C. *Veg. Hist. Archaeobotany* **23**, S37–S50 (2014).

93. Bayliss, A., Marshall, P., Richards, C. & Whittle, A. Islands of history: the Late Neolithic timescape of Orkney. *Antiquity* **91**, 1171–1188 (2017).

94. Martínková, N. *et al.* Divergent evolutionary processes associated with colonization of offshore islands. *Mol. Ecol.* **22**, 5205–5220 (2013).

95. Détroit, F. *et al.* Upper Pleistocene Homo sapiens from the Tabon cave (Palawan, The Philippines): description and dating of new discoveries. *C R Palevol* **3**, 705–712 (2004).

96. Samper Carro, S. *et al.* Somewhere beyond the sea: Human cranial remains from the Lesser Sunda Islands (Alor Island, Indonesia) provide insights on Late Pleistocene peopling of Island Southeast Asia. *J. Hum. Evol.* **134**, 102638 (2019).

97. Brumm, A. *et al.* Skeletal remains of a Pleistocene modern human (Homo sapiens) from Sulawesi. *PLOS ONE* **16**, e0257273 (2021).

98. Bellwood, P. & Hiscock, P. Australia and the Austronesians. in *The human past* (ed. Scarre, C.) 264–305 (Thames & Hudson, London, 2013).

99. Anderson, A. Crossing the Luzon Strait: Archaeological Chronology in the Batanes Islands, Philippines and the Regional Sequence of Neolithic Dispersal. *J. Austronesian Stud.* **1**, 25–44 (2005).

100. Simanjuntak, T. The Western Route Migration: A Second Probable Neolithic Diffusion to Indonesia. in *New Perspectives in Southeast Asian and Pacific Prehistory* (eds Piper, P., Matsumura, H. & Bulbeck, D.) 201–2 (ANU Press, Canberra, 2017).

101. Bellwood, P. *First Farmers*. (Blackwell Publishing, Oxford, 2005).

102. Blust, R. Subgrouping, circularity and extinction: some issues in Austronesian comparative linguistics. in *Selected papers from the eighth international conference on Austronesian linguistics* (eds Zeitoun, E. & Li, P.) 31–94 (Academia Sinica, Taipai, Taiwan, 1999).

103. Pawley, A. The Austronesian Dispersal: Languages, Technologies and People. in *Examining the farming/language dispersal hypothesis* (eds Bellwood, P. & Renfrew, C.) 251–273 (McDonald Institute, Cambridge, 2002).

104. Pawley, A. The origins of Early Lapita culture: the testimony of historical linguistics. in *Oceanic Explorations: Lapita and Western Pacific Settlement (Terra Australis 26)* (eds Bedford, S., Sand, C. & Connaughton, S.) 17–49 (ANU ePress, Canberra, 2007).

105. Paz, V. Island Southeast Asia: Spread or Friction Zone. in *Examining the farming/language dispersal hypothesis* (eds Bellwood, P. & Renfrew, C.) 275–285 (McDonald Institute, Cambridge, 2002).

106. Dewar, R. Rainfall Variability and Subsistence Systems. *Curr. Anthropol.* **44**, 369–388 (2003).

107. Denham, T., Ramsey, C. & Specht, J. Dating the appearance of Lapita pottery in the Bismarck Archipelago and its dispersal to Remote Oceania. *Archaeol. Ocean.* **47**, 39–46 (2012).

108. Clark, G., Petchey, F., Winter, O., Carson, M. & O'Day, P. New Radiocarbon Dates from the Bapot-1 Site in Saipan and Neolithic Dispersal by Stratified Diffusion. *J. Pac. Archaeol.* **1**, 21–35 (2010).

109. Addison, D. & Matisoo-Smith, E. Rethinking Polynesian origins: a West Polynesia triple-I model. *Archaeol. Ocean.* **45**, 1–12 (2010).
110. Irwin, G. & Flay, R. Pacific colonisation and canoe performance: Experiments in the science of sailing. *J. Polyn. Soc.* **124**, 419–443 (2015).
111. Sear, D. *et al.* Human settlement of East Polynesia earlier, incremental, and coincident with prolonged South Pacific drought. *PNAS* **117**, 8813–8819 (2020).
112. Wilmshurst, J., Hunt, T., Lipo, C. & Anderson, A. High-precision radiocarbon dating shows recent and rapid initial human colonization of East Polynesia. *PNAS* **108**, 1815–1820 (2010).
113. Hunt, T. & Lipo, C. Late Colonization of Easter Island. *Science* **311**, 1603–1606 (2006).
114. Dixon, R. B. The Long Voyages of the Polynesians. *Proc. Am. Philos. Soc.* **74**, 167–175 (1934).
115. Doran, E. Outrigger ages. *J. Polyn. Soc.* **83**, 130–140 (1974).
116. Couper, A. *Sailors and Traders: A Maritime History of the Pacific Peoples.* (University of Hawai'i Press, Honolulu, 2009).
117. Horridge, G. Origins and relationships of Pacific canoes and rigs. in *Canoes of the grand ocean* (eds Di Piazza, A. & Pearthree, E.) 85–105 (Archaeopress, Oxford, 2008).
118. Mahdi, W. The Dispersal of Austronesian boat forms in the Indian Ocean. in *Archaeology and Language III: Artefacts, languages and texts, One World Archaeology 34* (eds Blench, R. & Spriggs, M.) 144–179 (Routledge, London, 1999).
119. Bateson, F. Polynesian navigation. *Publ. Astron. Soc. Pac.* **71**, 187–193 (1959).
120. Lewis, D. Polynesian navigational methods. *J. Polyn. Soc.* **73**, 364–374 (1964).
121. Lewis, D. Voyaging Stars: Aspects of Polynesian and Micronesian Astronomy. *Philos. Trans. R. Soc. Lond. Ser. Math. Phys. Sci.* **276**, 133–148 (1974).
122. Di Piazza, A. A reconstruction of a Tahitian star compass based on tupaia's 'Chart for the Society Islands with Otaheite in the center'. *J. Polyn. Soc.* **119**, 377–392 (2010).
123. Sharp, A. Polynesian navigation to distant islands. *J. Polyn. Soc.* **70**, 219–226 (1961).
124. Finney, B. Myth, Experiment, and the Reinvention of Polynesian Voyaging. *Am. Anthropol.* **93**, 383–404 (1991).
125. Wright, W. & Wright, E. Submerged Boat at North Ferriby (Plates V-VI). *Antiquity* **13**, 349–354 (1939).
126. Wright, E. V. & Wright, C. W. Prehistoric Boats from North Ferriby, East Yorkshire. *Proc. Prehist. Soc.* **13**, 114–138 (1947).
127. Wright, E. & Churchill, D. The Boats from North Ferriby, Yorkshire, England, with a review of the origins of the sewn boats of the Bronze Age. *Proc. Prehist. Soc.* **31**, 1–24 (1965).
128. Barker, H. & Mackey, C. J. British Museum Natural Radiocarbon Measurements II. *Radiocarbon* **2**, 26–30 (1960).
129. Wright, Hedges, Bayliss, A. & Noort, V. New AMS radiocarbon dates for the North Ferriby boats - A contribution to dating prehistoric seafaring in northwestern Europe. *Antiquity* **75**, 726–34 (2001).
130. Wright, E. V., Hutchinson, G. R. & Gregson, C. W. A Fourth Boat-Find at North Ferriby, Humberside. *Archaeol. J.* **146**, 44–57 (1989).
131. Wright, E. V. & Switsur, V. R. The Ferriby 5 Boat Fragment. *Archaeol. J.* **150**, 46–56 (1993).
132. Van de Noort, R., Middleton, R., Foxon, A. & Bayliss, A. The 'Kilnsea-boat', and some implications from the discovery of England's oldest plank boat remains. *Antiquity* **73**, 131–135 (1999).
133. Switsur, V. R. & Wright, E. V. Radiocarbon Ages and Calibrated Dates for the Boats from North Ferriby, Humberside—A Reappraisal. *Archaeol. J.* **146**, 58–67 (1989).
134. Chapman, H. P. & Chapman, P. R. Seascapes and Landscapes—the Siting of the Ferriby Boat Finds in the Context of Prehistoric Pilotage. *Int. J. Naut. Archaeol.* **34**, 43–50 (2005).
135. Coates, J. The Bronze Age Ferriby Boats: Seagoing Ships or Estuary Ferry Boats? *Int. J. Naut. Archaeol.* **34**, 38–42 (2005).
136. Van de Noort, R. *et al.* Morgawr: an experimental Bronze Age-type sewn-plank craft based on the Ferriby boats. *Int. J. Naut. Archaeol.* **43**, 292–313 (2014).
137. Alcock, S. & Cherry, J. The Mediterranean World. in *The human past* (ed. Scarre, C.) 472–517 (Thames & Hudson, London, 2013).
138. Fitton, L. *Minoans.* (The British Museum Press, London, 2002).
139. Cherry, J. The emergence of the state in the prehistoric Aegean. *Proc. Camb. Philol. Soc.* **30**, 18–48 (1984).
140. Warren, P. The Miniature Fresco from the West House at Akrotiri, Thera, and Its Aegean Setting. *J. Hell. Stud.* **99**, 115–129 (1979).
141. Bonn-Muller, E. First Minoan Shipwreck. *Archaeology* **63**, 44–47 (2010).
142. Parkinson, W. & Galaty, M. Secondary States in Perspective: An Integrated Approach to State Formation in the Prehistoric Aegean. *Am. Anthropol.* **109**, 113–129 (2007).
143. Starr, C. The Myth of the Minoan Thalassocracy. *Hist. Z. Für Alte Gesch.* **3**, 282–291 (1955).
144. Castleden, R. *Mycenaeans.* (Routledge, London and New York, 2005).
145. Mountjoy, P. A Bronze Age Ship from Ashkelon with Particular Reference to the Bronze Age Ship from Bademgediği Tepe. *Am. J. Archaeol.* **115**, 483–488 (2011).
146. Pulak, C. The Uluburun shipwreck: an overview. *Int. J. Naut. Archaeol.* **27**, 188–224 (1998).
147. Pulak, C. The Uluburun Shipwreck and Late Bronze Age Trade. in *Beyond Babylon: Art, Trade, and Diplomacy in the Second Millennium B.C.* (eds Aruz, J., Benzel, K. & Evans, J.) 289–305 (Metropolitan Museum of Art, New York, NY, 2008).
148. Monroe, C. Sunk Costs at Late Bronze Age Uluburun. *Bull. Am. Sch. Orient. Res.* **357**, 19–33 (2010).

149. MacPherson, H. The Development of Cosmological Ideas. *Pop. Astron.* **21**, 78–84 (1913).
150. MacPherson, H. The cosmological ideas of the Greeks. *Pop. Astron.* **24**, 358–369 (1916).
151. Dicks, D. *Early Greek Astronomy to Aristotle.* (Cornell University Press, Ithaca, NY, 1970).
152. Evans, J. *The History and Practice of Ancient Astronomy.* (Oxford University Press, Inc., New York, NY, 1998).
153. Hadjidaki, E. Underwater Excavations of a Late Fifth Century Merchant Ship at Alonnesos, Greece : the 1991-1993 Seasons. *Persée* **120**, 561–593 (1996).
154. Lynch, D. Visually discerning the curvature of the Earth. *Appl. Opt.* **34**, H39–H43 (2008).
155. Kristiansen, K. & Larsson, T. *The Rise of Bronze Age Society.* (Cambridge University Press, Cambridge, 2005).
156. Beck, C. Criteria for "amber trade": The evidence in the eastern European Neolithic. *J. Balt. Stud.* **16**, 200–209 (1985).
157. Shaw, I. Egypt and the outside world. in *The Oxford history of Ancient Egypt* (ed. Shaw, I.) 314–329 (Oxford University Press, Oxford, 2000).

12: Early metallurgy

1. Michaelis, A. R. The Enigmatic Seven. *Interdiscip. Sci. Rev.* **7**, 1–3 (1982).
2. Bruce, I. A. F. Theopompus and Classical Greek Historiography. *Hist. Theory* **9**, 86–109 (1970).
3. David, B. *et al.* A 28,000 year old excavated painted rock from Nawarla Gabarnmang, northern Australia. *J. Archaeol. Sci.* **40**, 2493–2501 (2013).
4. Samuels, L. E. Australia's contribution to archaeometallurgy. *Mater. Charact.* **29**, 69–109 (1992).
5. Craddock, P. From Hearth to Furnace : Evidences for the Earliest Metal Smelting Technologies in the Eastern Mediterranean. *Paléorient* **26**, 151–165 (2000).
6. Roberts, B., Thornton, C. & Pigott, V. Development of metallurgy in Eurasia. *Antiquity* **83**, 1012–1022 (2009).
7. Birch, T., Rehren, T. & Pernicka, E. The metallic finds from Çatalhöyük: a review and preliminary new work. in *Substantive Technologies at Çatalhöyük* 307–316 (2013).
8. Radivojević, M., Rehren, T., Farid, S., Pernicka, E. & Camurcuoğlu, D. Repealing the Çatalhöyük extractive metallurgy: The green, the fire and the 'slag'. *J. Archaeol. Sci.* **86**, 101–122 (2017).
9. Bar-Yosef Mayer, D. & Porat, N. Green stone beads at the dawn of agriculture. *PNAS* **105**, 8548–8551 (2008).
10. Radivojevic, M. *et al.* On the origins of extractive metallurgy: new evidence from Europe. *J. Archaeol. Sci.* **37**, 2775–2787 (2010).
11. Scarre, C. Holocene Europe. in *The human past* (ed. Scarre, C.) 392–431 (Thames & Hudson, London, 2013).
12. Anthony, D. *The Horse the Wheel and Language: How Bronze-Age Riders from the Eurasian Steppes Shaped the Modern World.* (Princeton University Press, Princeton, NJ, 2007).
13. Chapman, J., Higham, T., Gaydarska, B., Slavchev, V. & Honch, N. The social context of the emergence, development and abandonment of the Varna Cemetery, Bulgaria. *Eur. J. Archaeol.* **2–3**, 159–183 (2006).
14. Matthews, R. The Rise of Civilization in Southwest Asia. in *The human past* (ed. Scarre, C.) 432–471 (Thames & Hudson, London, 2013).
15. Garfinkel, Y., Klimscha, F., Shalev, S. & Rosenberg, D. The Beginning of Metallurgy in the Southern Levant: A Late 6th Millennium CalBC Copper Awl from Tel Tsaf, Israel. *PLOS ONE* **9**, e92591 (2014).
16. Maddin, R., Muhly, J. D. & Wheeler, T. S. How the Iron Age Began. *Sci. Am.* **237**, 122–131 (1977).
17. Lechtman, H. & Klein, S. The Production of Copper–Arsenic Alloys (Arsenic Bronze) by Cosmelting: Modern Experiment, Ancient Practice. *J. Archaeol. Sci.* **26**, 497–526 (1999).
18. Radivojević, M., Rehren, T., Kuzmanovic-Cvetkovic, J., Jovanović, M. & Northover, P. Tainted ores and the rise of tin bronzes in Eurasia, c. 6500 years ago. *Antiquity* **87**, 1030–1045 (2013).
19. Thornton, C., Lamberg-Karlovsky, C., Liezers, M. & Young, S. On Pins and Needles: Tracing the Evolution of Copper-base Alloying at Tepe Yahya, Iran, via ICP-MS Analysis of Common-place Items. *J. Archaeol. Sci.* **29**, 1451–1460 (2002).
20. Yener, K. Strategic industries and tin in the ancient near east: Anatolia updated. *TUBA-AR* **12**, 143–154 (2009).
21. Lechtman, H. N. Arsenic Bronze: Dirty Copper or Chosen Alloy? A View from the Americas. *J. Field Archaeol.* **23**, 477–514 (1996).
22. Pigott, V. The acquisition of tin in Bronze Age southwest Asia. in *Metallurgy: Understanding How, Learning why: Studies in Honor of James D. Muhly* (eds Betancourt, P. P. & Ferrence, S.) 827–861 (INSTAP Academic Press, Philadelphia, PA, 2020). doi:10.4324/9781315193359-34.
23. Berger, D. *et al.* Isotope systematics and chemical composition of tin ingots from Mochlos (Crete) and other Late Bronze Age sites in the eastern Mediterranean Sea: An ultimate key to tin provenance? *PLOS ONE* **14**, e0218326 (2019).
24. Craddock, P. T. The composition of the copper alloys used by the Greek, Etruscan and Roman civilizations: 3. The Origins and Early Use of Brass. *J. Archaeol. Sci.* **5**, 1–16 (1978).
25. Higham, T., Bronk Ramsey, C., Owen, D., Pike, A. & Hedges, R. Radiocarbon dates from the Oxford AMS system: Archaeometry datelist 32. *Archaeometry* **49**, S1-60 (2007).

26. Slavchev, V. The Varna Eneolithic Cemetery in the Context of the Late Copper Age in the East Balkans. in *The lost worlds of Old Europe: The Danube Valley 5300 - 5000 BC* (ed. Anthony, D.) 193–212 (Institute for the Study of the Ancient World, New York, NY, 2010).

27. Renfrew, C. Varna and the social context of early metallurgy. *Antiquity* **51**, 199–203 (1978).

28. Gopher, A., Tsuk, T., Shalev, S. & Gophna, R. Earliest Gold Artifacts in the Levant. *Curr. Anthropol.* **31**, 436–443 (1990).

29. Craddock, P. Production of Silver across the Ancient World. *ISIJ Int.* **54**, 1085–1092 (2014).

30. Lucas, A. Silver in Ancient Times. *J. Egypt. Archaeol.* **14**, 313–319 (1928).

31. Gilead, I. The Chalcolithic Period in the Levant. *J. World Prehistory* **2**, 397–443 (1988).

32. Oy, H. West Anatolian mining in Early Bronze Age (3000-2000 BC). *J. Am. Heart Assoc.* **4**, (2017).

33. Kagan, D. The Dates of the Earliest Coins. *Am. J. Archaeol.* **86**, 343–360 (1982).

34. Cahill, N. & Kroll, J. H. New Archaic Coin Finds at Sardis. *Am. J. Archaeol.* **109**, 589–617 (2005).

35. Melitz, J. A model of the beginnings of coinage in antiquity. *Eur. Rev. Econ. Hist.* **21**, 83–103 (2017).

36. Konuk, K. *et al. XRF Analysis of Several Groups of Electrum Coins.* (The American Numismatic Society, New York, NY, 2020).

37. Grover, A. & Pandit, M. Ancient gold mining activities in India-An overview. *Iran. J. Earth Sci.* **7**, 1–13 (2015).

38. Kenoyer, J. The Indus Valley Tradition of Pakistan and western India. *J. World Prehistory* **5**, 331–385 (1991).

39. Miller, D. Ideology and the Harappan Civilization. *J. Anthropol. Archaeol.* **4**, 34–71 (1985).

40. Zhang, R., Pian, H., Santosh, M. & Zhang, S. The history and economics of gold mining in China. *Jiaodong-Type Gold Depos.* **65**, 718–727 (2015).

41. Bogucki, P. *The Origins of Human Society.* (Blackwell Publishing, Oxford, 1999).

42. Van der Mieroop, M. *A History of the Ancient Near East.* (Wiley-Blackwell, Chichester, 2016).

43. Kool, J. The Old Assyrian Trade Network from an Archaeological Perspective. (University of Leiden, 2012).

44. Postgate, N. *Early Mesopotamia: Society and Economy at the Dawn of History.* (Routledge, London, 1994).

45. Erb-Satullo, N. L. The Innovation and Adoption of Iron in the Ancient Near East. *J. Archaeol. Res.* **27**, 557–607 (2019).

46. Dodson, J. *et al.* Early bronze in two Holocene archaeological sites in Gansu, NW China. *Quat. Res.* **72**, 309–314 (2009).

47. Sun, W. *et al.* Origin of the mysterious Yin-Shang bronzes in China indicated by lead isotopes. *Sci. Rep.* **6**, 23304 (2016).

48. Bagley, R. Shang archaeology. in *The Cambridge History of Ancient China* (eds Loewe, M. & Shaughnessy, E.) 124–231 (Cambridge University Press, New York, NY, 1999).

49. Thorp, R. Erlitou and the search for the Xia. *Early China* **16**, 1–38 (1991).

50. Liu, L. & Xu, H. Rethinking Erlitou: legend, history and Chinese archaeology. *Antiquity* **81**, 886–901 (2007).

51. Chang, K. China on the eve of the historical period. in *The Cambridge History of Ancient China* (eds Loewe, M. & Shaughnessy, E.) 37–73 (Cambridge University Press, New York, NY, 1999).

52. Li, S., Li, Y., Zhu, R. & Wang, H. Analysis of Lead Smelting Technology in the Early Bronze Age Based on Smelting Slag from the Central Plains of China. *Metals* **13**, 435 (2023).

53. Buchwald, V. *Handbook of Iron Meteorites Their History, Distribution, Composition and Structure.* (University of California Press, Oakland, CA, 1975).

54. Huntington, P. A. M. Robert E. Peary and the Cape York Meteorites. *Polar Geogr.* **26**, 53–65 (2002).

55. Appelt, M. *et al.* The cultural history of the Innaanganeq/ Cape York meteorite. *Tech. Rep.* **2015** (2015).

56. Pringle, H. New Respect for Metal's Role in Ancient Arctic Cultures. *Science* **277**, 766–767 (1997).

57. Buchwald, V. F. On the use of iron by the Eskimos in Greenland. *Mater. Charact.* **29**, 139–176 (1992).

58. Hastrup, K. The End of Nature? Inughuit Life on the Edge of Time. *Ethnos* **88**, 13–29 (2023).

59. Flegontov, P. *et al.* Palaeo-Eskimo genetic ancestry and the peopling of Chukotka and North America. *Nature* **570**, 236–240 (2019).

60. Gurney, O. *The Hittites.* (Penguin Books Ltd, London, 1990).

61. Muhly, J. D., Maddin, R., Stech, T. & Özgen, E. Iron in Anatolia and the Nature of the Hittite Iron Industry. *Anatol. Stud.* **35**, 67–84 (1985).

62. Cordani, V. The Development of the Hittite Iron Industry. A Reappraisal of the Written Sources. *Welt Orients* **46**, 162–176 (2016).

63. Cooke, S. & Aschenbrenner, S. The Occurrence of Metallic Iron in Ancient Copper. *J. Field Archaeol.* **2**, 251–266 (1975).

64. Merkel, J. & Barret, K. The adventitious production of iron in the smelting of copper' revisited: metallographic evidence against a tempting model. *J. Hist. Metall. Soc.* **34**, 59–66 (2000).

65. Cline, E. *1177 BC: The Year Civilization Collapsed.* (Princeton University Press, Princeton, NJ, 2014).

66. Bell, C. The merchants of Ugarit: oligarchs of the Late Bronze Age trade in metals? in *Eastern Mediterranean metallurgy and metalwork in the second millennium BC: a conference in honour of James D. Muhly, Nicosia, 10th-11th October 2009* (eds Kassianidou, V. & Papasavvas, G.) 180–187 (Oxbow Books, Oxford, 2012).

67. Childs, S. T. & Killick, D. Indigenous African Metallurgy: Nature and Culture. *Annu. Rev. Anthropol.* **22**, 317–337 (1993).

68. Connah, G. Holocene Africa. in *The human past* (ed. Scarre, C.) 350–391 (Thames & Hudson, London, 2013).

69. Humphris, J., Charlton, M., Keen, J., Sauder, L. & Alshishani, F. Iron Smelting in Sudan: Experimental Archaeology at The Royal City of Meroe. *J. Field Archaeol.* **43**, 399–416 (2018).
70. Pringle, H. Seeking Africa's First Iron Men. *Science* **323**, 200–202 (2009).
71. Holl, A. F. C. Early West African Metallurgies: New Data and Old Orthodoxy. *J. World Prehistory* **22**, 415–438 (2009).
72. Breunig, P. & Rupp, N. An Outline of Recent Studies on the Nigerian Nok Culture. *J. Afr. Archaeol.* **14**, 237–255 (2016).
73. Franke, G. A Chronology of the Central Nigerian Nok Culture — 1500 BC to the Beginning of the Common Era. *J. Afr. Archaeol.* **14**, 257–289 (2016).
74. Deme, A. & McIntosh, S. Excavations at Walaldụ: new light on the settlement of the Middle Senegal Valley by iron-using peoples. *J. Afr. Archaeol.* **4**, 317–347 (2006).
75. Lane, P. The 'moving frontier' and the transition to food production in Kenya. *Azania Archaeol. Res. Afr.* **39**, 243–264 (2004).
76. Crowther, A., Prendergast, M., Fuller, D. & Boivin, N. Subsistence mosaics, forager-farmer interactions, and the transition to food production in eastern Africa. *Quat. Int.* **489**, 101–120 (2018).
77. Prendergast, M. *et al.* Ancient DNA reveals a multistep spread of the first herders into sub-Saharan Africa. *Science* **365**, eaaw6275 (2019).
78. Williamson, K. & Blench, R. Niger-Congo. in *African Languages: an Introduction* (eds Heine, B. & Nurse, D.) 11–42 (Cambridge University Press, Cambridge, 2000).
79. Diamond, J. & Bellwood, P. Farmers and Their Languages: The First Expansions. *Science* **300**, 597–603 (2003).
80. Blench, R. New Developments In The Classification Of Bantu Languages and Their Historical Implications. in *Datation et Chronologie dans le Bassin du Lac Tchad* (eds Barreteau, D. & Graffenried, C.) 147–160 (ORSTOM, Paris, 1993).
81. Vansina, J. New Linguistic Evidence and 'the Bantu Expansion'. *J. Afr. Hist.* **36**, 175–195 (1995).
82. Holden, C. Bantu language trees reflect the spread of farming across sub-Saharan Africa: a maximum-parsimony analysis. *Proc. R. Soc. B* **269**, 793–799 (2002).
83. Bellwood, P. *First Farmers*. (Blackwell Publishing, Oxford, 2005).
84. Schoenbrun, D. We Are What We Eat: Ancient Agriculture between the Great Lakes. *J. Afr. Hist.* **34**, 1–31 (1993).
85. Philippson, G. & Bahuchet, S. Cultivated crops and Bantu migrations in Central and Eastern Africa: A linguistic approach. *Azania Archaeol. Res. Afr.* **29–30**, 103–120 (1994).
86. Phillipson, D. Language and Farming Dispersals in Sub-Saharan Africa, with Particular Reference to the Bantu-speaking Peoples. in *Examining the farming/language dispersal hypothesis* (eds Bellwood, P. & Renfrew, C.) 177–187 (McDonald Institute, Cambridge, 2002).
87. Childs, T. Style, Technology, and Iron Smelting Furnaces in Bantu-Speaking Africa. *J. Anthropol. Archaeol.* **10**, 332–359 (1991).
88. Diamond, J. *Guns, Germs and Steel*. (Chatto & Windus, London, 1997).
89. Hansen, S., Montero-Ruiz, I., Rovira, S., Steiniger, D. & Toderaş, M. The earliest lead ore processing in Europe. 5th millennium BC finds from Pietrele on the Lower Danube. *PLOS ONE* **14**, e0214218 (2019).
90. Yahalom-Mack, N. *et al.* The Earliest Lead Object in the Levant. *PLOS ONE* **10**, e0142948 (2015).
91. Waldron, H. A. Lead Poisoning in the Ancient World. *Med. Hist.* **17**, 391–399 (1973).
92. Cilliers, L. & Retief, F. Chapter 14 - Lead Poisoning and the Downfall of Rome: Reality or Myth? in *Toxicology in Antiquity* (ed. Wexler, P.) 221–229 (Academic Press, Cambridge, MA, 2019). doi:10.1016/B978-0-12-815339-0.00014-7.
93. Delile, H., Blichert-Toft, J., Goiran, J.-P., Keay, S. & Albarède, F. Lead in ancient Rome's city waters. *PNAS* **111**, 6594–6599 (2014).
94. Ávila, A., Mansilla, J., Bosch, P. & Pijoan, C. Cinnabar in Mesoamerica: poisoning or mortuary ritual? *J. Archaeol. Sci.* **49**, 48–56 (2014).
95. Martín-Gil, J., Martín-Gil, F. J., Delibes-de-Castro, G., Zapatero-Magdaleno, P. & Sarabia-Herrero, F. J. The first known use of vermillion. *Experientia* **51**, 759–761 (1995).
96. Caley, E. & Richards, J. *Theophrastus on Stones*. (The Ohio State University, Columbus, Ohio, 1956).
97. Alabiso, A. Perspectives of Chinese architecture under the Qin Dynasty. *Riv. Degli Studi Orient.* **69**, 447–466 (1995).
98. Stone, R. Archaeologists Seek New Clues to the Riddle of Emperor Qin's Terra-Cotta Army. *Science* **325**, 22–23 (2009).
99. Higham, C. Complex societies of East and Southeast Asia. in *The human past* (ed. Scarre, C.) 552–593 (Thames & Hudson, London, 2013).
100. Rickard, T. The Use of Meteoric Iron. *J. R. Anthropol. Inst. G. B. Irel.* **71**, 55–66 (1941).
101. Vaughn, K. J., Grados, M. L., Eerkens, J. W. & Edwards, M. S. Hematite mining in the ancient Americas: Mina Primavera, A 2,000 year old Peruvian mine. *JOM* **59**, 16–20 (2007).
102. Aldenderfer, M., Craig, N., Speakman, R. & Popelka-Filcoff, R. Four-thousand-year-old gold artifacts from the Lake Titicaca basin, southern Peru. *PNAS* **105**, 5002–5005 (2008).
103. Burger, R. & Gordon, R. Early Central Andean Metalworking from Mina Perdida, Peru. *Science* **282**, 1108–1111 (1998).

104. Graffam, G., Rivera, M. & Carevič, A. Ancient Metallurgy in the Atacama: Evidence for Copper Smelting during Chile's Early Ceramic Period. *Lat. Am. Antiq.* **7**, 101–113 (1996).

105. Cooke, C., Abbott, M. & Wolfe, A. Metallurgy in Southern South America. in *Encyclopedia of the History of Science, Technology, and Medicine in Non-Western Cultures Vol. 2* (ed. Selin, H.) 1658–1662 (Kluwer Science, Dordrecht, 2008).

106. Gallardo, F., Vidal-Montero, E., Ballester, B., Blanco, J. & Guzman, G. Desert travels in the Atacama: making place through movement (c. 2500-1500 cal BP). *J. R. Anthropol. Inst.* **28**, 152–177 (2022).

107. Moseley, M. *The Incas and Their Ancestors: The Archaeology of Peru.* (Thames & Hudson, London, 2001).

108. Van Buren, M. & Mills, B. H. Huayrachinas and Tocochimbos: Traditional Smelting Technology of the Southern Andes. *Lat. Am. Antiq.* **16**, 3–25 (2005).

109. Eichler, A. *et al.* Ice-core evidence of earliest extensive copper metallurgy in the Andes 2700 years ago. *Sci. Rep.* **7**, 41855 (2017).

110. Gordon, R. B. & Rutledge, J. W. Bismuth Bronze from Machu Picchu, Peru. *Science* **223**, 585–586 (1984).

111. Abbott, M. B. & Wolfe, A. P. Intensive Pre-Incan Metallurgy Recorded by Lake Sediments from the Bolivian Andes. *Science* **301**, 1893–1895 (2003).

112. Hosler, D. & Macfarlane, A. Copper Sources, Metal Production, and Metals Trade in Late Postclassic Mesoamerica. *Science* **273**, 1819–1824 (1996).

113. Webster, D. & Evans, S. Mesoamerican civilization. in *The human past* (ed. Scarre, C.) 594–639 (Thames & Hudson, London, 2013).

Index

By the same author

Humans: from the beginning

In just a few years, our understanding of the human past has changed beyond recognition as new discoveries and advances in genetic techniques overturn long-held beliefs and make international news.

Drawing upon expert literature and the latest research, *Humans: from the beginning* is a rigorous but accessible guide to the human story, presenting an even-handed account of events from the first apes to the rise of the first cities and civilisations. Along the way, we learn about the emergence of modern human behaviour, prehistoric art, early modern human migrations from Africa, the peopling of the world, and how farming and agriculture replaced hunter-gathering.

Humans: from the beginning is written for the non-specialist, but it is sufficiently comprehensive and well-referenced to serve as an ideal 'one-stop' text not only for undergraduate students, but also for postgraduates, researchers, and other academics seeking to broaden their knowledge.

ISBN: 978-0-9927620-7-0 (paperback) 978-0-9927620-8-7 (Kindle)

Prehistoric Investigations

How do you infer the existence of a hitherto-unknown human species from a fragmentary finger bone? Why do we walk on two legs? Were Neanderthals really dimwitted? How did a small, solitary predator become the world's most popular pet? What was the ancient link between languages spoken in places as far apart as Iceland and India?

These are just some of the questions faced by those seeking to unravel the secrets of the vast period of time that predates the last six thousand years of 'recorded history'. In addition to fieldwork and traditional methods, paleoanthropologists and archaeologists now draw upon genetics and other cutting-edge scientific techniques.

In fifty chapters, *Prehistoric Investigations* tells the story of the many thought-provoking discoveries that have transformed our understanding of the distant past.

ISBN: 978-0-9927620-6-3 (paperback) 978-0-9927620-5-6 (Kindle)

Astronomy: from the beginning

The incredible story of how we learned about the Universe, from the earliest prehistoric observations to the first telescopes. Early astronomy ranks among the greatest achievements of the human intellect. But how did astronomers of the pre-telescopic era make accurate observations of the Sun, Moon, and planets, and predict their movements? And how can we uncover the ancient knowledge of societies that left few or no written records? The answers are in this fascinating book, which explores the history of astronomy, from prehistoric times to the Renaissance and the birth of modern science. Its coverage of these topics is even-handed, accessible, and avoids sensationalism, and avoids sensationalism. While aimed at the general reader, it is also fully referenced for students and academics.

ISBN: 978-1-9162964-2-8 (paperback) 978-1-9162964-1-1 (Kindle)

www.ingramcontent.com/pod-product-compliance
Lightning Source LLC
Chambersburg PA
CBHW080325270326
41927CB00014B/3097